AF506037

CREATING A WORLD ON PAPER

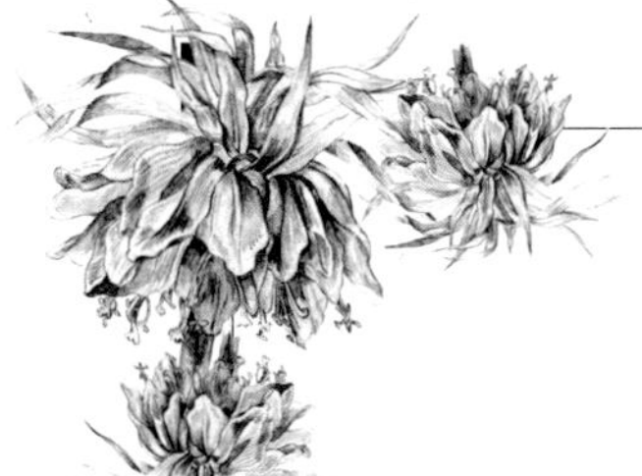

CREATING A WORLD ON PAPER

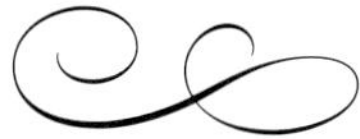

Harry Fenn's Career in Art

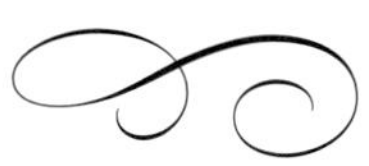

SUE RAINEY

UNIVERSITY OF MASSACHUSETTS PRESS

Amherst and Boston

ISBN 978-1-55849-979-9

Designed by Sally Nichols
Set in Granjon and Shelley Andante Script
Printed and bound by Thomson-Shore, Inc.

Library of Congress Cataloging-in-Publication Data

Rainey, Sue.
Creating a world on paper : Harry Fenn's career in art / Sue Rainey.
    pages cm. — (Studies in print culture and the history of the book)
Includes bibliographical references and index.
ISBN 978-1-55849-979-9 (cloth : alk. paper) 1. Fenn, Harry, 1838–1911. 2. Artists—United States—
Biography. 3. Fenn, Harry, 1838–1911—Criticism and interpretation. 4. Arts and society—United
States—History—19th century. 5. Arts and society—United States—History—20th century. I. Title.
N6537.F39R35 2013
741.6092—dc23

                              2012043583

British Library Cataloguing-in-Publication Data
A catalogue record for this book is available from the British Library.

Publication of this book has been aided by a grant from the Wyeth Foundation for American Art
Publication Fund of the College Art Association.

For the descendants of Harry Fenn, who have always

known their ancestor deserved to be remembered and

have helped me tell his story.

Contents

My interest in Harry Fenn dates back almost thirty years, to when I realized that many of the most attractive nineteenth-century prints of American scenery and cities offered in print shops were his compositions, often taken from disbound copies of the two-volume *Picturesque America.* The luminosity of that book's steel engravings and the variety and charm of its wood engravings intrigued me. I decided to examine how these images were made and their impact on their period, the 1870s.

Because Fenn was the first and most prolific of the artists who contributed to *Picturesque America,* I wanted to find out all I could about him. At first I found very little. About 1982 I learned from Maureen O'Brien, then curator of collections at the Montclair Art Museum, that some of Fenn's descendants still lived in Montclair, New Jersey, where he died in 1911. In the fall of 1983, I was thrilled to meet Fenn's granddaughter Dorothy van Antwerp Walters and Jean F. van Antwerp, the widow of Fenn's grandson Donald van Antwerp. Both welcomed me into their homes and showed me several of Fenn's works that had been passed down in the family as well as a brief account of his life written by his son.

Over the next decade, as the article I planned to write gradually grew into my 1994 book, *Creating "Picturesque America": Monument to the Natural and Cultural Landscape,* I kept in touch with these gracious women, who have since died. I also made contact with William V. Abt, Dorothy Walters's son and Fenn's great-grandson, who has generously allowed me to reproduce in this book several of his grandfather's artworks, some of Fenn's childhood sketches, and photos from a family scrapbook. I am immensely grateful to Bill, who is also an artist, for offering information, assistance, and encouragement when it must have seemed I would never complete this project.

In 2008, after writing about two other illustrators who were colleagues of Fenn, John Douglas Woodward and Mary Hallock Foote, I asked myself if I was tired of

Fenn or if I might want to write about his entire career. In looking through my voluminous files, I found new energy and enthusiasm: clearly, this artist was imaginative, creative, adaptable, indefatigable, and highly influential. His works shaped how many people viewed the world, popularized illustrated publications, and expanded the field for others. His story needed telling, and I wanted to tell it.

Since 2008 I have had the pleasure of being in touch with several other Fenn descendants who have also shared their artworks and knowledge with me. I am most grateful for their help and interest in their ancestor's life and work.

Many others have provided invaluable assistance on this decades-long journey: Marjorie Balge-Crozier encouraged me to study *Picturesque America* thirty years ago and read and commented on an early version of the manuscript for this book; Richard Crozier, an accomplished painter and champion of his artistic forbears, offered advice and cheered me on; and Georgia Barnhill, curator of graphic arts emerita, American Antiquarian Society, read the manuscripts and provided helpful suggestions on both projects. I am grateful to Helena Wright, curator of graphic arts at the National Museum of American History, for research leads and suggestions, especially on the role of photography in this period; and Stephen P. Rice, professor of American studies, Ramapo College of New Jersey, for his tough and insightful critiques. Anne Chestnut has been my guide through the mysteries of digital technology for many years. Daniel Bluestone helped with genealogical research and sections related to architecture. Raymond and Jane Gill contributed in many ways, especially by finding Fenn's grave in Evergreens Cemetery. Jonathan Flaccus shared my interest in Fenn and located many of his works, both drawings and prints. An anonymous reader solicited by the University of Massachusetts Press offered valuable suggestions that guided my revisions, and the press's staff has been most helpful. Thanks also to Robin Karson, Mike McCue, Bill Brandt, W. Dale and Rose Marie Horst, Paul Worman, and Alexander W. Katlan for information, suggestions, and encouragement.

Fenn's known works and few extant letters are scattered in various museums, libraries, and private collections. I am grateful to the individuals and institutions that have granted permission for these works to be reproduced and to the librarians and curators who have provided assistance over the years, especially my friends in the Albert and Shirley Small Special Collections Library at the University of Virginia; the Montclair Art Museum; the Prints and Photographs Division of the Library of Congress; the Archives of the American Watercolor Society; the Salmagundi Club; Cooper-Hewitt, National Design Museum; and the Montclair Public Library.

I am very grateful to the College Art Association for the generous support of a Wyeth Foundation for American Art Publication Grant, which provided funds for the illustrations.

In the chapters that follow, I present what I have been able to discover about Harry Fenn's remarkable career, with an emphasis on how his works in illustrated periodicals and books contributed to American culture. I fully expect that this renewed attention will lead to more discoveries about his life and work.

Sue Rainey

Creating a World on Paper

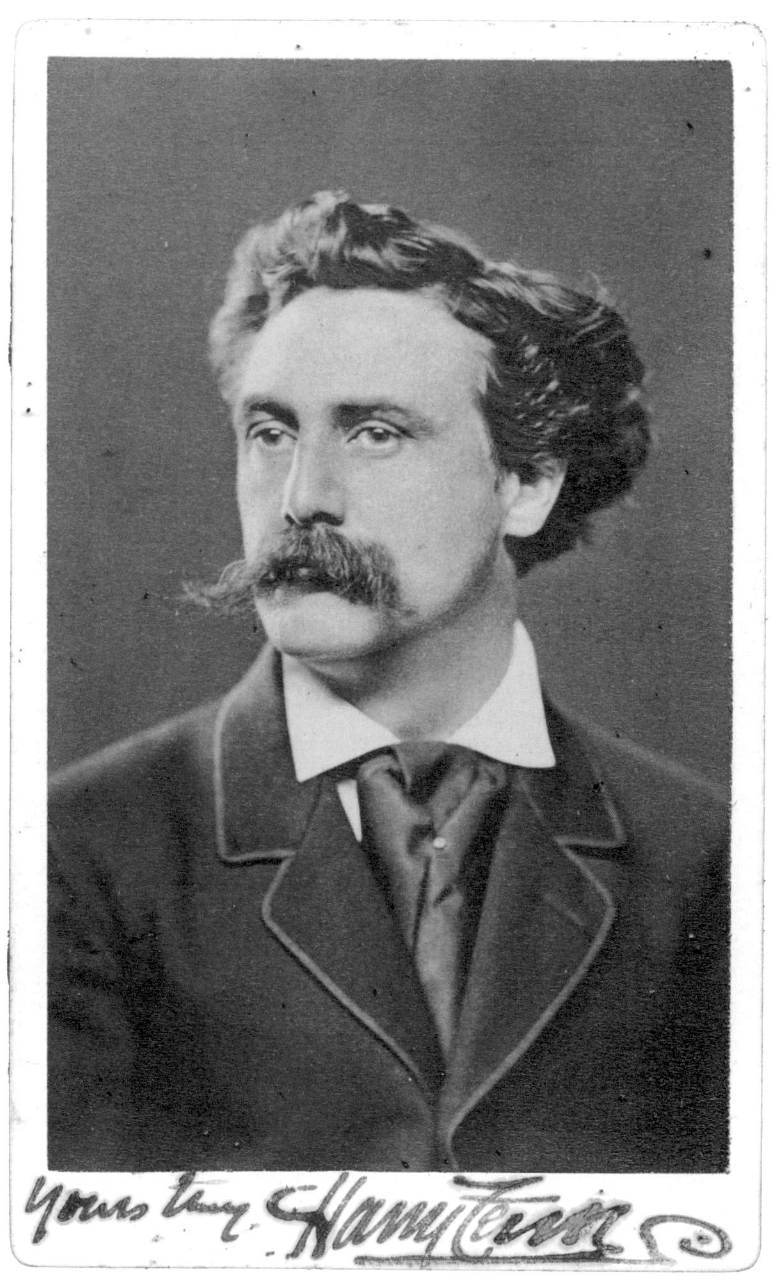

Harry Fenn's carte de visite, signed, ca. 1863. Photo by L Suscipj, Rome.
(Courtesy of Paul Worman Fine Art, New York.)

I

Early Life in England and New York

H ARRY FENN WAS A CONSPICUOUS presence in the world of American art in the latter half of the nineteenth century. In this period before photographs could be printed on the same page as type, a wide public looked to him and his colleagues for depictions of scenery, cities, and social and political life reproduced in periodicals and books. Fenn's dynamic and appealing compositions set a high standard. They built pride in America's scenic landscapes and urban centers, informed a curious public about foreign lands, and fostered an appreciation of printed pictures as artworks accessible to a growing middle class.

In 1875 the power of Fenn's pictures was clear to the younger artist James Henry Moser. He and another aspiring art student in Ohio pored over Fenn's images of Virginia's Natural Bridge in the book *Picturesque America* (fig. 1.1). Twenty-five years later Moser recalled how they "lingered night after night . . . over Fenn's exquisite and truthful drawings" of the famous geologic wonder. They even copied one such image "with Chinese fidelity" until they "knew the drawing and the text by heart." Resolving to see the bridge for themselves, they took a train to Lynchburg and then walked the fifty-eight miles to its base. Moser credited that monumental publication, which contained more than nine hundred images of the scenery and cities of the United States, many created by Fenn, with generating "the enthusiastic interest the youth of that time took in this country of ours and landscape art."[1] In 1879 the prominent art critic S. G. W. Benjamin assessed Fenn's impact similarly: "Under the guidance of his facile pencil how many have been instructed in art, and learned of the varied loveliness of this beautiful world!"[2]

These assessments of the influence of both *Picturesque America* and Harry Fenn are not overblown. The highly successful two-volume work, published in

THE NATURAL BRIDGE, VIRGINIA.

WITH ILLUSTRATIONS BY HARRY FENN.

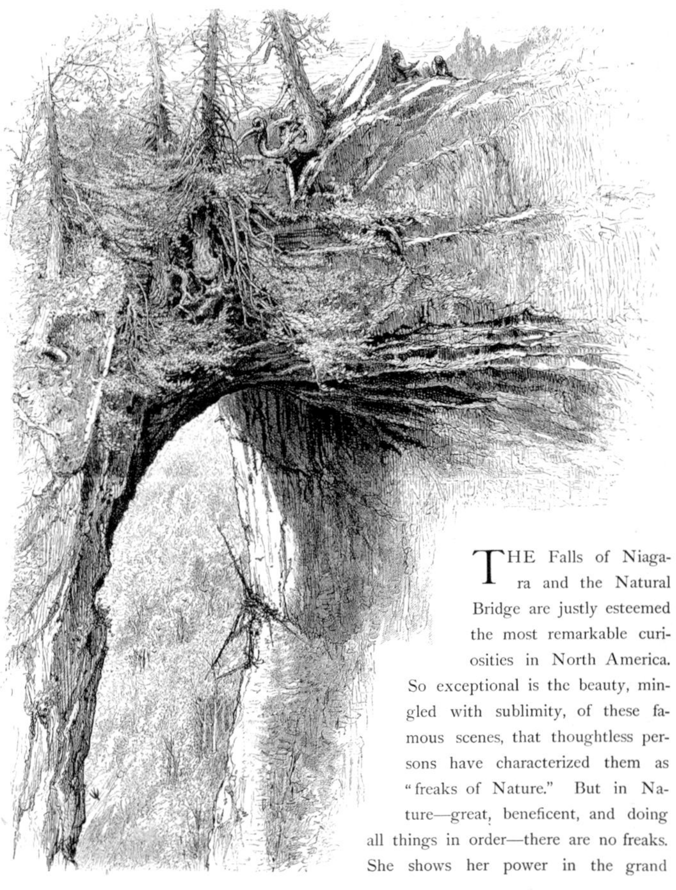

THE Falls of Niaga-
ra and the Natural
Bridge are justly esteemed
the most remarkable curi-
osities in North America.
So exceptional is the beauty, mingled with sublimity, of these famous scenes, that thoughtless persons have characterized them as
"freaks of Nature." But in Nature—great, beneficent, and doing
all things in order—there are no freaks.
She shows her power in the grand

1872–74 by New York's D. Appleton and Company, presented the most comprehensive portrayal of the American landscape to date, and Fenn was its primary and
most prolific contributor. His skillful, dynamic renderings of landscapes, plants,
and architecture contributed much to shaping popular images of this country and,
eventually, of many other parts of the world as well. In a period when printed pictures increasingly affected public opinion, his art exerted an influence that lasted
for at least a quarter century—from 1867, when a gift edition of John Greenleaf

Early Life in England and New York

Whittier's *Snow-Bound* featuring Fenn's illustrations appeared to wide acclaim, through the early 1890s, when almost every issue of the most prestigious illustrated magazine, the *Century,* contained reproductions of his work. The appeal of his early, well-delineated drawings led to assignments in locations throughout much of the United States, Europe, and the Middle East. His successes built upon one another until he became one of the first artists publishers thought of when they needed pictures of American or European landscapes or of ancient sites in Egypt or the Islamic world. In addition, his skill at rendering both architecture and plants of all sorts established him as a leading illustrator in those realms. A comment by the Romantic poet James Russell Lowell testifies to this perception: when mourning the loss to the axe of his favorite willow trees—the inspiration for "Under the Willows"—Lowell found himself wishing that Fenn "had sketched them at least."[3]

As the number of printed images increased exponentially, Fenn was positioned to reach a national market through magazines, newspapers, and books, helping to construct the "shared reality of information and desire" that was a hallmark of the emerging mass culture.[4] In a period of rapid economic expansion and cultural aspirations focusing on improved education and greater cosmopolitanism, Fenn flourished. His work for *Picturesque America* and the two highly successful Appleton publications that followed, *Picturesque Europe* (1875–79) and *Picturesque Palestine, Sinai and Egypt* (1881–83), was widely seen as playing a significant role in promoting public education and advancing culture. The prominent clergyman and editor Lyman Abbott credited their publisher with serving the community by developing "a genuine taste for pure, true art" while banishing "from the home the rude and coarse engravings and the tawdry chromos which in times past have so often furnished the sole art treasure of the American household." Furthermore, the illustrations in these books would teach "young and old" to love nature as well as art, for the true artist is a "seer" who introduces and reveals the natural world to others. They would also "teach not merely the student and the reader, but even the careless glancer at pictures, something respecting his own land and other lands. They broaden his horizons. They render more catholic his spirit, and more cosmopolitan his mind. No household can have such works as these lying on its center-table and have its children grow up wholly provincial."[5]

Fenn's colleagues also appreciated his key role within the world of American illustration. In 1892, when Fenn was fifty-five years old, the writer and artist F. Hopkinson Smith, speaking through the persona of "the Doctor" in his book *American Illustrators,* called Fenn "the Nestor of his guild"—the wise old warrior and statesman who guided those who followed. He based his high opinion on not only the quality of the *Picturesque America* imagery but also the book's "enormous financial success." As "the first illustrated publication on so large a scale ever attempted," it demonstrated "the commercial value of pictures" and "paved the way" for later illustrated works. According to Smith, soon "there were not enough artists to go around." If Fenn's efforts had instead been "a dead failure," some "distinguished illustrators" of his day might have been "measuring tape at Macy's."[6]

Although later generations of prominent illustrators most frequently prepared images for literary texts, depicting the characters in fiction and poetry, in Fenn's day—before photographs largely replaced artists' renderings of scenery and cities—illustration encompassed all types of pictures. Furthermore, as the primary means of delivering pictures to the public, illustration played an important role in the fine arts. In 1891, the art editor W. Lewis Fraser advised students that it "presented the most promising field" for careers in art.[7]

The field that Fenn helped expand remained the one he confidently and enthusiastically occupied until the end of his life; indeed, five of his illustrations appeared in the *Century* in April 1911, the month he died. In addition, he regularly painted and exhibited watercolors and participated in artists' associations. Yet, unlike some other painters who chafed at the need to earn a living by illustrating, Fenn apparently found the process of preparing images for books and periodicals to be fulfilling. In the mid- to late nineteenth century, the art world was less hierarchical than it would later become, although painting in oils always garnered the highest prestige. Especially in the 1870s and 1880s, many artists experimented with a variety of media for both illustrations and exhibition artworks, including watercolor, ink, etching, and pastel. Fenn's progression from wood engraving to drawing for illustration and painting in watercolors evidently resulted in a satisfying sense of achievement. By contrast, an artist obligated to turn from painting to illustrating to pay the bills, as happened to Fenn's colleague John Douglas Woodward, was less happy with the change.

Working as an illustrator was especially challenging in this period of fast-changing technology, a time not unlike today. As various new media replaced wood engraving, Fenn continually mastered the skills required to adapt to the latest reproduction processes. He was also flexible enough to try new fashions in technique and composition. This creative adaptability allowed him to flourish during an unusually long and prolific career and to produce images that have come to be iconic, such as his views of Natural Bridge and St. Augustine, Florida. Furthermore, his work set a standard for landscape, architecture, and nature imagery that was unable to be matched by the early attempts to reproduce photographs using the halftone process.

Early Life in England and New York

By focusing on Fenn's works—of which there were at least a thousand reproduced in widely distributed periodicals and books—and giving attention to his currently known exhibition watercolors, in this book I reconstruct the history of how and why he was valued in his own time. I also endeavor to explain why he is now being rediscovered after a century of neglect. Despite the nearly ubiquitous presence of his illustrations in the latter half of the nineteenth century, Fenn was largely forgotten in the decades after his death, when illustration came to be thought of as commercial art rather than fine art. The entire realm of printed pictures was largely overlooked during much of the twentieth century, when most art historians focused on oil painters, especially those with avant-garde approaches.[8] Fenn created few oil paintings, most likely because commissions for illustration occupied his time, and, when he chose to paint, he preferred watercolor for its speed and portability.[9] His many appealing watercolors are either scattered in public and private collections or unlocated. Although several of his works have appeared in exhibitions, no show has focused primarily on his output.[10] Only since the 1970s, as scholars have sought to understand how people in earlier periods viewed themselves and to explore the historical and cultural significance as well as the artistic merit of printed images, has Fenn's work received attention.[11] Here I explore and reassess his life and artistic career to enhance our understanding of the role of printed images in the emerging national consumer culture. I also seek to highlight the juggling act often required of artists to survive and, indeed, thrive, as Fenn was able to do. His story and his contributions will also illuminate the concerns and interests of the American public in this period when the United States first rose to political prominence and economic leadership.

Early Life in England

The man whose images would become familiar to so many Americans was English by birth. He was born Henry Fenn on September 14, 1837, in Richmond, Surrey, on the banks of the Thames southwest of London. At the time, Richmond was a small town with several historic estates, but it became increasingly linked to the capital after the arrival of the railroad in 1846.[12] Harry, as he was called, was the son of James Fenn, a grocer and tea dealer, and Eliza Biggs Fenn, who died in May 1838, before his first birthday. He had two brothers: James, who was five years older, and William, two years older, who died at the age of four.[13] His father's sister Ann lived with the family as housekeeper and no doubt also served as surrogate mother.

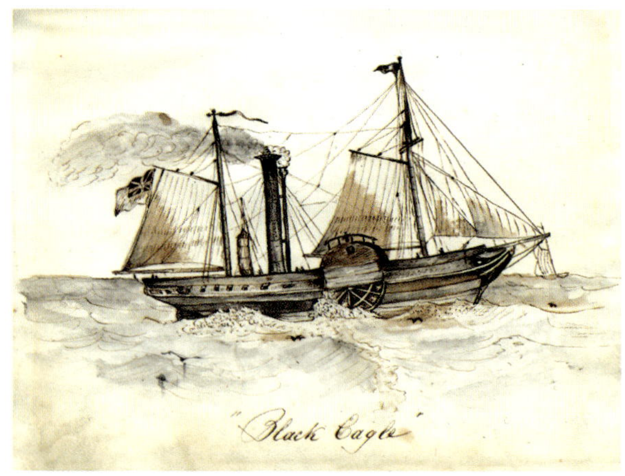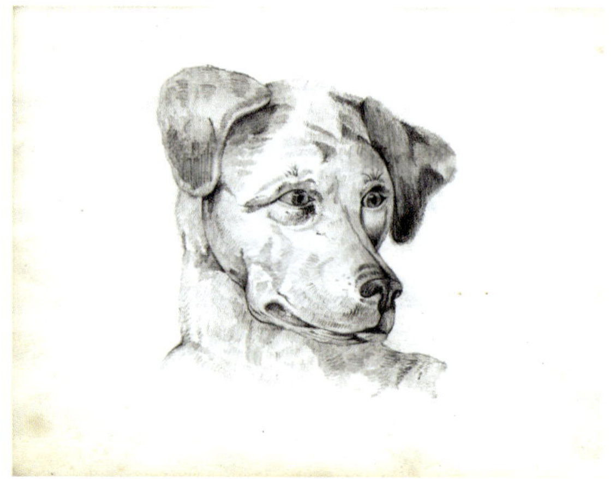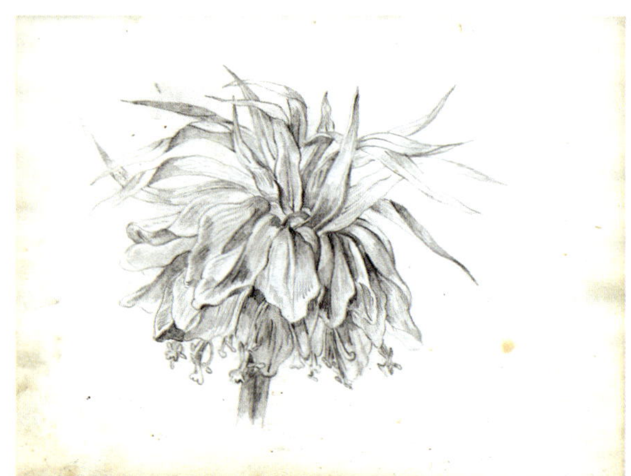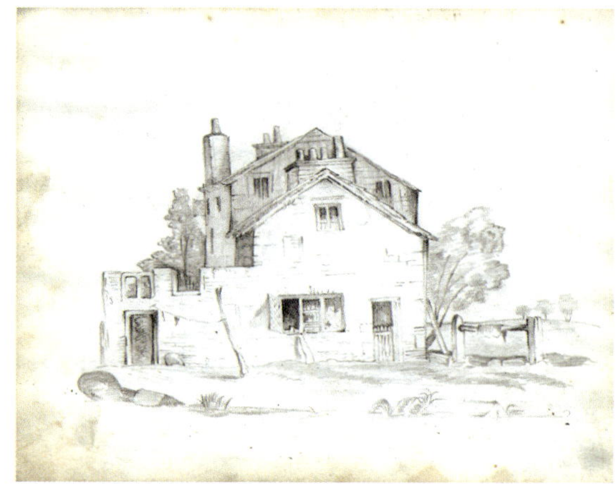

1.2 Harry Fenn, drawings from childhood sketchbook. (Courtesy of William V. Abt.)

Young Harry's schooling was likely in Richmond and Isleworth, the neighboring town to the west. He showed an early aptitude for art and had lessons from a local teacher.[14] A sketchbook of his drawings dated 1845 indicates that by eight or ten years old he had developed impressive skill at copying prints and drawing animals, plants, people, boats, and buildings (fig. 1.2).[15]

Source material on Fenn's early years is scarce. However, in 1910, near the end of his life, he related an experience from his youth that proved to be a turning point. In "The Boy and the Bishop," an article he wrote for the children's magazine *St. Nicholas* (fig. 1.3),[16] Fenn describes how, as a twelve-year-old boy, he attempted to paint one of the ancient oaks in Richmond Park, the former royal hunting ground near his home and likely a favorite retreat. Even at this young age, he was already engaged in depicting a particular species, the approach promoted by John Ruskin

Early Life in England and New York

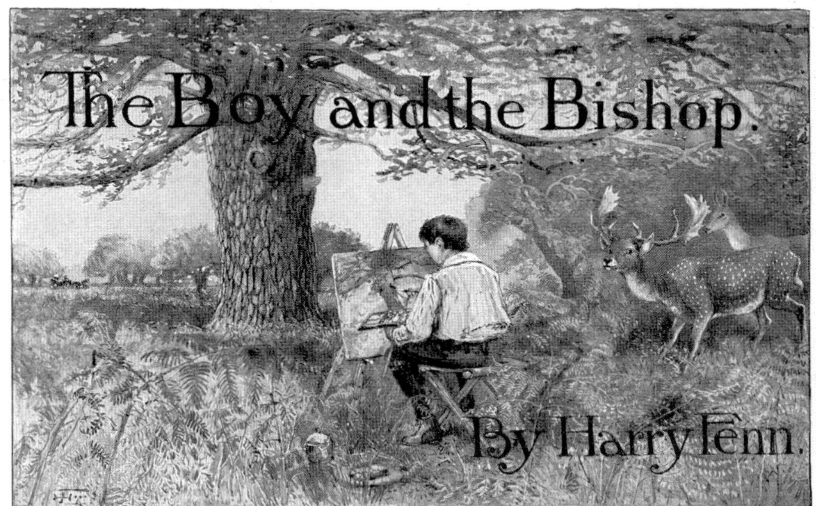

1.3. Harry Fenn, title illustration for "The Boy and the Bishop." *St. Nicholas,* June 1910, 705. Halftone, 3 9/16" x 5 3/4".

THIS is not a chronicle of an infant phenomenon, but just a true story of a bishop, and a boy whose life was largely molded by the following incident.

The oaks of England have always been celebrated, and I know of no finer sight than an ancient grove still in its prime, growing in a sunny glade of Richmond Park. One characteristic of this forest, and I can recall a score of them, is that each individual tree seems to have had a chance. It has all the room it wants to spread sidewise, stretches its great arms wide, its feet strike deep into the rich loam, and its proud head rises toward the sky, without let or hindrance, so that each is perfect in form, after its kind.

With youthful presumption and vanity (for I was just twelve, I remember), I had been wrestling with one of these monarchs of the forest, among the most difficult objects in nature to portray. I find with all my years of practise, the foreshortening of the branch of a tree often brings me up standing, but nothing daunts youthful impudence. My tools were a home-made easel, the cheapest kind of color-box to be bought in the toy-shop of a small English town, and brushes of the limpest. I had been engaged in this important work of art for three half-holidays (Wednesday and Saturday afternoon school did not then "keep" in England). I had been try-

ing to get every detail of trunk, bark, leaf, and branch. Bad as it all probably was, the careful study that I made of that oak-tree helped me my life through.

And, by the way, there is among the studies sold for the art schools of England, the reproduction of a pencil-drawing of a lemon tree, made in Sicily by Sir Frederick Leighton. It was the work of many days. In his lectures at South Kensington to young art students (where the original drawing is), he used to tell how many hours he spent upon it. Truly, it is a wonderful study. Every foreshortened branch and leaf, the markings and blemishes of the same, a perfect representation of a lemon tree. I heard him say in one of his talks: "I suppose many of you students in this day of impression look upon this elaborate drawing as a waste of time. I, on the contrary, think it time well spent, for when finished I felt sure I knew something, I may say, all, about a lemon tree, which has proved of life-long value to me in my finished pictures."

I recall this talk of Sir Frederick Leighton's to encourage the numerous young artists whose work I see from time to time in ST. NICHOLAS, enforcing careful conscientious drawing from nature to acquire skill in rendering; appreciation of good form and color; and to gather material for design. To compare small things with great, this careful study when I was a boy, brought

(1819–1900) as the way to artistic truth.[17] For three afternoons, he "had been trying to get every detail of trunk, bark, leaf, and branch," noting the kind of careful study that brought a "knowledge and love of the oak-tree" that "never deserted" him. His "tools were a home-made easel, the cheapest kind of color-box to be bought in the toy-shop of a small English town, and brushes of the limpest," and his company was only the "tame fallow-deer of the park." But late on the third day a "gorgeous carriage" pulled up and a gentleman and lady approached to see his work. After asking his name and age and where he lived, they went on their way. A few days later a package addressed to him arrived at the Fenn home. Inside were "a real grown-up artist's color-box, a half dozen silver-mounted brushes, and under the brushes a card inscribed 'With the best wishes of George Augustus Selwyn, Bishop of New Zealand.' Up to that day my education had all pointed to the life of a merchant, but the bishop was my destiny. . . . What he gave me was to him only a color-box. To me it was a heaven-sent sign, a symbol of sacred interest in my welfare. In my home I was only a little chap who liked to amuse himself with paints. After the bishop laid his hands upon me I felt myself dedicated to the work of transcribing the beauties of the world."[18]

Young Harry's timing for settling on such a vocation could not have been better. England's economy was flourishing, as symbolized by the 1851 Great Exhibition of the Works of Industry of All Nations, also known as the Crystal Palace Exhibition, in Hyde Park, and its continuation in 1854 in an even larger glass structure at Sydenham, south of London.[19] The period was also a propitious one for landscape artists. The Romantic poets, especially William Wordsworth, had popularized the notion that nature was a great teacher of moral and religious truths. The long-time hierarchy that ranked landscape painting below history painting and portraiture was changing, and more and more artists were heeding Ruskin's call to study and depict all aspects of the natural world—to particularize rather than generalize, as Sir Joshua Reynolds had prescribed. There was widespread interest in natural history—botany, geology, and meteorology—and collecting plant specimens, rocks, and fossils were popular pastimes. Fascination with travel in search of scenic views and places with historic associations was also strong, And artists such as J. M. W. Turner (1775–1851), Samuel Prout (1783–1852), David Cox (1783–1859), Copley Fielding (1787–1855), Clarkson Stanfield (1793–1867), and David Roberts (1796–1864) were exhibiting oil paintings as well as large watercolors of landscapes and cities of the British Isles, Europe, and beyond.

Since the watercolor medium had long been considered most appropriate for amateurs and primarily for coloring prints, its use for exhibition artworks was a new approach, one that would gain acceptance more slowly in the United States than in Britain. It did attract increasing numbers of professional practitioners after the development of improved papers and pigments. In addition to using translucent washes, Turner and other artists pioneered the use of opaque paints made by mixing watercolors and zinc oxide, or "Chinese white," with the Chinese white also applied for highlights.[20] By the time young Harry decided to become a painter, such

Early Life in England and New York

watercolors had gained favor with the British public and were exhibited frequently. Volumes illustrated with topographical views provided artists with another avenue for showing their work, and many of these same artists contributed to them. As publishers found a ready market for moderately priced books illustrated with intaglio engravings on steel, they began producing them in ever-growing numbers.

A thriving market also existed for books and periodicals illustrated with less-expensive wood engravings.[21] When the *Illustrated London News,* the first weekly newspaper to include numerous pictures, began publication in 1842, its front-page "Address" attributed great importance to this "illustrative art's" new uses: "To the wonderful march of periodical literature it has given an impetus and rapidity almost coequal with the gigantic power of steam. It has converted blocks into wisdom, and given wings and spirit to ponderous and senseless wood."[22] The demand for wood engravers grew when the Crystal Palace Exhibition and conflicts in Britain's empire such as the Crimean War spurred the *Illustrated London News* to feature more and larger illustrations.[23]

Although Harry wanted to transcribe "the beauties of the world," his business-minded father, apparently fearing that a career as a painter would be too risky, apprenticed him to one of London's leading wood engraving firms, Dalziel Brothers. Located on High Street in Camden Town, northwest of London, the firm was growing in step with the popularity of books illustrated with wood engravings. An apprenticeship there offered Harry, the son of a tradesman, access to a respected career related to the world of art that would likely provide steady and reasonably lucrative employment, despite his lack of a formal higher education.

The art of wood engraving had been revived in the late eighteenth century by Thomas Bewick (1753–1828) of Newcastle upon Tyne. Bewick's use of engraver's tools on the end grain of boxwood blocks, rather than the cross grain of planks of softer woods, yielded appealing images with fine detail and varied textures, primarily small vignettes of animals, birds, and rural life (fig. 1.4).[24] The process offered financial savings as well: printing from relief woodblocks—or, by the mid-nineteenth century, from electrotypes of the blocks—on the same press as letterpress type cost much less than printing from engraved metal plates or lithographic stones on heavier paper run through special plate presses. This new approach elevated the status of woodblock prints, formerly used for the cheapest, most ephemeral publications, and made them appropriate for good-quality books. It also fostered a change toward more integrated book design: whereas metal engravings were typically printed on separate sheets interleaved with the text, often requiring the reader to turn the book to view a horizontal image, wood engravings could be printed on the same page as the text.[25]

placed on a tree of a moft enormous fize, in the park, (after-
wards called the Hart-horn tree) accompanied with this infcrip-
tion :—

       " Hercules kill'd Hart o'Greece ;
       " And Hart o'Gre... ....'d Hercules."

   " The horns have been fince removed ; and are now at Julian's Bower, in the fame county."

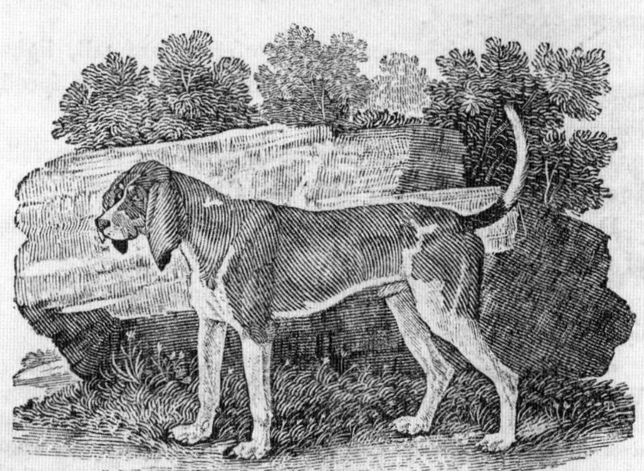

THE OLD ENGLISH HOUND

is defcribed by Whitaker, in his Hiftory of Manchefter,
as the original breed of this ifland, ufed by the ancient
Britons in the chafe of the larger kinds of game, with
which their country abounded.

    This valuable Hound is diftinguifhed by its great fize
and ftrength. Its body is long, its cheft deep, its ears
long and fweeping, and the tone of its voice is peculiarly
deep and mellow.—From the particular formation of its

Bewick had many apprentices, most of whom found their way to London.[26] One
of his favorite pupils, William Harvey (1796–1866), often worked with the Dalziels as a designer, and since he too lived in Richmond, he could have been a link
between the Fenn family and the Dalziels.[27] The principals of the firm, George and
Edward Dalziel (and, later, John and Thomas), served as art editors for several publishing companies and sometimes acted as publisher themselves. Their output had

increased exponentially over the years: in 1849 they produced 228 wood engravings; by 1851, the year of the Crystal Palace Exhibition, the number had risen to 1,621.[28] They commissioned designs from such artists as Harvey, Myles Birket Foster (1825– 1899), John Gilbert (1817–1897), John Tenniel (1820–1914), and, somewhat later, John Everett Millais (1829–1896), George John Pinwell (1842–1875), and Frederick Walker (1840–1875), among others. Departing from Bewick's so-called white-line technique, in which forms were distinguished by lines cut into the woodblock, the London artists, some of whom had trained as copper engravers, primarily used the black-line approach, in which a combination of lines and shading defined the sub-jects.[29] The designs were transferred in reverse to a woodblock, and the Dalziels' staff of skilled engravers cut away the white areas, leaving the lines and dark areas to receive the ink.[30] It was time-consuming, meticulous labor; the engraver typically worked under a magnifying glass, with the woodblock resting on a sandbag for easy maneuverability and a globe of water concentrating the light from a lamp. A set of tools could include perhaps six lozenge-shaped gravers or burins to cut lines of varying width; twelve tint tools for cutting parallel lines to indicate skies, water, or landscape features and textures; and several scoopers and chisels for removing the wood not drawn upon. When the engraving was completed, an electrotyped plate of the block was made for use in printing. These metal plates allowed minute lines to stand up to much longer press runs than the relatively fragile woodblocks, thus facilitating economies of scale.[31]

The Dalziel brothers began taking apprentices, or "pupils," in 1844. After the day's nine hours of engraving work, they offered them instruction in drawing, including perspective and anatomy from plaster casts. The Dalziels later recalled that "among those who availed themselves of these advantages were Harry Fenn and Charles Kingdon," two of their "earliest and very cleverest pupils."[32] The date Fenn joined the Dalziels is unknown, but it was probably in the early 1850s, at age fourteen or fifteen, soon after the Crystal Palace Exhibition. The apprentices' formal instruction would have been supplemented and enhanced by contact with the artists who created designs for the firm. In Fenn's case, an artist of special inter-est was surely the successful landscape painter and illustrator Myles Birket Foster, who was "a constant visitor" at the office and, as a youth, had also been a wood engraver's apprentice.[33] Even if Fenn did not rub shoulders with Foster, he saw his work, both on the woodblock and in print, and probably sought to emulate it.[34] Late in life, Fenn recalled that he "engraved many" of Foster's woodblocks and that Foster's method was to draw with "India ink or lamp black" upon the pre-pared whitened surface of the block and, when it was dry, to define the forms with lead pencil and accent the highlights with Chinese white. Fenn admired Foster's "wonderful penciling in the finish, full of detail but as free as a good etching" and found it "next to impossible to reproduce their delicate values with the graver."[35] As an illustrator, Fenn would use a similar approach when transferring designs onto the woodblock, and his early illustrations are frequently reminiscent of Foster's. The two artists were sometimes spoken of in the same breath after Fenn became a prominent illustrator.

Since the firm's practice was to sign all blocks simply "Dalziel," rather than with the specific engraver's name, we cannot identify Fenn's work. He might have engraved some of Foster's illustrations for the 1855 book *The Poetical Works of William Cowper* or *The Poets of the Nineteenth Century* of 1857, both edited by the Reverend Robert Aris Willmott and published by George Routledge and Company. The latter volume was larger and much more elaborate than the earlier one, and its illustrations were printed on the same pages as the text rather than separately. Foster supplied most of the landscapes, while William Harvey, John Gilbert, John Tenniel, John Everett Millais, and others provided the figures. Foster's designs in both books typically featured an oval vignette format with framing trees; less often he chose a vertical format arched at the top (fig. 1.5). Fenn would choose these same shapes for many of his early illustrations and later contributed to similar publications when American publishers began to issue elaborate gift books of poetry in the 1860s and 1870s.

During his years of apprenticeship, Fenn likely became familiar with earlier illustrated books that were greatly admired at the time, and some may have nourished his later work. These include editions of poetry by Samuel Rogers, Sir Walter Scott, and John Milton that were illustrated with vignettes after landscapes by the eminent painter J. M. W. Turner. Although the images in these books were steel engravings, they appeared on the page with lines of type.[36] Another source of inspiration may have been an 1848 edition of *Aesop's Fables* (published by J. Murray) in which John Tenniel's wood-engraved illustrations were harmoniously integrated with the text.[37]

As a favorite young apprentice and wood engraver in a high-profile and respected firm, Fenn must have developed a belief in his abilities and in the prospect of a successful career in illustration. Selling some of his own watercolors bolstered this confidence.[38] Yet, in 1857, when he was nineteen years old, he was still not ready to settle into a life with the company or, indeed, in London. He wanted to travel and experience new places—more of "the beauties of the world." When peace returned to England after the Crimean War, he decided to set out. The Dalziels recalled that

Early Life in England and New York

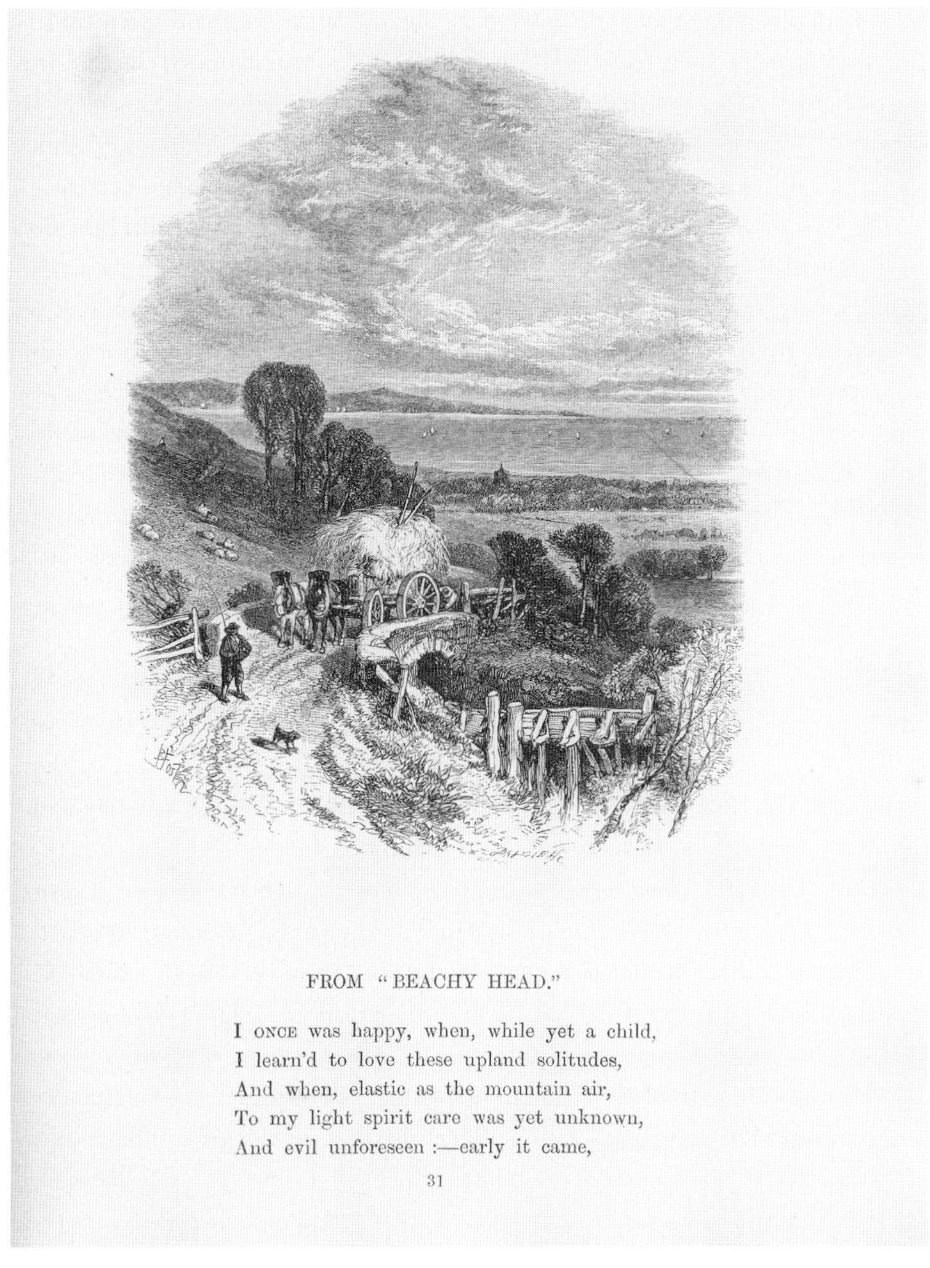

1.5. Birket Foster, illustration for "From 'Beachy Head,'" by Charlotte Smith. From Robert Aris Willmott, ed., *The Poets of the Nineteenth Century* (London: George Routledge, 1857), 31. Wood engraving by Dalziel, ca. 5" x 3 5/8". (Special Collections, University of Virginia Library.)

he and fellow apprentice Charles Kingdon "took ship to Canada, having determined to visit the principal cities there and in the United States."[39] Other reports mention that Fenn especially wanted to see Niagara Falls, then considered North America's most sublime scenic wonder: "When about nineteen he took his little box of sovereigns, and spread the contents in a row on his father's desk. He then surprised that gentleman by a request that he should make the row just as long again, in order that the aspiring artist could go to see Niagara."[40] The highly acclaimed London showing of Frederic Church's massive oil painting *Niagara* during the summer of 1857 may well have made his desire to see the falls irresistible. He would not see his father again, however, for James Fenn died before his son returned to England in 1862.

The two young men had a rough wintertime crossing of the Atlantic aboard a sailing vessel with only fifteen passengers; according to Fenn's son, it took more than a month instead of the usual ten days to two weeks, during which they ate mainly salt meat, hard tack, and potatoes.[41] No record exists of exactly how and when they made their way from their port of entry—probably Quebec City—to the United States, eventually settling in New York. Nevertheless, when the two artists arrived they found themselves in a place primed to put to use the skills and talents they offered. Their work experience with the well-known Dalziel firm no doubt lent a certain cachet to their resumes, and both met with enough success to lead them to stay in New York rather than return to England.

THE FIRST YEARS IN NEW YORK

At midcentury, New York was the largest city in the United States, with a population of more than half a million. It had overtaken Philadelphia and was vying with Boston as the country's leading printing and publishing center. Between 1840 and 1860, this industry was New York's fastest growing, aided by an increasing network of railroad lines that facilitated nationwide distribution of periodicals and books.[42] Public education was creating a demand for more reading material. Technological advances had reduced printing costs, especially faster, steam-driven rotary presses and machines for converting wood pulp into long rolls of paper, a cheaper alternative to paper made from rags. Cloth bindings also lowered the price of books.

Meanwhile, the early venture capitalists of publishing were gradually transforming their industry from small local firms to large companies equipped with their own printing plants capable of catering to a national market.[43] Most prominent among these was Harper & Brothers, which by 1855 occupied two large fireproof buildings in lower Manhattan, one on Cliff Street and the other facing Franklin Square, known as Printing House Square because the major newspapers were produced there. The firm had launched *Harper's New Monthly Magazine* in 1850, motivated in part by the desire to promote their books. When the magazine's wood-engraved illustrations proved to be a key attraction, the publishers included more

Early Life in England and New York

such imagery. The success of *Harper's Monthly* would in turn inspire other firms to launch illustrated periodicals, especially in the later 1860s, after the Civil War, thus increasing demand for illustrators and wood engravers.[44] In 1838 the number of engravers was estimated at only twenty; by 1870 there were about four hundred.[45]

Several publishers (Harper & Brothers among them) also produced illustrated editions of some of America's best-selling fiction, including an 1853 printing of *Uncle Tom's Cabin* with images by Hammatt Billings, published by John P. Jewett, and the works of James Fenimore Cooper illustrated by Felix Octavius C. Darley, printed by W. A. Townsend and other firms. Whereas earlier American wood engravers—such as Alexander Anderson, who introduced Thomas Bewick's white-line method to the United States, and his pupil Abel Bowen—had typically engraved their own designs, by the 1850s artists such as Billings and Darley specialized in designing for the engravers.[46] One observer who clearly considered such printed pictures "art" wrote: "Few persons not in the 'world of art' have any idea of the multiplied uses of the beautiful process [of wood engraving]"—from mechanical drawing to landscape to history and fiction—"nor how cheaply any required work can be done."[47] Another telling example of the enthusiasm for pictures at this time appeared in the *Pictorial National Library:* "Pictures are often more intelligible, instructive and inviting than words. . . . They attract the child, they allure the listless and unthinking, they speak to the wise and the serious. . . .They improve the taste, instruct the eye, assist the perceptive faculties, strengthen the memory, please the fancy, and often touch the heart when words would be powerless."[48] And in 1857 the *Cosmopolitan Art Journal* observed the current "'illustration' mania" having the effect that "nothing but 'illustrated' works are profitable to publishers; while the illustrated magazine and newspapers are vastly popular."[49]

Fenn's arrival was thus extremely well timed. When he and Kingdon got to New York in 1857, demand was high not only for artists who could design illustrations but also for wood engravers. Moreover, the field was not yet overcrowded. Engravers were needed to prepare the printing blocks for two large circulation weeklies and an ever-increasing number of illustrated periodicals and books. The first highly successful national illustrated paper, *Frank Leslie's Illustrated Newspaper,* was hitting its stride, despite a rocky beginning in 1855 and the financial panic of 1857, which had led to the demise of several periodicals.[50]

Frank Leslie was the pseudonym of Henry Carter (1821–1880), an immigrant from England who had arrived in New York in 1848, as had many others fleeing Britain and Europe after the unsuccessful attempts at reform that year. Leslie had supervised the engraving department of the *Illustrated London News,* whose use of numerous pictures provided a model for his own newspaper as well as several others.[51] He first worked briefly in Boston as an engraver for *Gleason's Pictorial Drawing-Room Companion,* a sixteen-page weekly launched in 1851 that was sold by subscription for $3 a year.[52] Leslie launched the *Illustrated Newspaper* in New York from his firm's offices on Frankfort Street in lower Manhattan, near Printing House Square. Circulation was initially disappointing but, by 1857, had increased dramatically after a reduction in price from ten cents per issue to six, and from $4 to $3 a year, and the addition of coverage of sensational murders and prominent national events.[53] That same year, Harper & Brothers launched a competing illustrated newspaper, *Harper's Weekly,* whose circulation grew dramatically during the Civil War.

Fenn's first jobs in New York were as a wood engraver, and in 1857 and 1858 he did some work for *Frank Leslie's Illustrated Newspaper.*[54] Many years later the artist would recall how, in his "young days," when he "was connected with an illustrated newspaper," the staff engravers would produce a large block of some newsworthy event: "Should there occur a railway accident, a shipwreck or fire, if it was of sufficient importance, it was depicted in black and white water color upon a two page boxwood block made up of a number of small pieces bolted together. The engraving is to go to press in the early morning; the drawing is laid on its face and with hammer and cold chisel the big block is knocked into twenty pieces. Twenty men go to work on it, and work the night through—imagine the result."[55] Fenn's description explains how large images required assembling a block from many small squares, since boxwood trunks were small and yielded end-grain surfaces only about two to four inches square.[56] Leslie had no doubt learned this approach at the *Illustrated London News.* Distributing individual squares to many engravers to complete allowed *Leslie's* and *Harper's Weekly* to depict events in a timely fashion, but it is remarkable that the pictures were as effective as they are. Sometimes a thin white line reveals where blocks were joined.

Fenn also worked for the Harper firm as a wood engraver around 1860, according to an account he wrote late in life.[57] Even as a young worker there, when charged with engraving "a portrait of a newly imported Arab stallion"—at a time when interest in horse breeding and racing was keen—he was confident and flexible enough to try an approach that seemed novel and risky to his supervisor. Though the drawing on the block was deemed "beautiful," it was "useless for the purpose of engraving," since the artist, T. C. Carpendale, had painted the horse with fragile Chinese white "against a dark foliage background." According to Fenn, "the head of the department was in despair," for both men knew that the "moment a graver

Early Life in England and New York

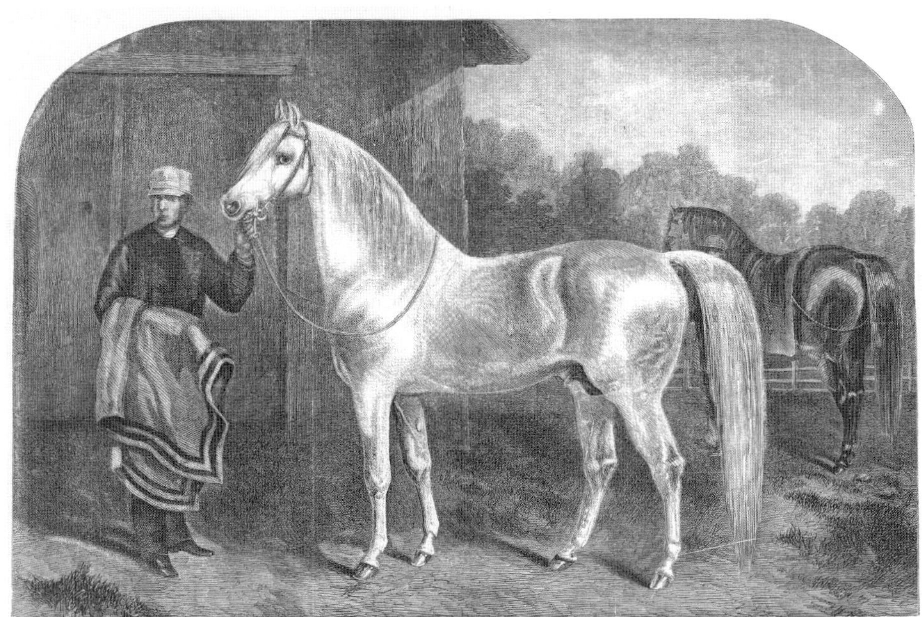

1.6. Engraved by Harry Fenn, after T. C. Carpendale, "Our Horse Show.—the Arab Horse Calif of Cairo, the Property of Judge Jones." *Harper's Weekly*, December 22, 1860, 812. Wood engraving, 9 1/8" x 13 3/4". (Special Collections, University of Virginia Library.)

entered any part of the quadruped a piece of the drawing the size of a dime would fly off."

Fenn's solution was to "make some notes and sketches of the values, etc.," and then to make "a very fine outline of the forms of the horse" on the block with "a lozenge graver." While the manager was out, he washed all the paint off the block and, after it was dry, "blacked the huge block with an ink ball, producing a field of polished ebony"; his outline of the horse showed in fine white lines. Next, he created the horse's "silvery coat" by "drawing with the graver." The full-page wood engraving that appeared in the December 22, 1860, edition of *Harper's Weekly* is almost certainly the one Fenn recalled making; it appears to bear an *H* and part of an *F* in the lower right (fig. 1.6). In creating white lines on a black background, Fenn was aware that he was using the white-line approach of Thomas Bewick, whom he called "the father of modern wood engraving."[58]

This account suggests that Fenn was a skilled and clever engraver. Certainly his knowledge of wood engraving would serve him well as he gradually realized his ambition to become a designer rather than an engraver. Other engravings by him have not been identified, but he could have engraved views of early Civil War battles based on photographs or sketches by those who had been at the scene. While working as an engraver, he probably also sought opportunities to draw on the woodblock, if only to do the mechanical work of supplying backgrounds or "laying out perspectives" on large blocks before they were divided into pieces.[59] Fenn may also have engraved for the prominent New York engraving firm of Nathaniel Orr & Company, which, beginning in 1860, prepared wood engravings to illustrate the early Beadle's Dime Novels, among many other works. Some of Fenn's earliest published artwork may have been designs for these popular adventure stories for boys, for he was hired as one of the Beadle illustrators, according to Albert Johannsen in his book on the publisher.[60]

During his early years in the United States, Fenn lived in Brooklyn, which had become a city in 1834. The town had grown dramatically after the Erie Canal increased shipping through the Port of New York and large numbers of immigrants, primarily from northern and western Europe, settled there. By 1860, with a population of 266,000, it was the nation's third largest city, after New York and Philadelphia.[61] It was also home to a lively circle of artists and illustrators who had relatively easy access via ferry to the area of lower Manhattan where printers and publishers had established their offices. Fenn sought to attract business by listing himself as "engraver" in the Brooklyn City Directories from 1859 to 1862. He gave his address as 335 Adelphi Street, a large three-story brick structure that was the home of the parents of the young woman he would marry in 1862. Most likely he was a boarder there. From 1859 through May 1861, Fenn gave only this residential address, but for June 1861 through May 1862 he added a business address, Franklin Square, the so-called Printing House Square where Harper & Brothers was also located.[62]

Fenn's first years in the United States coincided with the tumultuous controversies that, by 1861, erupted into armed conflict between the North and the South. Lacking evidence of Fenn's attitudes or experiences, we can only assume that as someone involved with newspaper illustration he was surely aware of the latest events. But, as the painter Worthington Whittredge remembered of New York during the war, "strange to say, [the war] had less effect upon art than upon many things of more stable foundations."[63] Artists' receptions continued apace, and the National Academy of Design even completed its new Venetian Gothic building on Twenty-third Street while the war raged on. Like most other artists and engravers, except for the "Special Artists," as they were called, covering the war for illustrated newspapers, Fenn likely focused on his work and personal life. He continued his study of art by attending the Graham Art School, where some of Brooklyn's artists volunteered to teach free classes.[64]

Started in 1852 in a rented room at the Brooklyn Institute on Washington Street, the school was named for Augustus Graham, an Englishman who had become

Early Life in England and New York

wealthy in the city and, in 1824, helped found the Brooklyn Apprentices Library Association, which became the Brooklyn Institute in 1843. Winter evening classes "from the Life and Antique" were held beginning in 1858.[65] Fenn may have studied with or known such wood engravers as Henry Walker Herrick (1824–1906); Benjamin F. Childs (1814–1863), who had become superintendent of engraving for the American Tract Society in 1850; and the artist and illustrator Charles Parsons (1821–1910), who was hired as art director at the Harper firm in 1863 and later became Fenn's friend and a fellow resident of Montclair, New Jersey.[66] In an 1860 report of the Brooklyn Institute, Herrick, "President of the Graham avenue School," stated that students met twice a week to "draw from the nude figure and from draped models" and that classes had "no fixed teacher, but the older members instruct the younger."[67]

Fenn, aged twenty-five in 1861, working in Manhattan as an engraver and living in and attending art classes in Brooklyn, was an attractive young man with prospects and an appealing personality. He was described as "a man of quick and artless emotions, with an eye that missed nothing, and with a spontaneous charm of manner that sorted admirably with his singularly handsome face."[68] In 1861 or '62 he married the daughter of his Brooklyn landlord.[69] Marian (Mary) Tompson was born October 20, 1842, to Elizabeth Jane (1803–1901) and William M. Tompson (1804–1890); both her parents had emigrated from England as adults.[70] Her father was an engraver on silver, and her uncle, Samuel Tompson, an engraver on steel. Mary was remembered by her son as a beautiful woman and an accomplished pianist. Her siblings were Julia, an older sister, and brothers Thomas and William Jr. The Civil War claimed William's life, but Thomas became "one of the members of a large wholesale dry goods firm of New York City" and apparently bought some of his brother-in-law's artworks.[71]

Fenn's watercolor drawing of the brink of the Horseshoe Falls, dated 1862, suggests the couple made a wedding trip to Niagara; the groom chose to depict how tourist facilities were marring the renowned site, a common complaint at the time (fig. 1.7). Soon after their marriage they sailed for England. By this time Fenn's ambition had expanded, and he was determined to abandon wood engraving for drawing and painting. Before setting sail, he took the decisive step of giving away "all his gravers, informing his fellow workers that he intended thereafter to use only pencil and brush."[72] The first of his published illustrations with an established date, titled "Breaking of the Ice at New York: A View from the East River," shows he had already acted on this intention. The full-page image appeared in the *Illustrated London News* on March 29, 1862; Fenn had either taken the sketch for it with him

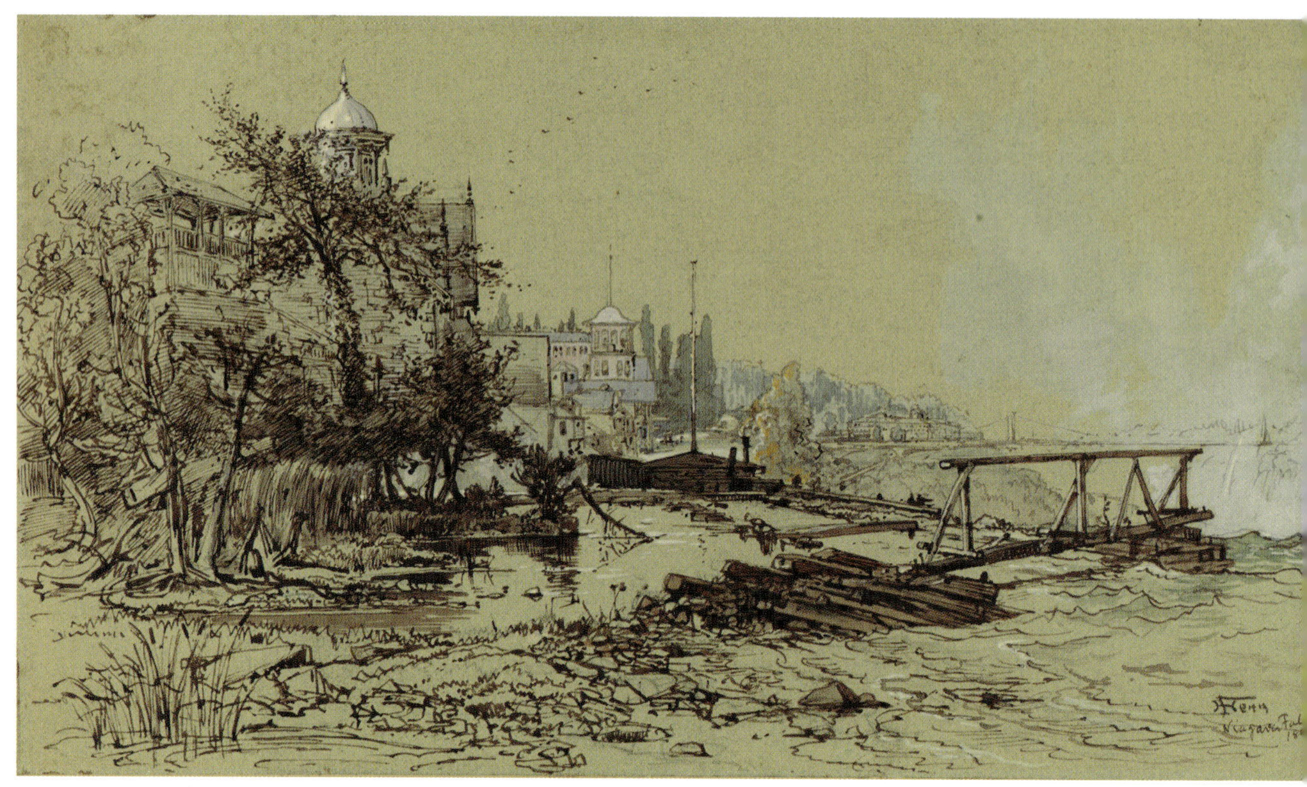

1.7. Harry Fenn, *Niagara Falls,* 1862. Watercolor, 10" x 17 3/4". (Smithsonian American Art Museum, 1967.136.9. Gift of Orrin Wickersham June.)

to England or sent it ahead. The brief accompanying text, which Fenn probably wrote, points out that this "striking scene," which "takes place annually," occurs when the ice breaks in the upper Hudson, and the ferry boats look strange "to a person new to America," appearing more like a "floating house, or even a street."[73]

The couple's first stop was to visit with Fenn's aunt Ann, who had helped raise him. Fenn's son later recalled a family story about their arrival in Richmond. Apparently, they hired a man at the station to deliver their trunks to Ann's address but never again saw him or their luggage, which contained most of their clothes and wedding presents.[74] Their first child, Alice Maude, was born in Richmond on August 20, 1862. In keeping with his new career goal, Fenn took advantage of the opportunity to study painting in Europe, considered essential training for aspiring artists; unfortunately, no details of his tour are known. The watercolors he exhibited after his return to the United States provide the only record of this period and indicate that he visited the Castle of Chillon, on Lake Geneva, as well as Florence, the Gulf of Spezia, and Rome.

Early Life in England and New York

The family returned to the United States by 1863. At first they lived in Brooklyn, presumably with Mary's family. There, on December 6 of that year, she gave birth to twin sons, Horace William, who died July 2, 1864, and Walter James, who became an illustrator and lived until 1961. In these years of establishing and expanding his family, Harry Fenn launched his career as an illustrator and watercolor painter.

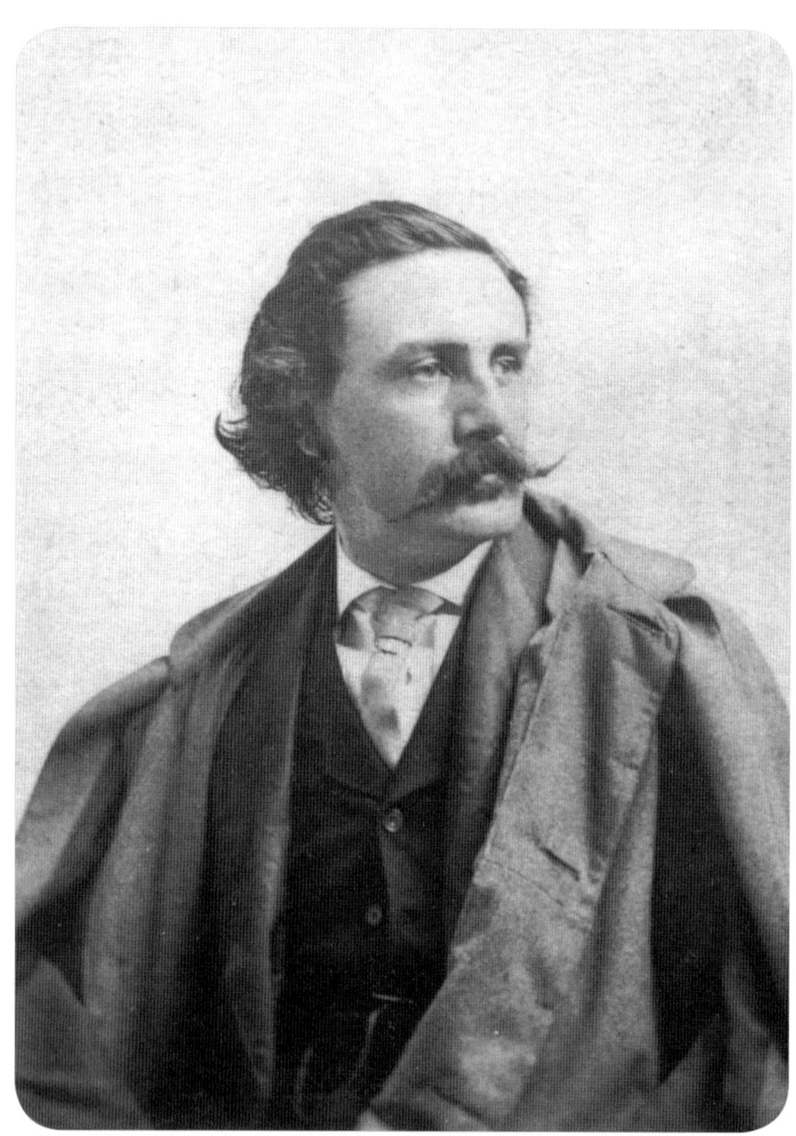

2.1. Photograph of Harry Fenn by J. Wallace Black, Boston.
(Courtesy of William V. Abt.)

Gaining Recognition as an Illustrator and Watercolor Painter

ENN WAS ABLE TO FULFILL his intention to abandon wood engraving and establish himself as a sought-after illustrator in the last years of the Civil War and the period immediately after. At this time, many Americans endeavored to find solace for their grief, honor the lost, lay animosities to rest, and focus attention on the reunited nation and its outstanding scenery, improved urban amenities, and abundant natural resources. They desired pictures of these subjects and expected to find them in periodicals and books, having grown accustomed to seeing timely images of battle scenes and other current events in the illustrated weeklies; indeed, during the war, the circulation of both *Harper's Weekly* and *Frank Leslie's Illustrated Newspaper* had soared. Many Americans newly arrived in the country's growing cities also sought images and poetry that would help them reconnect to the beauty of nature and the rural homes they had left behind.

In these years, Fenn moved along his career path, from illustrating a privately published book to working for the leading publishers of American literature. Similarly, he progressed from being one in a long list of contributing artists for several publications to serving as the sole illustrator of an important book of poetry. He also made professional contact with the poet John Greenleaf Whittier (1807–1892), the first of several famous writers he would come to know well. At the same time, in keeping with his ambition to be recognized as a painter, he began to exhibit his watercolors and, with several more prominent artists, participated in the founding of the American Society of Painters in Water Colors (later the American Watercolor Society). About 1865 he and his growing family moved across the Hudson River to Montclair, New Jersey, a town already becoming known as an artists' colony. In a house on Park Street, two more daughters were born: Florence Bessie, on July 2, 1865, and Lillian Marian, on March 1, 1867.

In 1864, soon after returning from England, Fenn received several assignments, apparently with the help of Nathaniel Orr, head of the New York engraving firm Nathaniel Orr & Company, considered by some to be the best in the United States; it was in Orr's office, at 52 John Street, that many artists and engravers congregated.[1] Fenn had done engraving and design work for Orr before his extended stay in England. Now, with Orr as intermediary, he produced several drawings and watercolors to serve as the basis for illustrations in a publication memorializing the prominent Hartford inventor and arms manufacturer Samuel Colt, whose revolving-breech pistol had been widely used in both the Mexican War and the Civil War, who had died in 1862, at age forty-six. The limited-edition tribute book, published in 1866 at great expense by Colt's widow, Elizabeth Jarvis Colt, was titled *Armsmear: The Home, the Arms, and the Armory of Samuel Colt; A Memorial* and edited by Henry Barnard.[2] For some of the images, Fenn worked from photographs, but he also visited Colt's estate; his watercolor of Armsmear's house and grounds is straightforward and full of detail (the painting is now in the collection of the Wadsworth Atheneum). At this point Fenn's style was restrained and precise, which obviously pleased Colt's widow, for she expressed her satisfaction in several letters to Orr.[3] The vignette Fenn designed for the title page is very much in the manner of Birket Foster, full of picturesque details and dramatic light effects (fig. 2.2).

Perhaps also through Orr, the American Tract Society engaged Fenn to prepare illustrations for several of its many publications for children. This large publishing concern, located at 150 Nassau Street in New York, helped supply the market for Sunday school literature that had developed in the 1830s as various Protestant denominations sought to improve religious and moral instruction.[4] In 1865 Fenn contributed three full-page illustrations, treated as plates and printed on heavier paper with blank versos, to *The Glen Cabin; or, Away to the Hills* by Caroline Cheseboro (1825–1873).[5] His vignettes depicted boys lost in a snowstorm and their family in dramatic mountain settings. For the society's December 1864 *Child's Newspaper* Fenn drew an image of the Freedmen's Village, located in Arlington Heights, Virginia, on property formerly owned by General Robert E. Lee. The image included the school, "Providence Home" for the aged and infirm, and several figures.[6]

In the mid-1860s, as the Civil War drew to a close, publishers were quick to prepare books related to the conflict, especially as seen from the Northern viewpoint.

Gaining Recognition

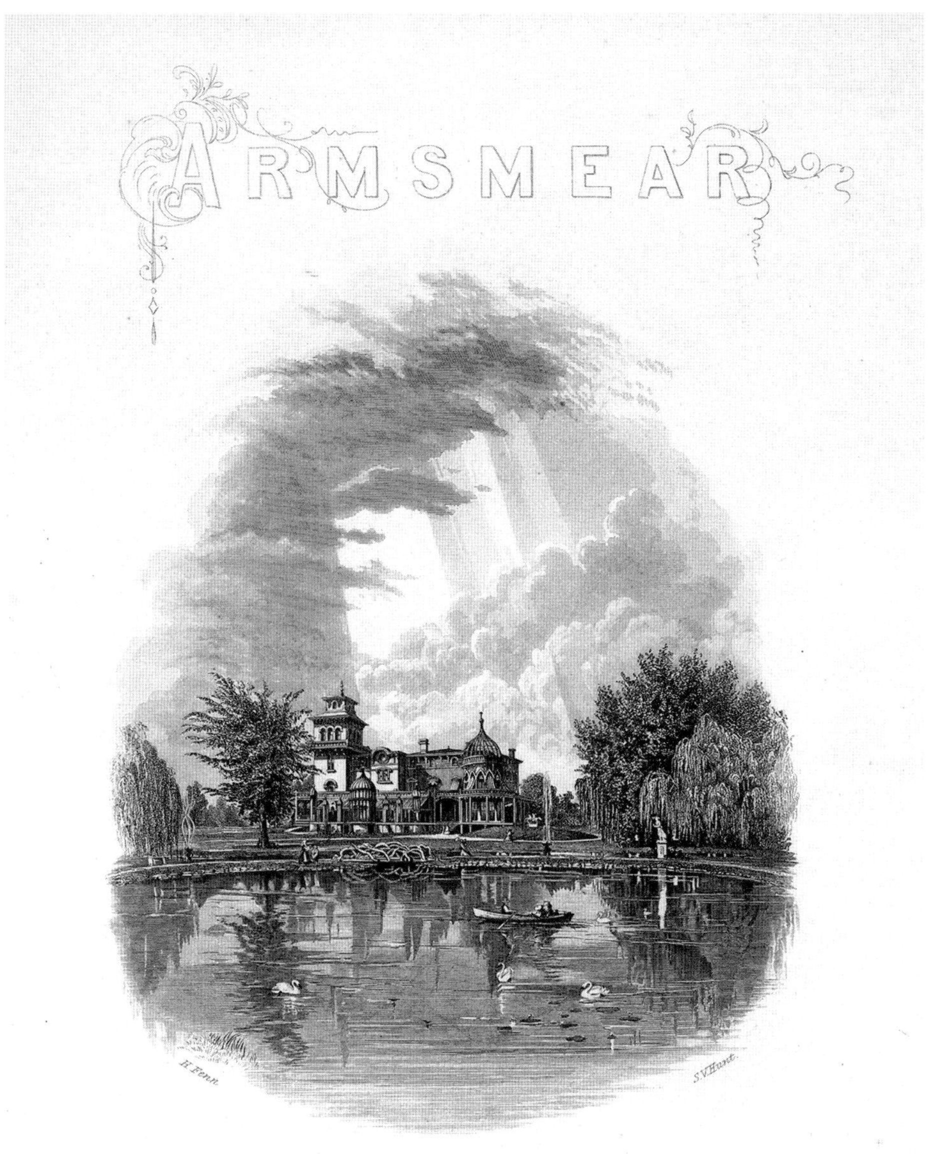

2.2. Harry Fenn, title page. From Henry Barnard, ed., *Armsmear: The Home, the Arms, and the Armory of Samuel Colt; A Memorial* (New York: [Alvord, printer], 1866). Steel engraving by S. V. Hunt, vignette approx. 5" x 3 3/4". (Special Collections, University of Virginia Library.)

Boston's Ticknor and Fields, the leading publisher of American literature in this period (including the most prestigious literary magazine, the *Atlantic Monthly*), released a selection of John Greenleaf Whittier's poems indicting slavery and celebrating emancipation and the nation's ideals. *National Lyrics* (1865) included ten illustrations, two of which Fenn signed using his monogram: an *F* overlapping an *H*. (The other illustrators were George G. White and Charles A. Barry.) For

"The Farewell of a Virginia Slave Mother to Her Daughters Sold into Southern Bondage," Fenn used a then-popular format, and one Birket Foster often used as well, of a circle broken at the bottom, in this case by tall grasses.[7] The image of a swamp included two small female figures with downcast faces standing beneath a large tree covered with Spanish moss, which illustrated the poem's refrain:

> Gone, gone—sold and gone,
> To the rice-swamp dank and lone,
> From Virginia's hills and waters,—
> Woe is me, my stolen daughters!

The image is appropriately bleak but also quite stiff and lifeless, perhaps partly the fault of the wood engraver, Charles Kingdon, with whom Fenn had traveled to the United States in 1857. Fenn's other signed work in the book illustrates "The Song of the Negro Boatman," Whittier's 1862 verse in dialect set within the longer, standard English "At Port Royal," which was inspired by the Union capture of a South Carolina port and the effort of Northern abolitionists to educate former slaves, now considered contraband. Fenn's image, showing large ships and a small rowboat crowded with dark, tiny figures, is only marginally successful. Perhaps for those familiar with the boatman's song, which had been set to music and became popular as a call for emancipation, the depiction was clear enough.[8]

A larger-scale publication related to the war was Frank B. Goodrich's *Tribute Book: A Record of the Munificence, Self-Sacrifice, and Patriotism of the American People during the War for the Union* (1865), which contained 147 illustrations. To expedite the completion of such heavily illustrated projects, publishers often asked for contributions from a long list of artists. In this case, Fenn provided drawings, as did such older, better-known illustrators as F. O. C. Darley (1822–1888), Augustus Hoppin (1828–1896), John McLenan (1827–1866?), Hammatt Billings (1818–1874), and H. W. Herrick, who was probably Fenn's teacher at the Graham Art School. Younger artists who would soon become famous, such as Thomas Nast (1840–1902), also participated. Fenn's fifteen designs, probably based on sketches or photographs and all engraved by N. Orr & Company, hold their own among those by his more established colleagues. An especially dramatic depiction is "The George Griswold, Laden with Breadstuffs," showing the vessel in stormy seas, which serves as the opening for chapter 11, "International Relief." Fenn again used a circular format, here broken by swirling waves (fig. 2.3). Orr's firm also engraved many of the illustrations for *The American Conflict: A History of the Great Rebellion in the United States of America,*

Gaining Recognition

2.3. Harry Fenn, "The George Griswold, Laden with Breadstuffs." From Frank B. Goodrich, *The Tribute Book: A Record of the Munificence, Self-Sacrifice and Patriotism of the American People during the War for the Union* (New York: Derby & Miller, 1865), 383. Wood engraving by N. Orr & Co., approx. 5" x 4 1/4".

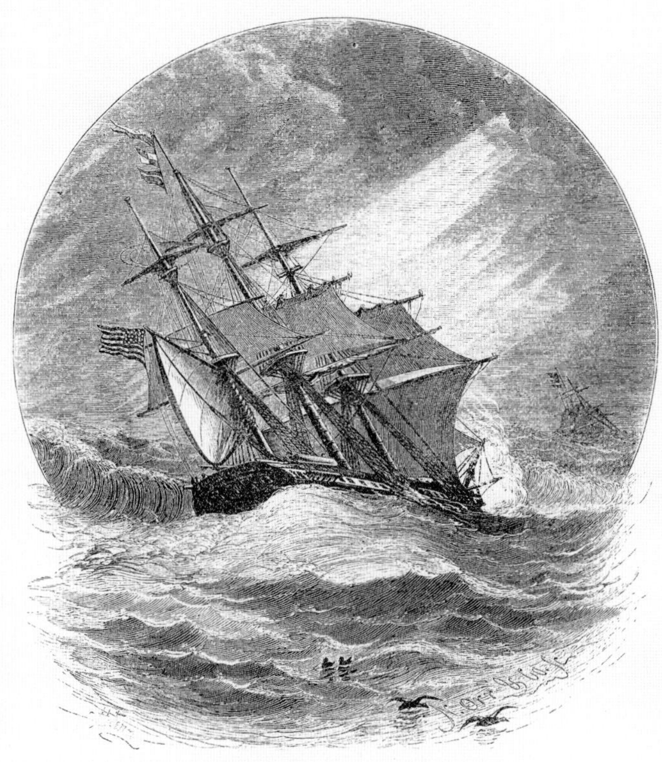

A STATE of things in the manufacturing districts of England, which had long been looked upon as inevitable, in consequence of the scarcity of cotton and the stagnation of American markets, existed, especially in Lancashire, in the summer and fall of 1862. In July, the large manufacturers began to close their mills, and in October one half of the operatives were out of employment,

1860–'65 (1866) by the antislavery advocate Horace Greeley. Fenn contributed six views, including two of Fort Sumter and one of Fredericksburg, Virginia.[9]

Fenn's other early commissions were related to the ongoing, recently intensified interest in exploring the North American continent and beyond; these were precursors of later assignments that would send him around the United States and to many other parts of the world. Work on the transcontinental railroad, which had slowed during the war, gained new impetus after 1865, opening the West to more settlers and travelers. In 1867 Fenn contributed to a hefty publication featuring the western states and territories, Albert D. Richardson's *Beyond the Mississippi;* issued by subscription from the American Publishing Company of Hartford, it sold ninety thousand copies in four years.[10] Fenn's six designs made a respectable showing among the more than two hundred by various artist-illustrators and depicted places that would have been strikingly unusual to audiences in the East: "The Taos Pueblo," "Mount Shasta, California," and "The Grizzly Giant," a huge sequoia tree. Since he had not yet traveled west, Fenn must have based these images on photographs or sketches done by others. Another minor assignment for two drawings that were also based on photographs or sketches was completed for Isaac I. Hayes's *Open Polar Sea: A Narrative of Discovery toward the North Pole in the Schooner "United States"* (1867).

Photographs often served as source materials for illustrators in this period. Fenn would use them throughout his career, although he often traveled to make on-site sketches as well. Working from this medium was challenging. In his 1896 manual *The Illustration of Books,* Joseph Pennell warned aspiring illustrators that there was "nothing in the world more difficult to work from" than photographs because, as he explained, "one is confused by endless unimportant, unselected details; the point of view is never that which one would have selected."[11] Whether or not Fenn shared this view, he was later admired for treating photographs "interestingly" and taking out the "trifling detail" when translating them into drawings.[12]

In 1868 Fenn once again worked with Nathaniel Orr, this time on a project related to the increasing interest in touring scenic sites to contemplate the beauties of nature and connect with divine creative power. Years earlier, Orr's firm had prepared illustrations for a guide to Trenton Falls, near Utica, New York, that had first been published in 1851 by George P. Putnam; now that the Utica and Black River Railroad provided easier access to the falls, Orr thought a new edition was warranted. To stress the site's increased accessibility, for the 1868 edition Orr added new images by Fenn that showed elegantly dressed tourists viewing the falls. In his redesign of a subject that an artist named Müller had drawn for the original edition, Fenn more fully delineated the trees, rock ledges, and waterfall and made the sightseers much more fashionable (fig. 2.4).[13]

Among the illustrations retained from the earlier book were some that combined images and text in interesting ways. These designs, by "Heine, Kummer and Müller," otherwise unidentified but presumably German artists, could have given Fenn ideas for moving beyond the conventions favored by Birket Foster. The page repro-

 Gaining Recognition

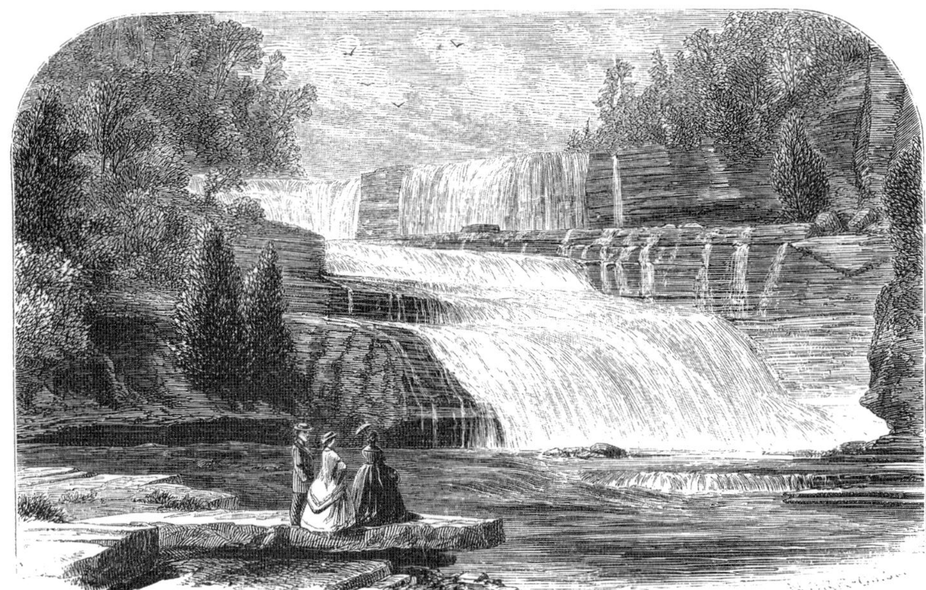

2.4. Harry Fenn, "High Fall." From N. Parker Willis, ed., *Trenton Falls, Picturesque and Descriptive* (New York: Published for the proprietor by N. Orr, 1868), 20. Wood engraving, approx. 3 1/8" x 4 1/2".

duced here as an example (fig. 2.5) includes comments by the popular journalist and travel writer Nathaniel Parker Willis about the way female visitors to the falls, with their "flowing skirts" and "picturesque bonnets and parasols," enhanced the scenery, especially if their clothes were colorful. Fenn could have seen other examples of designs juxtaposing text and image at Orr's office, notably those by John A. Hows for William Cullen Bryant's book of poetry *A Forest Hymn,* engraved by Orr.[14]

WORK FOR TICKNOR AND FIELDS

Although the publishers of most books to which Fenn had thus far contributed were either recently established or church-related, he soon took on more work for the highly respected firm of Ticknor and Fields, located in Boston, where American literature had initially flourished. This was the first instance of Fenn's skill and resourcefulness resulting in an ongoing relationship with a leading publishing house, the kind of opportunity he was able to exploit repeatedly as he became better known. Ticknor and Fields (and its later incarnations) would play an important role in Fenn's career by commissioning work that brought him much acclaim, especially designs for several volumes of poetry, and which led to his friendship with the popular poet John Greenleaf Whittier. In a time when poems were read aloud

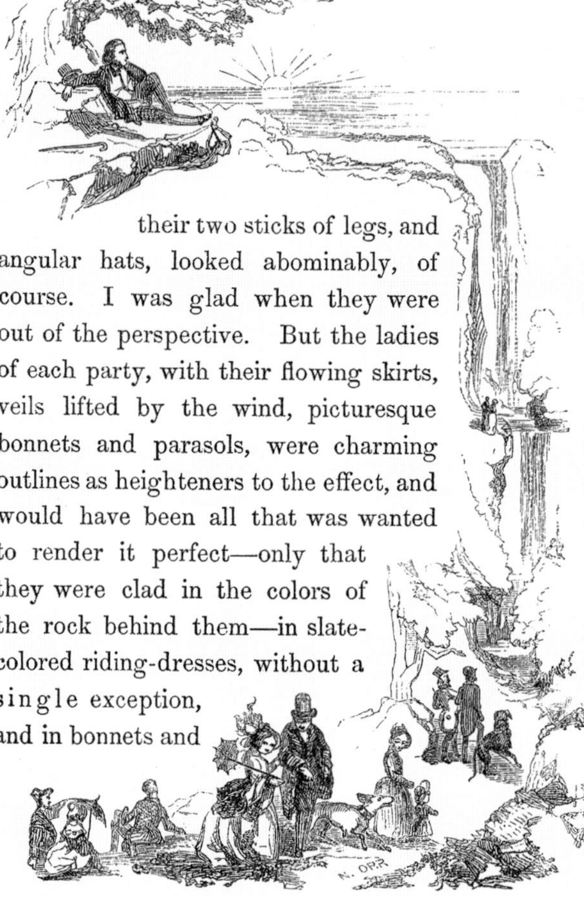

2.5. Heine, Kummer, and Müller, page illustration. From Willis, *Trenton Falls,* 75. Wood engraving by N. Orr & Co., approx. 4 1/4" x 2 1/2".

their two sticks of legs, and angular hats, looked abominably, of course. I was glad when they were out of the perspective. But the ladies of each party, with their flowing skirts, veils lifted by the wind, picturesque bonnets and parasols, were charming outlines as heighteners to the effect, and would have been all that was wanted to render it perfect—only that they were clad in the colors of the rock behind them—in slate-colored riding-dresses, without a single exception, and in bonnets and

in the family circle and memorized in school, the firm already had experience producing illustrated books of poetry, including an 1855 edition of Henry Wadsworth Longfellow's *Golden Legend,* with illustrations by Birket Foster;[15] Tennyson's *Enoch Arden,* with illustrations by Darley, W. J. Hennessy, the painter Elihu Vedder, and a young John La Farge, printed for the 1864 holiday trade;[16] and *Gems from Tennyson,* issued in late 1865, which reused some illustrations by British artists from an

1857 edition of Tennyson's poems published by Moxon in London, supplementing them with designs by such well-known American artists as John Kensett, Samuel Colman, F. O. C. Darley, William Trost Richards, and Winslow Homer.[17]

After Whittier's *National Lyrics,* Fenn's next work for Ticknor and Fields was for the firm's new monthly children's magazine, *Our Young Folks,* designed to engage and entertain young readers and thus to compete with more didactic, moralistic publications, such as those produced by the American Tract Society. In 1866, its second year, Fenn furnished several illustrations, including some meticulous nature studies of particular plants and rocks that were very much in the Ruskinian tradition (fig. 2.6). These early examples document his considerable knowledge of plant life and reveal a lifelong passion, as attested to in a much later account describing how he shared his knowledge and love of nature with a child, perhaps one of his daughters:

> 'Nearly forty years ago,' writes one who was herself his companion in the adventure, 'he took a little child sleighing through the Jersey hills, and to the accompaniment of the Russian chimes on the mountain pony, he described to her the summer garb of every little brown spear and snow-laden seed-cup which rose above the snow crust. He showed her how wonderful a setting they made for the ice-jewels of winter, what lovely blue shadow-patterns they drew on the snow, and how the trees all displayed their true character even without their green robes. Thus was the miracle of seeing wrought in the child, but when they came home in the December twilight, she only thought she had been to fairyland.'[18]

For the magazine's September 1866 issue, Fenn designed the title page for Harriet Beecher Stowe's story "Little Pussy Willow," which combined close-ups of plants, distinctive lettering and initials, and a rural scene. It is an early American example of an elaborate chapter opening akin to the work of English and German illustrators from the 1840s and 1850s.[19] (Additional Fenn illustrations for *Our Young Folks* are listed in Appendix 1.) In 1867 he provided a graceful frontispiece of irises for a gift edition of Longfellow's *Flower-de-Luce* and an opening illustration for Stowe's poem "A Day in the Pamfili Doria," to be included in *Religious Poems.*[20] The latter is by far the most attractive illustration in the book. By combining the poem's title with trees and figures relaxing near a fountain and a sunset streaming down on the dome of St. Peter's Basilica, tiny in the distance, Fenn has created an image in keeping with Stowe's mildly anti-Catholic message that the "Ave Maria bell" they hear from "that strange and ancient city" seems to be "calling the nations to prayer" and for "meaning" to "come back again" to worship.[21] During these months Fenn was often in the Ticknor and Fields office. His work

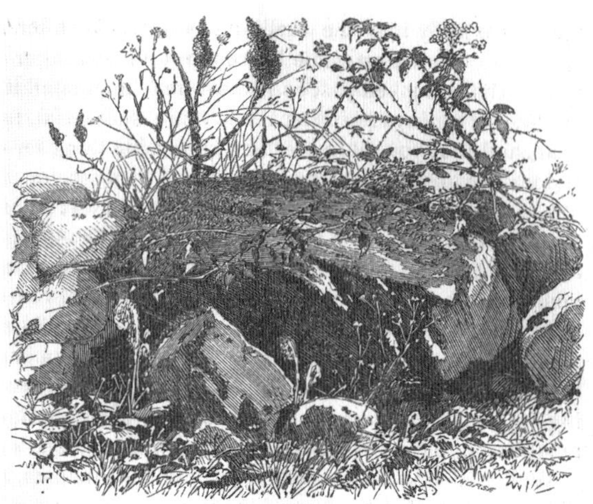

2.6. Harry Fenn, illustration for "The Four Seasons" by Lucretia P. Hale. *Our Young Folks,* June 1866, 363. Wood engraving, 2 5/16" x 2 3/4".

clearly impressed the head of the firm, the flamboyant promoter of American literature James T. Fields (1817–1881), as well as the newly arrived manager of the art department, A. V. S. Anthony (1835–1906), for the two men took the unusual step of commissioning him to be the sole illustrator of a special gift edition of Whittier's nostalgic poem *Snow-Bound.*[22] When first published by the firm in 1866, the lyrical narrative had struck a chord with Americans remembering their own childhoods and yearning for the simpler life of the farm after the trauma of the Civil War and in the face of growing industrialization and urbanization. In a sense, enhancing the poem's text with Fenn's images strengthened its impact as a foundational myth of the Anglo-Saxon population of the rural Northeast, at a time when the challenge of incorporating other groups into civil society was clear. The new edition came out in late 1867 for the Christmas trade, although the title page carried a date of 1868. In a prefatory note, Whittier commended Fenn's illustrations for their "faithfulness" to "the spirit and details of the passages and places" in his ballad.

Many years later Fenn revealed the considerable lengths required to achieve this faithfulness. His account in "The Story of Whittier's *Snow-Bound*" appeared in the April 1893 issue of *St. Nicholas* magazine, soon after the beloved poet's death. Fenn shed light on both his own passion to do a thorough, accurate job and the friendship that grew between him and Whittier. He describes how Fields, who thought the poem had "a picture in every line" and would make a perfect holiday gift, sent Fenn to Whittier's home in Amesbury, Massachusetts, to interview him and "gather material in the locality for illustrations." The shy Whittier met Fenn "rather coolly" and soon advised him to walk up the hill to see the view instead of "wasting" time with him. When he returned, Fenn greeted Whittier with "enthusiastic explanations" of what he had seen: the willows along the river and "the sunset sky." Whittier, Fenn remembered, "made no reply, but his eyes flashed for a moment, and he handed me a volume, turning to a certain page and stanza, where I found almost word for word, the effect I had described to him. The ice was broken; we saw a little alike."[23]

Still, Whittier urged Fenn to use his imagination rather than to visit his birthplace, the scene of the poem. By 1867 Whittier's boyhood home in nearby Haverhill was so changed that the sixty-year-old poet did not even want the artist to see it. Fenn insisted, however, claiming that Fields had ordered him to go. He eventually persuaded the immigrant woman renting the house to remove the modern stove and expose the original cranes in the hearth and to let him retrieve some old furniture from the attic. Then he sketched "till nightfall." Returning to Whittier, he opened his sketchbook "at the page illustrating the kitchen interior. The effect was startling; his face quivered; he started to his feet, and hastened around the study table, the sketch-book in his hands, and the tears running down his cheeks, crying, 'How did thee do it? how did thee do it? 'T is just as we knew it nearly a half-century ago!'"[24] During the week Fenn spent with Whittier they became close friends, and Fenn and his wife later visited Whittier's home several times. The poet also became Fenn's champion and promoted his work to Fields (discussed in the next chapter). He is reported to have commented, "What I would give, if I could see all Harry sees!"[25]

Fenn's illustrations for *Snow-Bound* established him as an important artist and illustrator. The diminutive volume is often described as "the first gift book published in America," and, although this claim is false, its persistence suggests the book's impact on a public hungry for images. Compared with *The Tribute Book* and the 1865 edition of Whittier's *National Lyrics,* both of which displayed the work of an array of illustrators, Fenn's *Snow-Bound* benefited from harmony of style combined with variety of subject and format. He later described his method of preparing the small illustrations: "All the drawings were made in water color on boxwood blocks, many of them not more than two inches square containing a dozen figures, all doing their various stunts with the left hands, so that they should come right when reversed in printing."[26] His method was probably similar to that of Birket Foster as Fenn had described it, using watercolor ranging from black to white and defining shapes with pencil.[27] Two skilled engravers, A. V. S. Anthony and William J. Linton (1812–1897), the latter a prominent English engraver who had recently immigrated to the United States, effectively inter-

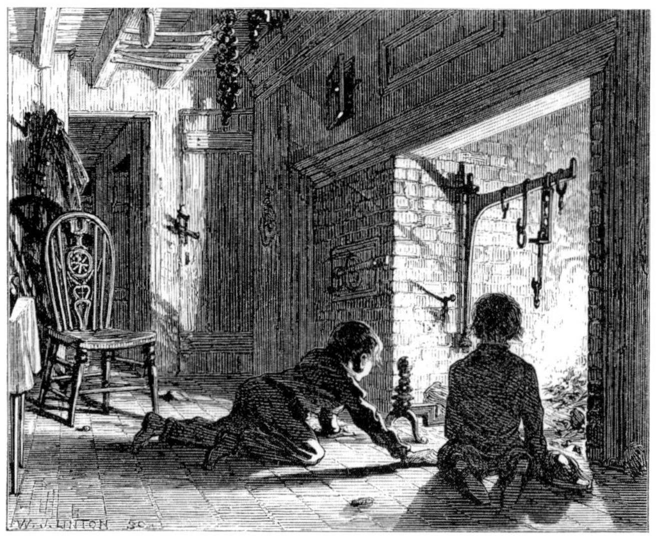

2.7. Harry Fenn, [Fireplace]. From John Greenleaf Whittier, *Snow-Bound; A Winter Idyl* (Boston: Ticknor and Fields, 1868), 18. Wood engraving by A. V. S. Anthony, 2 11/16"x 3 5/16".

preted Fenn's varied textures and contrasts, especially the appearance of snow on dark objects.

Fenn's designs represented a giant step forward compared to his pair of images for Whittier's *National Lyrics,* completed just two years earlier. His delicate but energetic compositions skillfully depicted the farm children's special activities both outdoors and inside after a deep snowfall. The small figures are expressive, even though he included few faces (facial features were difficult for a wood engraver to interpret, especially on such a small scale). Fenn's image of two children watching a fire in the hearth where he had exposed the old cranes (fig. 2.7) embodied Whittier's words,

> Beyond the circle of our hearth
> No welcome sound of toil or mirth
> Unbound the spell, and testified
> Of human life and thought outside.

More specifically, the vivid contrasts designed by Fenn and interpreted by Linton's adroit engraving capture the intense light of the fire igniting "the ragged brush" and "knotty forestick." As Whittier described the scene:

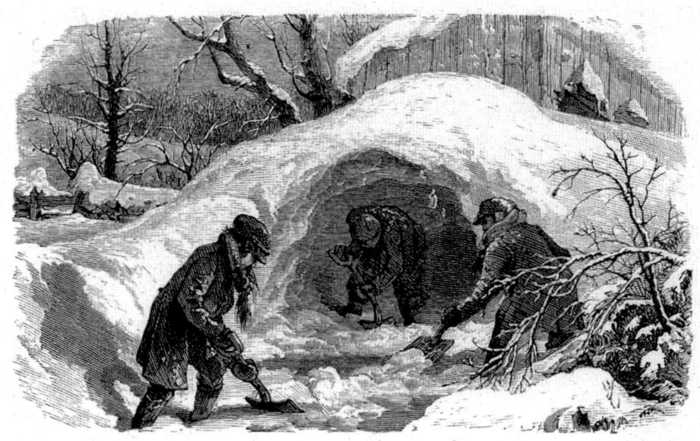

2.8. Harry Fenn, [Building Igloo]. From Whittier, *Snow-Bound*, 14. Wood engraving by A. V. S. Anthony, approx. 2" x 3 1/4".

then, hovering near
We watched the first red blaze appear
Heard the sharp crackle, caught the gleam
On whitewashed wall and sagging beam,
Until the old, rude-fashioned room,
Burst, flower-like into rosy bloom;

Each illustration conveyed part of the narrative, enhancing Whittier's words, as in figure 2.8, where the boys, "With mittened hands, and caps drawn low, / to guard our necks and ears from snow," shoveling "where the drift was deepest, made a tunnel walled and overlaid / With dazzling crystal." In the facing illustration they are shown having "reached the barn with merry din / And roused the prisoned brutes within."

The book apparently opened the eyes of many Americans to the possibilities of wood engravings as artworks, just as Bewick's and, later, the Dalziels' publications had already done among British audiences. In an October 10, 1867, *New York Times* article titled "New Publications," they were praised as "worthy of the best English work." A review in the December 13, 1867, *Chicago Tribune* stressed that *Snow-Bound*'s illustrations, although "mainly in miniature," "show the beautiful effects that can be worked up in wood at the hands of a good engraver." Furthermore, the reviewer states: "Art has been too long confined to the canvas and to steel and copper. These engravings show that there are possibilities in wood worthy the attention of any artist. . . . wood can express both a photographic similarity, and even a feeling and sentiment closely akin to oils, and that, too without the great auxiliary of color."

Other highly favorable reviews brought attention to Fenn's skills as an illustrator. A critic for the *New York Times* wrote: "The illustrations and the poem fit together so perfectly, forming a beautiful and harmonious whole, that one can hardly be said to have read 'Snow-Bound' unless he has read it in this edition."[28] In his 1880 "History of Wood-Engraving in America," W. J. Linton described several gift books from the 1860s and praised *Snow-Bound* as "the daintiest gift-book of them all," with its forty small drawings representative of Fenn's "early careful work."[29] And in 1882, when an exhibition of engravings on wood at the Museum of Fine Arts, Boston occasioned a retrospective look at the holiday editions publishers had produced over the years—"the pretty little volumes that made many a heart happy at Christmas time a dozen years ago"—a reviewer in the *Critic* mused of *Snow-Bound:* "It was this volume, if we mistake not, more than any other, which gave rise to a number of books of a similar kind, . . . Mr. Fenn began a movement in this country which has produced a host of imitators of more or less merit, who copy his style but are devoid of his artistic skill and delicate feeling for nature."[30]

Snow-Bound was also admired for its exceptional printing and attractive binding of dark green cloth stamped in gold, decorated with Fenn's design of the "well-curb with a Chinese roof." The paper was heavy, and the type large and well spaced. The prices were $5 for the cloth binding and $9 for the "Turkey Morocco" leather binding, quite substantial amounts at the time.[31] This book, and the many others that publishers would later produce illustrating familiar poems, was seen as a work of art; presenting it as a gift or displaying it on the parlor table attested to one's good taste and cultural aspirations.

Such praise brought Fenn widespread attention from the public and other artists, and at least one, Will H. Low (1853–1932), sought out his help. After becoming a successful illustrator, Low recalled that as a young man he admired Fenn's works in *Our Young Folks* and wrote him to ask "how he drew a moonlight." Fenn invited him to his Montclair studio, where Low saw "the beautiful things in illustration."[32] Fenn's generosity toward this young artist is in keeping with the few accounts of his sunny disposition and positive attitude. As his son-in-law described him: "He wanted nothing more to make him exuberantly and completely happy than the satisfaction of his sense of beauty. . . . [H]e was never more delightful and vivacious than when describing the scenes he had visited in his many wanderings. He could sketch with words as well as with brush and pencil, and not only saw with joy, but could visualize what he saw for those around him."[33]

Fenn's success with *Snow-Bound* would soon garner commissions from an ever-widening circle of publishers, but first came additional assignments for Ticknor and Fields. Working again from photographs, Fenn drew numerous illustrations for *A Journey in Brazil* (1868) by the prominent scientist Louis Agassiz. He also provided three calendar decorations for the firm's 1868 *Atlantic Almanac,* edited by Oliver Wendell Holmes and Donald G. Mitchell; his crisp black and white designs for June, August, and October stand out among the other mostly monochromatic contributions. In 1869, the year Ticknor and Fields became Fields, Osgood and Company, Fenn prepared illustrations for the Reverend William H. H. "Adirondack" Murray's *Adventures in the Wilderness,* a collection of tales about camping in the Adirondacks that popularized the region as a vacation destination.[34] Through his contributions to this book, which endorsed the therapeutic value of adventure in the wilderness (with the assistance of a hired guide who carried equipment, set up camp, and cooked), Fenn was identified with a cultural movement that legitimized play and robust leisure activities.

In *Work and Play* (1864), the clergyman Horace Bushnell had struck blows against the Protestant work ethic, insisting "nothing fires or exalts us, but to feel the divine energy and the inspiring liberty of play."[35] Murray, the minister of Boston's Park Street Congregational Church, and other liberal clergy had replaced Calvinism's emphasis on depravity and original sin with more optimistic beliefs in humanity's ability to intuit essential truths and to choose a moral course of action based on the intuitive "moral sense" or "conscience." They further maintained that, freed from superstition, dogma, and tradition, each individual human spirit would thrive and recognize the eternal in all things. Murray wrote of one of the Adirondack lakes: "I know of nothing which carries the mind so far back toward the creative period as to stand on the shore of such a sheet of water, knowing that as you behold it, so it has been for ages."[36] Although no details of Fenn's religious beliefs are known, except that he participated in churches of the Congregational denomination in Montclair, his response to nature's wonders was clearly similar to Murray's, and his enjoyment of fishing, hunting, and vacations at the seashore indicate that he relished play.

WORK FOR NEW CLIENTS

In 1868 Fenn's work also began to appear in the publications of the leading New York firm Harper & Brothers, whose art director was Charles Parsons, Fenn's colleague in the new American Society of Painters in Water Colors and a fellow resident of Montclair. Their friendship could only have helped Fenn gain commissions.[37] For the September 12, 1868, *Harper's Weekly,* he designed a full-page

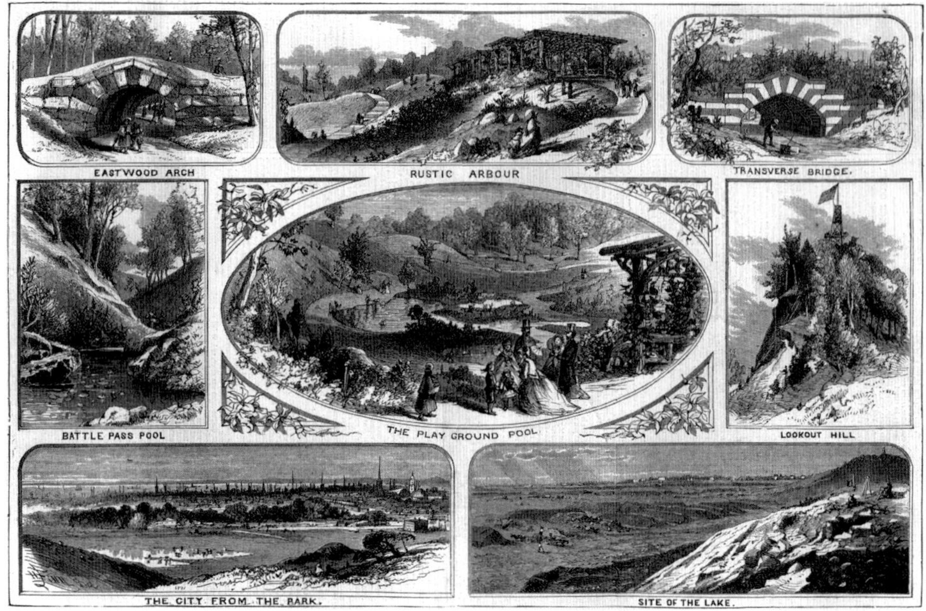

composite of scenes in Prospect Park, the huge public space in Brooklyn that had been under development since 1861 and recently opened to the public (fig. 2.9). Fenn's charming but highly conventional design contrasts greatly with the composites he created for the *Weekly* some twenty years later (see, for example, figs. 5.32, 5.33, and 5.34). For *Harper's New Monthly Magazine,* he illustrated the lead story for March 1868, "The Minnesota Pineries." His opening image of horses pulling a sled piled with huge logs through the snow is larger, more striking, and better engraved than most pictures in the magazine at the time. In the fall of 1869, his landscape images continued to stand out in the pages of *Harper's Monthly,* including views of western scenery, especially "Above the Shoshone Falls" (September), and of Brazil, notably "Entrance to the Harbor [Rio]" (October) and "Small Cascade, Tijuca" (November), all based on photographs.[38]

Also for the October 1869 *Harpers Monthly,* he produced several illustrations for an article that clearly demonstrates the period's interest in geologic tourism—both to understand earth's history and to be in touch with creative forces. "The Helderbergs" depicts New York's third mountain chain—after the Adirondacks and the Catskills—west of Albany. The writer, a very young Verplanck Colvin (1847–1920), would later oversee the geological survey of the Adirondacks and push for establishing a forest preserve there. He describes the Helderberg region—with its fossil-filled limestone cliffs that were "once the shell-covered bed of an ocean"—as appealing for hiking, viewing waterfalls, exploring caves,

Gaining Recognition

gathering fossils, and recalling legendary events of the Revolutionary War. Fenn depicted the cliffs, waterfalls, and caves with considerable precision, and in the foreground of "The Dome" he included an artist with easel and umbrella, a conventional device he would employ often to emphasize both the accuracy of the image and its value as an artistic subject (fig. 2.10).[39]

With his increased prominence as a result of *Snow-Bound* and other illustrations for well-known writers, Fenn's client base expanded in 1869 to include two new illustrated periodicals, *Hearth and Home* and *Appletons' Journal of Literature, Science and Art.* Fenn's drawing "A New-Jersey Farm-Scene" appeared on the front page of the March 6, 1869, *Hearth and Home,* a weekly published in New York "for the farm, garden, and fireside." It depicted "picturesque bits" of "old-style farm life" that were "slowly passing away," such as an iron bucket, a hollowed-out log for a trough, and haystacks. The result was an even more blatant nostalgia than that evoked by the *Snow-Bound* images. The first of Fenn's many contributions to *Appletons' Journal*—which was launched on April 3, 1869—appeared in the fourth issue, dated April 24. D. Appleton & Company, New York's second largest publishing firm, after Harper & Brothers, was founded in 1831 by Daniel Appleton (1785–1849); in 1869 it was directed by his eldest son, William Henry Appleton (1814–1899), with the assistance of his four brothers, John Adams, Daniel Sidney, Samuel Francis, and George Swett.[40] Fenn's close association with the company, which will be discussed at length in chapter 3, continued for the next fourteen years—a collaboration that would lead to success and acclaim for both the firm and the artist.

EXHIBITING WATERCOLORS AND FOUNDING A SOCIETY

Fenn had used watercolor for years, sometimes for preliminary sketches and, when he had time, for finished paintings. The medium, long considered impermanent and most appropriate for amateurs, was still struggling to gain an appreciative audience—and a share of the art market—in the United States. Although most likely the majority of his income always came from his work destined for publication, Fenn continued to produce, exhibit, and sell paintings throughout his career. Furthermore, he was an advocate for watercolor, promoting it as worthy of respect and patronage.

In the few years since returning from his visit to England and Italy in 1862–63, determined as he was to paint and draw rather than engrave, Fenn sought to exhibit and sell his watercolors. He submitted his work to various exhibitions and attracted at least one patron beyond the family circle. In 1864, he placed two watercolors in a show at the National Academy of Design: *The Old Basello [sic] Florence* and *The*

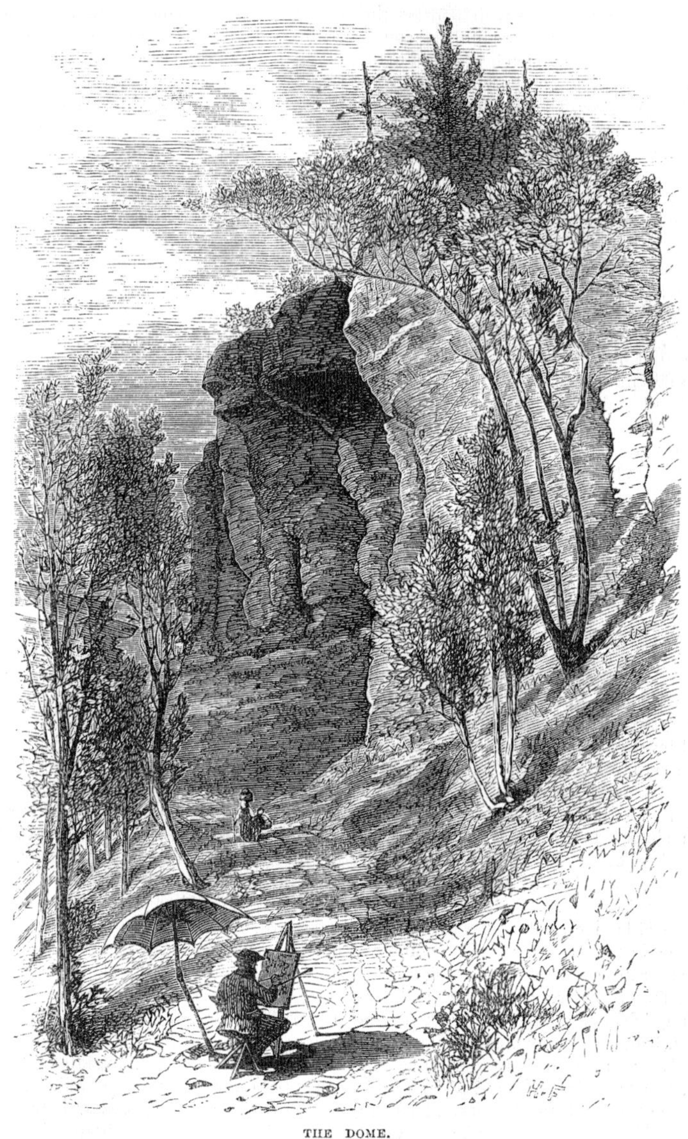

2.10. Harry Fenn, "The Dome," in "The Helderbergs" by Verplanck Colvin. *Harper's Monthly*, October 1869, 659. Wood engraving, 6 3/4" x 3 7/16".

Temple of Saturn [in the Roman Forum] (both unlocated).[41] Perhaps it was there that his work came to the attention of Colonel Henry Thomas Chapman, a young Union veteran and art collector from Brooklyn who bought several of Fenn's paintings. In the Brooklyn Art Association's show that December, one of the watercolors that Fenn exhibited, *Castle of Chillon,* was lent by H. Chapman; the other, *Carpara*

[Carrara?] Mountains—from Via Reggia [Viareggio?] was lent by W. W. Thompson, probably Fenn's father-in-law (with an incorrect middle initial).[42]

By the winter of 1866–67, when Fenn participated in the Artists' Fund Society exhibition at the New York Academy of Design, two of the works he showed were owned by Colonel Chapman: *Margate* and *The Bargello, Florence* (probably *The Old Basello* exhibited in 1864).[43] The latter was likely the painting of "the stairway of an old public building in Florence" described as follows in an article on Chapman's "fine private collection": "The combination of warm brown and reddish tones with scattering grey ones is excellently treated. The picture shows much power and careful study, the artist working faithfully at it before the very walls, day after day."[44] Although none of these early works have been located, two early examples suggest his abilities at this time. An unfinished painting of Florence with coloring similar to the one described shows the care Fenn took in depicting both architecture and the lively street life, as well as his skill in creating dramatic perspective (fig. 2.11). Another, perhaps earlier, watercolor of the Norman staircase in Canterbury, with a date that appears to be 1860, shows Fenn using looser brushstrokes and less detail while experimenting with lights and shadows (fig. 2.12).

The exhibition of the Artists' Fund Society in the winter of 1866–67 was especially noteworthy for the unusually large number of watercolor paintings on display and proved to be something of a turning point. A review by Stillman S. Conant in *Galaxy* magazine praised Charles Parsons's works at length and tersely mentioned that the works of Fenn and a few others "added interest and value to the exhibition." Yet Conant went on to comment that the exhibition, the largest of watercolor paintings ever gathered in the United States, was an important event regardless of the quality of the works. Unlike in England, where watercolor paintings were admired and sought after, the medium had been "totally neglected in this country," partly because of its difficulty: "An unskillful dauber in oils can produce pictures which take better with the general public than anything he could do in water colors, which require greater delicacy and precision, and more accurate knowledge of nature and of methods to make them acceptable. . . . Even the best efforts of our men in this branch of art have been treated with mortifying and unjust neglect."[45]

Conant's preference for works more akin to Turner's watercolors rather than meticulous representations of nature was clear when he noted the "perfection of imitation" but deficiency of "imagination" in the "studies or sketches," not "pictures," of John William Hill and his son John Henry Hill. Neither did the works of Dante Gabriel Rossetti, the English Pre-Raphaelite, or his American

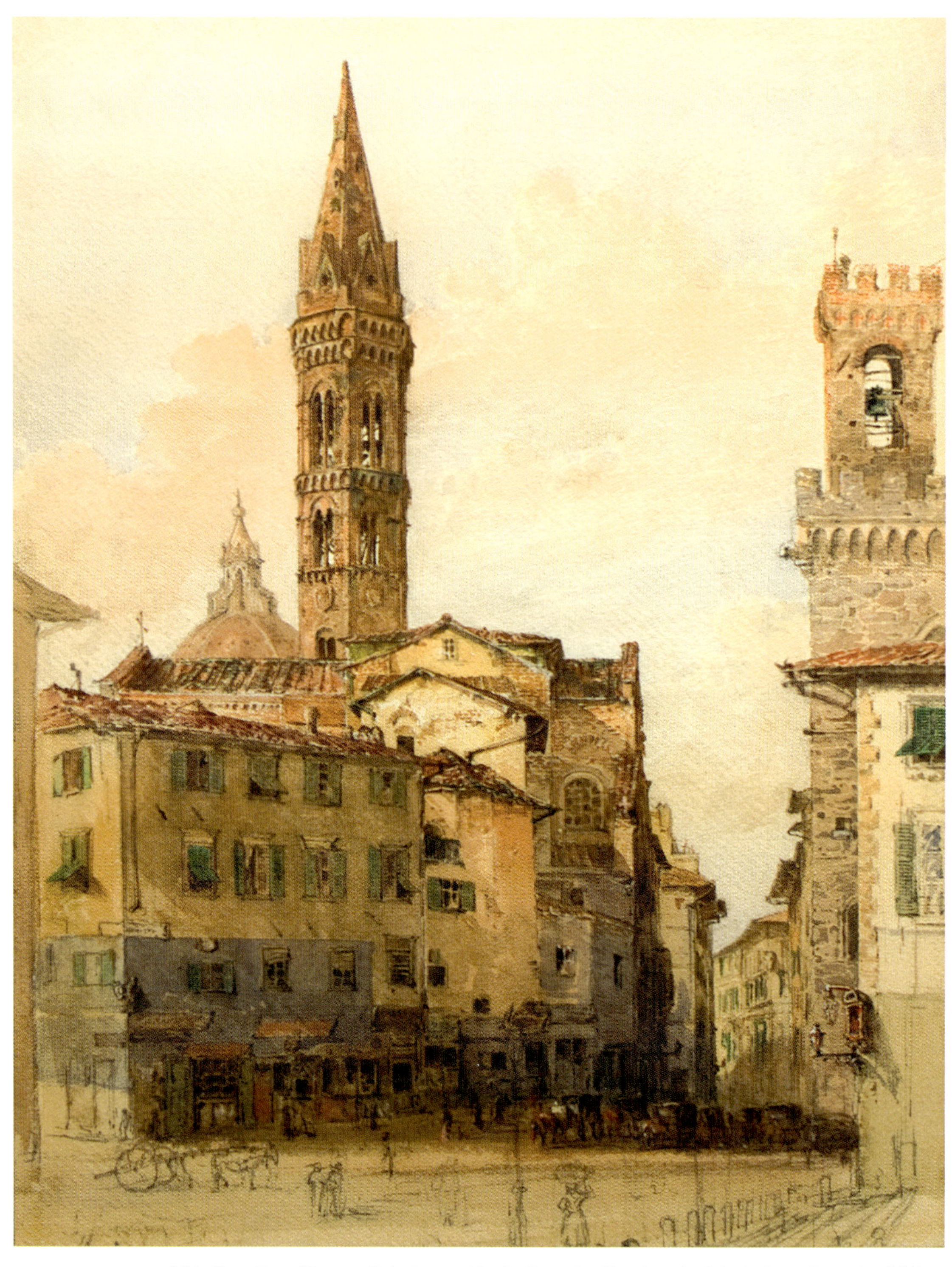

2.11. Harry Fenn, [Florence, Italy: tower of Badia Fiorentina Church on the left, the Bargello on the right]. Watercolor, approx. 18" x 13 1/2". (Private collection.)

counterparts impress him. Nevertheless, Conant asserted, the exhibition served the intended purpose of awakening interest in watercolor painting: "Hundreds of people were for the first time made aware that a water-color painting was better than a 'colored engraving,' or a chromo-lithograph; that depth of tone, richness of color, and exquisite delicacy of finish, can be obtained in water color as well as in oils."[46]

While this exhibition was on view, Fenn would join with others in a new organization intended to end the "unjust neglect" of watercolor painting and enhance its status by exhibiting admirable works and educating the public about the medium's durability. On December 5, 1866, eleven artists gathered to establish the American Society of Painters in Water Colors. They included Samuel Colman, who was elected president, William Hart, Alfred Fredericks, and William H. Thwaites (who designed for Nathaniel Orr and owned works by Fenn[47]). Fenn was among the ten additional artists who attended the second meeting, on January 2, 1867, and were elected to membership, including Jasper F. Cropsey, R. Swain Gifford, Napoleon Sarony, Charles Parsons, T. C. Farrer, and Henry Van Ingen. The group was mixed in terms of age, prestige, and experience in different media (and in the extent to which they are remembered today). Colman, Hart, and Cropsey were National Academicians, whereas Fenn and Parsons were primarily illustrators. The members began planning their first exhibition, and at the February meeting they added additional members and elected a hanging committee.

The society's first exhibition opened December 21, 1867, in the ornate, new National Academy of Design building at Twenty-third Street and Fourth Avenue. It ran for three months, in conjunction with the academy's winter exhibition, which included oil paintings and sculptures recently returned from the Exposition Universelle in Paris. Among the landscapes in oil, Frederic Church's *Niagara* and Albert Bierstadt's *Mount Hood* were conspicuous. A reviewer in the February 1, 1868, *Round Table* commented that the show, together with the first annual collection of the American Society of Painters in Water Colors, constituted "the cheapest and best by far of all the entertainments in town."

This exhibition occurred just as Fenn was receiving accolades for his *Snow-Bound* illustrations, and he was one of six watercolor painters mentioned in an early notice in the *New York Times,* along with "Samuel Colman, William Hart, Boughton, Smilie [*sic*]," and "W. I. Thomas."[48] Fenn showed three Italian subjects and one English view: *Toilers of the Sea* and *Pietra Santa Lucca* (Pietrasanta is a town near Lucca), which were for sale, and *Sketch Near Genoa* and *Church Porch,*

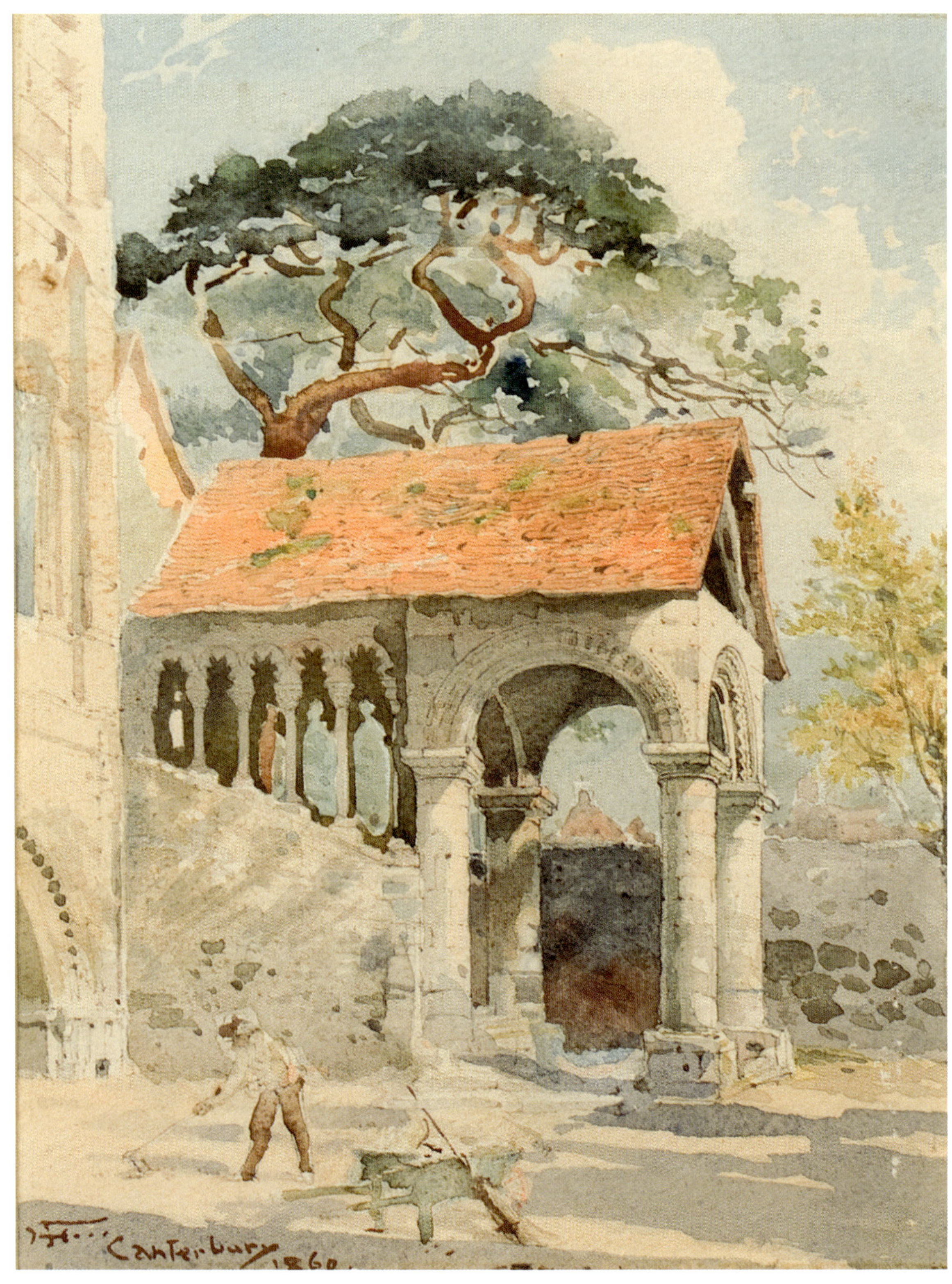

2.12. Harry Fenn, [Norman staircase, Canterbury], 1860? Watercolor, approx. 7 1/2" x 5 1/2". (Private collection.)

Levington, England, both owned by J. T. Fields, principal in the firm of Ticknor and Fields (an indication that his patrons now included his primary publisher). The *Round Table* singled out William Hart's landscapes for particular praise while giving Fenn attention and moderate approval. Yet the comments clearly show that Fenn was known for his wood engravings and that seeing his work in color came as something of a shock:

> Mr. Harry Fenn claims full recognition of his abilities. Several of his drawings are on show, having all considerable merit, while one at least is altogether admirable. We first come across him in 590, "Pietra Santa Lucca," and recognize at once an unusual crispness and sparkle, with a certain cleanness of touch as though he were used to drawing for an engraver. Yet he is not a happy colorist; and in this composition of figures, houses, and remote mountains his gradations of distance are not well preserved, while his touches for effect, legitimate for the pencil but not for the brush, are decidedly too frequent. But there is in him, we say, such a vigor and precision, that he must take a high place among us. His best bit is a small picture in the East Room, 378, "Toilers of the Sea," a coast scene, with fishing boats drawn up on a beach, and a sailor lad mending his nets beside one of them. It is extremely clever. Hypercriticism can perhaps only object to a certain want of ruggedness in outlines and of mellowness in hue. There is possibly, for the fisherman's trade and materials, somewhat too much of spick-and-span newness and sharp cutting. Is this the result of practice on box-wood for engravers?[49]

Since these works are unlocated, it is impossible to assess the critic's comments. One Fenn painting now at the Montclair Art Museum matches the description of *Toilers of the Sea,* but its 1868 date raises the possibility that it is, instead, the work shown the next year at the society's second annual exhibition: *Study of Boats, Porto Venice, Gulf of Shezzia,* owned by Samuel Wilde (fig. 2.13). (Whoever transcribed the title for the National Academy of Design records misinterpreted Fenn's handwriting, for the site is Porto Venere on the Gulf of La Spezia.[50]) Perhaps Fenn created a new, slightly different work, trying to correct the shortcomings of color and line to which the *Round Table*'s reviewer objected. Regardless, the painting's preponderant colors of peach and blue-green seem unnatural (considering the gray stone of the cliffs and church), and the distant mountains are indistinct.

At the same exhibition, the four other works Fenn exhibited included two American subjects titled as studies—*A Winter Study, Montclair, N.J.* and *A Twilight Study, Near Portland, Me.*[51] Exhibiting less-finished works as studies was becoming more common in this period.[52] Exhibitions were also beginning to

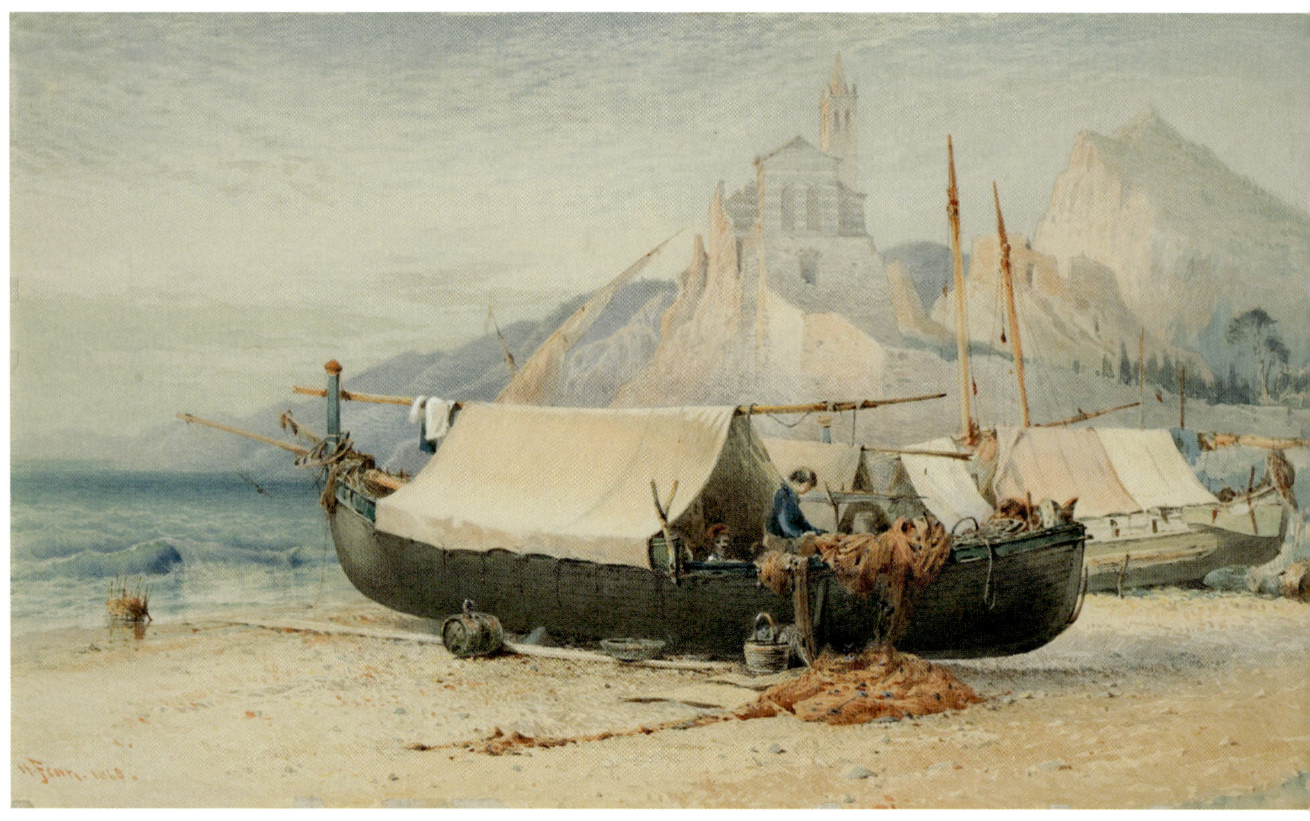

2.13. Harry Fenn, *Fishing Boats,* 1868. Watercolor on paper; sheet 9 1/8" x 15".
(Montclair Art Museum, Bequest of Mary Ellen Wilde, 1913.16.)

include illustrations, and proofs of some that Fenn had created for Henry Ward Beecher's celebrated book *Life of Jesus, the Christ* were displayed at the winter 1868 show, in the section devoted to the academy.[53]

For the society's third annual exhibition, in the winter of 1869–70, Fenn was still mining his Italian studies for subjects, exhibiting *A Study Near Florence* and *Roman Grist-Mill on the Tiber,* along with *Study of Wild Pigeons.*[54] (See Appendix 2 for a complete list of Fenn's contributions to the society's exhibitions.)

After participating actively in the founding of the American Society of Painters in Water Colors, Fenn quickly expanded his illustrating career in late 1869 and early 1870. With major assignments from the Appleton firm to illustrate poetry and depict scenery, discussed in the next two chapters, he had little time to paint watercolors for exhibition. Beginning in 1870–71, with the society's fourth annual exhibition, and continuing for the next decade, his contributions were drawn mainly from his travels for the Appleton firm to fulfill commissions for the

 Gaining Recognition

"Picturesque America" series and the subsequent book as well as for his next two commissions, *Picturesque Europe* (1875–79) and *Picturesque Palestine, Sinai and Egypt* (1881–83). These projects were so time-consuming that he had little opportunity to seek out additional subjects. Yet they brought other rewards, including travel and increasing skill, income, and prestige.

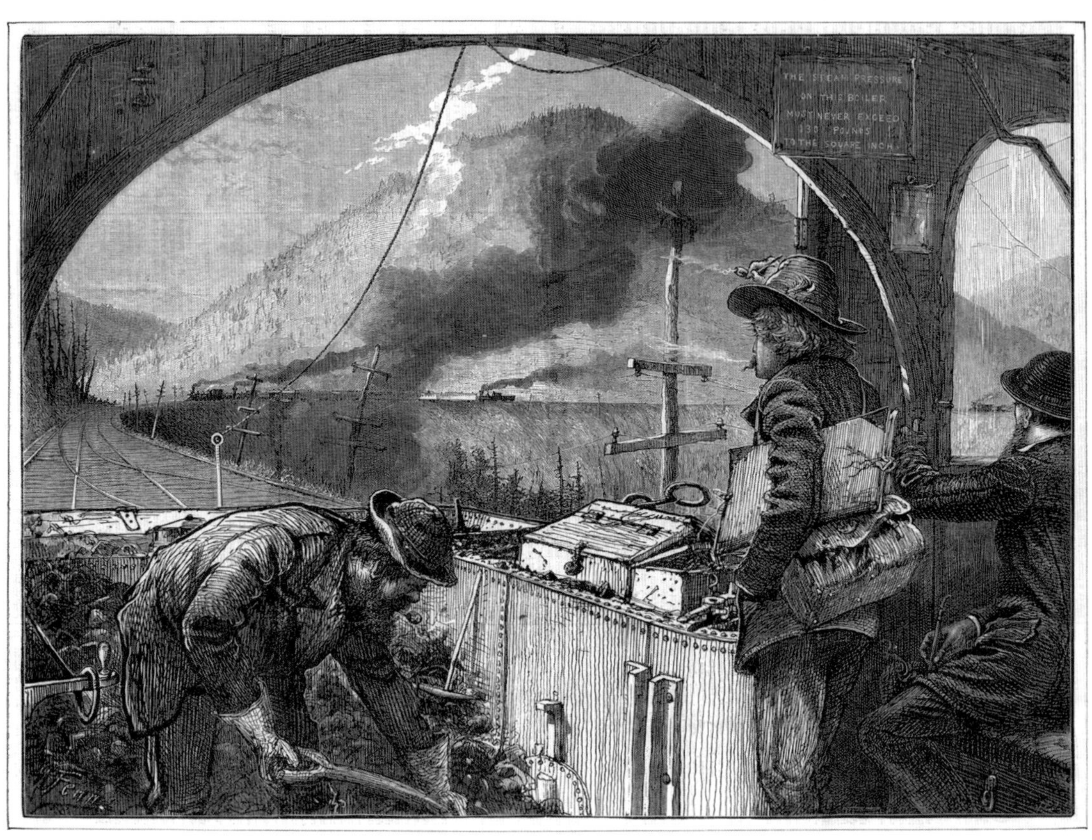

3.1. Harry Fenn, "On the Way to Pittsburgh,—Great Bend on the Alleghenies." *Every Saturday*, March 4, 1871, 200. Wood engraving by J.L.L.[?], 8 3/4" x 11 3/4".

3

Poetry and "Picturesque America"

FENN CONTINUED TO DEVOTE MOST of his time to preparing designs for illustrations, a surer means of supporting his growing family than completing paintings that might or might not sell. His projects in the late 1860s and early 1870s, commissioned by various publishers, ranged from one page for a periodical to hundreds of images for a book so successful that it gave rise to a series of large-scale illustrated books offered by subscription. In a few years, his approach evolved from highly conventional compositions to bolder, more dynamic designs. Furthermore, his works contributed in many ways to building or reinforcing pride in America's cultural and artistic accomplishments—including illustrated books—as well as its scenic wonders and impressive, orderly cities.

GIFT BOOKS OF POETRY

In this period, and throughout his career, Fenn accepted commissions to illustrate books of poetry by some of the nation's best-known writers. His own success with the late 1867 edition of *Snow-Bound* played an important role in creating this market, and after 1868 American firms began publishing an increasing variety of poetry books illustrated with new artwork by American artists. Publishers were responding not only to the popularity of *Snow-Bound* but also to criticism of the all-too-familiar practice of reusing electrotypes of wood engravings already published abroad, especially in England. For example, the December 1, 1869, issue of the *American Literary Gazette and Publishers' Circular,* the journal of the book trade, called for publishers to cease "manufacturing books out of all sorts of odds and ends" and instead commission original designs from American artists and engravers. This challenge also implied that such efforts would foster the needed development of skilled engravers in this country and that successfully competing with England and Europe in the cultural arena of illustrated books was a significant goal.[1]

Fields, Osgood, and Company (the successor to Ticknor and Fields) was already convinced of the value of original illustrations, based on the reception that *Snow-Bound* had received. For the 1869 Christmas trade, the company issued an edition of Whittier's *Ballads of New England* featuring landscapes by Fenn and other subjects by eight additional artists. The list of illustrations identifies the designer of each work and notes that A. V. S. Anthony was responsible for the engravings.[2] Fenn provided head- and tailpieces for all but one of the poems, signing his compositions in the block with "H. Fenn" or a monogram entwining his two initials. The latter would become his most distinctive signature, with the *F* extending more boldly over the years. As David Tatham notes in his 1992 book *Winslow Homer and the Illustrated Book,* the landscapes in *Ballads of New England,* "similar in size and tonality throughout . . . give the book unity," whereas "the differing styles of the figure artists provide coherent variety."[3]

Although the reputations of some of the figure artists already surpassed Fenn's, or soon would, including Winslow Homer and F. O. C. Darley, several critics found Fenn's work the most appealing. In the December 1869 *Atlantic Monthly,* William Dean Howells began a long review with the following assessment: "The most charming illustrations in this beautiful book are the pictures of Mr. Fenn, who in studies of the very scenes described by the poet has reproduced all the moods and sentiments of the New England landscape: the pathos of the rainy and cloudy coasts, the tender serenity of the river-bordered fields, the life and brightness of the villages, the sadness of the lonely farm, the solemnity of the hill-side graveyard." He continued: "There is not only fidelity to spirit and letter in Mr. Fenn's work, but there is in its great variety the clear impress of individuality, without the least mannerism"; indeed, these works employ few of Birket Foster's conventional devices. The "hill-side graveyard" Howells mentions illustrates "The Countess," a poem about a young village woman who dies after a blissful year of marriage to a French émigré. A large stone bridge frames the distant graveyard in Fenn's tiny but complex composition, which is full of intersecting diagonals enhancing the illusion of depth (fig. 3.2).

Admiration of Fenn's perceived ability to imbue ordinary rural landscapes with a variety of sentiments appropriate to the text, while maintaining "the clear impress

Poetry and Picturesque America

of individuality," was in keeping with the growing appreciation of French Barbizon-style landscapes. Rather than the expansive, sublime
subjects of Frederic E. Church and Albert Bierstadt, some American artists were choosing to
depict everyday subjects and gentler, relatively
flat landscapes in particular light and weather
conditions.[4]

An even more enthusiastic writer for the
Independent thought Fenn's illustrations for
Ballads of New England "almost surpassed" his
pictures for *Snow-Bound,* and that "never was
poet more happy than Whittier in his illustrators." The writer raved: "Harry Fenn, you are
a darling! Or, at any rate, your pictures are all
darlings. How with a few inky lines you reveal

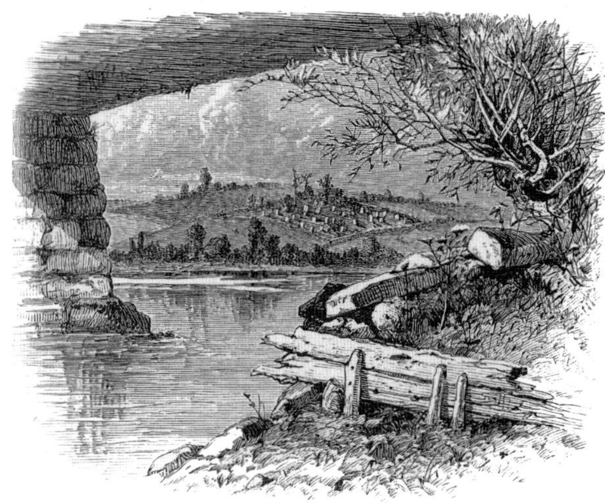

3.2. Harry Fenn, illustration for "The Countess." From John
Greenleaf Whittier, *Ballads of New England* (Boston: Fields,
Osgood, 1870), 51. Wood engraving by A. V. S. Anthony,
approx. 2 3/8" x 3".

to us, . . . the bloom and brightness of the summer hills; . . . the lilies on the pond;
the pansies, saucy in the grass. . . . All the pictures are beautiful; but Harry Fenn's
are beautifulest."[5]

The favorable reviews continued in the January 1870 *Putnam's Magazine,*
whose critic judged that "Mr. Fenn has borne away the palm from all his brother
artists. . . . His forte is landscape, and seascape, if we may invent the word, a
walk of art which seems peculiarly his own." The critic praised many of Fenn's
small head- and tailpieces—several of which were seascapes—but found Homer's
figures "foreign," being "native only to Japan and the regions thereabout," and
Darley's compositions "clever but mannered," showing no "growth" over "ten
years ago." Such comments suggest that although preferences had not yet caught
up with Homer's spare use of contours and flat picture plane most had moved
beyond Darley's overwrought detail and nervous line.[6]

Whittier was once again pleased with the illustrations. After seeing the proofs,
he wrote to James T. Fields: "The beauty of the engravings almost makes me
ashamed of the verses they illustrate."[7] He recognized "the scenery familiar from
boyhood," especially in the images for "Cobbler Keezar's Vision," "Wreck of
Rivermouth," "The Playmate," and "The Countess," all of which included landscapes by Fenn. The publisher featured Whittier's commendation at the beginning of the book, as had been done in *Snow-Bound.*

Pleasing and befriending so respected and beloved a figure would have valuable

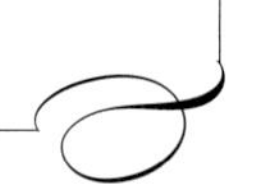

repercussions for Fenn. To prepare illustrations for *Ballads of New England,* he once again visited the scenes of the poet's boyhood.[8] Perhaps on that same journey and at Whittier's suggestion, Fenn and his wife traveled to the bleak Isles of Shoals, nine miles off the coast from Portsmouth, New Hampshire. There, the well-known poet Celia Thaxter (1835–1894) presided over a salon of visiting artists and writers in her parlor on Appledore Island, where her family ran a hotel. Whittier was a close friend of Thaxter and her husband, Levi, and no doubt facilitated Fenn's acceptance into the heady summer community, which at times in the late 1860s and 1870s included William Dean Howells, Sarah Orne Jewett, James T. and Annie Fields, James Whitcomb Riley, Harriet Prescott Spofford, and the painters William Trost Richards, Alfred Thompson Bricher, William Morris Hunt, and, later, Childe Hassam, who painted her lush flower garden repeatedly.[9]

Whittier's August 22, 1869, letter to Thaxter relates that the Fenns had recently visited him after returning from her hotel, reporting: "They had a delightful time on the island, and thank thee for it from full hearts." Whittier then provided a rare description of Mary Fenn: "Mrs F is a dear good woman,—I had a talk with her on serious matters—the great questions of life and duty—our relations to God and our hopes and fears of the future; and was struck by her calm faith and simple trust—her tender reverence, and all comprehensive charity."[10] Fenn had made some drawings or watercolors on the island, for Whittier also mentioned a "White Island" picture, and on November 11, 1869, he thanked Thaxter for a picture titled "Driftwood Fire," which he considered one of "Fenn's best."[11] Fenn would eventually publish several images of the Isles of Shoals and may have visited there often.[12]

Whittier's letters from 1869–71 show two instances of his promotion of Fenn for an illustration project. The first, in a letter dated February 12, 1870, involved a new poem Whittier wrote in response to a request from James T. Fields, who was planning a gift book of poetry to be released later that year. Whittier told Fields that his poem would "be difficult to illustrate" but that he knew of "no one who could do it, however, so well as Harry Fenn."[13] Fields acted in accord with Whittier's advice (although he might well have chosen Fenn anyway). When *Winter Poems by Favorite American Poets* appeared that December, Whittier's poem celebrating a world transformed by snow and ice, titled "The Pageant," was illustrated by Fenn, whose designs depicted rather literally such lines as "The gleaming tree-bolls, ice-embossed, / Hold up their chandeliers of frost" (fig. 3.3). Perhaps to achieve greater harmony than in *Ballads of New England,* this time the publishers hired one artist to prepare all the images for a specific poem.[14] In addition to "The Pageant," Fenn supplied designs for Longfellow's "Woods in Winter," and Sol Eytinge Jr. (1833–1905)

Poetry and Picturesque America

illustrated Whittier's "In School-Days," primarily with figure drawings. Winslow Homer, Alfred Fredericks, C. C. Griswold, W. J. Hennessy, Jervis McEntee, and Homer D. Martin provided illustrations for poems by Longfellow, William Cullen Bryant, James Russell Lowell, and Ralph Waldo Emerson.

In reviewing the book, one reader who kept an eye on the publishing industry commented in *Every Saturday* (also published by Fields, Osgood) that much had changed from a few years earlier, when Americans "looked to the presses of England and France for our more expensive and elaborate illustrated books." The lack "of artistic facilities which left us dependent on foreign publishers no longer exists," the reader says, and "in evidence of this" cites the very volumes discussed here (*Snow-Bound, Ballads of New England, Winter Poems*) as well as *Song of the Sower* (discussed below) and Scribner's edition of Elizabeth Barrett Browning's *Lady Geraldine's Courtship* (1870), illustrated by W. J. Hennessy.[15] A reviewer in *Harper's Monthly* highlighted the rivalry between American and European productions, praising Fenn's "exquisite landscapes" that appeared in another Scribner publication, *Songs of Home* (1871), and stating that "no French or English artist could have excelled his 'First Snow Fall,' for instance."[16]

In his second promotional effort, Whittier suggested that Fenn's works should accompany Celia Thaxter's writings. After her four-part essay titled "Among the Isles of Shoals" appeared to much acclaim in the *Atlantic Monthly* between August 1869 and May 1870, Whittier wrote to her on June 10 about Horace Greeley's admiration of her writing and mentioned that Mary Fenn was also "enthusiastic in praise of the same papers" and wanted "to see them in a volume with Harry's illustrations" (Fenn's wife was also a promoter of his work).[17] By July 1871, Thaxter was anticipating that the essays would be published in book form, and on July 24 Whittier again recommended his friend: "Some half a dozen of Fenn's pictures should go with them."[18] In 1873 Osgood issued *Among the Isles of Shoals* with four illustrations by Fenn. Upon receiving a copy, Whittier praised both the writing and the pictures in a letter to the *Atlantic*'s editor William Dean Howells, noting that Thaxter's descriptions of scenery had "all the charm of Thoreau and White of Selborne," and Fenn's frontispiece was "the most effective piece of wood

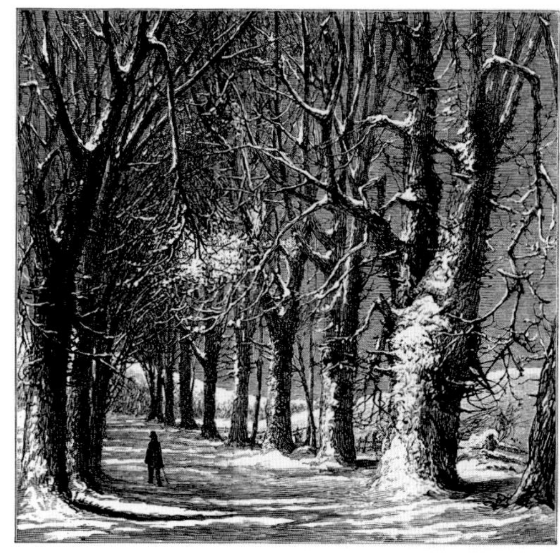

3.3. Harry Fenn, "Virgin snow-paths glimmering through / A jewelled elm-tree avenue," in "The Pageant" by John Greenleaf Whittier. From *Winter Poems by Favorite American Poets* (Boston: Fields, Osgood, 1871), 14. Wood engraving by A. V. S. Anthony, 3 3/4" x 3 13/16".

engraving" he had ever seen. Its "water and sky," he enthused, were "wonderfully well done. Fenn the artist, and Anthony the engraver, have here wrought their best."[19] The small, delicate engraving does effectively depict the light through cirrus clouds reflected on the water, but Whittier's extreme response suggests he was not keeping up with the plethora of fine wood engravings being produced by 1873.

The poetry collections published in these years by the large and respected firm of D. Appleton & Company also demonstrate the shift from reusing imported images to commissioning original artworks by American artists. The firm's gift book for the 1868–69 holiday season was *Wood-Side and Sea-Side,* which gathered poems by English and American writers and featured illustrations by several artists, including Birket Foster and William Harvey, which were probably reused from earlier English publications.[20] Within the next two years, however, the firm had changed its approach and switched to using original designs by American artists. The timing suggests that Appleton had also been stung by the criticism leveled at U.S. publishers for relying too heavily on electrotypes of engravings from abroad.

For holiday giving in 1870 and 1871, Appleton offered new editions of two of William Cullen Bryant's long-familiar poems that garnered much praise, *The Song of the Sower* (1871) and *The Story of the Fountain* (1872). The focus is on the images more than the poetry, for both books feature relatively large wood engravings on every page accompanied by only a few lines of text; the tissue guards separating the pages enhance the special quality of the illustrations, and a list in the front of the books identifies the artist and engraver of each. Fenn, by now a regular contributor to *Appletons' Journal,* joined many other artists, including Winslow Homer, W. J. Hennessy, John A. Hows, Granville Perkins, and C. C. Griswold, in providing designs in a great variety of formats and styles, which were then engraved by the "best engravers in the country."[21] (Although the resulting lack of overall harmony is striking today, perhaps contrasts enhanced interest for the era's viewers.)

In keeping with the growing taste for decorative cloth bindings, Appleton offered *The Song of the Sower* bound in green cloth, stamped with gold and black borders and shafts of wheat, for $5. Even the critic for *Scribner's Monthly,* published by a competing firm, was impressed: "Among the exquisite reproductions of familiar poetry that have appeared of late years from the American press there has not been a more magnificent volume than *The Song of the Sower,* just published by Messrs. D. Appleton & Co. . . . there are forty-two engravings . . . of the utmost beauty, delicacy, and tenderness. . . . what could be finer than the old barn on page 15, which Fenn has drawn and Karst engraved with such truthfulness

   Poetry and Picturesque America

in every line? Or where shall we find a more faithful drawing than Homer's factory girl on page 29, which the same engraver has cut from the block?"[22] For his
design, Homer included conventional figures and used line work to create the
background, producing effects that apparently found more favor than his earlier
illustrations for *Ballads of New England.*[23]

The image by Fenn singled out for praise—that of an old barn covered with
birds (doves, perhaps) and a fallen trunk providing shade for a sow and piglets—
embodies picturesque conventions. Far different is Fenn's response to Bryant's
lines about supplying grain: "For those whose toiling hands uprear / The roof-
trees of our swarming race." His image of construction under way in a city, with
scaffolding and huge stone blocks (fig. 3.4), is unlike anything he would later
draw for *Picturesque America,* whose city views feature impressive buildings and
elegant public spaces. This example effectively shows how illustrating poetry
often called forth subjects different from those Fenn would select for himself;
nevertheless, he was able to imbue them with interest and drama. Near the end of
the poem, his design to illustrate Bryant's lines about sending wheat "Wherever,
o'er the waiting earth, / Roads wind and rivers flow" strains to include everything
(fig. 3.5): a separate small panel shows the plant growing, and a larger, irregularly
shaped image—similar to his later views of the Palisades of the Hudson in *Picturesque America* (see fig. 3.27)—depicts a grain wagon at the top of a cliff and barges
on the river below. Clearly, in this period Fenn understood his role in illustrating
a poem to involve creating quite literal depictions of the text.

Building upon the success of *The Song of the Sower,* for the 1871 holiday season
Appleton published *The Story of the Fountain,* a matching volume of Bryant's
poetry to which Fenn contributed twenty-four of the forty-two images.[24] The
company's advertisements gave him pride of place, stating, "Drawings by Harry
Fenn, Winslow Homer, Alfred Fredericks, John Hows and others."[25] In its green
cloth binding, stamped in gold with four oval medallions and decorative elements
recalling Charles Eastlake's architectural ornaments, it sold for $5; a version in
full morocco leather cost $8. The book met with great acclaim, as evidenced by a
review in the *Christian Union,* which effused: "Any rational being who will look
at the initial cut (from the pencil of Harry Fenn and the graver of Harley), where
the sage and bard is represented *subtegmina fagi* [in the shade of the beech], in the
very act of catching the divine impulse from the fountain that flows at his feet,
will buy the volume incontinently for that alone."[26]

The speaker in Bryant's poem, while along the stream's banks, muses on the flow
of history as progress, from violent warfare between Indian tribes to the coming of

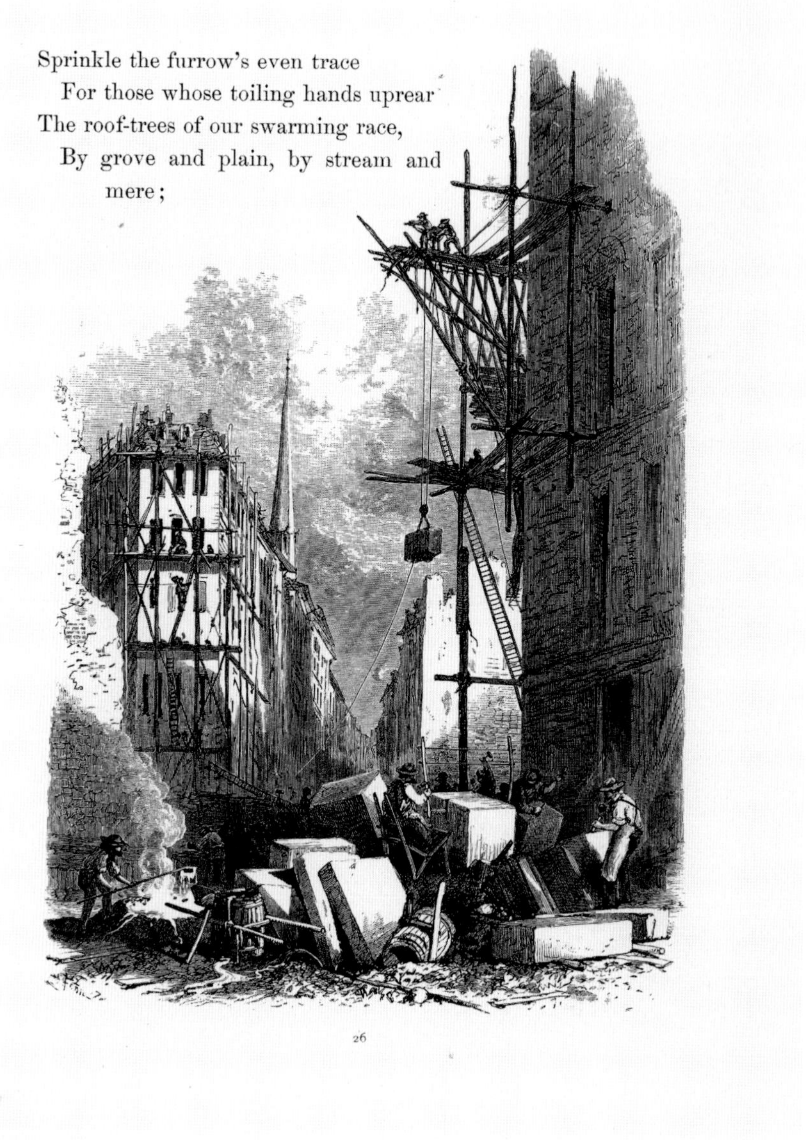

settlers who farmed in peace. Near the end, however, the sage wonders whether the stream will be degraded by future misuse. In responding to the lines "Will not man / Seek out strange arts to wither and deform / The pleasant landscape which thou makest green?" Fenn created one of his darkest illustrations: a view of railroad construction above a nightmarish industrial landscape (fig. 3.6). This disturbing vision of the possible consequences of growth in transportation and industry, likely

Poetry and Picturesque America

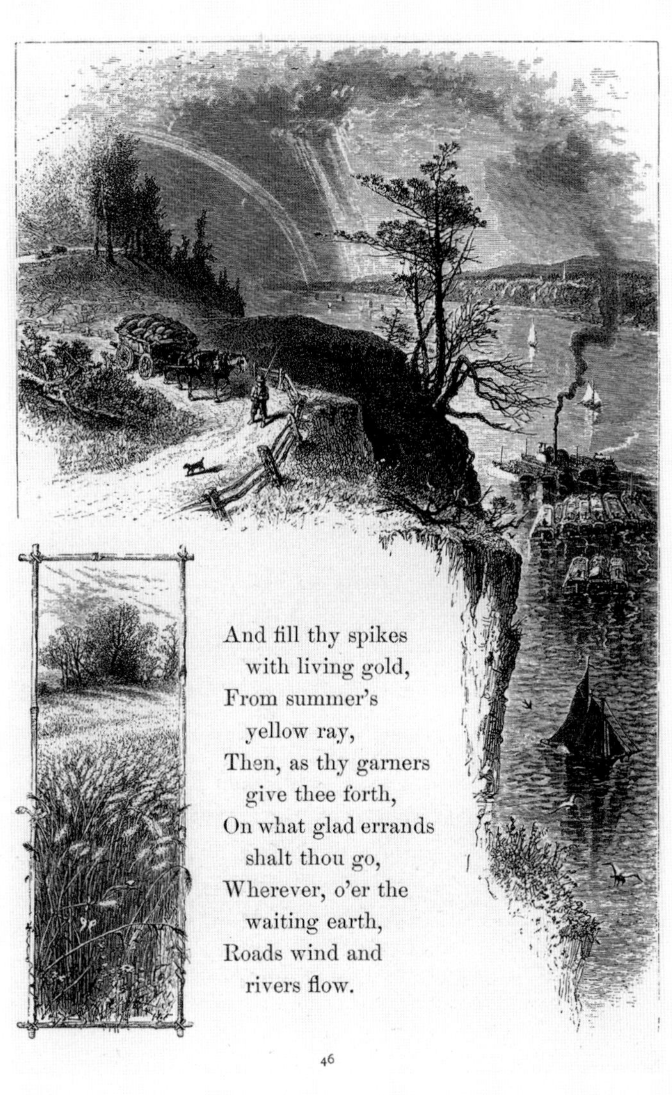

inspired by his visit to Pittsburgh in early 1871, is unique among Fenn's poetry illustrations.

Despite the image's inherent pessimism, a sweeping endorsement of the book and its illustrations appeared in the *Saturday Evening Gazette:* "The Messrs. Appleton deserve the thanks of all Americans who take pride in the artistic triumphs of their native land, and may lay the flattering unction to their souls that they have produced

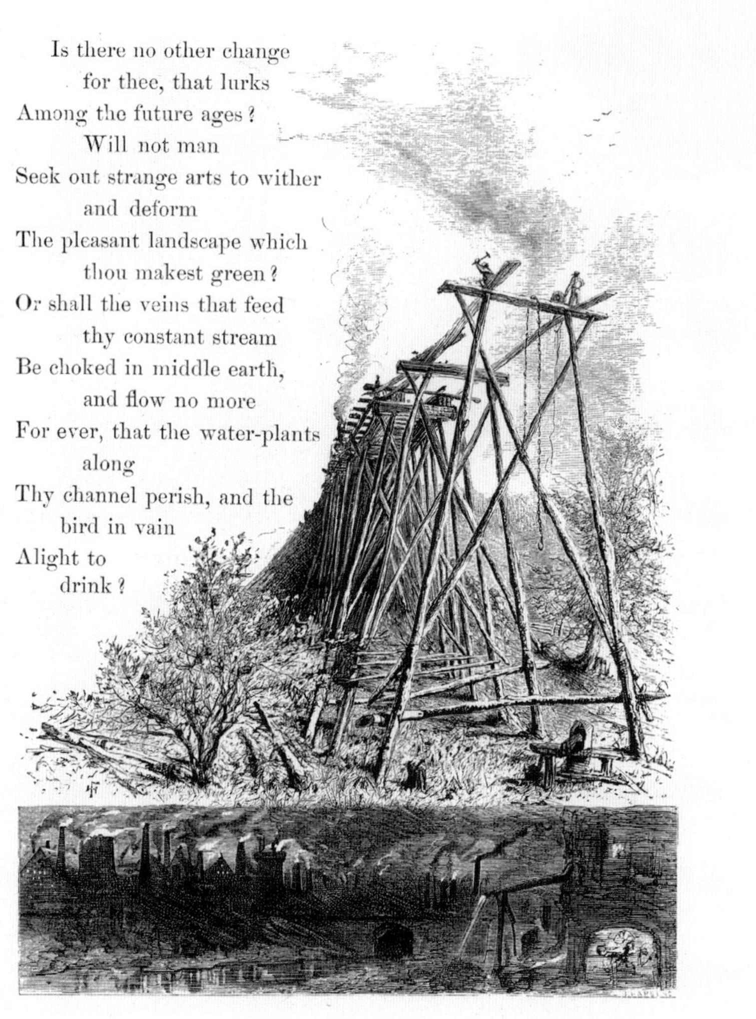

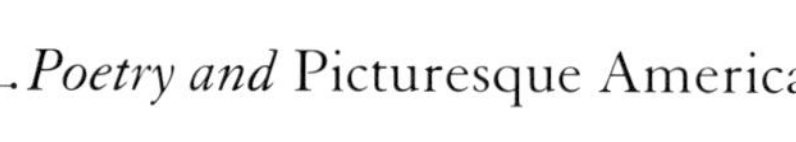

the best illustrated work that has ever been issued here."[27] Such high praise must have encouraged the firm to plan additional illustrated works, which indeed they did.

FENN AND D. APPLETON & COMPANY

Fenn's business relationship with the Appletons preceded his contributions to their two highly touted gift books of the early 1870s. It began soon after the firm

Poetry and Picturesque America

launched the weekly *Appletons' Journal of Literature, Science and Art* in April 1869, at ten cents a copy. The magazine's 11-by-8-inch format was larger than *Harper's Monthly* but smaller than *Harper's Weekly*. Its emphasis on literature and art—notably, works by American writers and artists—set it apart from the illustrated newspapers reporting current events, and the inclusion of science seemed appropriate for the firm that had published Charles Darwin's and Herbert Spencer's works in the United States.[28] In addition, its weekly appearance distinguished it from such literary monthlies as the *Atlantic, Harper's, Putnam's,* and *Lippincott's.*

No doubt the Appletons hoped to promote their other publications in this new periodical, as the New York firms of Harper and Putnam and Philadelphia's Lippincott did in theirs. But they also aimed to engage in the loftier mission of civilizing the newly reunited and ever-expanding nation. Like Harper, which designated *Harper's Weekly* as the "Journal of Civilization" on the masthead, Appleton was motivated by the confidence that evolution rendered progress inevitable. Spencer's works, published by Appleton in the early 1860s, supported this optimism by maintaining that environment, rather than Darwin's natural selection, determined character and mind.[29] Civilization advanced by filling the environment with the beauty and culture that would, in Kathleen Pyne's words, "reshape foreign peoples in the mold of ideal types—patterned after Anglo-Saxon Protestants."[30] Spencer's framework for understanding the world was reassuring to many because, even though it incorporated the latest scientific theories, it left room for the divine or, in Spencer's term, "the Unknowable."

In launching its own illustrated magazine, the Appleton firm thus joined what was becoming an important cultural movement in the visual arts to foster evolutionary progress. The journal would help educate and assimilate the nation's population scattered across the vast continent, including non-English-speaking immigrants, through the dissemination of pictures, primarily inexpensive wood engravings. One commentator described an illustrated periodical as "the art gallery of the world. Single admission, ten cents," and a writer in the *Hartford Times* noted that "a really *good* illustrated paper is a greater *educator* of the popular taste than any painter, however great."[31]

Furthermore, the text and images of widely circulated periodicals enabled many to experience a sense of belonging to a community of readers who shared familiarity with the up-to-date information presented in their pages. Over time, the contents of these publications helped a diverse populace imagine, or conceptualize, their society and make sense of and find their way in unfamiliar and increasingly complex urban settings.[32] Publishers responded to the public's avid interest in such magazines by sometimes advertising the day, and even the hour, when a new issue would be available.[33]

The new *Appletons' Journal* stressed the novelty and artistic value of its illustrations, claiming that many were fine enough to be framed. The wood engravings were frequently well designed and skillfully engraved, often of better quality than those prepared in haste and printed on thin paper for the weekly newspapers. Moreover, the trim size allowed for larger, more striking images than those in the monthlies. The new magazine also sought to distinguish itself from the era's other illustrated periodicals by offering an "Illustrated Supplement" each week: either a steel engraving, a large fold-out "cartoon" engraved on wood, or an "Art Supplement" containing wood engravings illustrating a popular topic, such as New York City or European gardens. The occasional inclusion of steel engravings also distinguished the *Journal* from most other current periodicals and linked it with the earlier tradition of costlier books illustrated with such engravings.

After preparing for the magazine's launch since at least the previous summer, the Appletons published the first issue on April 3, 1869. They wasted no time in enlisting the young artist whose illustrations for *Snow-Bound* had received such acclaim the year before. In the April 24 issue, two small views by Fenn appeared in the "New York Illustrated" art supplement, and more appeared in subsequent issues as the series on New York continued. (The entire series was published as a book in late 1869.) Fenn's illustrations for it were more dynamic in both style and format than those by most of the other contributors. His foldout "View of Castle Garden and New York Bay" was the featured cartoon in the *Journal*'s seventh issue, on May 15, 1869.

His illustrations in the first year also included the steel engraving "West Point and the Highlands" on September 11; another foldout, this one of Fairmount Park in Philadelphia, on September 25; a front-page harvest scene titled "October" on October 23; and two wood engravings of noticeably superior quality, "The Cape Ann Cedar Tree" and "Star Island, Isles of Shoals," on October 9 (fig. 3.7). This last, clearly the result of Fenn's visit to the islands that summer, was one of the more striking images the *Journal* had included; it is a forceful rendering of the prominent rock formation and an appealing group of well-dressed picnickers, presumably including the artist stretched out on a rock taking a break from his sketching post.[34] These commissions offered Fenn a chance to design on a larger scale, and in several his technique is looser, with fewer lines and greater use of the white of the paper than in most of his illustrations for poetry.

Fenn's works constituted a significant contribution to the *Journal*'s artworks from its earliest months, as did designs by Homer, Darley, and Alfred R. Waud, who had distinguished himself as a Civil War artist for *Harper's Weekly*.[35] But just as the new

 Poetry and Picturesque America

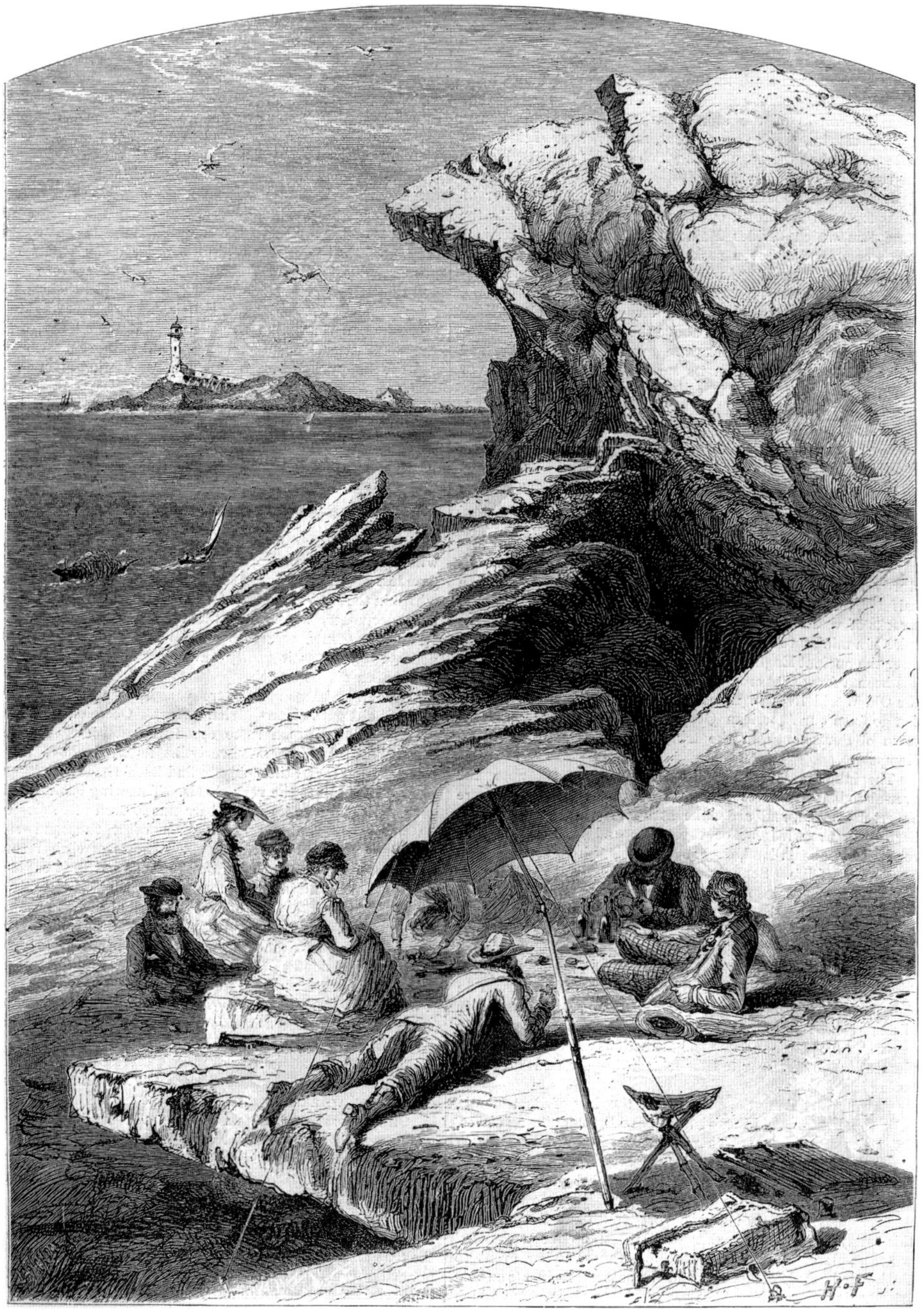

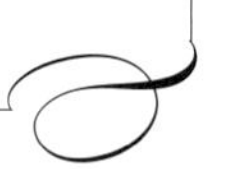

3.7. Harry Fenn, "New England Coast Scene.—Star Island, Isles of Shoals." *Appletons' Journal,* October 9, 1869, 241. Wood engraving, 9 1/4" x 6 3/8".

Journal began to receive favorable attention, the competition increased. More established rivals—notably *Frank Leslie's Illustrated Newspaper, Harper's Weekly,* and *Every Saturday*—announced plans to produce better illustrations. In addition, the *Aldine Press* increased its art coverage and touted "the Unequalled Excellence" of its "Woodcut Illustrations," with considerable justification. Not to be outdone, the new *Scribner's*

Monthly, scheduled to launch in November 1870 under the editorship of Josiah Gilbert Holland (1819–1881), the best-selling author of *Bitter-Sweet* and *Kathrina* (1867), boasted that it would have "the finest illustrations procurable at home and abroad."[36]

With such formidable competition, *Appletons' Journal* needed something special to attract and maintain subscribers. The initiative chosen by George S. Appleton (1821–1878), the brother credited with "fine artistic taste," and staff editors was a series on the "the most unfamiliar and novel features of American scenery"—titled "Picturesque America," it would feature illustrations by Harry Fenn.[37] It was this series that would lead to dramatic changes in Fenn's career.

The "Picturesque America" Series in *Appletons' Journal*

Although from today's perspective the theme of "picturesque America" might sound less than compelling, in 1870 it was an extremely timely and appealing subject. As the nation began to recover from the terrible devastation of the Civil War, travel for pleasure, business, and culture was once again a possibility, notably to the southern states and the West via the transcontinental railroad, newly completed in May 1869. Furthermore, the project's association with traveling "in search of the picturesque," a favorite pastime of the British upper classes in the late eighteenth century and still a popular activity in nineteenth-century America, appealed to a growing middle class seeking to associate themselves with cultural refinement through an appreciation of art and nature. This was just the audience *Appletons' Journal* hoped to attract.

Much of the enjoyment of this sort of touring involved the search for natural or cultivated landscapes that conformed to conceptions of the beautiful, the sublime, and the picturesque—aesthetic categories long established in art and literature and so familiar by the mid-nineteenth century that they needed no explanation. The *beautiful* was characterized by the smooth curving lines, harmony of color, and limited size of pastoral landscapes and calm lakes, scenes that evoked feelings of peace and contentment.[38] The *sublime,* in contrast, was characterized by vast height or depth, darkness, or powerful motion. Such scenes aroused feelings of awe or wonder; they could take one's breath away and cause the heart to skip a beat. But, viewed from a safe distance, towering peaks, deep canyons, roaring waterfalls, and dramatic storms could provide a thrill or *frisson* of terror.[39] The *picturesque* was less extensive in scale than the sublime and much easier to discover in the landscapes of Britain and the eastern United States. It was characterized by irregular form, rough texture, pleasing variety, and contrasts of light

Poetry and Picturesque America

and dark and often included ruins or gnarled trees, suggesting the passage of time. Its effect was to arouse curiosity and interest, and thereby provide delight. It was this type of scenery the medium of wood engraving, with its dependence on line, texture, and contrast, was best suited to depict. Yet, as the project developed, Fenn and the other contributing artists would, of course, include many scenes that could be considered beautiful or sublime as well.

Earlier paintings, prints, and books of topographical views had already established several sites as part of the canon of American scenery, such as Niagara Falls, the Hudson River and its Palisades, the Catskills and the White Mountains, Trenton Falls, Lake George, and Natural Bridge. Concentrating on the most impressive and accessible places, primarily in the Northeast, the most notable among the books were the English import *American Scenery* (1837–1839), with steel engravings after designs by the British artist William H. Bartlett (1809–1854) and text by the popular American writer Nathaniel Parker Willis, and *The Home Book of the Picturesque* (1852), which reproduced works by several leading American landscape painters.[40] In *Appletons' Journal,* a new series featuring "the most unfamiliar and novel" scenery promised to expand the catalogue of picturesque sites and thus inform and guide tourists while fostering pride in the nation's scenery.

Much of the United States abounded in cascading streams, rock formations and caves, and trees with twisting trunks and intricate foliage. Whenever possible, the series would emphasize the historical associations that made these scenes more picturesque, such as crumbling buildings, old wagons and boats, and idealized rural characters. By presenting copious evidence that the New World's cultural landscape was full of picturesque interest, it would help to diminish the long-standing inferiority complex with regard to the Old World's preponderance of historical sites and artifacts. Its scope soon expanded beyond scenic beauties to include America's civic amenities, agriculture, industry, and natural resources, contributing to the growing pride that culminated in the celebration of the nation's one-hundredth birthday at the Centennial Exposition, held in Philadelphia in 1876.

The series enabled many who had had little opportunity to travel to visualize places they had only heard of and incorporate them into their concept of the United States. Although some had access to images of American scenery and cities through art exhibitions or photographs, especially the stereographic views selling for $1.50 to $6.00 a dozen that had become a popular addition to many parlors and lending libraries, neither of these offerings could adequately satisfy the curiosity of large numbers of Americans.[41] Nor could the lithographic prints published by Currier & Ives and other firms, which frequently presented bird's-eye views of cities or idealized images of scenery. Nothing proved as accessible and as ubiquitous as the wood engravings that entered homes via popular periodicals. The frequent articles about particular regions attest to their appeal, such as those in *Leslie's* "Across the Continent" series and *Every Saturday's* "Graphic America," both from 1870. Further evidence lies in the fact that the artists who traveled to these regions to prepare drawings were treated as celebrities, with their comings and goings reported in the press.

The editors of *Appletons' Journal* had given attention to some of America's scenic features even before deciding to commission Fenn to depict them. In the magazine's first issue, a column titled "Matters of Science and Art" had implored painters to extend their reach, an echo of the earlier challenge to landscape artists issued by Alexander von Humboldt in his book *Cosmos* that had sent Frederic Church to the Ecuadorian Andes in the 1850s.[42] The column chided American painters for repeating "year after year pictures of the Catskills, the White Mountains, and the Adirondacks" and Lake George "while the Blue Ridge of Virginia and the mountain scenery of North Carolina seem never to have been visited by our painters."[43] The *Journal's* October 1869 issue featured "Novelties of Southern Scenery," an article written and illustrated by Charles Lanman (1819–1895), who claimed that in "treasures" of mountain scenery the southern states were "not one whit behind the Northern States," for they could boast of fourteen peaks higher than Mount Washington, "the king of the North."[44]

Clearly, the editor thought it was time to expand the imagery of American scenery to new subjects, but Fenn receives credit for the idea of using the *Journal's* pages to do so, according to an incident recounted in at least two sources. The setting was a social gathering that included some of the Appletons as well as Fenn, who overheard "an Englishman sneeringly say that the scenery of America had nothing picturesque about it." Since arriving in the United States some twelve years earlier, Fenn had apparently come to identify with the American landscape enough to leap to its defense, for he "remarked in the hearing of the heads of the house, 'If they will make it worth my while, we will show the young man if there is any thing picturesque in America.'"

Looking back on his life, Fenn might well have counted this remark as one of his most fortunate utterances. A few months later, he received a letter from the Appletons "asking him to come over and talk to them about that suggestion he had made," and this discussion led to a major commission.[45] Beginning in May 1870, the Appletons sent him on a tour of the South, which Fenn reported was "a great education in rapid outdoor sketching," although apparently not

Poetry and Picturesque America

until some months later was the decision made to create a series called "Pictur-esque America."[46] The first announcement of Fenn's assignment appeared in the "Table-Talk" section of the August 27, 1870, issue. It was the first of many notices that would enhance Fenn's reputation as a landscape artist:

> Let us say, . . . that, convinced the South offered fresher fields than elsewhere for the picturesque, we dispatched, last May, that accomplished artist, Mr. Harry Fenn, on a sketching-tour through the Southern country. Mr. Fenn ascended the St. John and Ocklawaha Rivers, Florida, traversed Georgia, the Carolinas, Eastern Tennessee, and Virginia, and has returned with his folio filled with a series of the most striking and beautiful sketches conceivable. These will go at once into the hands of our best engravers, and will soon give new interest and variety to the pages of the Journal.[47]

In the months when Fenn was traveling and his compositions were being engraved, the *Journal* continued to publish several views of the American land-scape, as it had from the beginning, drawn by other artists, including the painters W. L. Sonntag and George H. Smillie, both associated with the National Acad-emy.[48] Clearly, Fenn had competition, yet he was the one selected for this new, more ambitious project.

With the October 29, 1870, issue, just as the new *Scribner's Monthly* entered the market, *Appletons' Journal* recast the announcement, without naming Fenn, to promote a more comprehensive series not limited to the South. It noted that a "specially dispatched" artist was gathering material "for a series of papers to be called PICTURESQUE AMERICA consisting of splendidly-executed views of the most unfamiliar and novel features of American scenery accompanied with suitable letter-press."[49] In the next issue, a longer announcement identified the artist as "Mr. HARRY FENN, one of our most accomplished draughtsmen," and again men-tioned his travels in the South and his portfolio bulging with sketches that were now in the hands of the best engravers.[50]

The choice of where to send Fenn probably elicited considerable discussion. The desire to present fresh subjects and "the most unfamiliar and novel features" could well have suggested Florida, western North Carolina, and other parts of the South; however, the continuing turmoil over reinstating the former Confederate states into the Union, the presence of federal troops in several southern states, and growing Klan violence aimed at excluding African Americans from participation in civil society may have given the publishers pause.[51] In the few years since the close of the Civil War, the South had barely begun to recover economically from the devastation, yet northerners were curious about its scenic features and historic cities, not to mention its business opportunities. Florida in particular was receiving attention as a desirable destination for both adventure (hunting, fishing) and recuperation; Harriet Beecher Stowe and her husband had bought a winter home in Mandarin in 1867, and the October 1870 *Harper's Monthly* featured the article "Six Weeks in Florida" by George Ward Nichols.

The Appletons likewise saw an opportunity not only to appeal to readers' curiosity but also to develop a southern market for their journal. The "Picturesque America" series opened on November 12, 1870, with an article titled "The St. John's and Ocklawaha Rivers, Florida," with twelve illustrations by Fenn in a variety of sizes and formats. On his journey on the rivers, recently accessible by steamboat routes, Fenn had been accompanied by the writer T. B. Thorpe (1815–1878), a frequent contributor to the *Journal* and author of *The Hive of the Bee-Hunter* (1854), a collection of tales about alligator shooting, bear hunting, and fishing. Both the images and the text were printed on calendered paper, which was smoother than the rest of the magazine's pages and yielded sharper impressions of the wood engravings. A writer in the *Christian Advocate* was mightily impressed by the quality and wondered: "How the Appletons can furnish such illustrations on toned paper for ten cents is simply incomprehensible."[52]

Although swamps had long been viewed as unhealthy and forbidding, Fenn's images connected them with the picturesque aesthetic through association with the cycles of nature—growth and decay—and the device of a river journey, a classic way to experience the picturesque.[53] Thorpe exclaimed that from their steamboat "a picture of novel interest presented itself at every turn."

Despite its setting in an atypical semitropical location, Thorpe's account is a model of landscape description in the picturesque mode as English, European, and American writers had been practicing it for decades. Noting that "the pencil of the artist has heretofore scarcely touched" Florida, he contrasted the aridity and desolation of the "open tropical landscape" with the "recesses of the swamp," where they found flowers, vines, and gigantic trees "as nowhere else to be seen." Fenn depicted the scene Thorpe described of "an old dead cypress . . . covered with innumerable turkey-buzzards, which are waiting patiently for the decomposition of an alligator" (fig. 3.8), as well as a large white crane "seizing upon the young of the innumerable water-snakes which everywhere abound." As they steamed along the Ocklawaha River at night, the glow from burning pine-knots in iron cages lit up the trees and streamers of Spanish moss, reminding Thorpe of "banners amidst Gothic architecture." He also recounted meeting two "Florida

Poetry and Picturesque America

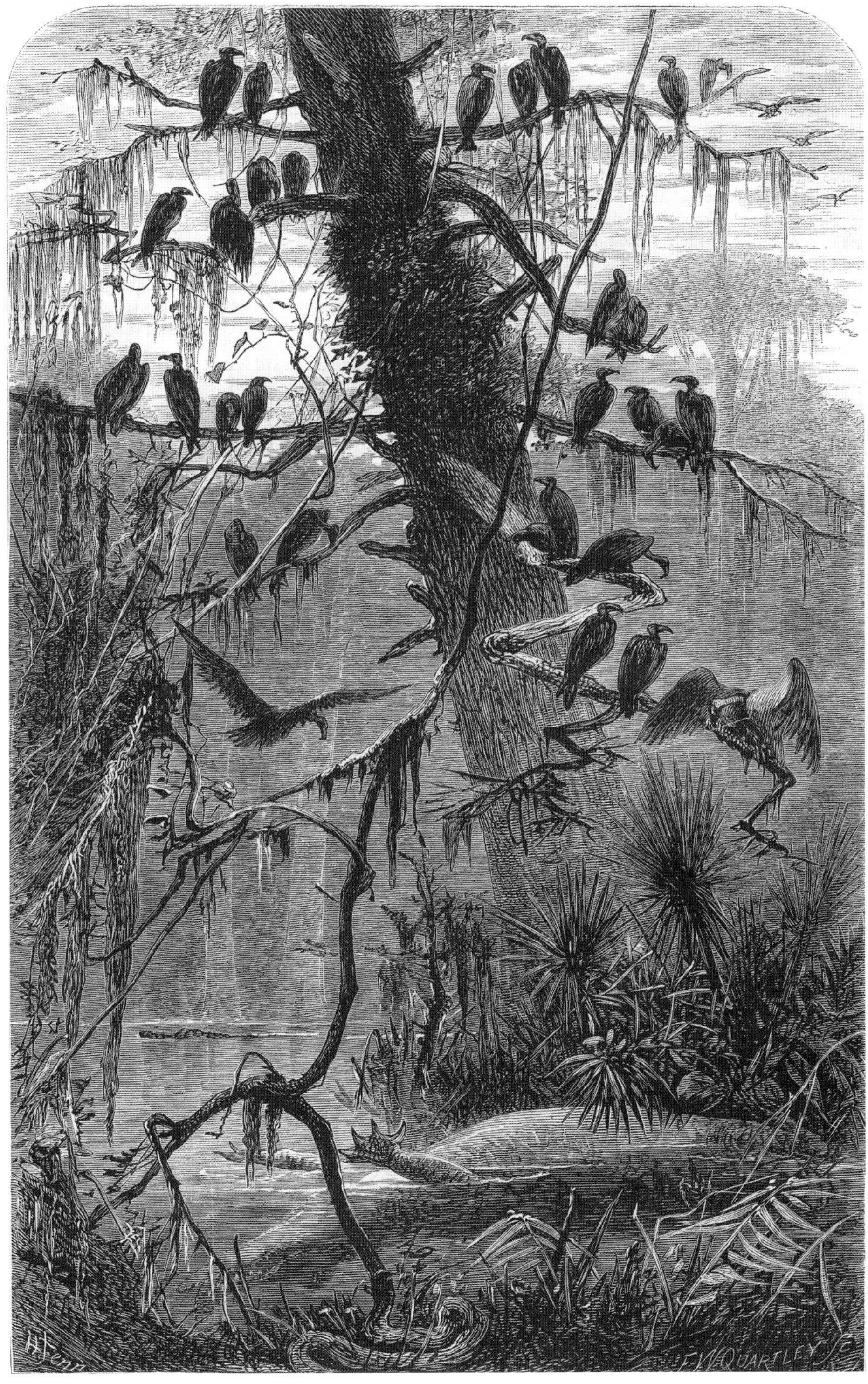

3.8. Harry Fenn, "Waiting for Decomposition." *Appletons' Journal,* November 12, 1870, 581. Wood engraving by F. W. Quartley, 8 3/16" x 5 1/16".

crackers" making cypress shingles near their hut, "the very model of the pictur-esque," which were illustrated by Fenn.[54]

Both the November 26 and December 17 issues contained two of Fenn's wood engravings of scenes in western North Carolina, printed on calendered paper. The accompanying text emphasizes the number of the state's mountains that were taller than New Hampshire's Mount Washington and celebrates the French Broad River, "whose wild and romantic course . . . abounds in the most picturesque and beautiful scenery," including "gorges of fearful height," huge cliffs, and weird and fantastic masses of rocks.[55] Fenn's illustrations " 'The Lov-ers' Leap'—at Early Sunrise" (fig. 3.9) and "Chimney Rock, Hickory-Nut Gap, North Carolina" (fig. 3.10) are typical of his depictions of mountains, in which he used low viewpoints and exaggeration to make the landforms appear taller while relying on light and shadow to reveal the contours of the towering rock formations. These natural wonders were of great interest at the time, and his pre-cise representation of their layers and fissures tells of sedimentation and erosion occurring over millions of years, in keeping with the theories of Charles Lyell.[56]

As the general public came to embrace the notion of the earth's antiquity, adjusting their understanding of the biblical account of creation in six days to allow for the passage of eons, many people saw rocks as the best evidence of divine providence at work in the planet's formation. As a result, rock hunting and cave exploring became popular pastimes. The Lovers' Leap illustration also includes a curving road and artist's umbrella and easel (although the artist is not visible), motifs similar to ones in "The Dome," an earlier Helderberg image (see fig. 2.10). Fenn often used adaptations of his own or others' compositions, as will be dis-cussed in later chapters.

After this impressive opening, the "Picturesque America" series continued in the pages of *Appletons' Journal* for the next year and a half, but with less careful preparation and fanfare. Detailed accompanying texts appeared less frequently, and soon the calendered paper was used only for full-page wood engravings and then not at all.[57] These cost-cutting measures suggest *Appletons' Journal* was not as successful as the firm had hoped, and perhaps the publishers cut back on com-missions involving travel as well. For a few months, Fenn was the only illustra-tor for the series. His striking images of Natural Bridge appeared on February 11, 1871, but with the February 25 issue, the "Picturesque America" designation began to be applied to work done by other artists as well. The first was a front-page illustration by Paul Dixon captioned "Picturesque America.—A Nook on the Hudson."

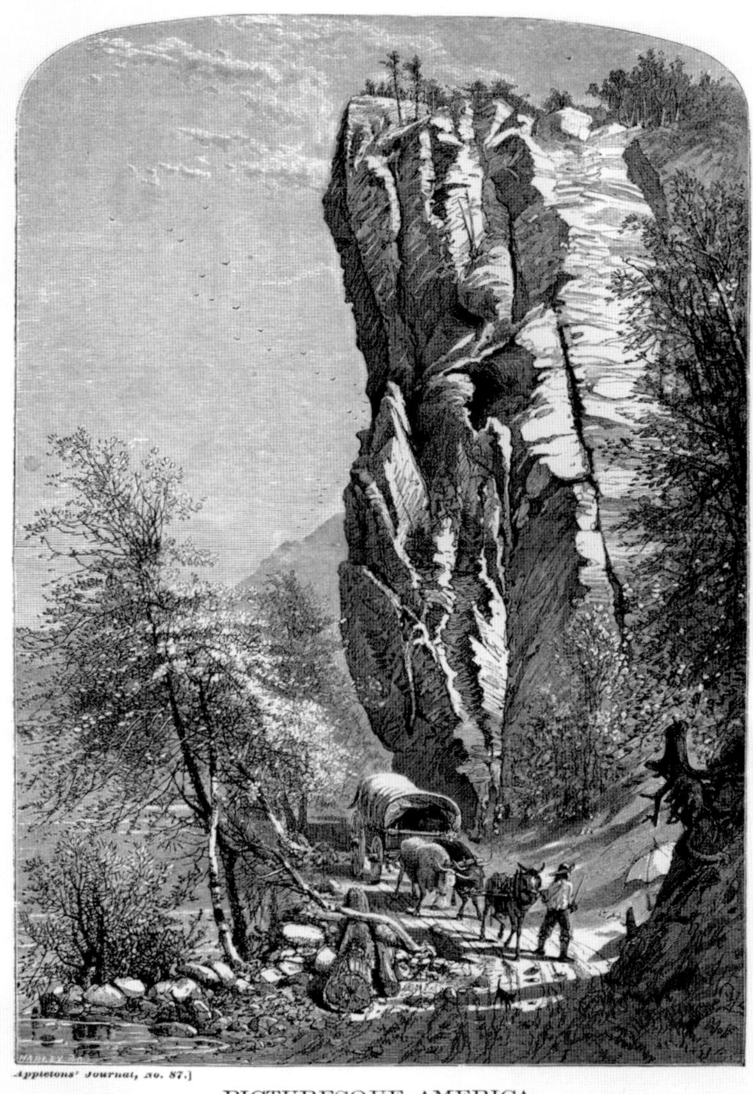

PICTURESQUE AMERICA.

ON THE FRENCH BROAD RIVER, NORTH CAROLINA.

"THE LOVERS' LEAP"—AT EARLY SUNRISE.

3.9. Harry Fenn, "Picturesque America. On the French Broad River, North Carolina. 'The Lovers' Leap'—At Early Sunrise." *Appletons' Journal,* November 26, 1870, Extra Sheet, No. 87. Wood engraving by [Joseph S.] Harley, 8 15/16" x 6 3/16".

The change did not pass unnoticed in a time when critics regularly reviewed the contents of periodicals. The March 9, 1871, "Periodicals" column in the *Philadelphia Inquirer* noted that the February issues of *Appletons' Journal* were "brilliant as usual," with "superior" engravings, especially "the views of Picturesque America"; the writer admired Fenn's "very fine" Natural Bridge images but

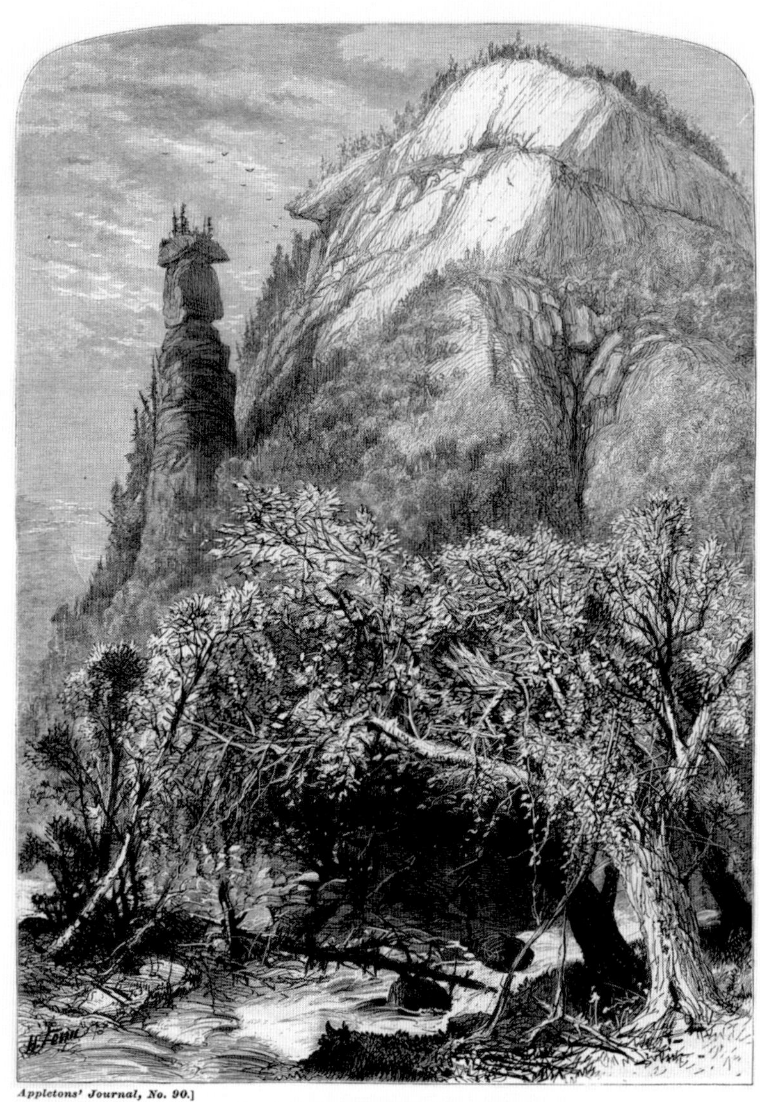

PICTURESQUE AMERICA.

CHIMNEY ROCK, HICKORY-NUT GAP, NORTH CAROLINA.

considered Dixon's treatment of the Hudson "hardly so happy as it might have been." Indeed, with its ground-level frontal viewpoint, little foreground interest, and predominantly gray tone, it *was* dull compared with Fenn's. For the rest of 1871, Fenn's work, including views of Yosemite that he based on photographs, appeared alternately with images of New Hampshire by A. C. Warren and of Nevada by Alfred R. Waud.

Poetry and Picturesque America

The *Every Saturday* Interlude

One reason the Appletons turned to other artists at this time was that Fenn had been enticed away in early 1871 by the publisher of *Every Saturday,* who invited him to travel with the magazine's writer and art director, Ralph Keeler (1840–1873), to the booming industrial city of Pittsburgh and the Pennsylvania oil fields. Published by James R. Osgood, the latest incarnation of the firm that had published *Snow-Bound,* this competing journal was increasing its emphasis on American features illustrated by American artists. Fenn was probably motivated by loyalty to the firm that had boosted his career so dramatically or the offer of higher pay (or both), although possibly he was dissatisfied with some aspect of his arrangement with *Appletons' Journal.*

Regardless, the February 11, 1871, *Every Saturday* announced "a series of papers illustrating points of scenic and industrial interest in the United States, on a grander scale than has ever been undertaken by any pictorial newspaper," an obvious challenge to the "Picturesque America" series.[58] Fenn's illustrations for articles titled "The Taking of Pittsburgh" and "Sketches in Oil" appeared from March 4 to April 1, 1871. His striking self-portrait, which shows him with portfolio in tow gazing out the back of the train at the Great Bend on the Alleghenies (see fig. 3.1), attests to his growing confidence and celebrity. His wide mustache, longish hair, and hat with a feather signaled that he was an artist, but a practical, active one, dressed casually in a rumpled wool jacket rather than a smock or velvet coat; the smoke trailing from his mouth and the pipe in his right hand conveys the train's fast movement.[59]

Fenn's new assignment could hardly have been more different from his travels for *Appletons' Journal* in search of the most appealing scenery and historic sites, such as old water-powered mills. Pittsburgh, the so-called Iron City, was known throughout the world for its rich coal deposits, technological advancement, and nearby oil fields in development since 1859. Fenn was now charged with depicting blast furnaces, rolling mills, and glassworks that spewed dirty smoke across the area where the Allegheny and Monongahela rivers merged to form the Ohio. Keeler found the city's sights exciting and picturesque; he once reported the "pyrotechnic display" after the tapping of a blast furnace to be as grand "as ever delighted the eyes of a victorious sovereign."[60] Fenn's smoke-filled image titled "The Levee" (March 25) (fig. 3.11), so unlike any of his designs for "Picturesque America," suggests the drama and intensity of this industrial area, as do some of his views of the oil fields, such as "Point Hill from French Creek," which shows

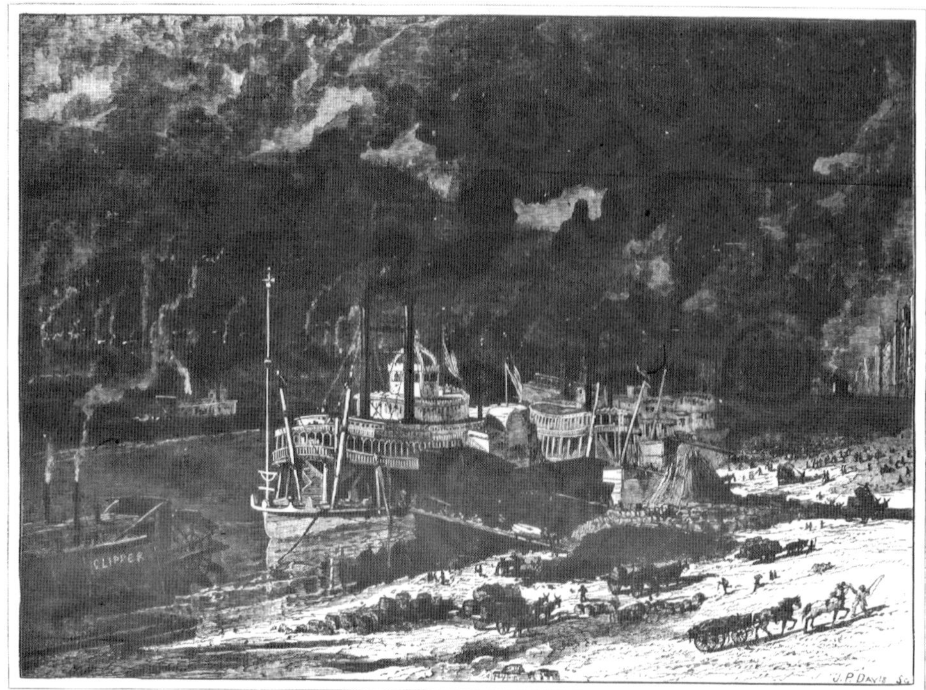

3.11. Harry Fenn, "Pittsburgh Sketches, —The Levee." *Every Saturday*, March 25, 1871, 273. Wood engraving, 9" x 12".

a hillside covered in derricks spewing smoke.[61] These images are similar to the dark vision of a possible future Fenn created for *The Story of the Fountain,* issued in 1872 (see fig. 3.6), although the writers' outlooks differ greatly. Since Fenn most likely visited Pittsburgh before beginning work on illustrations for Bryant's poem, what he saw there probably shaped his response.[62]

Fenn's interior views of factories show figures tending huge furnaces, casting steel ingots, and using a steam hammer, while Keeler's texts explain these operations in detail[63] and present a rosy picture of workmen who "seem to be as independent and almost as prosperous as their employers."[64] Both artist and writer also give attention to people besides mill workers: "A Family Coal Mine" is a strangely cheerful image of poor children scrambling for coal to heat their home,[65] and Fenn's two portraits of General Andrew Jackson, M.D., a local African American who had accompanied Pittsburgh's Duquesne Grays regiment in various wars and appeared regularly on horseback in military parades, depict a dignified figure at odds with Keeler's description of him as the object of laughter.[66] Since it is unknown whether Fenn completed his drawings before or after Keeler wrote the text, it is hard to judge whether he was intentionally departing from Keeler's narrative. Despite the poor quality of the engraving and printing in *Every Saturday* (compared to *Appletons' Journal*), a writer

Poetry and Picturesque America

in the *Literary World* considered Fenn's illustrations for "The Taking of Pittsburgh" article to be "among the best . . . ever seen in an American periodical."[67]

Return to *Appletons' Journal*

Soon Fenn was back at work for the Appletons. On the back page of the magazine's March 25, 1871, issue a conspicuous notice read: "The publishers of APPLETONS' JOURNAL have the pleasure of announcing the completion of arrangements by which Mr. HARRY FENN will for a time give his professional services exclusively to the prosecution of the series of views entitled 'PICTURESQUE AMERICA,' which for a few months past has been a conspicuous and attractive feature in the JOURNAL."[68] The announcement was repeated on April 1 and 8. No records have been found to shed light on the arrangements that enticed Fenn to work exclusively for the *Journal.* Better pay was probably a factor; another may have been anticipated travel with Oliver Bell Bunce, the editor overseeing the project who would also write several texts about their journeys. Fenn may well have realized that more coherent and interesting articles resulted from joint travel, as he had experienced with Thorpe for the *Journal* and Keeler for *Every Saturday.*

The March 25 issue announcing his return to the "Picturesque America" series included two full-page illustrations of historic East Hampton, Long Island, which Fenn perhaps based on sketches made the previous summer or fall. The contrast could hardly be greater between these images of old windmills, with carts and geese in the foreground, and those of iron making in Pittsburgh. The depictions counteracted the familiar criticism that the American landscape lacked historic associations and reinforced the text's claim that, of all the places on Long Island "that date back to the seventeenth century, none so now retains the customs and relics of the past in their perfectness as East Hampton" (fig. 3.12).[69] The windmills, which would become a familiar subject for artists in various media, are typical of the emphasis on picturesque older technologies rather than newer ones that characterized the series and, later, the book.

In April and May, more Fenn-designed views were published of Florida (April 22), Savannah (April 8), and the French Broad River in North Carolina (May 20).[70] Sometime in March, perhaps even before the announcement of Fenn's return to the *Journal,* he and Bunce had traveled by steamer from New York to Charleston, and in April the two men visited Lookout Mountain and Chattanooga. These journeys yielded outstanding articles. For his depiction of cities, Fenn drew old buildings and bustling harbors. His views of St. Augustine feature

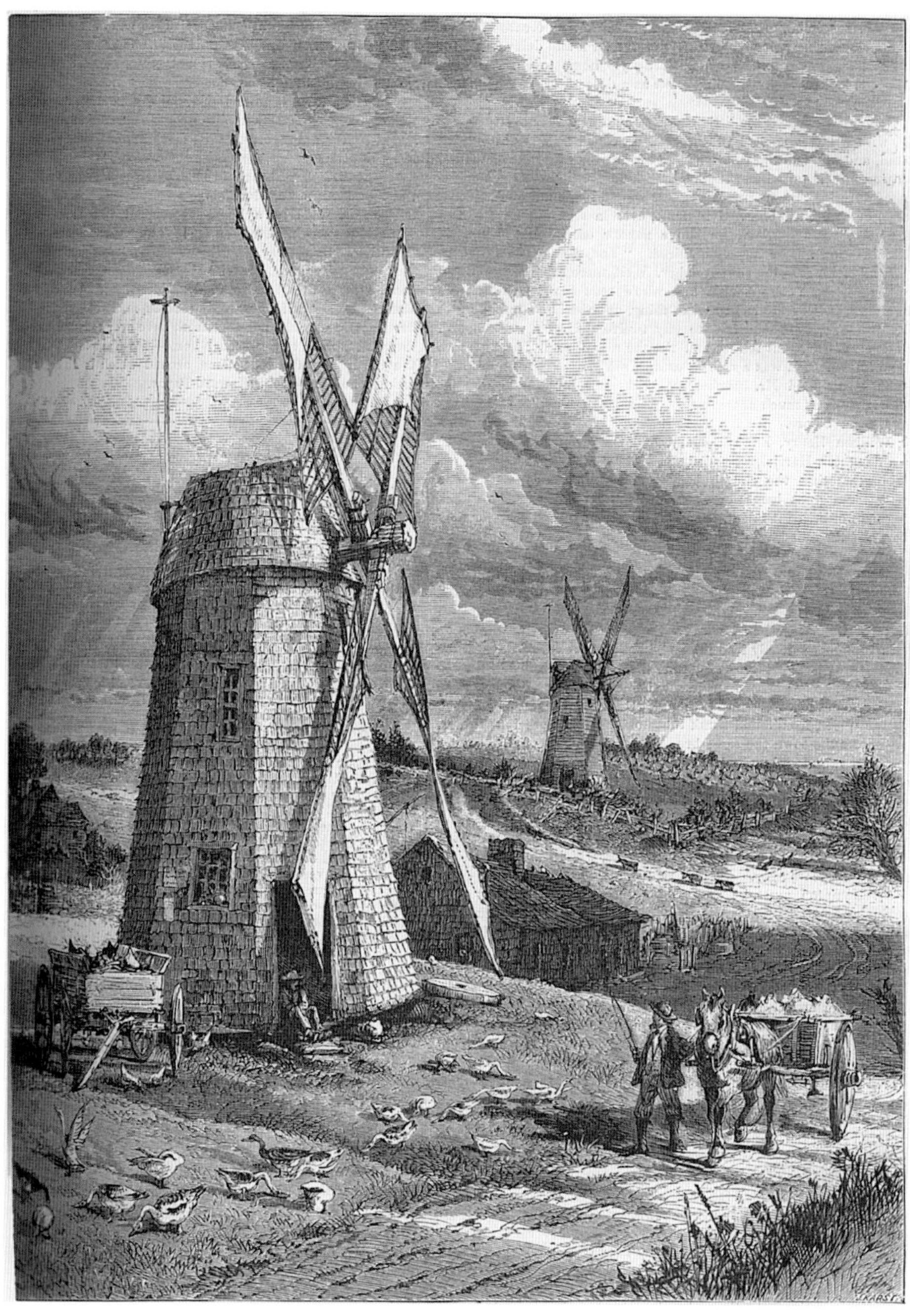

the picturesque architecture in the "oldest European settlement in the United States," which the text claimed "resembles an old town of Spain or Italy more than anyplace else in America." For Charleston, Bunce's text discussed buildings associated with the war—Fort Sumter and the ancient, well-loved but damaged customs house—whereas Fenn's illustration from the belfry of St. Michael's

Poetry and Picturesque America

Church (fig. 3.13) transformed the evidence of past conflict through the prism of the picturesque approach. Framing the view through a tower, with a black boy and playful pigeons in the foreground, Fenn emphasized the timeless charm of the old city. For Chattanooga, which had suffered heavy war damage and looked, in Bunce's words, "like a new colony" during its period of rebuilding, Fenn chose to depict scenes along the river, including the ferry landing, rather than the city itself. Only in "Canal, Richmond" did he draw a war-damaged building adjacent to a canal and across from "ramshackle porches of the negro tenements" in the Virginia city. Commenting on the illustration (February 3, 1872), Richmond native John R. Thompson noted "how much more effective in the hands of the artist is dilapidation than tidiness, and a ruin than a perfect structure."

Several times in his illustrations for the series, Fenn tried a distinctive type of composition that would become one of his favorites in this period and probably helps explain the contemporary appeal of his

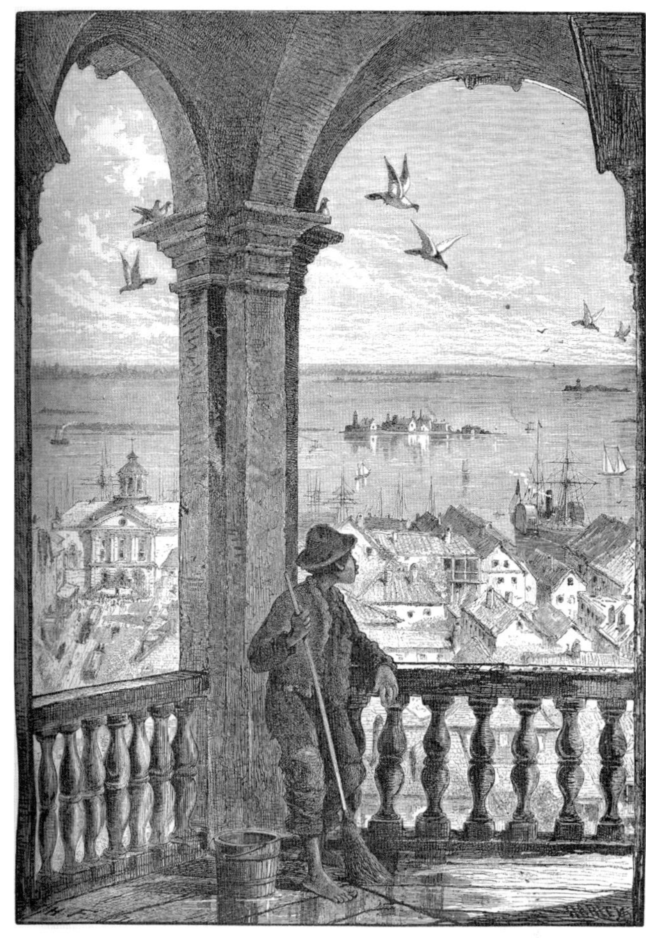

3.13. Harry Fenn, "A Glimpse of Charleston and Bay, from the Tower of St. Michael's Church." *Appletons' Journal*, July 15, 1871, 73. Wood engraving by [Joseph S.] Harley, 8 15/16" x 6 7/16".

work. The first instance is the opening image for the article on Natural Bridge (fig. 3.14), in which the text steps down the lower right of the page, below the title Fenn drew as part of the wood engraving, accentuating the height of the arched opening. In this version, compared to the one in the book (see fig. 1.1), Fenn made the bridge seem even taller by the inclusion of two tiny figures beside the creek below. (The book's format of wider margins required cropping the image and eliminating the figures.) The juxtaposition of text and picture, the irregular vignette shape, and the intricate lines depicting the rock formation and vegetation in impressive detail—beautifully drawn by Fenn and engraved by Joseph Harley—resulted in a striking page.

The design contrasted markedly with the usual rectangular, square, or oval

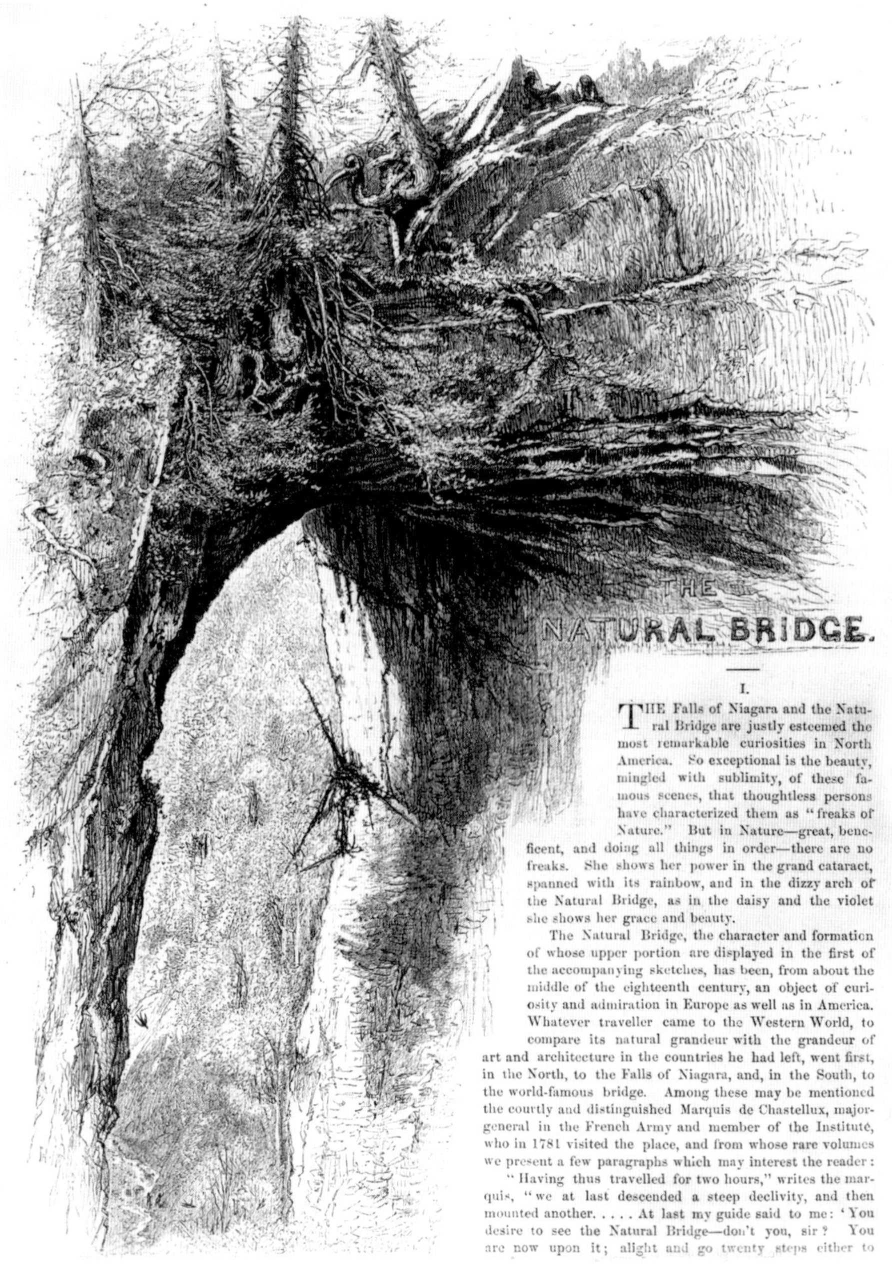

THE NATURAL BRIDGE.

I.

THE Falls of Niagara and the Natural Bridge are justly esteemed the most remarkable curiosities in North America. So exceptional is the beauty, mingled with sublimity, of these famous scenes, that thoughtless persons have characterized them as "freaks of Nature." But in Nature—great, beneficent, and doing all things in order—there are no freaks. She shows her power in the grand cataract, spanned with its rainbow, and in the dizzy arch of the Natural Bridge, as in the daisy and the violet she shows her grace and beauty.

The Natural Bridge, the character and formation of whose upper portion are displayed in the first of the accompanying sketches, has been, from about the middle of the eighteenth century, an object of curiosity and admiration in Europe as well as in America. Whatever traveller came to the Western World, to compare its natural grandeur with the grandeur of art and architecture in the countries he had left, went first, in the North, to the Falls of Niagara, and, in the South, to the world-famous bridge. Among these may be mentioned the courtly and distinguished Marquis de Chastellux, major-general in the French Army and member of the Institute, who in 1781 visited the place, and from whose rare volumes we present a few paragraphs which may interest the reader:

" Having thus travelled for two hours," writes the marquis, " we at last descended a steep declivity, and then mounted another. . . . . At last my guide said to me: ' You desire to see the Natural Bridge—don't you, sir ? You are now upon it; alight and go twenty steps either to

images, sometimes with arched tops and open bottoms, that filled the pages of *Appletons' Journal* and other periodicals, and it can be seen as a forerunner to the Aesthetic movement's emphasis on beautiful and more harmonious book design. Fenn used this approach several more times in the "Picturesque America" series, including in the openings for the articles "On the Tennessee" (October 14, 1871)

Poetry and Picturesque America

and "Richmond, Historic and Scenic" (February 3, 1872), as well as for the illustration "The James, above Richmond" in the Natural Bridge article. The pages have a more integrated look than do most American illustrated books of poetry, in which there is often little connection between image and text.

Fenn would later use the same approach to great effect in many of his illustrations for the book *Picturesque America,* sometimes recasting subjects from the journal in new compositions that combined image and type to yield a dramatic page. One example is his redesign of the rectangular illustration "Mount-Pisgah Inclined Plane" (January 28, 1871), which shows a gravity railroad at the mining and transportation center of Mauch Chunk (now Jim Thorpe), Pennsylvania, that gave a thrilling ride to visitors, including Fenn and Bunce. For the book, Fenn changed the image to an irregular vignette with room for type on the left, steepened the descent, and placed the car on the declining track rather than at the bottom (figs. 3.15, 3.16). The outcome was an appropriately exhilarating opening page. This approach to effectively combining text and image did not pass unnoticed by other artists who later contributed to the project, including John Douglas Woodward, who created "Arched Rock," an image similar to Fenn's Natural Bridge opening for the first page of the article "Mackinac."[71]

Picturesque America as a Book in Parts

By early 1872 D. Appleton & Company had decided to discontinue the "Picturesque America" series in its journal and instead begin publishing a subscription book of the same title, to be enhanced with steel engravings as well as wood engravings. We can only surmise that the decision was based primarily on finances. Although the series had been well received, evidently it had not enabled the *Journal* to secure as large a subscription base as the firm had wanted. Moreover, rival periodicals were attempting to improve their own pictures, and some even offered competing series to attract subscribers. For example, *Harper's Weekly* was featuring Thomas Nast's cartoons, and *Every Saturday* was publishing striking wood engravings, many by Winslow Homer, depicting New Englanders engaged in outdoor activities. Both *Harper's Monthly* and *Scribner's Monthly* regularly included articles on regions of the United States, often the same ones featured in *Appletons' Journal. Scribner's* promoted their landscape artist, Thomas Moran, who accompanied the Hayden expedition to Yellowstone in the summer of 1871, through advertisements hailing "The Wonders of the West" from "the famous pencil of T. Moran."[72]

Later that year, the *Aldine,* which had dropped "Press" from its title and added

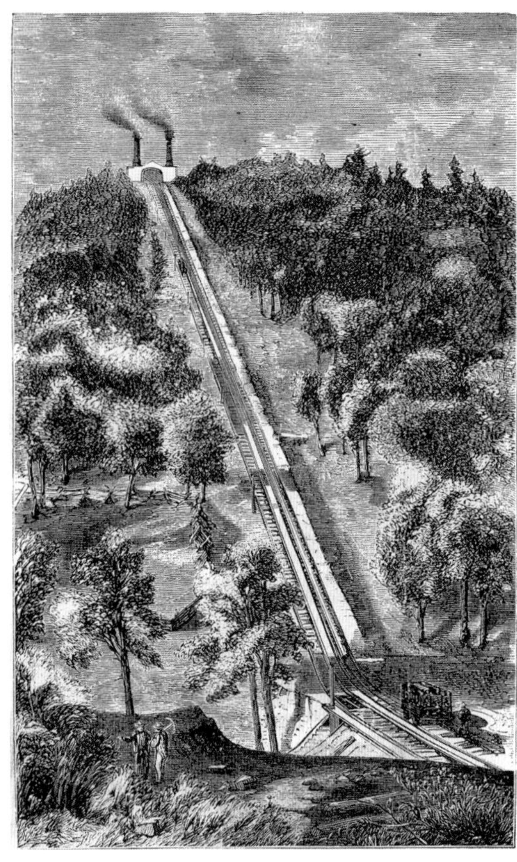

3.15. Harry Fenn, "Mount-Pisgah Inclined Plane." *Appletons' Journal,* January 28, 1871, 94. Wood engraving, 5 7/16" x 3 1/4".

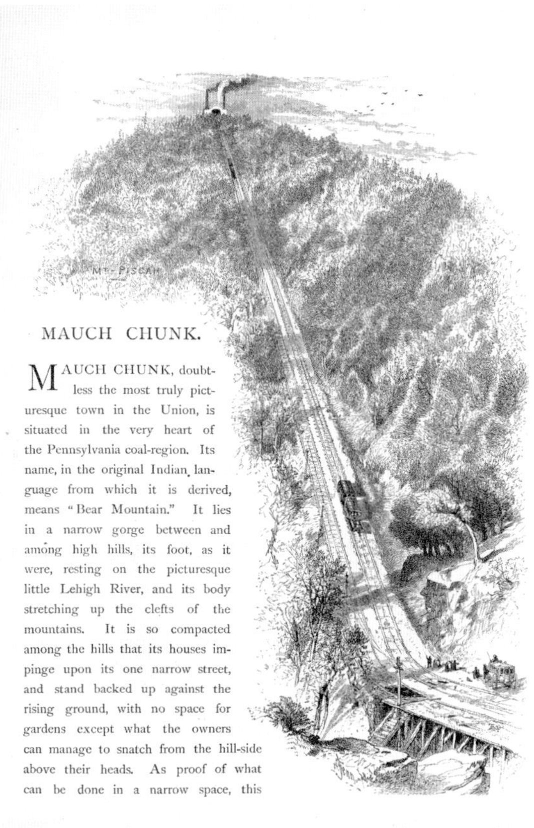

3.16. Harry Fenn, chapter opening for "Mauch Chunk." *Picturesque America,* 1:109. Wood engraving, approx. 9" x 6".

a subtitle—*The Art Journal of America*—and was lauded for the high quality of its large-format wood engravings, announced in its prospectus for 1872 the inauguration of a series depicting the "glories of the unrivaled scenery of our country." Claiming that previous attempts by other illustrated periodicals had "proved miserable failures—mere caricatures or topographical diagrams"—the *Aldine* embraced its mission "to reveal the undiscovered beauties" of the American landscape. The list of participating artists included W. T. Richards, William Hart, George and James D. Smillie, Granville Perkins, and F. O. C. Darley, attesting once again to the involvement of oil painters in illustration projects. The Appleton firm must have understood the difficulty of competing with such initiatives.

The firm's decision to focus on a subscription book rather than continue the magazine series was a wise one. The publishers enlisted William Cullen Bryant, at the time the "most distinguished resident of the city, referred to and honored as [New York's] first citizen," according to the historian Allan Nevins, to lend his name as editor.[73] Besides being one of America's best-known poets and the long-time respected editor of the New York *Evening Post,* Bryant was linked to art through his leadership of the committee working to found the Metropolitan Museum of Art and to the Appleton firm through many publications. His name could only add prestige to the project, although there is scant evidence that he played much of a role besides reading the text and writing a preface.[74]

Looking back in 1898 at a century's worth of American illustration, Arthur Hoeber stressed the significance of moving to a subscription book while acknowledging how tastes had changed twenty-five years later: "In 1872, . . . the Messrs. Appleton made a departure of an epoch-creating order that caused more or less of a popular sensation. This was the issuing of the first of the important illustrated subscription books, of which many were to follow and become such a source of profit to the trade. The volume was *Picturesque America,* and was perhaps the first book to contain large woodcuts. . . . Now they seem thin and feeble in almost every way, although then they were considered by the public at large as masterpieces of the draughtsman's and the wood engraver's art."[75] Subscription sales in these years were often more lucrative than bookstore sales, for canvassing agents could reach rural areas and towns that lacked bookshops or libraries.[76] The advantage of being able to pay in small increments rather than one lump sum was attractive to many subscribers, and the financial commitment enabled the firm to invest heavily in illustrations with less risk than publishers of earlier similar projects had assumed, often with disastrous results.

Appleton's hope that the appeal of an impressive two-volume work, elegantly designed and bound, would be great turned out to be justified. Many with sufficient means were evidently persuaded that such a magnificent book celebrating the scenery and cities of the United States, through artworks made by Americans, would signal their sophistication and culture. Canvassing agents supplied with sample pages spread out across the country to sign up subscribers for the entire work, to be distributed bimonthly in forty-eight parts over a two-year period. By June 1872 the first installment was ready. Each part, which cost fifty cents and featured a steel engraving, was enclosed in a pale blue cover adorned with the title, *Picturesque America; or, the Land We Live In,* and an image of an artist's palette and brushes. The text and wood engravings were printed on smooth off-white paper measuring 12 1/2 by 9 1/2 inches, with generous leading between the lines of type. When all the parts had been received, the subscriber could return them to Appleton for binding in one of several differently priced options or take them to a local binder.

The series in *Appletons' Journal* had covered only a few regions of the country, albeit some of the most novel and unfamiliar ones. The massive *Picturesque America* project would ultimately provide the most comprehensive coverage of the entire continental nation to date (although some hard-to-reach areas were omitted). Fenn would continue as its most prominent and prolific contributor, traveling to make sketches through early 1873 and illustrating twenty-four of the book's sixty-five sections. At the same time, however, Bunce also hired other artists to prepare illustrations. Some, like R. Swain Gifford, Thomas Moran, James D. Smillie, and William Hart, had already made or planned trips to far-flung areas only recently accessible by railroad. Others, such as John Douglas Woodward, Granville Perkins, Alfred R. Waud, W. L. Sheppard, and William Hamilton Gibson, were commissioned to travel and sketch on-site, as Fenn had been assigned to do. It is not surprising that no female artists participated in the project, although several female writers did; during this period, the working conditions of a landscape artist or illustrator—painting or drawing outdoors, sometimes living in a tent—were considered "obviously impossible for a woman," especially an unmarried one.[77]

For areas that were still relatively inaccessible, such as the Yellowstone region and the Rocky Mountains, Bunce obtained some of the photographs taken by William H. Jackson on the expeditions led by Ferdinand V. Hayden, which the artists then used as sources for their illustrations—Fenn for Yellowstone and Moran for the Rocky Mountains.[78] The halftone process that allowed photographs to be printed on the same page as text had yet to be developed, and the use of photographs as illustrations was complicated and expensive, for it involved mounting them on separate sheets and inserting them between the pages of type.[79] Furthermore, most critics and intellectuals still thought of photography as a craft derived from technology that lacked the emotional intensity of true art. In his preface to *Picturesque America,* Bryant pointed out this perceived deficiency, saying: "Photographs, however accurate, lack the spirit and personal quality which the accomplished painter or draughtsman infuses into his work."[80]

When Fenn or another of the hired artists returned with a full portfolio, there was great excitement at the Appleton firm as Bunce eagerly looked at the drawings and "gave vent to his admiration with loud praise" while the rest of the staff looked on. He then selected the drawings to be included in the book and, by his own account, often rejected two-thirds of the work if the artist had not hunted "for the most interesting alone."[81] Bunce also made suggestions for improvement, as did Fenn and some of the engravers.[82] Looking at the finished book, it is clear that Bunce's goal was to present positive views that would foster collective pride

   Poetry and Picturesque America

and unity and demonstrate the emergence of the United States as a world leader. He was highly selective in choosing images that dispelled long-held negative attitudes, including charges that the United States lacked ancient monuments, that its coasts were low and dull, that it had no majestic mountains like the Swiss Alps, that its countryside was unkempt rather than "groomed" like England's, and that its cities were inelegant and its people rude, devoid of taste, and mainly interested in money. Furthermore, it is clear that he, and probably the artists as well, avoided depictions of such contemporary problems as the unhealthy conditions of immigrants living in crowded cities, the plight of homeless children, strikes by laborers, and the destruction of landscapes by timbering and mining.

Once Bunce had selected an image, the artist redrew it in reverse on a whitened woodblock. (During this period, photography was beginning to be used to transfer an image to the block, but this procedure was not followed for *Picturesque America*.) In an article he wrote in 1909, Fenn explained how he went about preparing a woodblock for the engraver, and the accompanying reproduction of "On the Oklawaha River, Florida" (fig. 3.17) shows the effect he was trying to achieve:

> When I first came in touch with the craft, an illustrator needed to be an expert. He had to know how to prepare the smooth hard surface of the boxwood block, so that it would have sufficient tooth to take the pencil marks clearly. This was usually done by gently rubbing a fine piece of pumice stone, with plenty of water upon the block; then a preparation of finely pulverized Bath brick and Chinese or flake white was rubbed over the surface, then wiped off with the palm of the hand and allowed to dry. Then a delicate drawing of India ink or lamp black was made upon this prepared surface, the forms accented when dry with lead pencil and Chinese white to accent the high lights, etc. This was the method adopted by the celebrated English illustrator Birket Foster.[83]

Although we cannot be certain whether figure 3.17 shows Fenn's original watercolor sketch, a photograph of a uncut woodblock, or a later rendering to demonstrate the media he used on the woodblock, it does help us visualize how he drew in ink and Chinese white to guide the engraver and used watercolor to depict a night scene.[84]

Drawing on the block was slow, painstaking work that was hard on the eyes, especially if the artist attempted to lay down intricate guidelines for the wood engraver to use in creating tonal effects. Smillie's diaries show that reworking designs and preparing blocks for the book's section titled "St. Lawrence and the Saguenay" consumed most of his studio time from August to December 1873.[85]

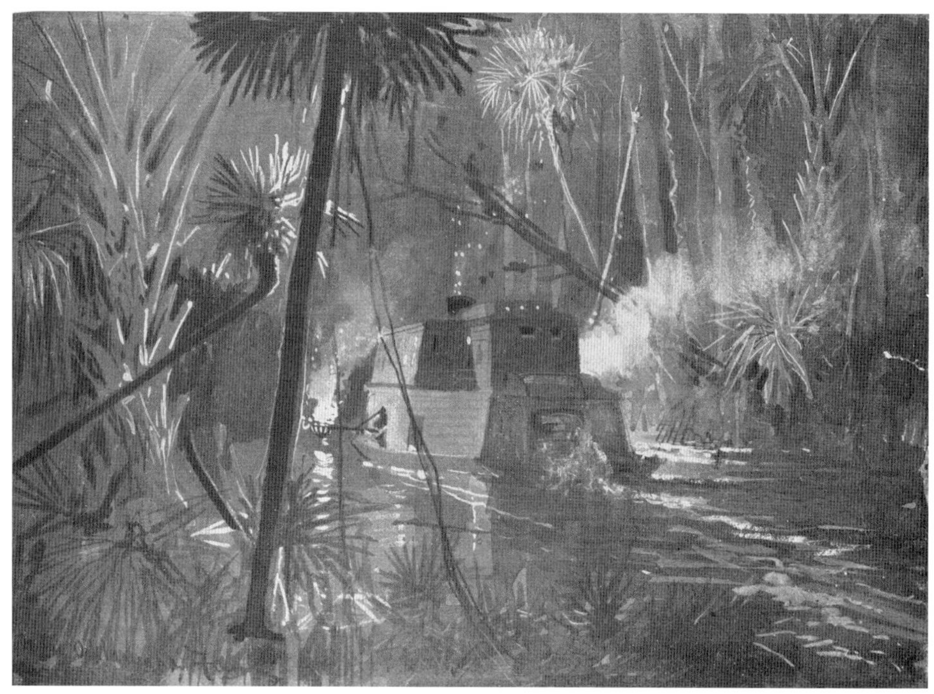

Because little written documentation exists and the drawings on the blocks were destroyed in the engraving process, it is difficult to know exactly what techniques were used by the artists. When finished, each typically signed the block in reverse with his last name, initials, or a distinctive monogram (as Fenn used) on the lower-right side, to appear lower left in the print.

The artists were normally paid for each completed drawing on the block. Records of payments made to Fenn are lacking, but Smillie's diaries record that he received $35 for full-page blocks and $25 for half-page blocks; a composite of Montreal views netted him $45. The artists were also reimbursed for travel expenses and paid a travel stipend. The amount may have varied based on the artist's prestige, for Smillie received $250 for a trip of fifteen working days up the St. Lawrence and Saguenay, whereas the younger artist William Hamilton Gibson expected only $40 a week on his second commissioned trip. Even this sum was respectable, considering that weekly salaries for the era's newspaper editors ranged from $25 to $60, and reporters generally earned only $20 to $30 a week.[86]

In comparing the wood engravings created from Fenn's and Moran's illustrations with those of the other contributors, it seems clear that the artists who had training as wood engravers or experience designing for and exploiting the quali-

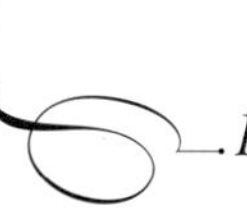

82   *Poetry and* Picturesque America

ties of that medium were more successful than were the novices in drawing on the block in a way that aided the engraver to produce an attractive image. They knew how to represent form through line and shading and probably took the time to lay down fine lines in various configurations to guide the engraver in representing surfaces and shadows. Painters who worked in oil or watercolor often had great difficulty producing effective designs for wood engraving because, without color, their works lost "form and light and shade" and were "stale, flat, and muddled," according to the engraver A. V. S. Anthony.[87] Some of the works copied after designs by R. Swain Gifford and William Hart show these characteristics.

Some scholars have commented that, as reinterpreted by engravers, the works by the different *Picturesque America* artists are indistinguishable and, too frequently, have a monotonous gray tone. However, several characteristic differences and qualities distinguish them. Fenn's works most often show his use of a loose bold line, strong movement through diagonals, and skill in manipulating tones from black to white. In contrast, Woodward's works display a tighter line, with short pencil strokes, and the frequent use of carefully rendered trees to determine the overall shape of the compositions. Perkins's works generally have a horizontal arrangement, with a calm, rather static effect, and Waud's, although always competent, are matter-of-fact and less dramatic than Fenn's. The drama of Moran's illustrations is often heightened by turbulent skies similar to Turner's.

Many skilled engravers worked on *Picturesque America*—some thirty-two names can be counted. They usually signed their surname or initials, sometimes followed by "Sc." (for *sculpsit,* "he or she engraved"), to appear at the lower right of the print. The type of engraving required fell midway between "fine" and "coarse" work, which was seen as an important advantage by the engraver William J. Linton. In *The History of Wood-Engraving in America,* published in 1882, Linton bestowed high praise on *Picturesque America*'s illustrations, to which he contributed: "The imperial quarto size of the page gave scope to the engraver; and there was no more need either for the weakening refinement of small book-work or for the haste of newspaper requiring. The best landscapes engraved in this country (and nothing of later years in England will equal them) are to be found here."[88] The quality of the wood engravings varies. Those by Joseph S. Harley, F. W. Quartley, and W. J. Linton are usually of high quality, whereas those by John Filmer, and (James H.?) Richardson are frequently characterized by areas of dull gray and indistinct forms.[89]

For the forty-eight steel engravings—those more expensive intaglio prints on heavier paper that would link the project to the still-prestigious tradition of books of topographical views—the firm reused some that had already appeared in

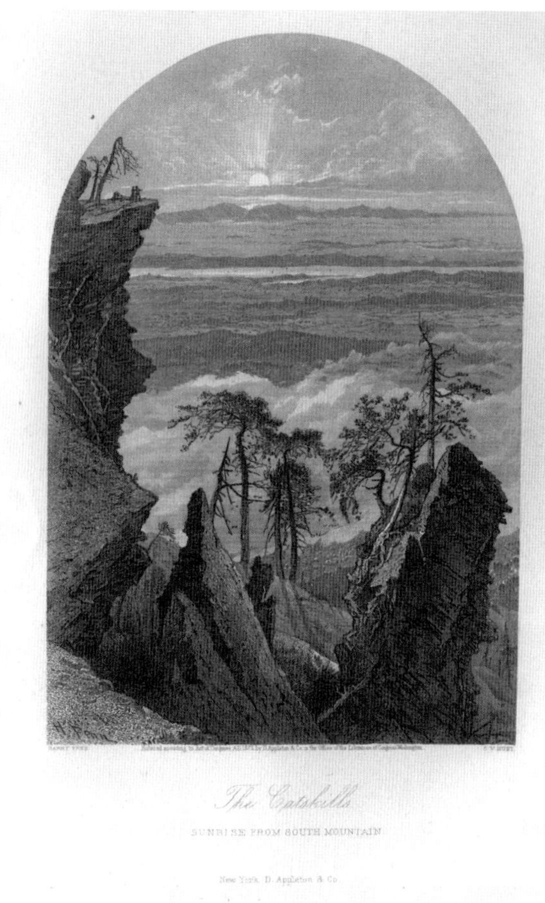

3.18. Harry Fenn, "The Catskills. Sunrise from South Mountain." *Picturesque America,* 3:opp. 127. Steel engraving by S. V. Hunt, approx. 8 5/8" x 5 11/16".

Appletons' Journal and paid to have plates made based on new works by Fenn, Woodward, and other participating artists.[90] These intaglio engravings excelled at depicting tone rather than line, and in most cases the original works they approximated were paintings in watercolor or oil. One example is Fenn's watercolor titled *Richmond from the James,* which was reproduced in *Picturesque America* as a steel engraving by Robert Hinshelwood.[91] In preparing the intaglio plate, Hinshelwood used sharp metal burins or gravers and acid (as in the etching process) to incise lines so fine as to be largely imperceptible to the naked eye (unlike wood-engraved lines and stipple). The different densities of black ink held within the lines yielded a variety of effects of light and dark, sometimes quite luminous. The engraver S. V. Hunt achieved impressive atmospheric effects in engraving some of Fenn's watercolor images, for example, the low clouds in "The Mount Washington Road" and "The Catskills. Sunrise from South Mountain" (fig. 3.18).[92] Producing steel engravings was time-consuming and required special printing presses that applied great pressure to force the ink from the incised lines onto the dampened heavy paper. It is no wonder, then, that Appleton included many more wood engravings than steel, some nine hundred in all.

The opening pages of volume 1 were designed to show the publication's scope. Fenn's dramatic frontispiece is a panorama of Niagara Falls, America's most famous scenic attraction, engraved on steel by Hunt. This image faces the steel-engraved title page, with Fenn's view of an unnamed waterfall, identified only as "Cascade in Virginia" (fig. 3.19), signaling that hitherto unknown and unheralded bits of scenery would be included along with familiar sites. His oval vignette, with letters seemingly crafted from twisted branches and a depiction of an artist at work (surely a self-portrait, considering the wide mustache), aptly embodied popular picturesque conventions and conspicuously drew attention to his identification with the series. Next came a complete letterpress title page and

Poetry and Picturesque America

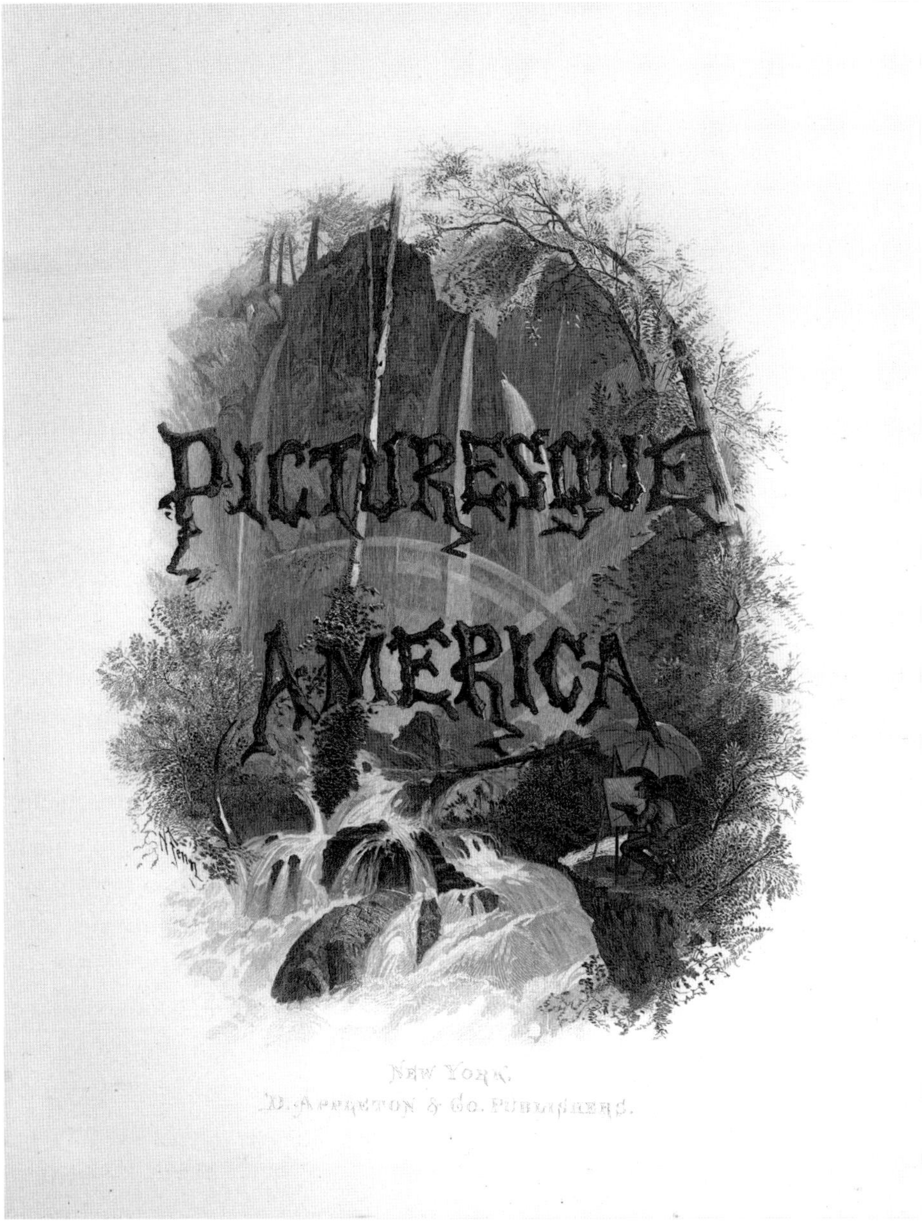

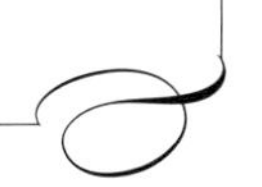

3.19. Harry Fenn, engraved title page ("Cascade in Virginia"). *Picturesque America,* vol. 1. Steel engraving by R[obert] Hinshelwood; page 12 1/2" x 9", image approx. 9" x 7".

preface. The first article, consisting of new material, is Bunce's "On the Coast of Maine," illustrated by Fenn with images of waves breaking on cliffs, dramatic evidence that America's coastlines were not flat and dull—at least not these. Other illustrations show elegantly dressed ladies and gentlemen admiring the cliffs and disembarking from boats with the help of guides (fig. 3.20).

The text and imagery provided a model of the leisurely touring by the cultural

Poetry and Picturesque America

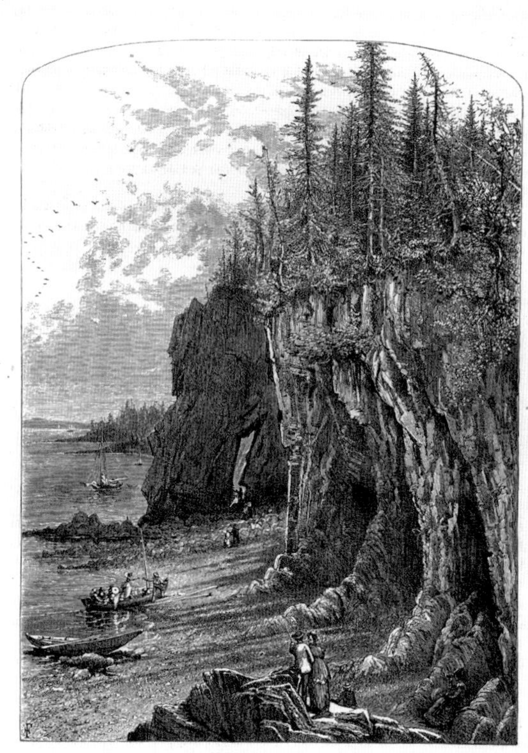

3.20. Harry Fenn, "The Cliffs near 'The Ovens.'" *Picturesque America*, 1:[5]. Wood engraving, 8 7/8" x 6 7/8".

elite in which the traveler in search of the picturesque viewed rock formations from the most impressive viewpoints and in all kinds of weather, including fog, with the attendant "dissolving views," and storms lending "extreme grandeur," or sublimity, to the experience (1:8, 10). Thus, the first section served as a keynote for the publication's approach to touring. The jump from Maine to Florida in the second section, and then to the West Coast with "Up and Down the Columbia" illustrated by R. Swain Gifford, vividly demonstrated the geographical range.

The opening pages of volume 2, by contrast, highlight the cultural amenities and industries that are also featured in *Picturesque America*. The frontispiece is a steel engraving of A. C. Warren's "New York from Brooklyn Heights," and the steel-engraved title page shows Fenn's rendering of the Capitol in Washington, D.C., with its newly completed dome towering above the letters of the book's title (fig. 3.21). The monumental architecture gave evidence that the nation's capital at last had parks and civic buildings comparable to those in London or Paris; furthermore, it conveyed the reassuring message that democracy and civilization were compatible—that orderly, well-dressed citizens knew how to appreciate the amenities built by public dollars—in a time when the violent excesses of the Paris Commune raised questions about where democracy might lead.

The volume's first article, "Highlands and Palisades of the Hudson," opens with Fenn's dramatic view "Poughkeepsie and Its Foundries at Night" (fig. 3.22), in which the foundry and two tiny workers silhouetted by a glowing fire are contained within a circular composition, reassuring viewers that the impact of such industries on the landscape was minimal. Etching-like masts of ships on either side soften the image, as does the small daytime panorama of Poughkeepsie below. The effect of this composite is vastly different from the views of Pittsburgh that Fenn created for *Every Saturday* in the way it distances the scene of work and highlights the page as an artistic construction.

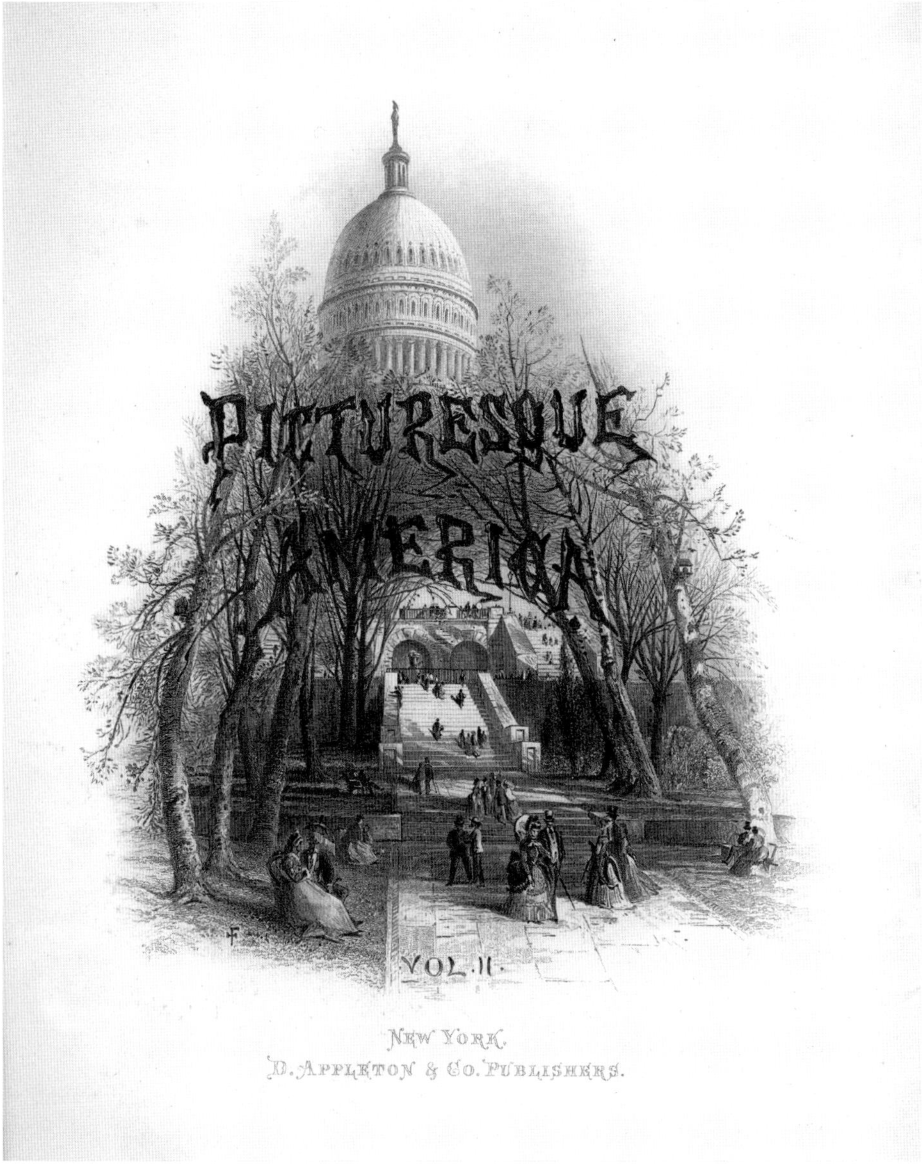

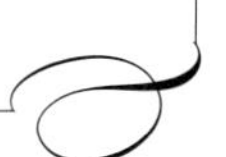

3.21. Harry Fenn, engraved title page ("Dome of the Capitol"). *Picturesque America*, vol. 2. Steel engraving by E. P. Brandard; page 12 1/2" x 9", image approx. 9" x 7".

Although Fenn's compositions were sometimes conventional, such as the circular scene of haying and traditional agriculture that opens the section on the White Mountains,[93] his growing reputation for fresh viewpoints prompted the editors to select him to create images of places already so familiar that they might elicit yawns rather than curiosity. He illustrated many sites that had long been both tourist destinations and artistic subjects, including the White Mountains, Niagara Falls, Trenton Falls, the Highlands and Palisades of the Hudson, the Catskills, Lake George and Lake Champlain, Mount Mansfield, the Adiron-

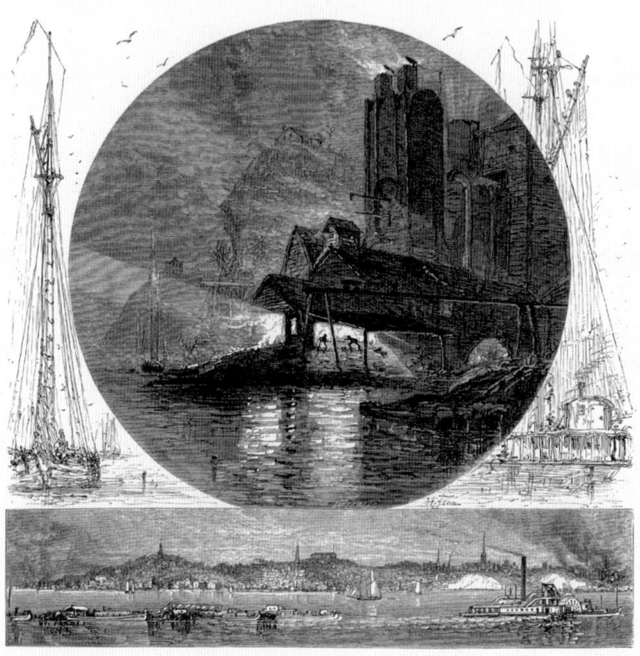

PICTURESQUE AMERICA.

HIGHLANDS AND PALISADES OF THE HUDSON.

WITH ILLUSTRATIONS BY HARRY FENN.

TO those who are willing to accept such unobtrusive companionship as we have to offer, in this artist's voyage among the noblest scenes of our most beautiful and perfect American river, we must say at the beginning that we shall not follow the tra-

dacks, Watkins Glen, and New York and Boston. In addition, he covered Weyers Cave in Virginia, the Cumberland Gap, and the new Yellowstone National Park.

His three images of Catskill Falls differ greatly from Thomas Cole's 1826 painting and provided fresh views of the famous site: "First Leap of the Falls" (2:120) focuses on tourists experiencing the upper falls from a viewing platform above and the rock ledge behind the falls; the full-page "Catskill Falls" (fig. 3.23) shows the whole falls with no interceding foreground and a much greater volume of water and more turbulence than in Cole's painting, emphasizing that nature's power continues

    Poetry and Picturesque America

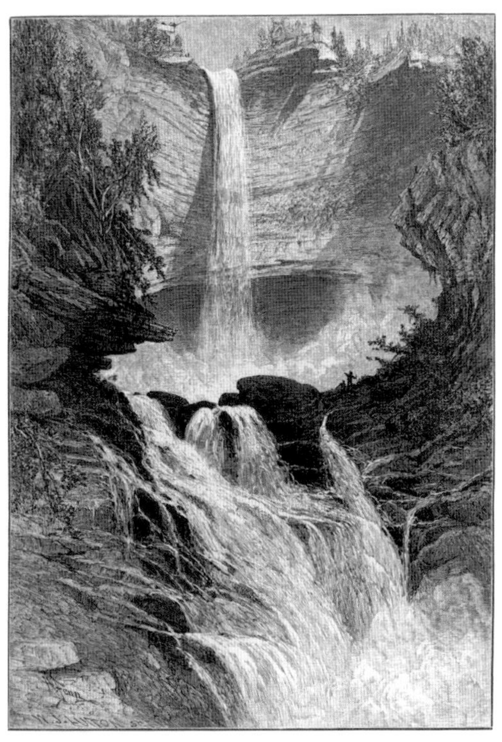

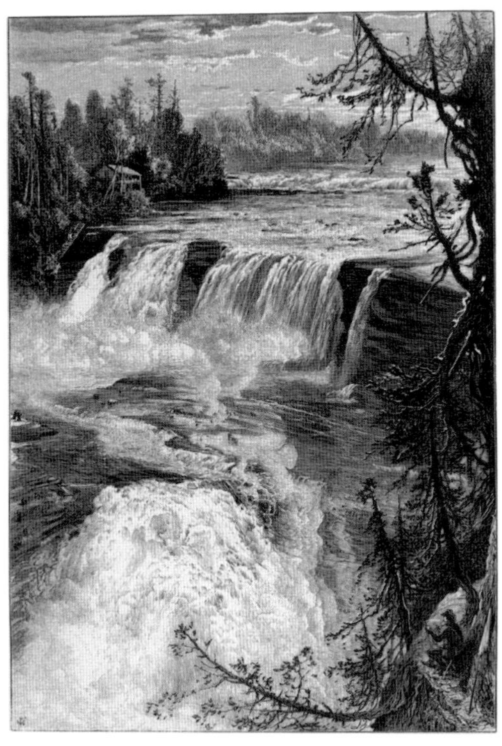

3.23. Harry Fenn, "Catskill Falls." *Picturesque America*, 2:121. Wood engraving by W. J. Linton, 9 3/16" x 6 3/16".

3.24. Harry Fenn, "General View of Trenton Falls, from East Bank" (with self-portrait lower right). *Picturesque America*, 1:454. Wood engraving by James Langridge, 9 1/8" x 6 1/4".

to erode the rock ledges; and in "Under the Catskill Falls" (2:123), Fenn shows himself balanced on a walking stick gazing in awe at the sheet of water. These illustrations were fresh in some ways but still very much in the picturesque mode, unlike Winslow Homer's "Under the Falls" in the September 14, 1872, *Harper's Weekly,* in which two stylishly dressed young women, also leaning on walking sticks, stare at the water with a bored look, suggesting a mocking attitude toward picturesque touring similar to that in Mark Twain's *Innocents Abroad* (1869). In a sense, *Picturesque America* epitomized an era that would come to an end in the next decade or so.

A comparison of Fenn's views of Catskill Falls and his 1868 view of Trenton Falls (see fig. 2.4) shows how much more adept he had become in using line and tone to depict falling water, rock formations, and trees. Furthermore, contrasting the earlier image of that popular and much-depicted site with those he created for *Picturesque America* highlights how dramatically his approaches to composition had changed. In "General View of Trenton Falls, from East Bank" (fig. 3.24), he used a high viewpoint from the right side to show the river's approach, made the lower falls drop out of the frame, and inserted a series of striking conifers along the

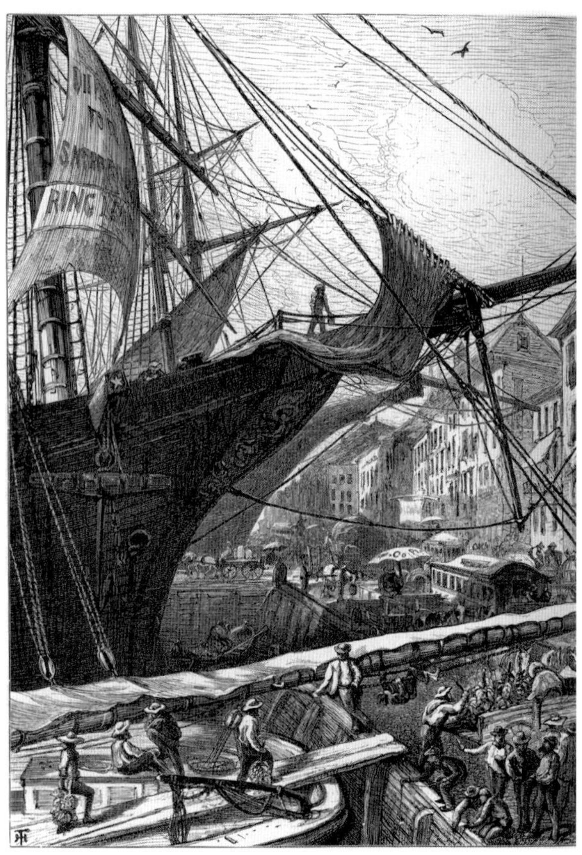

3.25. Harry Fenn, "A New-York River-front." *Picturesque America*, 2:550. Wood engraving by W. J. Palmer, 9 1/8" x 6 1/4".

right edge, defining the foreground and establishing a precarious, exciting viewpoint for the reader, far above the depiction of the artist sketching on a small ledge at the lower right. No wonder readers found Fenn's images fresh and appealing.

In his views of New York City, also a popular artistic subject and increasingly a central symbol of the nation's commercial and cultural life, Fenn drew a lively close-up titled "A New-York River-front," with the bow of a ship looming over a wharf where some men work and others relax (fig. 3.25)—one of the few images of work in a city scene—and "A Glimpse of Fifth Avenue," showing Fenn gazing through the "tower of the novel, Oriental-looking synagogue" (Temple Emanu-El) at "the highway of fashion" below (fig. 3.26), described by Bunce as "one unbroken line of costly and luxurious mansions."[94] Bunce often used superlatives to stress New York's sophistication: "No city has an avenue of such length," he said, and New York's Central Park is "unapproached in this country and unexcelled abroad" in its "union of art with Nature" (2:555, 557).

Picturesque America also depicted the parks and open spaces of America's cities, including the rural cemeteries on their outskirts, and the private family parks and "castle-like mansions" of the new suburbs. In describing Boston's Back Bay, the writer G. M. Towle admired "the domestic luxury and architectural display" brought forth by "persistent thrift in commerce, and busy competition in the active walks of life" (2:238). Such attitudes coincided with those of the Reverend Henry Ward Beecher, who compared the successful businessman to the great elm tree in the social garden and maintained that stately homes and gardens benefited the entire community by providing examples of beauty that educated and elevated the poor.[95] Thus, *Picturesque America* presented a model of residential luxury to strive for—one that Fenn would realize for himself in the 1880s.

Another example of Fenn's use of a fresh viewpoint for a familiar sight can be seen in "The Palisades," the rock formation bordering the Hudson River across from New York City that had figured in countless paintings and prints. The

Poetry and Picturesque America

high vantage point shows the steep cliffs dropping precipitously to the river below, and a rock jutting from the right provides a viewing platform for the reader (fig. 3.27). F. W. Quartley's masterful engraving interprets Fenn's use of both line and shading in an image blessedly free of the overall gray tone that often made wood engravings dull. This illustration exemplifies how Fenn used compositional devices such as jutting rocks or fallen logs placed diagonally in the foreground to increase the illusion of depth, an approach that may have been inspired by the radically three-dimensional landscapes and cityscapes viewed through the popular device known as the stereoscope. Stereographic images impressed the general public and probably increased appreciation of close observation and dramatic depth in all types of subjects, prompting many artists and photographers to aim for greater three-dimensionality in their compositions.[96] Fenn's creative use of such techniques, as well as his penchant for steep verticals and narrow passages, may have been influenced by photography.[97]

In his views of the White Mountains of New Hampshire, Mount Mansfield in Vermont, and the Adirondacks in New York State, all areas that artists frequently treated in panoramic vistas, Fenn included several views of vacationers at play, either fishing, hiking, or boating. This emphasis was in keeping with the writings of such liberal Christian clergymen as Horace Bushnell and W. H. H. "Adirondack" Murray, who promoted leisure and adventure in the wilderness as a means not only to mental and physical health but also of being in touch with "divine energy."[98] In "Emerald Pool, Peabody-River Glen," Fenn shows himself taking a break from his easel to catch a fish in the White Mountains (fig. 3.28), and he depicts climbers on a rough

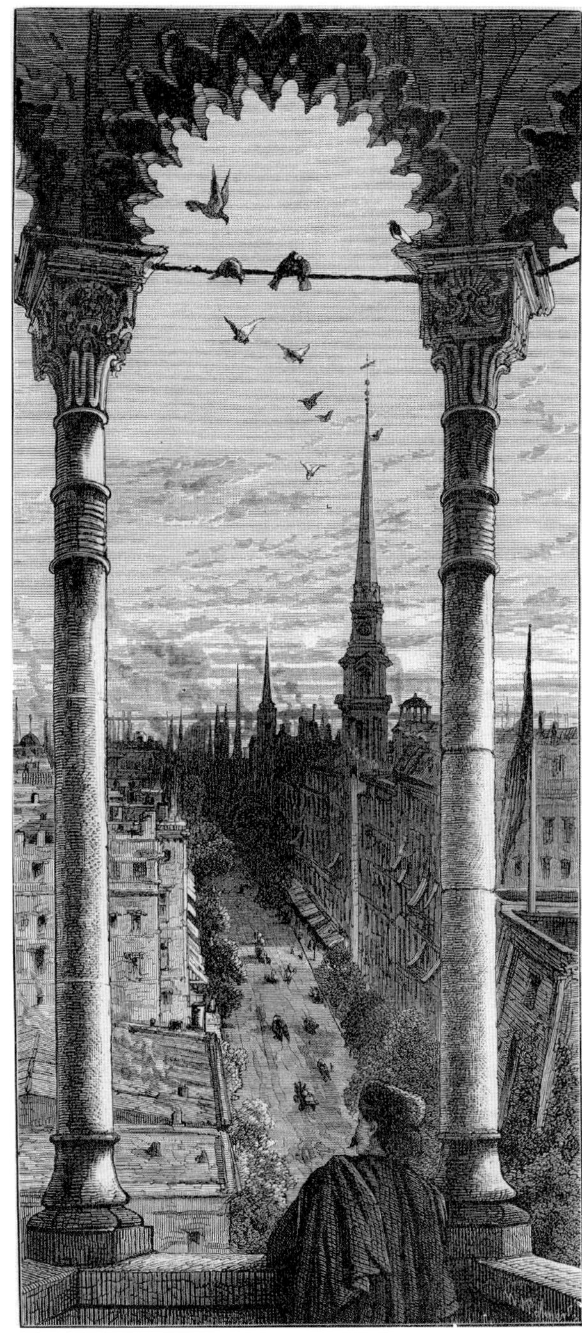

3.26. Harry Fenn, "A Glimpse of Fifth Avenue." *Picturesque America,* 2:555. Wood engraving by W. J. Palmer, 9 1/16" x 3 7/8".

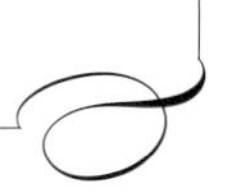

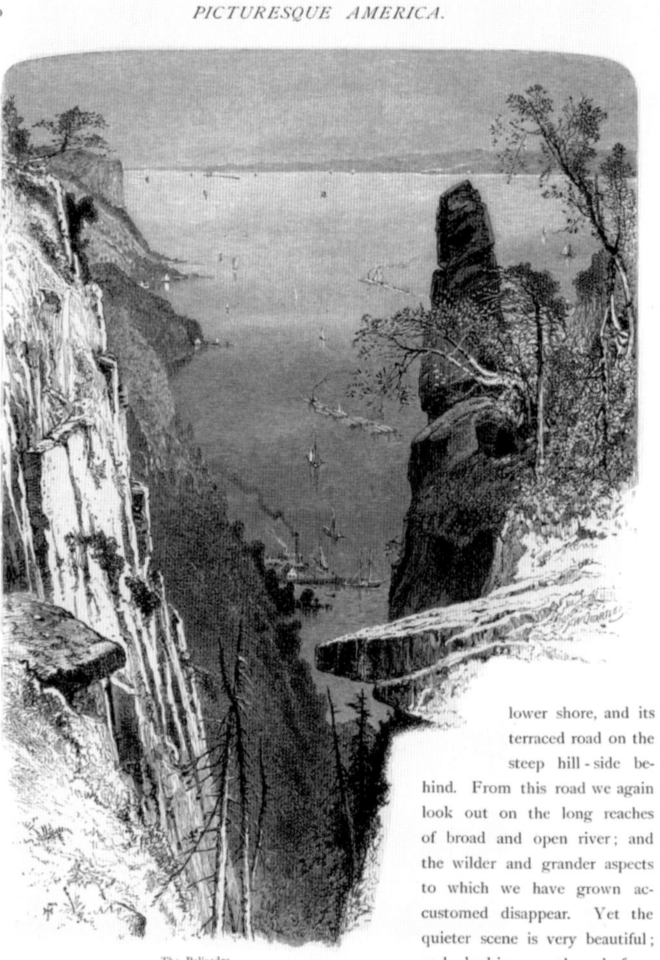

trail in the Adirondacks in "The Indian Pass" (2:432). Other images of mountain-eers, such as those at Mount Mansfield in "Climbing the Nose" (2:283), are illus-trative of the then-popular "mountain fever" fed by features in various periodicals describing the expeditions of Britons John Tyndall and Edward Whymper in the Swiss Alps, the recent surveys in the Sierra Nevada and the Rocky Mountains, and Clarence King's *Mountaineering in the Sierra Nevada.*[99] It is usually men who popu-

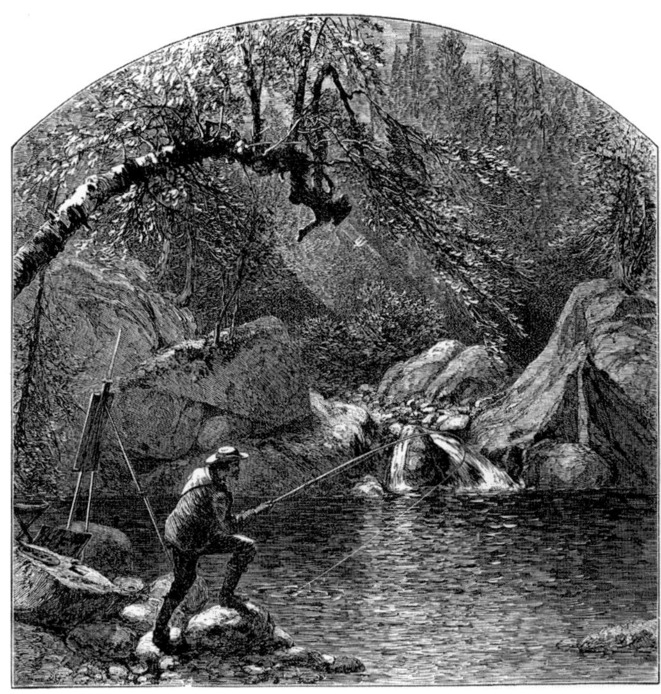

3.28. Harry Fenn, "Emerald Pool, Peabody-River Glen." *Picturesque America,*
1:166. Wood engraving, 6 7/16" x 6 7/16".

late these scenes of strenuous activity; women in the mountains tend to be shown on horseback ("The Descent of Mount Washington," 1:158) or being helped up a trail by male companions ("Cliff above Dismal Pool," 1:170).

While *Picturesque America* shows most of the scenic attractions in the East as comfortably accessible, equipped with paths, benches, bridges, boats, stagecoaches, and hotels, its views of the West emphasize wilderness and sublime scenery as yet untouched by civilization. Some of Fenn's images of Yellowstone include small male figures exploring the sites; women tourists appear only in Smillie's views of the more accessible Yosemite Valley. The artists show few means of conveyance besides horses. Figures of American Indians are featured in several sections, suggesting circumstances before the arrival of European settlers.

Disregarding settlements, farms, herds of cattle, mines, and mills, Fenn and the other artists focused almost entirely upon the mountains, rock formations, waterfalls, canyons, giant trees, and dramatic coastlines of the West. The writers, in turn, extolled their wonders. In his text, Burlingame claims that "far from the railway route" in California's Sierra Nevada "there is Alpine scenery" as grand as Switzerland's (2:198). The journalist J. E. Colburn says of the Grand Canyon: "None of

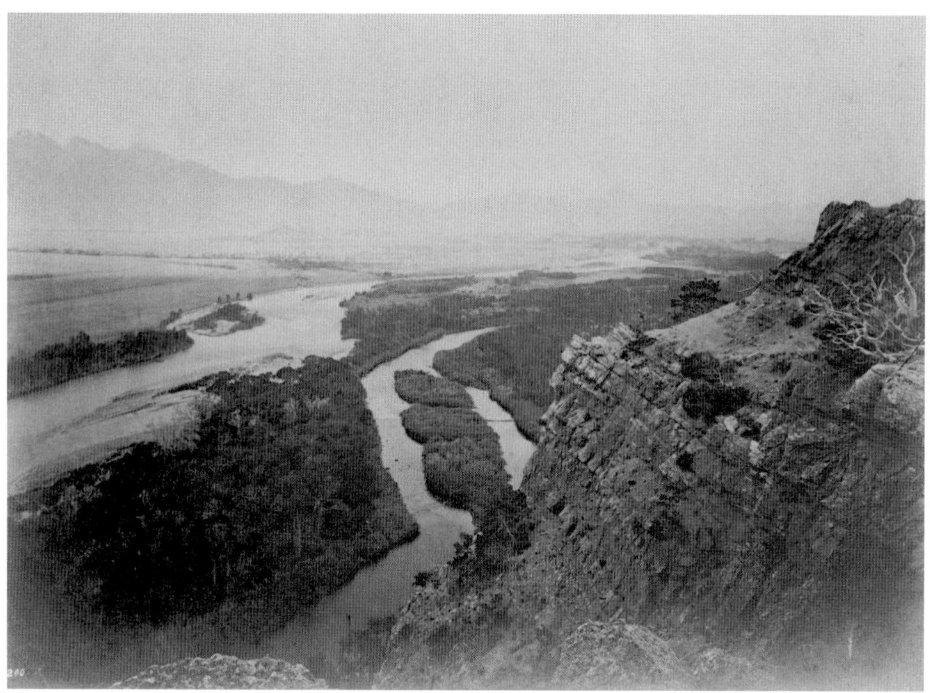

3.29. William Henry Jackson, [Valley of the Yellowstone, 1871]. Photograph. (Library of Congress Prints and Photographs Division, Washington, D.C.)

the works of Nature on the American Continent . . . approach in magnificence and wonder the cañons of the Colorado." He further describes "creeping out carefully on the edge of the precipice" to look down "directly upon the river, fifteen times as far away as the waters of the Niagara are below the bridge" (2:503, 510).

No town or city in the vast expanse between St. Louis, Missouri, and Oakland, California, is depicted in *Picturesque America*. Moran does include a memorable image of well-dressed strollers in his illustration "The Oaks of Oakland," but even the sophisticated, thriving city of San Francisco, then rivaling New York in hotels and theaters, receives scant attention. Where the writers conveyed enthusiasm for advancing development and greatly appreciated the conveniences of hotels, the artists celebrated the region's largely untouched wilderness and suggested by their subjects that nature's sublimity and progress could coexist without conflict.[100]

In 1872, just as *Picturesque America* was appearing in parts, the federal government established the nation's first national park, Yellowstone, demonstrating its intention to preserve special and unique regions as public lands for all to enjoy. Because the new park was still difficult to reach, Fenn used photographs by William H. Jackson, official photographer of the expedition led by Ferdinand V. Hayden, as a starting point for his illustrations. This approach was one he fre-

Poetry and Picturesque America

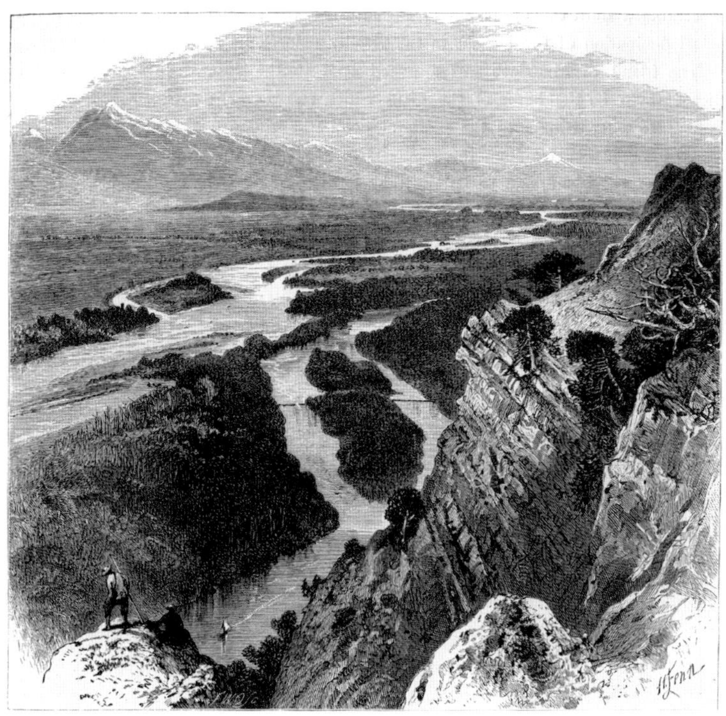

3.30. Harry Fenn, "The Yellowstone." *Picturesque America*, 1:292. Wood engraving,
6 1/4" x 6 5/16".

quently turned to in his later career, and a close look at his transformation of one
of Jackson's pictures shows just how much artistry was involved (figs. 3.29, 3.30).
By adopting a higher viewpoint and a vertical format, Fenn increased the image's
depth and drama. He heightened interest by delineating detailed stratifications in
the cliff face and conveyed the enormous scale of the scene by placing two figures
in the foreground and a tiny boat sailing far below. He drew the river winding
much farther in the distance than is shown in the photograph's faint background,
and he enhanced the contrast between bushes, water, and open land to create a
more interesting—and indeed more picturesque—image. Likewise, he turned
the overexposed background shapes into snow-capped mountains and enhanced
the blank expanse of pale gray sky with areas of clouds.[101] Clearly, working from
a photograph was not a matter of simple copying: it involved selecting format,
viewpoint, lighting, focus, and details. Although few of the photographic sources
for Fenn's later illustrations have been located for comparison, his approach in
transforming them would have been similar.[102]

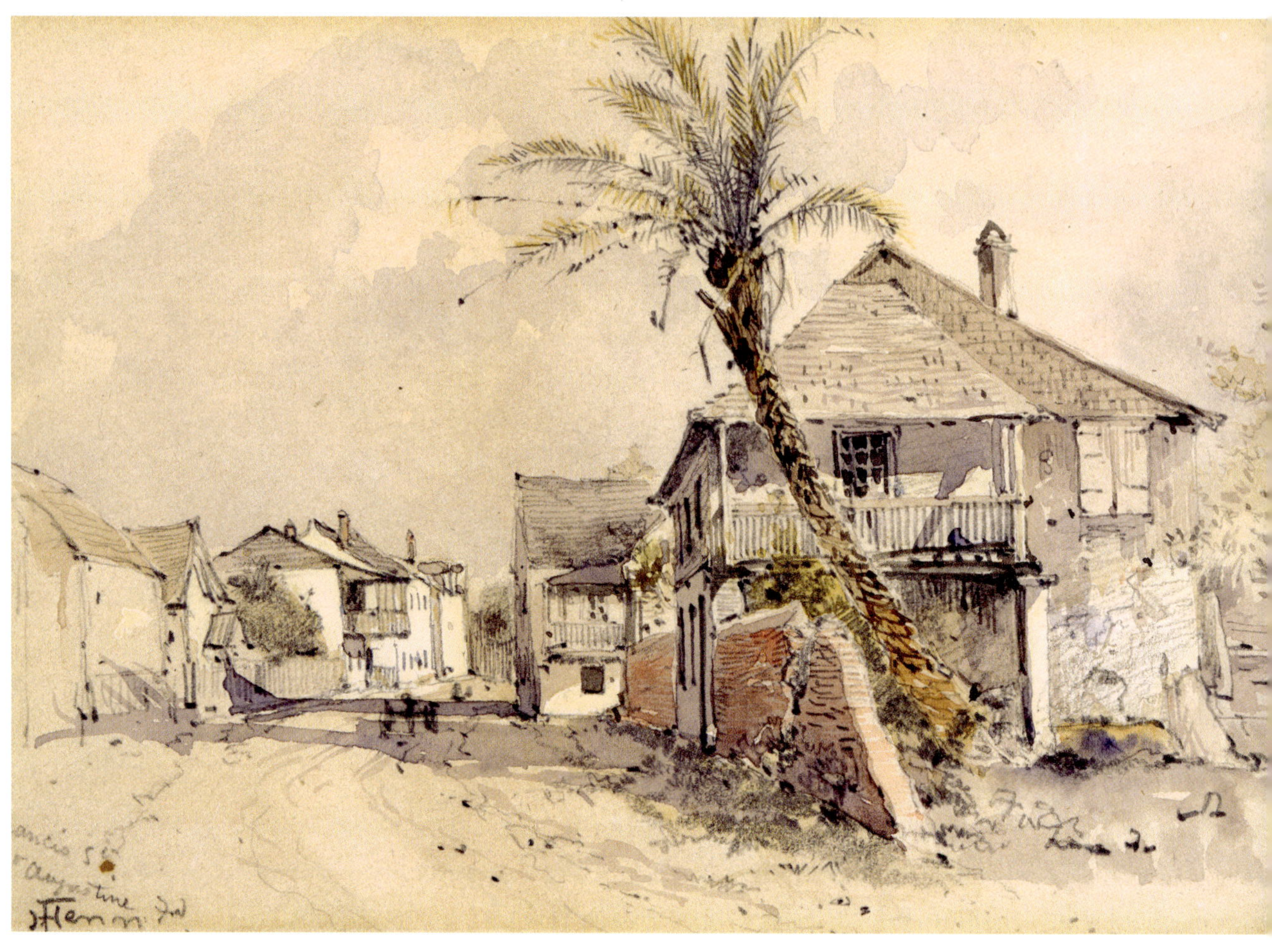

3.31. Harry Fenn, *Francis Street, St. Augustine, Florida,* ca. 1870. Watercolor over graphite; sheet 4 3/4" x 7". (Montclair Art Museum, Gift of Eleanor Hines. 1982.35.)

Fenn's Original Works Relating to *Picturesque America*

Despite the *Picturesque America* commission being Fenn's most important to date, the paper trail of his original artworks is sparse. The likeliest reason is that sketches were usually discarded once they had been redrawn on the woodblocks.[103] The valued product was the illustration printed from the engraved block or, more precisely, an electrotype of the block. Fortunately, a few of Fenn's works related to the project are now preserved in museums and help shed light on his working methods and increasing skill as an artist.

From these works we learn that Fenn sometimes used watercolor, or a combination of graphite and watercolor, for his on-site sketches. In this practice he differs from some of the later artists who worked on *Picturesque America,* notably John

Poetry and Picturesque America

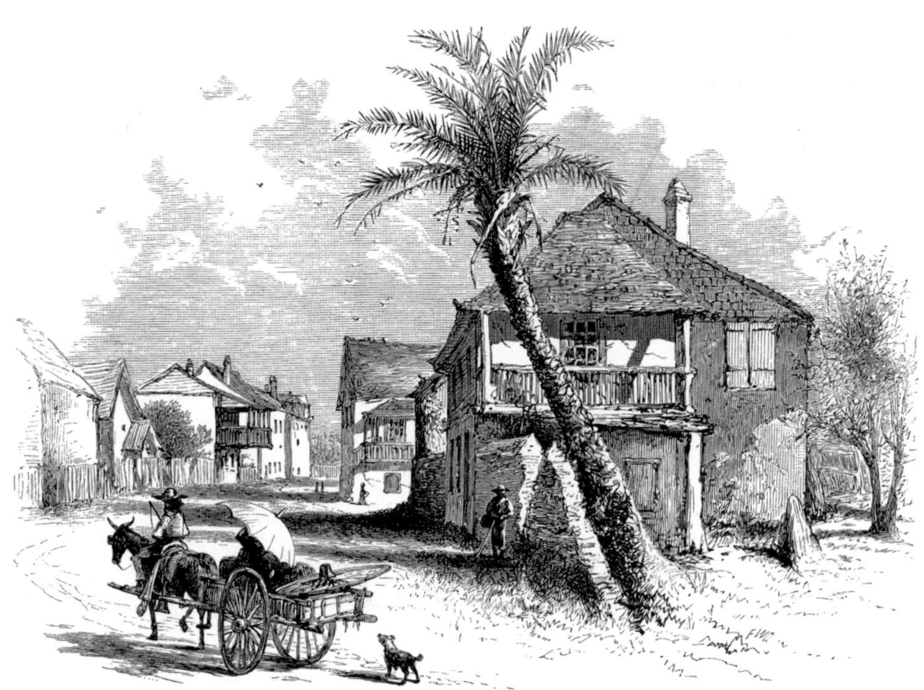

Douglas Woodward and Alfred R. Waud, whose extant sketches are done primarily either in graphite or in graphite with Chinese white.[104] A pair of small watercolors by Fenn in the Montclair Art Museum apparently served as the basis for two of his Florida illustrations that appeared in both *Appletons' Journal* and *Picturesque America;* one was the study for "Bar Light-House, Mouth of St. John's River" (1:20).[105] Comparing the images shows that, in keeping with picturesque conventions, Fenn enlivened the woodblock version through the addition of such details as clouds, dramatically shaped plant materials in the foreground, and turtles heading toward the beach. He also made alterations that resulted in a more pronounced diagonal movement from foreground to background. The other watercolor was the basis for "St. Francis Street, St. Augustine," to which Fenn once again added picturesque details, including birds, a mule-drawn cart carrying a figure shaded by an umbrella, and a dog (figs. 3.31, 3.32). He also assumed a higher viewpoint and increased the image's three-dimensionality by inserting figures of diminishing size and making the buildings on the left smaller, so that they appear farther away.[106]

The use of figures in this illustration is typical of the series and the book that followed: they provide scale and foreground interest and are often shown engaged in traditional tasks or admiring the view. Acting as a stand-in for the viewer, they draw us into the image and model an appreciation of nature's wonders. Faces, which were difficult to engrave at a small scale, are rarely depicted in detail. In most of the images, with the exception of some that show African Americans in the South or laborers, the American population appears to be homogeneous and well dressed.

One of Fenn's illustrations of Charleston focuses on an African American woman and her children selling sweet potatoes and shows none of the negative stereotyping typical of this period (1:203); it could have been based on a photograph, as was the case with some of his images featuring people. He almost certainly used a photograph—perhaps one of the popular stereographs of genre scenes—when he placed the same pair of African American boys gazing squarely at the viewer in illustrations of St. Augustine (1:187) and North Carolina (1:145).[107] This reliance on outside sources may indicate that Fenn felt he needed help depicting the features of people unfamiliar to him, especially since he seldom took time to sketch individuals while traveling.

Another work related to a *Picturesque America* illustration is the watercolor titled *Niagara Falls* (Smithsonian American Art Museum), which was discussed earlier as possible evidence that Fenn and his wife traveled to the New York attraction after their wedding. Although dated 1862, the painting appears to have served as a source for Fenn's later illustration titled "The Brink of the Horseshoe." A comparison of the two images (figs. 3.33 and 1.7) reveals how he diminished the disorderly array of logs and shrubs, placing much of the messy foreground in dark shadows, to create a more harmonious, if less interesting, composition. Obviously, when Fenn completed the work in 1862, his aim was different from the goal embraced a decade later for the *Picturesque America* images. The earlier work is more in keeping with frequent complaints about how the famous natural wonder had been degraded by commercial tourism than it is an attempt to show its sublimity.

Other, more highly finished watercolors related to Fenn's work for the "Picturesque America" series suggest that either he sometimes remained at a site long enough to complete a detailed painting or he later reworked an on-site sketch to create a new work suitable for exhibition or sale. One example is *The Cypress-Shingle Yard, Ocklawaha River, Florida,* a watercolor dated 1870 in the collection of the Metropolitan Museum of Art. It features the same subject as one of the illustrations in the initial "Picturesque America" magazine installment on Florida, including the lean-to that his traveling companion Thorpe had found so picturesque.[108] It may be one of the paintings Fenn exhibited at the fourth annual exhibition of the American Society of Painters in Water Colors in 1870–71, perhaps the one described in the catalogue as "no. 509 Sketch on the Ocklawaha River, Florida."

Another watercolor now owned by the New-York Historical Society was clearly the basis for an illustration. It is extremely close in its details—down to the birds

Poetry and Picturesque America

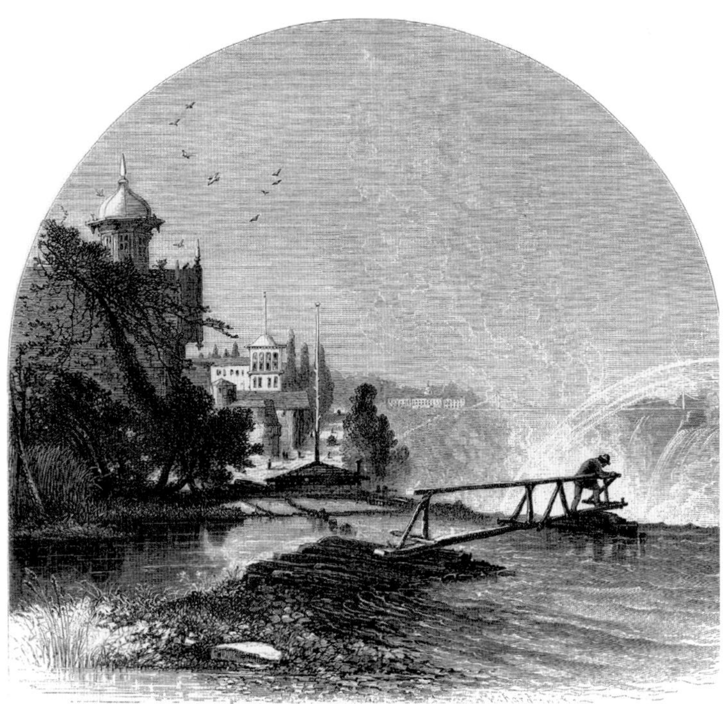

3.33. Harry Fenn, "The Brink of the Horseshoe." *Picturesque America*, 1:433. Wood engraving, 6 1/4" x 6 3/8".

flying in the upper left—to the wood engraving titled "Picturesque America.— East Hampton, L.I.—View from the Church Belfry" that appeared in the March 25, 1871, *Appletons' Journal* (figs. 3.34, 3.35). This could be a case where Fenn completed his rendering, including precise details, on the spot. The images have minor variations in the sky and horizon. The most striking difference is the much greater contrast in the engraving between the wooden structure of the belfry and the sunlit view it frames—a good example of how Fenn compensated for the lack of color.

The Success of *Picturesque America*

Picturesque America was extremely successful financially, despite the panic of 1873 touched off by the bankruptcy of the financial giant Jay Cooke and Company, which led to the failure of railroads, banks, and other businesses. It also succeeded in achieving its cultural aims. It fostered pride not only in America's landscapes and cities but in American artists, engravers, and publishers as well. Its highly positive images, so many of which were created by Fenn, filtered out disturbing signs of change—large factories, crowded cities, poor immigrants, and the destruction of forests and moun-

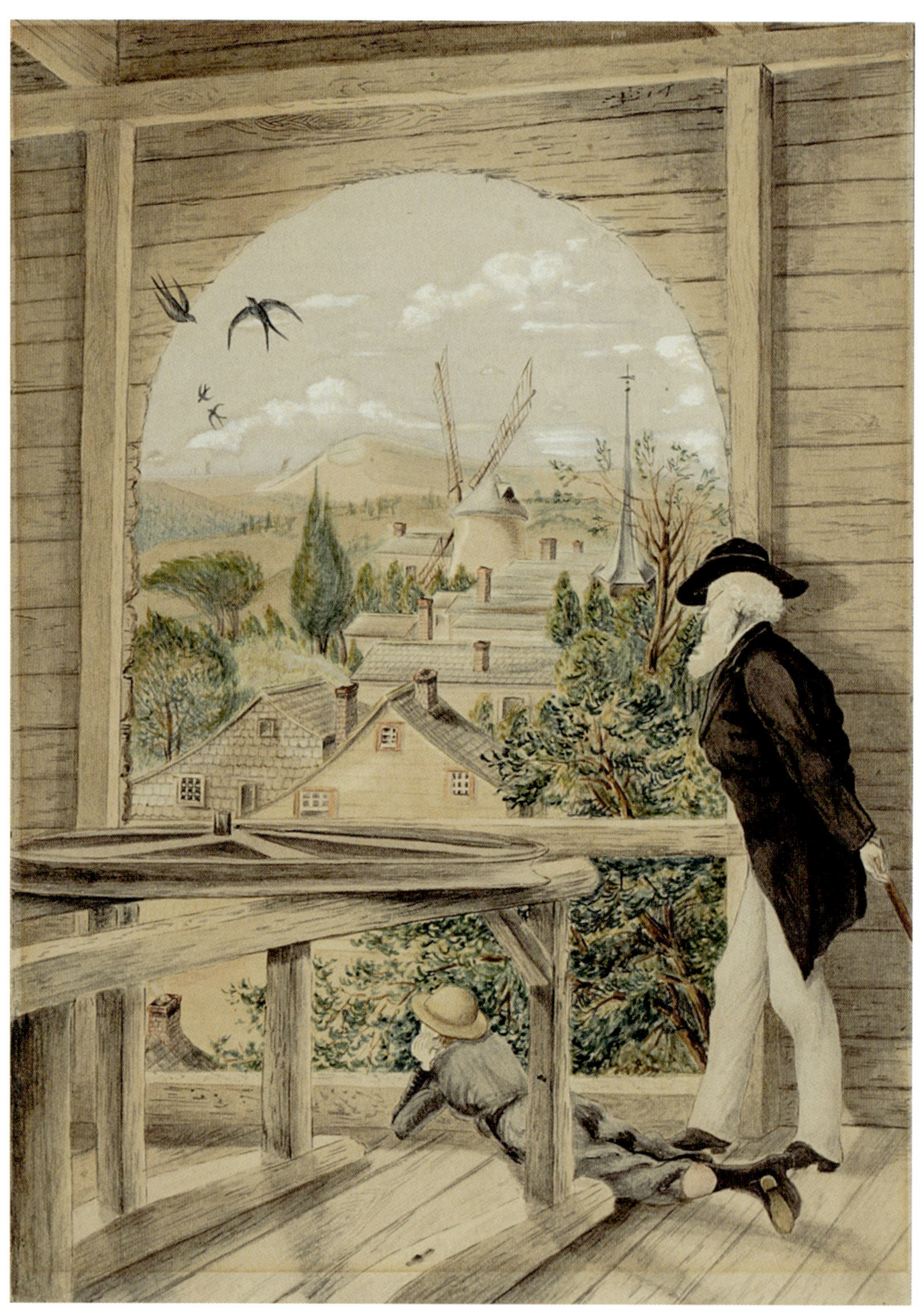

3.34. Harry Fenn, *East Hampton, from the Church Belfry*, ca. 1872. Watercolor, gouache, black ink, and graphite on card, 11 5/8" x 9 1/8". (Collection of the New-York Historical Society, acc. no. 1980.45.)

tains by logging and mining—and reassured many people that the United States was still picturesque. It set forth didactic models of leisurely touring that would yield spiritual benefits, of orderly behavior and fashionable dress appropriate for the public spaces of cities, and of the most admired dwelling type, elegant suburban mansions.

By displaying the book prominently on the parlor table, Americans could align themselves, symbolically at least, with those who appreciated art and nature and had time and money enough to travel in search of the picturesque. In addition, support of this renowned, large-scale art project provided families of moderate means a way to become patrons of art, just like the wealthiest Americans. Most important, it enabled citizens to construct and identify with a national self-image based on reconciliation of North and South and incorporation of the West. Its graphic testimony of the variety, uniqueness, and potential wealth of the American landscape and the advanced civilization of its cities both promoted and reinforced a resurgence of nationalism rooted in the homeland

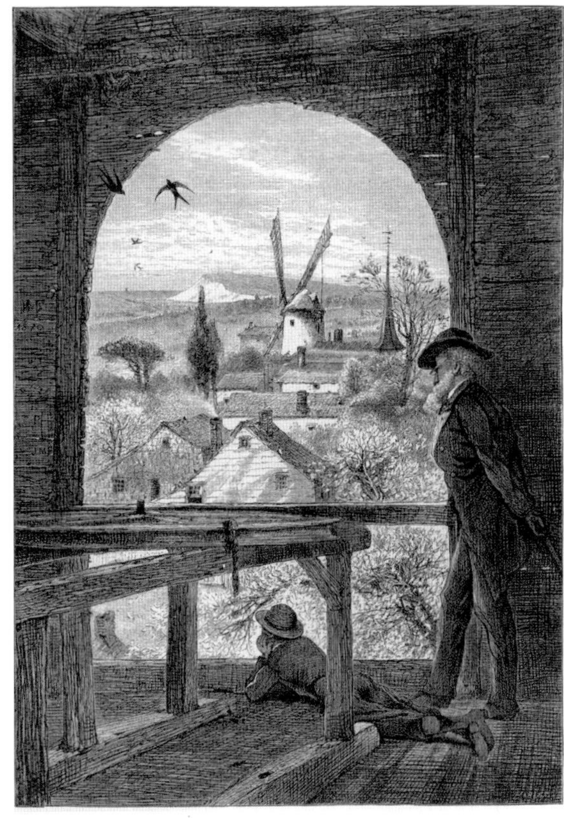

3.35. Harry Fenn, "East Hampton, from the Church Belfry." *Picturesque America*, 1:253. Wood engraving by [Joseph S.] Harley, 8 7/8" x 6 1/8".

rather than in institutions of democracy, as would have been the case in the years before the Civil War.[109]

Success in the United States led to subscription sales in England beginning in 1873 under the imprint of Cassell, Petter, Galpin and Company. The admiration of the British press shows how far American publications had come from a few years earlier, when publishers had relied on reusing illustrations from English books. The London *Graphic* called it a "magnificent work," of which the publishers, the editor, Bryant, and the "principal artist, Mr. Harry Fenn . . . may well be proud." The article went on the say that it was "satisfactory to find that art is so highly appreciated in the United States." It continued: "We hope that the English publishers will look to their laurels. Surely there is a public sufficiently appreciative to make it a profitable enterprise to issue work in England of this high class, instead of the poor-looking photographs of used up engravings which do duty with us now."[110]

In the publishers' exhibit at the 1876 Centennial Exposition in Philadelphia, D.

Appleton & Company displayed a specially bound edition of *Picturesque America* alongside its first book, the three-inch-square *Crumbs from the Master's Table,* issued in 1831. The pairing had the desired effect, for René Fouret commented in the "Report of the French Commission" that *Picturesque America* compared favorably with similar works published in France and England and could, "from a typographical and artistic point of view, be considered the best of all original publications from the American press."[111] It was again displayed at the 1878 Exposition Universelle in Paris in the collective exhibit by American publishers, and shortly afterward an abridged and reorganized version was published in French under the title *L'Amérique du Nord pittoresque.*[112] An 1883–85 German publication, *Amerika in Wort und Bild* by Friedrich von Hellwald, reused approximately half the wood engravings in *Picturesque America.*[113] Appleton's successful publication also inspired the Toronto firm Belden Brothers to issue *Picturesque Canada* as a subscription book in an almost identical format from 1882 to 1884. The primary artist for this work was F. B. Schell, but a few works were contributed by *Picturesque America* artists including Fenn, whose eight designs could have been based on photographs or studies already in his portfolio.[114]

By April 25, 1880, a member of the Appleton firm reported that forty thousand copies of *Picturesque America* had been sold and $2.4 million collected by subscription agents.[115] For many years, additional bound sets were sold, and in 1894 Appleton published a shorter, less expensive, revised edition.[116] Fenn's prominent contributions to this high-profile project brought him increased attention and established him as a leading—perhaps *the* leading—illustrator of the American landscape. James Henry Moser's testimony that Fenn's Natural Bridge images compelled him and his friend to seek out the site is a strong endorsement of the power of his published works. After this project, he never again lacked assignments.

EXHIBITING WATERCOLORS, 1870–73, INCLUDING A "MASTERPIECE"

Even with a heavy workload involving travel and preparing woodblocks for engravers, Fenn continued to participate actively in the American Society of Painters in Water Colors, having several paintings accepted for its annual exhibitions.[117] In these years, the subjects of most of his submissions derived from his journeys for "Picturesque America," either the series or the book. The society's fourth annual exhibition, in 1870–71, disappointed some critics, although works by A. F. Bellows and James Smillie received considerable praise.[118] Fenn's paintings included three Florida subjects. *The Convent Gate, St. Augustine, Fla.* may well have been similar to the skill-

Poetry and Picturesque America

fully rendered illustration "The Convent Gate" that appeared in *Appletons' Journal* on July 1, 1871 (fig. 3.36), which was striking in its effective use of spare line and the white of the paper to depict sunlit stucco walls. *Coquina Quarry, Anastasia Island, St. Augustine* may also have resembled a wood engraving with the same title that appeared in the same issue of the *Journal* (1:195). And, as mentioned previously, entry no. 509, *Sketch on the Ocklawaha River, Fla.,* could be the painting of the cypress-shingle-makers' camp that is now in the collection of the Metropolitan Museum of Art.

Whatever the subject of this so-called sketch, a *Chicago Tribune* reviewer found it "dreamy and delicate." Yet the writer gave more attention to Fenn's "more characteristic picture, 'The Home of Howard Payne'" in East Hampton, Long Island. Payne was the composer of the 1823 song "Home, Sweet Home," so popular during the Civil War. Fenn depicted the exterior and interior of his boyhood home for the *Journal* and, later, *Picturesque America* (1:254, 255). The interior image, full of shadows and intricate lines representing wood and stone, showed the old fireplace with a kettle hanging down, a cat on the floor,

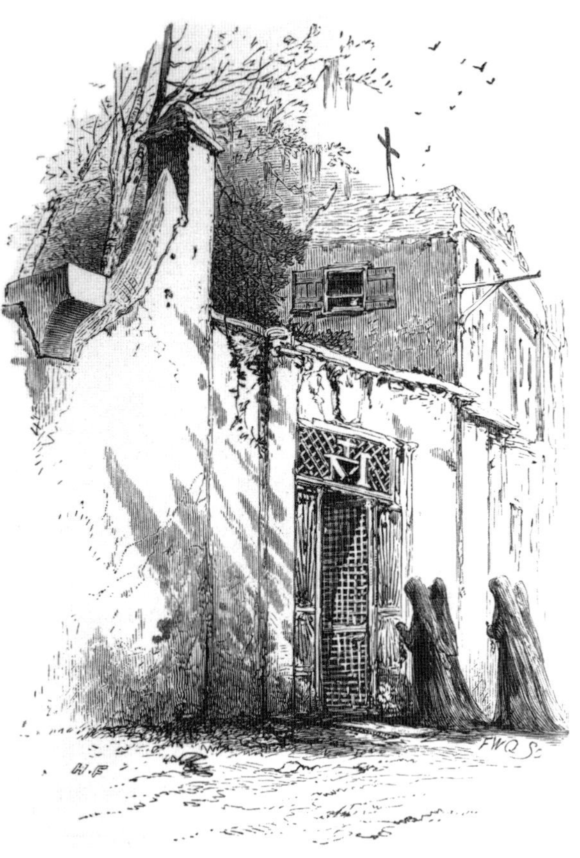

3.36. Harry Fenn, "The Convent-Gate," in "Scenes in St. Augustine." *Appletons' Journal*, July 1, 1871, 18. Wood engraving by F. W. Quartley, 4 5/8" x 3 1/8".

and a partial view of an adjoining room where a woman sits by a window. Although Fenn's exhibition watercolor (fig. 3.37), now in the Montclair Art Museum, is of the same fireplace, it is a much more focused and appealing composition, suggesting that in painting it he reworked whatever sketch or sketches he had drawn on-site. The reviewer's pronouncement that this piece was more characteristic of Fenn probably had to do with the picturesque subject, full of nostalgia, similar to the fireplace image in *Snow-Bound*. The writer's next comments about the painting's power are on the mark: "A flood of sunshine entering the door and casting upon the ashy hearth a sort of mocking gleam; the peculiar expression of absence haunting the room, gave a touching little side view of one early recollection of the author of 'Home, Sweet Home.'"[119] This work, as well as *The Convent Gate, St. Augustine, Fla.,* would be among those Fenn exhibited at the 1876 Centennial Exposition in the section devoted to the American Society of Painters in Water Colors.

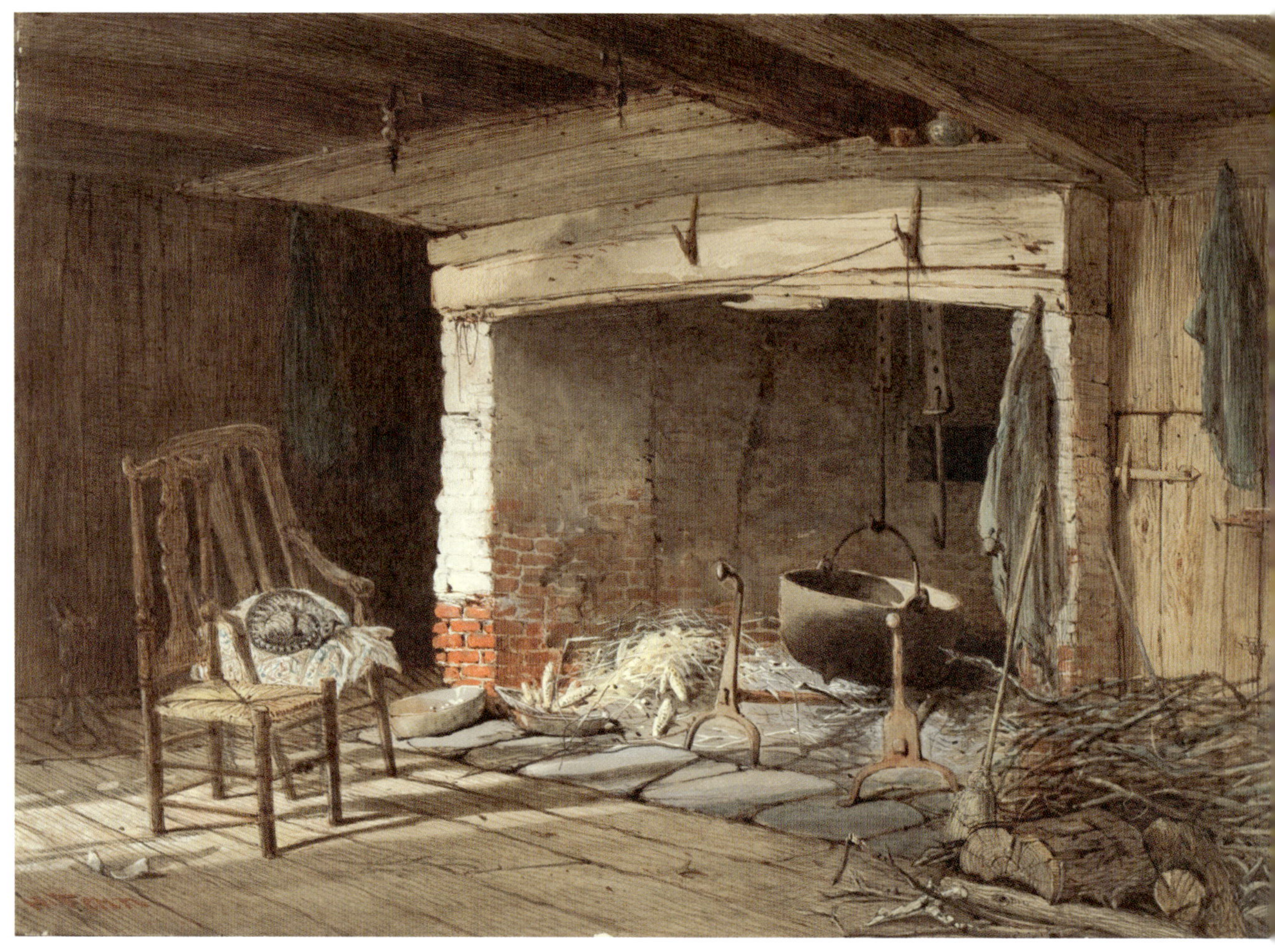

3.37. Harry Fenn, *Old Fireplace,* ca. 1870. Watercolor on paper, 10" x 14 1/4". (Montclair Art Museum, Bequest of Mary Ellen Wilde, 1913.14.)

At the fifth and sixth annual watercolor exhibitions, in 1871–72 and 1872–73, Fenn continued to exhibit a variety of landscapes related to the "Picturesque America" project, including views of Florida, Niagara Falls, and Watkins Glen, New York. (See Appendix 2 for a listing.) Susan Nichols Carter's review of the fifth annual show in *Appletons' Journal* gave particular attention to Fenn, describing his "Sketch" as "a good study of the head of a colored woman"—a rare instance of a portrait by Fenn (this work is unlocated). Carter gave more space to Fenn's painting *The Mouth of the St. John's River [Florida],* which she said attracted "a good deal of attention."[120]

Fenn's work gained more prominence at the sixth annual show, which took place after *Picturesque America* had begun to be published in parts in mid-1872.

   Poetry and Picturesque America

His *Goat Island, Niagara* was hailed as a "masterpiece." Although the title does not match that of a wood engraving in the book, it probably relates to a sketch he made while on assignment. This "masterpiece" may well have been the unusually large 1871 painting titled *Goat Island* that was included in the November 9, 1911, auction of eighty-two works by Fenn to settle his estate after his death. It measured 30 inches wide by 19 inches high (much larger than his typical size of about 20 by 12 inches) and was described as a "pen and ink and wash drawing," suggesting it was ink and white gouache rather than full watercolor.[121] The March 22, 1873, *Appletons' Journal* noted with pride that the artist for *Picturesque America,* Harry Fenn, "whom common consent places at the head of our landscape draughtsmen on wood," had been praised in the New York *Evening Mail* for his "brush-finished drawings in pen and ink" and quoted the comments:

> Goat Island is his masterpiece, and a masterly masterpiece it is. The rush of the water, the glistening rocks, the substance of the bowlders, are all perfectly rendered; while the tree-trunks are full of sylvan power and rugged strength, and the delicate interlacery of their mingled branches is interpreted with that confused individuality so difficult of attainment, but so easy of acknowledgment. This is a wonderful picture, and we are sure that, when Mr. Fenn has studied figures and becomes accustomed to the *technique* of water-colors, he will make a name in that branch of art which at present he only uses as an adventitious assistance.[122]

We can only surmise Fenn's reaction to this praise of his "masterpiece," conveyed with the assumption that he was unused to watercolor, a medium in which he had practiced and exhibited for several years and that he helped promote as one of the early members of the American Society of Painters in Water Colors. If *Goat Island* was indeed monochromatic, that helps account for the critic's comments. It could also be that Fenn had just then come to the critic's attention as a result of *Picturesque America.*

Whatever Fenn's reaction, his successes would soon lead to an extended stay in England to work on additional Appleton commissions—first *Picturesque Europe* and then *Picturesque Palestine, Sinai and Egypt.* Once again, he was fortunate, for he did not suffer from the panic of 1873, which led to five years of economic depression, making it more difficult for artists to earn a living in the United States. Living abroad and steadily employed, Fenn avoided these troubled times, and his career in illustration flourished.

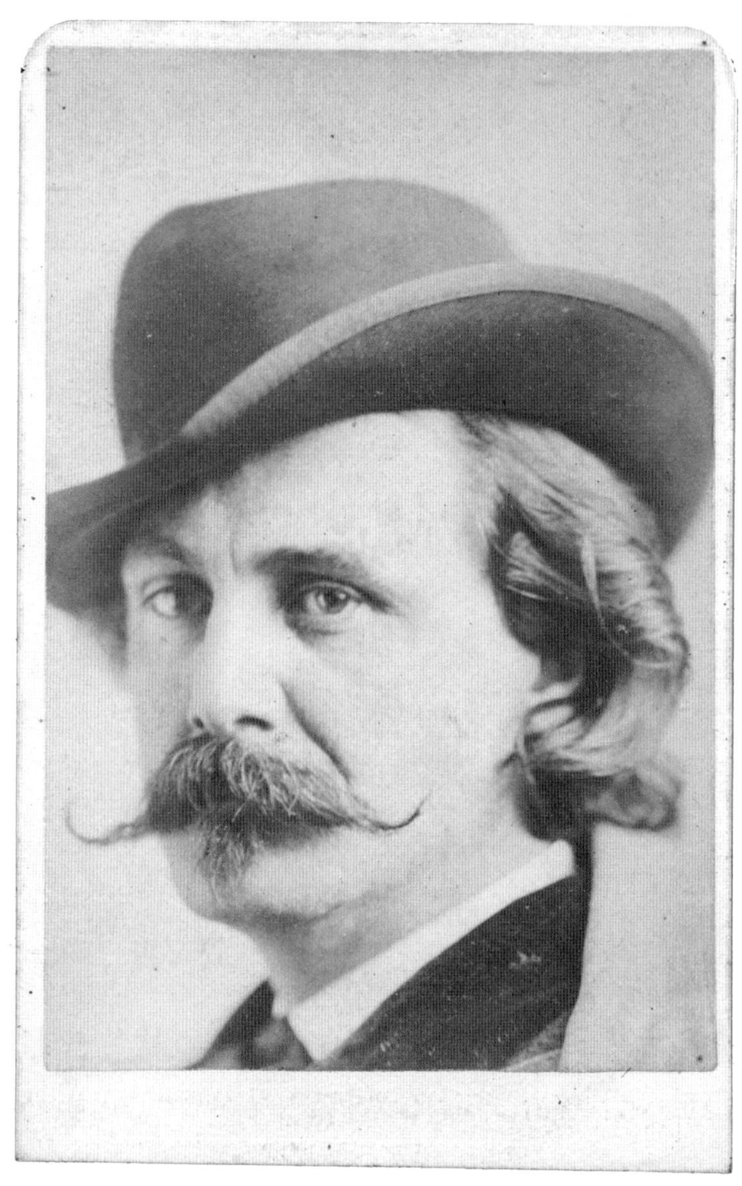

4.1. Carte de visite of Harry Fenn, ca. 1873. (Courtesy Paul Worman Fine Art, New York.)

4

Years Abroad—

"Picturesque Europe" and

"Picturesque Palestine"

ROM 1873 TO 1881 FENN lived abroad and traveled as the quintessential artist in search of the picturesque. Soon after Appleton began publishing *Picturesque America* in parts in mid-1872, it became clear that the book's combination of text and images was a winning formula. In fact, it was so successful that the firm involved Fenn in two successors—*Picturesque Europe* and *Picturesque Palestine, Sinai and Egypt*—produced in an identical format and using the same printing technologies. With their expensive steel engravings—among the last to appear in any major publication—and more numerous wood engravings in the picturesque mode, these books offered just enough innovation in layout and design to seem fresh and to appeal to a wide audience. Nevertheless, tastes were changing and many painters were turning away from picturesque and sublime landscapes to figural subjects and depictions of ordinary outdoor scenes shown in specific seasons or under particular atmospheric conditions.

After many *Picturesque America* subscriptions had been sold and a number of parts, or fascicles, had been distributed, the Appletons decided to publish a companion volume titled *Picturesque Europe.* The announcement, which appeared inside the wrapper of part 43 of *Picturesque America,* stated that the new book had been in preparation for some time; another notice in part 45 added that the projected date for beginning publication was January 1, 1875 (which proved overly optimistic). Clearly, the pride in American scenery and cities fostered by *Picturesque America* had helped lay to rest feelings of inferiority and led many subscribers to want a comprehensive visual survey of Europe as well. The growing sense of belonging to an Atlantic community, combined with the resurgence of interest among many Americans in their Anglo-Saxon heritage, enhanced the appeal and fostered the success of the book, especially its sections on Britain and Northern Europe. The same growing confidence prompted the United States to sponsor its first world's fair, the 1876 Centennial Exposition in Philadelphia, to which nations were invited to present their cultures, peoples, and accomplishments.

Like the organization of the fairs, the visual display of *Picturesque Europe* and, later, *Picturesque Palestine, Sinai and Egypt* presented and ordered the regions of the world as a spectacle to be experienced by viewing.[1] The books were late examples of "the visualization of the travel experience," in which scenic tourism replaced the opportunity to meet and converse with others as the primary motivation to travel.[2] By enabling readers to feel familiar with the areas depicted, they likely encouraged them to plan on, or at least dream of, visiting some of these places. Fenn's contributions to both works would enhance his reputation and garner praise for American illustrated publications both in the United States and abroad.

To further their ambitious new project, in 1873 the Appletons sent Fenn and his wife, their son, and three daughters to England, even as the engraving, printing, and perhaps even writing continued on *Picturesque America*. In some ways, moving to England must have seemed to Fenn like a homecoming, but it also meant leaving behind treasured colleagues in New York whom he would miss, as revealed in an undated letter to Nathaniel Orr: "I have not heard from any of the fellows in an age."[3] The family stayed in the country for eight years, living in several different locations, as Fenn came and went as necessary for his assignments. At one time Fenn kept a studio at 5 Blandford Place, Park Road, in northwest London, not far from Baker Street station, and in 1874 the family lived in Margate, a seaside resort to the east of the city. They also rented rooms at Gräfenberg House, New Barnet, Hertfordshire, on the north side of London, the location of a Victorian Turkish bath where Fenn's wife may have taken a cure in the dry air, which was thought to be therapeutic.

Mary Fenn suffered from recurring health problems; in a September 18, 1871, letter to Celia Thaxter, Whittier wrote that she had been "very ill" and was undergoing a "water cure" at Clifton Springs, in New York.[4] Fenn expressed concern for the "condition" of his "poor dear wife" in an undated letter thanking a Mrs. Holmes for her kindness during the episode:

> You don't know what a comfort it is to me, to have the knowledge that there is a kind and loving heart near her to say a word of sympathy now and then. As you say, you know full well "the heart of a sick wife and mother" and know also, how hard such a painful separation is from your dear loved ones at home and how they all miss, and long for you.
>
> Dear Mrs. Holmes please advise me what you think I had better do about

Years Abroad

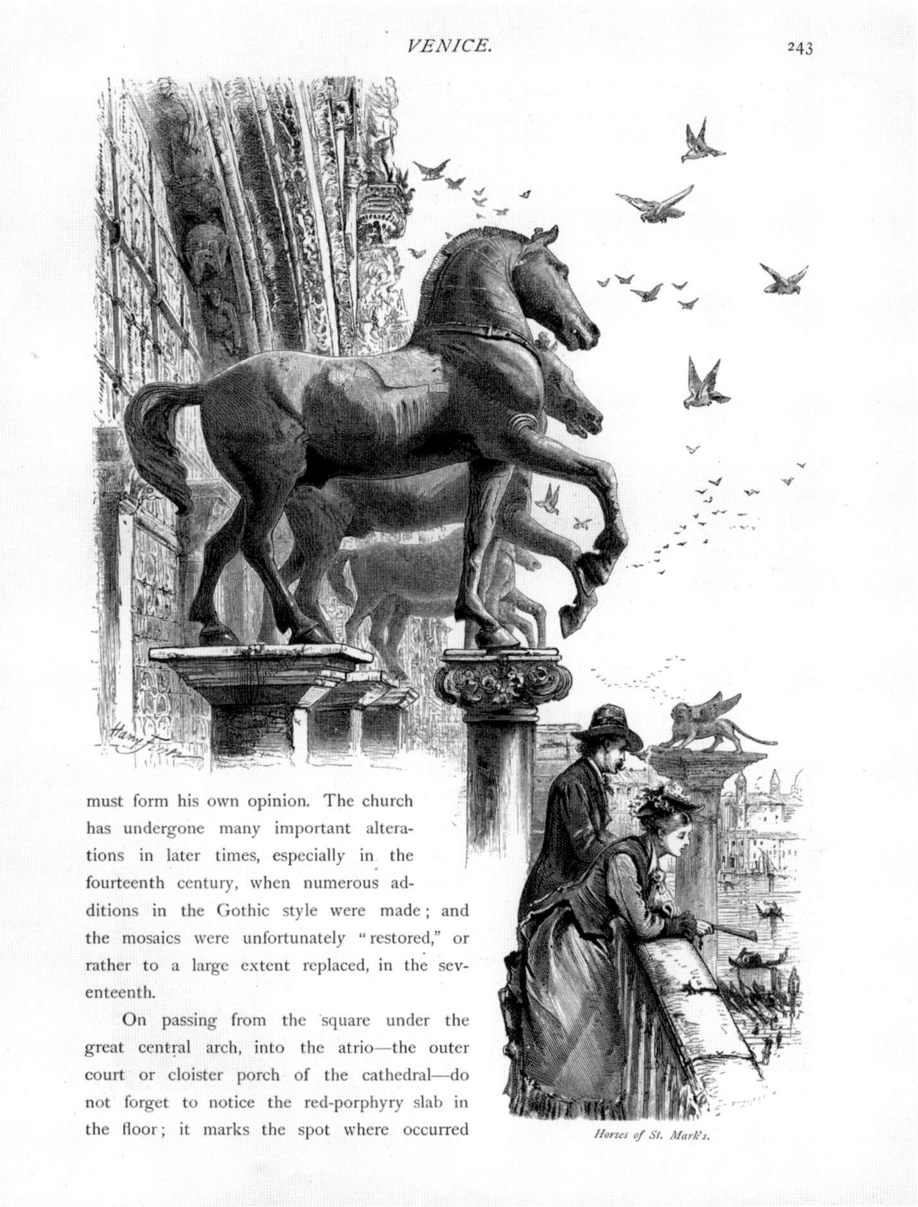

4.2. Harry Fenn, "Horses of St. Mark's" (with self-portrait and portrait of his wife). *Picturesque Europe*, 2:243. Wood engraving, approx. 9 1/2" x 6 1/2".

my wife's case, let her remain a while longer, or try and bring her home as soon as she can be moved.[5]

After moving to England, however, Mary Fenn was apparently well enough to travel with her husband, for he drew the two of them in Venice enjoying the view from the balustrade at St. Mark's Basilica, rendering the portrait of his wife with great care (fig. 4.2).

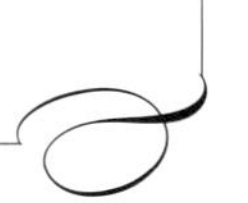

Another letter from their time in England shows Fenn's interest in his daughters' welfare. In it, he expresses that he and his wife were "not quite satisfied with the school" the girls were attending in Baldock, and he asks Nathaniel Orr about a school his daughters had attended in Brussels.[6] By mid-1876 the Fenns were renting rooms in Hampstead Heath, a pleasant residential area near a hillside park overlooking downtown London that was favored by many artists and writers.[7] By 1880 they were living in a farmhouse near Haslemere, in Surrey, where their daughter Hilda Marguerite was born.

In early 1874 *Appletons' Journal* called readers' attention to the fact that Harry Fenn was in England, and it quoted a letter revealing the artist's strong feelings about Americans' lack of appreciation for watercolor paintings. Fenn noted the high prices that such works had attained at the summer exhibition of the Water-Color Society in London and wrote: "There is one little fact . . . pertaining to this exhibition that I should like the American water-color despising public to know: a drawing by young [Frederick] Walker, thirty inches by twenty, has sold for twelve hundred pounds sterling. This is about his usual price, and there are many who get almost as much."[8] That amount must have been the equivalent of $6,000 at the time, for the *Philadelphia Inquirer* countered that, on the contrary, "Americans admire and treasure" watercolors. The notice continued: "It may be true that six thousand dollars is a higher price than has ever been paid in this country for a single water color, but this is owing to the simple fact that no painting of the class in question of such great value has yet been offered to the American picture-buying public—a public that is desirous of possessing choice water colors, and admires the masterly productions that have flowed so freely upon them from the studio of Mr. HARRY FENN."[9]

Despite his discouragement with the American public, Fenn continued to submit watercolors to the American Society of Painters in Water Colors exhibitions, but not as regularly as before. In 1874 and 1876, he exhibited works he had completed before leaving for England. At the society's seventh annual exhibition, in 1874, he showed a painting that was listed as being owned by his mother-in-law: *Blue Beads and Her Court,* a genre scene of a small child (perhaps one of his daughters) seated at a table "stringing turquoise-hued beads, and . . . decorating a group of dolls."[10] One reviewer said that Fenn, "hitherto known by his pleasing landscapes, has a charming bit of genre, a child with a table full of toys."[11] The three artworks that Fenn exhibited at the 1876 Centennial Exposition—*Old Fireplace of the Author of "Home Sweet Home," Old Convent Gate, St. Augustine, Florida,* and *Study of Boats*—had been included in the society's earlier exhibitions.[12]

For its 1878 annual exhibition, Fenn apparently sent works from England, for

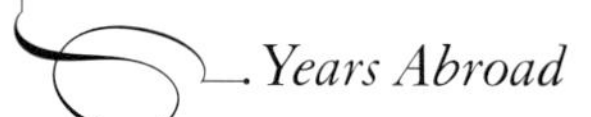

Years Abroad

he is credited with two new paintings, *Carrigan Head, Donegal, Ireland* and *The Lower Soko, Tangiers, Morocco*. He had depicted Carrigan Head in a wood engraving in *Picturesque Europe*'s section on the west coast of Ireland (1:326). Although no record of a visit to Morocco has been found, he could have traveled there via a short boat ride from Gibraltar, which he covered for *Picturesque Europe*. (A painting of Tangier dated 1881 lends weight to this possibility.) The *Art Journal* noted that *The Lower Soko* was "admirable in its tone of colour and aerial lightness."[13] That Fenn participated only intermittently in the society's exhibitions while he was in England is not surprising, considering his heavy workload at the time.

PICTURESQUE EUROPE

Before Fenn's arrival, the Appletons had arranged for the joint publication of *Picturesque Europe* with Cassell, Petter & Galpin, a large London firm that had maintained a New York office since 1860 and published the British edition of *Picturesque America*.[14] C., P. & G., as it was known, had found success issuing illustrated works at reasonable prices, particularly *Cassell's Illustrated Family Paper* (1853–1867), *Cassell's Illustrated Family Bible* (1859), and, in the 1860s, editions of Milton's *Paradise Lost* (1866), Dante's works, and *The Fables of La Fontaine* (1867), all illustrated by the popular French artist Gustave Doré. From 1869 to 1875 it published six volumes of *Illustrated Travels: A Record of Discovery, Geography, and Adventure,* edited by H. W. Bates, and beginning in 1872, *Old and New London* by Walter Thornbury, also in six illustrated volumes. The firm appeared to be an exceptionally appropriate partner for Appletons' grand undertaking, and it played the primary role in the production of the book. Since the writers, many of the artists, and the engravers were British, it seems clear that C., P. & G.'s staff selected them, rather than Appletons' editor Oliver Bell Bunce or other staff members, although the Appletons initiated the publication, determined the format, and hired Fenn to work on it.[15]

Although the earliest notices announcing *Picturesque Europe* that appeared in the London *Times* failed to mention Fenn by name, he played an important part in the project, which from the beginning gave more attention to the images than to the text. Of the sixty-seven sections, Fenn contributed to forty-two and was the sole illustrator of ten, more than any other artist. He almost certainly contributed the greatest number of illustrations, although it is impossible to count them accurately since many of the wood engravings are unsigned.

The American and British editions of *Picturesque Europe* contain noticeable differences. In the former, the British writers were omitted from the table of contents, a departure from *Picturesque America,* whose writers had been included there. The only person named was the editor, Bayard Taylor (1825–1878), a well-known American journalist, travel writer, lecturer, and poet who was appointed U.S. minister to Germany in 1878; he was also listed on the title page and mentioned in related advertising. The British edition did not cite Taylor as editor or contain his preface, which was aimed at American readers, but it did include the names of the writers at the end of each article. The American and British editions also differed in the arrangement of the articles, the engraved title pages, and the total number of volumes.

As might be expected, this joint British-American publication on Europe gave greatest attention to the British Isles. In Appleton's three-volume work published for its American audience, volume 1 and the first five sections of volume 2 treated Great Britain and Ireland. Other regions that received attention were those that had been part of the traditional Grand Tour and were still favorite and relatively accessible destinations for British and American travelers: France, Switzerland, Italy, and the German states. Parts of Spain were also covered in five sections, whereas Norway, Sweden, Belgium, Holland, Austria, and Greece received less attention, and only one section was devoted to Russia.

In his preface to the American edition, Taylor set the keynote for expecting and identifying differences between the American and European landscapes. He stressed that because climatic disparities yield various types of vegetation and atmospheric conditions, "the same form of mountains which, in our Northern States, would be covered with birch and hemlock, generally wears an even mantle of heather in Scotland, and is brilliant with box and arbutus in Italy."[16] He further notes that, in Europe, "Primeval woods"—the "forests which have never even been touched by man—are so rare as to be curiosities" and goes on to assert that so many Americans are interested in Europe's historic landscapes because these places are associated with their heritage. The American's "ancestors may have ruled in the feudal piles, built the venerable abbeys and minsters, or inhabited the quaint medieval dwellings which still line the shadowy streets of old English or Continental towns. The past of his own stock comes vividly back to him in the pictures of these objects" (1:v). These words reveal Taylor's typically limited concept of the meaning of *American* as well as the contemporary interest among his compatriots in their Anglo-Saxon and Teutonic origins.

From the beginning, the Appletons emphasized that *Picturesque Europe* would give great attention to historic sites. An announcement for the new book that appeared on the covers of parts 43 through 46 of *Picturesque America* read: "In this work the innumerable old ruins, the splendid cathedrals, the ancient abbeys, the monuments of art scattered everywhere, will secure more varied subjects than in our own country, where the artist has little more than scenes of Nature to inspire his pencil."[17] In this case, their desire to tout the new publication resulted in language that ran counter to their earlier insistence that America, too, had picturesque historical sites. In volume 1, some sections are even organized by types of historic architecture rather than geographical areas—and carry such titles as "English Abbeys," "Old English Homes," and "Cathedral Cities."

The text is also full of history, with many of the writers dwelling at length on the political, military, and religious events that had marked the various regions. Their frequent references to specific images suggest that the writers had access to the wood engravings (or the drawings for them) while preparing their descriptions. A brief overview of the text and images shows that, just as the language of *Picturesque America* was shaped to promote pride in U.S. landscapes and cities, the British writers of *Picturesque Europe* used superlatives in describing the distinctive elements of their own patrimony. Windsor Castle, for example, takes first place among the royal palaces of Europe (1:1); "nowhere are the combinations of rolling hills and winding valleys more attractive" than in Warwickshire (1:58); and "no other country" has "such a wealth of picturesque ruins" of monastic buildings as England (1:246).

As in *Picturesque America,* views of rivers, lakes, waterfalls, mountains, rock formations, and dramatic coasts are prominent in *Picturesque Europe.* The writers praise the scenery of many other regions besides Britain, such as the Italian lakes, the fjords of Norway, the Jura Mountains, and Lake Geneva. The English enthusiasm for mountain climbing finds expression, especially in "The High Alps" section. The text also gives tips on finding the best viewpoints, as it did in the earlier book. In the section on Toledo, Spain, for example, the writer advises: "Let those who would thoroughly realize its picturesqueness descend with the artist to the river's edge," an invitation that Fenn's image confirms (3:31). Other writers stress the drama of viewing scenic features during storms or at sunrise or sunset, and they pass judgment on what is picturesque: one states that the "epithet picturesque applies more properly" to the caves and forests of the Jura than to any other district (3:429), whereas another notes that "modern civilization is not picturesque" in Switzerland, where the "march of 'improvement' is now so rapid . . . that no one can dare say how long any relic of antiquity will be spared" (3:211).

As in *Picturesque America,* the artists avoid showing recent "improvements," focusing instead on older structures and traditional types of agriculture, industry, and transportation. They also depict the people of different regions, often wearing ethnic dress. Compared with *Picturesque America,* the images and text of *Picturesque*

Europe pay relatively little attention to major cities. Paris is not included (perhaps because it was still recovering from the Franco-Prussian War and the Commune), and the only scenes of London are distant views from the Thames. Edinburgh, Rome, Amsterdam, Naples, and Moscow receive some attention, while Athens and Constantinople are each depicted in several engravings. (These were surely based on photographs, since the Russo-Turkish War had made travel to these cities too risky.[18])

In addition, numerous comments show that the writers felt themselves to be part of a superior culture. Most have a strong preference for Protestant religions and exhibit an anti-Catholic bias, as was also common in the United States in this period. For example, the writer responsible for describing the towns of Halberstadt and Nuremberg, where the population had converted to Protestantism during the Reformation, finds their buildings much superior to the "squalid and tumble-down walls" in "so many prince and priest ridden communities" (2:272–73). Others describe the descendants of the Moors in Murcia, Spain, "as idle and apathetic as the veriest Oriental drugged with *hasheesh*" (2:390), the Jews of Poland as not "pleasant to behold," and Warsaw as "colorless" and "depressing" (3:397–98). They view the peoples of southern Europe as backward and warn of the inconvenience and danger of travel in Calabria and Sicily, in southern Italy (3:160). Greece is "a country of sickening contrasts," with its glorious past but so little progress since independence that "the want of inns and roads, and the prevalence of brigandage" keep travelers away.

By contrast, thanks to its railroads, "sleepy" Spain is "awakening," although the writer complains that "Spaniards are not hospitable by English and American standards" (3:22). Moscow has also become accessible by train, and the Turks have been roused to modern progress and built trams, omnibuses, and railways in Constantinople (3:308), but beware "the Bazar," which has many robbers (3:313). The inclusion of Turkey, England's ally in the Crimean War, is not surprising, but the attitude expressed in the last line of the book, as the section on the Danube closes with passage through the "Iron Gates," shows how qualified it was: "We pass, if not into Asia, at least into a mongrel and unpicturesque Europe" (3:491).

Even before Fenn's arrival in London in 1873, C., P. & G. began working to produce the more than one thousand illustrations planned for the book; the first three sections were illustrated by British artists. Fenn's earliest contributions appear in the fourth and fifth sections, "Warwick and Stratford-on-Avon" and "The South Coast, from Margate to Portsmouth." The order in which regions containing his illustrations appear in the book suggests that his first sketching journeys were to England, Scotland, and Ireland, and he eventually covered Spain, much of Italy,

Years Abroad

and parts of Switzerland and Germany.[19] His travels in Italy began in the winter of 1875 and were completed before late February 1876, as indicated by the writer and art critic Lucy H. Hooper, wife of the American ambassador in Paris, who reported in *Appletons' Journal* that she had "seldom passed a keener hour of art-enjoyment" than when viewing the "fine" watercolor sketches of Italy and Sicily that Fenn had created for *Picturesque Europe*.[20] She clearly appreciated the unusual viewpoints and dynamic, often diagonal, compositions; her somewhat awkwardly worded praise of Fenn's ability to "lend to scenes hackneyed by dent of reproduction an entirely fresh and novel aspect by dent of originality in treatment" provided an advance endorsement of the new project.

Information about Fenn's work-related trips during this period is scarce. An obituary written by his English son-in-law, the journalist Sidney Brooks, makes us wish we knew more, especially about his excursion to Italy and Sicily. Brooks claimed that Fenn was "captured by Sicilian brigands and soon after thrown into an Italian prison, where he spent some days before the British consul could persuade the officials that a traveler with Garibaldi's card in his valise was not necessarily a dangerous revolutionary."[21] When back in London, Fenn worked hard on his illustrations, spending from 9 a.m. to 2 p.m. and from 3 p.m. to 7 p.m. in his studio, according to a letter he wrote to Nathaniel Orr in mid-1876. Yet another letter suggests that he relished his travels: "I am still working away on P.E. Spent the whole of last winter in Italy and Sicily fetching up at Malta, and should like to be doing the same at this moment for of all the beastly weather I have ever experienced this is about the worst. However, I am off to Spain in a week or two where I hope to again make acquaintance with the sun."[22]

Fenn was paid £20 a week when traveling, quite a respectable sum at the time.[23] It is unknown what he was paid for his drawings on the block. As the work progressed, however, Fenn and his younger colleague John Douglas Woodward, who joined the project in 1876, became dissatisfied with C., P. & G. In a letter dated 1878, Woodward complained of "the penny saving way of these shoddy people," that is, the principals of the firm, who made them wait in a "dirty office" and "groaned over every item of expense."[24] The two men would be pleased when Appleton chose a different partner for its next project, *Picturesque Palestine, Sinai and Egypt*.

Picturesque Europe's sixty steel plates (plus the three title pages in the American edition) were engraved by some of the most respected men in this specialty; printed on heavy paper, the steel engravings reproduced works by several English artists including Birket Foster (Fenn's mentor at the Dalziel firm), a German painter named Carl Werner, and Fenn and Woodward. Foster contributed seventeen

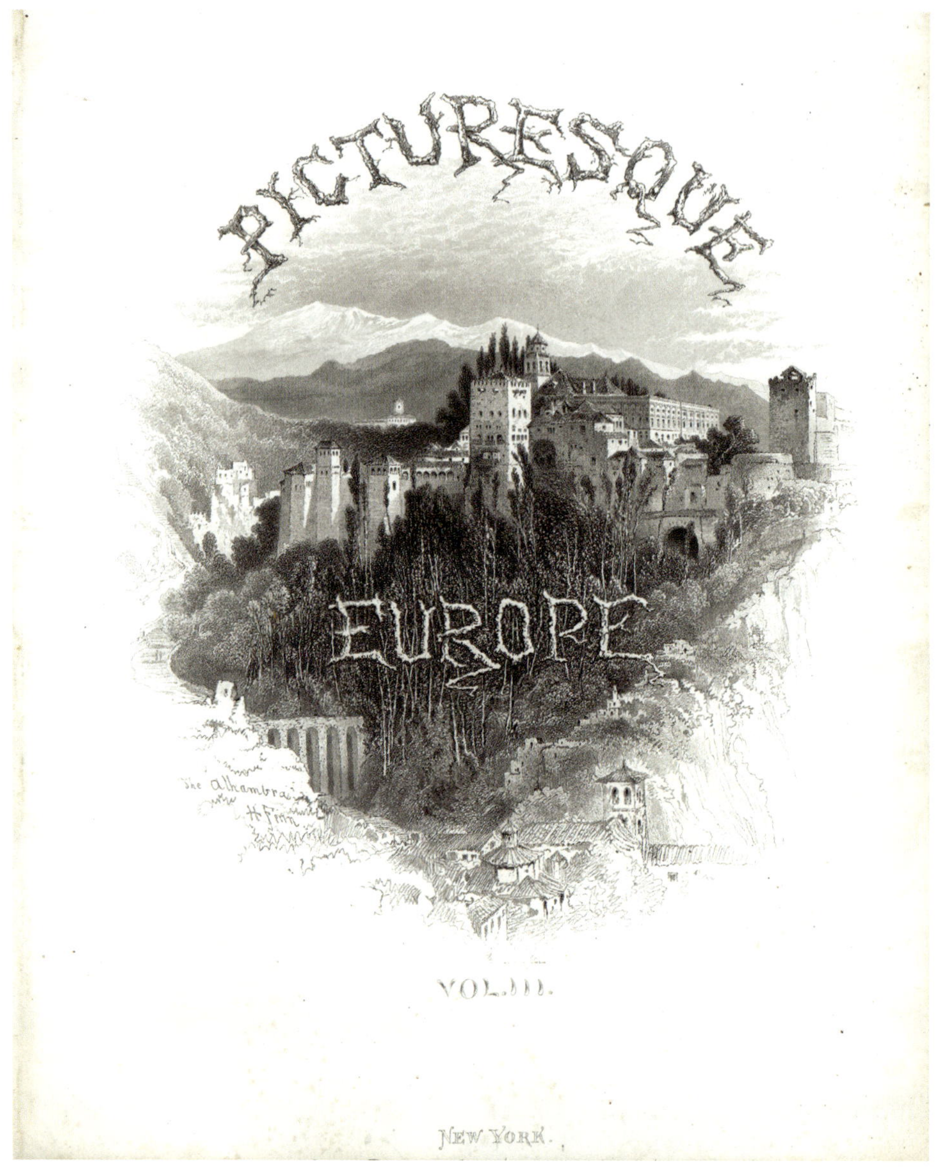

views, including one titled "The Thames from Richmond Hill," the area where Fenn grew up. Perhaps the successful younger artist, who had made his mark in the United States and returned to England for this project, crossed paths with Foster at the C., P. & G. offices. Despite Fenn's earlier admiration of Foster, it is clear that he had since departed from the approach of not only Foster but also the other British artists, as an examination of the steel engravings reveals.

In volume 1, all the plates except the two by Fenn are straightforward landscape views presented more or less from ground level. By contrast, Fenn's "Rocks

Years Abroad

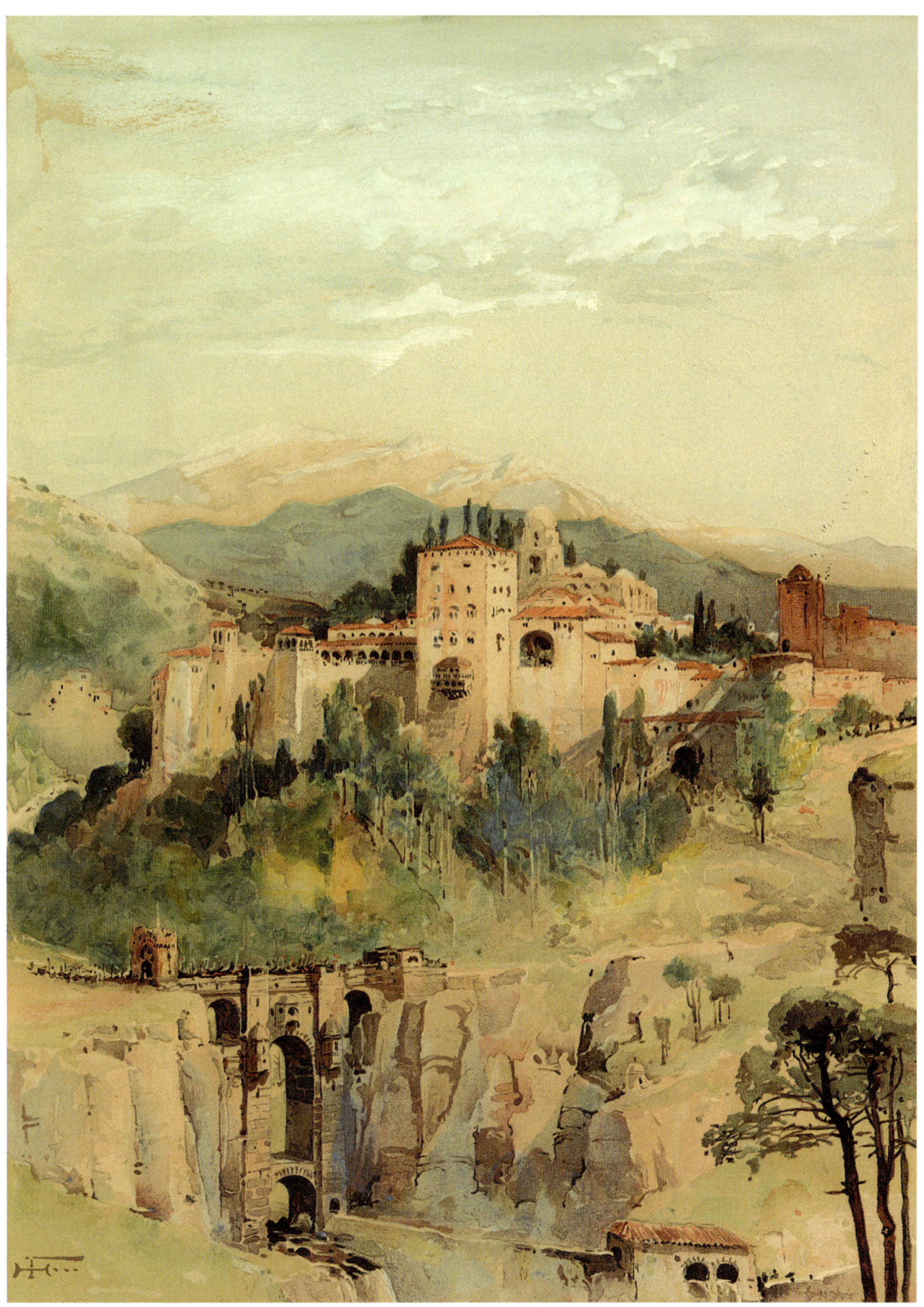

4.4. Harry Fenn, [The Alhambra and Sierra Nevada], ca. 1875. Graphite, watercolor, and gouache, approx. 14" x 10". (Private collection.)

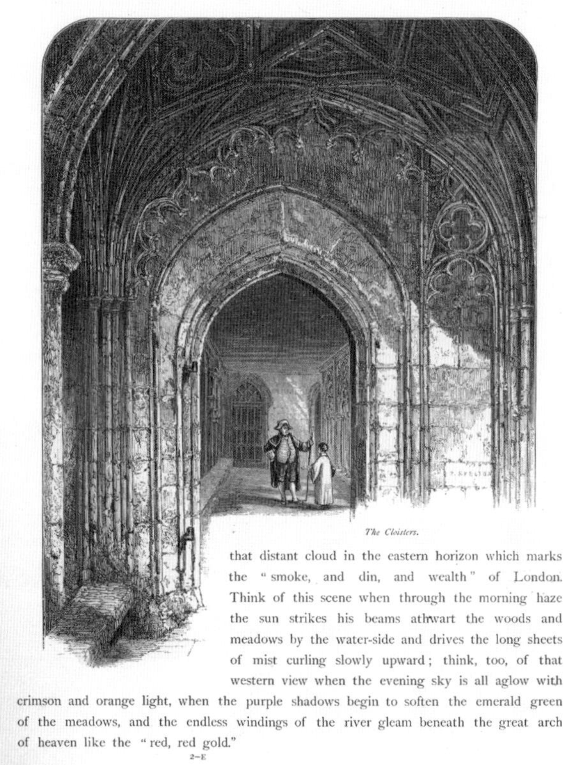

4.5. P. Skelton, "The Cloisters." *Picturesque Europe*, 1:9. Wood engraving, approx. 7 3/4" x 5 15/16".

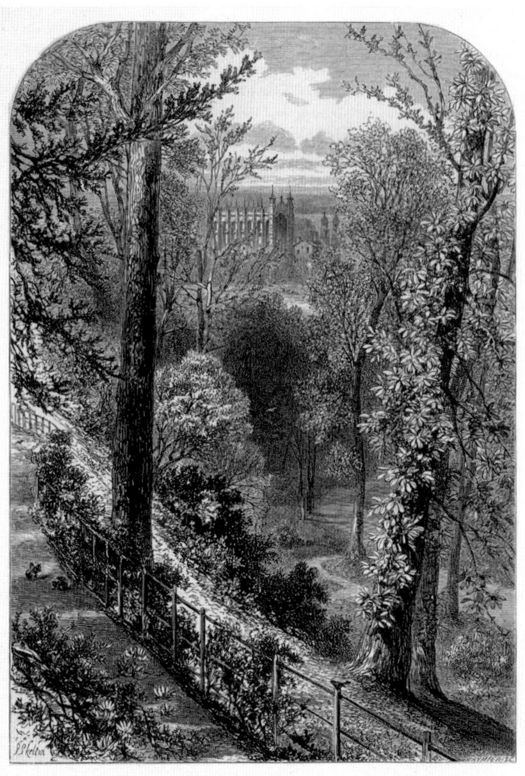

4.6. P. Skelton, "The Slopes, Windsor." *Picturesque Europe*, 1:13. Wood engraving by Whymper, 9 1/8" x 6 1/4".

at Ross" and "The Bent Cliff" have high viewpoints, resulting in more dramatic compositions. Fenn also designed an ornamental steel-engraved title page for each of the three volumes of Appleton's edition. These striking opening pages feature a calligraphic treatment of the titles, whose letters are made to look like gnarled wood, combined with a scene related to the contents of each volume. In volume 3, which contains sections on Spain, the curved letters of *Picturesque* embrace a vignette of the Alhambra, in Granada, with the Sierra Nevada Mountains in the distance (fig. 4.3). An extant watercolor of the same subject seen from a slightly different angle may be an example of Fenn's plein-air work or his reworking of one or more sketches (fig. 4.4).

Several of the English artists who contributed designs to be engraved on the woodblocks were well-established landscape specialists. They included William Henry James Boot (1848–1918), who had illustrated several periodicals and books published by C., P. & G. and would be elected a member of the Royal Society of British Artists in 1884; Percival Skelton (fl. 1850–1880), who specialized in coastal

Years Abroad

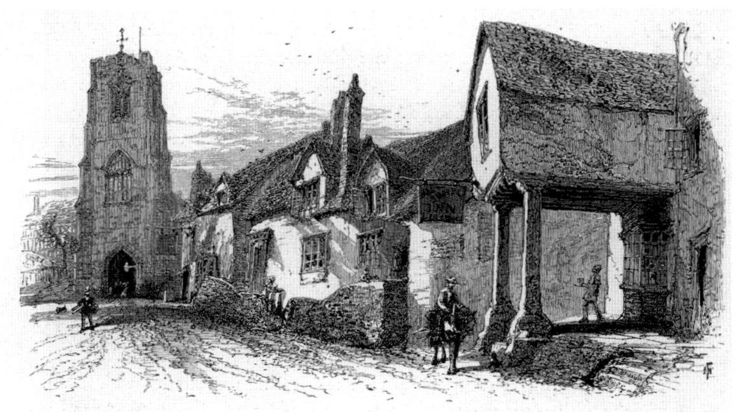

4.7. Harry Fenn, "West Gate, Warwick." *Picturesque Europe*, 1:58. Wood engraving, approx. 3 1/4" x 6 3/8".

scenes and landscape and figure illustrations; Edward Monson Wimperis (1835–1900), who had studied with Birket Foster and worked extensively for the *Illustrated London News* before turning to watercolor painting; Richard P. Leitch (1827–1882), who illustrated books of poetry and had been sent to Italy by the *Illustrated London News* in 1859; and Thomas Leeson Rowbotham (1823–1875), an engraver, lithographer, and painter who taught drawing at the Royal Naval School, Greenwich, had illustrated *English Lake Scenery* (1875), and, with his father, had published *The Art of Landscape Painting in Watercolours* (1850).

Certainly, these artists had much experience depicting landscapes in easel, or rectangular, formats as well as vignettes. Yet, the illustrations in the first sections of *Picturesque Europe* (before Fenn's work begins to appear) show that they were attempting to follow one of the approaches Fenn had used so effectively in *Picturesque America*—combining irregularly shaped images with blocks of type—without quite understanding how to do so effectively. For example, on page 9 of Appleton's American edition (fig. 4.5), the jagged lower edge of text confuses and conflicts with, rather than complements, Skelton's image (see also 1:5 and 12). Moreover, the artists were sometimes not as successful as Fenn in drawing on the block in a way that resulted in an attractive wood engraving. Skelton's design titled "The Slopes, Windsor" (fig. 4.6) is a visual jumble of details of different textures; and later in the volume, the engraved lines in "Ellen's Isle" (1:400) draw attention to themselves rather than enhance the image.

After Fenn joined the project, many of his designs offered models of more appealing, more dramatic compositions. His first wood engraving in volume 1, "West Gate, Warwick," which opens the "Warwick and Stratford-on-Avon"

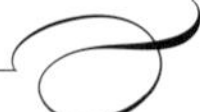

rock, locally called killas, which often passes into a dark, almost black rock, containing much of the mineral hornblende. The intermediate and principal part is composed of serpentine, generally of a dark olive-black color, but in the neighborhood of the Lizard, and of the eastern coast, inclining more to red and green, often beautifully mottled and veined. From the various quarries in it come the polished shafts and columns, the slabs and ornaments, now becoming so deservedly popular, especially in architectural decorations.

At the northeast extremity of this great serpentine district is a huge block of the igneous rock called *gabho*, of a bluish-gray color, which, if not too costly from its hardness, would, I believe, when polished, also make a very handsome decorative stone. Besides its geology, this district is the headquarters of a very remarkable flora, characterized by a number of plants found hardly anywhere else in the British Isles, such as the tamarisk, the autumn squill, the *Genista pilosa*, and the *Erica ragans*, or Cornish heath. The last is hardly to be found off the serpentine, but is there extraordinarily

The " Frying-Pan."

section, shows an effective use of the vignette format, with striking perspective and light effects that take advantage of the white of the paper (fig. 4.7). In addition, his use of irregular shapes for the image interlocking with type was usually skillful enough to instruct others (1:83, 86, 232, 337), as in "The Frying Pan" (fig. 4.8), where it seems as if the viewer can approach the high point directly above the type. In later sections, the British artists, especially Leitch and Rowbotham, became more adept at producing designs similar to Fenn's. Most of the wood engravings for the book were done by the London firm of Josiah Wood

Whymper (1813–1903), and their uneven quality no doubt relates to the skill of the various engravers as well as the artists.[25]

Fenn's status among his fellow artists was surely enhanced when the January 1877 issue of Appleton's *Art Journal* printed two of his illustrations before their appearance in volume 2 of *Picturesque Europe:* "Island of St. Giulio, Lake of Orta" and "Off the Rialto" (fig. 4.9), the famous bridge over Venice's Grand Canal. The writer praised the artist's distinctive approach, saying: "Mr. Fenn has a very happy faculty of seizing upon unconventional points of view in a scene. . . . Often as the 'Rialto' has been painted and engraved, every one must admit that Mr. Fenn has succeeded in making as fresh and striking a picture as if the place were new to the world of Art. Mr. Fenn unites boldness with delicacy to a remarkable degree. He seizes upon a point of view with great courage and dash, puts in his effects in a large and broad manner, and yet does not lose delicacy of detail, nor does he lack in finish of execution."[26] The writer much preferred

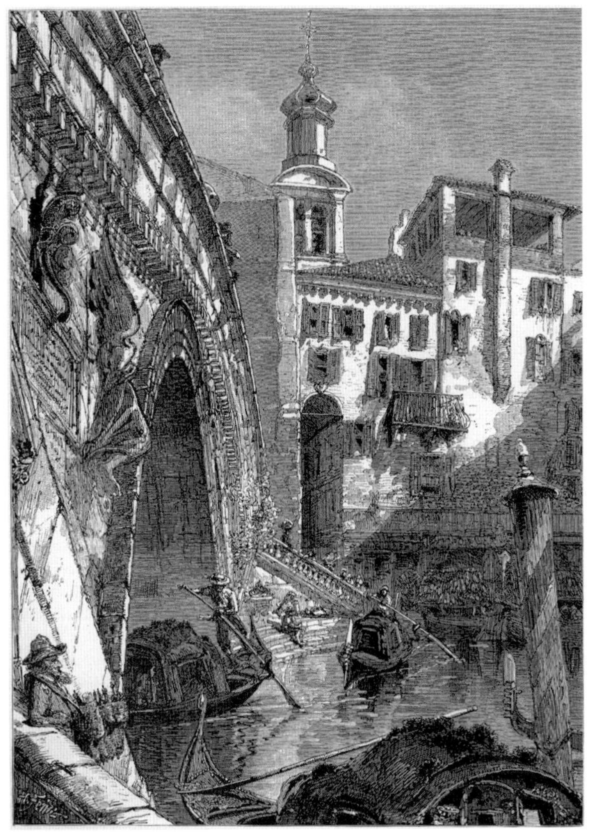

4.9. Harry Fenn, "Off the Rialto." *Art Journal* (New York), January 1877, 21. Wood engraving, 9 1/4" x 6 7/8".

Fenn's drawings to the "dreary monotony of photographic views" lacking in "spirit" and "expression." The boldness of viewpoint and composition is obvious when comparing Fenn's image of the Rialto with a second, entirely conventional frontal view that appears two pages later in the same section on Venice ("The Rialto," 2:231). To contemporary viewers, Fenn's work was dynamic, with bold strokes and unusual compositions that conveyed individuality while showing good technique, that is, "finish of execution."

The work of the two Appleton artists, Fenn and Woodward, was appreciated by their English employers. In 1876, after completing a few months' worth of work on *Picturesque Europe,* Woodward wrote home that C., P. & G. had encouraged him to stay and promised "no end of work," leading him to comment that "there seems to be a great scarcity of good draughtsmen in England."[27] Of course, the quality of the designs and the engravings varies greatly; sometimes the foreground figures in Fenn's compositions are unattractive, with thick, dark outlines

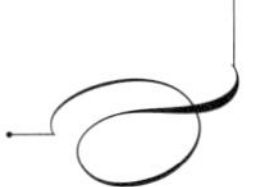

bathing. All round lie softly-sloping hills covered with carefully-tended vines; towers of churches and other buildings rise in all directions; and on the opposite side of the river, on its steep, precipitous rock, is the fortress of Marienberg, rising like Ehrenbreitstein over Coblentz, or Buda over Pesth. The cathedral is remarkable for its monuments of bishops, varying in age and taste from the sleepful, trusting repose of the earlier pastors, to the awkward and exaggerated attitudes of their late successors. Monuments of prince-bishops, like those of popes, are apt to vary in size and splendor with the number of nephews and the fortune which they leave behind them. On the site of the martyrdom of St. Killian is built

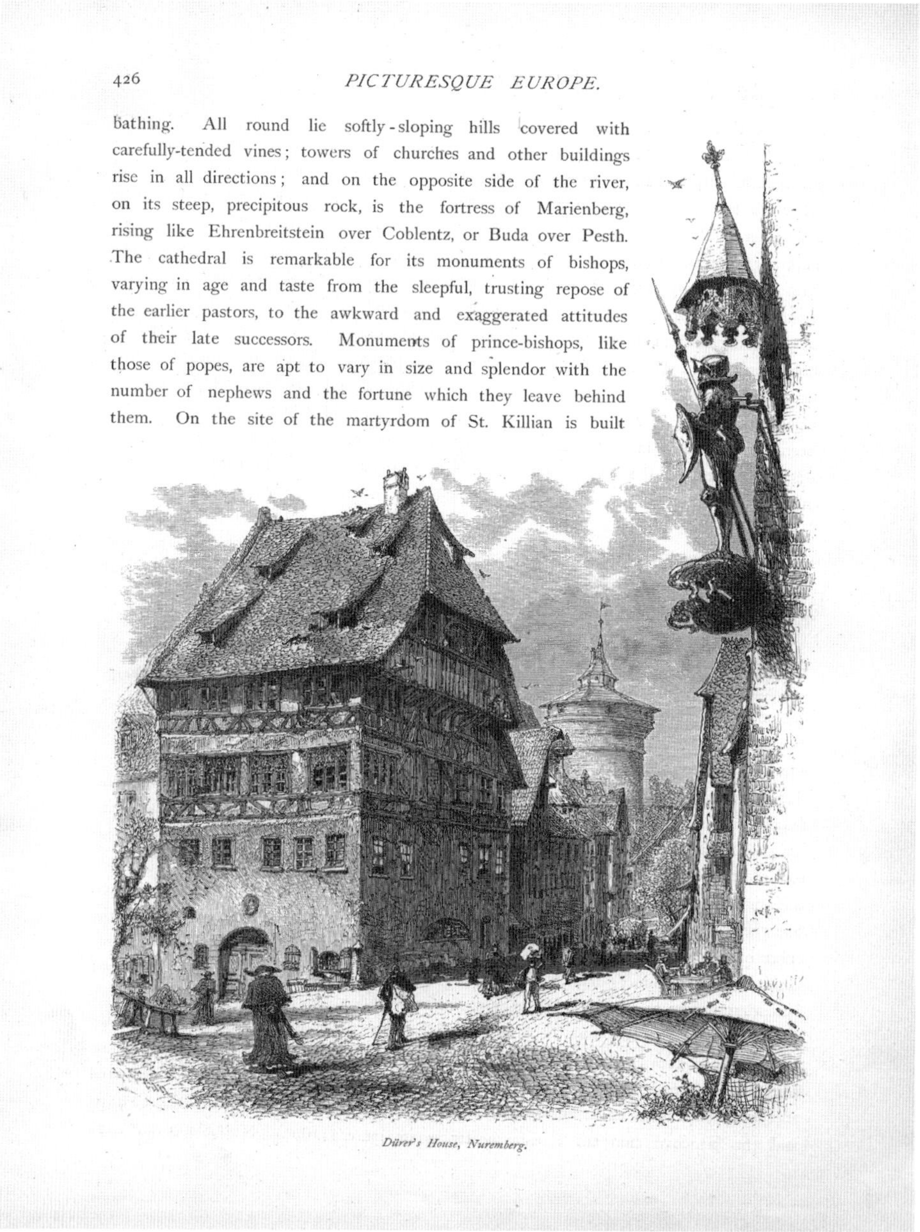

Dürer's House, Nuremberg.

that contrast with the weight of other lines (perhaps the fault of the engraver). In addition, it is obvious that both he and Woodward sometimes used photographs to aid in the depiction of foreground figures or entire scenes, as Fenn had done in *Picturesque America.*[28]

    Fenn's assignments required him to draw all types of scenery—mountains,

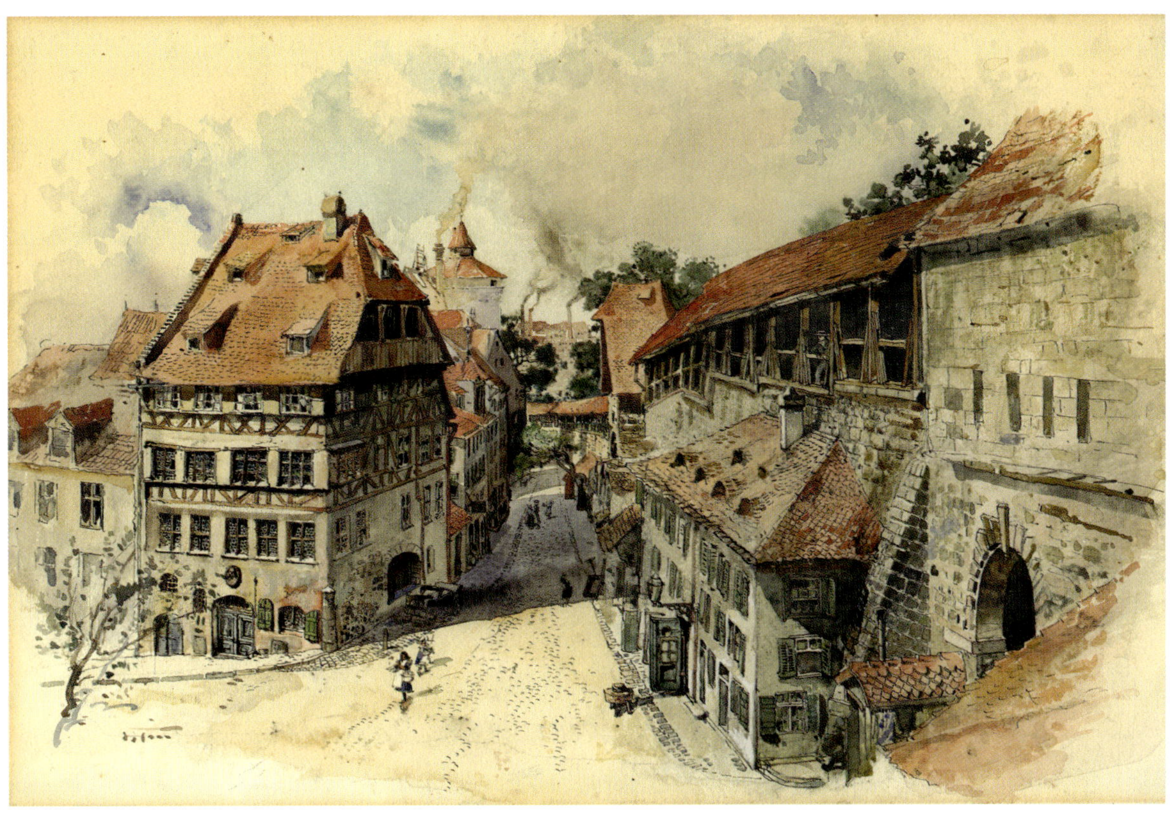

4.11. Harry Fenn, *Albert Dürer's House from the Walls of Nurnberg*, ca. 1875? Ink, wash, and gouache on paper on board, 12 1/4" x 17 1/2". (Private collection.)

lakes, waterfalls, rivers, rock formations—and to focus particularly on historic architecture. He drew the Coliseum in Rome; the Alhambra and the Great Mosque of Córdoba, in Spain; Warwick Castle and Anne Hathaway's cottage in England; and Albrecht Dürer's House in Nuremberg, Germany. Although the preliminary drawings for such images were often destroyed, a surviving highly finished watercolor similar to his precisely rendered illustration "Dürer's House, Nuremberg" (figs. 4.10, 4.11) raises questions about Fenn's working methods. Might he have painted this watercolor on-site while sketching for *Picturesque Europe,* realizing that its expansive format was unsuitable for the book? Or did he prepare the watercolor later, based on his sketches, using a different format and including many more buildings? The brightly colored painting may have similarities to some of those in the first annual exhibition of the American Society of Painters in Water Color that were criticized for their inharmonious color.

The publishers must have thought Fenn was especially adept at capturing

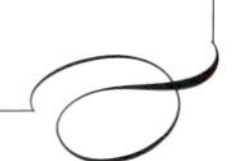

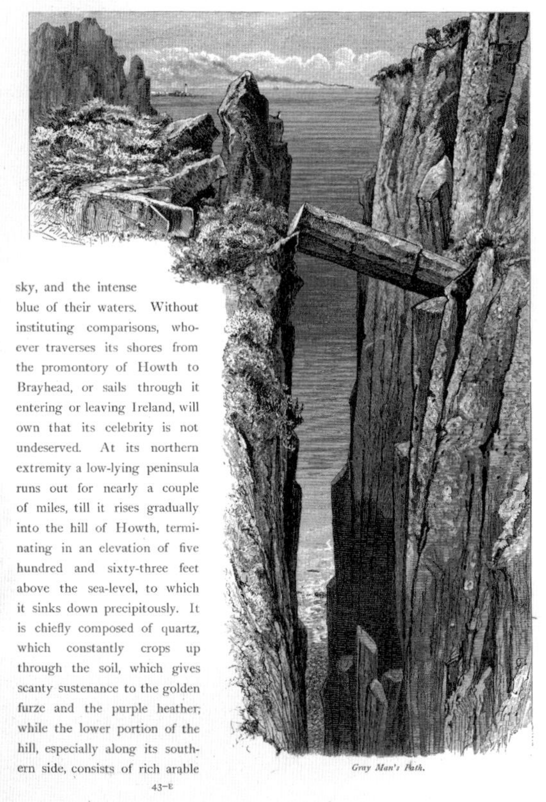

4.12. Harry Fenn, "Gray Man's Path." *Picturesque Europe*, 1:337. Wood engraving by Whymper, 9 1/4" x 6 1/4".

coastal scenery, for they made him solely responsible for illustrating the sections titled "The Land's End" and "The West Coast of Ireland" and asked him to contribute to those on the south coast of England and "The West Coast of Wales." Many of these designs are striking compositions offering a dramatic perspective, as in "Gray Man's Path," which shows a trail near Fair Head in Ireland. The writer describes it in sublime terms as "a deep, wild chasm, which strikes one with a feeling of awe almost amounting to horror, dividing the headland sheer down over two hundred feet" (figs. 4.12, 4.13). A watercolor corresponds almost exactly to the wood engraving, again prompting us to wonder whether Fenn made the painting on-site and used it as his source for the illustration or if a sketch he made on-site became the basis for both works.

A venture as large as *Picturesque Europe* required time to produce, and more than two years passed between the time Appleton sent Fenn to England and the release of the book's first part in the United States, in late 1875 (probably December).[29] In the meantime, the Appletons warned their patrons not to be deceived by another publisher that had taken advantage of the delay to issue a similarly titled book consisting of reused steel plates of European sites.[30] The American edition of *Picturesque Europe* was issued monthly in parts priced at fifty cents apiece, with light brown paper covers printed with the title and a circular image of Europa seated on a bull. *Picturesque Europe* matched *Picturesque America* in format, but it was longer, more than 1,400 pages, and consequently included a larger number of wood and steel engravings.

The prospectus that appeared on Appleton's early part covers touted the work as "the most Complete and elegantly Illustrated Work on Europe ever produced" and called special attention to the originality of the artworks: "THE ENGRAVINGS OF THIS WORK ARE ALL NEW, having been executed from sketches by American and English artists, who for two years past have been traveling over every part of Europe, in order to secure accurate and the latest views of picturesque places." It also explained

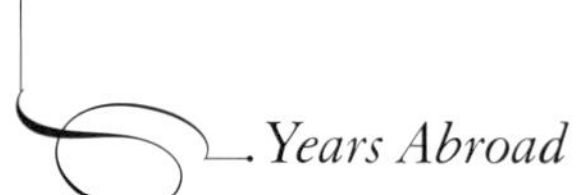

Years Abroad

that the book would "probably be completed in Sixty Parts" (the actual number) and *"positively* not exceed Sixty-six Parts" (doubtless a tactic to reassure subscribers concerned about the total cost). The salesman's sample book prepared by Appleton to solicit subscribers contained parts 1 and 2, as well as eight additional steel engravings. Exhibitors at the 1876 Philadelphia Centennial Exposition who wished to demonstrate the superiority of their printing presses printed some of the book's illustrations as examples; the *New York Times* reported: "The printing of such delicate work, requiring as it does the greatest accuracy of adjustment and extreme regularity of working of the press, can only be executed on presses of the highest class, design, and construction."[31]

By late 1879 the publication in parts was complete and Appleton offered the book, well timed for holiday giving, in three volumes bound in full morocco leather at $54 and half morocco leather at $48. The *Chicago Daily Tribune* called it "the most beautiful book that the present holiday season has produced."[32] The *New York Times*

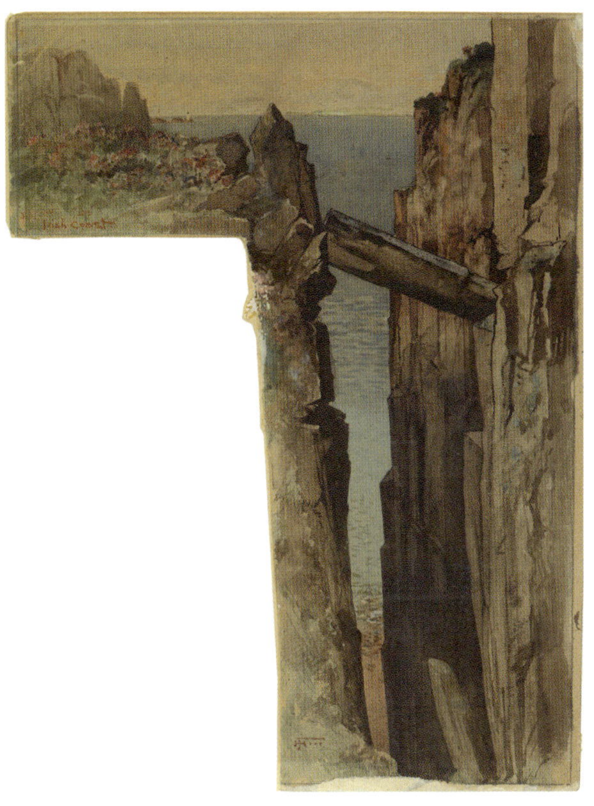

4.13. Harry Fenn, *Irish Coast*, ca. 1873–74. Watercolor and gouache, approx. 19 1/4" x 14". (Courtesy of Richard Fenn van Antwerp.)

reviewer agreed, commenting that the publishers had spared "no cost or labor" and that *Picturesque Europe* "was a direct result of the popular favor given" to *Picturesque America,* but its "scope [was] larger and its rank more serious."[33] On December 16, 1879, the London *Times* published a long description of volume 3, extolling the beauty and variety of the subjects and "the admirable management of tone, in the play and relief of light and shadows" in the illustrations. The writer cites several of the English artists by name; although Fenn was not mentioned, his "Calvary Carlsbad" (3:268), a moonlight view of crosses on the Dreikreuzberg, was praised as "one of the most poetical conceptions in the volume."

In London, Cassell, Petter & Galpin began issuing their edition of *Picturesque Europe* in early February 1876, with parts priced at two shillings, sixpence each.[34] The first bound volume was ready for the Christmas trade in December of that year.[35] For its customers, C., P. & G. divided the book into either five or ten volumes. The five-volume set was offered at ten pounds, ten shillings. One version of the ten-volume edition was the most expensive work the firm had ever offered: the large-paper edition sold for twenty guineas (one guinea equaled one pound, one shilling) bound in cloth and fifty guineas in red morocco and stamped in gold and black, with a different image on the front cover of each volume.[36] *Picturesque Europe* continued to be advertised and sold for many years in England; C., P. & G.'s successor, Cassell & Co. offered a five-volume "Popular Edition" in 1900.[37] A Spanish version was published 1882–83.[38]

On June 25, 1880, Cassell, Petter, Galpin, and Co. (the slight name change indicates that the company had taken on additional partners) engaged the firm of Christie, Manson & Woods to auction off "the whole of the original water-colour drawings" made for the steel engravings in *Picturesque Europe,* along with other artworks, an indication that these were considered the property of the publisher. The sale catalogue gave most attention to the project's senior painter, proclaiming in large type: "Including Seventeen Works of Birket Foster." The names of the other artists, including "H. Fenn" and "H. D. [*sic*] Woodward," appear in small type. Not surprisingly, Foster's works brought the highest prices, ranging from around forty to seventy pounds, followed by those of the other well-known English artists, such as Leitch. Fenn's works sold for only a few pounds, with "Monte Pellegrino, Palermo" attaining the highest price, "10/10," presumably ten pounds, ten shillings.[39]

THE *PICTURESQUE PALESTINE* PROJECT

By September of 1877, with the publication of *Picturesque Europe* well under way but far from complete, the momentum of the "picturesque" series seemed unstoppable. Appleton made plans for yet another sequel—*Picturesque Palestine, Sinai and Egypt* (often shortened to *Picturesque Palestine*) to be illustrated by Fenn and Woodward from on-site drawings.[40] The two artists were the obvious choices, given that they were already in England and had the requisite skills and experience. Once again, Appleton partnered with a London firm, this time the venerable Virtue and Co., presided over by James S. Virtue after the death of his father, George H. The publisher of numerous works notable for their landscape illustrations, including *American Scenery,* Virtue had already featured the Holy Land and Egypt in its lavish monthly *Art Journal,* in which Charles Boutell's "Exploration of Palestine" series appeared in 1868–69.[41]

A book on Palestine, Sinai, and Egypt had long been envisioned by George S. Appleton, the force behind *Picturesque America* and *Picturesque Europe,* who rec-

 Years Abroad

ognized its appeal but did not live to see its completion. He knew that such a publication would help satisfy the intense curiosity that many Americans and Britons felt about these regions located at the eastern end of the Mediterranean and thought of as the Holy Land by Christians, Jews, and Muslims.[42] This interest was fed by myriad stories and travelers' accounts, artists' renderings, and stereographic views, from the folktales recounted in the *Arabian Nights* to the paintings of William Holman Hunt and Frederic Church.[43]

In both the United States and Britain, cultural, religious, and political concerns converged to create a keen demand for information about this part of the world. Protestant Christians in both countries were eager to enhance their presence in the Holy Land, to gain followers, and to identify and preserve the sites of events in their religion's sacred history. The huge success of William McClure Thomson's best seller *The Land and the Book; or, Biblical Illustrations Drawn from the Manners and Customs, the Scenes and Scenery, of the Holy Land* (1859), whose sales ranked second only to *Uncle Tom's Cabin* in the latter half of the nineteenth century, shows the fascination with accurate identification of sites.[44] *Picturesque Palestine, Sinai and Egypt* would be the most comprehensive visual survey of the region yet to appear, offered in a format much more affordable than its most important predecessor, *The Holy Land, Syria, Idumea, Arabia, Egypt and Nubia* (1842–49), which commanded a high price due to its hand-colored lithographs after drawings by David Roberts.[45]

Picturesque Palestine arrived at a time when Protestant Christians felt that accurate depictions of the historic region would enable them to explain and understand the Scriptures and preserve their beliefs. In an increasingly rationalistic and scientific age, challenges to the Bible's authority and historical accuracy were growing ever louder. New studies by philologists and cultural historians revealed languages and civilizations older than those of the Hebrews, calling into question the biblical chronology. Geologic theories about the earth's formation over millions of years, not the six days described in Genesis, led some to question their beliefs or become agnostic; such had been the effect of Darwin's theories about the origins of species through natural selection, published in the United States in 1859 by Appleton to much fanfare as well as outrage.[46] Many people were able to maintain their conviction that geology revealed God's handiwork by readjusting their notion of the length of a biblical "day" to encompass eons. In addition, some leading scientists followed Herbert Spencer in accepting Jean-Baptiste Lamarck's ideas about adaptation to the environment as the process of evolution, which they found compatible with teleology and a natural order set in motion by God.[47]

At the same time, science's emphasis on the value of empirical observation buttressed the widely held expectation that studying the topography of the Holy Land would lead to the identification of the physical sites of important events and thus authenticate biblical accounts (although some were aware even then that this approach could neither prove nor disprove questions about miracles and revelation). One example that caused great excitement was the 1868 discovery of the Moabite Stone, which bears an inscription corroborating a biblical reference to the Kingdom of Moab.[48]

In Britain, the liberal Anglican priest Arthur Penrhyn Stanley, who later wrote the introduction to *Picturesque Palestine,* encouraged free inquiry into biblical subjects and the questioning of traditional sites. His 1856 book *Sinai and Palestine in Connection with Their History* established him as Britain's foremost authority on the Holy Land and became the indispensable companion of all British travelers (and, indeed, of Woodward and Fenn). In 1865 Stanley and others founded the Palestine Exploration Fund (PEF) to aid in the exploration of Jerusalem and other Holy Land sites because, they claimed, "no country more urgently requires illustration." This development would, in effect, unite key religious and political interests and have considerable repercussions for *Picturesque Palestine,* whose contributing writers often had connections to the PEF.

The PEF's findings received much press coverage in the United States, especially as travel to the Holy Land increased after the Civil War. (The first organized American tourist excursion there was the 1867 one in which Mark Twain took part and later satirized in his best seller *The Innocents Abroad; or, The New Pilgrims' Progress.*) In 1871 Appleton published some of the PEF's earliest reports in *The Recovery of Jerusalem* by Charles W. Wilson and Charles Warren, two royal engineers.[49] Similarly, the British Ordnance Survey's attempt to identify Mount Sinai, where Moses received the Ten Commandments, was reported in the June 17, 1871, *Illustrated Christian Weekly,* with illustrations by Fenn that he had based on photographs. On April 29, the same weekly published an article on Warren's excavations of Jerusalem's old city wall in which the writer asserted that there was more interest in that city than in "any other . . . in the world." The article's title, "The Crusade of the Nineteenth Century," expressed the contemporary notion that western Christians—equipped with surveyor's tools, "sextant, and theodolite, and compass"—were undertaking a crusade to "wrest" from "lying priests, and patriarchs, and effendis [encompassing Roman Catholics, Eastern Orthodox Christians, and Turks] the truth which the rubbish of ages and the false reverence of superstition combine to conceal."[50]

 Years Abroad

Such rhetoric suggests the proprietary attitude so common among western Protestants at this time that their knowledge of the region and their ability to travel there to explore and map it gave them power over it.[51] In 1870 the American Palestine Exploration Society was formed to complement the PEF, and its mission is telling: to counteract "modern skepticism" through "the illustration and defense of the Bible." As expressed by the society's chairman at the outset: "Whatever goes to verify the Bible history as real, in time, place, and circumstances, is a refutation of unbelief."[52]

Picturesque Palestine answered this call for the illustration of lands described in the Bible. Its own prospectus, which appeared on the back of early part covers, expresses sentiments close to those of the leaders of the PEF and American Palestine Exploration Society: "There is no country in the world so especially interesting as that in which the momentous events of Bible History were enacted. At the same time there is no country which so urgently requires illustration, to enable us rightly to understand the incidental references to it in the Scripture narrative." Undoubtedly, Appleton expected that a publication so in keeping with contemporary concerns would find a large audience. And choosing to publish jointly with an English firm could only strengthen the project, considering the interests of the British public and the lead the PEF had taken in exploration of the Holy Land. That the book could be viewed as defending the Bible must also have appealed to the solidly Episcopalian Appleton family, possibly helping to counterbalance the company's publications that seemed to attack the Bible, including the theories of Darwin and Huxley.[53]

Political concerns also contributed to the demand for information about these regions. The interests of Britain, with its closer geographical proximity and history of direct involvement in military conflicts in the eastern Mediterranean, were more overt than those of the United States and grew stronger as the British Empire expanded. Its chief rivals were first Russia and then France, two countries that had long maintained a conspicuous presence in the Holy Land as protectors of traditional Christian sites. A primary goal of British foreign policy was to sufficiently dominate the eastern Mediterranean to keep routes open to India, preventing Russia from territorial expansion and checking French influence. The PEF's efforts to map and explore the region, using military officers trained as surveyors on loan from the Corps of Royal Engineers, could provide legitimate cover for reconnaissance of Russian and French activities, including the building of the Suez Canal, completed in 1869. John James Moscrop explains that this effort had wide appeal, for "the appearance of a group of military Christian heroes

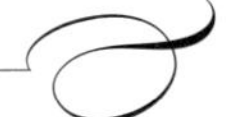

fighting for and working for God, the Empire and the commercial and military prosperity of Britain matched well the mood of an age that saw Britain, her Empire and her armies as divinely blessed."[54]

Although the United States had been less directly involved in the region, its leaders recognized that expansion of commerce in the Mediterranean was vital to the nation's economy.[55] After 1830, the U.S. Navy began maintaining a presence along Palestine's shores; in 1832 the still-young nation initiated a consular presence in Palestine and established a full consulate in Jerusalem in 1856.[56] With the close of the Civil War, American expansion was focused on the west, toward the "new Eden" of California and the Pacific; nevertheless, the transcontinental railroad was completed the same year as the Suez Canal, and California and Palestine, in Hilton Obenzinger's view, were "at the far geographic poles of the same explosive process of expansion and identification."[57]

The role of *Picturesque Palestine, Sinai and Egypt* in shaping Americans' and Britons' images of these places was significant. It would become a widely disseminated and admired visual survey of regions whose Muslim and Jewish residents had neither the means nor the desire to represent themselves pictorially, given their interpretation of the Second Commandment as prohibiting human representations in art. By assuming considerable knowledge of the Bible, focusing on attractive landscape features and picturesque ruins, and selectively ignoring then-recent changes and residents' true circumstances, the book interpreted these regions as survivals from ancient times and thus distanced viewers from the reality of the era. The cultural significance of such interpretations still reverberates in today's unresolved conflicts over the rights to these lands.

Fenn and Woodward played a key role in the project from the beginning. Their designs—for both the wood and the steel engravings—became the heart of the book, and they began working on them long before the editor or writers were selected. They also exerted more control over the imagery than previously; they were responsible for supervising the engravers (many of whom were based in New York and had contributed to *Picturesque America*) and authorized to accept or reject their work.[58] For the two men, this was a plum commission, but not necessarily one to which they had aspired (unlike Church and the British artists Roberts, Hunt, and David Wilkie, who had chosen to make their own artistic pilgrimages to the Holy Land). In fact, Woodward made it clear in several letters that, had he not needed the income, he would have declined the challenging assignment.

His letters, written primarily on Sundays to his wife and mother, are a rich source of information, offering the rare opportunity to consider the artists' expe-

Years Abroad

riences firsthand and informing us about their methods, their attitudes toward their work, and their pleasures and disappointments. The letters also remind us repeatedly of the dangers and inconveniences of travel in this period, when sea voyages were risky, roads were inadequate or nonexistent, infections were frequently life threatening, and communication by mail took weeks or months. They reveal that the life of the traveling artist in search of the picturesque, often viewed as exciting and novel, could sometimes be tedious and difficult.

Through Woodward's letters, we know that Fenn was pleased with the change in publishers and thought that Virtue was "disposed to do the thing in a more gentlemanly manner than C.P/&G."[59] Fenn had completed his work for *Picturesque Europe* in the fall of 1877 and was eager to leave for the Holy Land as soon as possible, but Woodward needed more time to put his drawings on the blocks. Both the artists and the publishers also had concerns about the spread of the Russo-Turkish War and whether England would enter the conflict on the side of Turkey, its ally in the Crimean War; if not, Middle Eastern travel might become more dangerous.[60] Their departure was delayed until early February 1878, and in the meantime the two artists became better acquainted. Although they had both worked on the two previous "picturesque" publications, they had never traveled together. Woodward, the younger, less-established artist, worried that Fenn might preempt the choice subjects. But as he came to know his colleague, these concerns were allayed and their collaboration proved extremely amiable.

First Trip to the Holy Land, 1878

Before departing, Fenn and Woodward met with James Virtue and his partner Frederic Daldy to plan their trip. Virtue invited them to his estate, Oakland Park, on the banks of the Thames below Richmond—not far from Fenn's childhood home—to "look over his books, photographs &c of Palestine and to talk over the business arrangements."[61] Seeing which sites earlier artists and photographers had selected and how they had depicted them provided some preparation for the journey. Next, following Virtue's and Daldy's advice, they made their travel arrangements through representatives of Thomas Cook and Sons, the well-known firm that had begun organizing tours to the Holy Land shortly after the opening of the Suez Canal.

Both men expected Virtue to be more generous than Cassell, Petter & Galpin, but they had to fight for higher wages; salary negotiations were still unresolved even as they prepared to embark. In an eleventh-hour standoff, the artists refused to go unless their demands were met. Finally, Virtue agreed to their terms, and on February 15, 1878, Fenn and Woodward boarded the steamship *Zambesi* off Southampton. The wood engraver Josiah Wood Whymper, who had held a farewell supper in their honor, no doubt "with an eye to future work," also saw them off. (Whymper was likely disappointed, for the artists were not pleased with his work on *Picturesque Europe* and sent little his way).[62] On a ship full of military men and their wives on their way to India, "with a crew of Lascars" in "red turbans and baggy breeches," they soon reached Gibraltar. Fenn knew it well, having sketched the peninsula for *Picturesque Europe,* and proceeded to show Woodward around.[63]

The cruise through the Mediterranean was quite a lark as Woodward describes it to his wife in a letter dated February 22, 1878: "It seems like another world after smoky London, so bright, warm, and pleasant. We lounge on deck under the awnings, smoke, read, play cards, and tell yarns all day . . . our table is very good. . . . We always eat pickled ginger and Bombay Duck with the curry." As they approached Malta, Woodward speculated that the war would have little effect on Palestine but noted that "the Turks are naturally feeling very bitter against England now, and we are traveling under British protection." Still, he reassured her, "We will be well taken care of, for Cook would not let any of his tourists run any risk if it could be prevented, and especially the representatives of two such well-known publishing houses."[64]

Their ship reached Port Said, Egypt, about February 28, and the men spent three days in the Hôtel des Pays, just at the mouth of the Suez Canal, waiting for a steamer to Joppa (Jaffa). They observed the teeming street life, with vendors of all sorts, and sketched "quaint groups of oriental figures." In this environment completely new to them, the two specialists in picturesque landscape focused on people. Like most other western travelers, including the writers for *Picturesque Palestine,* they assumed that the dress, dwellings, and activities of the residents had persisted through the centuries; this view was in keeping with Stanley's comment that "the unchanged habits of the East render it a kind of living Pompeii."[65] It was a way of seeing only the picturesque exterior—or of not really seeing the people themselves. Fenn and Woodward would continue to make quick sketches of clothing and activities to fill in the foreground of their compositions for *Picturesque Palestine,* whose illustrations featured many more figures than the two earlier books (fig. 4.14).[66] Yet, despite this new focus on people, neither Fenn nor Woodward would attempt to depict specific biblical narratives, as biblical illustrators and some English painters had done before them.

Years Abroad

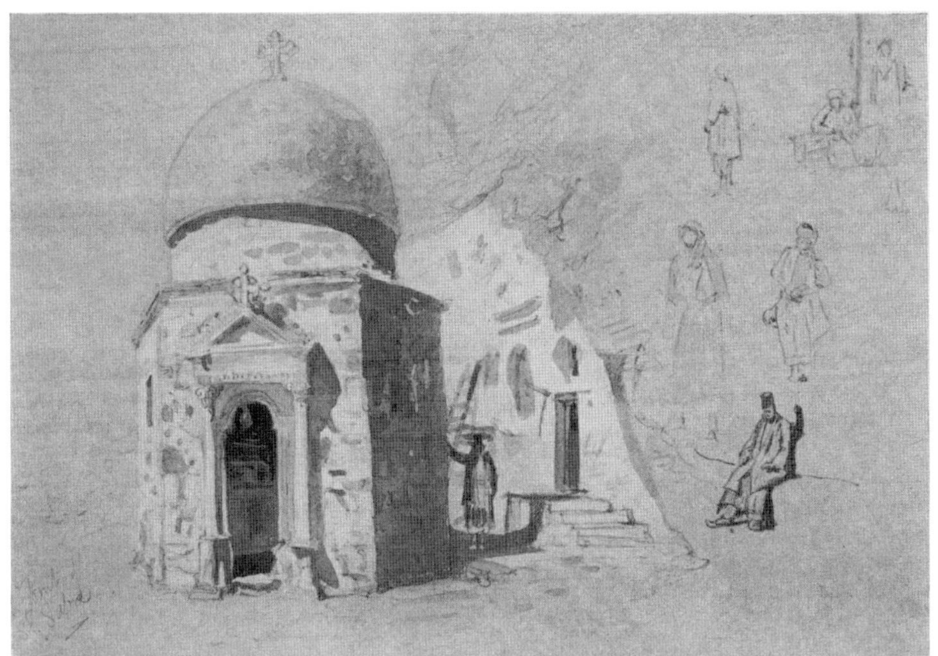

Cook's dragoman, or guide, met their ship in the waters off Jaffa and escorted them through a chaotic scene of "natives" in boats vying for passengers. (See Fenn's illustration in 2:128, for a rare depiction of their travel experiences.) In Jaffa they stayed at the Hotel Jerusalem, amid the orange groves of the German Colony north of the city, and that evening met with Cook's agent Rolla Floyd, an American who had settled in Palestine and become a prominent tour organizer.[67] As they embarked on their tour through the Holy Land, these artists so adept at seeking out and depicting the picturesque in the United States and Europe faced new challenges. Their charge, which differed from that for the earlier books, was to represent those sites associated with biblical history, many of which were piles of rubble in barren landscapes. To render them as picturesque would require considerable ingenuity. Furthermore, they were traveling through a region mostly lacking in tourist infrastructure, circulating among peoples whose cultures were unfamiliar and who were sometimes hostile to them as Christians and as artists.

Despite such drawbacks, they often received special treatment and were provided with more services than they were accustomed to. In an April 7, 1878, letter to his wife, written on their first extended tenting excursion in Jericho, for which they were accompanied by armed soldiers, Woodward expressed some of the paradoxes of travel in the region. Initially, he was impressed by the camping arrangements: "Our tent is magnificent, as water tight as a house and as finely decorated as the Louvre. The beds are very comfortable and the cooking Parisian. There is nothing to add to our comfort that the dragoman or cook cannot produce. We eat from the finest china and silver, have pickles, jam, and all preserved fruits. . . . In fact, our camp is a perfect hotel in all of its appointments, for us two. We have eight men, including the soldiers, and ten horses and mules."[68]

Yet there were annoyances, too, as noted in a letter dated one week later (April 14): "Notwithstanding the novelty and pleasure in some respects or that will be in looking back to such a journey as this, the present is not always so. You can form no idea of the glare and heat from these bare white hills—a perfect barren, treeless wilderness of desolation and at nights the braying of the donkeys, howling of dogs and chattering of camp servants keeps you awake." He then went on to describe the flies in the soup and the fleas in their beds and the thousands of children pestering their roadside camp.

Another unique aspect of this journey was the questionable authenticity of sites traditionally associated with biblical narratives. Woodward and Fenn, like most Protestant visitors, were aware of the controversies and highly skeptical of many of the Roman Catholic and Eastern Orthodox traditions. Nevertheless, they took care to accurately represent the appearance of such sites. In Jaffa, where they sketched the house of Simon the Tanner, the traditional place of the apostle Peter's "vision commanding him to preach the gospel to the Gentiles," Woodward referred to Stanley, writing, "Stanley considers . . . the site as having been truly identified. The house, though, cannot be the original one."[69] While sketching the building, Woodward and Fenn attracted so much attention that each needed a dragoman with a big stick by his side to keep the crowd away.[70] Such was their introduction to the way the local residents would treat them: some scowled, while others thought it a good joke to be sketched.

When a "strapping" twenty-one-year-old named Francis who had helped fend off beggars in Jaffa asked to accompany them on their travels, the artists agreed. Francis was a Lebanese Christian with knowledge of English and French as well as the local languages, and he had a rather condescending attitude toward Muslims. As their "man Friday," he sharpened pencils, washed color boxes, lit their pipes, and took on the difficult task of finding models.[71] His attitude may have played a role in how local residents responded to the artists.

Fenn and Woodward next rode on horseback to Jerusalem, where they had the "largest and best room" at the Mediterranean Hotel, next to the pool of Hezekiah and opposite the Tower of David.[72] From there they could sketch figures in the

   Years Abroad

market. On their first Sunday in the city, they went to the Church of the Holy Sepulcher during a "high festival of some kind." Woodward, accustomed to more restrained Protestant worship, was bothered by "all sorts of dirty people talking incessantly" and "the cat squalling of the priests . . . making the most unearthly din I ever heard." With mocking irony reminiscent of Twain, he commented, "For convenience, I suppose, the priests had placed the spot[s] connected with the death of Our Lord under *one* roof and near each other. Mt Calvary is upstairs in the gallery and has three holes in the floor where the crosses stood. After all this mockery and humbug, we went to the English Church [Christ Church, built in 1842] on Mt. Zion, and it was a great relief to attend a service so simple and beautiful."[73] Despite this reaction, their depictions of the Church of the Holy Sepulcher are dignified and respectful (1:19, 21).

Later that day, they ascended the Mount of Olives, where the view extended to the Jordan River and on to the Dead Sea. They read aloud the description in their guidebook, "Murray"—almost certainly the 1875 edition of the popular *Handbook for Travellers in Syria and Palestine,* written by the Reverend Josiah L. Porter and published in London by John Murray. They also read related parts of the New Testament, including the sayings Jesus uttered there.[74] (The index in Murray's guide, which listed biblical passages relevant to each site, would have made these easy to find.) Woodward was moved by the sight of the unchanged hills and valleys and wrote that Jesus's words, when read on the Mount of Olives, "have a realization that they would never have read anywhere else."[75] Fenn, a Congregationalist and regular churchgoer, likely had a similar reaction. He clearly made use of Murray's index, as indicated by a watercolor drawing of Caesarea Philippi on which he noted in ink the site's biblical references as listed in the book; the ancient town, now called Banias, was the site of the Transfiguration in the gospels of Matthew and Luke and where Jesus said of Peter, "upon this rock I will build my church." This drawing, one of Fenn's few works from this trip that have been located, is now in the collection of the Metropolitan Museum of Art.[76]

In Jerusalem, the "Sheik of the Mosque" came to see them and, pleased by baksheesh from their guide Rolla Floyd, gave them liberty to sketch the Dome of the Rock but insisted that a soldier accompany each of them. Even thus protected, Woodward reported that women abused him in "choice Arabic" and boys threw stones and called him "a dirty dog of a Christian."[77] Nevertheless, he was distressed by the poverty he saw everywhere and by the lepers, to whom he gave pennies and oranges as alms and to persuade them to let him sketch in peace.[78]

After about two weeks in Jerusalem, Fenn and Woodward made a brief trip

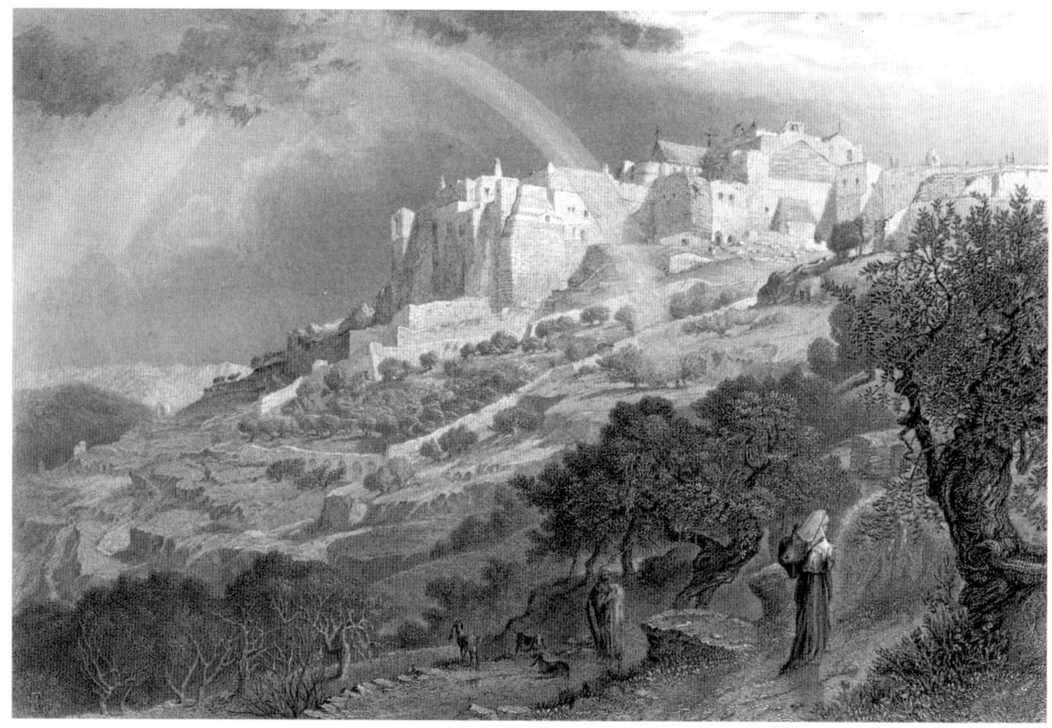

4.15. Harry Fenn, "Church of the Nativity, Bethlehem." *Picturesque Palestine,* 1:opp. 123. Steel engraving by J. J. Crew, 9" x 12 1/2" .

on horseback to Bethlehem, during which they were pelted by rain and hail. They found the town "quite picturesque" but "surrounded by so much that is tawdry and by so many squabbling priests, that there is nothing to impress one with a feeling of awe or reverence."[79] Nevertheless, the steel engraving titled the "Church of the Nativity, Bethlehem," after Fenn's design, is highly picturesque, with gnarled olive trees in the foreground and a jumble of ancient walls perched on the steep hill (fig. 4.15). It is also clearly intended to evoke reverence, as indicated by a rainbow—considered a sign of God's grace—arcing across the cluster of buildings. Several pages later Fenn's images on facing pages contrast the later embellishment of the traditional site of Jesus's birth, the Chapel of the Nativity in Bethlehem's St. Mary's Church (1:128), with a depiction of a simple residence titled "An Example of a Peasant's Home, With Its Manger, in a Village of Palestine" (1:129), in which an arch, mirroring the earlier rainbow, frames the humble manger beside which cows stand.

Next, the artists traveled to Jericho, the Jordan, and Mar Saba, accompanied by

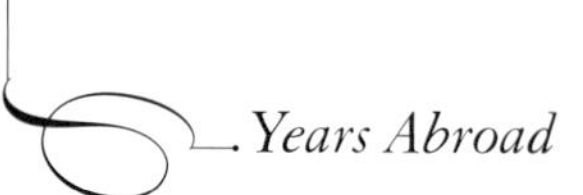

Years Abroad

their retinue of soldiers, servants, and camping equipment. The pressure to work quickly and make many sketches is clear from Woodward's letters. On a Monday afternoon, they arrived at Mar Saba, the ancient Eastern Orthodox monastery on the cliffs of the steep ravine of the Kedron, which, although not a biblical site, was often considered one of the most picturesque places in the Holy Land.[80] They "spent the balance of the day looking around and selecting subjects to draw" and left the next day around noon.[81] In that time, Fenn had made at least four detailed drawings of various subjects (1:150, 153, 155, 158) and Woodward had completed at least three, as evidenced by the published images.

A close look at the wood engraving "Entrance to the Cave of St. Saba" (fig. 4.16) shows that Fenn created a dynamic, irregularly shaped composition with intersecting diagonals and then arranged the text to wrap around it. He skillfully exploited the medium through his relatively spare use of line, except in the shadows, and by retaining ample white space to depict bright sunlight reflecting off the various surfaces.[82] Although their time at Mar Saba was brief, Fenn and Woodward chose their subjects well: the variety of views—at close range, from below, and toward a distant horizon—produced a group of images that struck viewers as being fresher and more thorough than earlier ones of this well-known site. They were hailed as "the best drawings we have yet seen of that extraordinary fortress and retreat," according to the London *Art Journal*.[83]

At their next stop, the Cave of Adullam, "where David was hid with his followers," Fenn fell in a hole, jarring himself. While he was "lying under an olive tree on a mattress" to recover, he and Woodward were "besieged by people with old clothes to sell." The artists eventually bought garments to take back with them; once back in London, Woodward asked his wife to pose in them so that he could add foreground figures on the woodblocks; Fenn may have done the same.[84]

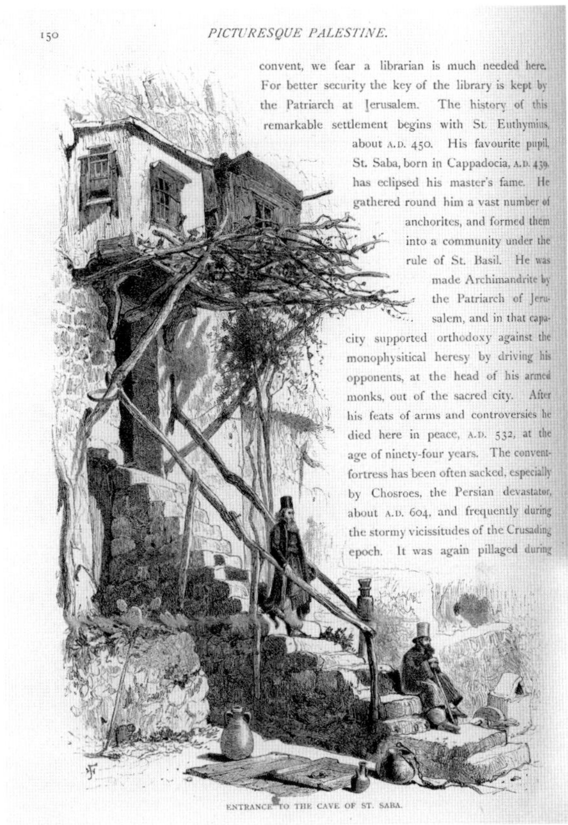

4.16. Harry Fenn, "Entrance to the Cave of St. Saba." *Picturesque Palestine*, 1:150. Wood engraving by Whymper, approx. 9 1/2" x 6 1/2".

After sketching more places near Jerusalem, they headed north toward Damascus; on the way, they would visit Bethel, Shiloh, Nablus, Nazareth, Tiberias, and the Sea of Galilee. On their second day out, they sent a muleteer back to Jerusalem for letters and cut short their work in order to return to camp and read them; Fenn had none and "was dreadfully blue for a while." They found Nablus "the most picturesquely situated town" they had yet seen, but, knowing its reputation for hostility toward Christians, neither wanted to sketch the mosque. They drew straws, and Woodward got the task. Entering the city accompanied by Francis and a soldier, he was surrounded by a large crowd who pushed to follow him as he entered a house near the mosque. The owner, "a very decent sort of Mahomedan" who allowed him to draw from the rooftop in exchange for baksheesh, shut out the crowd. Still, "boys threw stones" and "women and girls reviled" them for the three hours they were there.[85] Yet, as was typical, both Woodward's drawing and the wood engraving based on it, "Entrance to the Great Mosque (Jamia El Kebir), Nablus" (1:245), give no hint of strife. In it, a young man waters a plant on the rooftop, and groups of men rest and talk near the mosque's doorway.

By the time the group reached Nazareth, Fenn and Woodward were twelve weeks into their journey and counting the days until they could head back home. Woodward, clearly at a low point, wrote:

> I am so tired of drawing mud hovels perched up on hill tops and rejoicing in Biblical names—but of all disappointing places this is the worst. The people are very civil and pleasant—but the town new and unpicturesque and at every step or turn—some Catholic humbug—there is so much (chiefly Roman Catholic) . . . lying about holy places that instead of inspiring me with any feeling of reverence—or awe—the opposite effect is produced. If I stay much longer in the Holy Land I will doubt every event recorded in Holy Writ, at least the Roman Catholic version of it. Never have the least desire to come here. The scenery is barren and vile beyond description.[86]

Despite Woodward's discouragement with the barren scenery, mud hovels, and "unpicturesque" towns, both he and Fenn were skilled at selecting subjects and including details to create a pleasing image. For example, Fenn's illustration titled the "Mosque at Nazareth" (fig. 4.17) combines varied architectural forms, picturesque plant growth, and two groups in the foreground, described in the long caption as: "A Bedouin bargaining with a seller of fruit, and a group of stonemasons at work, with their hammers characteristically in their left hands." Fenn may have based the people on one or more photographs, an approach both artists used when adding distinctive figural types to the foreground of their designs—not surprising given their time constraints, the hostility they often encountered, and their unfamiliarity with traditional crafts and customs.

When working from photos, the artists often made the figures larger than those in figure 4.17, and sometimes made them the main subject (see, for example, 1:27, 44). A comparison of the wood engravings in *Picturesque Palestine* and the travel photographs produced by the Beirut-based Bonfils firm, which at the time were sold in Jerusalem and Cairo, reveals that Woodward copied from several of them, and Fenn probably did as well. As was true in *Picturesque America,* the use of photographs is evident when an identical figure or group appears in illustrations of different places or when individual figures are shown frontally, looking directly at the viewer.[87]

When confronted with bare hills and piles of rubble, the men quickly learned to enhance the foreground with a fragment of a ruin, an interesting tree, or groups of animals or people, often shown engaged in activities unchanged since biblical times: women drawing water, carrying jugs, or grinding grain; men plowing or riding burros and camels; Bedouins on horseback. To enhance the interest and three-dimensionality of their images, both artists frequently used framing devices (arches, windows, overhanging trees) or added drama to a sky with the addition of storm clouds, rainbows, or light effects, another convention of picturesque imagery. They also combined imagery and type in varied ways, as they had done in the earlier books in the series.

In addition, for *Picturesque Palestine,* Fenn and Woodward frequently introduced variations in scale and more than one viewpoint in a single image while manipulating the picture plane—effects that photography could not achieve, which was perhaps part of their illustrations' appeal. In one striking example by Fenn, "Traditional Site of Bethpage, The House of Figs," a distant landscape view is seemingly held by fig branches, in effect flattening the picture plane of the

4.17. Harry Fenn, "Mosque at Nazareth. A Bedouin bargaining with a seller of fruit, and a group of stonemasons at work, with their hammers characteristically in their left hands." *Picturesque Palestine,* 1:275. Wood engraving by WHM, approx. 9 1/2" x 6 3/8".

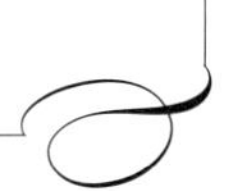

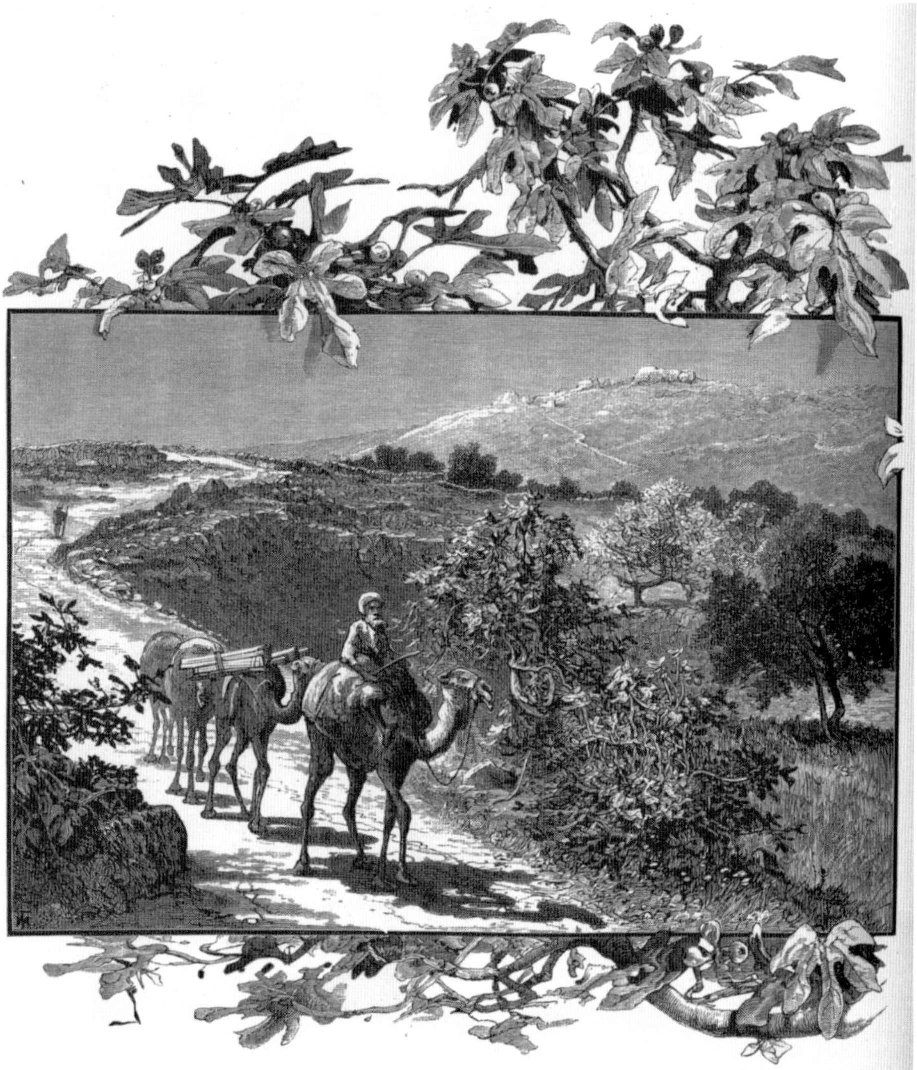

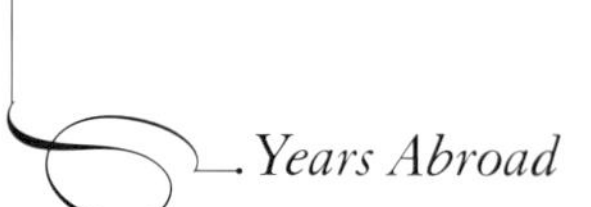

TRADITIONAL SITE OF BETHPHAGE, THE HOUSE OF FIGS.

On the ridge which leads from the Mount of Olives to the hill above Bethany.   Fig-trees grow by the wayside, and branches of the **fig-tree** border the picture.

landscape while emphasizing the lifelike three-dimensionality of the branches (fig. 4.18).[88]

An interesting variation of this device is a simultaneous exterior and interior view, as in figure 4.19. The exterior view shows the wall where visitors seeking admission to the Convent of St. Catherine, in Sinai, would place a letter in a basket let down from the "pent-house," as it is called in the caption; overlapping this view is a darker rectangle showing the interior and a monk letting down the rope. Such overlapping images created dynamic pages, where parts of an image seemed

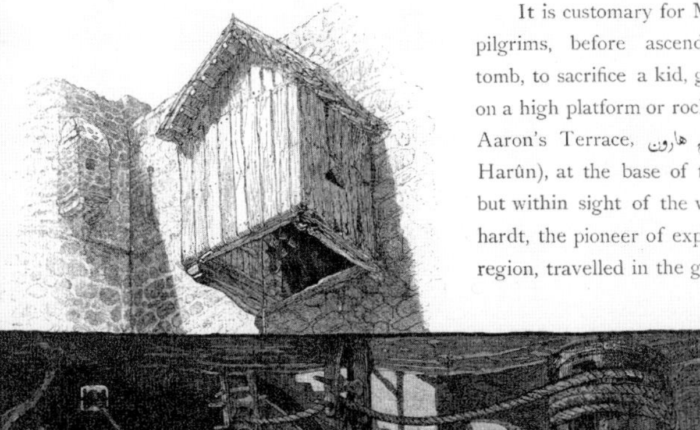

It is customary for Mohammedan pilgrims, before ascending to the tomb, to sacrifice a kid, goat, or sheep on a high platform or rock ledge called Aaron's Terrace, صطوح هارون (Settûh Harûn), at the base of the mountain, but within sight of the wely. Burckhardt, the pioneer of explorers of this region, travelled in the guise of a poor Mohammedan pilgrim, and hired a guide east of Petra to lead him through the city to Aaron's shrine that he might sacrifice there, and thus it was that he contrived to see the wonders of the valley. The guide led him to Aaron's terrace. Burckhardt killed the goat at a spot where he observed a number of heaps of stones. While he was in the act of slaying the animal his guide called out, " O Harûn, look upon us! it is for you we slaughter this victim! O Harûn, protect and forgive us! O Harûn, be content with our good intentions, for it is but a lean goat! O Harûn, smooth our path, and praise be to the Lord of all creatures! " This

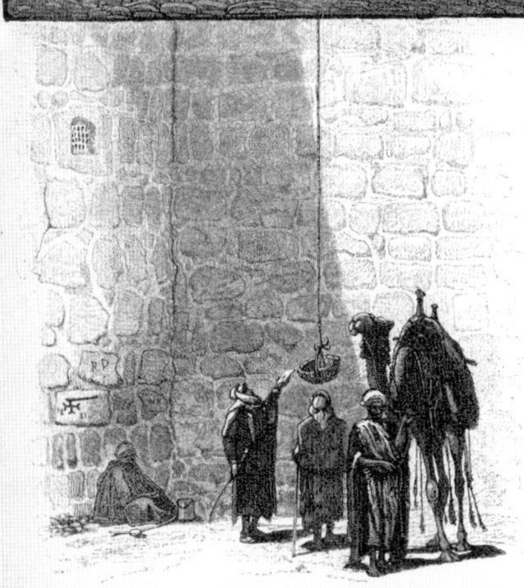

LETTER OF ADMISSION TO THE CONVENT OF ST. CATHERINE.
'ormerly travellers were drawn up into the convent through the pent-house shown above; now, however, if the letter thus received is found satisfactory they are admitted by a side door.

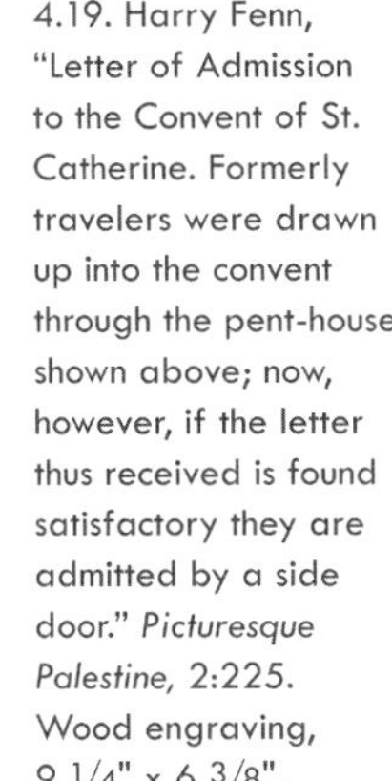

4.19. Harry Fenn, "Letter of Admission to the Convent of St. Catherine. Formerly travelers were drawn up into the convent through the pent-house shown above; now, however, if the letter thus received is found satisfactory they are admitted by a side door." *Picturesque Palestine*, 2:225. Wood engraving, 9 1/4" x 6 3/8".

to come forward while other parts receded. Similar approaches had been used by Japanese artists since midcentury and were becoming popular in Europe, notably for the decoration of porcelain.[89] Regardless of whether Fenn and Woodward had seen such works, their strategies proved highly effective. Reviewers of the freshly released first parts of *Picturesque Palestine* were pleased and surprised to find pictures that presented a less desolate region than they had come to expect.

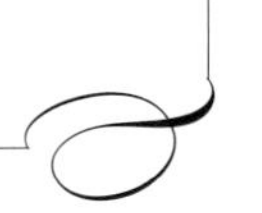

Picturesque Europe *and* Picturesque Palestine

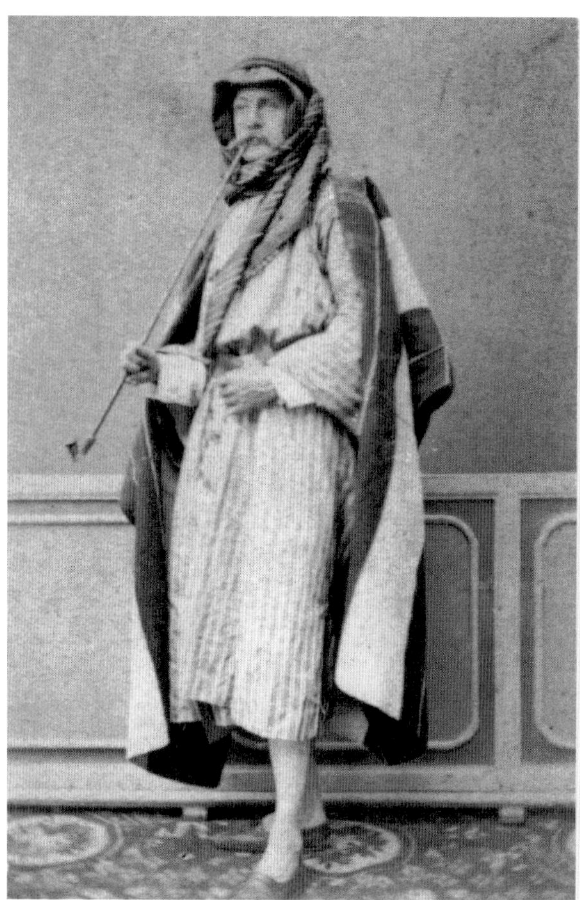

4.20. Photograph of Harry Fenn in Arab cloak, ca. 1878–79. (Courtesy of William V. Abt.)

According to one critic in the London *Times,* the lands depicted in the book retained much beauty, and Jerusalem much "stateliness."[90]

After suffering a low point at Nazareth, the artists' moods improved during four pleasant days at Capernaum, on the Sea of Galilee (or Lake of Gennesaret). Contrary to their expectations and the warnings in their guidebook, they were not bothered by insects, and Woodward, remembering the events of Jesus's life that had occurred there, found that this region and the Mount of Olives evoked the greatest "feeling of reverence" of all the places he had seen in the Holy Land. Two weeks later, after an arduous journey over roads that he described as "mere goat tracks," they arrived in Damascus, "a wonderfully picturesque place" with "bazaars so tempting" that Woodward feared they would be ruined by their "outlays." [91]

For the book, Fenn drew the gold- and silversmith's bazaar (1:393). His description of a watercolor painting of the same subject, in a later undated letter, reveals that he was a highly curious and engaged traveler who learned and retained much from his journeys: "All those queer silver trinkets you see on the tray are not only sold but *made* in that smoky old place. . . . The fellow with the bellows like a concertina is melting silver in a little clay hat looking thing. . . . The divisions like church pews . . . are rented for the dealers in silver trinkets. Then the interesting dickering that is going on between the Bedouin woman and the old jeweller."[92]

Next the group traveled to the Roman remains of Baalbek (now in Lebanon), where for three days their tents were pitched in "the court of the Great Temple," according to Woodward. He reported that after working all day, he and Fenn would take their "Arab cloaks" and "long pipes and wander through the ruins, or sit for hours on some fragment of former grandeur and enjoy the marvelous effects of light and shade, or pass the time telling yarns" (fig. 4.20).[93] Twenty years later, Fenn would recall these same experiences in an article he wrote for

St. Nicholas magazine titled "There Were Giants in Those Days," in which he described arriving "after ten hours in the saddle" too tired and hungry to admire the ruins. That night, however, he was "almost overcome" when he saw the full moon "flooding the snowy peaks of Lebanon" and "the six huge columns" that seemed to reach "the very stars." He suggested that his young readers "imagine a stone about three times the size of a railroad freight-car" being "carried two miles from the quarries, and hoisted many feet from the ground."

Although local legend held that the walls were "the work of Solomon, assisted by the genii," Fenn reported the most plausible theory of the time: that an inclined plane was built at the great stone, and then thousands of men were forced to drag it up to its place in the wall.[94] One of Fenn's few known original drawings from the trip is a rough pencil sketch of massive columns (fig. 4.21) that he made on the back of a watercolor and pencil drawing of the coast at Caesarea (suggesting that paper was scarce). Comparing this drawing to the wood engraving "The Fallen Column, Ba'albeck" (fig. 4.22), we see that Fenn has rendered the nearby standing columns taller, making the fallen structure loom even larger.

The artists next went to Beirut and then set sail back to Port Said, postponing a trip to the Cedars of Lebanon until the next year because of heavy snow in the mountains. In Beirut, Fenn received word that one of his daughters was dangerously ill with typhoid fever, forcing the party to head back as quickly as possible. Fenn traveled to Marseilles by steamer and then by rail to Paris. Upon arrival in London, he learned that his youngest daughter was also "not expected to live," and then his wife fell ill as well. What a relief it must have been when they all recovered.[95]

London Interlude

Soon both artists would be saddened to learn of the July 7, 1878, death of George S. Appleton, the man so instrumental in supporting the "picturesque" series. Yet the project continued despite this setback. William W. "Willy" Appleton, son of William Henry Appleton, another of the original founders, crossed the ocean to meet with Fenn and Woodward and settle arrangements for the book. Woodward commented that Appleton "complimented" their sketches "highly," and when they told him about the beauty of the flowers in Palestine, he suggested they "introduce them throughout the book." They did so in interesting ways that are often suggestive of the contemporary craze for pressing botanical specimens in scrapbooks. (See, for example, figure 4.23, "Ma'yan Musa, the Spring of Moses,"

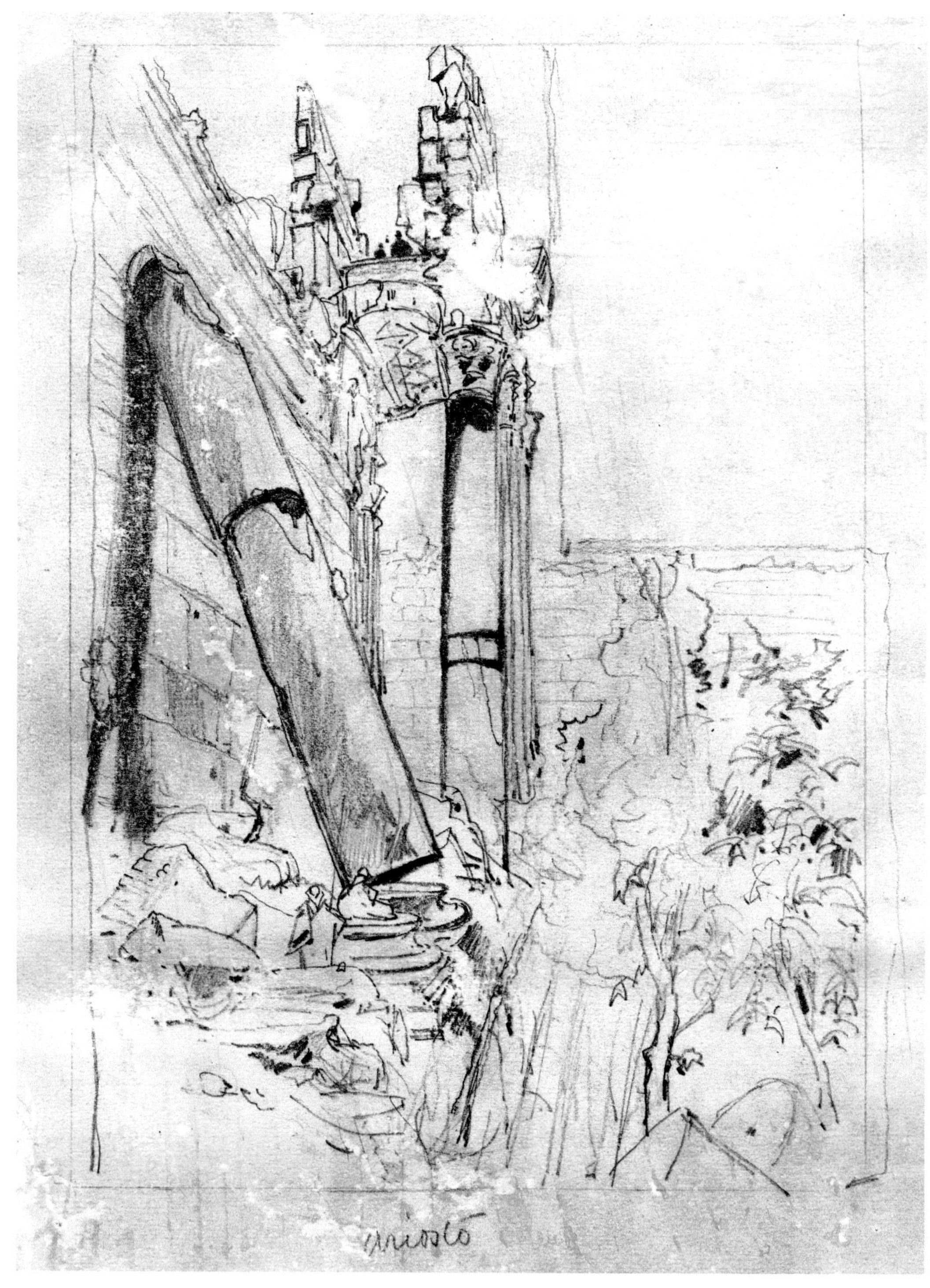

4.21. Harry Fenn, drawing for "The Fallen Column, Ba'albek," ca. 1878. Graphite, 9 1/2" x 6 1/2". (Private collection.)

4.22. Harry Fenn, "The Fallen Column, Ba'albek. In the peristyle on the south side of the Temple of the Sun, where only four connected columns remain *in situ*. Several shafts have fallen from the temple platform into the little orchard below." *Picturesque Palestine*, 1:460. Wood engraving by E. B. Badoureau, 9 1/2" x 6 1/2".

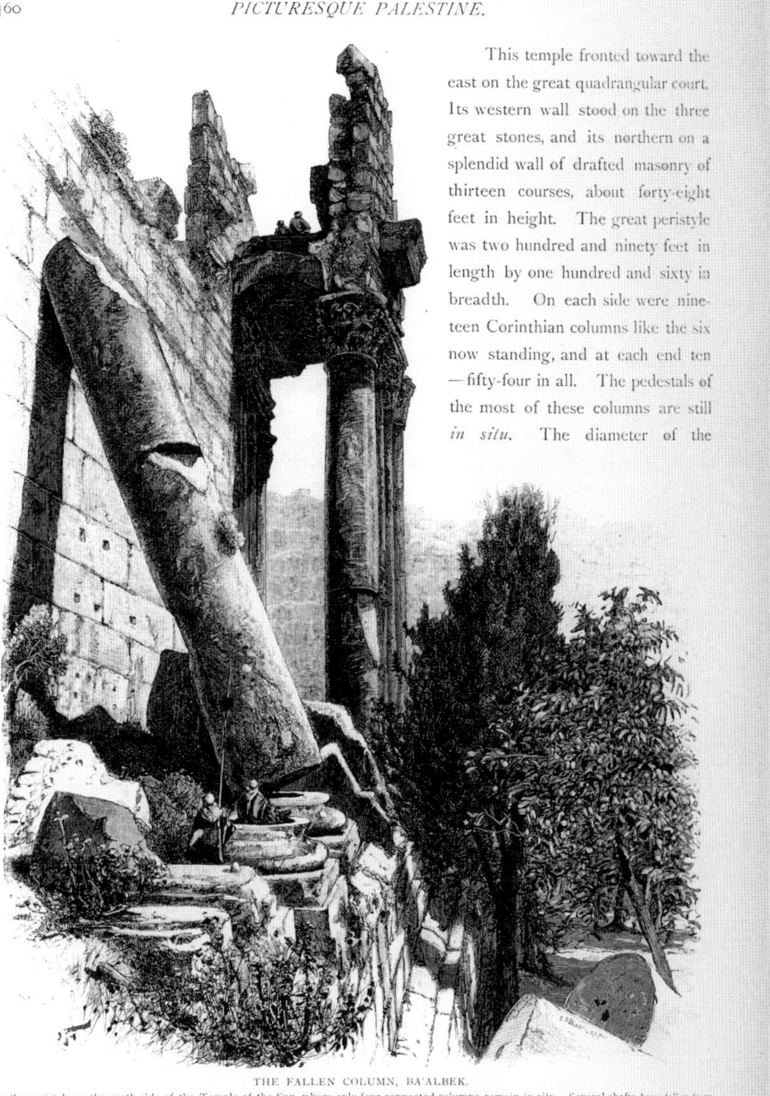

This temple fronted toward the east on the great quadrangular court. Its western wall stood on the three great stones, and its northern on a splendid wall of drafted masonry of thirteen courses, about forty-eight feet in height. The great peristyle was two hundred and ninety feet in length by one hundred and sixty in breadth. On each side were nineteen Corinthian columns like the six now standing, and at each end ten —fifty-four in all. The pedestals of the most of these columns are still *in situ*. The diameter of the

THE FALLEN COLUMN, BA'ALBEK.

In the peristyle on the south side of the Temple of the Sun, where only four connected columns remain *in situ*. Several shafts have fallen from the temple platform into the little orchard below.

in which Fenn introduced a fern extending from a wide gray frame and overlapping the page.) Then the two artists met with Virtue and Daldy to look over the sketches and select those that would be suitable for steel engravings. The publishers praised their work, which "had far exceeded their expectations as to subject, variety, style, and so forth," and said that they would leave decisions about the next trip in the artists' hands.[96]

After such a positive meeting, Fenn and Woodward were shocked a few weeks

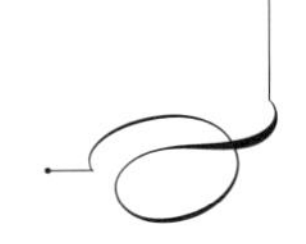

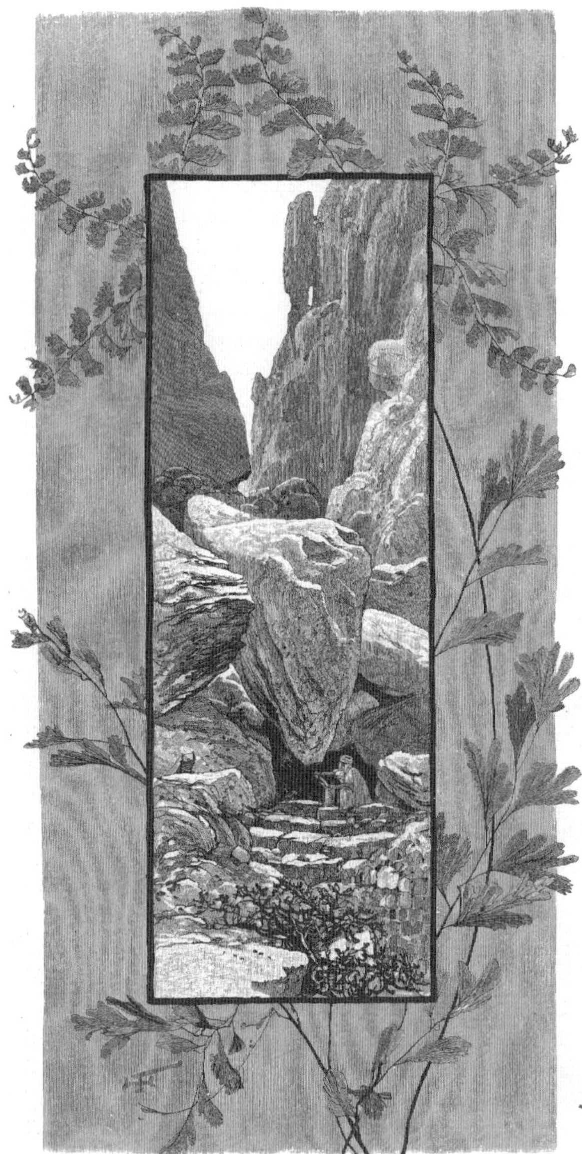

4.23. Harry Fenn, "Ma'yan Músa, the Spring of Moses, Sinai. At this spring, rising up in a cool shady rock-grotto, the Bedawin believe Moses to have watered Jethro's flocks." *Picturesque Palestine,* 2:354. Wood engraving, approx. 9 1/2" x 4 3/4".

later to read the newspaper report announcing the failure of Virtue and Co. Although they continued working on their drawings, they had "orders not to give out any engraving" and must have wondered whether the project would proceed as planned. Even the careers of these successful illustrators, both associated with two well-known publishing houses, were not free of risk. Eventually the firm's creditors agreed that carrying on the business would be the best means of regaining financial solvency. By early September, "Mr. Appleton Sr." and Daldy assured them that "everything had been satisfactorily arranged": the publishers still wanted them to go to Egypt and Sinai and then to Jaffa to complete the book.[97]

Fenn and Woodward set their departure date for January 7, 1879; in the meantime, they worked on their drawings and watercolors for the book's steel engravings. On December 29, Woodward complied with a request from the Appletons to visit Arthur Penrhyn Stanley, then dean of Westminster Cathedral, who had just completed a successful lecture tour in the United States and was as well known there as in Britain for his book *Sinai and Palestine* (1856). They wanted Woodward "to show [Stanley] the sketches and to try to interest him enough in the book to get his consent to edit it." Clearly, the pictures were the priority in this project from the beginning—work on the book had already been under way for more than a year, and still no editor had been commissioned (and probably no writers had, either). Stanley "seemed pleased with the drawings" but consented to write only a preface; ultimately, his brief introductory text was titled "Introduction."[98]

 Years Abroad

Second Trip to Egypt, Sinai, and the Holy Land, 1879

For their second journey, the artists chose a different route, traveling by train to Marseilles and then by steamer to Port Said. The first leg of the trip was not without complications: the train from Paris got stuck in a snowdrift for nine hours; shivering and hungry, the passengers were finally rescued, but Fenn and Woodward had to abandon their baggage and missed their boat. They were eventually able to board another vessel and arrived at the Hotel du Nil in Cairo on January 19. On their first morning there, Francis and one of their earlier dragomen appeared, having somehow heard they were coming.[99] The four of them "hired donkeys" and "galloped about all the day," according to Woodward, who was quick to provide his assessment of their new destination in a letter dated the day after their arrival: "Cairo seems to be a very picturesque place, but we will be able to get so many good photographs that I think we can hasten the work here by using them."[100] Yet, a watercolor by Fenn of shoe vendors in Cairo's bazaar (fig. 4.24), painted with subtle colors and displaying myriad details but an unfinished foreground, appears to have been made on the spot rather than from a photo. In the corresponding wood engraving titled "In the Shoe Bazaar," however, some of the figures Fenn added to the foreground were probably based on photographs (fig. 4.25).[101]

For a Nile trip scheduled in advance, they booked passage on the steamer *Mehalah* and stayed in "one of the largest and best" staterooms. Woodward reported spending much time on deck, making sketches of the picturesque boats "with their large shoulder of mutton sails." They enjoyed the journey, but Woodward was disappointed in the temples, perhaps because few had yet been excavated from the sand. "I have not seen anything from an artistic point of view that impressed me so much as Baalbeck," he wrote to his wife on February 9. The same letter mentions that the American consul at Luxor, an Egyptian, had heard that he and Fenn were working on a book and insisted they join him for an elaborate dinner, hoping they would mention him in their book. Before heading to the Sinai Peninsula, they visited the pyramids. Woodward described how they were assisted by "boosters," pushing them up the steep outside and down the slippery inside and demanding baksheesh for "bringing us in some water . . . for giving me a boost over a bad place . . . for lighting my pipe . . . for sitting on my coat . . . even a bill from the 'Doctor' for, of all things, feeling my pulse!"[102]

Their caravan for the Sinai trip started out a few days ahead, and they joined the camp "by rail at Suez." The group, arranged this time not by Cook but by a dragoman named Nijm, consisted of "thirteen camels carrying water from the

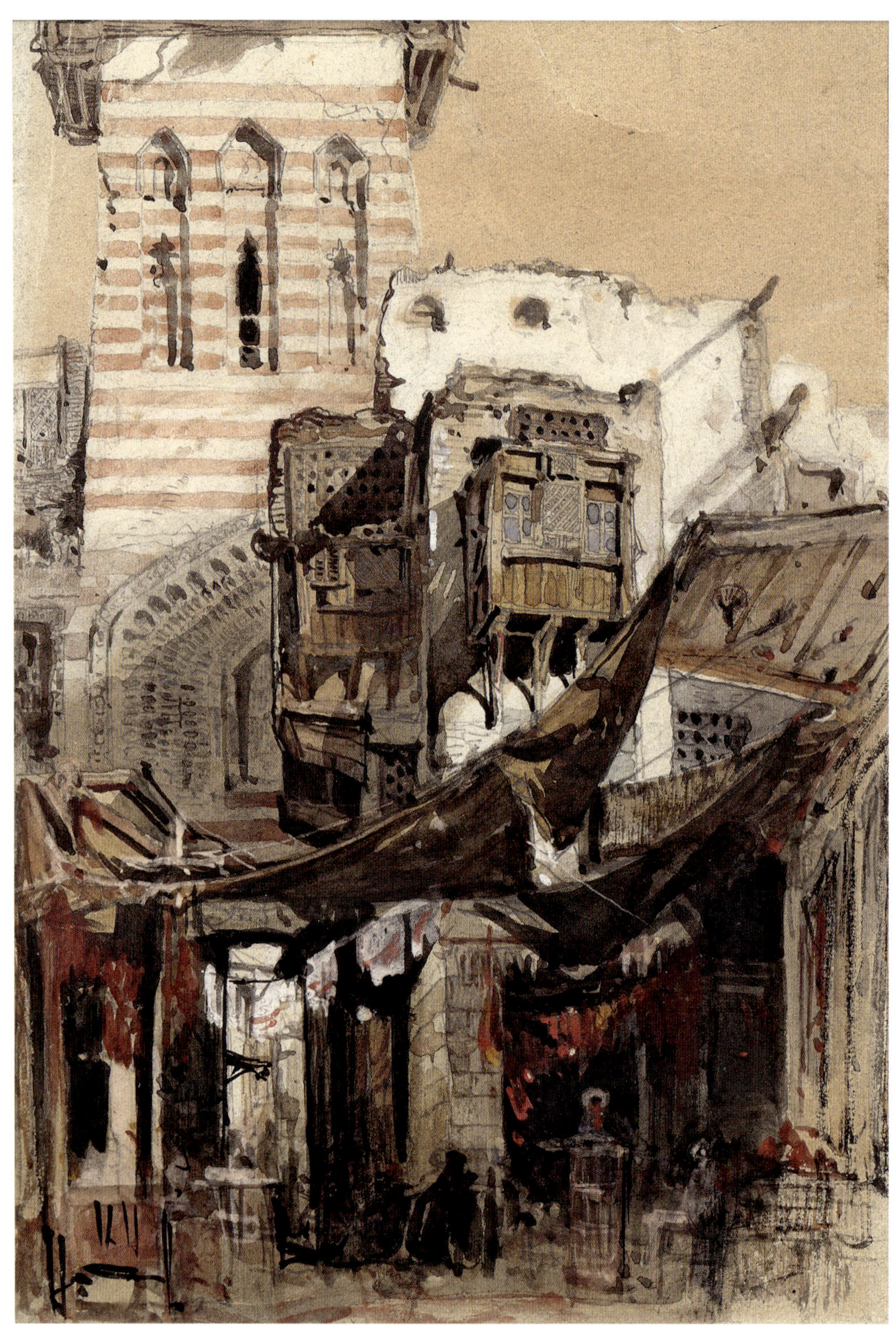

4.24. Harry Fenn, *Cairo's Shoe Bazaar*, ca. 1879. Watercolor and gouache over graphite on wove gray-blue paper, 9 1/2" x 6 1/2". (Courtesy of William V. Abt.)

Nile, enough to last to Mt. Sinai, coops of turkeys and chickens," and an assortment of "new tents."[103] Their month on the peninsula proved exceedingly difficult—Woodward wrote that it was "the most trying trip" he had ever made.[104] It was extremely cold, and he was so sick that he could make only rough sketches to be finished later. For ten days the group was without water "fit for a pig to drink."[105] When they returned to Ayun Musa, across the bay from Suez, "their camp was ordered to stay in quarantine," which Woodward felt was probably just "red tape to extract baksheesh." They decided to escape by boat at night.[106] This escapade evidently became one of Fenn's favorite stories—perhaps embellished in the retelling—for a friend recalled it thusly after Fenn's death: "Once, when returning from months in the desert, he found himself held up in quarantine and unable to cross to Port Said. He had promised to deliver some sketches by a certain date, so he chartered a sailing boat with a crew of reckless Arabs, and just before dawn ran the blockade under a rain of shot from the shore."[107]

From Port Said, they sailed to Jaffa and this time visited sites in southern Palestine. They decided not to go all the way to Beersheba, because doing so would have taken four days and they could rely on photographs for the one well they needed to sketch. They were disappointed in Hebron, where they "could scare up only six subjects, try as [they] might." Eventually, they reached the wilderness of Engedi, on the Dead Sea, "the worst part" of their journey because of "swarms of scorpions" and occasional hostile Bedouins. They were accompanied by guards led by "Sheik Abas," a former soldier from Hebron, who used his gun to stand down Bedouins demanding tribute money for passing through the area and drawing water from a well.[108]

By April 20 they were once again in Bethlehem and found it much changed from the previous year, with many new buildings. Woodward said: "Strange as

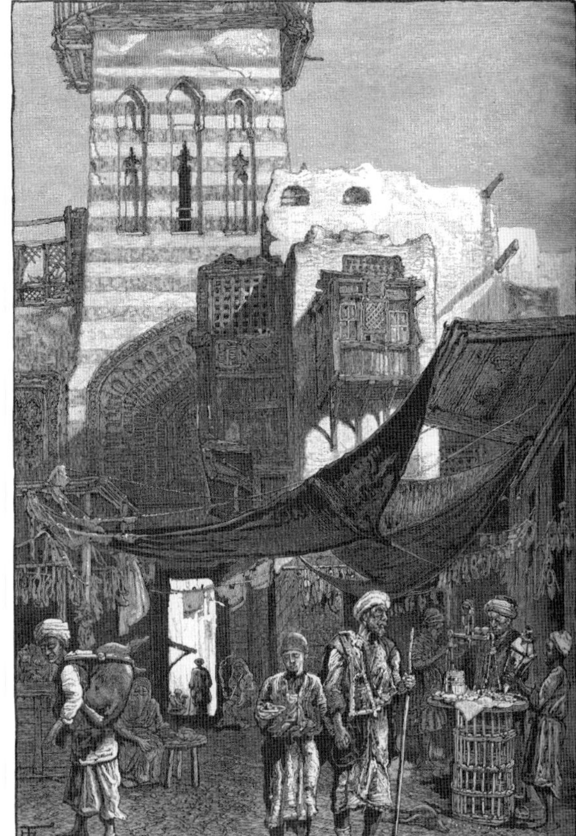

4.25. Harry Fenn, "In the Shoe Bazaar. This was formerly a school, an interesting building now in a very dilapidated condition. The gateway, however, is still preserved." *Picturesque Palestine,* 2:376. Wood engraving, 9 1/2" x 6 1/2".

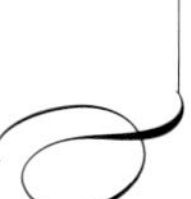

it may seem we never find anything worth doing in Christian villages like this
and Nazareth. They lack the dirt and squalor and picturesqueness of Oriental Mohammedan towns."[109] They then traveled north again, visiting sites connected with Samson and Elijah, expressing considerable irritation at having to
retrace some ground because of the "imperfect list of places" given them the year
before.[110] Woodward was behind in his work and concerned about quickly finish-
ing the requisite number of sketches so that they could head back. By May 14 they
were in Beirut, and from there they took a twelve-day trip by horseback to the
Cedars of Lebanon.

Recounting their journey later in a *St. Nicholas* article titled "Silk & Cedars: A
Scramble in the Lebanons," Fenn claimed he almost lost his life when the trail
passed the "very edge of the cliff" over a smooth rock, and his horse, "who was
very fond of admiring the scenery instead of paying attention to his business,"
slipped. Fortunately for Fenn, the easily distracted animal was also agile: "One,
if not both, of his hind legs went over the edge, and there was nothing more
substantial than air for a thousand feet below. However, the wiry little beast
scrambled cat-like up on the shelving ledge again; but it was a narrow escape."
In the mountains of Lebanon, the silk culture—terraces or "hanging gardens"
of mulberry plants—immediately attracted Fenn's attention. He shared with the
magazine's young readers his lifelong interest in silkworms, noting that when he
was a boy it was "a fad among the young folks to raise silkworms." He explained
the caterpillar's life cycle, from eggs to worms to cocoons, which are picked and
"spun into hanks." Then Fenn described the cedars, the four hundred or so trees
in the grove they visited, one of only eleven left from "an enormous unbroken
forest in the time of King Solomon." He compared the destruction of the forest to
Americans' cutting of the California redwoods.[111]

After descending from the mountains, Fenn and Woodward boarded a steamer
in Beirut and, via Port Said and Alexandria, made their way to Venice. After a
brief look around the Italian city, they ventured on to Paris, where Woodward,
who longed to give up illustration for painting, visited the Salon exhibition. By
mid-June the men were back in London.[112]

Completing the Project—Text and Images

Both artists spent much of the next two to three years working up their sketches
as illustrations on the woodblocks or as watercolors to serve as the basis for steel
engravings. Woodward was eager to return to the United States as soon as pos-

sible and did so in late summer of 1879. From his home in South Orange, New Jersey, with easy access to New York City, he continued his illustration work and supervised the engraving, as he and Fenn had been hired to do. Fenn and his family stayed on in England until 1881.

The publishing firms would eventually engage an editor, Colonel Charles W. Wilson, "formerly Engineer of the Palestine Exploration Society" and then–consul general in Asia Minor (Anatolia), as well as several writers who had spent considerable time in the regions they covered in the book. The group included British clergymen, PEF explorers, and four American clergymen who had served as missionaries; during the next three to four years, the writers prepared their articles, sometimes referring to the illustrations and sometimes not. The different sections of the book vary greatly in quality and interest, from Mary Eliza Rogers's lively accounts of visiting in Islamic homes to the dry pronouncements of the Reverend Selah Merrill about barren hills and filthy people.[113] Their texts would deliver on the promise stated in the book's prospectus to include "the very latest results" of the "most important explorations" by British and Americans teams. Yet, with regard to two of the most debated questions—the location of Jesus's tomb and of Mount Sinai—they did not take a stand, perhaps to ensure that the book's appeal remained wide.[114]

The writers' responses to their experiences of the Holy Land were, of course, shaped by the values they and their cultures embraced. Their cultural baggage included preferences for the picturesque aesthetic, Protestant Christianity as the highest expression of religious faith, and Western social mores emphasizing education, industriousness, and the rule of law. Both the writers and the artists were keenly aware that the Holy Land no longer flowed "with milk and honey"; still, they viewed the "degradation" not as proof of divine retribution, as had some earlier, more Evangelical writers, but as the result of natural causes such as earthquakes and erosion, historic battles, and the current oppressive Ottoman rule (2:150–54; 1:192, 315, 428).

Faced with barrenness and desolation, the writers stressed nature's continuity in landforms, bodies of water, and vegetation. They described the sites of events recounted in the Bible—the broad plains where battles had taken place, caves that had served as hiding places, and wells, lakes, and rivers connected with the stories of the Patriarchs and Jesus. Where possible, they emphasized picturesque and sublime views; according to the writer of "Northern Galilee," for example, "those who enjoy landscapes as seen from the summits of mountains will find a greater number of opportunities of that kind in Palestine than in almost any other country." Yet the religious associations made such views special, as from a hill near Nazareth where "every object in that wonderful panorama was familiar to our Lord" (1:311). The artists, of course, drew many such vistas, just as they had on previous assignments.

The bare mountains and rock formations of the Sinai Peninsula—"the Alps unclothed," according to one writer—where the Hebrews had wandered after the Exodus from Egypt and Moses had experienced God's presence on Mount Sinai, were of particular interest, and almost one-third of volume 2 is devoted to this region. In an age eager to understand geologic history and just becoming familiar with the strata of America's Grand Canyon, the bare rocks, "with innumerable veins of the most brilliant hue," held great appeal, like "some gigantic geological model map" (2:255). Thus, in addition to their important religious associations, the exposed strata were viewed by the writers as evidence of divine creation. The cumulative effect of the artists' numerous images of the Sinai Peninsula (despite their lack of color) coincided powerfully with the text's emphasis on creative power and scenery "both strange and grand." (Even in black and white, several of the steel engravings manage to suggest vivid colors; see especially 2:opp. 303).

Like the artists, the writers assumed that the dress, customs, and occupations of the local residents had persisted through the centuries. One found the harvest customs he observed near Bethlehem to be "a practical commentary on the Book of Ruth" (1:132); several images show threshing (1:opp. 201, 227), although none attempted to specifically represent the Boaz and Ruth story. Another asserted that "brick-making goes on in the same manner as when Israel built the house of Pharaoh" (2:364), and on the same page a wood engraving after a design by Fenn shows the process. Some of the writers were repelled by the dirt and squalor that the artists found pictur-esque, and they described villagers as "degraded and filthy" (1:307). While the artists looked for quaint differences, the writers admired those people who seemed most like themselves: the relatively small groups of Christian residents whom they perceived as superior in many ways to their Muslim neighbors. They found the women of pre-dominantly Christian Bethlehem "the best-looking" in Palestine, probably owing to "the Norman blood in their veins" (1:133), and admired the "energy and enterprise of the villagers educated by the Greek and Latin priests" (1:228). In general, the writ-ers commended what they considered evidence of progress, such as new schools and hospitals and the proposed railroad to the Euphrates valley (2:18), precisely the types of changes and new construction the artists largely avoided.

Where the artists' representations of worship by people of different faiths were uniformly respectful, the writers' attitudes toward religious and ethnic groups varied greatly. They were kinder toward the "higher classes" of Muslims in Jerusalem than to the Turks, who were found "very inferior to the Arabs in education and capacity" (1:118). Bedouins received negative treatment in the text (2:281–85) but more positive visual representations, likely because the artists found these tribesmen armed with spears and riding on horseback to be highly picturesque (1:405, 418, 424). Both the writers and the artists admired Islamic architecture for its pleasing intricacy of form and ornament and saw in it a kinship with Gothic architecture.[115]

Although they wrote approvingly of Islamic rituals of prayer and the practice of charity, some writers were critical of parts of the Koran and the culture's treatment of women. In the images, peasant women are frequently shown at their tasks, wearing loose clothing and with their faces uncovered. By contrast, the few depictions of "ladies" show them veiled, often seated on a donkey or horse, and accompanied by an attendant. In that these shrouded figures are mysterious, they can be associated with the tradition of orientalist paintings, but that the women are shown in public rather than in their homes or harems is an important difference.[116]

The writers' attitudes toward the priests of the Eastern Orthodox church are so negative that one assumes they stem partly from continuing rivalry with Russia and the animosities that persisted from the Crimean War, when Britain and France had battled Russia as Turkey's allies. The writers found the "Greek" priests at Mar Saba to be ignorant, even illiterate (1:151), and were repulsed by the frenzied scramble to touch the Holy Fire in the traditional Easter ritual at the Church of the Holy Sepulcher (1:23–28).

In general, the British writers were more favorably disposed toward the region's Jewish residents. This attitude was in keeping with the widespread expectation that Jewish peoples would eventually reclaim their ancient homeland; in the meantime, the British consulate acted as their protector, as the French had long done for the Roman Catholics and the Russians for Orthodox Christians.[117] One writer's comment that "all civilized races . . . look away to Judea as the fatherland of their religion" (1:334) shows the contemporary interest in the history of religions and the recognition of the heritage shared by Judaism and Christianity. The publishers clearly hoped to reach a Jewish audience.[118]

Although *Picturesque Palestine* is not overtly political, through its writers' endorsement of change and progress in the Holy Land it lent support to the notion that the governing regime should be brought to an end. A clear reference to this stance can be found in a statement by Charles Wilson in the opening section of the book, which notes a widespread belief among Muslims in Palestine that "their own tenure of the country is drawing to a close" and that

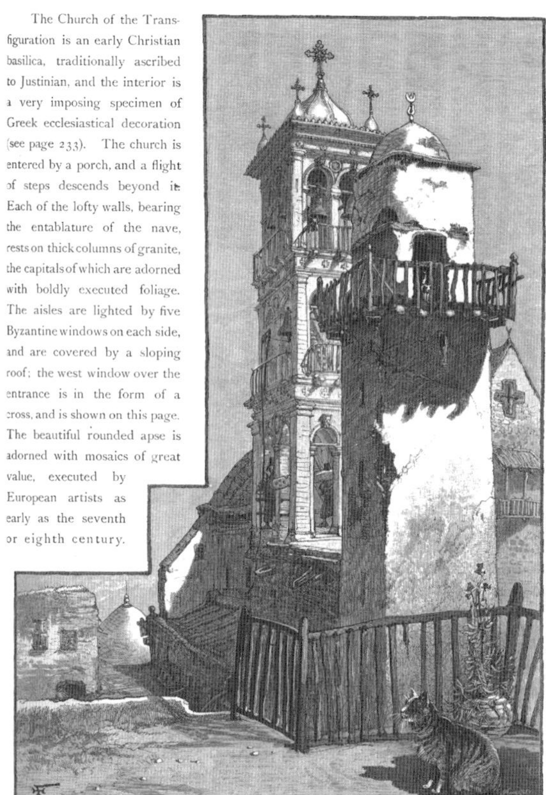

4.26. Harry Fenn, "The Crescent and the Cross. The belfry of the church and the minaret of the mosque, standing so near to each other within the convent walls, produce a singular effect, and strange to say the former is of very recent construction, while the latter dates from an early period." *Picturesque Palestine*, 2:235. Wood engraving by Quartley, 9 1/2" x 6 1/2".

Christians will recapture the city of Jerusalem (1:70). Graphic testimony of Christianity's claim to the Holy Land may be seen in Fenn's illustration "The Crescent and the Cross" (2:235), which shows a damaged minaret beside a more recently constructed church belfry within the walls of the Convent of St. Catherine (fig. 4.26). In fact, British troops would enter Jerusalem in 1917, during World War I, overcoming the resistance of Turkish and German forces, and in 1920 the League of Nations would establish the British Mandate for Palestine, whose purpose was to establish a homeland for the Jewish people.[119]

More clearly than any political implications, however, the text and pictures of *Picturesque Palestine* testified that knowledge of the region—through on-site exploration or armchair travel—could illuminate many aspects of the Scriptures through an understanding of the region's topography and the customs of its people, and that this familiarity could enrich a person's religious and aesthetic life. The book also conveyed much about the culture that produced it: an Anglo-American Protestant Christianity that valued the Holy Land primarily for its potential to buttress a faith being eroded by new scientific and historical findings. It viewed many of the region's current inhabitants as illegitimate interlopers. At the same time, these Western Christians, with their knowledge of the region's history and ancient languages and their new techniques of surveying and excavating, assumed a proprietary right to visit, explore, and map the area and to judge what was needed to improve or develop it. They also claimed the right to interpret and re-present these lands as part of their own heritage—an attitude that led to the creation of the popular Palestine Park at the Chautauqua Assembly in New York State, with its miniaturized topographical replica that visitors could walk through dressed in "oriental" garb, and the inclusion of an eleven-acre "Jerusalem" at the Louisiana Purchase Exposition in St. Louis, Missouri, in 1904.[120]

 Years Abroad

In packaging this book as the third installment in a series focusing on the picturesque, the project had the effect (most likely unintentional) of placing this land, with its history vital to three religions, on a par with "picturesque America" and "picturesque Europe"; the emphasis on aesthetic criteria in some ways diminished and trivialized the region's sacred associations. The touting of the "entirely new" wood engravings derived "from sketches made on the spot" by "Eminent Artists" linked *Picturesque Palestine* with a long-admired tradition of landscape art; a purchaser could thus expect to reap the benefits of enhanced prestige for displaying an interest in both art and religion. In addition, the emphasis on the illustrations as works of art and their obvious visual appeal probably led many readers to focus on them rather than on the lengthy and rather dull text—much as many people do when leafing through coffee-table books today. The result could well have been that the overwhelmingly positive content of the images more effectively presented the region as a place little changed from biblical times than did the ambiguous musings of the writers.

Before publication began, in April 25, 1880, the *Chicago Tribune* printed an interview with William H. Appleton, then the company's senior member. He reminisced about some of Appleton's greatest successes, such as "Webster's Speller," which sold a million copies a year for forty years, and pointed out the high cost of bookmaking: "For example it cost us $138,000 to publish 'Picturesque America,' and that without adding the cost of printing." He went on to tout *Picturesque Palestine,* saying that the firm was "in process of making a book that will be in many respects superior to 'Picturesque America,'" and highlighted the role of the artists: "For the past two years we have had artists—Mr. Harry Fenn and J. D. Woodward—traveling through the Holy Land and making sketches for this book." He made an exciting story of it, claiming that some drawings were "made at the risk of the artists' lives" and that Woodward was "the first outsider ever admitted within the sacred walls [of the Mosque of Jerusalem], and he was obliged to have two soldiers, armed to the teeth, stand guard over him as he sketched. Even then his life was threatened, the people are so prejudiced against strangers."

Less than a year later, in early 1881, *Picturesque Palestine* began appearing in parts in the United States; the first of the four volumes issued by Virtue was available in London by that September, followed by the second volume sometime before December.[121] The book soon garnered praise. On March 21, 1881, the prominent American clergyman Henry Ward Beecher wrote: "If the work continues to be executed on the same scale it has been thus far, it will easily assume the very highest place over all the almost innumerable illustrated works upon Palestine."[122] A writer in the March 26, 1881, *Churchman* noted that "the multitude" who had dreamed of a pilgrimage to the Holy Land owed Appleton "their best thanks" for enabling them to "get almost as correct an idea of the holy places as if" they were seeing them with their "own eyes." And a reviewer in the London *Times* wrote, "If anything short of a visit to the scenes here described and illustrated could satisfy the desires of the Bible student, it would be some such publication as this."[123]

These sentiments were echoed by another American clergyman, Lyman Abbott, who was also editor of the *Christian Union.* According to him, the illustrations were "more life-like, and in the best sense more true, than reproductions from photographs. . . . The artist interprets Nature, and, if he be a true artist, gives her inward meaning as the photograph can not." Abbott went so far as to say of Palestine: "In some respects, to visit it by the aid of the artist and the author is better than to visit it in person, for one thus escapes the dirt, the discomfort, the wretchedness, the squalor, the ignorance, and the superstition which belong to the modern life of this romantic but unhappy and oppressed country."[124] Despite filtering out much of the messy reality of these complicated places, the book would in fact depict the Holy Land more comprehensively than any previous work.[125] With its nine hundred pages and more than six hundred illustrations, it was hard to ignore.

Even before publication of *Picturesque Palestine* was completed in late 1883, adaptations were being issued in France and Germany.[126] For the holiday trade that year, Appleton offered a gift edition in two volumes, which the *New York Evangelist* designated "at once the finest and most intrinsically valuable issue of the season, in this or any other country."[127] It sold well, and in subsequent years the number of travelers to the Holy Land and publications about the region increased dramatically.[128] Having established themselves as specialists on this part of the world, Fenn and, to a lesser extent, Woodward contributed illustrations to several of these later publications, and images from *Picturesque Palestine* were reused in several as well.[129] The project would have lasting repercussions for Fenn's career and enhance his image as an adventurous, well-traveled artist.

By 1880 Fenn and his family were living at Watts Farm in the village of Shottermill, near Linchmere, West Sussex. It was there that Fenn worked on his illustrations for *Picturesque Palestine* and that the couple's last child, Hilda Marguerite, was born on September 18, 1880. This home and its surroundings were described

Years Abroad

by Fenn's oldest daughter, Alice Maude, in two articles that appeared in the *Century* after the family's return to the United States. She described the move from "dear, dirty, smoky old London" to a rented farmstead, with its "long, low, red-tiled house of stone with great latticed windows and ivy-grown porch" that was "guarded by giant oaks" and offered a view of a "long green valley."[130] They decorated the house with Italian and Spanish sketches and Moorish rugs. The article had illustrations by her father, including one of his studio.

During their time there, they became familiar with rural life: sheep shearing, haying, broom making, and May Day festivals. The area had a rich cultural life that attracted artists, such as Birket Foster, Sir Lawrence Alma-Tadema, and George Henry Boughton, and writers, including Thomas Hardy and Gilbert White of Selborne. Their farm was a "ten minutes' walk beyond Brookbank," where George Eliot lived while writing *Middlemarch,* and just three miles away was Aldworth, Tennyson's grand house.[131] Many accounts of Fenn's life mention his friendship with Tennyson, and it seems likely they became acquainted at this time; he eventually illustrated some of the poet's works, including a special edition of *In Memoriam.* The two men were said to attend the same church, St. Laurence's, in nearby Lurgashall. According to Sidney Brooks, poets and nature lovers were drawn to Fenn, and he and Tennyson "would talk for half an hour over the wondrous qualities of color in a wheat field."[132]

A letter Fenn wrote to James Russell Lowell on February 18, 1881, suggests that he was ready to settle down and resume contact with his American friends. Fenn had heard from Alma-Tadema that Lowell was in London and said that it would be a "great pleasure to call upon" him. The letter continued: "Since last I had the pleasure of seeing you I have been a wanderer on the face of the earth, and should much like to know of the welfare of some of our mutual New England friends that I have not heard of for many years."[133]

Several months later, after living in the old farmhouse for about two years and in England for eight, the Fenn family—with five children ranging in age from one to nineteen—returned to New York. In that bustling center of publishing and art, Harry Fenn would be welcomed back by his colleagues and soon tapped for numerous commissions by a wide variety of publishers.

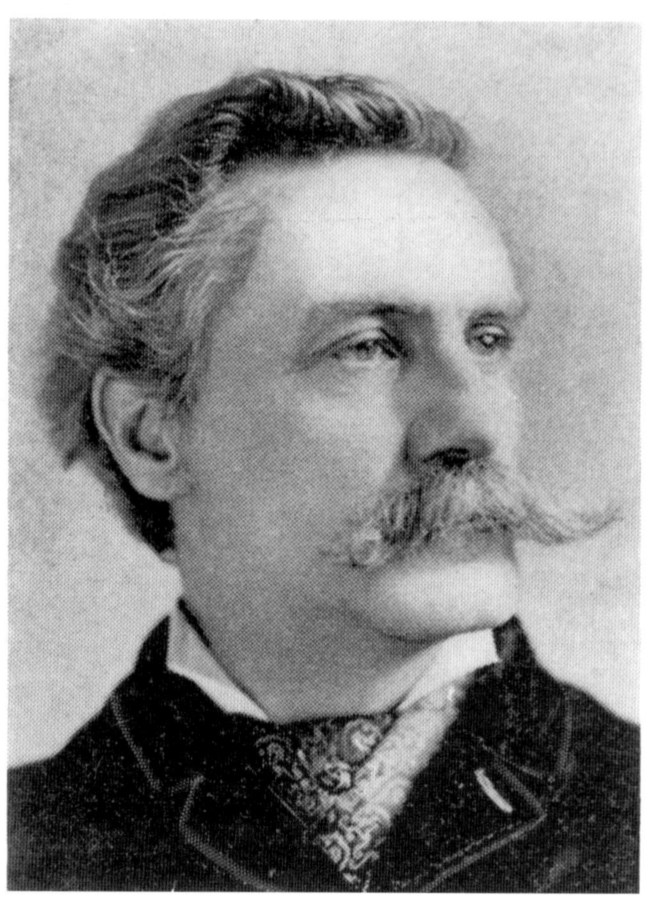

5.1. Photograph of Harry Fenn. From Francis Hopkinson Smith, *American Illustrators* (New York: Charles Scribner's Sons, 1892), 63.

5

New Clients,
New Technologies, and a
New Home—The 1880s

As Fenn worked to complete his illustrations for *Picturesque Palestine* and his daughter Hilda neared her first birthday, the family returned to the United States. Although a second transatlantic move must have been difficult and their loyalties divided between England and America, Fenn apparently anticipated many commissions and wished to establish a permanent home where he could spend most of his time. By late September 1881, the family was settled with Mary Fenn's parents on Adelphi Street in Brooklyn. Their three-story house, with the dining room and kitchen in the basement, a porch and garden in the back, and at least seven bedrooms, was large enough to accommodate them all.[1] Fenn soon resumed his professional activities in New York, listing himself as "artist" in the New York City directories for 1882–83 and 1883–84, with 16 West Twenty-third Street, near Fifth Avenue, as his studio.[2] His name does not appear in later directories, suggesting he was busy enough to no longer need to advertise his services.

The 1880s were indeed the high point of Fenn's career. Returning to New York after eight years abroad, he resumed his participation and leadership role in the American Water Color Society (so renamed in 1878), which had begun catering to a growing middle-class art market. His illustration career took a promising turn as well. After having spent years working exclusively for Appleton on two high-profile books, he soon found himself in demand for a plethora of projects with other publishers.

Within the fast-changing world of publishing, fresh approaches to wood engraving and new printing technologies were vying with the older processes. Fenn was a rare example of an artist whose illustrating career bridged these transitions seamlessly, just as he bridged two different generations. His peers, Thomas Moran, Winslow Homer, and others, had worked first as illustrators in the age of wood engraving, then largely abandoned illustration for painting and etching. By contrast, many members of the next generation of artist-illustrators, such as Joseph Pennell and Edwin A. Abbey, combined book and magazine illustration using the new technologies of line cut and halftone with production of etchings and paintings for exhibition and sale. Fenn thrived by embracing the emerging technologies as opportunities to display his work in a variety of published media, while he continued to paint exhibition watercolors. His familiar compositional strategies, presented by the new processes, continued to appeal to a wide audience, while works of his younger colleagues also found favor with those seeking fresh approaches.

In the years the Fenns had spent abroad, New York's position as the country's leading publishing center had solidified, increasing the demand for illustrators there. Its population had jumped to almost two million and included a growing number of America's wealthiest families, among them William Henry and Cornelius Vanderbilt II, who were constructing impressive mansions on Fifth Avenue. Yet the numbers of the city's poor—who lived in cramped, unhealthy tenements— were also on the rise, boosted by an influx of immigrants from Ireland. The city's congestion problems and social ills may have played a role in Fenn's decision to settle across the Hudson River. By early 1884, he had purchased a site in Montclair, the New Jersey town where the family had lived before their years in England.[3] He would have anticipated receiving a warm welcome there. While the family had been away, a local newspaper published an article in which Fenn was described as a "genial and lovable man" and an "eminent artist" who was "sorely missed" in "his adopted home," to which many wished his speedy return.[4] The house he built there during the next year would garner much attention for its distinctive asymmetrical facade, complete with gables and towers, and the Aesthetic-style interior decoration. It would also enhance his reputation as a highly successful artist-illustrator.

The Fenns returned to a United States in transition. Across the country, an ever-expanding market enjoyed access to national and international products and publications, fostering a more urban, cosmopolitan, commerce-based society. Sarah Burns has described this "rapidly urbanizing and incorporating society" as one in which "mass culture, spectacle, commercialism, and consumerism were fast becoming common denominators of modern experience."[5] The 1876 Centennial Exposition had introduced inventions such as the telephone and an improved telegraph and demonstrated that American innovators excelled in applying science to mechanical processes.[6] The proliferation of the nation's rail-

New Clients, New Technologies, New Home

roads—backed by government subsidies and attendant corruption—facilitated the growth of settlements, agricultural production, and an industrial economy in which national corporations were replacing regional firms. This new transportation network brought faster distribution of all types of goods, including newspapers and periodicals, to an increasingly literate public. At the same time, a lack of regulation allowed unfair pricing to prevail and enabled the so-called robber barons to establish monopolies, with John D. Rockefeller's Ohio-based Standard Oil Trust chief among them.

The South continued its slow recovery from the economic devastation caused by the Civil War, aided by investment from the North in the coal, timber, cotton, and pig iron industries, but enthusiasm for Reconstruction had waned; even as the old planter class and new entrepreneurs gained power, the Black Codes restricted African Americans' rights and liberties. Four new states joined the Union in 1881—North Dakota, South Dakota, Montana, and Washington—and new towns were cropping up west of the Mississippi, with cities like Chicago, Omaha, and Kansas City growing fast. To promote settlement and economic growth, the federal government had moved most of the Native American inhabitants of these regions to reservations, although some struggled to retain their traditional way of life, fighting the U.S. Army, most recently the Nez Perce tribe in 1877. In the Northeast, rural areas were losing population to cities whose steam-powered factories promised only long hours and low pay. Labor groups began to press for improved conditions, and the violence of the Great Railroad Strike near Philadelphia in 1877 shocked the nation. After strikers destroyed railroad cars and federal troops killed twenty-five employees, public opinion largely turned against the workers.[7] Further, just about the time the Fenns returned to the United States, its citizens were mourning the death of the new and promising president, James A. Garfield, on September 19, 1881, two months after he was shot by an assassin.[8]

These and other changes would shape publishers' choices of subject matter and, in turn, Fenn's assignments. He would prepare illustrations related to some of the more positive aspects of these changes and events, including reestablishing ties with the South through attention to historic homes of southern leaders and reconciliation between the former adversaries in the Civil War and featuring new architecture and other improvements in growing cities and suburbs. Somewhat later projects sent him to the West to document not only its recent developments but also its distant past. By partnering with the publishers of illustrated magazines, Fenn continued to contribute to their civilizing mission with his scenes of progress, order, and beauty.

A DIFFERENT ART MILIEU

In some ways Harry Fenn took up his career right where he had left off, but with an enhanced respect owing to the two conspicuous and successful projects in which he had participated after *Picturesque America*. Yet in his absence the art world had changed, with the emergence of new tastes and preferences in both painting and illustration. Art museums and art schools were being established in New York and throughout the country. The number of magazines devoted to the arts had tripled,[9] and many more art critics debated—with greater sophistication—which subjects and styles were appropriate for American artists. Fenn would play an active role in this world, just as he had before his time abroad, taking on fresh challenges and learning to work in different media.

With regard to subjects, the public was decidedly more interested in figure paintings and depictions of fields and forests, shown at particular times of day and in different seasons, that suggested a painter's intimate relation to nature. This approach—described by Peter Bermingham as an "effort to memorialize essential verities of the natural world in the face of accelerating change"—was inspired by the works of such French Barbizon painters as Jean-François Millet, Camille Corot, Théodore Rousseau, and Charles-François Daubigny.[10] There was less enthusiasm, among critics and collectors at least, for paintings of picturesque or sublime scenery, as seen in the works now lumped together as the Hudson River School. This shift had been stimulated by the Centennial Exposition, where some of Fenn's works were exhibited (although he did not attend). The critical response to the fair's Art Section was mixed, from Clarence Cook, who could hardly express his "disappointment" and "mortification" over the American display, to Susan Nichols Carter, who thought it "the best collection" of American works ever shown. Nevertheless, she, like many others, considered Great Britain's exhibit "superior to that of any other country represented" and especially admired the recent works by William Holman Hunt, Frederic Lord Leighton, and William Powell Frith showing "the passion or the toil of life."[11] Despite the conflicting opinions, the exposition undoubtedly served to strengthen both the interest of American art patrons in acquiring European works and the desire of aspiring American artists to study abroad.

In succeeding years, the debate grew more heated as fewer painters chose subjects that told a story, conveyed a moral, or depicted nature's magnificence as revelatory of divine creation. Instead, they focused on beauty of design and color, adopting bold techniques that called attention to the artist at work. Their

  New Clients, New Technologies, New Home

detractors decried this approach as "art for art's sake." American artists who had studied in Germany took inspiration from the Dutch masters, particularly Frans Hals (rediscovered by art historians in the late 1860s), and the Spanish baroque painters, especially Jusepe de Ribera and Diego Velásquez; they used bold brushstrokes to paint flatly lighted figures against dark backgrounds.[12] Those who had studied in France often emulated the highly finished canvases of French academicians or Jules Bastien-Lepage, whose paintings of figures outdoors in diffused light exhibited a careful control of color values.[13]

Upon returning to the United States, many of these artists became dissatisfied with the National Academy's exhibitions and training and founded a competing group, the Society of American Artists.[14] When their artworks were first exhibited in New York in 1877, some critics objected to what they saw as an overemphasis on technique. Within a few years, however, the subjects and styles of these artists had become more accepted. The prominent critic Sylvester Koehler thought their works heralded a new age in American art characterized by more thorough artistic training and greater technical sophistication and individuality.[15] Fenn was certainly aware of the changing tastes, for he soon associated with many of these younger artists in various organizations and assignments; in fact, one of his major clients was Richard Watson Gilder, the editor of the *Century Magazine* and husband of Helena DeKay Gilder, a founder of the Society of American Artists. Nevertheless, any changes in his approach to illustration were gradual and primarily in response to developments in engraving techniques and printing processes. It is harder to assess the effect of the newer styles on his watercolors, since so few have been located.

PARTICIPATION IN ART ORGANIZATIONS

After his return in 1881, Fenn participated actively in artists' organizations, especially the American Water Color Society, which continued to promote the medium as well as the American artists who used it. Although interest in the society's exhibitions had waned in 1871 and 1872, they received new energy beginning in 1874 thanks to the inclusion of plein-air sketches and works in "Black and White" (done for illustration) and the participation of Winslow Homer and younger artists such as Edwin Austin Abbey and Thomas Eakins.[16] The society's first exhibition after Fenn's return, the fifteenth annual held at the National Academy of Design in February 1882, was mainly well received. He and the other exhibitors must have been pleased when the *Harper's Weekly* reviewer proclaimed that "the best of the American productions" excelled "the best of the European specimens." The *Weekly* also published a double-page spread of small reproductions of works "from the Illustrated Catalogue"; of the forty paintings shown, twenty-two featured figures.

Other comments by the reviewer might well have given Fenn pause, perhaps prompting him to consider subjects closer to home and to aim for greater emotional content. He exhibited six works derived from his travels in the Holy Land and Europe: *A Day School in the Shoemaker's Bazaar, Damascus; The Rialto Market, Venice; The Market Place, Segovia, Spain; A Bit in North Wales; In an English Garden;* and *The Gate of Pardon, Seville Cathedral.* The critic, however, was pleased that the show represented "less gadding about in foreign parts than usual" and that painters were paying greater attention to "the neglected picturesqueness of the metropolis," as in "Mr. Hopkinson Smith's 'Under the Towers,'" a view of the Brooklyn Bridge, which was hung in "the place of honor." And in language suggesting works in the Barbizon mode, the writer also approved of landscapes in which the artist attempted "something better than the merely photographic or descriptive; something by which the interpenetration of the painter's emotions has become illumined with a ray of the ideal, something in which by a play of fine tones the real has become more or less transfigured."[17]

Of Fenn's six paintings, *The Gate of Pardon, Seville Cathedral* was illustrated in the exhibition catalogue; it looks similar to his *Picturesque Europe* illustration "The Gate of the Court of Oranges, Seville Cathedral" (3:136).[18] Despite one critic's objection, images such as this, in both books and exhibitions, fed the growing interest in architectural monuments around the world, as had architects' reports on their travels.[19] Fenn's only mention in a review of the show came from the *Art Amateur*'s often-acerbic critic Clarence Cook, who had harsh words for him and most of the other contributors. He found Fenn's "carefully worked-up drawings of Spanish and Oriental subjects without charm of color, and lighted apparently not by the sun, but by Jablochkoff," referring to the recently developed arc lamps called Jablochkoff candles used for nighttime lighting in cities.[20] Such criticism was not new to Fenn—similar accusations had been leveled at him after the society's first exhibition, in 1867–68—and his later paintings suggest that he worked toward achieving more harmonious color.

For the first time, the American Water Color Society's annual exhibition also included two rooms devoted to etchings, and seeing these prints may have sparked Fenn's interest in the medium. American artists had begun experimenting with this printmaking process while Fenn was still in England, and the

New Clients, New Technologies, New Home

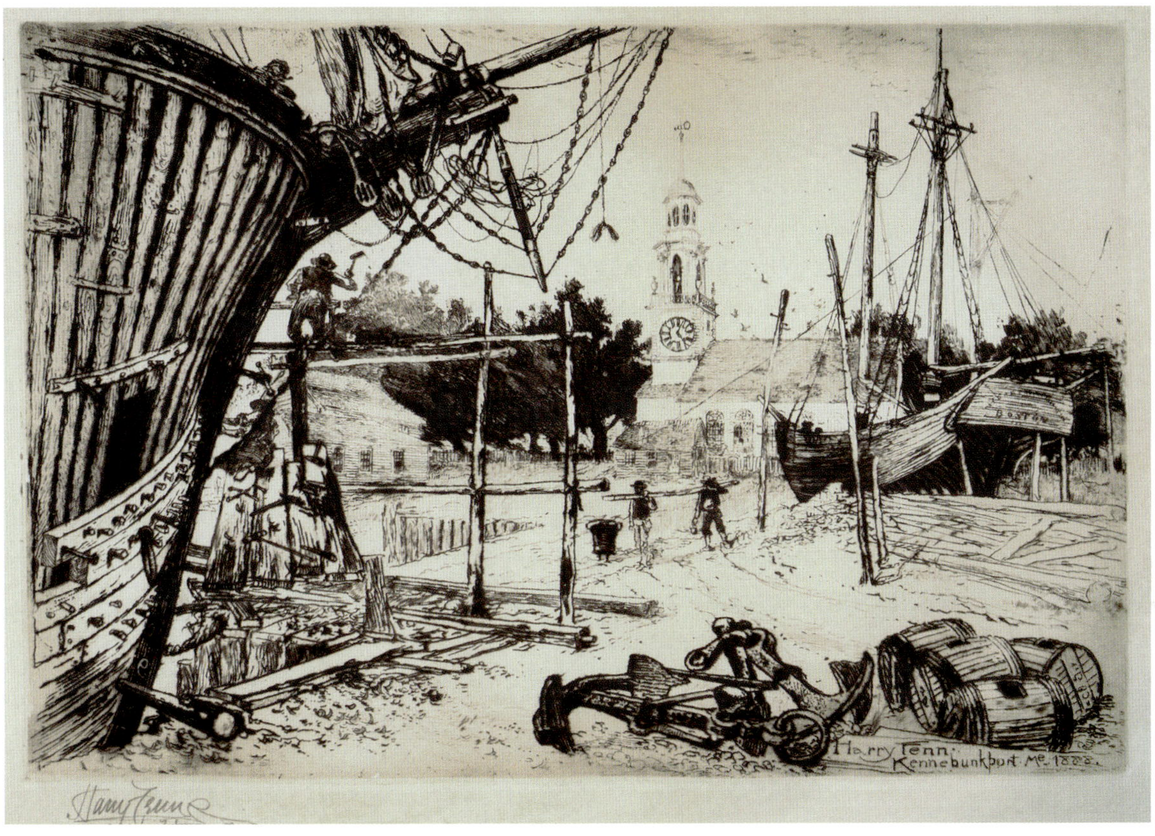

5.2. Harry Fenn, *Kennebunkport, Maine,* 1888. Etching, 10 3/4" x 15 3/4". (San Diego Museum of Art [http://www.TheSanDiegoMuseumofArt.org], 1942:109, gift of Mary L. Fenn.)

so-called etching revival had been gaining momentum since the founding of the New York Etching Club in 1877.[21] Its appeal lay in its autographic nature: unlike a wood engraving, an etching plate could be prepared by the artist alone, without the intervention of another hand. The aforementioned *Harper's Weekly* reviewer considered the show's examples "beyond question the noblest display ever seen of American genius in this department of the fine arts"—one that would provide a "public explanation of the esteem in which American etching has come to be held by the best judges in the Old World."[22] Fenn had at least one etching lesson soon after the exhibition, given on May 6, 1882, by James D. Smillie, an active participant in the revival.[23] Only a few etchings by Fenn have been located, however, including two views of shipyards—*Kennebunkport, Maine,* dated 1888 (fig. 5.2), and *Lobster Cove*—exhibited in the New York Etching Club's 1889 show at the National Academy of Design.[24] Although publishers at this time were producing a few books illustrated with etchings, Fenn is not known to have contributed to any such volumes.[25]

Fenn's renewed participation in the American Water Color Society was obviously welcome. On March 15, 1882, he was elected to the Board of Control, the group that selected works for exhibition, along with George H. Smillie, Thomas Moran, and F. S. Church. On November 15, he was appointed to the catalogue committee, as were Church and two members of the Society of American Artists who had studied in Munich, Henry Farrer and Walter Shirlaw.[26] Early in 1883 Fenn was put forward as a candidate for president of the society, but he eventually declined the nomination.[27] By this time, almost a decade after Fenn's 1874 complaint that the American public failed to appreciate watercolors, the status of watercolor painters had improved dramatically. The society's exhibitions were well attended, and, with prices relatively low compared to large works in oil, many moderately well-to-do collectors were able to purchase them. According to a *New York Times* writer: "The great successes of the Etching Club and Water-color Society are due to the spread of a love for the fine arts among persons of moderate means."[28] A *Harper's Weekly* review in February 1883 began with these words:

> That prosperous organization, the American Water-color Society, has just opened its sixteenth annual exhibition at the National Academy of Design, in the usual and reasonable expectation of selling a vast number of pictures— thirty thousand dollars' worth at least—and of having a good time generally. For some years, indeed, the American Water-colorist has been altogether the cheerfulest type of artist to be seen on this side of the Atlantic. The public buys his works, and attends the displays of them; and neither the beauty nor the fashion of the metropolis is scandalized by the question, "have you seen the Water-color Exhibition?". . . The American Water-colorist, not to put too fine a point on him, enjoys the most deserved artistic success in the city.[29]

Since Fenn had worked on the illustrated catalogue, he must have been pleased when the reviewer praised it as being "of more serious import than any of its predecessors." (The most noticeable difference is that several of the illustrations occupy an entire page.) One of Fenn's paintings illustrated in the catalogue, *Marshall's Creek, Pa.*, was larger than most, measuring 20 by 29 inches, and came with a higher price of $350. It featured a fisherman on a rustic bridge, with an oxcart and house on the far side of the creek. It was also among the sixteen selected to appear in *Harper's Weekly,* but little of its appeal can be discerned from the small black and white image reproduced therein.[30] (See Appendix 2 for titles of Fenn's other exhibited works.)

 New Clients, New Technologies, New Home

The responses to Fenn's use of color continued to vary widely. When *A Pennsylvania Bee Colony* was shown in London in the summer of 1883 alongside nearly one hundred watercolor works by American painters, it was praised as "perfectly delightful in its bright color and delicate effect."[31] Yet in a review of the 1884 American Water Color Society exhibition, at least one critic found the same painting's bright colors "inharmonious."[32] Another painting exhibited that year, *Market Scene, Tangier* (likely the work reproduced in fig. 5.3) does show modulations of color.[33] The minaret in the background and the rough market sheds in the middle ground are carefully painted in subdued but harmonious hues, and bits of turquoise, red, and orange provide highlights and interest; foreground details in deep shadow include a woman in full burka with only one eye visible. (As mentioned earlier, Fenn could have visited Morocco from Gibraltar, although no records of such a trip have been found.)

Fenn's participation was also welcome in the Salmagundi Sketch Club, a group founded in 1871 whose members included artists, illustrators, musicians, and prominent citizens. The club had begun mounting an annual *Black and White Exhibition* in 1878, and for the December 1881 event Fenn displayed three paintings: *A Study of Gorse; Coiling Heather and Study of Dead Bracken;*[34] and *In an English Garden;* he also exhibited the next three years.[35] (See Appendix 2.) By 1883, the club's exhibitions had attracted considerable attention; they presented a variety of media and techniques, including "India ink, etchings, engravings, drawings on wood, and illustrative work generally," as well as black-and-white oil paintings, for which there was currently a "rage," according to a reviewer in the *Brooklyn Daily Eagle*.[36]

While Fenn and his American colleagues participated in exhibitions of watercolors, drawings, and etchings, which found an appreciative audience among the moderately well-to-do, a more rarified market was competing with the annual exhibitions and established galleries to attract the business of the wealthiest Americans. The new corporate elite—those who had amassed fortunes in transportation, finance, real estate, and manufacturing—often preferred oil paintings by contemporary European artists to oils or watercolors by Americans. To satisfy the growing demand, the American Art Association began staging elaborate art auctions in 1883, and soon affluent collectors from across the nation were converging on New York to attend. The paintings were displayed in rooms resembling the homes of the rich, and the auction format allowed buyers to display their wealth and artistic taste in a more public and publicized way than the earlier practice of buying from dealers' galleries or artists' studios.[37] French paintings that achieved

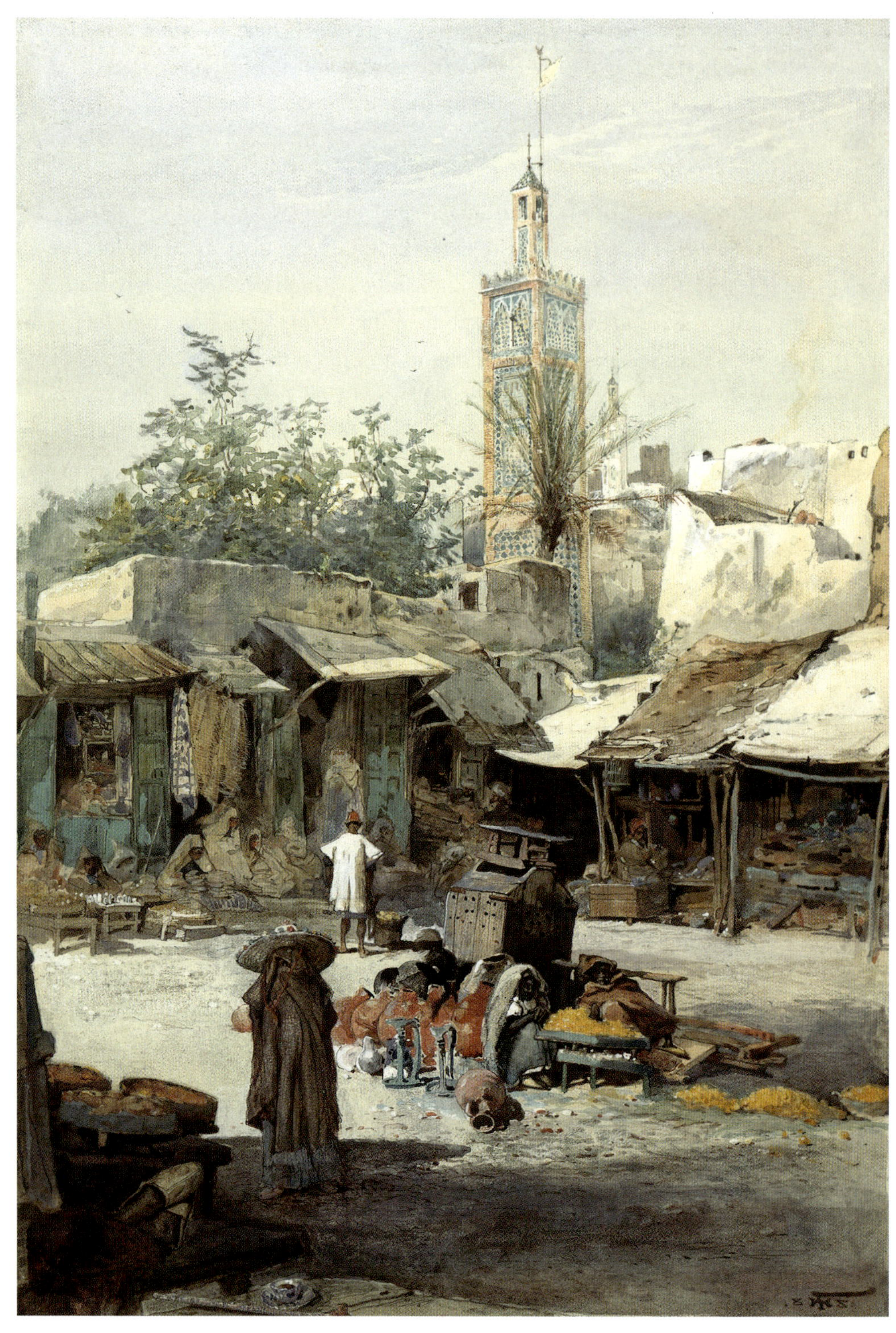

5.3. Harry Fenn, *Market Scene, Tangier*, 1881? Graphite, wash, and gouache on paper, approx. 18 1/4" x 12 1/4". (Private collection.)

record prices in the mid-1880s were Jules Breton's *Evening in the Hamlet of Finistère* ($18,200) and *The Communicants* ($45,500); Meissonier's monumental battle scene *Friedland, 1807* ($66,000); and, most spectacularly, *The Angelus* by Jean-François Millet (approx. $110,000).[38] John Ott has observed that "nostalgic scenes of village life by French realist, Barbizon, and academic artists heavily populated the roster of works at the very summit of value" and conjectured that images of hardworking peasants content with their lot would have appealed to those corporate leaders faced with protests and demands from employees.[39] Clearly, this segment of the art world was far different from the one in which Fenn participated.

CHANGES IN THE WORLD OF PERIODICALS

Soon after his return to New York, Fenn found time to take on other projects besides *Picturesque Palestine.* His success with Appleton's three massive publications had established his reputation, and he was one of the first artists publishers thought of when they needed scenes of landscapes or cities in the United States, the British Isles, Europe, or the Holy Land. Yet the world of illustrated periodicals had also changed while he was away, with new players and new techniques moving to the forefront; these shifts may have presented challenges at first but eventually served him well and furthered his career. *Appletons' Journal* and *Every Saturday* had ceased publication, and *Scribner's Monthly,* which had competed with the *Journal* and its "Picturesque America" series, had reorganized in 1881 under a change of ownership and a new name: *Century Magazine.* The owners wanted their periodical to be an instrument of "righteousness" that would deliver a "constant stream of refining influence."[40]

Building on the success of *Scribner's,* the *Century* soon became the leading illustrated monthly. Its editor, the poet and literary tastemaker Richard Watson Gilder, focused on history, travel, and literature. Its printer, Theodore Low De Vinne, improved the quality of wood engravings by using dry paper, better inks, and overlays that applied varying pressure to different parts of the image, thus avoiding a dull, uniform gray.[41] De Vinne was also the printer for the Century Company's children's magazine, *St. Nicholas,* which had absorbed *Our Young Folks* (purchased from Ticknor and Fields).[42] The use of a new rotary press built by R. Hoe and Company beginning in 1886 further increased printing speed and cut costs.[43] Another change that benefited all magazine publishers was Congress's 1879 authorization of low second-class mail rates for periodicals.[44] With the revenue from more advertisements helping to offset the expense of its many illustrations, the *Century*'s price remained affordable to many, at thirty-five cents an issue or $4 a year. The advertisements were printed in separate sections at the front and back of its thick monthly issues—approximately 160 pages total—and typically discarded before the volume was bound.

The *Century* would be the most successful of the illustrated monthlies during this period, and, although based in New York, it boasted a national circulation of 200,000 by the late 1880s.[45] *Harper's Monthly,* whose illustrations had improved in quality, was a close second at the same price. According to Theodore P. Greene, author of a 1970 book examining periodicals in this period, both magazines appealed to "those high-minded, educated, principled, professional and mercantile gentlemen of old families who looked with considerable distaste upon the political corruption and unscrupled industrial competition of the Gilded Age."[46] Neither gave much attention to the political or economic scene, although Gilder and the *Century* endorsed civil service reform.

American illustrated periodicals were admired abroad as well as at home and became a source of national pride for their excellence and relatively low cost. A writer for the *Critic* boasted in 1883: "There is no other country in the world that spreads periodically such an intellectual feast before its public. A bound volume of *Harper's* or *The Century* is as handsome a book as authors and artists can make. There is no publication printed that is as cheap as a copy of either of these magazines. A book containing as much in the way of letterpress or illustrations would cost two or three dollars at least."[47] Such periodicals continued to claim an important role in educating and uplifting a public now spread across the continent. The 1882 special Christmas issue of *Harper's Weekly* pointed out that, where the great artists of Europe had painted for popes and emperors, American artists drew for "all the people," and that exposure to the beauty of their works would play a "humanizing" and "refining part in American civilization and daily life . . . wherever the finely illustrated magazine or paper goes—and it goes everywhere: to the copper mines of Lake Superior, to the cattle ranch in Wyoming, to the Florida everglades, to the primeval forest beyond Katahdin."[48] Looking back at this period, Joseph Pennell wrote in his 1925 memoir, *The Adventures of an Illustrator:* "At that time Americans looked for art in *Scribner's* and *Harper's* as they think they have found it to-day in the movies and the comics."[49]

The prominence of the *Century, Harper's Monthly,* and Boston's venerable *Atlantic,* published without illustrations since 1857, is clear from the fact that their contents were regularly discussed in all types of regional and special-interest periodicals, from the *Manhattan* and the *Outing* to the *New England Farmer, and Horticultural*

New Clients, New Technologies, New Home

Register, and newspapers countrywide. To alert their eager audiences, the publishers would announce in advance the topics to be treated in the coming year, month by month, accompanied by the names of the writers and illustrators. The keen competition among these three monthlies was the subject of a fictionalized debate that appeared in the 1883 *Christian Union* based on the question: If you could have but one of the magazines, which would you choose? One friend prefers the illustrations and art features in the *Century,* saying, "Why some of its engravings are worth the price of the magazine ten times over." Another thinks *Harper's* has better writers and likes "The Easy Chair" column. The third, "the more philosophical of the circle," thinks that "a single number of the 'Atlantic' has more sound, substantial thought in it than a whole volume of your New York magazines. It is the wholesome oatmeal and roast-beef of the magazine diet; 'The Century' and 'Harper's' are the candied fruits." After further consideration of the merits of all three, however, the writer balks at choosing and concludes, "If I had but one choice, I should choose all three."[50]

The late 1870s and early 1880s saw the beginning of a new approach to wood engraving that was in keeping with the changing tastes; it was also more sympathetic to artists, especially those who had returned from Europe emphasizing individual styles, more vigorous brushstrokes, and looser handling. The guiding principle of the engravers embracing this approach was to faithfully reproduce an artist's work, attempting as much as possible to convey the look of the original medium, whether oil, pencil, ink, watercolor, pastel, charcoal, or etching. Their task was greatly facilitated by the process of photographically printing a reversed image of the artist's work directly onto the woodblock.[51] These engravers, including Timothy Cole (1852–1931) and several younger men and a few women, were collectively referred to as the New School of Wood Engraving; in 1882 they organized the Society of American Wood-Engravers, which held exhibitions and published portfolios of members' work, gaining admiration for wood engraving as an art form.[52] *Century* and other magazines featured their work, especially Cole's reproductions of paintings of the great European masters. Within little more than a decade, however, the halftone process would largely eliminate the need for their services.

Some older wood engravers disparaged the new approach and railed against it, especially William J. Linton, who had done much work for *Picturesque America.* Linton preferred to emphasize the engraver's artistry in creating more conventional lines that clearly depicted the subject.[53] Many artists appreciated the New School techniques, however, and magazine subscribers evidently approved as well. Looking back on this period of experimentation, one critic recalled that some viewed the changes "with amazement and no little foreboding," but

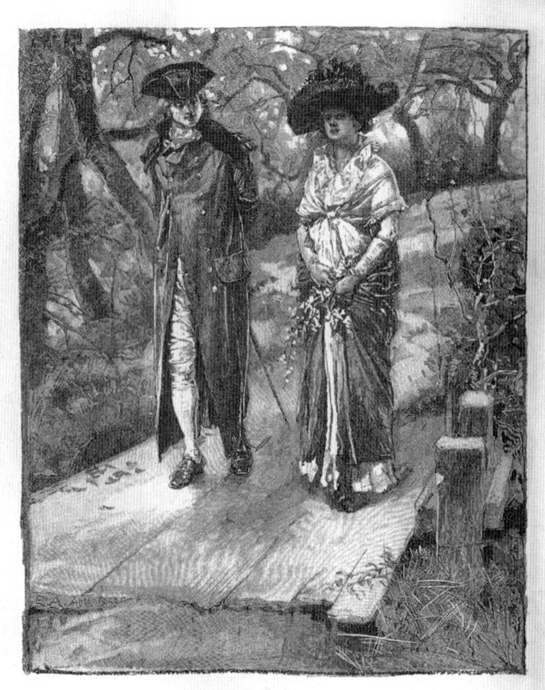

5.4. Edwin A. Abbey, frontispiece illustrating "Almond Blossom" by Margaret Veley. *Harper's Monthly*, April 1881, opp. 323. Wood engraving by Timothy Cole, 5 3/4" x 4 1/2".

eventually "there came to be pictures bearing the personal characteristics and art feeling of the men who designed them. . . . The artists were delighted and the public amazed."[54] The new approach was also admired abroad. The English critic Philip G. Hamerton wrote: "Now, whatever may be the differences of opinion about the desirableness of this imitative art, there can be no question that the Americans have far surpassed all other nations in delicacy of execution."[55]

An early commentary in the August 27, 1881, *Churchman* (a weekly magazine with ties to the Episcopal church) gives a notion of the new technique's appeal. The critic praised the frontispiece for the poem "Almond Blossom" (fig. 5.4), as drawn by the popular figure painter Edwin A. Abbey and engraved by Timothy Cole, in the August 1881 *Harper's Monthly*. The image was strikingly different from a conventional wood engraving: "It presents the effects of india-ink rubbed in with masterly carelessness, or the softness and tenderness of chalk or charcoal, or the mellow handling of the perfect lithograph. Indeed, properly mounted, it would almost pass for an autograph of Mr. Abbey himself; the engraver, in fact, surrenders himself unreservedly to the mood, caprice, and idiom of the designer."[56]

The New School wood engravers were often responding to artists' experiments with media and styles. Yet there were limits. The same critic who liked Abbey's "Almond Blossom" disapproved of the impressionistic images in the same issue designed by H. Bolton Jones and his brother F. C. Jones to illustrate "A Day in Africa," finding them characterized by "bad drawing, mussiness, unintelligible detail." The critic much preferred the illustrations for "The White Mountains," done in a more familiar style that conveyed "the spirit of Birket Foster and Fenn."[57]

For some audiences, the type of work Fenn had been doing for more than a decade was still appealing. During this period he continued to experiment with irregular page layouts and designs that combined two or more viewpoints, as he had for *Picturesque Palestine*. He would also take advantage of the New School

New Clients, New Technologies, New Home

engravers by creating works in watercolor, pen, and, apparently, charcoal or soft graphite for them to engrave. And when the technology of process line blocks was developed in the mid-1880s, he would experiment with large, bold ink drawings that could be photographed to prepare relief printing plates. Toward the end of the decade, when photogravure technology was applied to book illustration, Fenn would create works for that process as well.

FENN'S WORK FOR PERIODICALS, EARLY TO MID-1880s
Images of Europe and America for the *Century* and *Harper's Monthly*

The New York publishing world of the 1880s was larger and more competitive than in the late 1860s and early 1870s. Fenn chose to work as a freelance artist, accepting commissions from a wide range of publishers, especially the leading illustrated periodicals. For the next decade, he was most closely associated with the *Century,* to which he regularly contributed landscapes and architectural views. The Century Company's building was on Seventeenth Street at Union Square, some six blocks from Fenn's Twenty-third Street studio.[58] Although he was acquainted with the magazine's editor, Richard Watson Gilder, his main contact was probably Alexander W. Drake, who served as art director for both the *Century* and *St. Nicholas* for some forty years. He also oversaw the printing of images, "carefully revising the work of the overlayer, and taking to both overlayer and pressman, as guides to their work, not only the artists' fine proofs, but even the originals" to achieve tones that were as accurate as possible.[59] Drake was known for encouraging artists and holding engravers to a high standard. In the words of Joseph Pennell: "He has done more for the advancement of illustration than any man living."[60]

Among Fenn's illustrations for the *Century,* many depict places familiar from his years abroad or show his use of the graphic approaches he had honed while working on *Picturesque Europe* and *Picturesque Palestine.* An example of the latter can be seen in his first assignment for the magazine. For John Muir's article "The Bee-Pastures of California," which appeared in the June and July 1882 issues, several of his designs combine close-ups of flowers and plants with distant views, similar to several of his illustrations in *Picturesque Palestine* (see, for example, fig. 4.18). This type of image must have held appeal at the time, for many other illustrators used similar approaches. In one case the designer of a new edition of Owen Meredith's *Lucile* updated some of the illustrations by adding flower surrounds.[61]

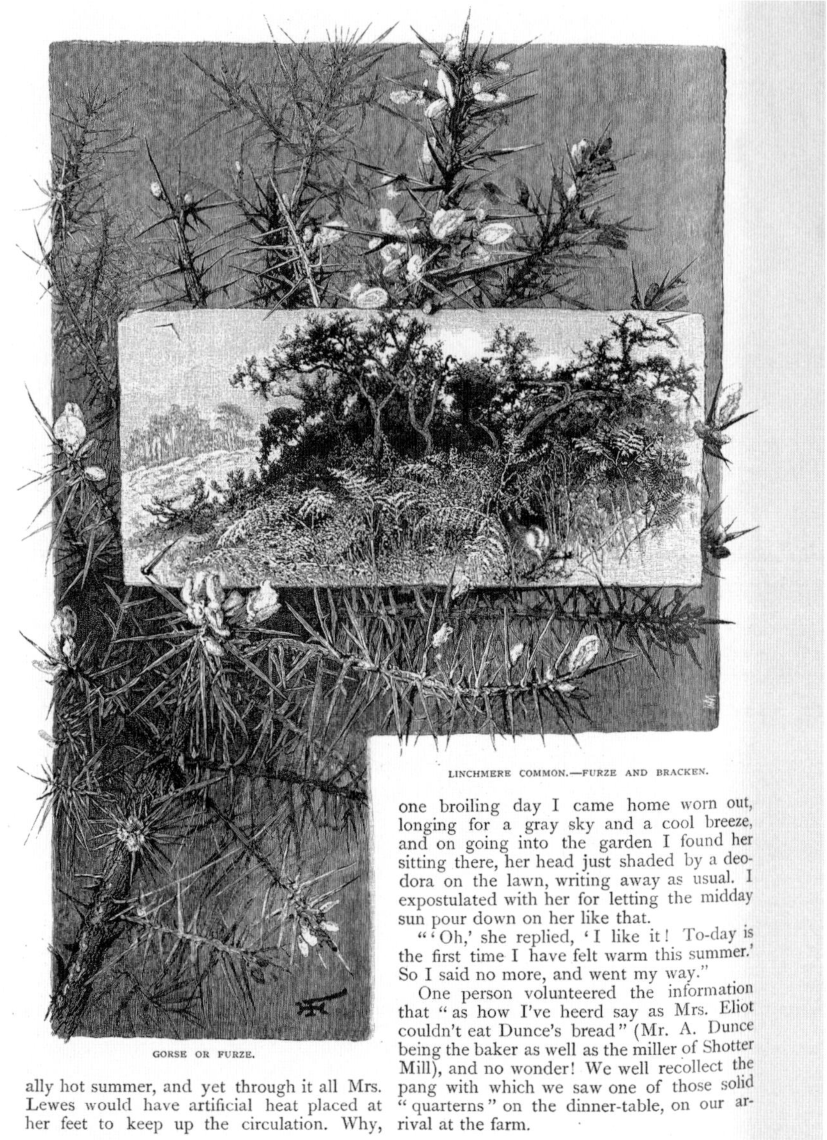

one broiling day I came home worn out, longing for a gray sky and a cool breeze, and on going into the garden I found her sitting there, her head just shaded by a deodora on the lawn, writing away as usual. I expostulated with her for letting the midday sun pour down on her like that.

"'Oh,' she replied, 'I like it! To-day is the first time I have felt warm this summer.' So I said no more, and went my way."

One person volunteered the information that "as how I've heerd say as Mrs. Eliot couldn't eat Dunce's bread" (Mr. A. Dunce being the baker as well as the miller of Shotter Mill), and no wonder! We well recollect the pang with which we saw one of those solid "quarters" on the dinner-table, on our arrival at the farm.

ally hot summer, and yet through it all Mrs. Lewes would have artificial heat placed at her feet to keep up the circulation. Why,

The subjects of many of Fenn's subsequent commissions suggest that *Picturesque Europe* had whetted, but not satisfied, the public's appetite for information on Britain and Europe. The August 1882 "Midsummer Holiday Number" of the *Century* opened with Alice Maude Fenn's aforementioned article "The Borderlands of Surrey," illustrated with her father's images of the area in England where they had last lived. The wood engravings, done by some of the New School engravers, interpreted the variety of media he had used in the originals. For example, "Linchmere Common.—Furze and Bracken" (fig. 5.5) shows Fenn's close-up watercolor-

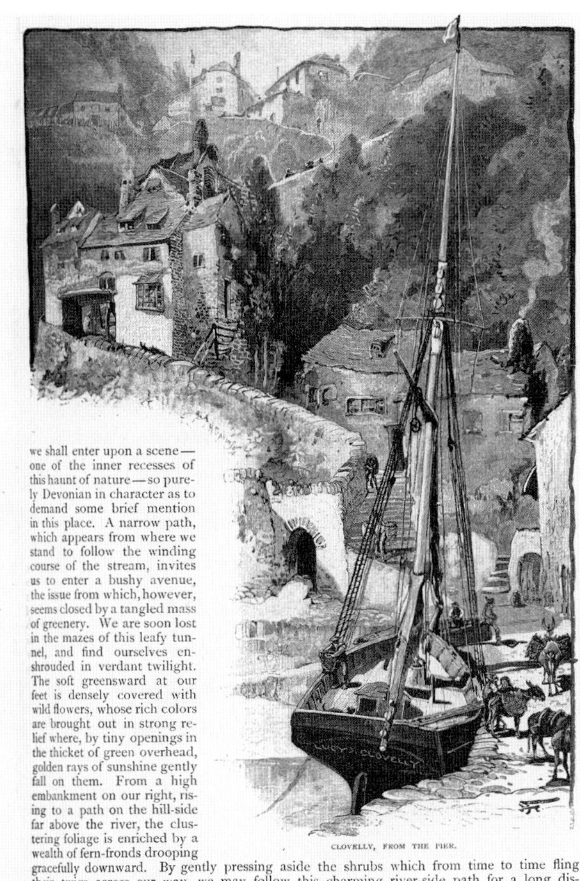

5.6. Harry Fenn, "Clovelly, from the Pier," in "The Fairest County of England" by Francis George Heath. *Century,* December 1883, 173. Wood engraving, approx. 7 1/2" x 5 1/4".

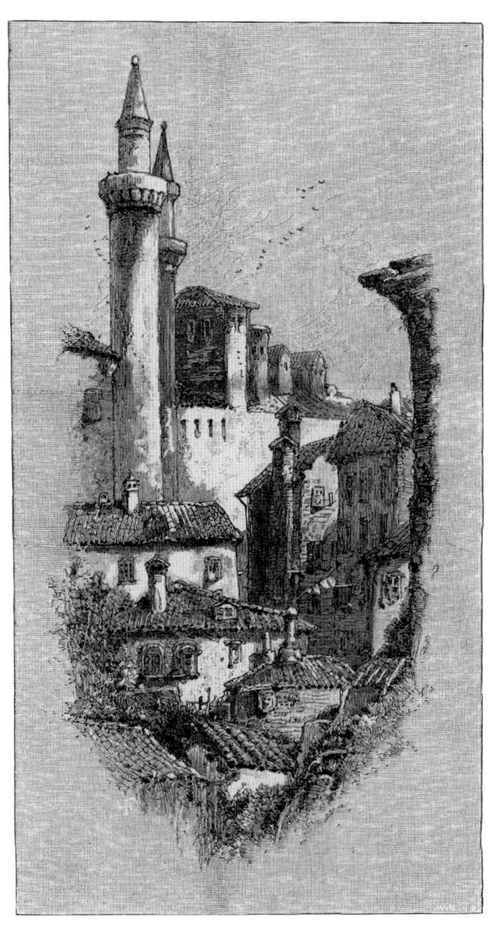

5.7. Harry Fenn, "In Urbino," in "Notes on the Exile of Dante" by Sarah Freeman Clarke. *Century,* March 1884, 751. Wood engraving, 6 6/16" x 3 3/8".

like image of gorse, or furze—depicted with trompe l'oeil precision—on a toned background, beyond which some of the long thorns extend onto the white of the page while others pierce a small pen-and-ink-like landscape, holding it in place.[62] The resulting intricate and overlapping planes create an image of great interest. To understand the much greater variety of effects achieved by New School wood engravers, compare this illustration with figure 4.23, "Ma'yan Musa, The Spring of Moses" from *Picturesque Palestine,* in which it is impossible to identify the media originally used to depict the inset landscape and surrounding fern.

Fenn illustrated another lead article set abroad—"The Fairest County of England," Francis George Heath's account of Devonshire—for the *Century*'s December 1883 issue. As engraved by Henry Davidson, his view titled "Clovelly, from the Pier" has the look of a watercolor (fig. 5.6). Again, a comparison with a conventional wood engraving, figure 3.25, "A New York River Front" from *Picturesque America,* high-

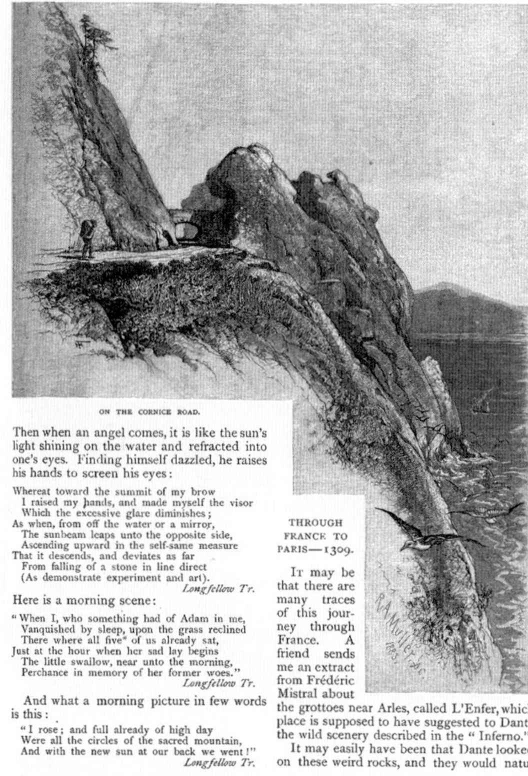

ON THE CORNICE ROAD.

Then when an angel comes, it is like the sun's light shining on the water and refracted into one's eyes. Finding himself dazzled, he raises his hands to screen his eyes:

Whereat toward the summit of my brow
  I raised my hands, and made myself the visor
  Which the excessive glare diminishes;
As when, from off the water or a mirror,
  The sunbeam leaps unto the opposite side,
  Ascending upward in the self-same measure
That it descends, and deviates as far
  From falling of a stone in line direct
  (As demonstrate experiment and art).
          Longfellow Tr.

Here is a morning scene:

"When I, who something had of Adam in me,
  Vanquished by sleep, upon the grass reclined
  There where all five* of us already sat,
Just at the hour when her sad lay begins
  The little swallow, near unto the morning,
  Perchance in memory of her former woes."
          Longfellow Tr.

And what a morning picture in few words is this:

"I rose; and full already of high day
Were all the circles of the sacred mountain,
And with the new sun at our back we went!"
          Longfellow Tr.

THROUGH FRANCE TO PARIS—1309.

It may be that there are many traces of this journey through France. A friend sends me an extract from Frédéric Mistral about the grottoes near Arles, called L'Enfer, which place is supposed to have suggested to Dante the wild scenery described in the "Inferno."

It may easily have been that Dante looked on these weird rocks, and they would natu-

* "Virgil, Sordello, Dante, Nino, and Conrad. And here Dante falls upon the grass, and sleeps till dawn. There is a long pause of rest and sleep between this line and the next, which makes the whole passage doubly beautiful. The narrative recommences like the twitter of early birds just beginning to stir in the woods." *From Longfellow, Translator's Notes.*

5.8. Harry Fenn, "On the Cornice Road," in "Notes on the Exile of Dante." *Century,* April 1884, 835. Wood engraving by R. A. Muller, 6 13/16" x 5 3/16".

lights the way Davidson's finely engraved lines convey the tones of a watercolor. Fenn's illustrations for "Among the Red Roofs of Sussex" (September 1885), a second article by his daughter about the region in which they had lived, were praised by a critic for the *Brooklyn Daily Eagle* as truly representing the "English atmosphere" and capturing "that moist, mellow quality that pervades the air of England, tempering the sunshine and giving softness and richness to color."[63] The critic also took note of Fenn's return, albeit a little belatedly: "It is a pleasure to find Mr. Fenn among the illustrators once more. He is a man of great cleverness, and beyond an occasional edginess of line in his figures there is little to carp at."[64]

For "Notes on the Exile of Dante," in the March and April 1884 issues of the *Century,* Fenn redrew sketches by the author and artist Sarah Freeman Clarke (1808–1896), a member of the Transcendentalist circle. It was one of many instances of Fenn reworking photographs or sketches of a region familiar to him. His designs show the range of media now available to illustrators and the varied effects that New School wood engravers were able to achieve. "In Urbino" (fig. 5.7) has the look of an etching, with the rectangular gray background surrounded by a black line delineating the paper on which it is printed, whereas "On the Cornice Road" (fig. 5.8), as interpreted by the many different types of lines and stippling of R. A. Muller, appears to have been drawn originally in soft graphite or charcoal. And "Rue du Fouarre, Paris" (fig. 5.9), with its dark shapes and soft lines, appears to reproduce an oil painting, a most unusual choice of medium for Fenn. With such variations in tone and detail, it's no wonder a public long accustomed to conventional wood engravings was amazed.

Other illustrations for Clarke's article dispensed with the services of a wood engraver altogether; instead, process line cuts were used. Faster and less expensive than wood engraving, this photoengraving method produced a relief metal plate from a photographic negative of an original ink drawing.[65] Fenn was highly skilled in pen and ink and embraced this emerging technology; his "Monte Reggione"

New Clients, New Technologies, New Home

(fig. 5.10) provides a good example of how it could reproduce crisp black lines. Together with the wood-engraving techniques of the New School, the process line cut opened up exciting possibilities in illustration, allowing artists to try a wider range of media and gain new appreciation of their abilities.

Fenn's assignments with other publishers also allowed him to draw upon his familiarity with the British Isles and the countries of Europe and, in turn, brought him attention from the press. Clearly, he did not share the fierce loyalty to the *Century* that Joseph Pennell recalled experiencing when he was just starting off as a staff artist: "I felt myself a most important factor in the success of The Century . . . and under no circumstances would I have worked for the rival [*Harper's Monthly*], nor would any of the Century artists."[66] For *Harper's Monthly,* Fenn prepared illustrations for W. H. Rideing's June 1882 article "Quaint Old Yarmouth" as well as a February 1883 article titled "The Wild Welsh Coast" by Wirt Sikes, the American consul in Cardiff.[67] Although the wood engravings in *Harper's Monthly* were similar to those in the *Century,* the printing quality was often less crisp and the tones less varied. Nevertheless, the *New York Times* praised Fenn's Welsh coast illustrations as "picturesque and striking to an extent rarely seen in the magazine work of the times."[68] A particularly striking example is "The Huntsman's Leap" (fig. 5.11), which recalls "Gray Man's Path," one of Fenn's images of Ireland from *Picturesque Europe* (see fig. 4.12). The *Critic*'s

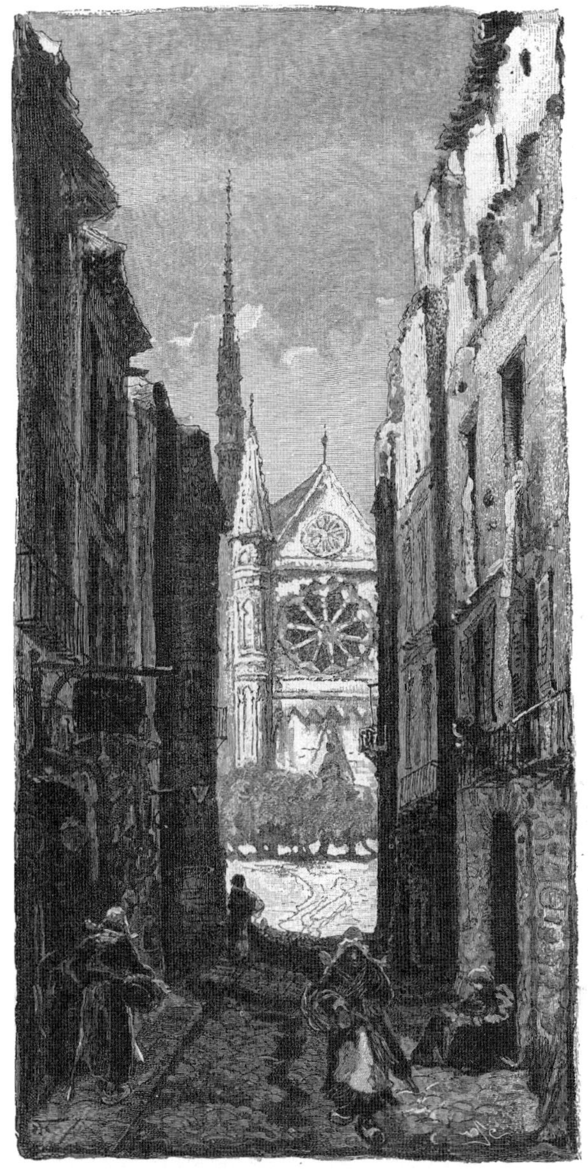

5.9. Harry Fenn, "Rue de Fouarre, Paris," in "Notes on the Exile of Dante." *Century,* April 1884, 836. Wood engraving, 6 7/8" x 3 1/4".

reviewer also approved of what he considered a "bolder style of drawing," noting that Fenn had "dropped altogether his Birket Foster mannerisms."[69] Whereas earlier critics had applauded the long-familiar style of Fenn's mentor, decades later others had come to view it as "too uniformly bright and pretty," and lacking in "strength."[70]

Other Harper commissions took Fenn back to favorite American haunts, demonstrating once again that appealing illustrations of a particular region often led

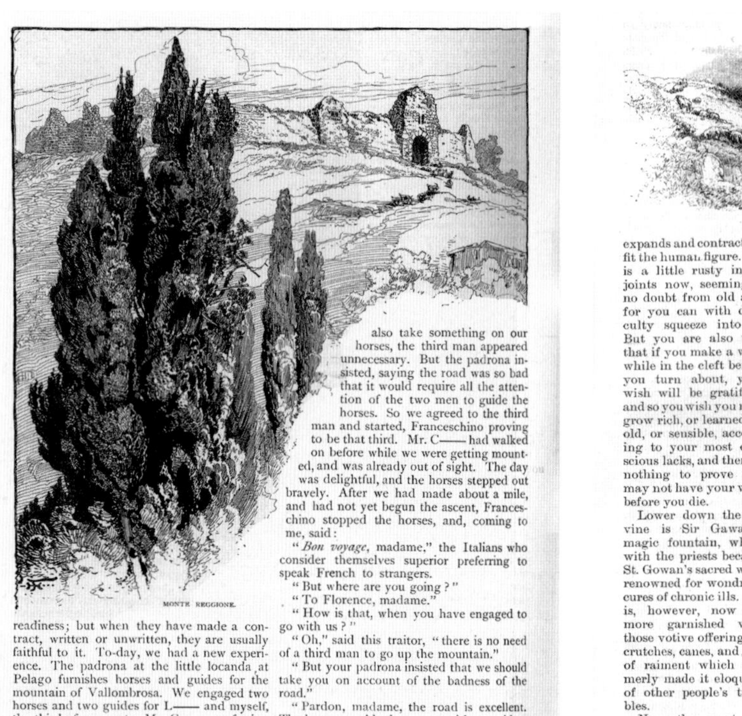

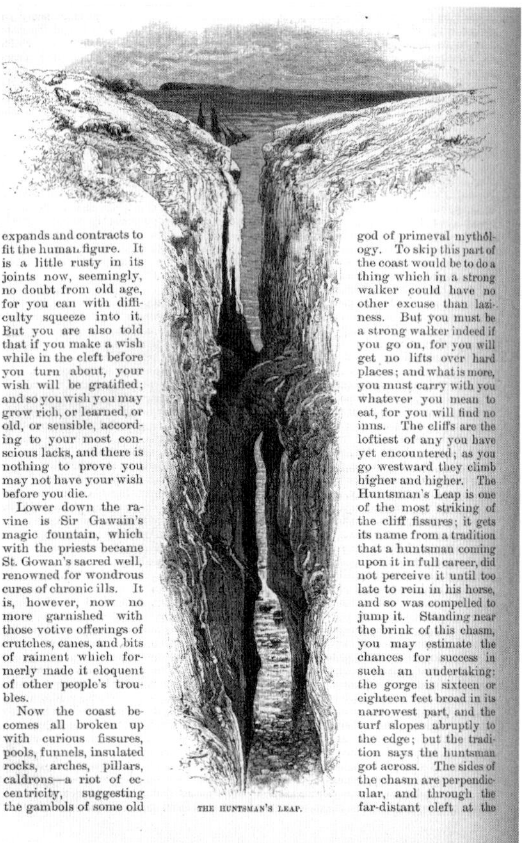

5.10. Harry Fenn, "Monte Reggione," in "Notes on the Exile of Dante." *Century*, March 1884, 740. Process line cut, 5 3/4" x 5 3/16".

5.11. Harry Fenn, "The Huntsman's Leap," in "The Wild Welsh Coast" by Wirt Sikes. *Harper's New Monthly Magazine*, February 1883, 348. Wood engraving, approx. 7 5/8" x 4 7/8".

to more professional opportunities. Instructions written by Fenn on his original drawings for some of these jobs suggest he frequently interacted with the engravers preparing the woodblocks, thus ensuring the best possible outcome. For the September 1883 *Harper's Monthly* he illustrated the Catskills, a region he had covered for *Picturesque America,* but the subjects he selected for Lucy C. Lillie's article were different, and in preparing them he used a variety of media. A note on his large, bold rendering for "Haine's Falls," done in brown and white watercolor (fig. 5.12), shows him taking advantage of the then-routine use of photography for transfer-ring images to blocks. To facilitate an addition he hoped to make, he wrote in the margin: "Please photograph it on a block that will give half an inch more at the bottom. I want to put a little more water."[71]

For the January 1884 *Harper's Monthly,* Fenn illustrated "The Quaker Poet," an article about his friend John Greenleaf Whittier written by another friend, Harriet

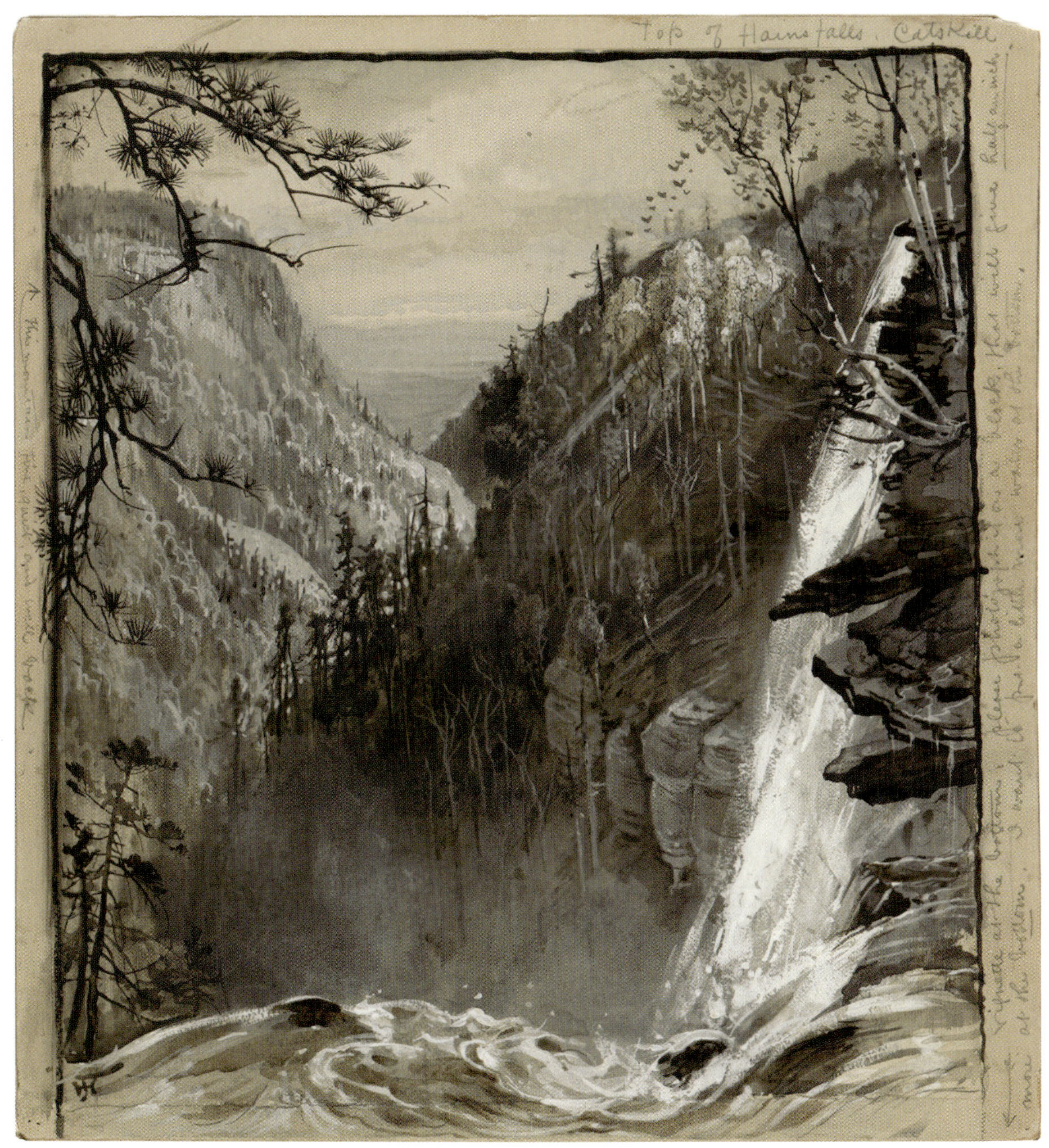

5.12. Harry Fenn, *Haine's Falls, Catskills,* ca. 1883. Wash drawing, monochromatic, board, 14" x 12 1/2"; image 13 1/2" x 11 1/4". (Cabinet of American Illustration, Library of Congress Prints and Photographs Division, Washington, D.C.)

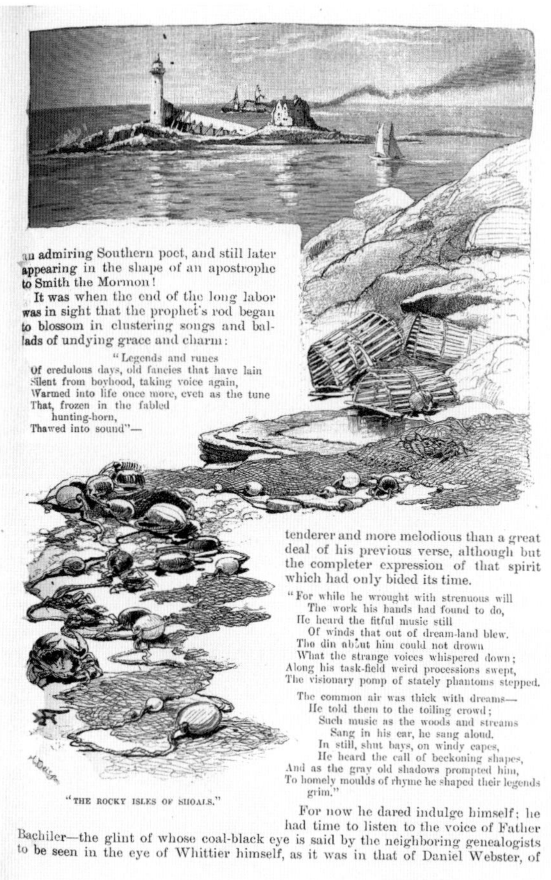

5.13. Harry Fenn, "The Rocky Isles of Shoals," in "The Quaker Poet" by Harriet Prescott Spofford. *Harper's Monthly*, January 1884, 177. Wood engraving by H. Deis, 7" x 4 3/4".

Prescott Spofford,[72] that offered him a chance to treat his old acquaintance Celia Thaxter's territory in a new way. "The Rocky Isles of Shoals" gives a distant view of the lighthouse on its tiny island from a rocky outcrop where nets and lobster traps wind down the page and through the type (fig. 5.13). For the July 1885 issue, he revisited (in his imagination at least) Mount Desert Island, Maine, through illustrations for the poem "Midsummer on Mount Desert," as well as the Adirondacks for an article titled "Ampersand" by Henry J. van Dyke Jr.—the first of several collaborations with this well-known minister and writer.[73]

Fenn returned to the Niagara Falls region to prepare illustrations for "The Neighborhood of the International Park," an August 1887 article by Jane Meade Welch that celebrated the recent establishment by New York State and Canada of a large park to protect the area surrounding the falls. Fenn's black, gray, and white watercolor *Thorn-Trees near Niagara* (fig. 5.14) includes his handwritten instructions to the wood engraver: "Cut the ground up & down very simple[,] quiet, giving all the importance to the 'Jagged Thorn Trees.'" Comparing this painting with the wood engraving (fig. 5.15) shows that Anderson did use vertical lines to depict the grassy foreground; but the less effective use of white space behind the trees renders the wood engraving less dramatic than Fenn's large wash drawing. For some of the other pictures for this article, wood engravers worked directly from images of photographs on the block, a taste of the great changes to come.[74]

Work for "Battles and Leaders of the Civil War"

Besides assignments to depict the scenery of the United States and other parts of the world, themselves indicative of a growing cosmopolitanism among subscribers, Fenn participated in an important project whose aim was national reconciliation. Beginning in 1884 he was a conspicuous contributor to "Battles and Leaders of

New Clients, New Technologies, New Home

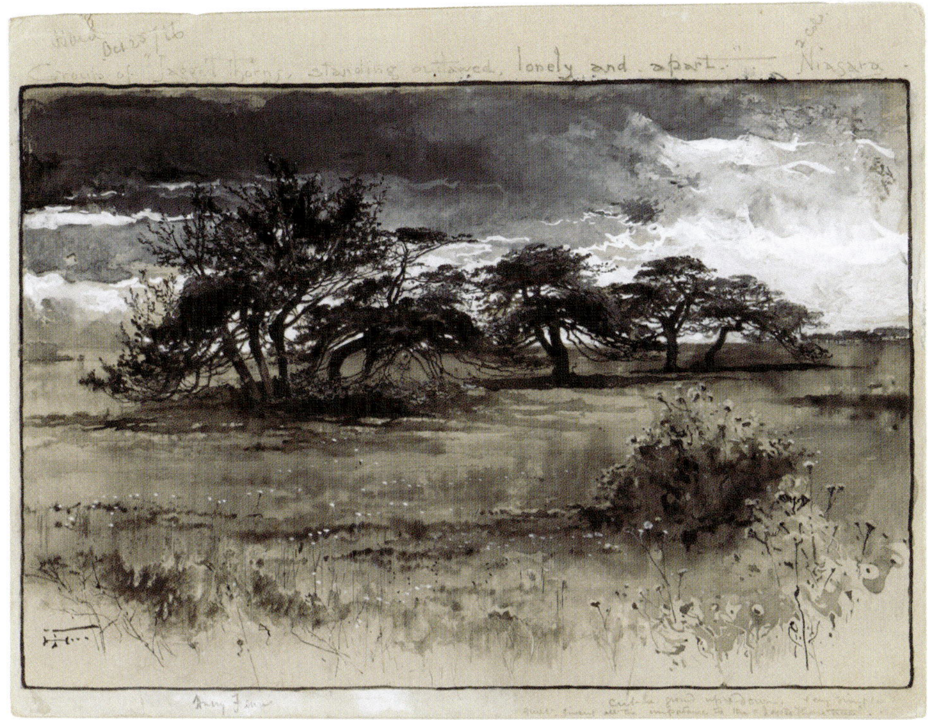

5.14. Harry Fenn, *Thorn-Trees near Niagara,* ca. 1887. Wash drawing on board, 11 3/4" x 14"; image 9 1/4" x 13 1/2". (Cabinet of American Illustration, Library of Congress Prints and Photographs Division, Washington, D.C.)

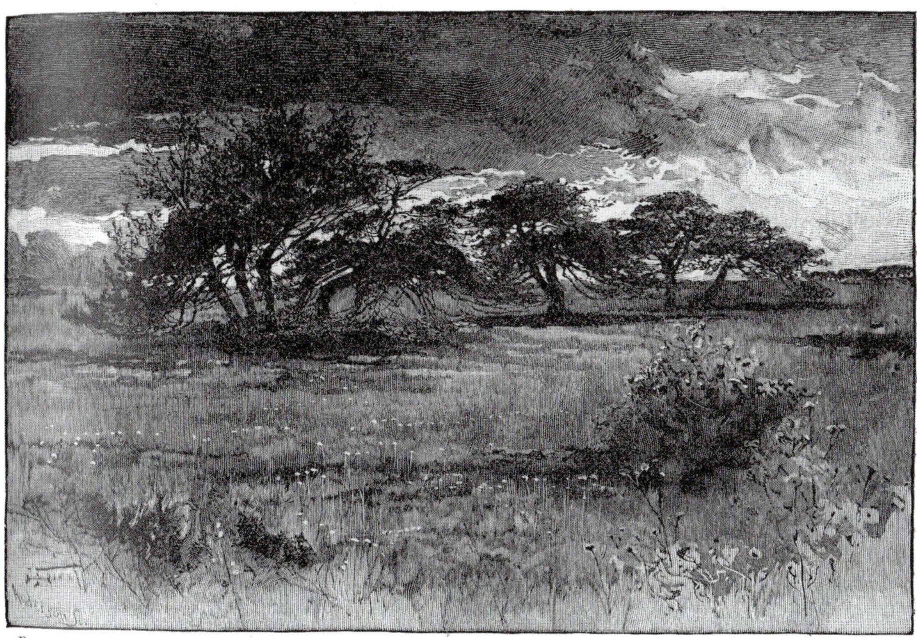

5.15. Harry Fenn, Thorn-Trees near Niagara," in "The Neighborhood of the International Park" by Jane Meade Welch. *Harper's Monthly,* August 1887, 337. Wood engraving by Anderson, 3 1/4" x 4 3/4".

the Civil War," a long-running series in the *Century* that was its most ambitious to date. Almost twenty years had passed since the war. The political turmoil of Reconstruction had quieted, and there was a growing interest in the events and meaning of this historic struggle. Many who had lived through that time of trauma and upheaval were ready to recount their experiences and make peace with former adversaries. Union and Confederate veterans were beginning to gather for commemorative events on battlefields, and publishers such as Kurz & Allison sold large chromolithographs of battle scenes to a public eager for visual reminders. The *Century*'s plan was to solicit reminiscences from commanders and soldiers on both sides of every battle and then publish these accounts accompanied by illustrations. The magazine's editor, Richard Watson Gilder, and his associates Clarence Clough Buel and Richard Underwood Johnson "rightly judged that articles celebrating the skill and valor of both sides would hasten the elimination of sectional prejudices and contribute toward reuniting the country by the cultivation of mutual respect."[75] Hoping to reach wide audiences in the South as well as the North, they avoided such divisive topics as race and slavery, thus likely excluding African Americans from the effects of a collective reconciliation.[76]

Gilder expected that the series would be "the most important thing, historically . . . in this century" and "a flank movement on all our rivals."[77] It was launched in November 1884 with the first installment, "The Battle of Bull Run." A few months later in his "Topics of the Time" column, Gilder wrote that although they had expected a cordial reception for their timely and "non-political discussion" of the war, they were "hardly prepared for the almost unbroken response of welcome which has greeted the enterprise, whether in the generous notice of the press, or in the large number of encouraging and helpful letters" arriving "from all sections of the country," all of which resulted in an "extraordinary increase of the circulation of the magazine."[78] Installments appeared from November 1884 through December 1887, during which time circulation doubled to a quarter million.[79] In 1888 the Century Company published the papers from the series, plus additional articles and illustrations, as a four-volume set titled *Battles and Leaders of the Civil War,* which sold more than 75,000 copies.

Illustrations for the series included portraits, maps, and battle scenes; these last were based on wartime or later drawings or photographs, which were reproduced as wood engravings or process line blocks. Fenn was prominent among a host of participating artist-illustrators, including J. O. Davidson, Theodore R. Davis, Edwin Forbes, Winslow Homer, Edwin J. Meeker, Joseph Pennell, William Ludwell Sheppard, Walton Tabor, Charles Vanderhoof, Alfred R. Waud, and John

New Clients, New Technologies, New Home

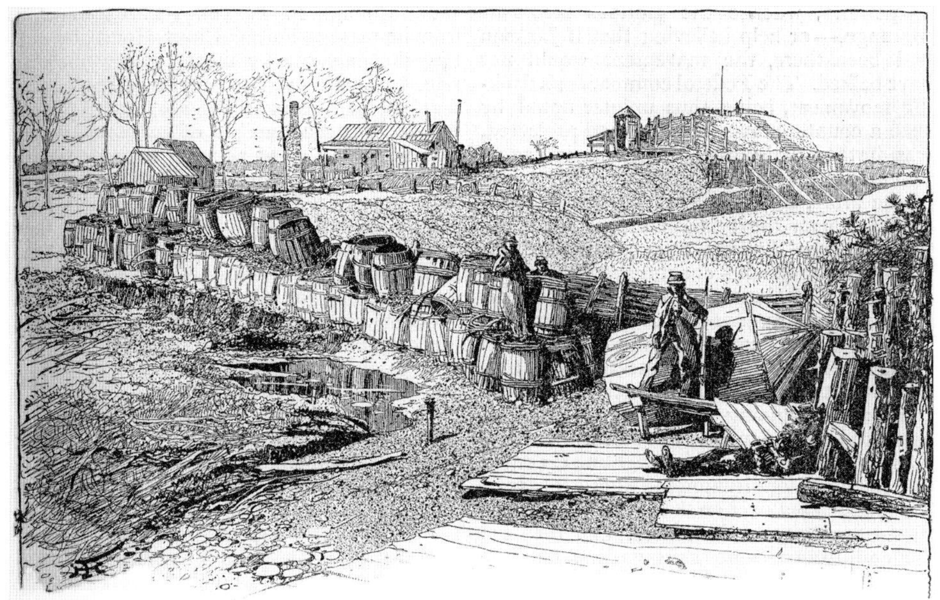

CONFEDERATE FORTIFICATIONS ABOUT MANASSAS JUNCTION.
[This view is from a photograph taken in March, 1862. It represents the works substantially as they were at the time of the battle.]

Douglas Woodward; a few of these men had fought in the conflict or served as special war artists for *Harper's Weekly* or *Frank Leslie's Illustrated Newspaper*.[80] For his many contributions, Fenn was able to choose the medium that best suited the subject, either ink (primarily line drawings, for buildings and trees), which were reproduced as process line blocks, or tonal watercolors (for landscapes), which were interpreted by wood engravers. His participation began with the opening article, G. T. Beauregard's account of Bull Run, to which he contributed four illustrations, basing two on photographs from 1862. "Confederate Fortifications about Manassas Junction" (fig. 5.16), which the caption claims represented "the works substantially as they were at the time of the battle," was printed at a much-reduced size from a process line block of Fenn's precise ink drawing.[81]

Typically, his drawings were two to four times the size of the illustrations made from them, in keeping with the needs of the new line cut process, which required larger originals to ensure that line quality was maintained at the smaller scale. In fact, the art instructor Ernest Knaufft (1864–1942) advised aspiring illustrators to make their originals "eight times as large as the illustration" and the lines "four times as far apart."[82] Fenn sometimes expressed concern about the quality of reproduction of his ink drawings. On one example, *Present Aspect of Gaines's Mill* (fig. 5.17), which is full of intricate brickwork, twigs, and sycamore seedpods, he wrote: "Get *this* as large as you can. The detail is so very fine that it will go for nothing if *very much reduced*." As

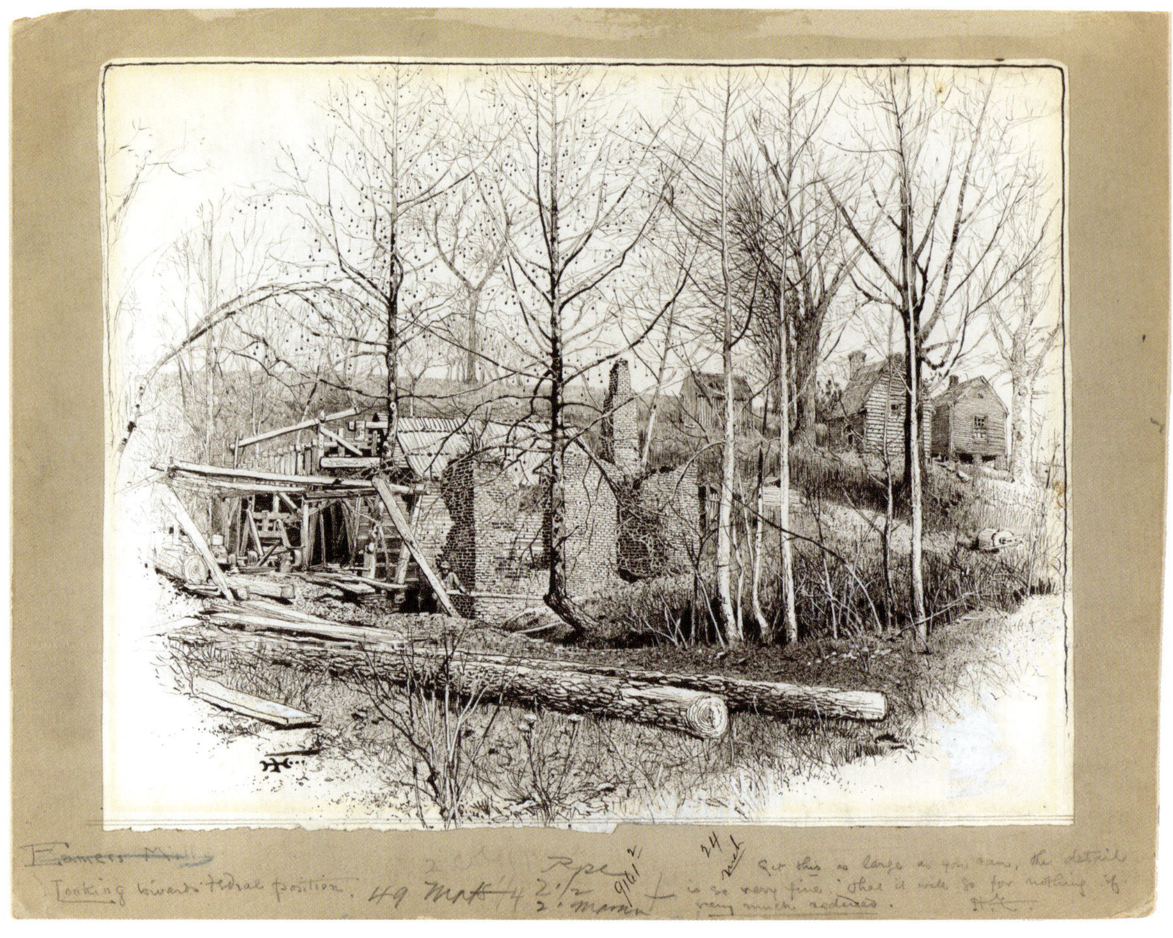

5.17. Harry Fenn, *Present Aspect of Gaines's Mill, looking East,* 1885. Pen and black ink, white gouache on off-white paper, lined on board, 10 1/8" x 12 3/4". (Cooper-Hewitt, National Design Museum, Smithsonian Institution, 1947-87-17. Gift of Willis M. Rose. Photo by Matt Flynn; Cooper-Hewitt, National Design Museum, Smithsonian Institution / Art Resource, New York.)

it appeared in the June 1885 *Century,* measuring 4 1/4 by 5 1/4 inches (reduced from the approximately 10-by-12 3/4-inch original), much was indeed lost. About "The Malvern House" (fig. 5.18), another of Fenn's precise ink drawings reproduced as a line block, a critic commented: "Fenn has an eye like a camera, especially for that most confusing of work, the drawing of branches in groups where trees interlock. His picture of 'Malvern House,' where he sees every brick and shingle, while at the same time his drawing preserves a certain breadth, is a notable instance of close observation."[83]

Fenn used a much different approach in depicting the battle of Belmont, in which the Union gun-boats *Tyler* and *Lexington* fired from the Mississippi River onto Confederate batteries at Columbus, Kentucky. For this scene, he produced a gouache

New Clients, New Technologies, New Home

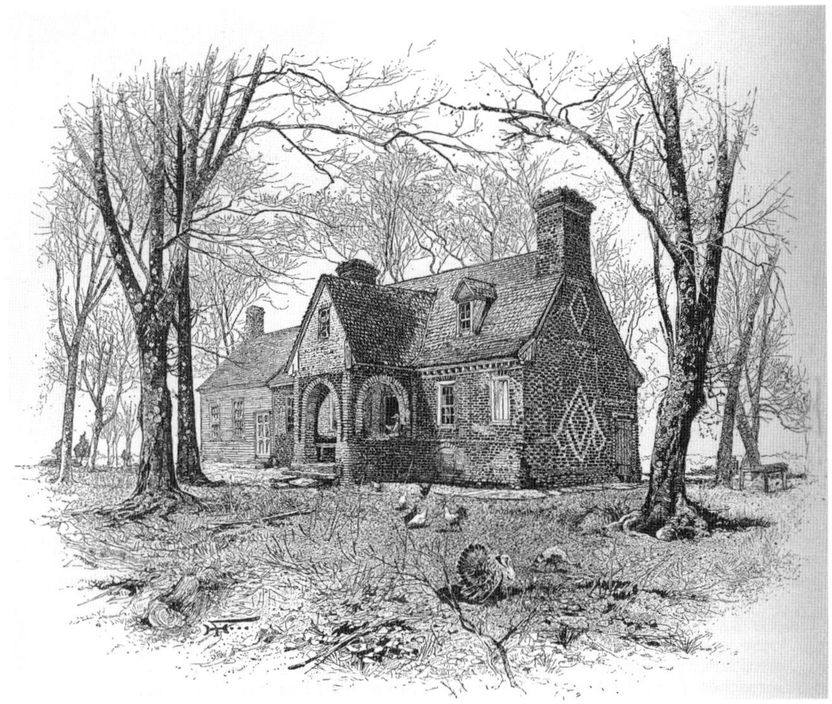

5.18. Harry Fenn, "The Malvern House. (Drawn by Harry Fenn, After Photograph by E. S. Anderson.)," in "The Last of the Seven Days' Battle" by Fitz John Porter. *Century*, August 1885, 620. Process line cut, 4 1/4" x 5".

watercolor in tones of brown, black, and gray, based on a contemporary sketch by Admiral Henry Walke, who also wrote the account (fig. 5.19). The watercolor was reproduced as a highly tonal wood engraving by Sylvester in January 1885. Another of Fenn's watercolors, *Defense of Cage's Ford,* includes dozens of soldiers sprawled in the foreground, a challenge that the artist and engraver executed well.[84]

Fenn continued to participate in the "Battles and Leaders" series until its completion in both the magazine and subsequent four-volume set, all while carrying out myriad other assignments. He was one of the project's earliest and most prolific artists, just as he had been for *Picturesque America,* once again contributing to an important cultural landmark. According to Civil War historian Bruce Catton, the work was crucial in healing the nation's wounds:

The noble *Battles and Leaders* collection of pictures and accounts . . . resolutely and without making a fuss about it treated the great tragedy as a matter of pride and loss for people of both sides. There was no attempt to draw a moral, to preach, or to urge mutual forgiveness; there was simply the unspoken assumption behind every paragraph and every picture that somewhere

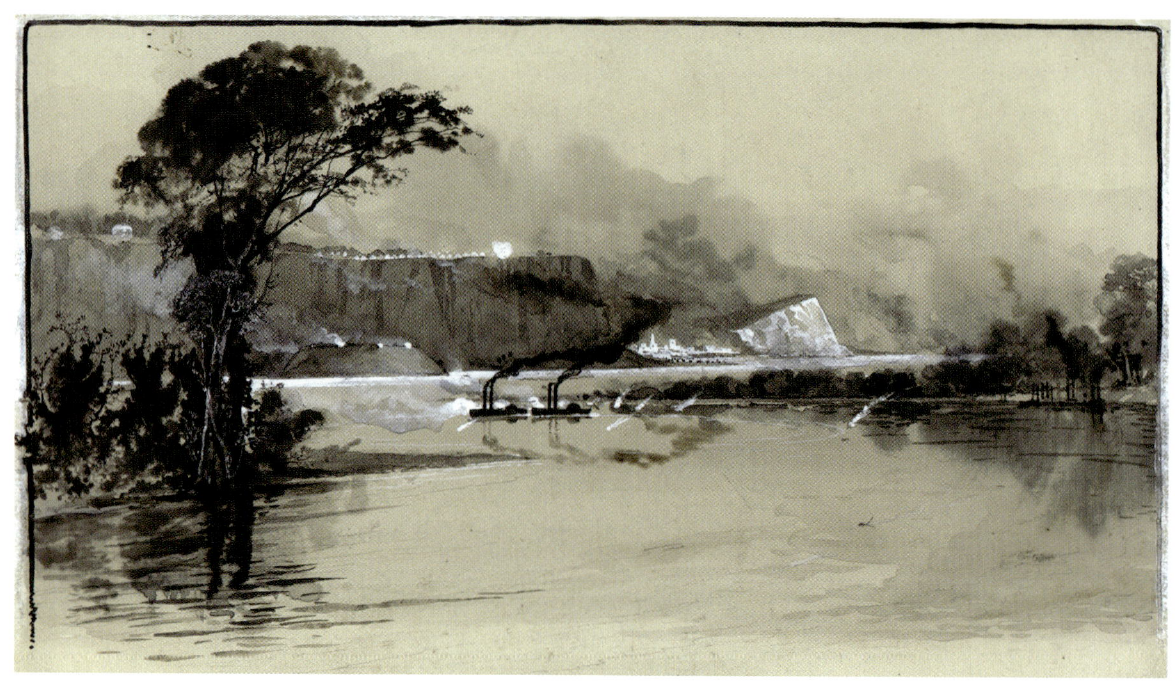

5.19. Harry Fenn, *Battle of Belmont*, ca. 1884. Graphite, wash, and gouache, 8" x 14 1/4". (Private collection.)

beyond guilt and beyond blame the people of America had fought to extricate themselves from an unendurable situation and, doing so, had established a better base for all future years.

These pictures helped to filter out the evil and the ugliness. If they unintentionally lent a tinge of romance to what was underneath everything a matter of unrelieved tragedy, it was a romance the country desperately needed.[85]

DEPICTING ARCHITECTURE

Fenn further contributed to American culture and confidence through his skillful renderings of architecture, a topic also receiving increased attention at the time. The *Century*'s art editor, Alexander W. Drake, often chose him to illustrate historic buildings for the "Battles and Leaders" series and later features on both historic and new buildings, and fellow illustrator Joseph Pennell wrote that his older colleague "might almost be said to have invented the artistic illustration of architecture in America."[86] The art critic Royal Cortissoz considered him one of the few artists whose depictions "added a true sense of architectural structure to the feeling for pictorial charm."[87]

Fenn typically departed from straightforward frontal views, choosing instead a high or low viewpoint combined with a diagonal or corner perspective that

New Clients, New Technologies, New Home

showed the full volume of a building. He drew freehand instead of using a straightedge and employed a wide variety of line weights. According to Pennell, Fenn used "a different line for each substance."[88] Highly skilled with perspective, he was able to successfully capture the recesses and projections of facades, avoiding dull, flat planes and showing the play of light on surfaces. He further enhanced interest by setting a building within its context. When the editor of *American Architect,* William Rotch Ware (1848–1917), organized a competition of the best pen and ink artists, Fenn's works were among the favorites, along with those of Francis H. Bacon and Wilson Eyre.[89]

The 1876 Centennial Exposition, a celebration of the nation's founding one hundred years earlier, had revived interest in the architecture and history of the colonial period and given impetus to a nascent preservation movement. One of the most popular exhibits at the Philadelphia fair—the "New England Log-House and Kitchen"—was an idealized space furnished with such heirlooms as a clock, cradle, desk, and spinning wheel. It sparked a fashion for collecting American antiques, to which the country's illustrated magazines responded throughout the next decade with features on historic architecture. As a prominent contributor, Fenn fostered this interest as well. For the *Century*'s March 1884 article "Old Public Buildings in America" by Richard Grant White (the scholarly father of architect Stanford White), Fenn prepared views of the Massachusetts State House in Boston as well as churches there and in New York, Wilmington, Delaware, and Montreal. "Old South Church, Boston" depicts the meeting house that had recently been saved from demolition but was still under threat; it was a building that, according to White, united "religious and patriotic associations" more than any other structure in America.[90] As was typical of his style, Fenn composed his ink and watercolor drawing using a high viewpoint and corner perspective (fig. 5.20). This and most of the other images were reproduced as wood engravings, although Fenn's "Old State House, Boston" appears to be a process line cut of an ink drawing. (See Appendix 1 for additional illustrations).[91]

In 1885 Fenn once again made a tour of the South, this time to draw historic buildings for the *Century;*[92] the popular nature writer John Burroughs accompanied him, at least in Kentucky. His images of the homes of several key statesmen and founding fathers appeared in 1886 and 1887: Henry Clay's Ashland in Lexington, Kentucky, where the current owner named a colt "Harry Fenn" in honor of the artist's visit (December 1886);[93] Thomas Jefferson's Monticello, near Charlottesville, Virginia, with the appearance of the images coinciding with the celebration of the one-hundredth anniversary of the framing of the Constitution (September 1887)[94]; and George Washington's Mount Vernon (November 1887).

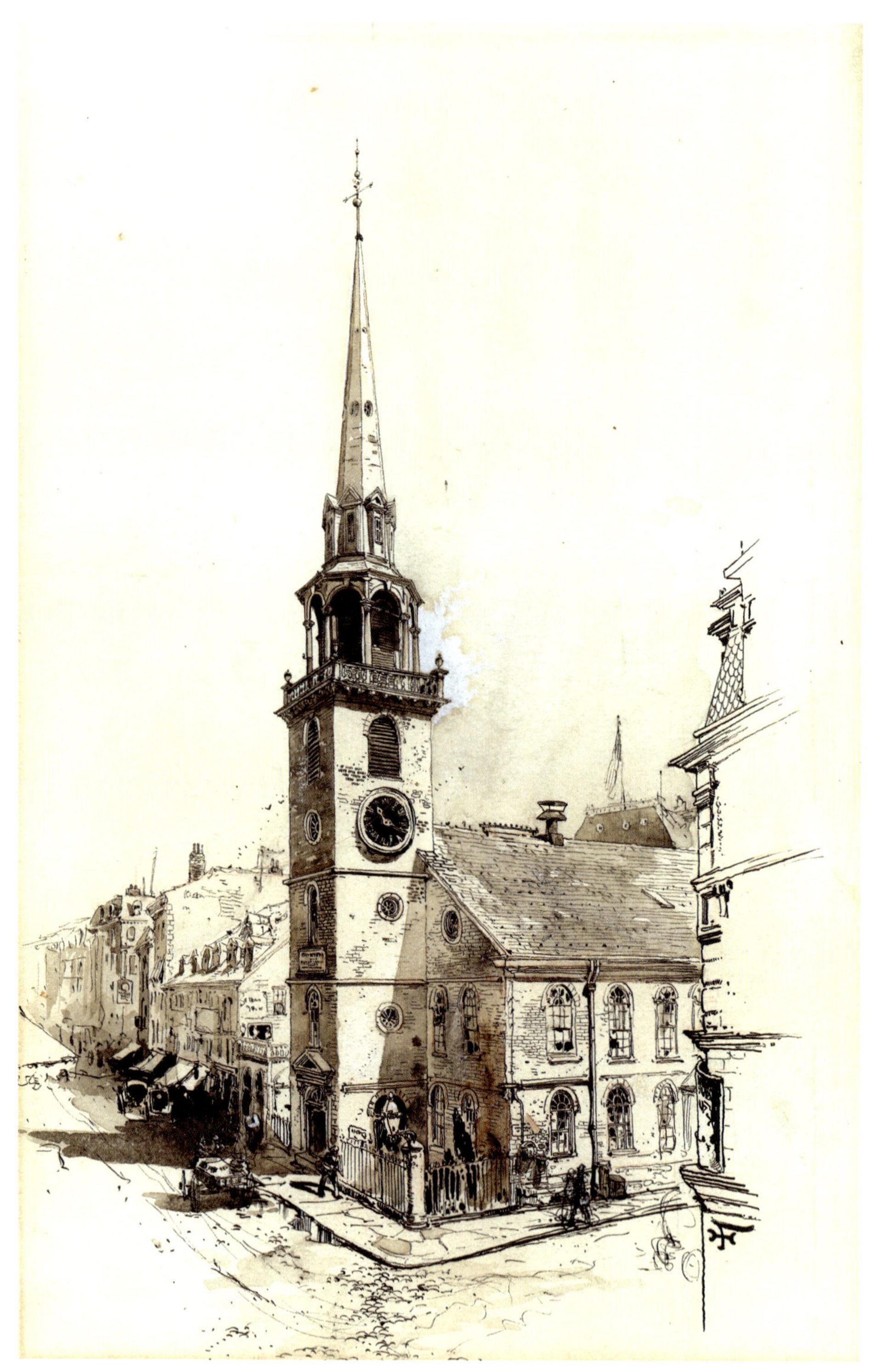

5.20. Harry Fenn, drawing for "Old South Church, Boston," ca. 1884. Pen, wash, and gouache on paper on board, 13" x 8 1/2". (Private collection.)

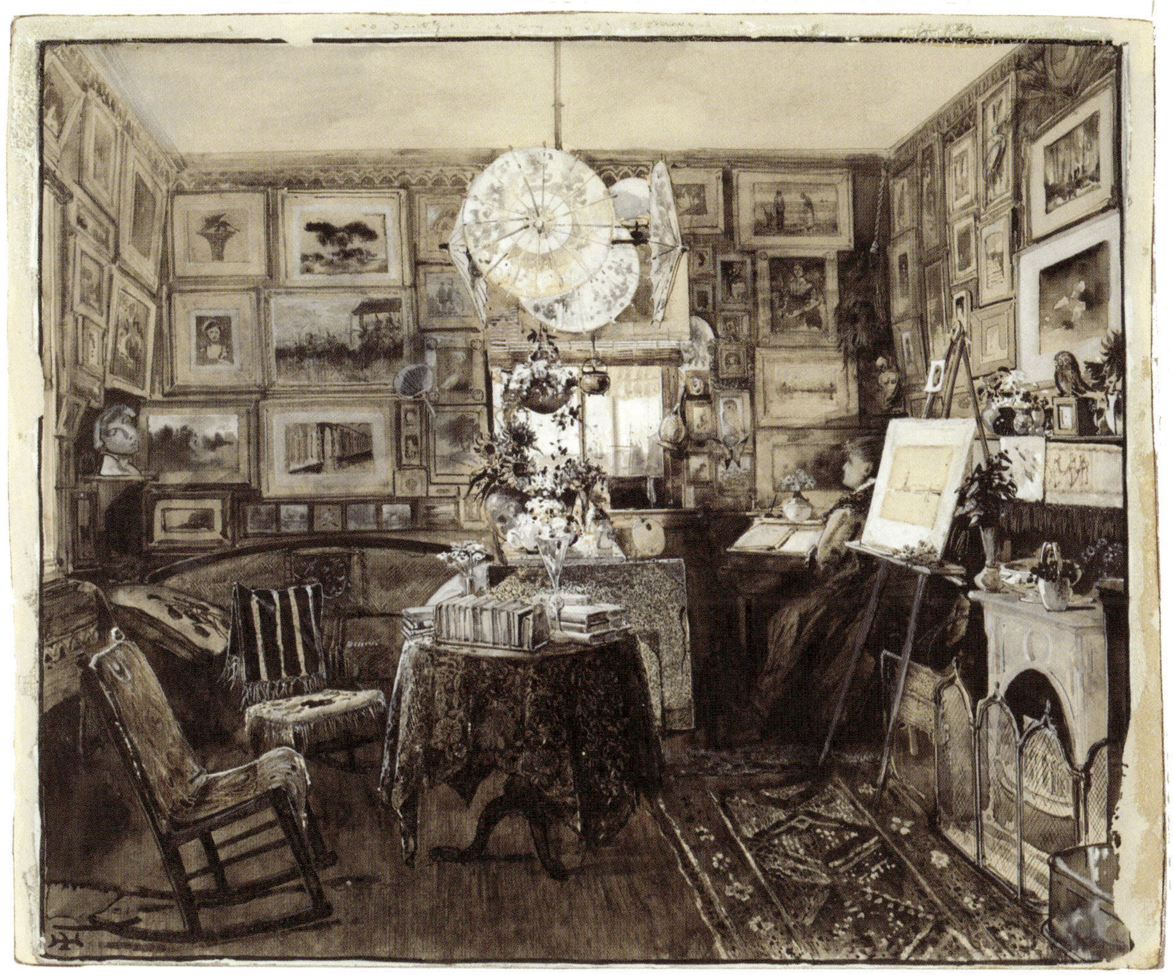

5.21. Harry Fenn, *The Studio* [Celia Thaxter's Study], ca. 1886. Black ink, watercolor washes, and opaque white, 11 3/4" x 14 1/4". (Montclair Art Museum, Gift of Mrs. Eleanor Seidler, 1964.23.)

For the November 1886 *St. Nicholas* magazine, Fenn provided six illustrations for Alice Wellington Rollins's article about Portsmouth, New Hampshire: "A City of Old Homesteads," which also gave attention to the nearby Isles of Shoals. In "Celia Thaxter's Study," his depiction of the parlor where his old friend entertained her guests, every inch is covered by paintings, statues, vases of flowers, Japanese parasols, and oriental rugs. Compared to Fenn's amazingly intricate ink and wash drawing (fig. 5.21), the resulting illustration shows the skill of the engraver but loses the subtleties of light and shading in the original, a further indication of why artists would have welcomed new techniques that replicated their work more precisely.

Fenn was frequently called upon to depict new buildings as well, for there was widespread interest in recent architecture and whether Americans were making progress in this realm. When S. G. W. Benjamin wrote about the then-current tendencies in architecture in his 1880 book *Art in America,* he was pleased that in the rebuilding after the fires in Chicago in 1871 and Boston in 1872 "groups of buildings or single structures have been erected which are at once elegant, commodious, and artistic." Further, the "profile" of American cities had "begun to partake of the picturesque character hitherto supposed to belong only to the Old World." Benjamin clearly admired the various styles that were growing in popularity, such as Romanesque and Gothic revival and French Renaissance, and used Boston's new Museum of Fine Arts as an example, with its fine composition of "clusters of spires and domes." In his opinion, "twenty years ago one would have looked in vain for any such harmonious outline of structural beauty in this country."[95]

When the art critic Mariana Schuyler van Rensselaer prepared a series for the *Century* designed to educate readers about good contemporary architecture, chiefly buildings by H. H. Richardson, titled "Recent Architecture in America," Fenn was among the many artists who contributed imagery.[96] His work was most conspicuous in the article "Churches" in the January 1885 issue. His seven illustrations are much more lively and interesting than the four by other artists, especially his views of Trinity Church, Boston. He prepared bold images of that church's massive tower and also its interior, with its sumptuous Aesthetic-style decoration designed by Richardson and John La Farge (fig. 5.22). The illustration, with its dramatic, almost triangular format, low viewpoint, complicated perspective, and use of a wide variety of lines, supports the author's comments that Trinity is "very unlike any of our previous efforts, as well as very striking, imposing, and beautiful."[97]

Fenn would continue to produce architectural views throughout his career, notably for the World's Columbian Exposition in Chicago in 1893 and the Pan-American Exposition in Buffalo in 1901. In so doing, he publicized and fostered pride in the excellence of America's built works.

FENN'S POETRY ILLUSTRATIONS IN THE EARLY TO MID-1880S

In addition to preparing what seems to be an exhausting number of periodical illustrations, in the early 1880s Fenn was also a prolific contributor to books, especially volumes of poetry. The success in the late 1860s and 1870s of such gift books as *Snow-Bound, The Story of the Fountain, The Song of the Sower,* and, indeed, *Picturesque America,* had encouraged publishers to expand their offerings. In December 1883, a review in the *Nation* of twelve illustrated books for the holiday trade noted that this "branch of art" had become "so large and in so many ways so important

 New Clients, New Technologies, New Home

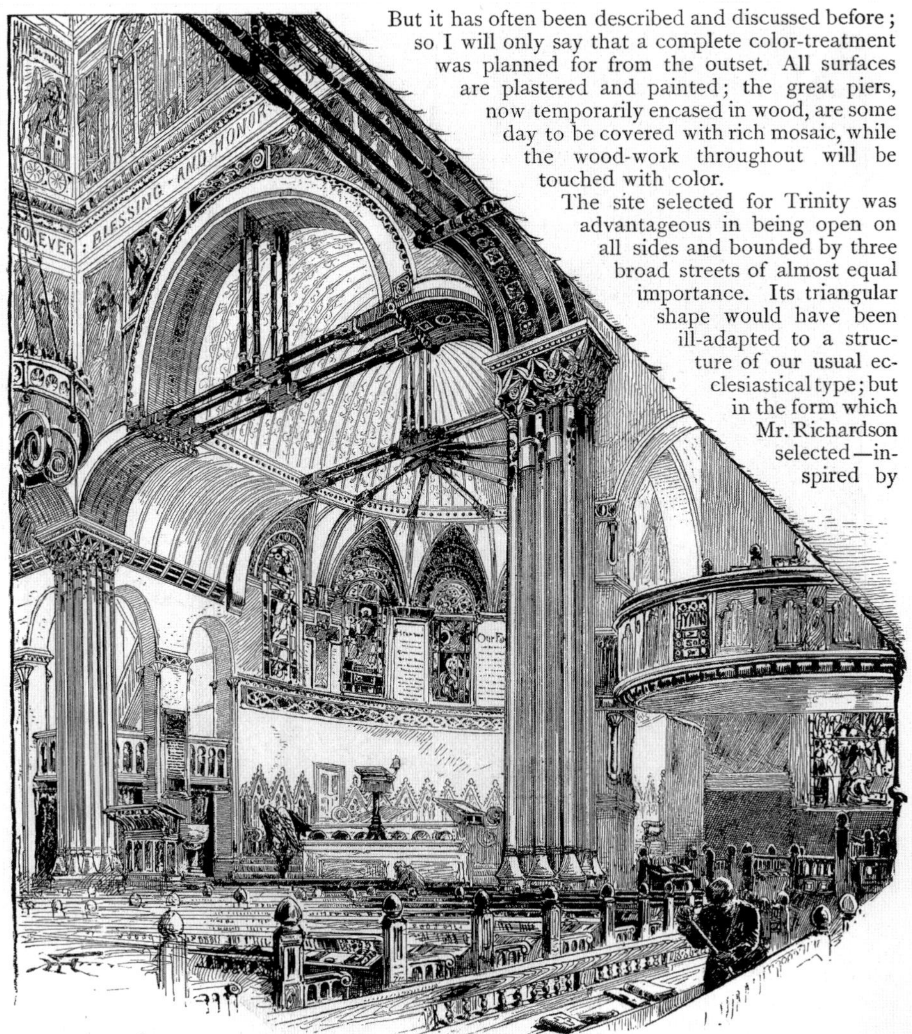

But it has often been described and discussed before; so I will only say that a complete color-treatment was planned for from the outset. All surfaces are plastered and painted; the great piers, now temporarily encased in wood, are some day to be covered with rich mosaic, while the wood-work throughout will be touched with color.

The site selected for Trinity was advantageous in being open on all sides and bounded by three broad streets of almost equal importance. Its triangular shape would have been ill-adapted to a structure of our usual ecclesiastical type; but in the form which Mr. Richardson selected —inspired by

5.22. Harry Fenn, "Chancel of Trinity Church, Boston," in "Recent Architecture in America. IV. Churches" by M. G. van Rensselaer. *Century,* January 1885, 330. Process line cut, 6" x 5 1/8".

as to demand and merit a larger and more systematic study than it has received . . . as the chief method of popularizing art."[98] For most books of poetry, publishers continued to engage several artists to provide designs. Fenn was among the major contributors to such publications as *The Cambridge Book of Poetry and Song,* editions of several of Tennyson's poems, and Jean Ingelow's *High Tide on the Coast of Lincolnshire,* little remembered today but popular as a recitation piece at the time.[99] He also contributed Egyptian scenes to an 1886 edition of Byron's *Childe Harold's Pilgrimage.*[100] (More titles appear in Appendix 1).

In late 1883, however, Fenn had the opportunity to once again be the sole artist for a book of poetry. The Boston firm of Roberts Brothers engaged him

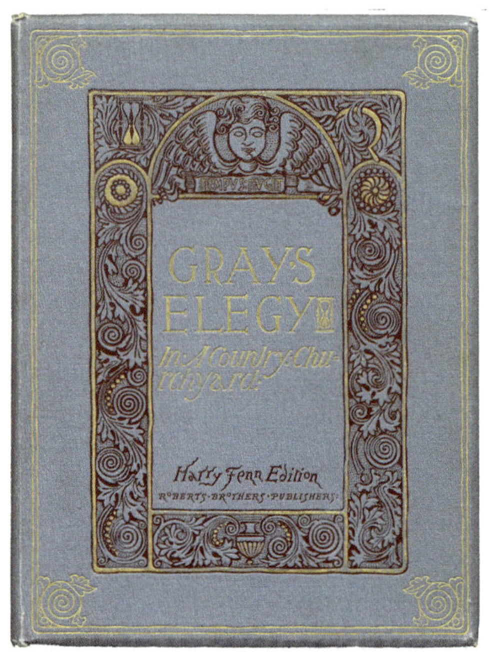

5.23. Front cover of Thomas Gray, *Elegy Written in a Country Churchyard,* Harry Fenn Edition (Boston: Roberts Brothers, 1884). Turquoise cloth stamped in gold and reddish brown, 9 3/8" x 6 7/8".

to illustrate Thomas Gray's perennial favorite *Elegy in a Country Churchyard,* first published in 1750 and frequently illustrated earlier in the nineteenth century, for example, by Birket Foster in 1853. In a highly unusual move, the publishers emphasized his contributions by stamping "Harry Fenn Edition" on the front cover in a distinctive, flowing typeface, giving him nearly equal billing with the author (fig. 5.23). Fenn prepared thirty designs, described above the list of illustrations as being "from sketches taken at Stoke Pogis, the scene of the poem," whose church he had depicted for *Picturesque Europe* (1:272). The book was printed on heavy paper and offered in two sizes, 7 3/4 by 5 1/4 inches and 9 3/4 by 7 inches, and at least three cloth colors—turquoise stamped in brown and gold, gray stamped in dark blue and silver, and yellowish green stamped in brown and gold—at $1.50 for the smaller size and $3.00 for the larger. More elaborate bindings were also offered.[101]

Fenn selected subjects from the poem's text ranging from shepherds to Gothic vaults to the ocean floor, rendering them in a wide variety of shapes and sometimes trying to integrate type and image. In at least one case, he designed images on facing pages to complement each other in a pleasing way, something he could do when he controlled the entire layout. In figure 5.24 the left-hand page illustrates the unseen richness of life in "dark, unfathomed caves of ocean," while the right-hand page shows the abundance of flowers "born to blush unseen." The almost mirror image of the format draws the two together harmoniously.[102] His other designs are also crowded with details, and the more tonal ones, reproduced as wood engravings, are often dark and heavy. The variety of subject and format is so extreme that the effect is rather jarring. Despite the book's prominence, it was not one of his best projects.

Opinions on Fenn's *Elegy* illustrations were split. The *Harper's Monthly* reviewer admired their "unity of sentiment" and "almost religious value," whereas the *Nation* found them "so literal in their adherence to the text as to be devoid of imaginative interest."[103] Such contrasting judgments foreshadow a more radical questioning of the value of illustrations that would lead, in the next century, to few or no such images appearing in books of poetry and fiction (except children's books). One critic had already railed against the "reprehensible waste of ability, time, and money": "If a story is the better for illustrations it is poorly or weakly written. . . . But the public are pic-

New Clients, New Technologies, New Home

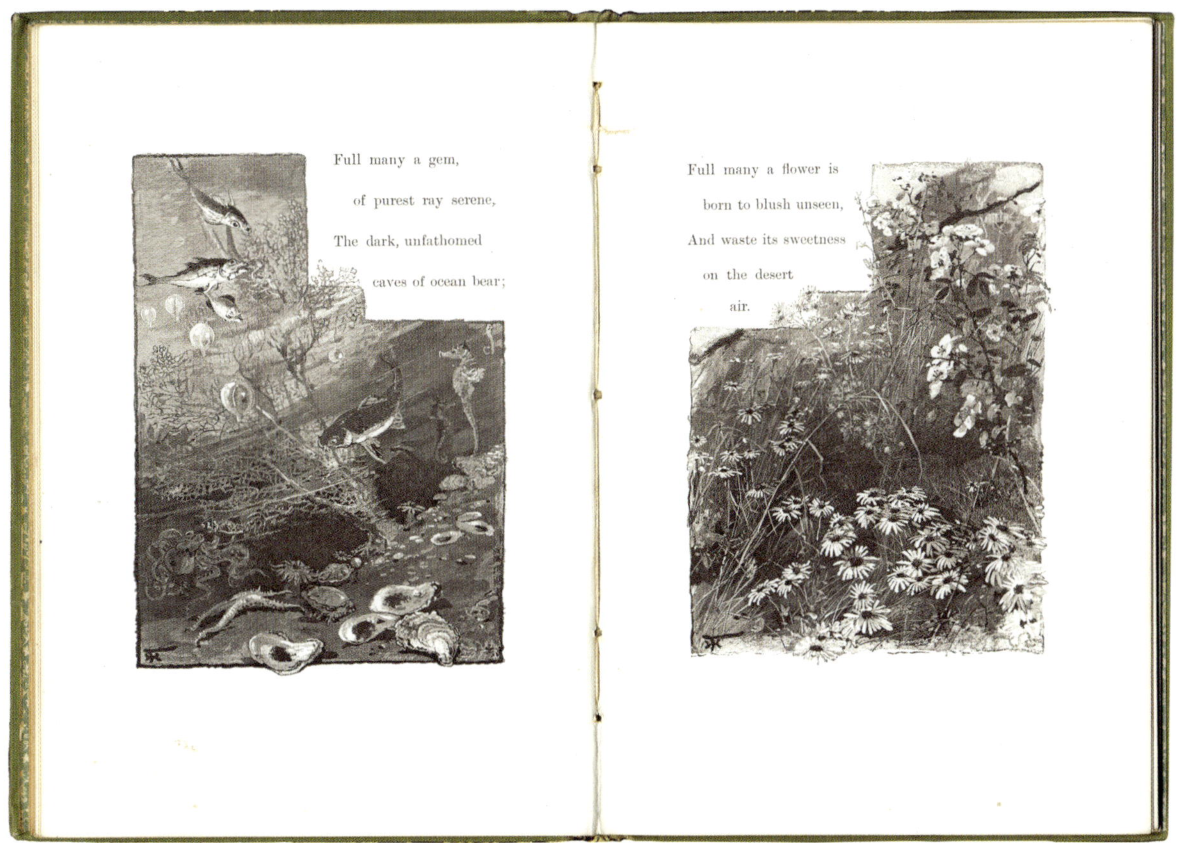

5.24. Harry Fenn, "Full many a gem, / of purest ray serene." From Gray, *Elegy*, n.p. Wood engravings by George T. Andrew; left, 4 13/16" x 3 3/8"; right, 4 5/8" x 3 1/4".

ture-crazed and demand their fill, and the broad, wide market of the million must be coddled and cosseted with pictures everywhere, quite like grown children."[104]

Gray's *Elegy* was clearly in vogue, for three illustrated editions were published in late 1883 alone. As one reviewer said of the revered poem: "It is so true to both general and individual experience that it grows all the time more human and more universal."[105] Perhaps its popularity can be explained in part by nostalgia for a simpler, preindustrial age and the traditions of rural life that were quickly disappearing, as well as its tribute to the worthy, though unhonored, dead of the churchyard and the leveling sentiment of its most famous line, "The paths of glory lead but to the grave." In recent years, genre paintings had been popular, especially those depicting American farmers by Thomas Waterman Wood and Eastman Johnson and French peasants by Jules Breton, in particular.[106] Another factor may have been the contemporary appeal of picturesque cemeteries located near large cities, like Mount Auburn in Boston and Greenwood in Brooklyn, which had come to be viewed as places to commune with nature and contemplate mortality.

Of the three editions published that year, Lippincott offered the most expensive; called "The Artists' Edition," it came in a larger format than the Fenn edition and was illustrated with designs by A. B. Frost, H. Bolton Jones, Woodward, and Thomas Hovenden, among others. This edition was preferred by critics for the *Nation* and *Dial,* though the *Harper's Monthly* reviewer found Fenn's "more unpretending" volume equal "in the perfection of its illustrations."[107] The third edition, published by Estes & Lauriat, was smaller and less expensive, with illustrations by Birket Foster, W. L. Sheppard, and others.

FENN'S NEW HOME IN MONTCLAIR

Despite such an intense work agenda, Fenn found time to take on a new project: the creation of a distinguished home for his family. In building a large, handsome residence—as several older, highly successful artists had done—Fenn would reinforce his reputation as a tasteful and accomplished artist, an image far removed from earlier stereotypes of the struggling artist in a garret studio. Although no specific records of his income have been found, it must have been substantial. Some hint of his prosperity can be gleaned from a March 22, 1887, article in Boston's *Daily Evening Transcript* claiming that "Harry Fenn, a pupil of Birket Foster, used to get $10,000 a year from the Appletons for his work on 'Picturesque America.' In American scenery drawing no one is his superior." The writer further speculated: "He probably earns $10,000 now by general work." (By one estimate, $10,000 in 1887 would equal approximately $244,000 in 2011.)[108]

Whatever his earnings, Fenn clearly felt secure enough to break ground on a large home in Montclair, New Jersey, where his family had rented before leaving for England. The town of around five thousand inhabitants offered good views and relatively clean air and was connected to Manhattan by rail and ferry. By early 1884 Fenn had bought property there, and by mid-1885 his sixteen-room house, called "The Cedars," was completed (fig. 5.25).[109] Fenn chose the architect Henry Edwards Ficken (1844–1929), originally from London, who kept an office on Broadway; his firm had drawn the plans for the Iron Pier at Coney Island and designed several prominent buildings in New York.[110] Ficken had also been a successful architectural draftsman before becoming an architect, a role in which Fenn may have known him.[111]

Fenn's house was distinctive, suggesting that the artist had strong opinions about what he wanted. The wooden building covered in cypress shingles, with

New Clients, New Technologies, New Home

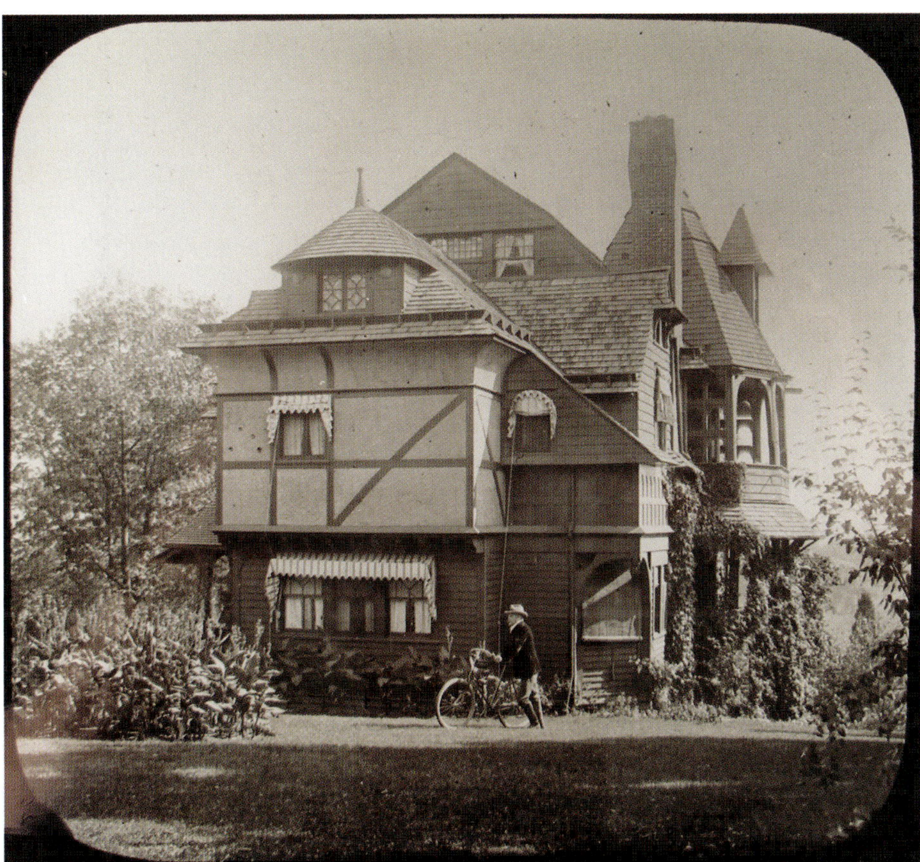

half-timbered sections, was reminiscent of the "style of architecture generally known as Early English," more recently termed *shingle style* (fig. 5.26).[112] The earliest mention of the house appeared in *Harper's Weekly,* which described it as "a commodious cottage quaint in outlines and proportions, both externally and internally," with "two stories and a gambrel roof" and "an open-timbers tower."[113] Its commanding view stretched from "Coney Island and the Highlands of the Hudson as far north as Peekskill," according to Lizzie W. Champney in her article in the *Century* titled "The Summer Haunts of American Artists." Fenn's year-round residence was included among the vacation homes of well-known artists from the previous generation who had built along the Hudson River, including Albert Bierstadt, Thomas Cole, Frederic E. Church, and John F. Kensett.[114]

For the article, Fenn drew his studio (fig. 5.27)—which Champney described as "directly under the roof"—filled with his sketches "whose subjects range 'from Florida to Egypt and from Warwick to Jerusalem,'" attesting to his far-flung travels. "Costumes of various Oriental and European peoples, relics of many

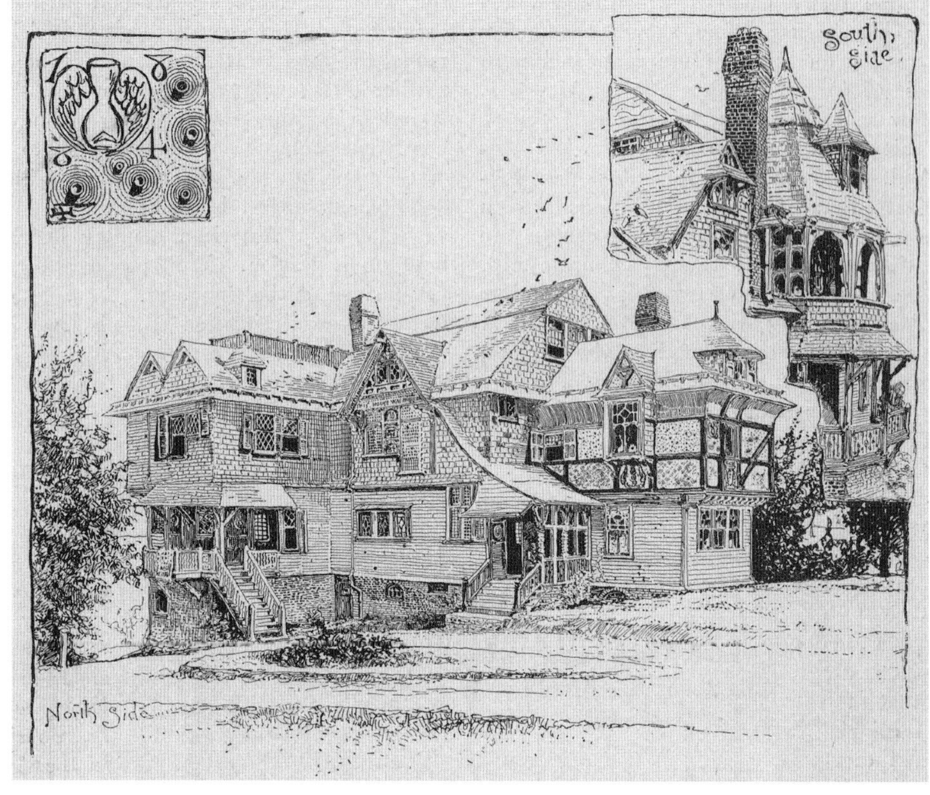

artistic pilgrimages," were also scattered about.[115] The decoration of the rest of the house, with Japanese, Moorish, and neo-Gothic touches, was similarly in the mode of the increasingly popular Aesthetic style, which combined decorative motifs—whether geometric or more naturalistic—and objects from many different cultures to create an artistic ensemble. This approach focused on the visual qualities of the items, dissociating them from their particular history and culture. It had been encouraged in Britain by William Morris's carpets, textiles, and wallpapers and in such books as Owen Jones's *Grammar of Ornament* (1856), Christopher Dresser's *Studies in Design* (1874–76), and Charles Locke Eastlake's *Hints on Household Taste* (1868), which became so popular in America that eight U.S. editions were issued between 1872 and 1886.[116] Fenn would have been familiar with this style of decoration from his years in England and had likely brought many decorative objects back from his travels. In addition, he probably would have seen images of such eclectic interiors in two recent publications: his friend Harriet Prescott Spofford's book, *Art Decoration Applied to Furniture* (1878), and *Artistic Houses,* published by Appleton for five hundred subscribers from 1883 to 1884.

   New Clients, New Technologies, New Home

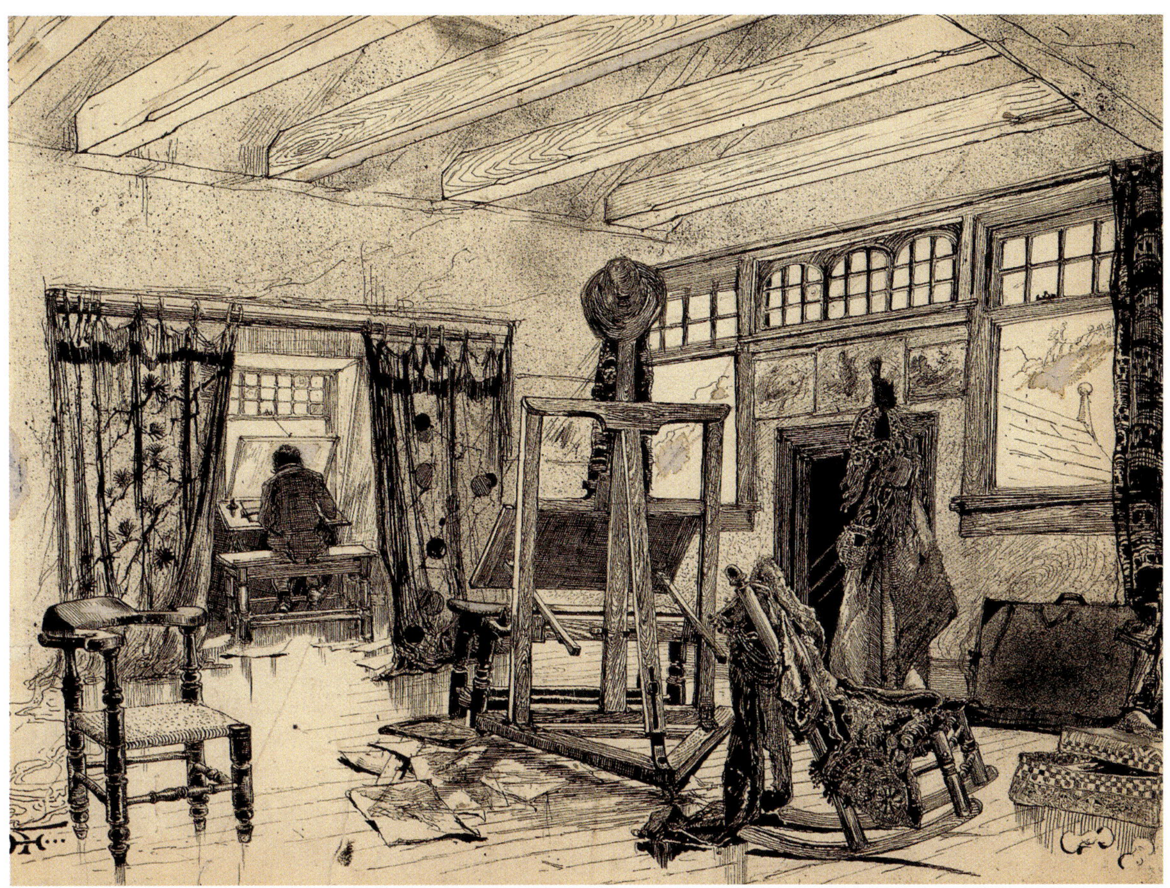

5.27. Harry Fenn, drawing for "Interior of Harry Fenn's Studio, Montclair, N.J.," in "The Summer Haunts of American Artists" by Lizzie W. Champney, *Century*, October 1885, 844. Pen and ink on illustration board, 16 3/8" x 21". (Courtesy of William V. Abt.)

Eclectic decoration was in keeping with the growing cosmopolitanism and desire to emulate European fashions, and many middle-class as well as wealthy Americans created Oriental "cosy corners" or other foreign-themed rooms, which were often akin to Fenn's images of domestic architecture in the Middle East and Europe.[117] The international marketplace at the 1876 Centennial Exposition in Philadelphia was an important impetus for this trend. Americans found the British displays of objects to beautify the home superior to local products, which led to a new emphasis on art training to improve American manufactures. Many visitors were also impressed by the Turkish and North African furnishings and fabrics in the national exhibits and bazaars.[118] But the biggest sensation was caused by the Japanese contributions. The displays of screens, porcelain, silks, glass, and bronzes (but no prints) generated enormous interest in that country's ancient craft traditions.[119]

The wide range of objects from around the world sold well and created a market that persisted for many years, as seen most conspicuously in expanding department stores such as Macy's in New York and Wanamaker's in Philadelphia.[120] Japanese touches such as lattices, matting, and lacquerware were often incorporated into interiors in the "artistic" or Aesthetic style, including in Fenn's house.

The Cedars received considerable attention in periodicals, indicative of the contemporary interest in not only the lives of artists as seers of visual taste who could lead the way but also their homes and studios, which could serve as models for interior decoration. William Merritt Chase's studio in the 51 West Tenth Street building in New York, as depicted in his paintings and in the press, had provided one such model for eclectic displays, as had Church's Hudson River valley home, Olana.[121] One of the later articles on Fenn's house contained a "walk through" narrative of the more public rooms, noting details of how he presented himself as well traveled and up-to-date through his use of the popular color yellow[122]: "From a hooded entrance porch one passes into a warm-toned vestibule, and then into a large, square hall with wainscots of wood and panels of matting. It is evident at once that Mr. Fenn has been a traveler, for the fruits of many lands surround the walls," including "cabinets and weapons and Moorish lamps" (figs. 5.28, 5.29). An arch "frames the fireplace nook," where "ivory blends with yellow," setting off "the rich tones of the Moorish plaques on the shelf." "Japanese lattice and yellow silk" cover the alcove's windows. "The white and gold fireplace" is decorated with amber tiles, and "Venetian glass and shells" adorn the mantel. On one side is a divan covered with a Moroccan rug and cushions and "about the rooms are bits of Chippendale, a sixteenth-century cabinet of ebony and ivory, and a table of fine Japanese lacquer." A portfolio of Fenn's sketches beckons guests, and the stairway leading to his studio is lighted by a ten-foot window, on which the artist has painted a "life-size dogwood tree in blossom."[123]

In participating so actively in the decoration of his home, Fenn was right in step with the Aesthetic movement's emphasis that artists should practice a wide range of media, from stained glass to ceramic painting to interior decoration.[124] Louis Comfort Tiffany and John La Farge were perhaps the most conspicuous examples of such diverse practice. Fenn would later engage in additional decorating projects, and his studio work area reflected the media he used regularly: "One corner is devoted to black and white, another to easel and color box," with a third corner devoted "to the etching table," surprising information considering how few of Fenn's etchings have been located.[125]

Just as Fenn took pains with the decoration of his house, so too did he attempt to control its image in the press by supplying drawings to accompany the articles describing it. In 1886 he prepared three illustrations for the *Magazine of Art*

New Clients, New Technologies, New Home

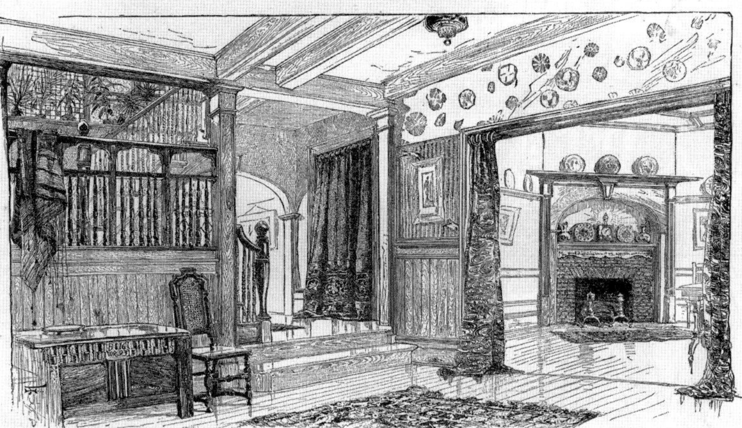

48 THE MAGAZINE OF ART.

cap of the two-storeyed piazza, which is really an adjunct of it. The attic under this roof is Mr. Fenn's studio, and the space under the cap of the tower is utilised for storing canvases, &c. Exteriorly, the woodwork of the cottage is painted a dark brown; the plastered surfaces, plainly indicated in the drawing, have, unfortunately, been disturbed by some meaningless incised forms, intended as ornament; but these may be easily covered up by a fresh coat of plaster. Some vines, which have

here a light salmon colour; and a frieze is simulated by placing, on a narrow shelf, a row of blue-and-white Delft and Spanish-Moorish platters. A few fine pieces of old Nankin blue-and-white porcelain may be admired on the mantelshelf of the dining-room; and a number of prints in red ink, after drawings by Mr. Burne Jones, occupy the remainder of the wall-space. The drawing-room is mostly in warm greys, corresponding with the Japanese *portière* with its pattern of waves and tortoises in black

IV.—THE HALL, LOOKING INTO THE DINING-ROOM.

only just been planted, will eventually hide a good part of the exterior surface in any case; and their fresh green will make an acceptable contrast with the brown and grey of the building.

The colour-effect of the interior is already all that could be wished for. Much of it is undoubtedly due to the artistic arrangement of Mr. Fenn's choice though small collection of *bric-à-brac*, and to the draperies of doors and windows. But, as it left the hands of the architect, Mr. Ficken, it must have appeared a pleasant and inviting interior. The wainscoting of the hall, its ceiling, and the woodwork of the stairs are of Georgia pine varnished to a fine golden hue, which strikes the keynote for all the three principal rooms. The wall above the wainscoting is a cream tint, with panelling of yellowish matting. In the dining-room (IV.) this last is replaced by the painted surface of the wall,

and white, and with the window of opalescent glass, and bookcases curtained with Japanese brocade. The unplastered brick of the hall chimney should be remembered when forming a conception of the harmony of warm, subdued tones furnished by the architect, to which Mr. Fenn has added little but blue and green and gold, his share of the decoration culminating in the tail of a magnificent stuffed peacock, which depends from its perch on the staircase window-sill. The over-mantel, as shown in the drawing, is in stamped and gilt Japanese leather.

The upper rooms are all in the same light golden-yellow tone; but each has its individual effect, due to its outlook or to its decoration, or to both. From a railed platform on the roof of the wing which contains the offices and the servants' rooms, a view may be had almost as wide as that from the summit of the neighbouring hill.   R. RIORDAN.

(published in London, Paris, New York, and Melbourne by Cassell & Company), which ran a feature on his house written by R. Riordan for the series "Artists' Homes." Letters reveal that he took care to render the exterior in a "bold open and picturesque manner" (see fig. 5.26) and requested better printing of an interior view, complaining of the proof: "The thinnest lines are now of the same value as the darks. It makes it look a little common" (see figs. 5.28, 5.29).[126]

That same year, the house was featured in *Artistic Country-Seats: Types of Recent American Villa and Cottage Architecture,* a rather elaborate book published in two

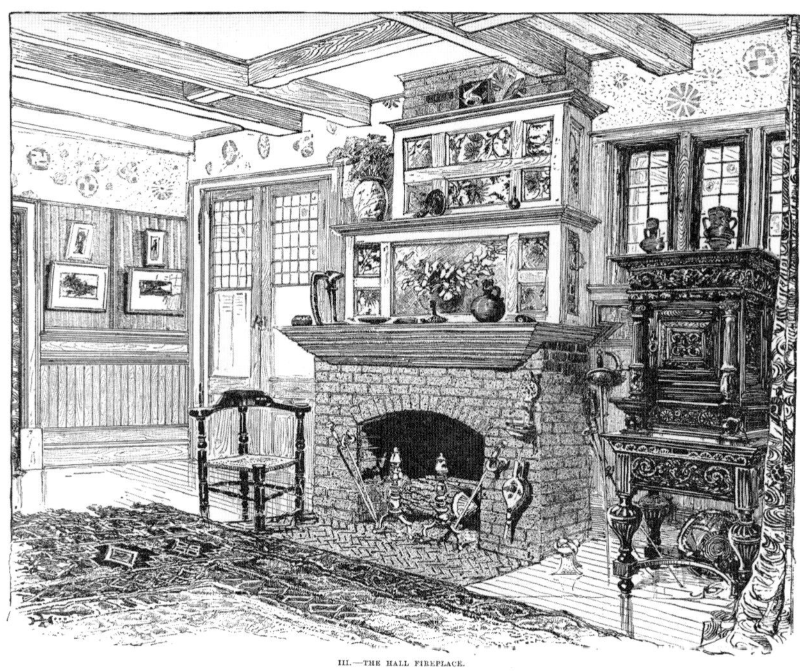

5.29. Harry Fenn, "III.—The Hall Fireplace," in "Artists' Homes," 47. Process line cut, 6 1/2" x 8".

volumes by Appleton. The editor, George William Sheldon, selected one hundred homes built during the past ten years "at a cost of from five thousand to five hundred thousand dollars" to be described and illustrated with a photograph of the exterior and a floor plan. Sheldon's preface clearly linked the "renaissance" in American architecture celebrated within the book to the Centennial Exposition and proudly stated that "a committee of architects from Great Britain," recently sent to assess American architecture, had found "in the country-seat the American architect's chief triumph."[127] As the third home featured, Fenn's "country-seat" was prominent. Sheldon reported the cost, "according to contract," as $8,250 and considered this "little expense" to have produced "so much beauty."[128] The inclusion of the Cedars in this and the several articles discussed earlier must have enhanced Fenn's reputation and status.

PERIODICAL ILLUSTRATIONS IN THE LATE 1880S

In the late 1880s, Fenn's commissions were related to many aspects of contemporary culture, current events, and developments in housing and technology. As the coverage of his own house shows, he was well known for his travels in the Middle East. In the wake of *Picturesque Palestine*'s success and the simultaneous

New Clients, New Technologies, New Home

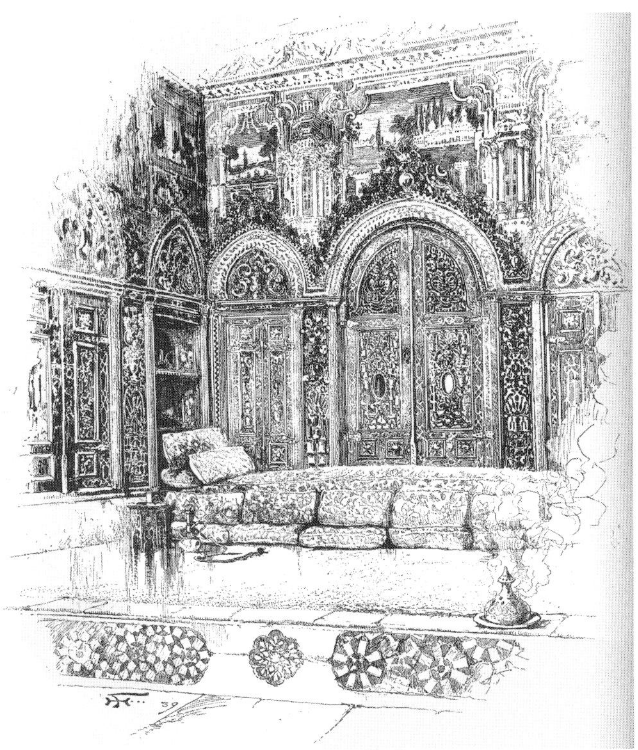

5.30. Harry Fenn, "An Arab Interior, Damascus," in "Tadmor in the Wilderness" by Frederick Jones Bliss. *Scribner's Magazine,* April 1890, 406. Process line cut, approx. 6 1/8" x 5".

publication of Lew Wallace's novel *Ben-Hur: A Tale of the Christ* (1880), which by the mid-1880s had become a phenomenal best seller, interest in the region was stronger than ever, and publishers naturally looked to Fenn and his colleague John Douglas Woodward for illustrations.[129]

In 1885 the *Century* ran a series by the Philadelphia photographer Edward L. Wilson on different parts of the Holy Land and asked Fenn to create illustrations based on the author's photographs, since the technology for printing photographs along with type was still unsatisfactory. The November issue opened with "A Photographer's Visit to Petra," which included thirteen illustrations signed by Fenn, one strikingly similar to Frederic Church's 1874 painting *El Khasné, Petra.* Subsequent articles by Wilson on the Sea of Galilee, Jerusalem, Sinai, and other areas, also illustrated by Fenn, Woodward, and others, appeared over the next four years.[130] Fenn and Woodward also prepared landscapes and architectural views for S. G. W. Benjamin's articles "The City of Teherân" for the December 1885 *Century* and "Mountaineering in Persia" for March 1886. Benjamin was the first U.S. minister to Persia (1883–85?) and a prolific writer on art and travel

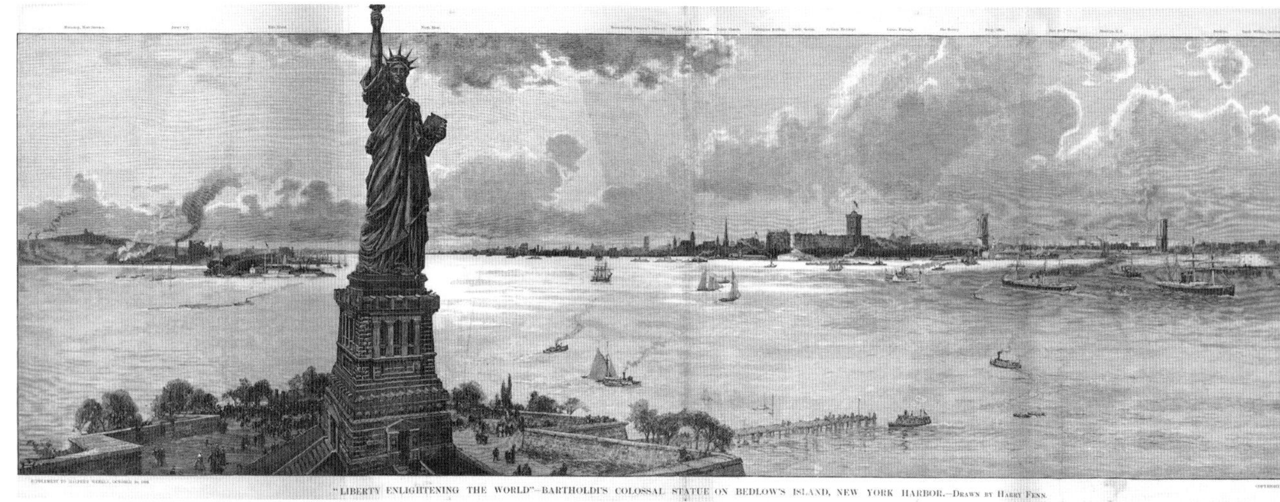

5.31. Harry Fenn, "'Liberty Enlightening the World'—Bartholdi's Colossal Statue on Bedlow's Island, New York Harbor.—Drawn by Harry Fenn." *Harper's Weekly*, October 30, 1886, supplement. Wood engraving, 14 3/4" x 40 3/4".

subjects. His article "A Glance at the Arts of Persia" (September 1886) was illustrated by Fenn and Irving R. Wiles, who did most of the figure drawings.[131]

Other commissions involving Middle Eastern topics included "The Amusements of Arab Children" for the January 1888 *St. Nicholas;* Fenn's images, which feature figures (rather successfully in the one on p. 176), were probably based on photographs.[132] For the August 1885 *Harper's Monthly* he illustrated "A Lunch with the Druzes," using his *Picturesque Palestine* image of Caesarea Philippi as a source for "Old Bridge at Banias."[133] In 1889 Fenn made a spectacular ink drawing titled "An Arab Interior, Damascus" (fig. 5.30), for an article in the April 1890 *Scribner's Magazine,* which is similar to some of the Damascene interiors he produced for *Picturesque Palestine.*[134]

Fenn's commissions for the large-format *Harper's Weekly,* where his friend Charles Parsons worked as art director, gave him the opportunity to design larger compositions that were often related to important current events.[135] An outstanding example is his striking, oversize fold-out illustration (14 3/4 by 40 3/4 inches) of the recently dedicated Statue of Liberty, "Liberty Enlightening the World—Bartholdi's Colossal Statue on Bedlow's Island, New York Harbor" (fig. 5.31), which appeared in the October 30, 1886, issue. Intended to demonstrate French–American friendship, this gift from France was originally planned for the centennial year, 1876, but construction was long delayed; its dedication, which occurred only after the expensive pedestal was completed, was a much-heralded event. In the wood engraving of Fenn's panoramic view of the harbor—extending from

New Clients, New Technologies, New Home

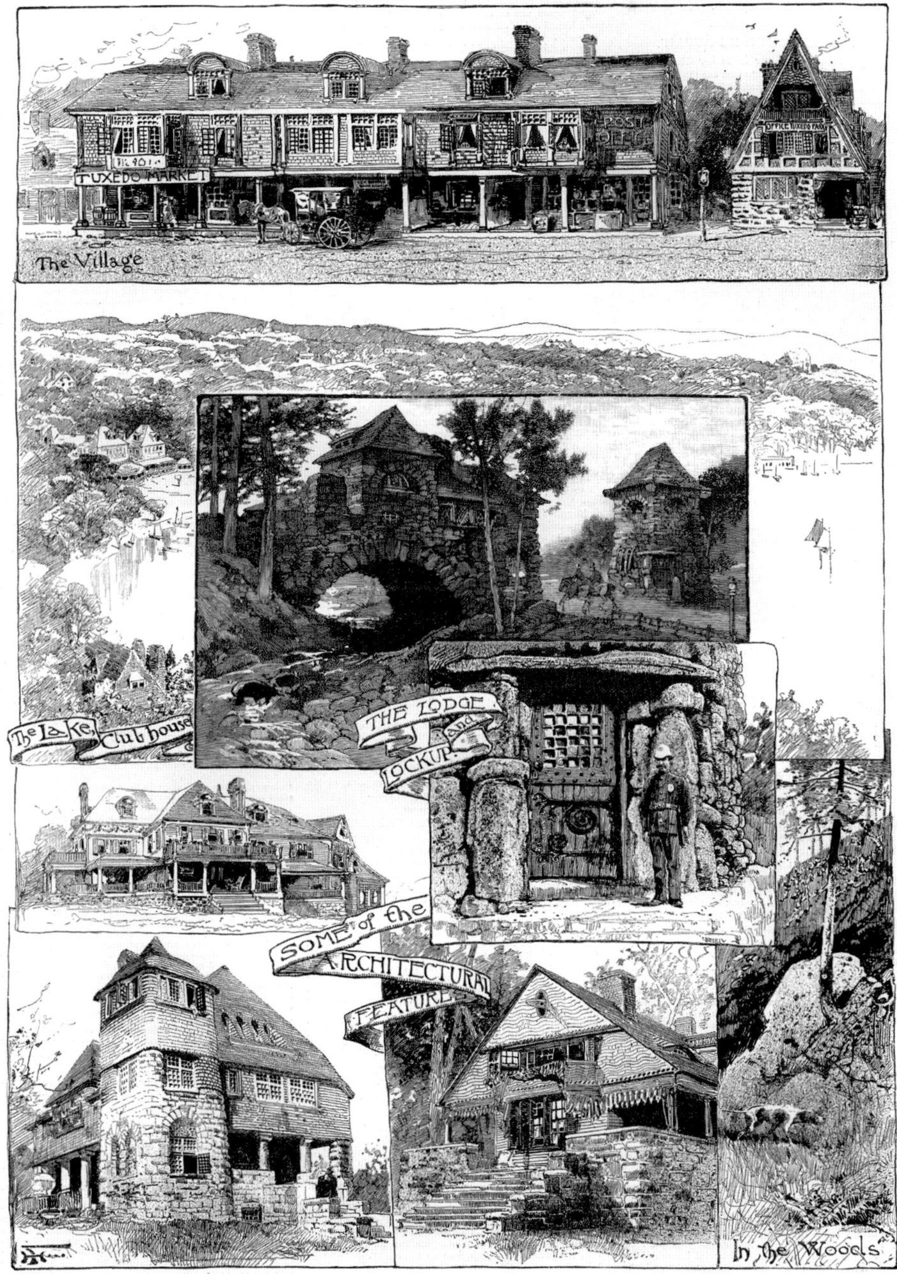

5.32. Harry Fenn, "Tuxedo Park.— Drawn by Harry Fenn from Sketches, and Photographs by Hill Brothers." *Harper's Weekly,* December 18, 1886, 824. Process line cut and wood engraving, 13 1/4" x 9 3/16".

New Jersey to Brooklyn—Liberty appears gigantic, with her torch breaking through the top frame and a crowd of small figures at the base.

Fenn also prepared numerous full-page designs for the *Weekly* that combined several small images into what may be called *composites;* such illustrations might also be termed *collages,* suggesting an arrangement of pictures in a scrapbook and in keeping with the appeal of illustrated magazines. According to Tom Gretton, "an assemblage of overlapping or interlocking sketches both delivered plenty and suggested inexhaustibility."[136] Like the periodicals themselves, such illustrations appealed to increasingly cosmopolitan consumers—both urban and rural—attracted by a wide range of choices. Fenn prepared three of these full-page designs of scenery and resort facilities near Saratoga Springs, New York, in 1883 (July 14 and 28, August 11) and many more in the late 1880s. His December 18, 1886, "Tuxedo Park, New York" showcases the new private resort community of the tobacco magnate Pierre Lorillard (fig. 5.32). The development reflected the influence of Japanese landscape traditions in the unprecedented way the stone and shingled buildings were placed among the forest and rock outcroppings of the 7,000-acre site with as little disturbance as possible.[137] Although working from photographs, Fenn created a distinctive composition by using a variety of viewpoints and a new style of titling, featuring his own calligraphy on panels that look like gently folded ribbons. Other composites of more distant places such as the Everglades, Mount Shasta, and San Antonio, also based on photographs, emphasize the pleasing variety of these sites. (See Appendix 1.)

Some of Fenn's later assignments for *Harper's Weekly* were related to the growing interest in other cultures, as the discipline of anthropology developed and put forth theories about a cultural hierarchy that progressed from savage to more civilized states, a notion that had already been popularized in the evolutionary theories of Herbert Spencer. His composite of pen drawings of Indians in "Around Behring's Straits" (February 12, 1887), with their boats and homes made of whalebones and walrus hides, includes several individuals or groups clearly based on photographs that are notable for the straightforward translation of the faces, without caricature or idealization. Alaska had belonged to the United States since 1867, and the accompanying text referred to its native peoples as "our arctic fellow-countrymen"; it suggested that the mother and child Fenn drew "may be taken, perhaps, for the sole residents of that locality whose portraits have reached the metropolis."[138]

The ancient culture of the American Southwest was also of interest, and for the May 18, 1889, issue Fenn created a double-page spread titled "Pre Historic Arizona" composed of thirteen overlapping pen sketches of ruins of Indian dwellings, painted rocks, and Spanish missions. Other assignments to depict foreign lands included "Corea, the Chosön Land" (January 12, 1889), which the writer, Charles Chaillé Long, secretary of the American legation in Seoul, said was "attracting the world's attention" as "one of the last of the undiscovered countries of the globe—the

New Clients, New Technologies, New Home

veritable *Ultima Thule*" (37); and images of Cairo
for the same writer's feature "The Nile Valley"
(December 21, 1889).

In mid-1887 the Harper firm gave Fenn a
chance to undertake a sketching project similar
to his work for *Picturesque America*—promoting
American scenery and travel—but with illustrations that had a very different look. From
July 16 through November 19, 1887, the *Weekly*
published a series of his views of the "watering-
places" along the New England coast. With the
decline of farming, lumbering, and fishing, the
region's economy was increasingly fueled by
tourism to places recently made accessible by
railroad. After religious leaders like William
H. H. "Adirondack" Murray and Henry Ward
Beecher began promoting vacations as essential to mental and spiritual health in the 1860s
and 1870s, it became a goal of most wealthy city
dwellers, as well as those who aspired to the middle class, to spend a week or a month each year
in the mountains or on the seacoast.[139]

The featured coastal resorts included Nahant, Marblehead, and Cape Ann, Massachu-
setts; Kennebunk, Camden, Castine, Mount Desert, and Bar Harbor, Maine; and
Campobello, New Brunswick. Compared to his *Picturesque America* images, these
illustrations give more attention to tourist facilities, both transportation and accom-
modations. Fenn composed pages with views of coastal cliffs, old boats and harbors,
and historic buildings, presenting the locales as appealingly picturesque. From the
varied look of the images, he prepared some pen drawings and some watercolors, all
of which were reproduced as wood engravings. The juxtaposition of different styles
and subjects sometimes works well but other times results in a confusing jumble
of difficult-to-read details. For example, in figure 5.33, "A Bit of New Hampshire
Coast," in which Fenn once again depicted the Isles of Shoals, his image of the cliff's
profile lower right stands strangely unconnected to any landform. Some of the later
installments in the series, such as "In and about Campobello, New Brunswick," are
more orderly and perhaps more visually pleasing, composed of a larger tonal work

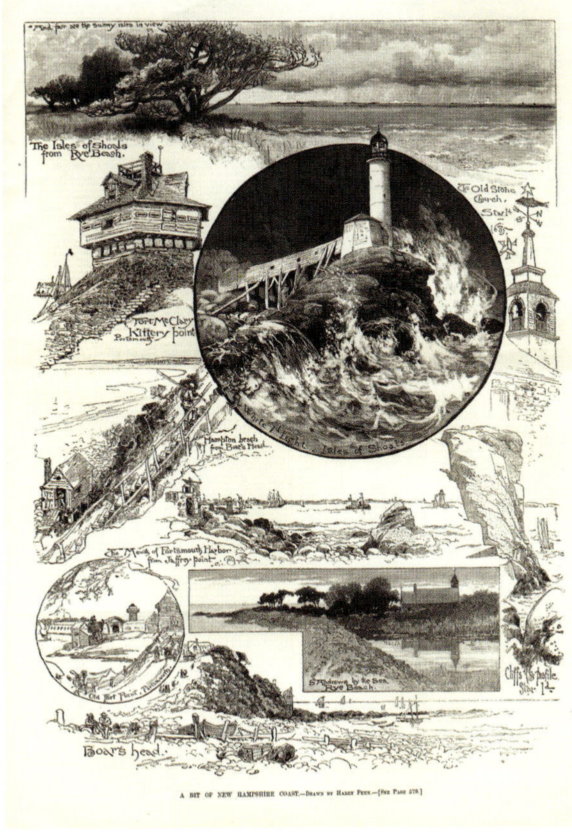

5.33. Harry Fenn, "A Bit of New Hampshire Coast.—Drawn by
Harry Fenn." *Harper's Weekly*, August 13, 1887, 581. Process line
cut and wood engraving, 13 1/8" x 9 1/4".

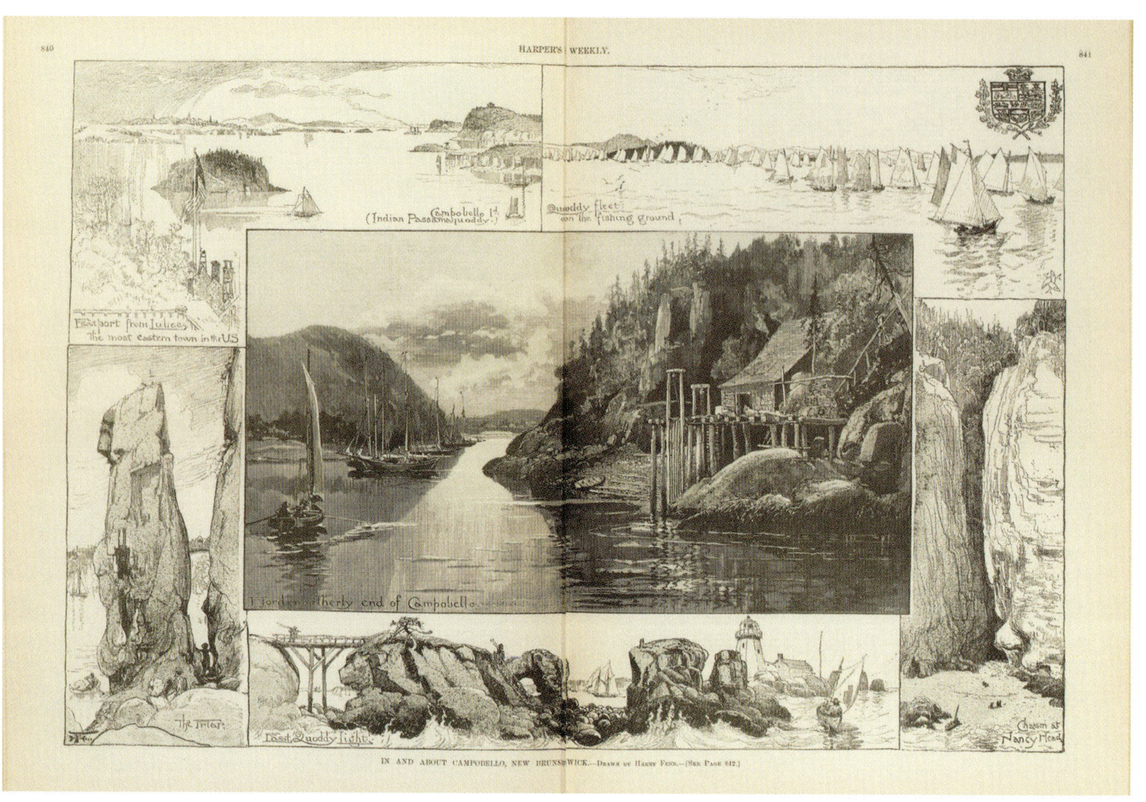

5.34. Harry Fenn, "In and about Campobello, New Brunswick.—Drawn by Harry Fenn." *Harper's Weekly,* November 19, 1887, 840–41. Wood engraving, 13 3/4" x 20".

in the center bordered by smaller, more sketchlike images (fig. 5.34). (See Appendix 1 for additional illustrations of summer vacation spots.)

Interest was also keen in the orderly growth of the nation's cities, and Fenn prepared an illustration for the January 26, 1889, *Harper's Weekly* titled "The Transformation of the West Side of New York City." In this case the writer of the accompanying article was unhappy about the "vulgar pretentiousness" of some of the new buildings, and thought Fenn had embellished reality: "The impression Mr. Fenn's drawings make of the architecture of the West Side is more favorable than that made by the buildings themselves, not merely because the objects depicted are 'helped' by his pencil, but also because they are selected."[140]

Fenn publicized and celebrated new transportation links and a planned technological improvement in an article he wrote and illustrated for the October 5, 1889, *Harper's Weekly.* Titled "From Owen Sound to Mackinac," it recounts his journey by ship from the Canadian town in southern Ontario to the Saint Mary's River near Sault Ste. Marie, where he had a glimpse of Lake Superior before

New Clients, New Technologies, New Home

venturing back to Mackinac Island in Lake Huron. This timely coverage proposed a new travel destination (the Canadian Pacific Railroad had increased its service thanks to larger and swifter boats feeding its rail lines) and pointed out that both the Canadian and U.S. governments were planning to spend "upward of eleven million dollars" to improve the Sault Ste. Marie Canal linking Lakes Superior and Huron, thereby increasing exports of grain and other commodities. As in his other articles, Fenn is clearly an engaged and informed traveler, and here he reveals his national pride as well. He points out that cargo will be able to pass "unbroken" from Duluth, Minnesota, to Liverpool, England: "Even now the boats in their short season carry a commerce greater than the Suez Canal for the year. And this, the largest lock in the world, is to be augmented by a far larger one now in the course of construction."[141]

THE LATER 1880S: EXPERIMENTS WITH BOOK DESIGN AND PROCESSES

In this period, publishers and reviewers, and in turn readers, began paying more attention not just to illustration but also to page design, typography, paper stock, and binding—in short, treating books as artistic objects. An early example wholly designed by an artist was *The Merry Adventures of Robin Hood* (Scribner's, 1883), for which Howard Pyle was responsible for the text, illustrations, binding, choice of type, and layout.[142] This flourishing of book design can be seen as both a reaction against industrialization and a part of the Aesthetic movement's desire to infuse everyday objects with beauty, thereby reaching, and refining, a wider public.

By 1885 ornamental borders reminiscent of past centuries and other cultures were a popular form of embellishment.[143] Sometimes pages were sent through a press twice to "take the impression of a decorative tint block" in a second color.[144] Publishers continued to offer both cloth and leather bindings but frequently added fancier options at higher prices; for example, James R. Osgood advertised an edition of Tennyson's *Princess* (1884), to which Fenn contributed, "with full gilt edges, in box" or in a wide range bindings: cloth, $6.00; full morocco or tree calf, $10.00; calf or morocco with inlaid mosaic patterns, $12.50; or crushed levant, with silk linings, $25.00.[145] Fenn would later contribute head- and tailpieces and three illustrations to Moncure D. Conway's *Barons of the Potomack and the Rappahannock,* a limited-edition book published in 1892 by the Grolier Club, an association of book collectors; 360 copies were printed on Italian hand-made paper, and three on vellum.

After the success of the "Harry Fenn Edition" of Gray's *Elegy* in 1883, Roberts

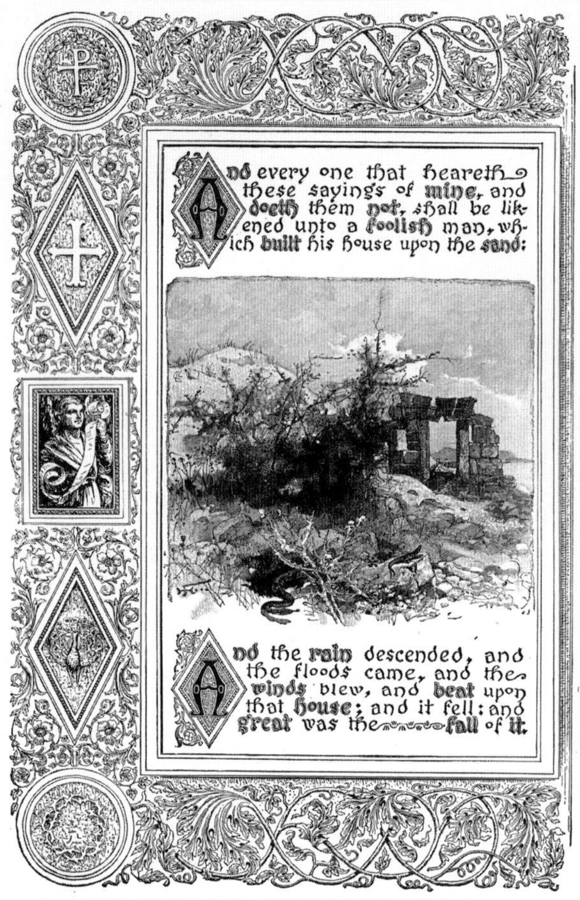

5.35. Harry Fenn, "Which built his house upon the sand." From *The Sermon on the Mount, Illustrated* (New York: Federal Book Co.; © Roberts Brother, Boston, 1885), n.p. Wood engraving by George T. Andrew; decorative borders by Sidney L. Smith; engrossed text by Charles Copeland; page 13" x 9".

Brothers engaged the artist again in 1885 to contribute to an elaborate edition of *The Sermon on the Mount* combining the text from the gospel of Matthew, written in Charles Copeland's calligraphy, and decorative borders by Sidney L. Smith. The book is a decidedly heavy-handed example of the era's deluxe editions. Contributing the figural subjects were the artist-illustrators W. St. J. Harper, Henry Sandham, F. S. Church, and J. A. Frazer. Fenn provided eight illustrations, primarily landscape and city views; his "'Mount of Olives,' from Jerusalem" appeared both in black and white inside the book and in color glued onto the front cover.[146] Some of Fenn's designs were clearly derived from *Picturesque Palestine* illustrations, but the one reproduced here (fig. 5.35) was not; this page was admired by the *Art Amateur*'s critic, who thought Fenn "contributed some of the best illustrations in the book." Though some reviewers admired such extensive decoration (one even called the book "a most perfect specimen of what is now called the book-maker's art"), others preferred simpler designs of "the good old-fashioned sort" and more attention given to the text.[147] Fenn's landscapes and seascapes of the simpler type were published in 1887 by Harper in *Bar Harbor Days,* a novel by Mrs. Burton Harrison, a popular fiction writer.[148] His last major poetry commission, an 1897 edition of Tennyson's *In Memoriam,* would be a more restrained example of the Aesthetic style.

In addition to fresh approaches to book design, publishers in this period experimented with other new technologies besides process line cuts. One that began to be used in the 1880s and 1890s was photogravure, an intaglio process akin to aquatint (it is sometimes called photo-aquatint) that used photography to make intaglio plates; capable of reproducing either photographs or tonal artworks, it yielded rich shades in black and white or sepia and required separate printing on heavy paper.[149] Fenn was one of many artists who contributed to a publication utilizing this process, *Picturesque California and the Regions West of the Rocky Mountains, from Alaska to Mexico.*

New Clients, New Technologies, New Home

Published in 1888 by James Dewing and Company of San Francisco, it was the most ambitious publishing project yet attempted by a Western firm, and its pages demonstrated the region's cultural amenities as well as its spectacular scenery.[150] The book was edited by the naturalist and writer John Muir and included contributions from many other California writers and artists. In addition to photogravures, this ten-volume tour de force displayed most of the printing technologies of the time, including etchings, wood engravings, line blocks, and photo-etchings.[151] For a book with the word *picturesque* in the title, Fenn was an obvious choice to contribute illustrations, as were such artists as Thomas Moran, Charles Graham, Thomas Hill, William Keith, and Julian Rix, all of whom had painted the West. Fenn must have worked from photographs, for he first traveled to California only in 1890; he contributed "Upper End of the Hetch-Hetchy Valley" (photogravure from a watercolor); "The Grizzly Giant"; and two views of the Hotel del Monte in Monterey.[152]

A long-standing goal of some printers and publishers was to print in full color, but the complicated color halftone process took years to develop. Before it was introduced widely, the publishing firm of Frederick A. Stokes printed four of Fenn's works in 1888 by chromolithography, a planographic process in use since midcentury. They illustrated *Bethlehem to Jerusalem,* a poem credited to George Klingle, the pseudonym of Georgiana Klingle Holmes, and were described on the title page as "facsimiles of water-color sketches . . . from studies made in the Holy Land by Harry Fenn."[153] The same images appeared again in Fenn's collaboration with the young artist Susie Barstow Skelding (1857–1934), whose many books of flower and bird illustrations had already been published by Stokes. In their first joint effort, titled *Bits of Distant Land and Sea,* the contrast between the two artists' work is great. Where Fenn's striking vignettes display his usual dramatic viewpoints, some with diagonal compositions and some with bold verticals (fig. 5.36), Skelding's show stiff, horizontal formats. The difference was noted by one reviewer, who found Fenn's works "immeasurably superior to the others in conception and technique."[154] "Church of the Nativity, Bethlehem" is like his steel engraving of the same site in *Picturesque Palestine* (see fig. 4.15), which he clearly used as a source; oddly, however, the colors in the book are soft pastels.[155] In November 1889, the Stokes firm mounted an exhibition at their Fifth Avenue store of watercolors prepared for their publications, including some by Fenn and Skelding.[156] This is one example among many of publishers either exhibiting Fenn's works or submitting them to displays organized by others, a practice that indicates the publishers not only owned the originals on which the illustrations were based but also valued them as artworks in their own right.[157]

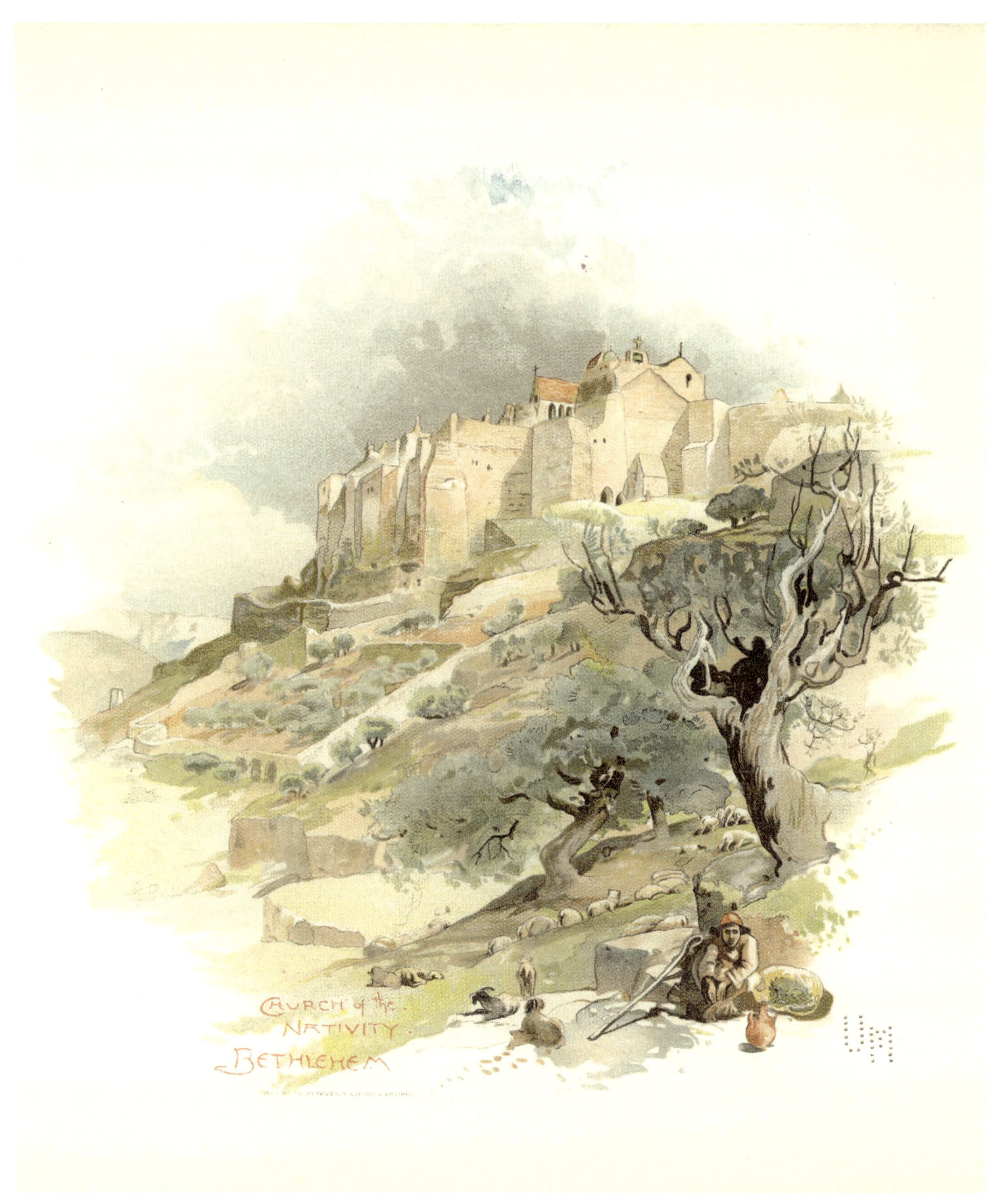

5.36. Harry Fenn, "Church of the Nativity, Bethlehem." From *Bits of Distant Land and Sea,* ed. and illus. Susie Barstow Skelding (New York: Frederick Stokes and Brother, 1888), n.p. Chromolithograph, 10 1/4" x 9 1/2".

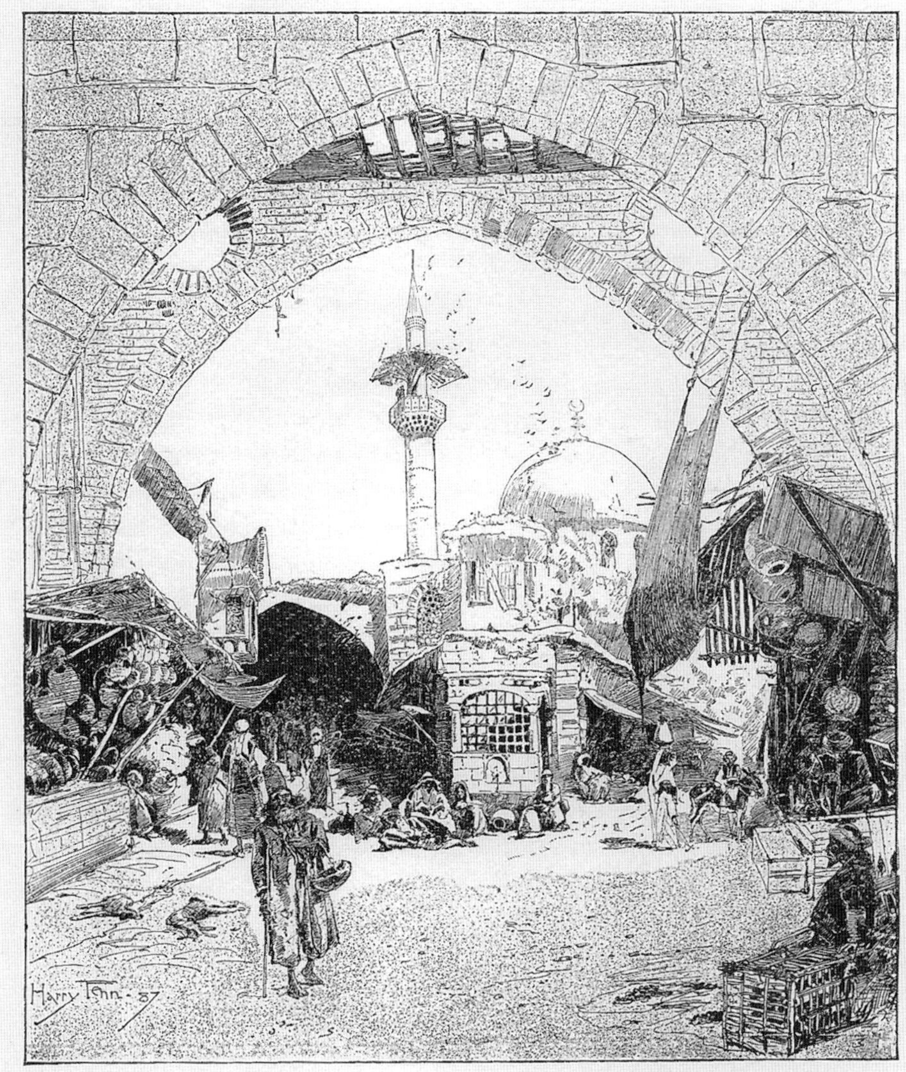

✳355—THE GREEN MOSQUE—24x29—HARRY FENN.

5.37. "✳355—The Green Mosque—24 x 29—Harry Fenn." From *American Water Color Society. Sixteenth Annual Exhibition. Illustrated Catalogue, New York, 1883.* Process line cut, 4 1/2" x 4".

SUCCESSES IN WATERCOLOR

Remarkably, even as he worked to complete such a plethora of commissions, Fenn also found time to produce watercolors for exhibition and sale. In fact, his paintings in the later 1880s often garnered more favorable comments than had his earlier work in the medium. In 1887 *The Green Mosque* ($300) was praised by reviewers of the American Water Color Society's twentieth annual exhibition; a small reproduction was included in the catalogue (fig. 5.37) as well as in the February 5 issue of *Harper's Weekly.* In the estimation of the *Weekly's* critic: "Mr. Harry Fenn is seen at his best in the present exhibition with an Oriental study, 'The Green Mosque,' a riotous wealth of Asiatic detail and color."[158] When the painting was shown in April at the Boston Art Club, another critic singled it out in language revealing a preference for more traditional works:

> Among these pictures Harry Fenn's "Green Mosque, Damascus" (No. 39), takes first place, for many reasons. It is, above all things, a picture, not a study. . . . The foreground of the picture is in shadow under a huge arch of rugged masonry; beyond is the full white light of an Eastern day falling on decrepit ruins and strange men and women, and flashing on the white bulb of a Saracenic dome and the vitreous blue of a slender minaret. Seen from a distance of about five feet, the work is a wonder of varied and beautiful color, rich and compact as an Oriental shawl. . . . The study of character is also very wonderful. . . . Technically the thing is masterly, not only in the ease of the handling, but in the truth of tones and of values, in the exactitude of the infinite textures, in the clear rendering of deep shadow and veritable light. . . . It is a good picture in every way.[159]

This was high praise, indeed, for his composition, light, color, and figure drawing, elements that some earlier critics had disparaged. From the small black and white reproduction, it is impossible to tell if this critic's praise is justified, but apparently Fenn's skill in handling color had improved. His painting *The Washing-Ground, Madrid,* exhibited at the society's 1888 show, received praise from several quarters as well, including a reviewer in the *Independent,* who described it as "a sparkling and spirited piece of work with a brilliant color scheme in which the stretches of snowy linen strike the most conspicuous note."[160]

Until this time, few of Fenn's works had featured figures; perhaps the strong preference for figural art in this period motivated him to depart from his usual approach. His "figure picture" titled *The Lone Hand* received mixed reviews when exhibited at the Brooklyn Art Association in 1885. As described by a *Brooklyn Eagle* critic, who liked it, it showed "a cavalier of the time of Charles the First . . . seated at a table" studying the cards in his hand. This critic considered Fenn, "the well known illustrator," as "equally happy in the painting of both figures and landscape" and praised the thoughtful expression and pose of the figure as well as the drapery, which displayed "the handling of a careful draughtsman and good colorist."[161]

New Clients, New Technologies, New Home

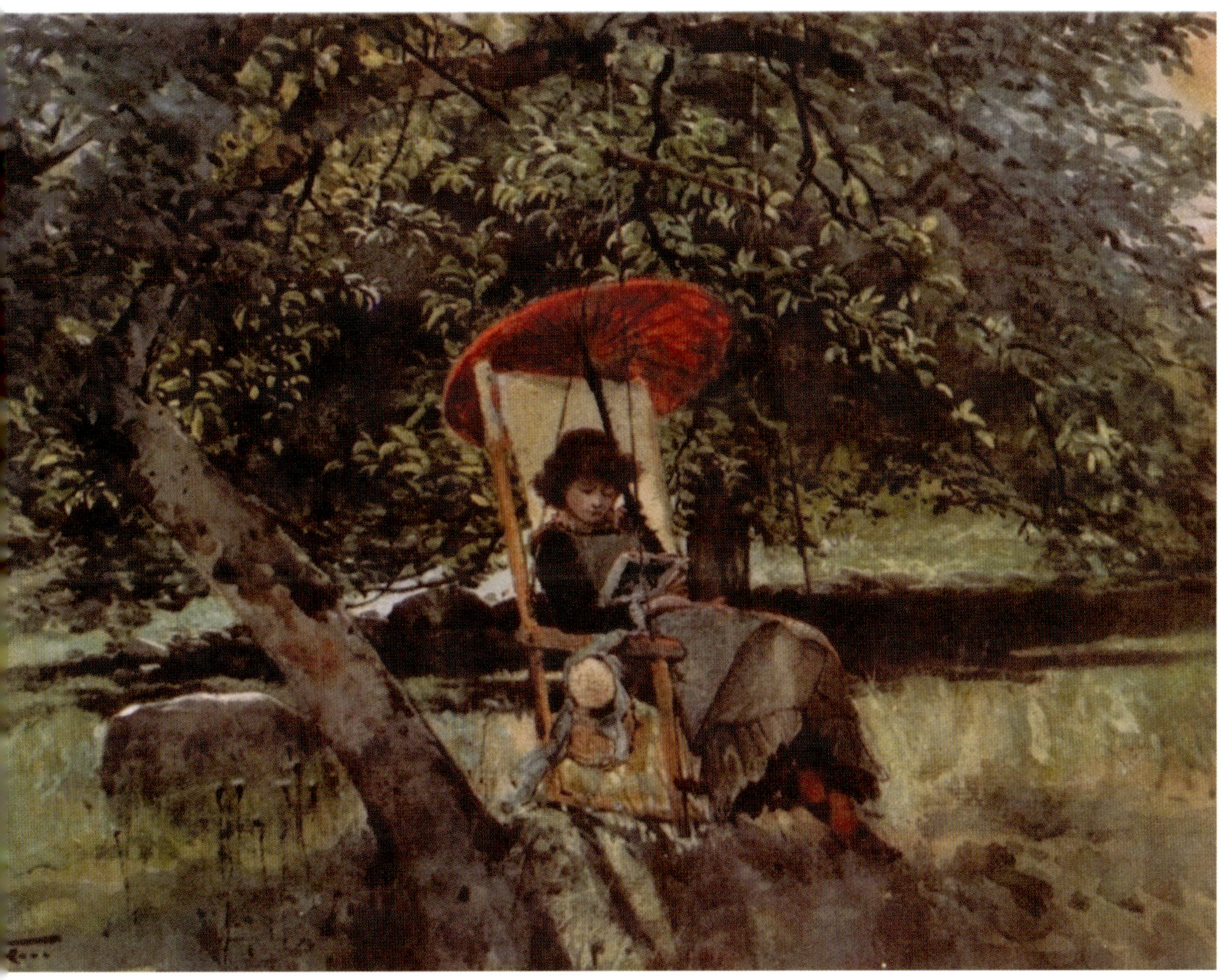

5.38. Harry Fenn, *Summer Afternoon*, n.d. Reproduced from *La Femme* (New York: Grand Central Galleries, 1983), 75. Watercolor on paper, 9" x 11 1/2".

Two other figure paintings featuring young women seated out-of-doors, perhaps one or more of his daughters, stand out among his works. In one, the woman is reading in a lawn chair shaded by a bright red Japanese umbrella (fig. 5.38).[162] The large tree filling the foreground and encompassing the seated figure creates a relatively flat space in which she seems to float. The other, titled *My Grandmother's Garden*, currently known only through its depiction in the catalogue of the 1890 American Water Color Society exhibition, shows a woman seated among hollyhocks and poppies, apparently meditating on the letter in her lap (fig. 5.39). Both

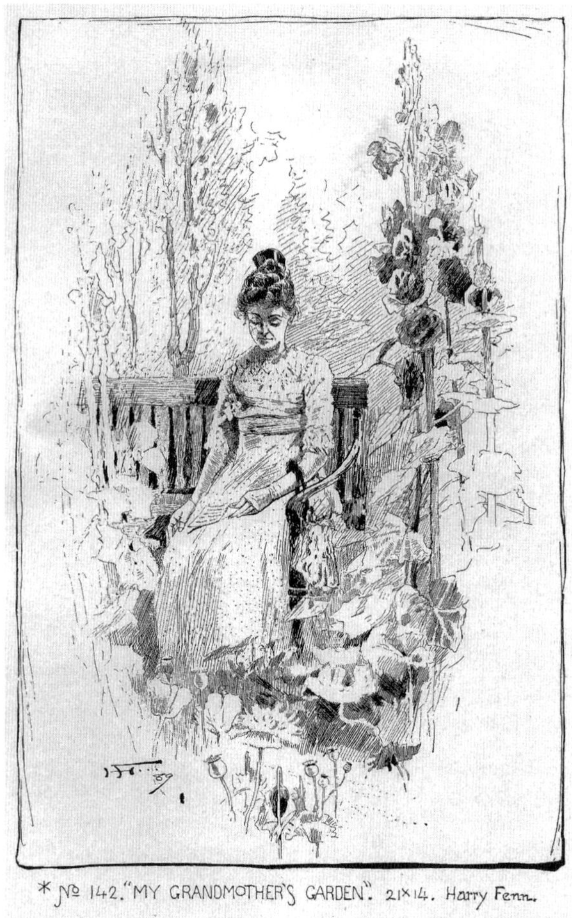

5.39. "No. 142. 'My Grandmother's Garden.' 21" x 14". Harry
Fenn." From *American Water Color Society. Twenty-third Annual
Exhibition. Illustrated Catalogue*. New York, 1890. Process line cut,
6 3/8" x 4 1/8".

paintings have parallels to many by other artists from the 1880s through the turn of the century that depict women indoors or out, reading or contemplating, suggesting the life of the mind and the spirit.[163] Perhaps if more figure paintings by Fenn come to light, an evaluation of his skills in this realm will be possible.

Throughout the 1880s Fenn's exhibition watercolors were illustrated frequently, both in the society's catalogues and in periodicals covering art, a confirmation of his prominence as a painter, considering the hundreds of works typically on display. *The Rialto Market* in Venice was pictured in the catalogue for the 1889 exhibition and was one of fifteen works illustrated in *Harper's Weekly* (fig. 5.40). Although the painting is unlocated, the little black and white depiction of it, when compared with his *Picturesque Europe* illustration of the same subject (fig. 5.41), serves as an example of how he altered earlier works when preparing watercolors for exhibition. In this case, he created the illusion of greater depth by pushing back the buildings and leading the eye through the piles of vegetables to a more ordered array of boats. In addition, he more precisely delineated the arches of the market, the buildings, and the church tower in the background while omitting details that made the illustration appear cluttered, such as the man in the foreground, the woman sitting in a chair, and the large sail. The bright sunlight reflecting on the arches and across the buildings also enhances the image's appeal.

Looking back at Fenn's career one hundred years after his death, it is clear that he reached a peak in the 1880s. From his mid-forties to his mid-fifties, he participated in scores of projects for the era's leading periodicals and publishers of poetry. Many reinforced the pride Americans felt in their country's scenery and tourist facilities; their growing cities populated with impressive new buildings and historic old ones; their cosmopolitan interests in other lands and cultures;

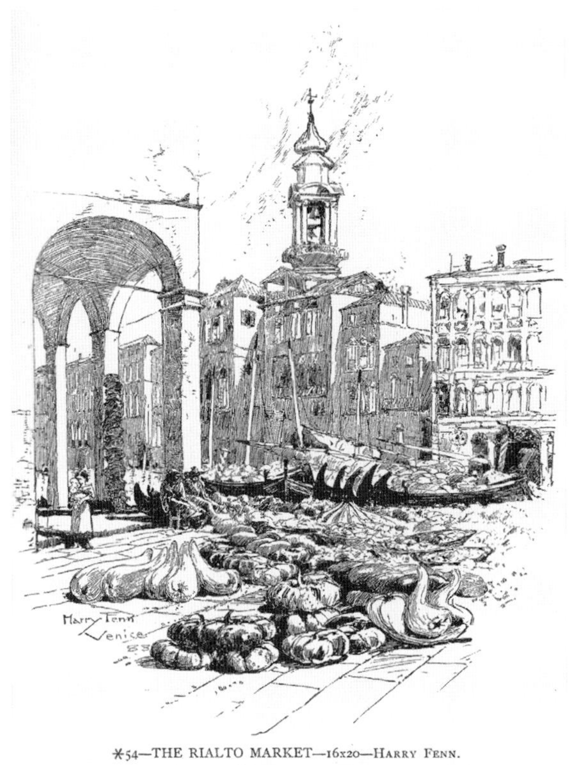

5.40. "*54—The Rialto Market—16 x 20—Harry Fenn." From *American Water Color Society. Twenty-second Annual Exhibition. Illustrated Catalogue. New York, 1889.* Process line cut, 5 3/4" x 4 1/2".

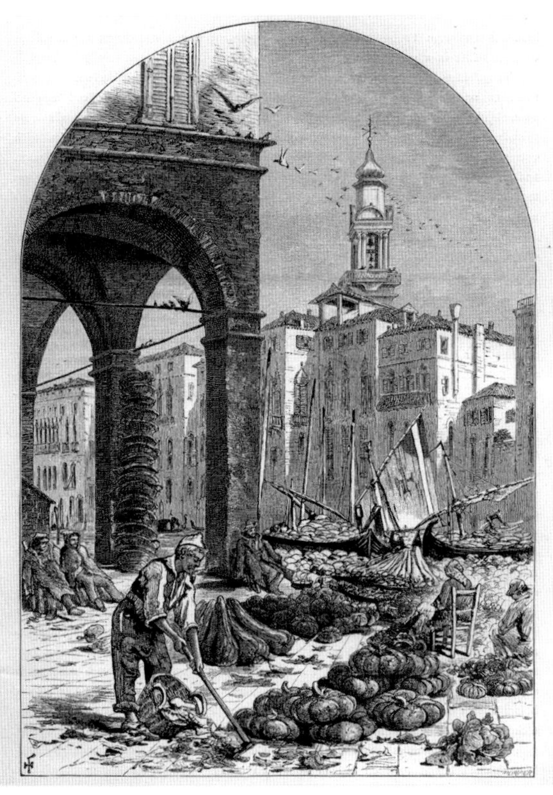

5.41. Harry Fenn, "Vegetable-Market on the Grand Canal, near the Rialto." *Picturesque Europe,* 2:233. Wood engraving by Whymper, 9 3/4" x 6 7/16".

and their compatriots' talents as artists, writers, and publishers. At the same time, Fenn produced a steady stream of watercolors for the popular exhibitions of the American Water Color Society as well as other organizations, which brought him increasing recognition as a painter. And in 1884–85 he completed his distinctive and much-admired home in a desirable New Jersey suburb. In a front-page story about Fenn that appeared in the September 1889 issue of the journal *American Bookmaker,* the writer stressed that the artist "has been as conscientious and manly as he has been persevering and industrious"—this at a time when some worried that newer notions of art for art's sake, or art divorced from spiritual values, would lead to social and political degeneration instead of wholesome activity.[164] He was also credited with an uncommonly long period of "successful work" producing imagery in the familiar, traditional styles that were reassuring and still admired by many audiences.[165] Clearly, Fenn was thriving in this period.

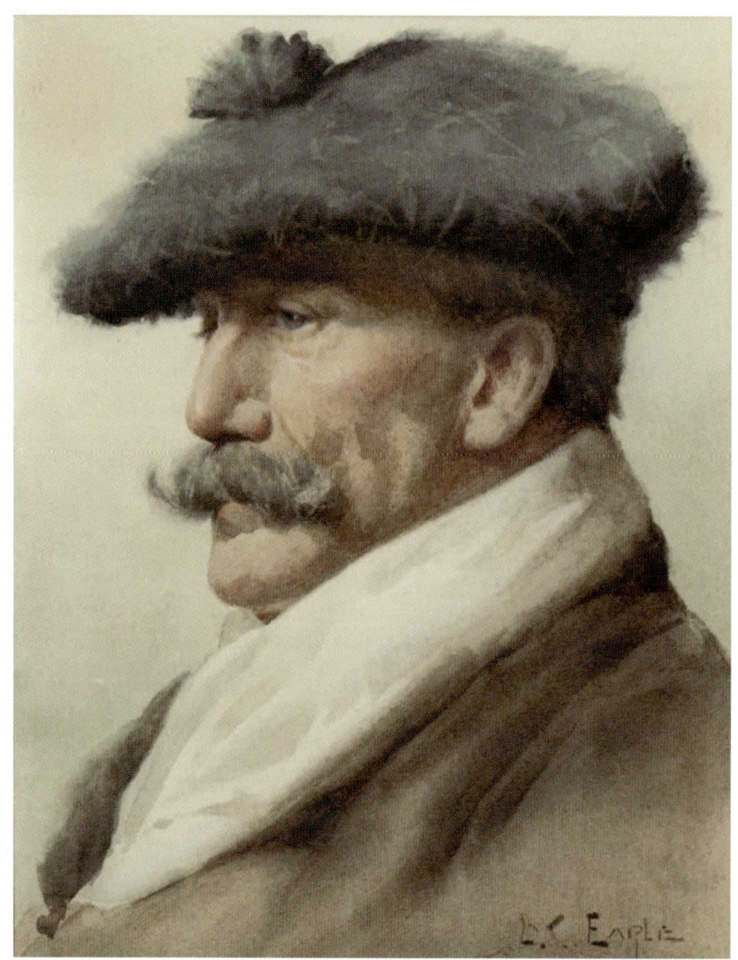

6.1. Lawrence C. Earle (1845–1921), *Portrait of Harry Fenn*, n.d. Watercolor on paper, 13" x 9 3/4". (Montclair Art Museum, Gift of Dr. Morgan Ayres, 1923,1.)

6

Challenges and Triumphs— The 1890s and Beyond

S THE END OF THE NINETEENTH CENTURY approached, the United States was greatly changed since Fenn's arrival in 1857. It was now one of the most prosperous and powerful nations on earth. Its population of more than seventy million, which stretched from coast to coast, was in closer contact than ever before thanks to the railroads, the telegraph, and the telephone. Experiments with a new mode of transportation, the automobile, were also under way. Cities located on railroad lines in the middle of the country were booming, and much of the nation's wheat, corn, and cotton was being shipped overseas.[1] More people now worked in manufacturing and mining than in agriculture. The American steel industry had outstripped England's, and, with the Bessemer converter and open-hearth process, it was poised to supply the necessary material to build infrastructure, from bridges and skyscrapers to water lines and sewer pipes.[2] As one American trade official would boast in 1900, "It seems almost incredible that we should be sending cutlery to Sheffield, pig iron to Birmingham, silks to France, watch cases to Switzerland . . . or building *sixty* locomotives for British railroads."[3] The 1898 Spanish–American War set the United States on the road to empire, and, after it secured territories that could serve as fueling stations across the Pacific, business interests pushed to expand trade with China, Korea, and Japan.[4]

Yet the growing materialism and widening divide between rich and poor troubled many people, especially as the numbers of immigrants increased; more than five million arrived between 1880 and 1890, many from southern and eastern Europe.[5] Workers organized to demand higher wages, but their efforts foundered against the power of big business, as when hired guards battled employees in the 1892 Homestead strike against the Carnegie Steel Company. The Pullman

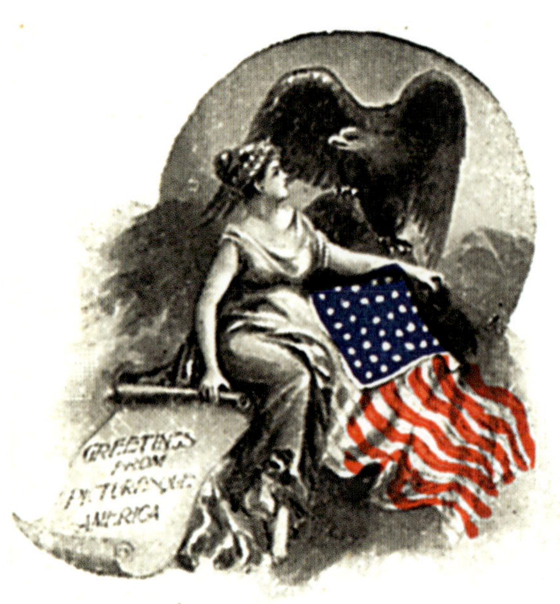

6.2. "Greetings from Picturesque America," detail of "private mailing card" from the series published by Arthur Livingston, New York. (Private collection.)

strike of 1894 against the Great Northern Railway was squelched only when President Grover Cleveland sent in federal troops. Such disruptions challenged confidence in inevitable progress, humanity's intuitive moral sense, and the ability of science and technology to improve the lives of all citizens, just as they raised fears that radical elements would overturn the social order.

In these years, Fenn continued to prepare works that celebrated scenery, promoted travel, and depicted not only aspects of history but also new initiatives in agriculture and transportation. He also took on assignments that publicized America's growth and expansion and provided glimpses of faraway lands and different cultures, such as China and Indonesia. Despite the great changes and problems troubling society, many of the attitudes that Fenn's art had always helped promote or reinforce were still current, including interest in experiencing Europe and the Middle East, whether through lectures, travel clubs, or actual travel, and especially pride in the American landscape and travel to see it.[6] Clearly, the mission of *Picturesque America* and similar projects had been effective. Indeed, in F. Hopkinson Smith's book *American Illustrators,* one speaker calls on artists to stop globetrotting and paint "American life and characteristics," for doing so will show that the country has "GOT the things to paint from." It proclaimed: "With a mountain and river scenery unrivaled on the globe; with rock-bound coasts breaking the full surge of an ocean; with forests of towering trees compared to which in girth and height the trees of all other lands are but tooth-picks; with plains ending in films of blue haze and valleys sparkling with myriads of waterfalls; with every type of the human race blended in our own . . . with a history filled with traditions the most romantic—Aztec, Indian and Negro . . . what do we want to go away from home to find something to paint?"[7]

Similarly, a ten-part series titled "Through Picturesque America, in One Hundred Views of Scenic Magnificence" occupied the centerfold of the *Ladies' Home Journal* for most of 1900. Each month the double-page spread was filled with ten photographs of notable places, with brief text by journalist and travel writer Luther L. Holden.[8] Although the technology, format, and audience were vastly

Challenges and Triumphs

different, the message was similar to that of *Picturesque America*. Other examples of the ongoing persistence of that cultural landmark include the use of the phrase "Picturesque America" on postcards, a newly popular product that was replacing travel letters. One series featured images of places throughout the country inset with an eagle, an American flag, and a woman holding a poster declaring, "Greetings from Picturesque America" (fig. 6.2).[9] By contrast, for many the ubiquitous concept of a "Picturesque America" had become old-fashioned, appropriate for jest and satire, as seen in two cartoons produced by Charles Dana Gibson in 1900. In one, the lovely "Gibson girls" are arrayed on the

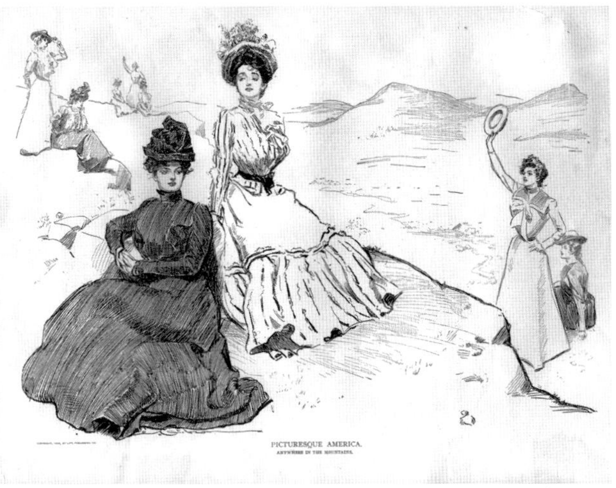

6.3. C. D. Gibson, "Picturesque America. Anywhere in the Mountains." From Charles Dana Gibson, *Americans Drawn by Charles Dana Gibson* (New York: R. H. Russell, 1900), n.p. Process line cut, approx. 9" x 12 1/2".

beach above the caption, "Picturesque America: Anywhere Along the Coast"; in the other, they are set in the mountains, above a similar title (fig. 6.3).[10]

Fenn remained extremely active in his artistic career—the consummate professional who sought and fulfilled myriad commissions and participated in artists' organizations and exhibitions. His reputation as an illustrator remained strong with the general public, and publishers still featured his name to promote their books and periodicals. Yet cheaper periodicals and wider use of the halftone process to print photographs was further transforming the world of illustration that Fenn had known so well. In addition, younger artists working in radically different styles were gaining greater attention and favor from the critics; some, like E. A. Abbey, Joseph Pennell, Frederic Remington, and Gibson, are better known today, whereas others, like Alfred Brennan and André Castaigne, are largely forgotten. Although Fenn was still mentioned in articles on contemporary illustration, his name more often appeared near the end than in the beginning, as did those of female illustrators.[11] An 1891 overview titled "Illustration and Our Illustrators" cited his work from "many years ago" on *Picturesque America* as "at the time quite the best thing of its kind that had been done in black and white in this country" while noting that the artist had "kept pace with the advanced methods of picture making."[12] Although Fenn was increasingly perceived as an elder statesman, his remarkable adaptability enabled him to persevere and continue to make significant contributions.

New Magazines, New Processes, and New Illustrators

The world of illustrated magazines would change and expand in the 1890s in ways that could scarcely have been anticipated when Fenn returned from England a decade earlier. New, more cheaply produced magazines were gaining a large share of the market. A prime example is the *Ladies' Home Journal,* which had launched in 1883 and cost only fifty cents a year; by 1890, it anticipated 600,000 subscribers at $1 a year.[13] For this and most of the other new magazines, advertising revenues offset manufacturing costs and allowed low subscription rates. (Designing images for ads would eventually become a lucrative field for some illustrators while undermining their prestige as fine artists; Fenn is not known to have worked in this field.) Fenn's major clients, the *Century, Harper's Monthly,* and *Scribner's Magazine,* had also gradually included more advertising in separate sections at the front and back. Because they continued to use many wood engravings, however, their expenses for illustrations remained high, and issues still sold for thirty-five cents each, or $4 a year. The *Cosmopolitan,* a magazine that competed with the three long-established general periodicals, started out slowly but gained readership after John Brisben Walker purchased it in 1889. He kept the price low—twenty-five cents—by selling much advertising and using primarily the new halftone process for illustrations; he also gave relatively more attention to science, politics, and world affairs.[14] Another low-priced illustrated periodical was *Munsey's,* which switched from being a weekly to a monthly in 1891.

By 1890, the halftone process, in which an image photographed through a cross-line screen was used to create a metal relief printing plate, had gained wide acceptance; it could reproduce both artworks and photographs. As Tom Gretton has described it: "The half-tone screen works by exposing a negative onto a sensitized zinc plate, interposing a glass screen on which a very fine grid of black lines has been made, turning the continuous tone into a pattern of dots of varying sizes but invariant tone."[15] To produce good-quality prints from the tiny raised dots required smooth paper to receive the ink. To meet this need, advances in paper manufacturing led to commercial-scale production of calendered paper, whose smooth and glossy surface also greatly improved the printing of wood engravings by allowing for greater tonal range and sharpness.[16] The Harper firm and the *Century* tried using a few halftones in 1884 and 1885. The cost saving compared to wood engravings was dramatic: whereas a full-page wood engraving cost around $300 to prepare, a halftone cost only $20. However, cross-line screens were difficult to make, and the early halftones often lacked sharpness and contrast. In 1890, the *Century* was still spending about $8,000 an issue on wood engravings. But that year, after Levy Brothers of Philadelphia began mass-producing good quality diamond-ruled cross-line screens, the use of halftones increased greatly in most major magazines.[17]

Lower-cost periodicals became even more appealing when the United States suffered a severe economic depression that began in early 1893 and continued for four years. The downturn was brought on by unregulated capitalism, especially the over-expansion of railroads with shaky financial backing. The Philadelphia and Reading Railroad was the first to declare bankruptcy, on February 23, 1893, and runs on banks, bank failures, and further railroad insolvencies followed. Unemployment soared, especially among industrial workers in cities, and farmers suffered as prices plummeted. Coinciding with these economic woes affecting all aspects of American life, something of a revolution occurred in magazine publishing, heralded by even lower prices and changes in content. S. S. McClure launched his illustrated monthly, *McClure's,* at fifteen cents an issue, and in response John Brisben Walker and Frank Munsey soon cut the prices of their magazines as well—*Cosmopolitan* to twelve and a half cents, and *Munsey's* to ten cents.[18] Within four months *Munsey's* circulation had skyrocketed from 20,000 to 200,000.[19]

While the older magazines still focused much attention on Europe and history, the newer ones gave more space to the contemporary American scene (the muckraking era would begin in *McClure*'s pages in 1902).[20] The latter aimed at a popular audience, offering fiction and accounts of exotic places and current celebrities, such as wealthy entrepreneurs and lovely actresses and society hostesses. The *Ladies' Home Journal* offered advice about fashion, home decorating, and entertaining. *Munsey's* regularly included reproductions of European paintings of female nudes and sharply differentiated itself from the cultural aims of the long-established leaders to educate and improve: "We aim to give you just what you want. Munsey's Magazine is not a class magazine, but a magazine for the people—the whole people, the great, broad, seventy million people. . . . Our thought is bent on determining your thought, your fancies and desires, rather than on the dream of an ideal magazine for an ideal people. Our aim has been to make a magazine for the people just as we find them—good, rich, healthy, buoyant human nature—not the pale porcelain variety."[21] Richard Ohmann, in *Selling Culture,* summarizes the appeal of these new, cheaper magazines: "They took from the weeklies the idea of a lively pictorial appearance, from these and a few of the monthlies a willingness to hustle ads . . . from the women's magazines and the mail order journals the idea of a very low price that would attract a large audience of people with only a little extra money to spend."[22]

These periodicals, as well as *Frank Leslie's Popular Monthly,* would gain an increasingly large share of the market; from the late 1890s through the early 1900s the circulation figures of the *Century, Harper's Monthly,* and *Scribner's* declined, and the magazines never regained their preeminence. In contrast, by April 1895 *Munsey's* circulation had jumped to 500,000 and by the end of the year *McClure's* reached 250,000, far exceeding the older leaders.[23] Many people were shocked when the Harper firm declared bankruptcy on December 4, 1899, and went into receivership. In the estimation of William Dean Howells, "It was as if I had read that the government of the United States had failed."[24] The bankruptcy resulted from more than just declining circulations, of course, but the world of magazine publishing was definitely in flux.

The periodicals that had played such an important cultural role for several decades had succeeded in attracting a large audience among the educated and relatively well off, but the reach of the newer magazines was unprecedented. Ohmann estimates that there were "no mass circulation magazines in 1885," but by 1900 about twenty existed. Furthermore, the total circulation of monthlies was "about 18 million in 1890, and 64 million in 1905," roughly "three copies for every four people, or about four to every household" in the United States.[25] As these publications disseminated information via words and images and encouraged purchases of nationally advertised products, they became key in the development of a common culture across the country. Since Fenn did relatively little work for these magazines, he would not play as vital a role in shaping images of the United States and the rest of the world as he had in earlier decades.

The proliferation of illustrated magazines created more opportunities for younger illustrators—with the demand attracting some from abroad—and soon trade magazines and professional societies were established to foster exchanges and help build careers. Publishers featured the artist-illustrators who were enlivening their pages and attracting audiences in articles and books; a prime example was Smith's *American Illustrators* (1892), in which the character known as "the Doctor" called Fenn "the Nestor of his guild" and gave him credit for popularizing illustration.[26] Charles Scribner's firm published elaborate folios of "proof impressions" from its most popular magazines in 1879 and 1881, highlighting the wood engravers as well as designers.[27] The *Quarterly Illustrator,* published in New York from 1893 to 1895, served as a directory for publishers and editors in search of illustrators, providing "a representative selection from all the great periodicals"; several of Fenn's works were reproduced in its pages.[28] This move toward greater professionalism was in part an attempt to maintain the status of illustrators as disseminators of fine art—removed from commercialism—even as the magazines' dependence on advertising and mechanical means

    Challenges and Triumphs

of reproduction increased.[29] In 1901 the Society of Illustrators was established to promote the profession by holding exhibitions and trying to improve business dealings with publishers. Fenn became a member.[30]

The younger illustrators who garnered attention and praise in the 1890s included many whose careers had begun to flourish in the previous decade and whose work filled the pages of the *Century* and Harper's periodicals alongside those of Fenn.[31] Several of them, according to Joseph Pennell, looked for inspiration to the works of the Spanish artists Mariano Fortuny (1835–1874), Daniel Vierge (1851–1904), and Martin Rico (1833–1880) and emulated many aspects of their styles. These included Fortuny's "use of short, broken lines, or, rather, the substitution of the spot for the line" and "the omission of the definite outline"; Vierge's "delicate modeling"; and Rico's "grace of line" and "brilliancy of light."[32] The illustrator W. A. Rogers recalled that he and his young colleagues in New York would gather weekly at Brentano's bookstore "to see what Vierge had to

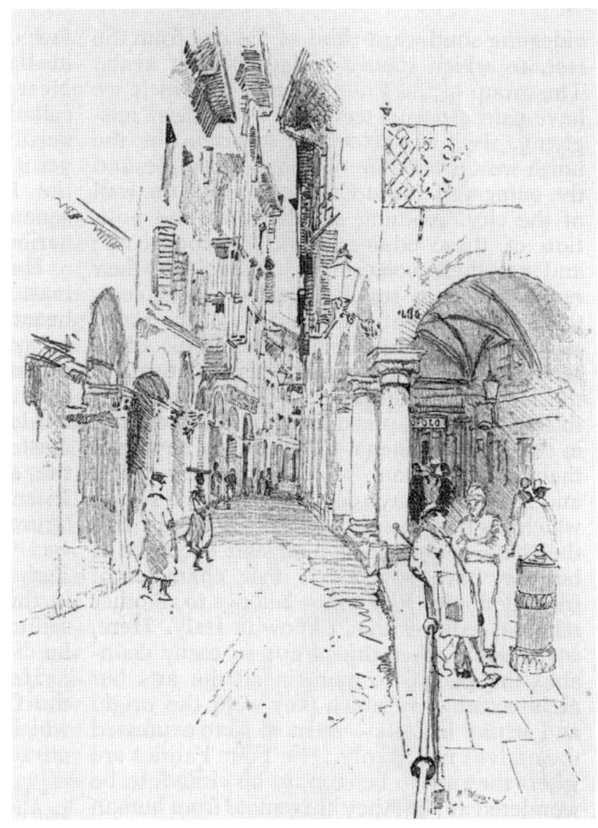

6.4. Joseph Pennell, "An Arcaded Street, Pisa," in "Tuscan Cities" by W. D. Howells. *Century*, October 1885, 895. Wood engraving, approx. 4 1/8" x 3".

offer" in the latest issue of the Paris newspaper *Le Monde illustré,* just off the steamship. They would crowd around Edwin A. Abbey, who held the paper, and comment "enthusiastically on the amazing effects of sunlight, where by the white paper's dazzle the great Spaniard had made magic somethings out of optical nothings. Then we would all disperse to our dens, there to dream dreams of being Daniel Vierges ourselves on some future day."[33] An article in the June 1893 *Century* titled "The Father of Modern Illustration: Daniel Vierge Urrabieta" by August F. Jaccaci describes Vierge as a great artist whose example had fostered advances in illustration by other illustrators as well as wood engravers during the previous twenty years.[34]

Pennell's early illustrations for the *Century*—images of European cities and scenery—show a variety of approaches similar to those of the Spanish artists. Many gave the impression of quickly drawn sketches, with relatively few lines and the white of the paper contributing to the composition (fig. 6.4); some were open-sided, irregularly shaped vignettes with dramatic perspective (for example, "Monument

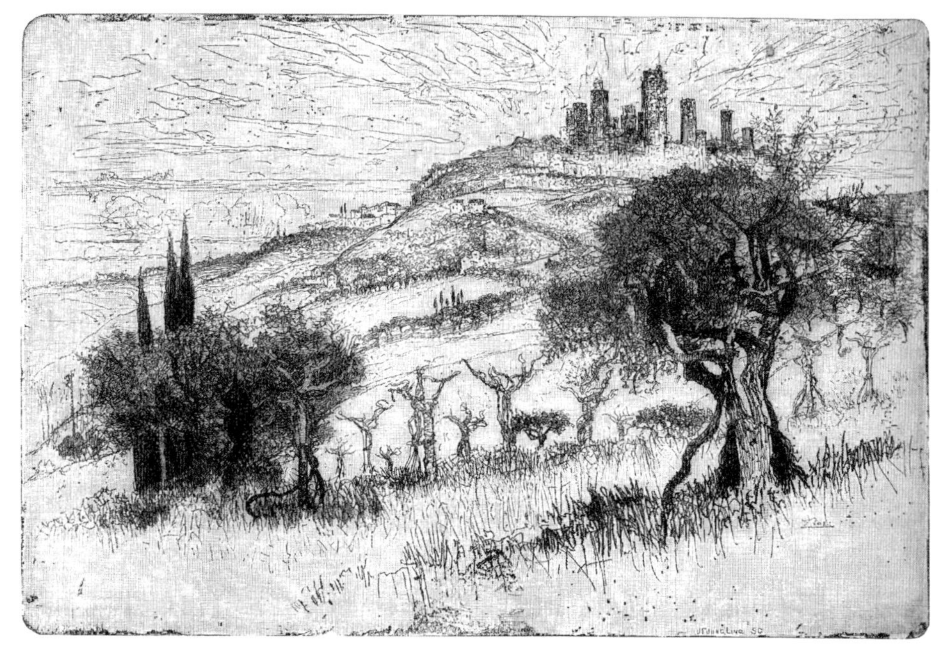

in Phoenix Park, From the River," December 1884, p. 176); others used a gray tone to set off the paper of the "etching" or "sketch" from the page, as Fenn had also done. The new approaches to wood engraving discussed earlier could effectively represent the various media that Pennell, Fenn, and other artists used. As etchings were gaining in popularity, one critic commented on how the wood engraver Frederick Juengling had managed to convey the look of that medium in one example by Pennell, "A Mountain Town" (fig. 6.5): "The things that wood engravers can do nowadays would startle old Bewick out of a year's growth, were he alive to see them." The illustration "might readily be taken for an etching itself. . . . The play of the needle along the copper in the outlining of the clouds and the little dots where the acid has cut through the varnish in the process of biting the lines have been reproduced with an exactitude almost photographic."[35]

As the world of illustration expanded to include cheaper periodicals and younger illustrators with different approaches, Fenn adapted to the increased competition by widening his client base and experimenting with compositions and techniques. For example, he created for *St. Nicholas* what was for him a noteworthy departure: "In the Clover" (fig. 6.6) shows a young boy lying in a meadow and accompanies Maurice Thompson's poem by the same name. With a high horizon line, large areas of few details, and relatively flat space, except for the wildflowers that break out of the picture frame, it has the look of an etching, but

   Challenges and Triumphs

its spatial arrangement resembles the compositions of some Japanese prints. Fenn was indeed
experimenting.

Moreover, he obviously did not think he
was above working for the newer magazines.
Although some ridiculed the *Ladies' Home Journal* as appealing to lowbrow women, he contributed at least two illustrations to the publication,
including a pen drawing titled "The Valley of
the Bow" of a site in western Canada, to accompany Lady Macdonald's article "An Unconventional Holiday" (September 1891).[36] As early as
June 1890 he was taking on assignments for the
Cosmopolitan as well. For the article "Soft Crabs,
Canvasbacks, and Terrapin," he prepared several
ink drawings with a distinctly Japanese look (fig.
6.7), especially seen in the decorative initial letter,
with its two-dimensional pattern, and an illustration titled "Shedding," with overlapping elements and an implied progression (fig. 6.8).[37] For
the May 1891 *Cosmopolitan* he composed architectural images for the article "The New Philadelphia" by Henry C. Walsh, including "The
Chestnut Street National Bank," a striking full-
page rendering from an unusually high, raking
viewpoint. He used a similar, although lower, viewpoint
for "The Cliff-Dwellers of New York," published in the
magazine's July 1893 issue (fig. 6.9).[38] (See Appendix 1
for other *Cosmopolitan* and *McClure's Magazine* illustrations by Fenn.)

DIFFICULTIES AND INITIATIVES: LETTERS
FROM THE 1890S

In this changed environment, with magazines using more
photographs and young artists meeting the demand for
illustrations, Fenn had to strive to maintain his position.

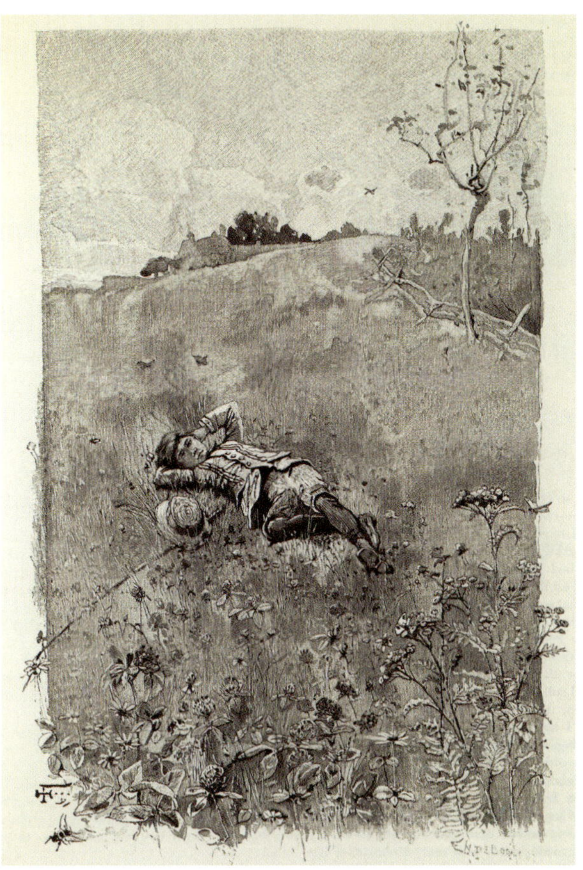

6.6. Harry Fenn, "In the Clover," for poem of the same title by
Maurice Thompson. *St. Nicholas,* July 1891, 711. Wood engraving
by [illegible], approx. 7 1/2" x 5".

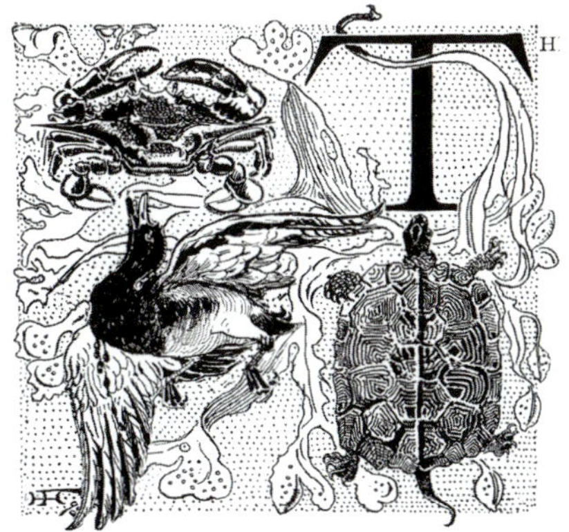

6.7. Harry Fenn, opening for "Soft Crabs,
Canvasbacks, and Terrapin" by Allan
Forman. *Cosmopolitan,* June 1890, 145.
Process line cut, approx. 3 1/8" x 3 5/16".
(Library of Virginia.)

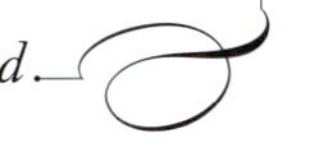

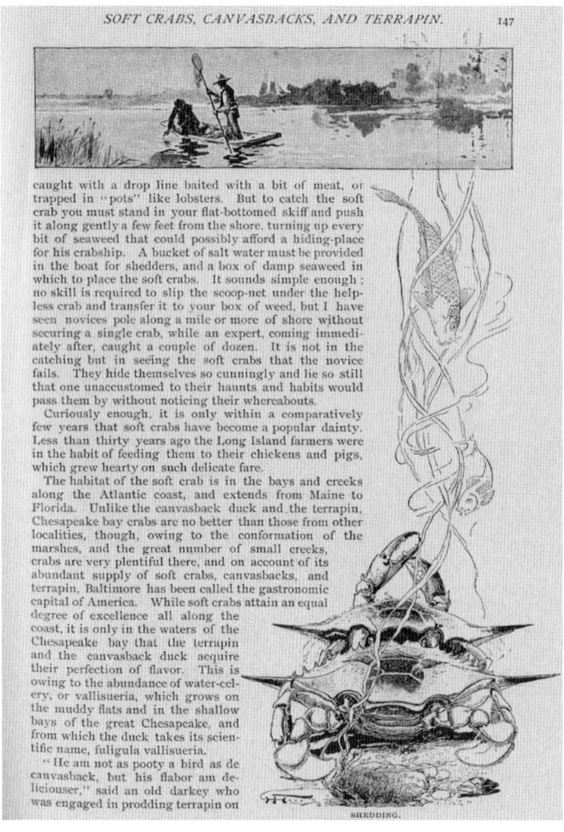

6.8. Harry Fenn, "Shedding," in "Soft Crabs, Canvasbacks, and Terrapin." *Cosmopolitan*, June 1890, 147. Process line cut, 7 3/4" x 4 3/4". (Library of Virginia.)

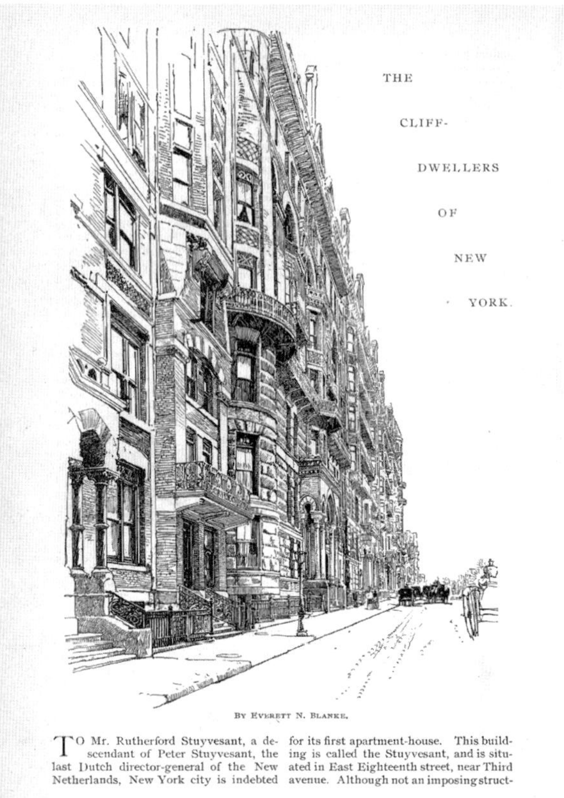

6.9. Harry Fenn, opening for "The Cliff-Dwellers of New York" by Everett N. Blanke. *Cosmopolitan*, July 1893, 354. Process line cut, approx. 7" x 4 1/4".

Several letters from the 1890s shed light on the challenges he faced as well as some of the indignities he suffered. Reviewing this correspondence before looking in detail at specific commissions will help explain his working methods and how he related to clients and colleagues. They also show that although most of the subjects Fenn illustrated at this stage were selected by an editor, publisher, or writer, he sometimes proposed topics as well.

The constant need to control expenses must have affected the way publishers of the older periodicals dealt with artists, and Fenn saw his commissions from some of them decline. He was not always given the choice assignments, as revealed by a most unusual, bitingly sarcastic letter to Arthur B. Turnure at the Harper firm in March 1892. In it, Fenn asked: "How can I resist such fascinating subjects? Well not being very busy you shall have them. But I wonder if I shall ever again get a batch from Harpers that I can 'do myself proud' on. 'A bad workman finds

 Challenges and Triumphs

fault with his tools' you will say—But it's hard to 'make a silk purse out of a sow's ear.' By the way you don't say what medium you want them in; pen I presume."[39] This query about medium stands out, especially in light of an earlier letter to F. B. Schell (art director at Harper after Charles Parsons's retirement), in which Fenn, writing about illustrations to be based on photos Schell had sent, says, "I think they will be nearly all pen."[40] In this case, at least, he made the decision about medium himself.

A preliminary layout in Fenn's hand for "Art in Modern Bridges," an article in the May 1900 *Century,* shows that his involvement with page design, which had started with *Picturesque America* and perhaps even earlier, continued throughout his life. For this article, he designed the opening (fig. 6.10) and, for succeeding pages, made quick sketches of bridges in various shapes and sizes arranged with blocks of type. Later he refined the sketches, as shown by comparing his layout sketch for "Karl's Bridge" with the page from the *Century* (figs. 6.11, 6.12).[41] In the article, the prominent architecture critic Montgomery Schuyler laments the absence of "art" in the design of most new bridges in America and calls for architects to work alongside engineers to create bridges that are both structurally sound and aesthetically pleasing. Fenn provided images of bad examples as well as some that Schuyler admired, including Washington Bridge over the Harlem River in New York City and the metal towers of the proposed North River Bridge over the Hudson, designed by Gustav Lindenthal but never built (fig. 6.13).

Fenn also occasionally suggested topics he thought worthy of illustration. Several letters to Schell indicate that when he took more initiative, he expected more compensation—although not much more. For a double-page composite for *Harper's Weekly* of scenes in Rimini, Italy (March 8, 1890), based on photos Schell had sent to him, Fenn's payment was $80.[42] Some months later, concerning a

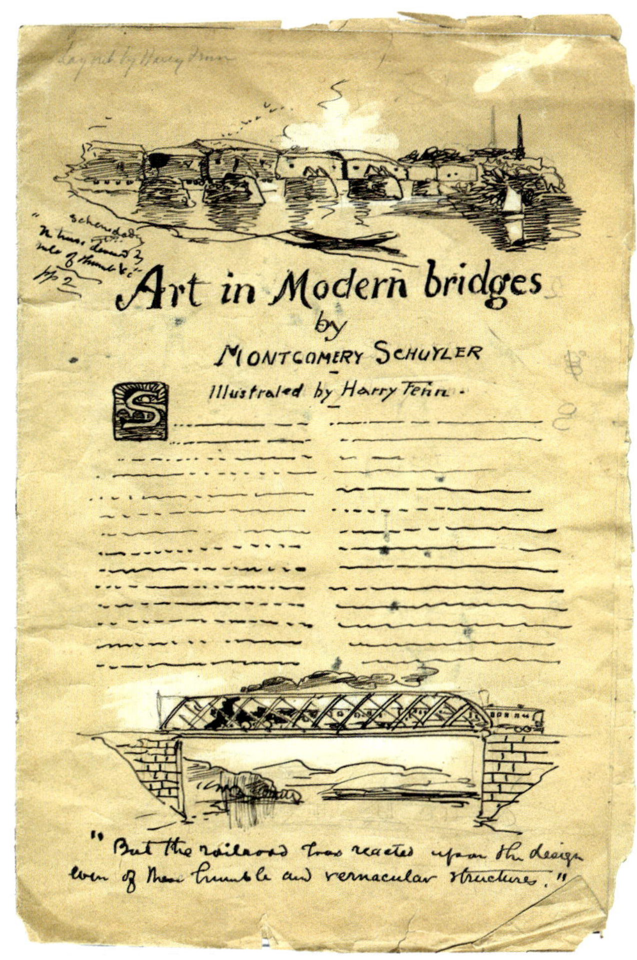

6.10. Harry Fenn, layout for "Art in Modern Bridges," first page. Ink and gouache; sheet 15" x 9 3/4". (Private collection.)

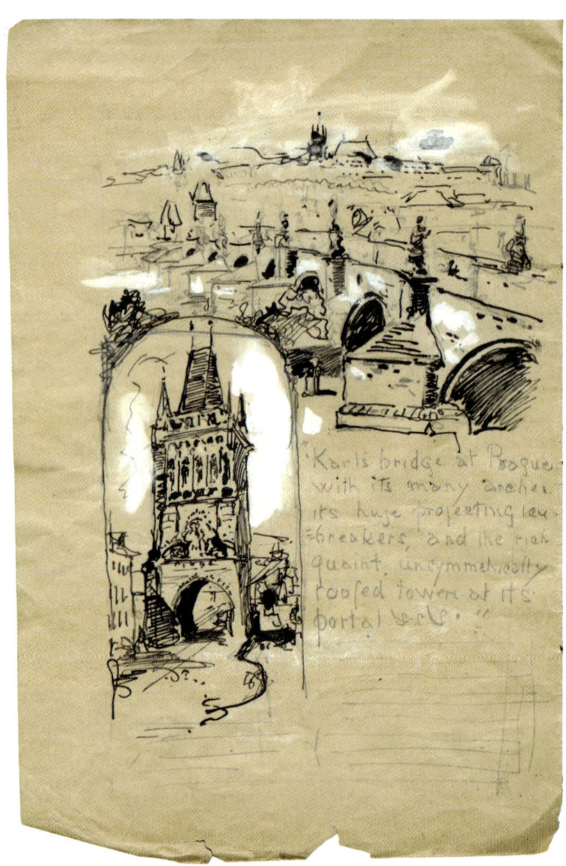

6.11. Harry Fenn, layout for "Art in Modern Bridges," second page. Ink and gouache; sheet 15" x 9 3/4". (Private collection.)

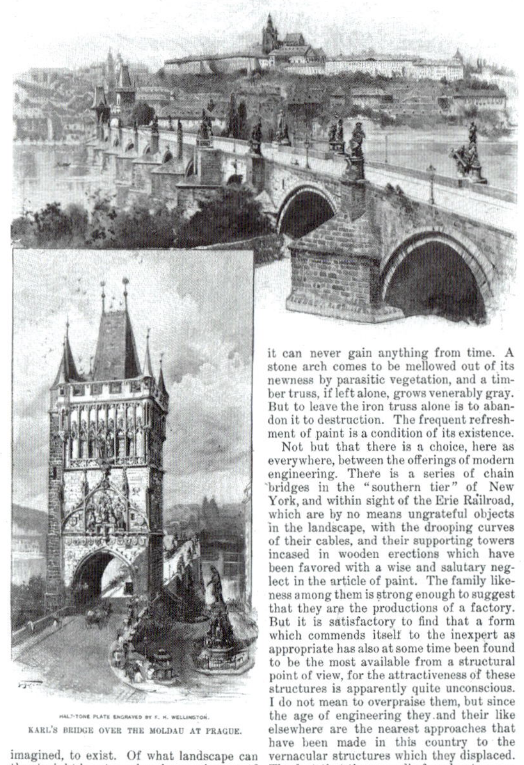

it can never gain anything from time. A stone arch comes to be mellowed out of its newness by parasitic vegetation, and a timber truss, if left alone, grows venerably gray. But to leave the iron truss alone is to abandon it to destruction. The frequent refreshment of paint is a condition of its existence.

Not but that there is a choice, here as everywhere, between the offerings of modern engineering. There is a series of chain bridges in the "southern tier" of New York, and within sight of the Erie Railroad, which are by no means ungrateful objects in the landscape, with the drooping curves of their cables, and their supporting towers incased in wooden erections which have been favored with a wise and salutary neglect in the article of paint. The family likeness among them is strong enough to suggest that they are the productions of a factory. But it is satisfactory to find that a form which commends itself to the inexpert as appropriate has also at some time been found to be the most available from a structural point of view, for the attractiveness of these structures is apparently quite unconscious. I do not mean to overpraise them, but since the age of engineering they and their like elsewhere are the nearest approaches that have been made in this country to the vernacular structures which they displaced. The fact that they are all of moderate span, and by no means *tours de force* from the engineering point of view, tends to assist this

HALF-TONE PLATE ENGRAVED BY F. H. WELLINGTON.

KARL'S BRIDGE OVER THE MOLDAU AT PRAGUE.

imagined, to exist. Of what landscape can the straight iron truss be a harmonious part? What stream, except the Styx, can it appropriately span? One of its misfortunes is that

14

6.12. Harry Fenn, "Karl's Bridge over the Moldau at Prague," in "Art in Modern Bridges" by Montgomery Schuyler. *Century,* May 1900, 14. Halftone plate engraved by F. H. Wellington, approx. 7 1/2" x 5 3/16".

composite titled "Recent Architecture in New Jersey" (*Harper's Weekly,* August 2, 1890), he wrote: "In a former arrangement with Mr. Parsons $85 was my charge for a page when I furnished the subject, hunted up the material[,] paid for photographs and so forth as in this case."[43] Unfortunately, we have no way of knowing if Fenn instigated other projects for the *Weekly,* although it seems likely that it was he who suggested a page of illustrations and a brief article he wrote about new exhibits of medieval ironwork at the Metropolitan Museum of Art (November 9, 1889). An 1895 letter to Richard W. Gilder at the *Century* shows Fenn suggesting a series on the writers of Essex County, Massachusetts—Longfellow, Whittier, Hawthorne, W. H. Prescott, and Louis Agassiz—with Harriet Prescott Spofford as a possible author. He pointed out to Gilder that "hosts of Essex Co. people in the far far west" would find such an article "vastly interesting, if we could make it *smell* strong *enough of the* soil."[44] No doubt Fenn made recommendations about images more often than texts, primarily in face-to-face consultations with art directors and, perhaps, authors as well. A letter to a staff member at the *Century* shows him following up a meeting with more suggestions for illustrating a series of articles on Alexander the Great, which eventually did appear in the magazine from November 1898 through October 1899. Recalling his own travels in the region of the ancient Greek conqueror's campaigns, he wrote:

> I forgot to mention to you yesterday what I think is the most interesting Alexandrian point in northern Syria. Some forty miles north of Beirut in a little bay at the mouth of the Dog [Doj] River is the place the hosts of Alexander swarmed en route for Egypt—On the rock cut . . . all the old Kings left their mark. Assyrian, Egyptian, Babylonian, and most interesting to you one by Alexander the great. . . . In the old rock cut road one can see the foot holes of the horses and the grooves worn by chariot wheels—I send you a rough sketch.[45]

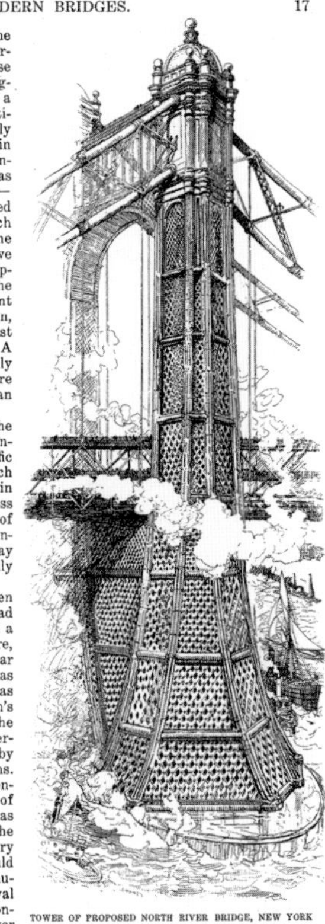

public wrangle over its site, and one of the competitive engineers recognized this opportunity in his design. Not the least praise that is due to the builders of the Washington Bridge is due to them for resisting a temptation which is found almost irresistible by engineers in general, and usually quite irresistible by American engineers in particular—the temptation to make an engineering record. The St. Louis Bridge was already completed when this was begun—completed with a clear span of five hundred and twenty feet. The temptation to stretch theirs out at least ten feet longer into "the biggest steel arch in the world" must have been very great. To have resisted the temptation and stopped ten feet short of "the record" is an evidence of the same restraint and moderation which, applied to the design, has made this architecturally so far the most successful of great American bridges. A modern metallic structure, "mathematically conceived," may, we see, attain a result more than Roman in power and more than Roman in beauty.

There are two works constructed at the very beginning of modern engineering—indeed, before the beginning of the scientific design of framed structures in metal—which offer a most exemplary contrast. It was in 1819 that Telford began the erection, across the Menai Strait, of a suspension bridge of a span, till then undreamed of, of five hundred and seventy feet. This was a highway bridge, which still survives and does its daily work, remaining a beautiful object.

It was a quarter of a century later when Stephenson, summoned to erect a railroad bridge over the same estuary, and within a few hundred yards of the earlier structure, devised and executed the Britannia tubular bridge, in which the extreme of ugliness was attained at a single bound. The year 1845 was the infancy of engineering, and Stephenson's work remains a feat of engineering in the ingenuity of the devices by which he overcame the mechanical difficulties imposed by natural conditions and artificial limitations. The "stiffening truss," by which modern engineering has facilitated the carrying of railroad-trains on suspension bridges, was unknown to him, and his solution of the problem was mechanically the best, very likely, that his time afforded. But he could have made nothing uglier if all the accumulated engineering experience of the interval had been at his command. No truss construction, however bizarre, not the cantaliver of Niagara or the "fish-belly" girders of

VOL. LX.—3.

TOWER OF PROPOSED NORTH RIVER BRIDGE, NEW YORK CITY. HEIGHT OF TOWER, 625 FEET; SUSPENDED SPAN, 2850 FEET. GUSTAV LINDENTHAL, ENGINEER.

6.13. Harry Fenn, "Tower of Proposed North River Bridge, New York City. Height of Tower, 625 Feet; Suspended Span, 2850 Feet. Gustav Lindenthal, Engineer," in "Art in Modern Bridges," 17. Process line cut of pen and ink drawing, 7 7/8" x 2 3/4".

Fenn did not hesitate to request favorable treatment, as when he wrote regarding his drawing of Newstead Abbey (for the October 1890 *Harper's Monthly*): "Reserve a tiptop engraver for me won't you. I have taken no end of pains with the drawing, and I think it will come out very well."[46] And when the writer Edward Eggleston complained that Fenn had not drawn the right kind of iceberg for his article, the artist defended himself with humor and politely requested payment: "Not being a Arctic explorer [I] don't know one from tother. I gave you the most picturesque conception of one that I could muster—And you will bear me out in the fact that not a word was said about the kind of ice-berg required. . . . Under the circumstances I don't think it quite fair that I should be the loser by the drawing. And there will have to be a new drawing made."[47]

Fenn's work in watercolor continued to be an important part of his life at this time, and he constantly sought an audience for his paintings, just as he did for his illustrations, through exhibitions in various venues. In 1893 he corresponded with William Macbeth, who operated the first commercially successful gallery in New York to show primarily contemporary American artists.[48] Fenn had recently received a medal at the Chicago World's Columbian Exposition, and when he sent Macbeth two watercolors to display, he asked in a postscript: "I wonder if it is worth anything to *us* in a business point of view that I am a Chicago medal man.—You know how that sort of thing affects *some* purchasers."[49]

Letters also reveal that after many months of work-related travel and time spent completing drawings in his home studio, Fenn would schedule some time off. During these vacations, he would often stay with friends who lived in appealing locales, as he had with Celia Thaxter on the Isles of Shoals in the late 1860s and 1870s. He spent part of his holidays working, whether on illustrations or watercolor paintings. In the summer of 1891, he was at the home of a Miss C. M. Pierce in Brant Rock, on the coast of Massachusetts, where he completed at least two watercolors.[50] In September he visited Harriet Prescott Spofford (1835–1921), the popular and prolific author of fiction that challenged stereotypes of women, at her home on Deer Island, near Newburyport, Massachusetts. Later that month Fenn was back at Brant Rock, where the duck hunting was so good he didn't want to leave, as he admitted in a letter to Schell: "I'm not ready to come away even now. The Brant ducks are passing along the coast now by the thousand, one man in a boat can bag 50 a day."[51]

In 1893 Fenn's family spent much of the summer at South Cliffs, the Block Island home of William A. Fisher, off the coast of Rhode Island. Fenn's letter of August 1893, in response to Macbeth's request for watercolors to display in his gallery, reveals that he had little time to prepare any. He wrote: "If I have anything more than I want for the W.C.S. and the water color club, I shall be very glad to put them in your hands. But I fear there will not be much this year. The publishers have kept me so busy with black & white all summer."[52] Yet he did produce at least one lovely watercolor of a lily pond (fig. 6.14), unusual in its wide format, limited color range, and lack of horizon. In 1895 Fenn may also have visited Monhegan Island off the coast of Maine. His watercolor painting "A Silvery Morning on the Coast of Maine" (1895) was exhibited that year at the annual exhibition of the Pennsylvania Academy of the Fine Arts, in Philadelphia.[53]

These letters help fill in the picture of Fenn as a busy, confident professional who met challenges with considerable grace and humor. They also show that he continued to do much work for the *Century* and Harper, his long-term major clients.

   Challenges and Triumphs

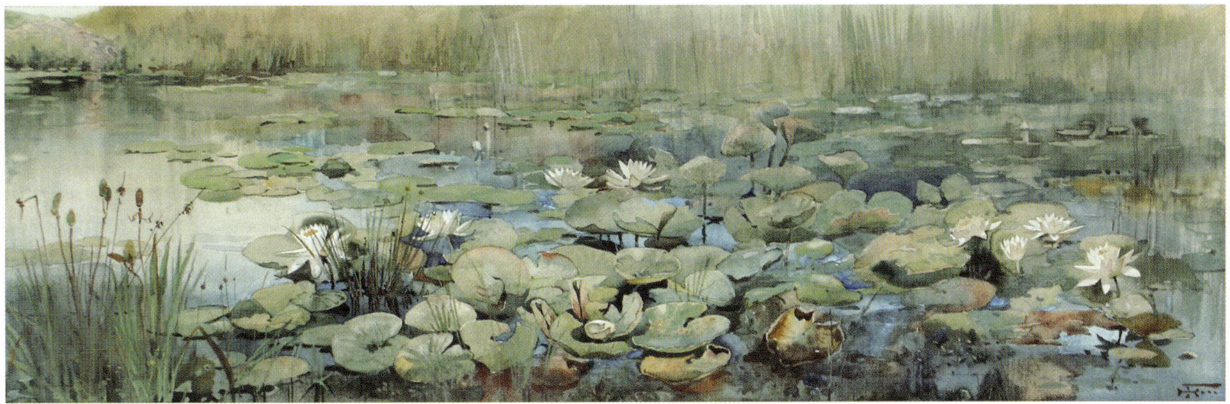

6.14. Harry Fenn, *A Block Island Pond*, 1893. Watercolor on paper, 6 3/4" x 20 1/2". (Cooley Gallery, Old Lyme, Conn.)

THE 1890S AND BEYOND

An overview of Fenn's illustrating projects in the late nineteenth and early twentieth centuries, with a closer look at specific examples, reveals how he responded to changing tastes, increased competition, and new technologies and highlights many of the subjects that were of keen interest to Americans. It also shows that publishers still sometimes used Fenn's name to attract customers. At the same time, however, they reduced costs by replacing wood engravings with either process line blocks or halftones with touch-up engraving, before eventually shifting to halftones alone. In addition, they increasingly chose to reproduce photographs rather than artists' original works. The exception was the *Century*'s editor, Richard Watson Gilder, who did not consider photography an art form and resisted using photos despite the savings, fearing their presentation of "reality" would threaten the magazine's mission to uplift and civilize.[54]

Illustrating California

In 1890 the *Century* engaged Fenn to provide images for its coverage of the settlement of California and the earlier Spanish presence there. Fenn had suffered from rheumatic gout for several months earlier that year and gone to Deal Beach, New Jersey, to rest and recuperate.[55] But by July he was well enough to undertake this new assignment involving extensive travel. This was his longest journey yet for the *Century*—taking him all the way to the West Coast and Southern California—and recalled his earlier worldwide journeys for Appleton's "picturesque" series.

Since the beginning of the gold rush in 1848, California's population had grown quickly, numbering 1.2 million by 1890; the state's large cosmopolitan city of San Francisco was often called the New York or Paris of the Pacific coast. With several rail lines completed, many settlers now arrived in "Pullman cars instead of 'prairie schooners'" and "built fine houses instead of log cabins," as T. S. van Dyke wrote in *Picturesque California*.[56] The appeal of mild weather, abundant sunshine, and thriving orchards, wheat fields, and vineyards attracted many to what was coming to be known as "our Italy."[57] In fact, for the November 1890 issue, *Harper's Monthly* was preparing an article about Southern California with that very title, written by Charles Dudley Warner. Editors at the *Century* would have been aware of their competitor's plans and must have judged that the time was ripe to give attention to the region's colorful history. Instead of focusing on the pleasant climate, fertile soil, and recent civic amenities, as Warner did, the *Century*'s articles concerned the history of "emigrants' trains," the discovery of gold, the early Spanish families, and the missions. Writers would join the likes of Hubert Howe Bancroft, who was chronicling the region's progress "from a wilderness into a garden of latter-day civilization."[58] In addition, they would reinforce romantic attitudes about the Mission era that had been fed by Helen Hunt Jackson's best-selling 1884 novel, *Ramona,* the first to be set in Southern California. It was the story of a beautiful young woman with an American Indian mother and a Scottish father, raised by a well-to-do ranching family of Spanish Californians, who harbored a forbidden love for an Indian man. The novel did much to stimulate tourist interest, with its descriptions of old missions and haciendas, but not as much as Jackson had hoped it would do to improve the treatment of American Indians.

Fenn's trip was announced in an August 16, 1890, article in the local news section of the *San Francisco Chronicle,* whose headline proclaimed: "An Eminent Artist. / Harry Fenn Arrives from New York. / He was a Month in Following the Old Overland Trail to California." The article went on to provide details of his travels while attesting to his continuing national reputation:

> Harry Fenn, the eminent New York artist, and one of the founders of the American Water-Color Society, arrived in the city last night and is a guest at the Palace Hotel. Mr. Fenn stands at the head of his profession as an illustrator for books and magazines, while his rare watercolors have attracted attention at every annual exhibit held in New York city for many years. Mr. Fenn is a college-bred man and a native of England, although a resident of this country for thirty-five years. He has traveled all over the world and journeyed for many years to make the remarkable illustrations for "Picturesque America," "Picturesque Europe" and "Picturesque Egypt and Palestine."

Challenges and Triumphs

Mr. Fenn's visit to California is for the purpose of making the illustrations
for a dozen or more articles to appear in a leading Eastern magazine illustrative of the early history and the settlement of California up to the days of the
gold excitement. To study the original color of the way of the Argonauts in
the early days Mr. Fenn left the railroad at North Platte over a month ago,
and has since journeyed overland, following the original trail to California.
In speaking of his trip Mr. Fenn said to a CHRONICLE reporter last night:
"I have followed the old California trail to San Francisco, traveling by foot,
bronco and wagon, crossing the Laramie peak, sleeping out of doors and
roughing it generally. Here and there I found relics of the early days, such
as old schooner wheels and old-fashioned horseshoes. I followed the trail to
General Bidwell's beautiful rancho at Chico. I will remain in California for
several months, and will make sketches of the old mansions and other objects
of historical interest. When my work is completed here I will visit Arizona
and Northern Mexico, and will make a special study of the Zuni Indians."

By October 27 Fenn was back in Montclair.[59] His extant drawings and published
illustrations suggest that he traveled widely in California but had abandoned
plans to visit Arizona and northern Mexico and study the Zunis.[60] The fact that
illustrations related to this journey appeared in the *Century*'s November 1890
issue, immediately after his return, indicates that he sent drawings and watercolors back to New York while en route.

Fenn's host at the 26,000-acre "beautiful rancho" at Chico, now known as the
Bidwell Mansion, was General John Bidwell (1819–1900), a well-known pioneer,
politician, and agricultural innovator who would write several of the articles
Fenn illustrated. Bidwell had led the first wagon train to California in a harrow-
ing journey in 1841, worked as the town of Sutter's business manager, founded
Chico, fought in the Mexican–American War, served in the California senate and
the U.S. Congress, and run for governor on the Prohibition ticket in 1880.[61] He
and Fenn probably discussed which subjects required illustration. For his article
"The First Emigrant Train to California" (November 1890) Fenn depicted the
Missouri River, the Laramie Range, "Monument Point, Salt Lake," "The Humboldt Palisades" and "The Humboldt Sink," and "Truckee Meadows," along the
trail.[62] The images show small wagons stretching across vast, desolate plains or
valleys, enlivened only by rock formations, prairie dog hills, and animal skele-
tons. Frederic Remington provided the drawings of trappers, pioneers, American
Indians, and buffalo, as he often did for the *Century* and Harper's periodicals. He
was currently in the limelight after two of his gigantic oil paintings had received
much attention—*A Dash for the Timber* at the 1889 National Academy of Design

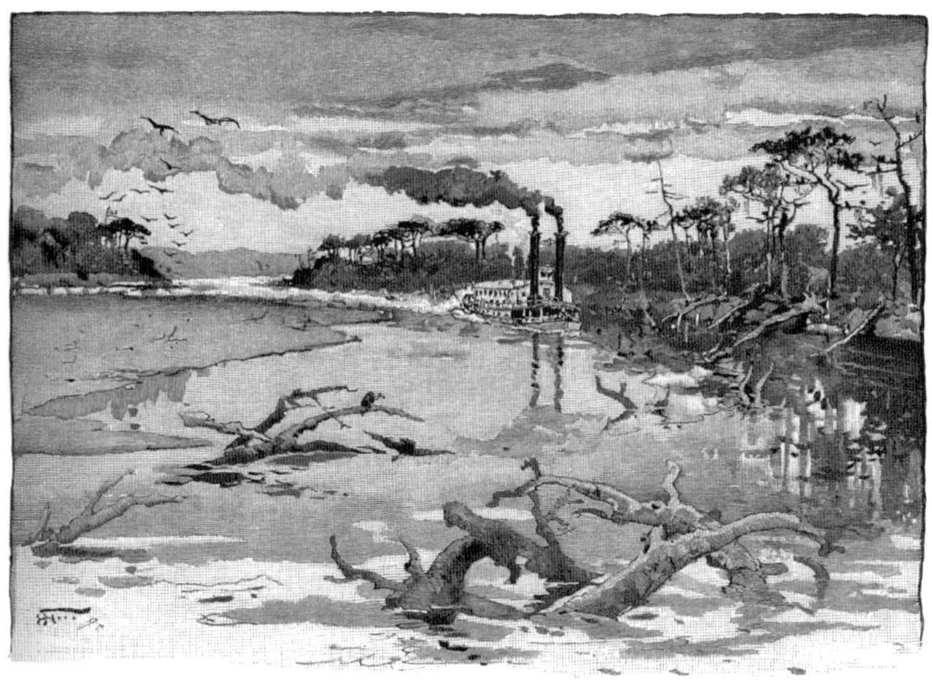

exhibition and *The Last Lull in the Fight,* which won a second-class medal at the Paris Exposition the same year.[63]

In this article and the ones that followed, the two processes used to reproduce the artists' works continued to be wood engraving and process line blocks, in about equal measure. As interpreted by the wood engravers, some of Fenn's images have the look of watercolors, especially "Low Water on the Missouri" (fig. 6.15). Others, such as "Monument Point, Salt Lake," are line blocks of ink drawings. The December *Century* led off with Bidwell's article "Life in California Before the Gold Discovery," with more of Fenn's watercolor renderings skillfully engraved to convey transparency, an effect seen especially in "Fort Ross."[64]

More images of California derived from Fenn's travels were used to illustrate two articles in the January 1891 *Century:* "Pioneer Spanish Families in California" by the California journalist Charles Howard Shinn, was illustrated with "The Scene of H. H.'s 'Ramona,'" Fenn's depiction of an old structure at the Camulos Ranch identified with Jackson's novel; and "The Missions of Alta California" by John T. Doyle. In the latter account, Doyle stressed the role of the Franciscan monks in bringing civilization to the Indians, whom he considered "originally of low intelligence and brutish habits," and described the "magnificent" ruins of the Mission of San Luis Rey as "a monument to the piety, devotion, industry, and disinterestedness

 Challenges and Triumphs

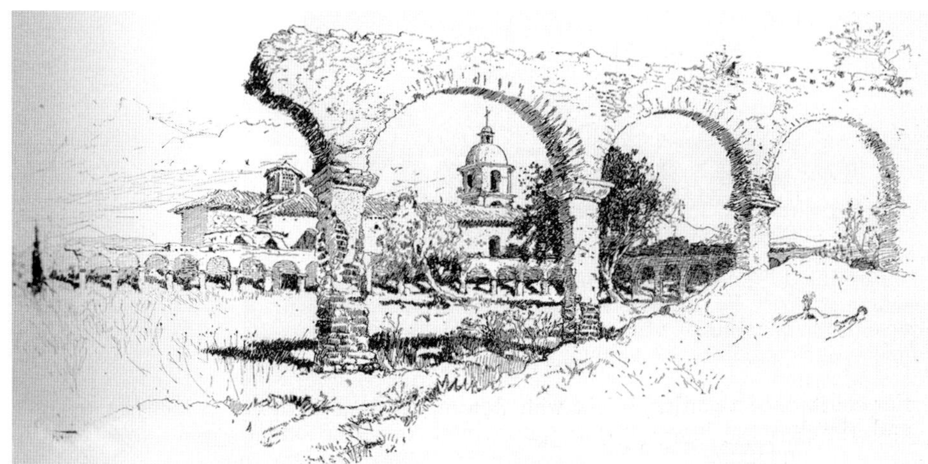

6.16. Harry Fenn, "The Mission of San Luis Rey, San Diego County," in "The Missions of Alta California" by John T. Doyle. *Century*, January 1891, 401. Process line cut of pen and ink drawing, approx. 2 3/8" x 3 1/2".

of the venerable monks . . . who were the first colonists of Alta California." Fenn's images of the sprawling, often-dilapidated buildings in their remote settings, such as "The Mission of San Luis Rey, San Diego County" (fig. 6.16), further romanticized the state's Spanish history.[65]

But these were not the only works by Fenn in the January 1891 *Century*. He was also the sole illustrator of the issue's lead article, "Along the Lower James," by Charles Washington Coleman, which featured two plantations on the James River in Virginia, Shirley and Brandon, as well as Jamestown; it was one of several *Century* articles depicting the romance of the Old South. The James River illustrations were derived from his 1885 trip through the South (in fact, the one of Brandon plantation is dated that year) and may well have been completed earlier, before his California trip. In all, the issue included thirty-one illustrations by Fenn, perhaps a record for him and certainly the culmination of his prominence in the 1880s. His output in these months seems to outstrip even his usual impressive productivity.

The *Century*'s California series continued throughout 1891 with articles on John Charles Fremont and the discovery and mining of gold. These were illustrated with landscapes by Fenn and additional subjects by such artists as Remington and A. C. Redwood.[66] The July 1891 issue reproduced several of Fenn's landscapes from his journey west to illustrate "Across the Plains in the Donner Party (1846)" by Virginia Reed Murphy, who as a child had survived the crossing and its gruesome descent into cannibalism by some members of the group.

Because of Fenn's substantial contributions to these articles, editors and publishers clearly began to view him as an expert on California and engaged him for related commissions, including "Picturesque Plant Life of California" for the October 1892

Century and "The Conquest of Arid America" for its May 1895 issue.[67] He also produced fanciful illustrations for a poem about the Sierra Nevada by Miles I'Anson, *The Vision of Misery Hill,* published by G. P. Putnam's Sons in 1891.

Fenn and the World's Columbian Exposition

In the early 1890s Fenn received several important commissions related to a major event of the period: the World's Columbian Exposition. In the years leading up to 1892, the four-hundredth anniversary of Columbus's arrival in the New World, interest had grown in holding another world's fair in the United States on the scale of the hugely successful Paris Exposition Universelle of 1889. Known for its iconic Eiffel Tower—with its open steel-girder construction—that exhibition had celebrated the centennial of the French revolution. Several cities including New York, St. Louis, and Washington, D.C., competed to host this event designed to promote the industry and products of the United State and international trade. Likely persuaded by a $10 million pledge from a committee of leading Chicago businessmen, the U.S. Congress chose, in April 1890, what was then the nation's second largest city and set 1893 as the year the fair would run. The goal of civic leaders was twofold: to showcase Chicago's dramatic recovery from the terrible fire of 1871 and to combat negative impressions that had resulted from the Haymarket labor uprising of 1886.[68]

After considerable controversy, Jackson Park on Lake Michigan was selected as the site. A local architectural firm headed by Daniel Burnham and John W. Root oversaw the design of the buildings; they, in turn, involved many of Chicago's and New York's leading architects as well as the eminent landscape architect Frederick Law Olmsted (who had helped with the site selection). Construction began in July 1891 and was nearly finished when the fair opened to the public on May 1, 1893. The white neoclassical buildings with uniform cornice heights, arranged around a large lagoon and canals, created a striking ensemble, and the 264-foot-tall wheel designed by George Ferris for the midway took its place as the most prominent structure on the horizon. This monumental national project, which brought together dozens of artists in the creation of a harmonious vision, was, as Sarah Burns has observed, "the greatest moment of artistic incorporation and integration into the mainstream of modernizing America."[69] Known as the "White City," the fair was a major boon to the era's City Beautiful movement, whose mission was to make America's urban spaces more attractive and efficient. It welcomed more than twenty million visitors to its grounds and earned a profit of $1.4 million.[70]

The great demand for illustrations generated by the fair helped Fenn to weather

 Challenges and Triumphs

the panic of 1893 and ensuing depression. He was hired to participate in several projects that promoted Chicago and the exposition, not only during the construction phase but also through the months of operation and the aftermath. Because he was still a leading illustrator of architecture, publishers of periodicals as well as large-format commemorative books used his name to sell their products. Although no records have been found to place Fenn in Chicago at the time of the fair, a newspaper article promoting one such volume indicates that he spent some time onsite. The article recounts that "for month after month" as the fair was being built, painters were "welcomed at Jackson Park, while Harry Fenn crowded his sketch books, and Childe Hassam covered many a glowing canvas, and Tom Moran and Frank Millet, and Bolton Jones and Blashfield and many another skillful artist haunted the scene in search of picturesque and beautiful effects."[71] Fenn could have worked from photographs, but it seems more likely that he would have taken advantage of his commissions to visit the blockbuster event.

Fenn's first fair-related project was to provide illustrations of buildings and the Chicago River for Captain Charles King's article "The City of the World's Fair," which appeared in the November 1891 *Cosmopolitan*. For "The Columbia World's Fair," an article by M. H. deYoung in that same magazine's March 1892 issue, Fenn contributed "The Lagoon," "Bird's Eye View of the Buildings," and "Entrance to Machinery Hall" (most likely using architects' renderings as his source).[72] Noteworthy for the history of illustration is that, just a little more than a year later, when the *Cosmopolitan* devoted almost its entire September 1893 issue to the fair all the images were photographs reproduced as halftones. However, the magazine did engage Fenn to illustrate William Dean Howell's account of the exposition, "Letters of an Altrurian Traveller," which ran in the December 1893 issue.[73]

It is also of note that the *Century* turned to artists other than Fenn for many of the fair views that illustrated its pages. Before the world's fair opened, a whole host of illustrators had made images based primarily on architectural drawings, and in May and September of 1893 the *Century* featured some extremely soft-focused scenes of buildings and fairgoers supplied by the young French artist André Castaigne (1861?–1929 or 1930), who had immigrated to the United States in 1890 (fig. 6.17).[74] For a Christopher Columbus–related piece that ran in the May 1893 *St. Nicholas* magazine, Fenn drew "The Convent of La Rábida," the nunnery near Huelva, Spain, where the explorer spent a restless night before heading west into the unknown on August 3, 1492. In a reenactment of the voyage on October 12, 1892, replicas of Columbus's three ships set out from there amid great ceremony, and Spain built a replica of the convent for its pavilion at the fair.[75]

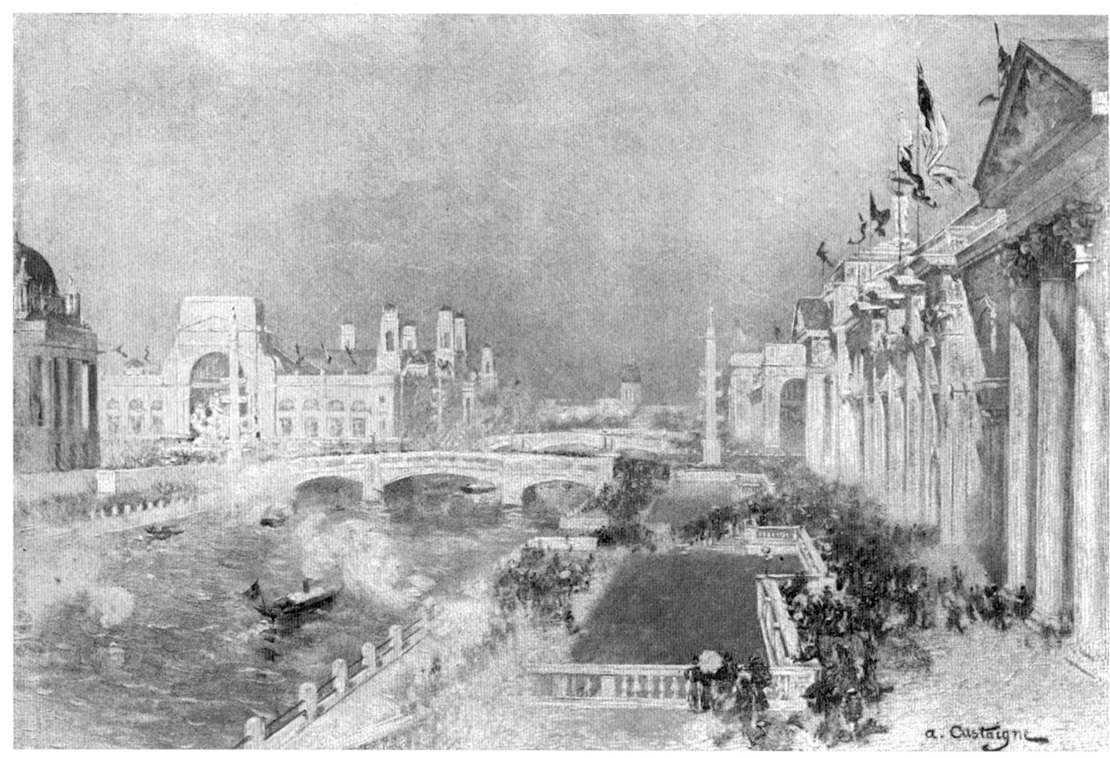

6.17. André Castaigne, "The World's Fair—Looking North from Lion Fountain," in "At the Fair" by M. G. Van Rensselaer. *Century*, May 1893, frontispiece [2]. Halftone plate, 4 15/16" x 7 5/16".

In the aftermath of the Chicago World's Fair, Fenn participated in two elaborate serial publications marketed as records of the great event: *World's Columbian Exposition: The Book of the Builders,* by Daniel Hudson Burnham and Francis Davis Millet, and *The Art of the World,* by the journalist and editor Ripley Hitchcock (1857–1918). The former had a complicated history. It was published in 1894 in either one or two volumes, with the plates issued separately, by the Columbian Memorial Publication Society of Chicago and Springfield, Ohio; it was also offered by several newspapers, including the *Washington Post,* the *Knoxville Journal,* and the *Dallas Morning News.* The *Post* advertised it as being issued in twenty-five parts at twenty-five cents each and listed Fenn's name first among the project's fifty-eight "Leading American Illustrators."[76] His contributions included preconstruction views—"The Site of Administration Building, March, 1891" and "The First Dredge, August 1891"—and a chromolithograph showing a finished area of the grounds, "The West Terrace from the Court of the Obelisk" (fig. 6.18).[77]

The massive folio titled *The Art of the World: Illustrated in the Paintings, Statuary,*

 Challenges and Triumphs

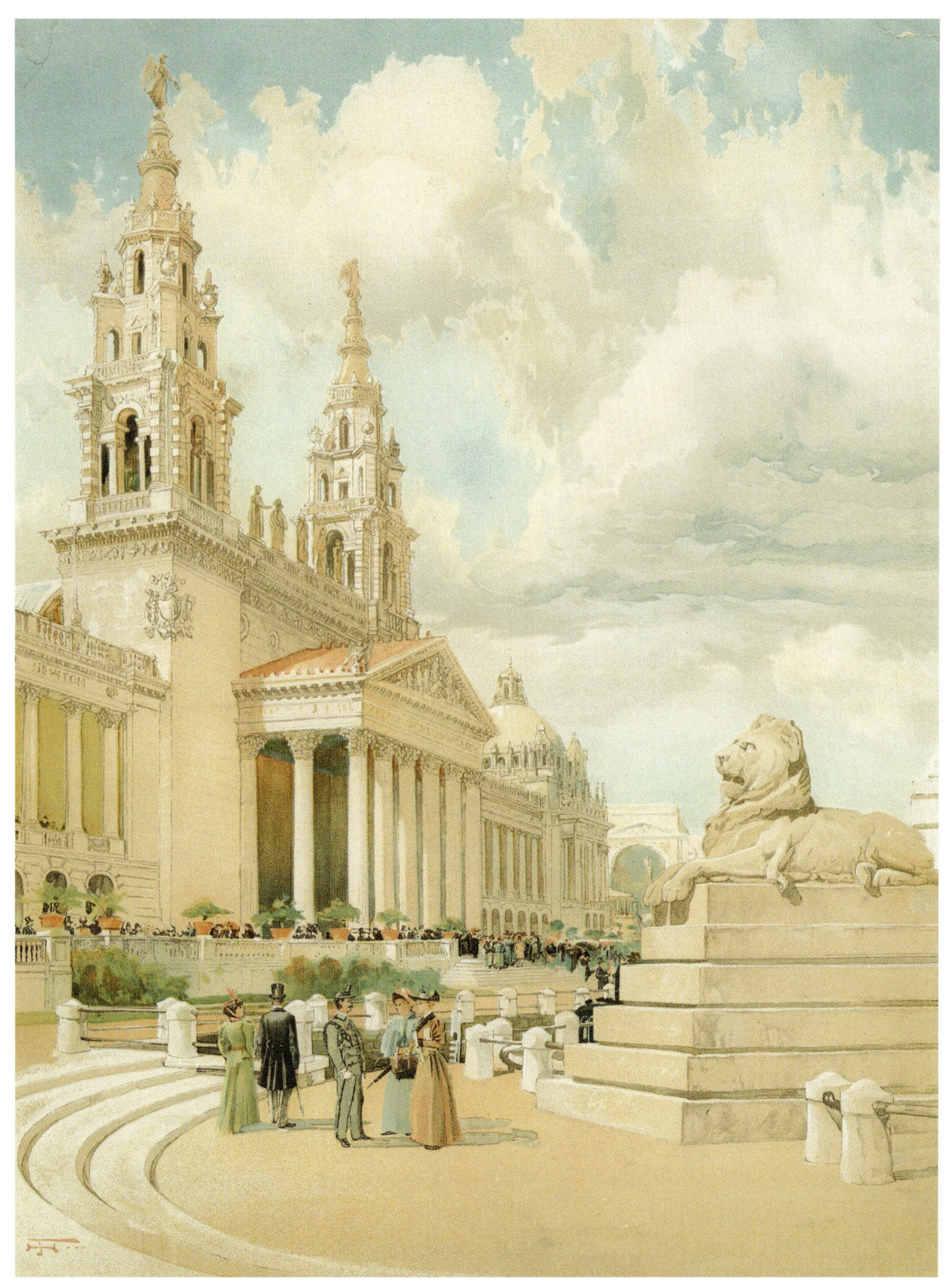

6.18. Harry Fenn, "The West Terrace from the Court of the Obelisk." From Edwin D. Weary and Daniel H. Burnham, *World's Columbian Exposition* (Chicago: Edwin D. Weary, 189–). Chromolithograph, 14" x 10 3/8". (The Newberry Library, Chicago. Case T 500-C1 W85.)

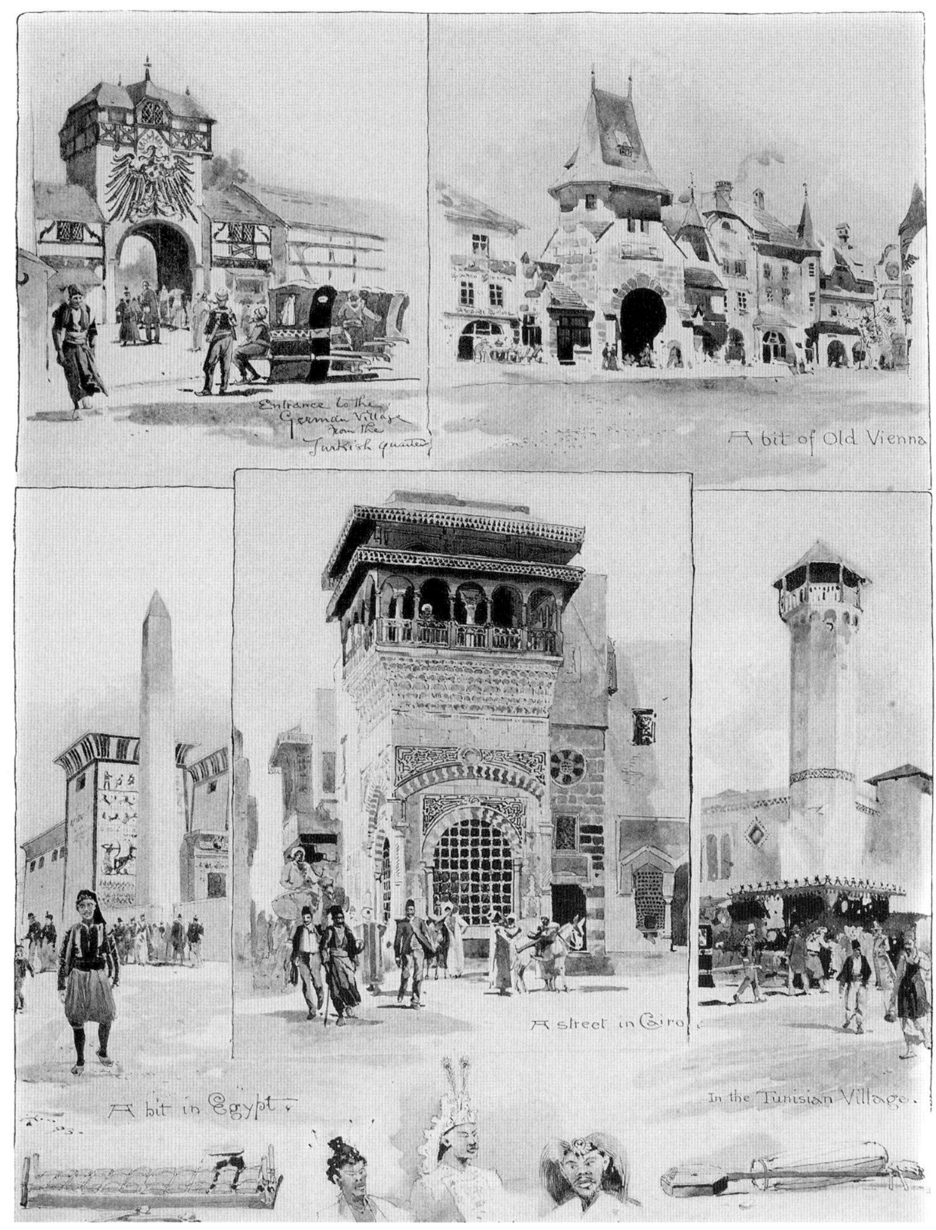

and Architecture of the World's Columbian Exposition was issued in 1895 by Fenn's old firm, D. Appleton and Company, in thirty parts selling for $1 each. Fenn designed the part covers, which included a medallion containing Columbus's head and a rendering of the Fine Arts Building.[78] Like *Picturesque California,* the book used many different processes to reproduce images of the buildings and exhibited artworks, including photogravures and typogravures in color and black

 Challenges and Triumphs

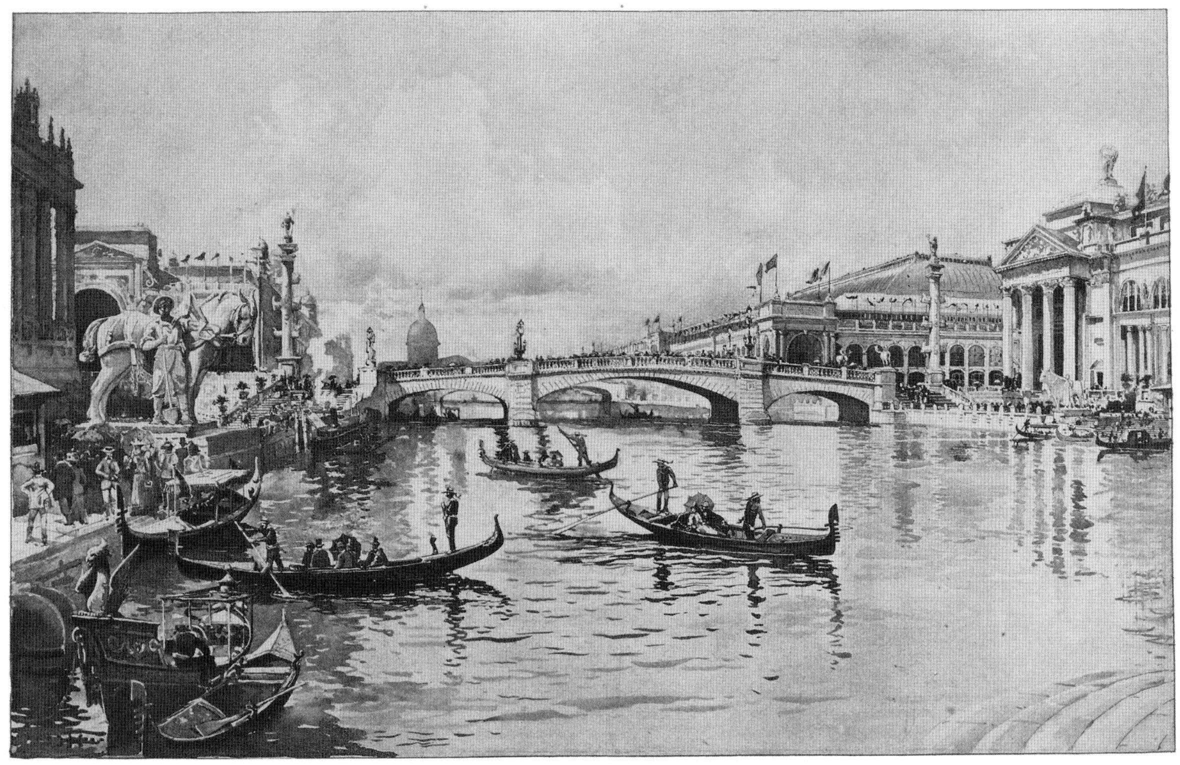

6.20. Harry Fenn, "View along the Canal from a point near the Obelisk with the Argricultural [*sic*] and Liberal Arts Buildings on the right, the Machinery and Electricity Buildings on the left, and the Illinois State Building in the Extreme Distance." From Hitchcock, *Art of the World*, 1:opp. xxiii. Photogravure; sheet 12 1/4" x 16 1/4". (Special Collections, University of Virginia Library.)

and white. None of Fenn's exhibited works appear, but he did provide full-page images of various parts of the elaborate White City: "Scenes in the Midway Plaisance" (fig. 6.19), a composite of attractions ranging from "A bit of Old Vienna" to "A street in Cairo" to a "Tunisian Village"; a photogravure of his watercolor "View along the Canal from a point near the Obelisk with the Agriculture and Liberal Arts Buildings on the right, the Machinery and Electricity Buildings on the left and the Illinois State Building in the extreme distance" (fig. 6.20); "The Woman's Building"; "A Group of State Buildings"; and "The California Building," with fruits and flowers trailing down the page in his familiar style. Not surprisingly, after such prominence illustrating architectural examples from the Chicago fair, Fenn was later called on to depict scenes from subsequent expositions: the Tennessee Centennial Exposition at Nashville in 1897, the United States Pavilion and the Publishers' Building at the Paris Exposition of 1900, and the fair in Buffalo in 1901, as will be discussed later in this chapter.[79]

Fenn also participated in the Chicago fair as an exhibitor. Nine of his works were shown in the exhibit "Pen and Ink, Charcoal, Black and White and Other Drawings," and he, along with twenty-one others, received a medal for "Works in Black and White." There was only one grade of medal, bronze, which was accompanied by "a diploma setting forth the points of excellence" in the artist's work.[80] The comments about this group of exhibitors, which appear in *History of the World's Columbian Exposition,* once again stress the key role of periodicals and their illustrators in the American art scene and count them as a reason for national pride:

> The collection of pen-and-ink and wash drawings was important and inter-esting, because in no country has work in black and white been more culti-vated or developed with such high results as in the United States. The monthly magazines fostered a demand and the improvements in the mechanical work of reproduction opened the artistic field for such work. Among nearly five hundred examples were Shakespearean illustrations of Edward [Edwin] A. Abbey, A. Castaigne's sketches of incident, humorous and figure subjects from C. D. Gibson, and some of the finest productions of Kenyon Cox, Harry Fenn, William Hamilton Gibson, E. W. Kemble, Alfred Parsons, Charles S. Reinhart, Frederick Remington, and others.[81]

Fenn's works were lent by two of his publishers, the Century Company and Charles Scribner's Sons, except for one drawing, which presumably was Fenn's own to lend. There is no record of whether Fenn participated in selecting the works, but such a scenario seems plausible. The original pen drawing "Sepulchres of Ferdinand and Isabella, Philip, and Joanna, in the Royal Chapel, Granada"—so appropriate, with its Columbus connection—shows his remarkable skill with the pen, particularly in the elaborate grillwork of the screen (fig. 6.21).[82] Fenn's other exhibited drawings are presently unlocated, but published versions of some of them show their appeal and range of media, for example, "Kiga" (fig. 6.22) and "The First Glimpse of the Khuzneh" (fig. 6.23), which brings to mind Frederic E. Church's 1874 painting of the same subject, *El Khazneh, Petra.*[83]

Books Experimenting with Halftones

Another of Fenn's projects in 1893 motivated in part by the Chicago World's Fair was *The Niagara Book.* Its preface points out "the lack of a good souvenir of Niagara Falls" and the "special relevance" of such a publication in "America's

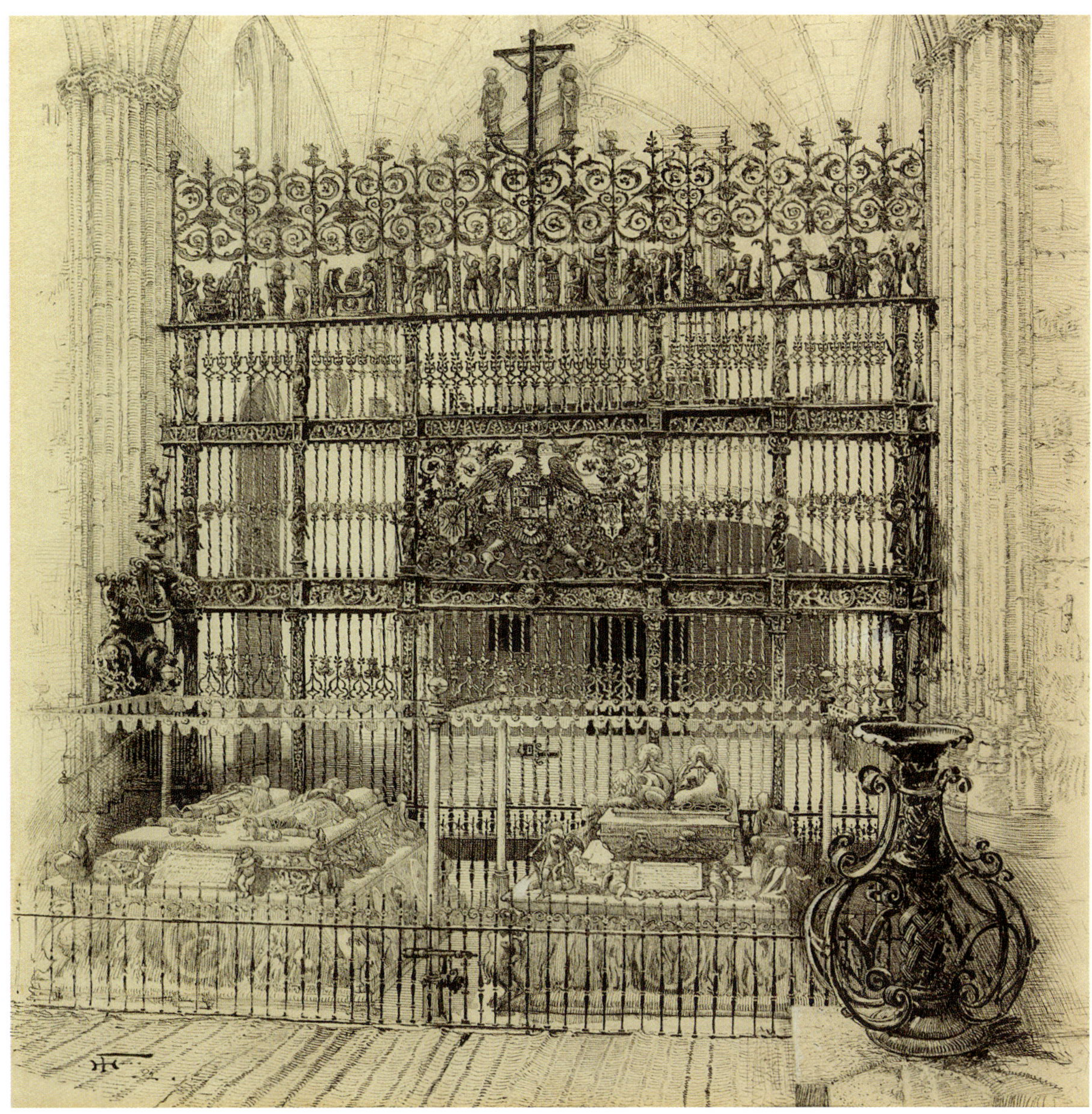

6.21. Harry Fenn, *Sepulchres of Ferdinand and Isabella and Philip and Joanna, in the Royal Chapel, Granada,* [1892]. Ink, approx. 12 3/4" x12 1/2". (Private collection.)

greatest anniversary year," suggesting it was designed to appeal to both American and foreign tourists on their way to or from the fair. The range of writers (among them W. D. Howells, Mark Twain, and Nathaniel S. Shaler) ensured that the book would be descriptive and entertaining while dealing with the history of the falls and the huge, multiyear project then under way to use its water power to

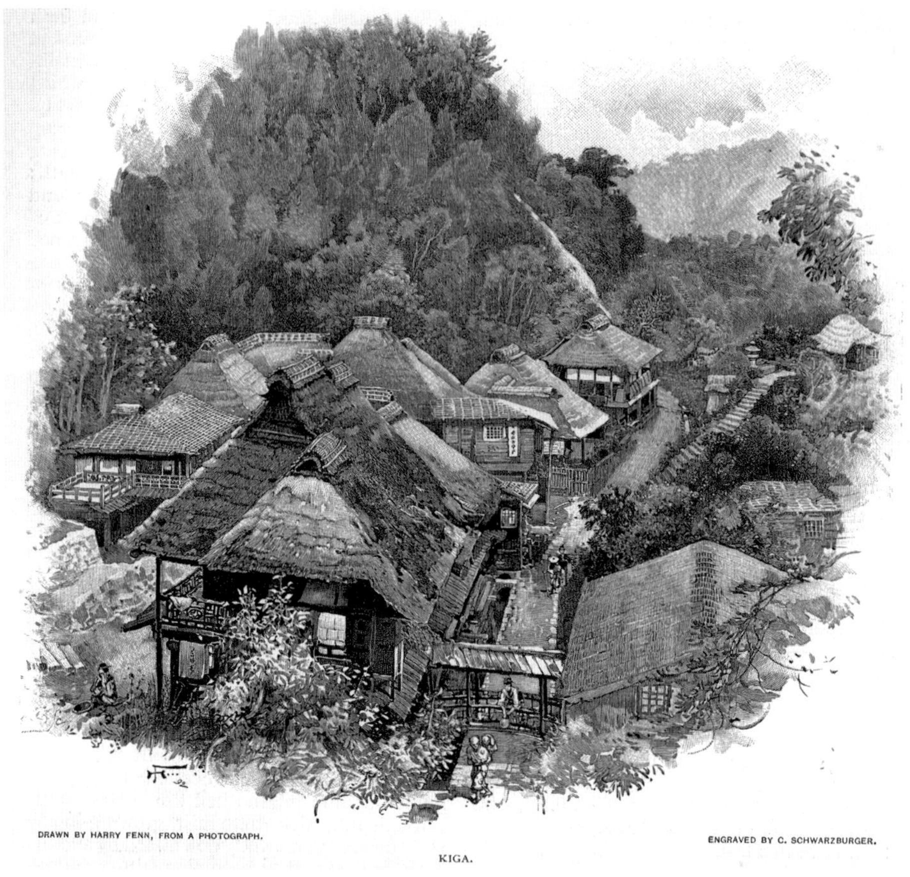

6.22. Harry Fenn, "Kiga," in "An Ascent of Fuji the Peerless" by Mabel L. Todd and David P. Todd. *Century,* August 1892, 487. Wood engraving by C. Schwarzburger, 4 7/8" x 4 7/8".

generate electricity. Fenn's contribution was also highlighted in the preface: "One of the greatest artists in the country has prepared the water-color sketches and the novel drawings from which the illustration plates are made."[84] These included a chapter opening for each of the essays as well as six grisaille watercolors, reproduced as black and white halftones. The *Critic*'s reviewer found the images disappointing, commenting that they "are either very slight or they have been more than usually ill-treated in the process employed to reproduce them."[85] Indeed, the halftones have little contrast and the drawings embellishing the chapter openings—presumably printed as line blocks—are pale and soft. These shortcomings were typical in the early years of the technology. Five of the original watercolors, which are much larger (10 by 14 inches, compared to approximately 3 3/4 by 5 inches in the book) and, with their sepia tones, more attractive, are in the collection of the Albright-Knox Art Gallery in Buffalo. Fenn's *View of the American Falls, from below the Cave of the Winds* is a dynamic image, full of crashing water and mist, with small figures struggling along the wooden walkway (fig. 6.24).[86]

Challenges and Triumphs

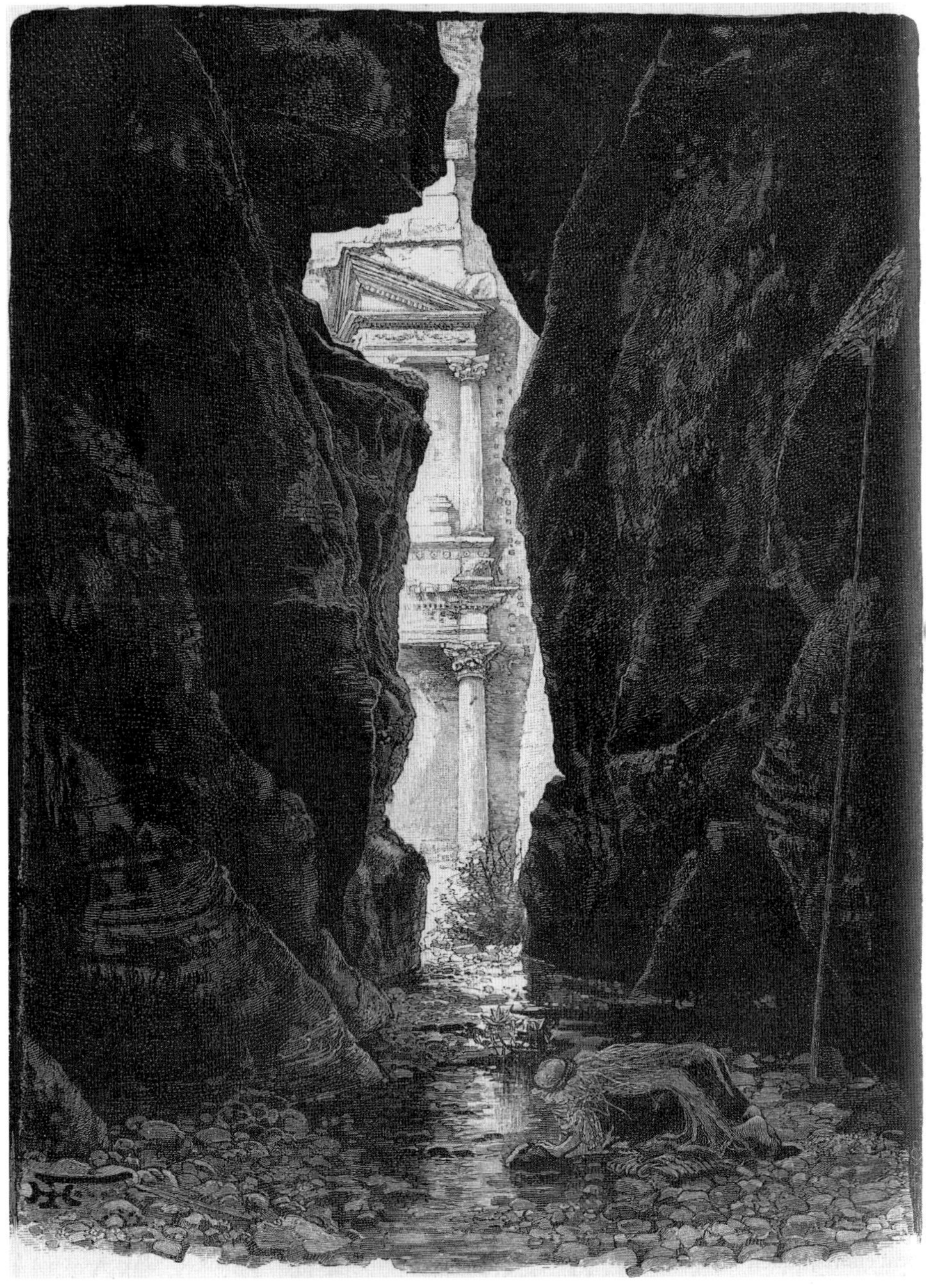

6.23. Harry Fenn, "The First Glimpse of the Khuzneh," in "A Photographer's Visit to Petra" by Edward L. Wilson. *Century,* November 1885, 8. Wood engraving, 7 1/4" x 5 1/4".

Publishers of books as well as periodicals were moving toward greater use of the halftone process to reproduce not only artworks, as in *The Niagara Book,* but also photographs. Still, they tended to highlight the artists' contributions rather than the photographs, recalling the way Appleton had earlier featured the steel engravings produced by that older, more prestigious technology rather than the more numerous

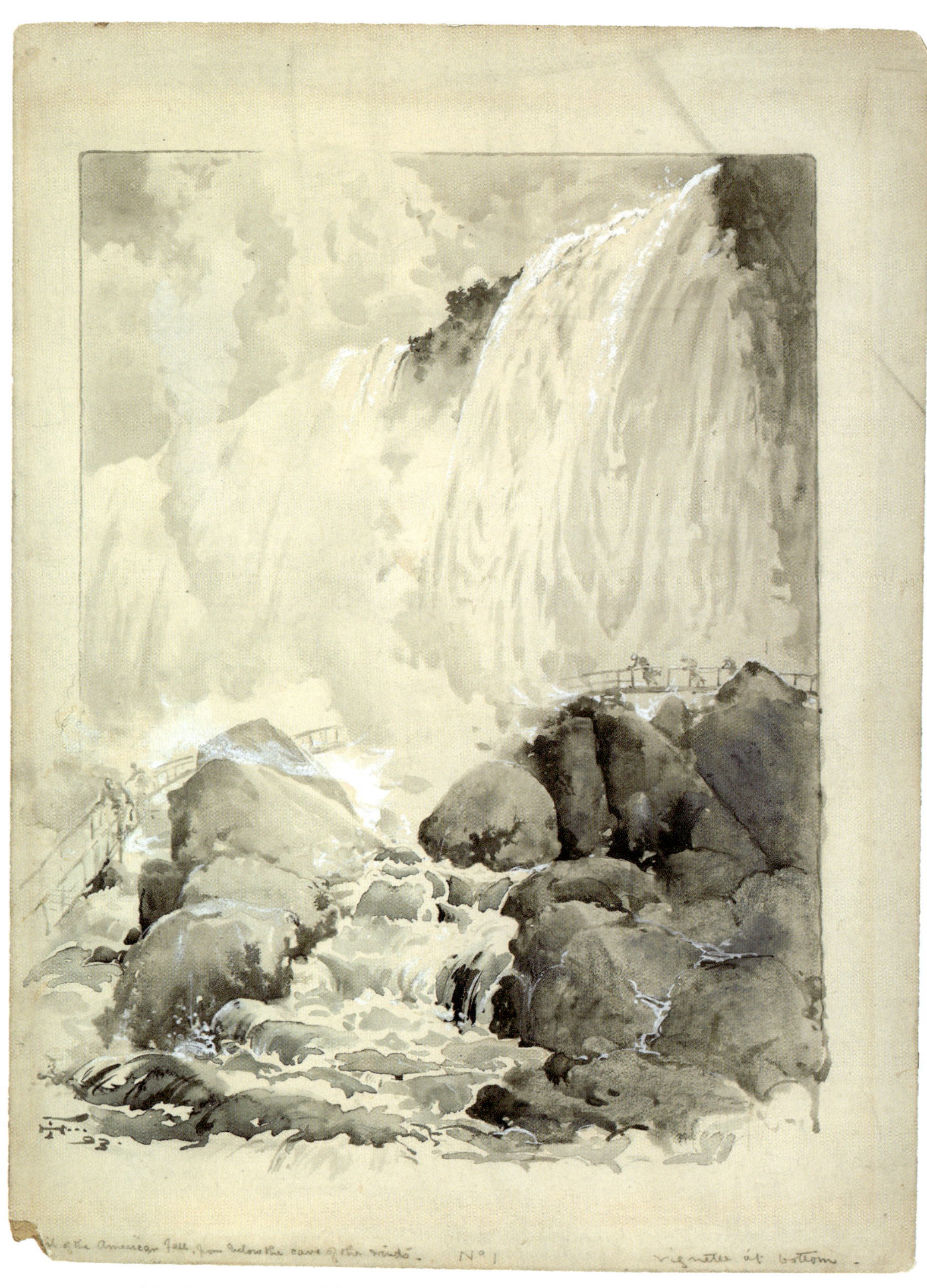

6.24. Harry Fenn, *View of the American Falls, from below the Cave of the Winds,* 1893. Watercolor on paper, 14 1/4" x 10 1/2". (Collection Albright-Knox Art Galley, Buffalo, N.Y. Gift of Mr. & Mrs. Roy J. Friedman, 1964. Photo: Albright-Knox Art Galley / Art Resource, New York)

wood engravings in *Appletons' Journal* and the "picturesque" series. When Fenn contributed to books illustrated primarily by halftones of photographs, the publishers featured his name on the title page and in advertising. An early instance was Appleton's 1893 *In the Track of the Sun* by Frederick Diodati Thompson, a member of the Union Club who wrote about his travels in Japan, China, India, Egypt, Palestine, and other regions. The title page stated, "with many illustrations by Mr. Harry Fenn and from photographs," but since Fenn provided only one of the seventy full-page illustrations, plus some initial letters, chapter openings, and tailpieces, his inclusion in the project can only be viewed as the token artist. The book met with some positive response, although the halftone process still needed improvement and many of the full-page photographs are blurry and lack contrast.[87] Clearly, travel books illustrated by artists, like Appleton's *Picturesque America* and its successors, were facing increased competition from photographs.

Work for Periodicals

Fenn continued to fulfill commissions for periodicals other than the *Century*. *Harper's Weekly* hired him to report visually on some of the new, large-scale engineering projects that denoted progress and were of great interest at the time—resulting in some of his duller composite images—while for *St. Nicholas* he created some of his more delightful experiments in layout and design. For the *Weekly* he depicted schemes to irrigate whole regions and build railroads: "The Water Miracle of Yakima, Eastern Washington" (May 19, 1894), "The Great Reservoir System of the Upper Mississippi" (January 9, 1897), and "Along the Line of the Peruvian Central Railroad, the Tallest in the World" (January 23, 1897).[88] Perhaps the editors hoped Fenn could use his legendary skills to make such projects picturesque, even while working from photographs. He also prepared composites of places that did in fact have such potential and were of interest as vacation destinations, including "Sketches in Bermuda" (April 27, 1895) and "Michigan's New State Park (July 20, 1895)," showing Mackinac Island (for which he appears to have turned to some of Woodward's *Picturesque America* illustrations). He also created seven attractive pen and ink vignettes of Guadalajara for an article titled "A Great Mexican State Capital" (January 27, 1900), one instance of the attention to Latin America that appeared in the press in the build-up to the Pan-American Exposition in Buffalo in 1901.

When the United States went to war in 1898, ostensibly to free Cuba from Spanish rule, Fenn was engaged more than ever in depicting current events, now reported more quickly than before via wireless telegraph and the telephone. Although one wonders if he considered such assignments potboilers, his images seem to contradict that idea. For example, shortly after Commodore George Dewey's ships destroyed the Spanish fleet in Manila on May 1, Fenn created an image of the battle for the May 14 *Harper's Weekly*—"from the descriptions of the conflict telegraphed from Manila and Hong-Kong"—that is action packed and full of drama. Because the "special artists" the *Weekly* had engaged were probably still en route to Manila, the art editor turned to Fenn, who delivered as required. He illustrated "Compostella Barracks, Havana, in 1898" from a photograph as well (May 4, 1901).

Harper's Weekly also called on Fenn when China became newsworthy as it underwent the Hundred Days' Reform, from June 11 to September 21, 1898; instigated by the young emperor Guangxu's edicts aimed at modernizing aspects of the government, the military, and the educational and economic systems, the movement was brutally put down by his aunt the empress dowager Cixi and members of the conservative ruling Manchu elite. Fenn drew the front-page image for the October 22 issue, "The Disturbances in China. Peking—The Forbidden City, as Seen from the Imperial City," based on "the only photograph known to have been taken of the prohibited Enclosure," and also contributed a lively composite, "Peking—Places of Interest in and about China's Capital." The brief, ironic accompanying text expressed the desire to know the dowager empress better "from a distance."[89]

Barely a year later, in October 1899, Fenn illustrated an article for the *Century* titled "The Streets of Peking" by Eliza Ruhamah Scidmore that described the city as "the most splendid, spectacular, picturesque, and interesting . . . in China." Working from photographs, he depicted many of its picturesque features, including "grimy, tattered old men" selling birds at a street fair. His original ink, wash, and gouache drawing in grisaille shows how skilled he had become at representing people, using light and shadow to define shapes and create interest (fig. 6.25). Reproduced as a halftone plate with added engraving and the title "Trained Birds," Fenn's image supported Scidmore's claim that Peking was an "incredible" and "surprising" place. It is interesting to note how the new halftone technology could reproduce Fenn's depictions of individuals more effectively than had the earlier images of people interpreted by wood engraving (see, for example, fig. 4.25), even when both were based on photographs.

As the *Century*'s editors called on him less often to illustrate entire articles, Fenn seems to have taken on more work in the 1890s for the Century Company's premier children's magazine, *St. Nicholas*. It is tempting to interpret this change

Challenges and Triumphs

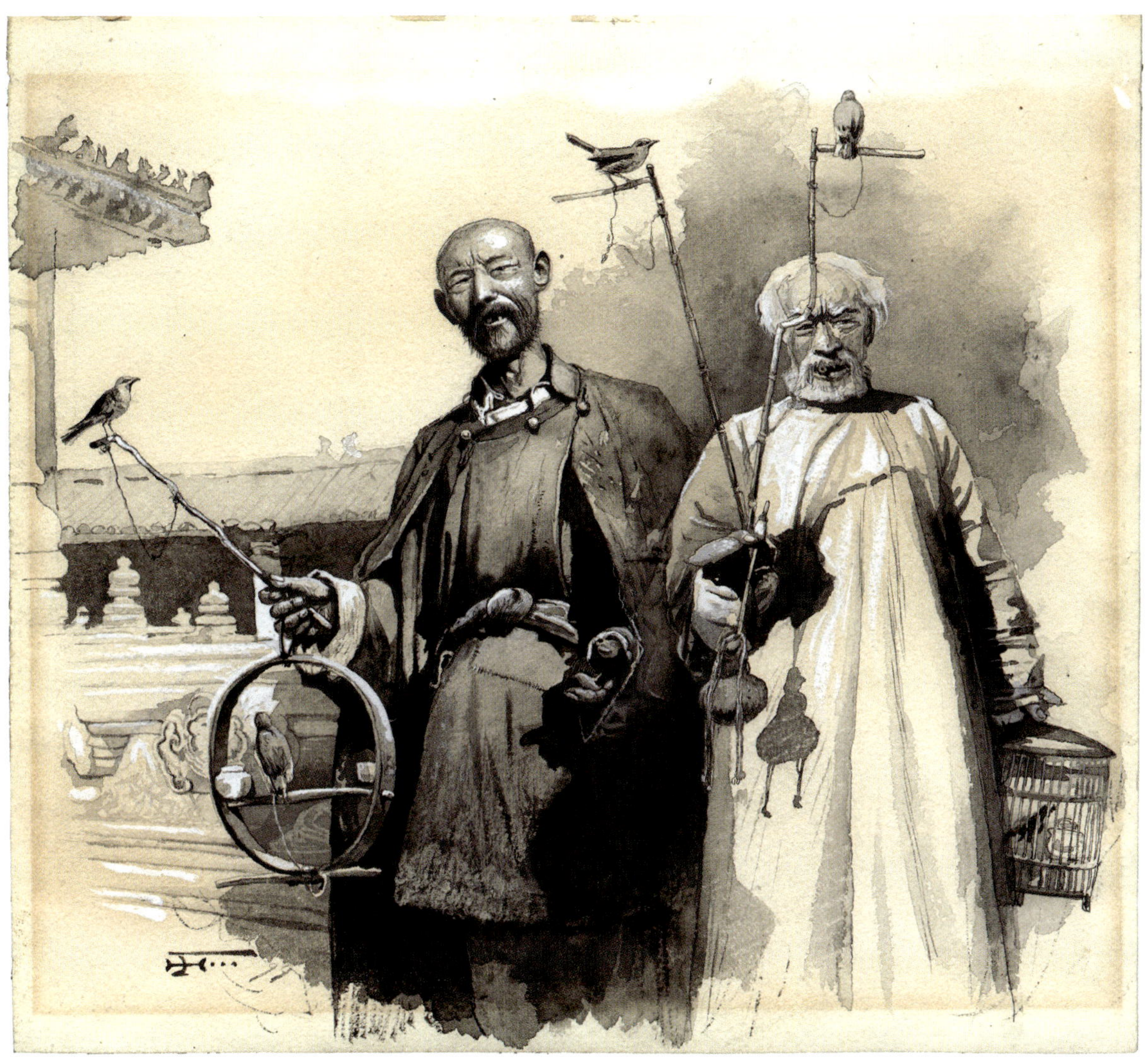

6.25. Harry Fenn, [Bird Sellers in Peking], 1899. Ink, wash, and gouache, 9 1/4" x 10". (For illustration titled "Trained Birds," *Century*, October 1899, 871.) (Private collection.)

as a demotion until one notes the other prominent artists who were also working for *St. Nicholas,* including Joseph Pennell, Childe Hassam, Frederic Remington, Jules Guérin, and E. W. Kemble, plus some of the most successful female illustrators, such as Mary Hallock Foote and Jessie Curtis Shepherd. Many well-known writers also contributed to the magazine, and its London edition was successful as well.[90] Fenn produced views of historical and contemporary American architecture and places he had visited in his earlier travels for the "picturesque" series, Boston, New Orleans, and Italy. *St. Nicholas* also hired him to illustrate articles and poems about plants and birds, including "A Talk about Wild Flowers" (June 1891) by John Burroughs and "Plants That Feed upon Insects" (June 1897). For the poems, Fenn designed attractive titles incorporating his own lettering and sometimes interspersed drawings with the lines of poetry, creating a fully designed page. (See Appendix 1 for additional *St. Nicholas* illustrations.)

In 1894 and 1895, Fenn participated in what must have seemed a rather mundane project for *St. Nicholas*—the creation of an illustrated page about each state, which, along with a poem by Garrett Newkirk, would help children remember facts about it. Fenn's illustrations frequently reused images that he or Woodward had made for *Picturesque America* and included as an aide-mémoire an object resembling the shape of the state (for example, the image of a saw for Tennessee). The publishers gathered these pages into a book called *Rhymes of the States,* released for the holiday trade in late 1896. One review called the book "Geography sugar-coated," and reactions to Fenn's illustrations varied from "ingenious" and "clever" to "attractive by their oddity."[91]

Fenn also worked for the magazine's rival, *Harper's Young People.* For the latter's October 20, 1891, issue he designed the information-packed composite "Bread and Bread-Making of Many Peoples"—illustrating "Syrian women grinding wheat" and "An American Flour Mill," shown as the most advanced method in the group—indicative of the contemporary interest in cultural comparisons. The October 27 issue included another composite, "Cheese and Cheesemaking," depicting up-to-date methods of this culinary craft

Ventures with Authorship and New Approaches—Modest and Bold

Fenn wrote as well as illustrated several articles for *St. Nicholas* in the 1890s, including "The Story of Whittier's *Snow-Bound*" (April 1893), discussed in Chapter 2. To prepare "Silk & Cedars: A Scramble in the Lebanons" (April 1897), he drew upon his travels to the mountains of Lebanon almost twenty years before, as mentioned in Chapter 4. For the article's title page, he created an elaborate design in ink, wash, and gouache that incorporates his own lettering (fig. 6.26). The abstract pattern of insect wings behind the letters gives way to vividly realistic silkworms and moths shown at different stages as well as the smooth, hard cones of the cedars, which Fenn described as "about the size and form of a well-grown Spitzenberge apple." The composition was striking and no doubt attracted the attention and curiosity of the boys and girls who saw it—and probably their parents as well. He recounted in detail his encounters in Tripoli and Lebanon with his "old friend" from his childhood days, the

Challenges and Triumphs

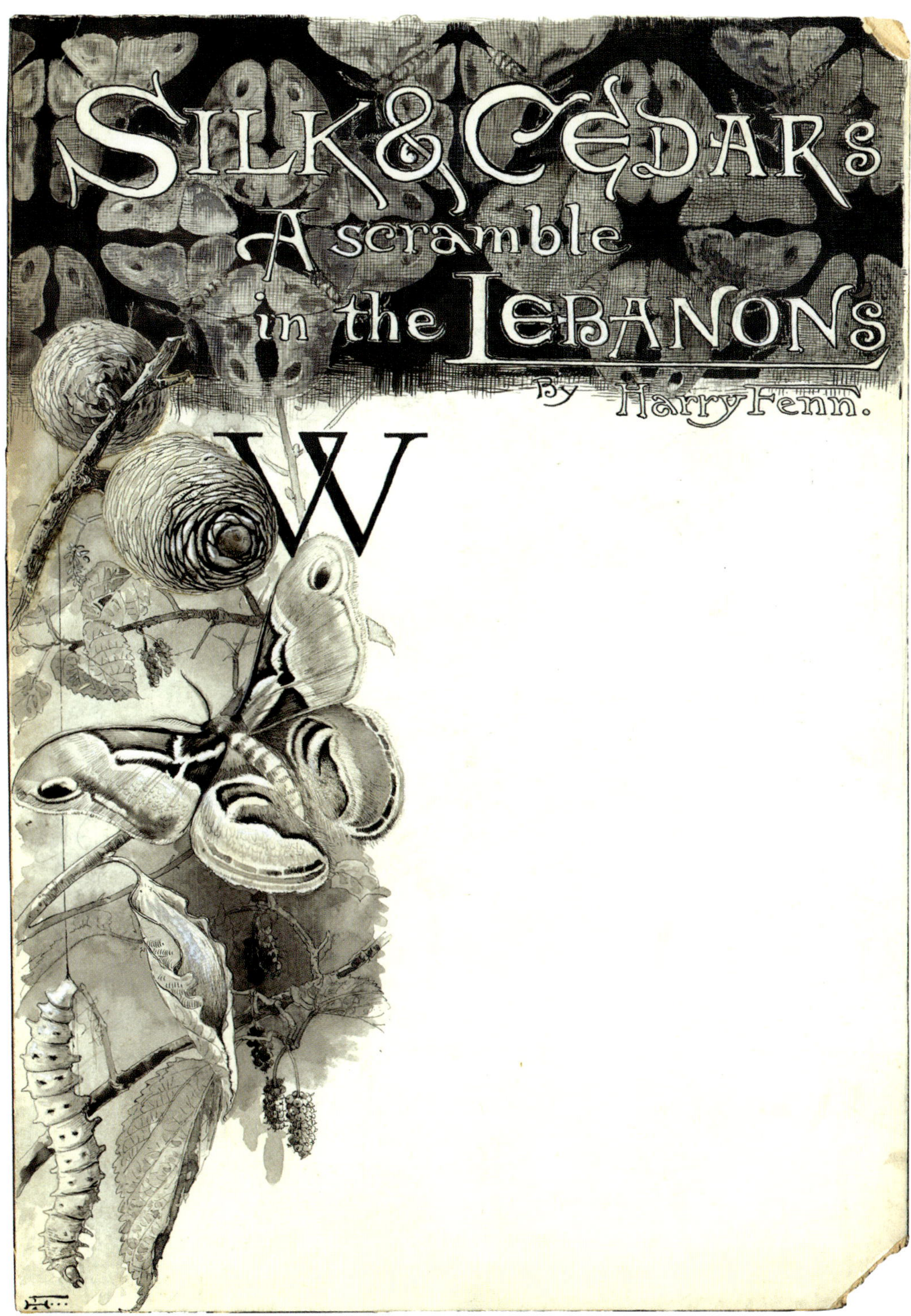

6.26. Harry Fenn, opening for "Silk & Cedars: A Scramble in the Lebanons." Ink, wash, and gouache, 18 1/4" x 12 1/2". (Private collection.)

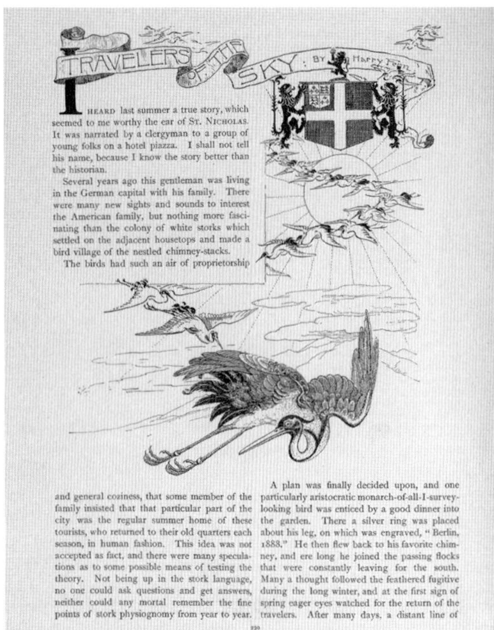

I HEARD last summer a true story, which seemed to me worthy the ear of St. Nicholas. It was narrated by a clergyman to a group of young folks on a hotel piazza. I shall not tell his name, because I know the story better than the historian.

Several years ago this gentleman was living in the German capital with his family. There were many new sights and sounds to interest the American family, but nothing more fascinating than the colony of white storks which settled on the adjacent housetops and made a bird village of the nestled chimney-stacks.

The birds had such an air of proprietorship and general coziness, that some member of the family insisted that that particular part of the city was the regular summer home of these tourists, who returned to their old quarters each season, in human fashion. This idea was not accepted as fact, and there were many speculations as to some possible means of testing the theory. Not being up in the stork language, no one could ask questions and get answers, neither could any mortal remember the fine points of stork physiognomy from year to year.

A plan was finally decided upon, and one particularly aristocratic monarch-of-all-I-survey-looking bird was enticed by a good dinner into the garden. There a silver ring was placed about his leg, on which was engraved, "Berlin, 1888." He then flew back to his favorite chimney, and ere long he joined the passing flocks that were constantly leaving for the south. Many a thought followed the feathered fugitive during the long winter, and at the first sign of spring eager eyes watched for the return of the travelers. After many days, a distant line of

6.27. Harry Fenn, opening for "Travelers of the Sky," a story by Harry Fenn. *St. Nicholas,* January 1894, 230. Process line cut, approx. 6 1/2" x 5 1/2".

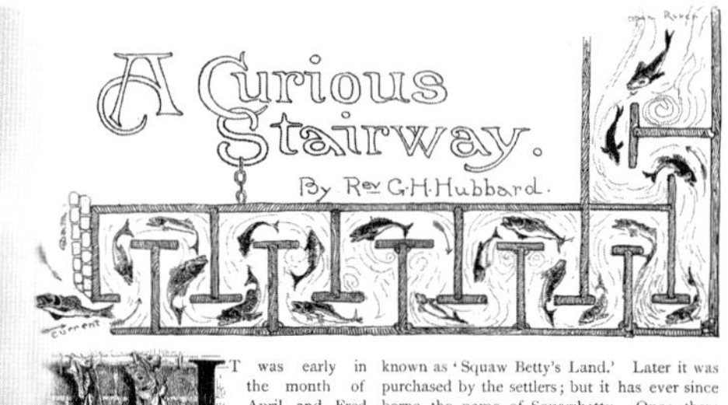
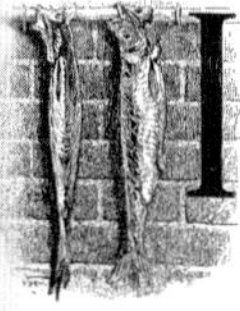

IT was early in the month of April, and Fred Kent was spending a few days with his uncle in Taunton. Fred's home was in a village among the mountains in New Hampshire, and, being only ten years old, he had not often traveled. This was his first visit to the State of Massachusetts, and he saw many things that were interesting.

One fine, warm day, his Uncle James drove up to the door, and said, "I'm going to drive into the country on business this morning. Would you like to go with me, Fred?"

Fred said he would, and went into the house for his hat.

"Where are we going?" Fred asked as he scrambled into the buggy.

"To Squawbetty," replied his uncle.

"Squawbetty!" echoed Fred. "That's a funny name for a village! Where in the world did they ever get such a name?"

"The name is n't so strange," was the answer, "when you know how it came to be given. When the town of Taunton was first settled, the land in what is now its east part was owned by an old Indian squaw named Betty, and was known as 'Squaw Betty's Land.' Later it was purchased by the settlers; but it has ever since borne the name of Squawbetty. Once there were large iron-works at the village; but they were burned down years ago. The village is a quiet place now. At present the only object of interest is a curious stairway that I am going to show you."

"Is it a stairway in one of the early settlers' houses?" said Fred. "I have read of hidden stairways in old castles, by which persons used to escape when the castle was captured. William Wallace had one leading to an underground passage that went from his home to an old monastery near by. Did the settlers of Taunton have such stairways to escape from the Indians?"

"Oh, no," said Uncle James, laughing at the notion. "This stairway is more curious than those; and it is out of doors, where everybody can see it."

"I guess I know what the stairway is like, then," Fred went on, for he was fond of guessing. "It can't be any more wonderful than one I saw once near home, cut out of the solid rock. We were having a picnic where the river runs in a deep cut between two high rocks, and the only way to get down to the riverside was by steps cut in the cliff. I guess your stairway is something of that sort."

"You will have to guess again, and then you won't guess right," said Uncle James mysteriously, but with a smile. "The stairway we

6.28. Harry Fenn, opening for "A Curious Stairway" by G. H. Hubbard. *St. Nicholas,* June 1896, 661. Process line cut, approx. 4 1/2" x 5 1/2".

silkworm, describing the steep terraces of mulberry plants, the bare trees with "not a single leaf" left by the "voracious worms," the way families relinquished their houses to the hatching worms that had to be fed and watched night and day, and finally the "picking," when neighbors were called in to help collect the cocoons before they were spun either there or in Tripoli or Damascus. Once again, we see Fenn as a knowledgeable traveler who can call up vivid memories to tell a good story.

Fenn also wrote and illustrated a brief but delightful piece, "Travelers of the Sky" (*St. Nicholas,* January 1894), about an attempt in Berlin to prove that storks returned to the same nests year after year. A silver ring engraved "Berlin, 1888" was placed on the leg of "one particularly aristocratic monarch-of-all-I-survey-looking bird"; the bird returned to the same chimney the next spring with, to the surprise of the banders, a second ring engraved "India sends greetings to Berlin."[92] For the story's opening page, Fenn combined the title and illustration of storks zigzagging through the sky to create a page with a highly asymmetrical, Japanese look (fig. 6.27). The banner-like strip enclosing the title and author's name is a device Fenn would use repeatedly. Among Fenn's other distinctive openers for *St. Nicholas* (June 1896) is "A Curious Stairway" (fig. 6.28), the Reverend G. H. Hubbard's story about a boy's visit to a fish stairway that enabled herring to bypass a milldam on the Taunton River in Massachusetts. Fenn's lettering and rather abstract, two-dimensional rendering from above creates an enticing page. And his opening for "How Plants Spread" (November 1896) again combines his lettering with a fanciful depiction of dandelion seeds blown from a seedpod.[93]

Fenn also began to experiment with the lighter

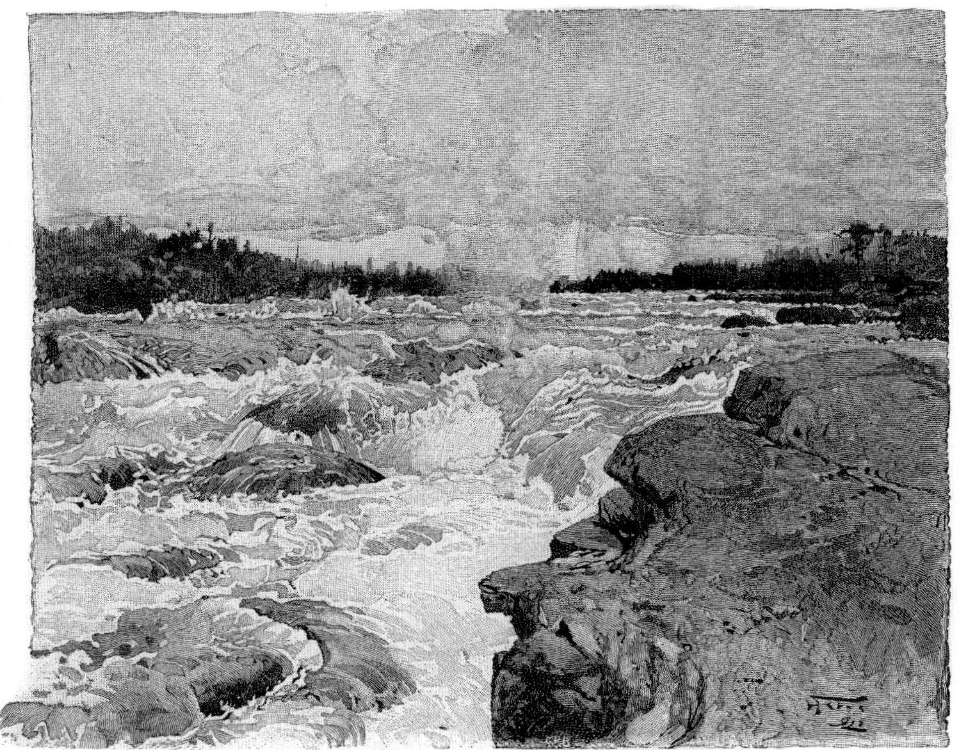

6.29. Harry Fenn, "Rapids above the Grand Falls," in "The Grand Falls of Labrador" by Henry G. Bryant. *Century,* September 1892, 649. Halftone with wood engraving by G. P. Bartle, 4" x 4 3/4".

styles that were gaining in popularity, opting for fewer dark shadows and less contrast, an approach seen especially in his work for the *Century.* He sometimes used watercolor in a more impressionistic manner than he had earlier. One example is his Labrador view for the September 1892 issue, "Rapids above the Grand Falls. (From a Photograph Taken 250 Feet above the Brink)" (fig. 6.29), engraved by G. F. Bartle, which uses the white of the paper effectively.[94] Another successful interpretation from less than two years later, this time reproduced by the halftone process, is "Lourdes during a Pilgrimage.—The Grotto Is Seen below the Apse of the Church" (fig. 6.30).

In landscape illustrations, Fenn increasingly used softer, less distinct forms. This shift may have been prompted by the comments of critics who admired the works with less contrast being produced by Castaigne, Pennell, and some other younger artists, which were similar in style to such painters as George Inness, James McNeil Whistler, Dennis Miller Bunker, and John Henry Twachtman. Though their works varied greatly, many of them conveyed, through soft focus and ethereal colors, an otherworldly transcendence or mystery. According to Kathleen Pyne, in Whistler's paintings "forms so dematerialized and veiled

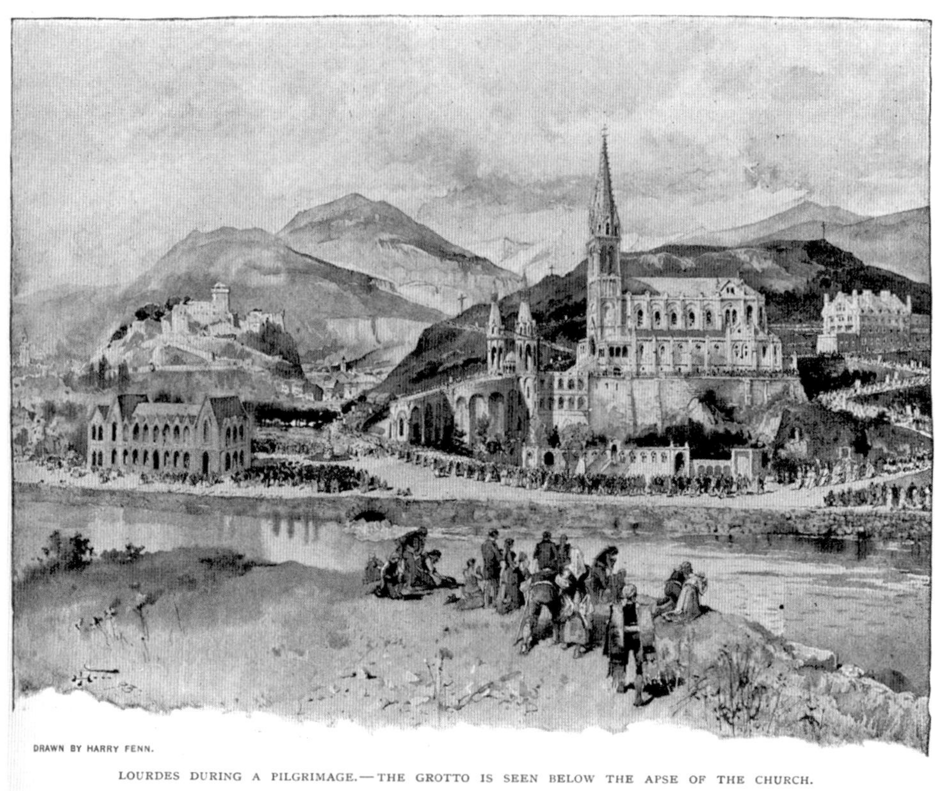

LOURDES DURING A PILGRIMAGE. — THE GROTTO IS SEEN BELOW THE APSE OF THE CHURCH.

suggested to Americans the painter's mystical experience of the world as essence." Furthermore, "the possibility that some transcendental plane of experience could be verified held out an escape from the nihilism in the idea of this world as a finality in itself—a pessimism with which Darwin's evolutionary studies were identified."[95] The discovery of X rays in 1895–96 would only increase interest in exploring depths under the surface and invisible to the eye.

In the May 1894 *Art Amateur,* a writer offering instruction for the student reader contrasted works in the April 1894 *Century* by "that veteran illustrator" Fenn with Castaigne's series in the same issue titled "From the Old World to the New," illustrating an immigrant family's journey. The writer was critical of Fenn's darks and shadows, his "exaggerated contrasts," in his five illustrations for "A Summer Month in a Welsh Village" by Susan Nichols Carter, including "The Stream above the Village" (fig. 6.31). Although granting that Fenn's compositions could "hardly be surpassed" and his treatment of "masses" "might almost be called scientific," the writer wrote: "The dark masses lack air, and the light masses would be vastly improved by 'graying.'" In sum, this critic much preferred Castaigne's drawings, in which "the light is admirably diffused" throughout (fig. 6.32).[96]

Challenges and Triumphs

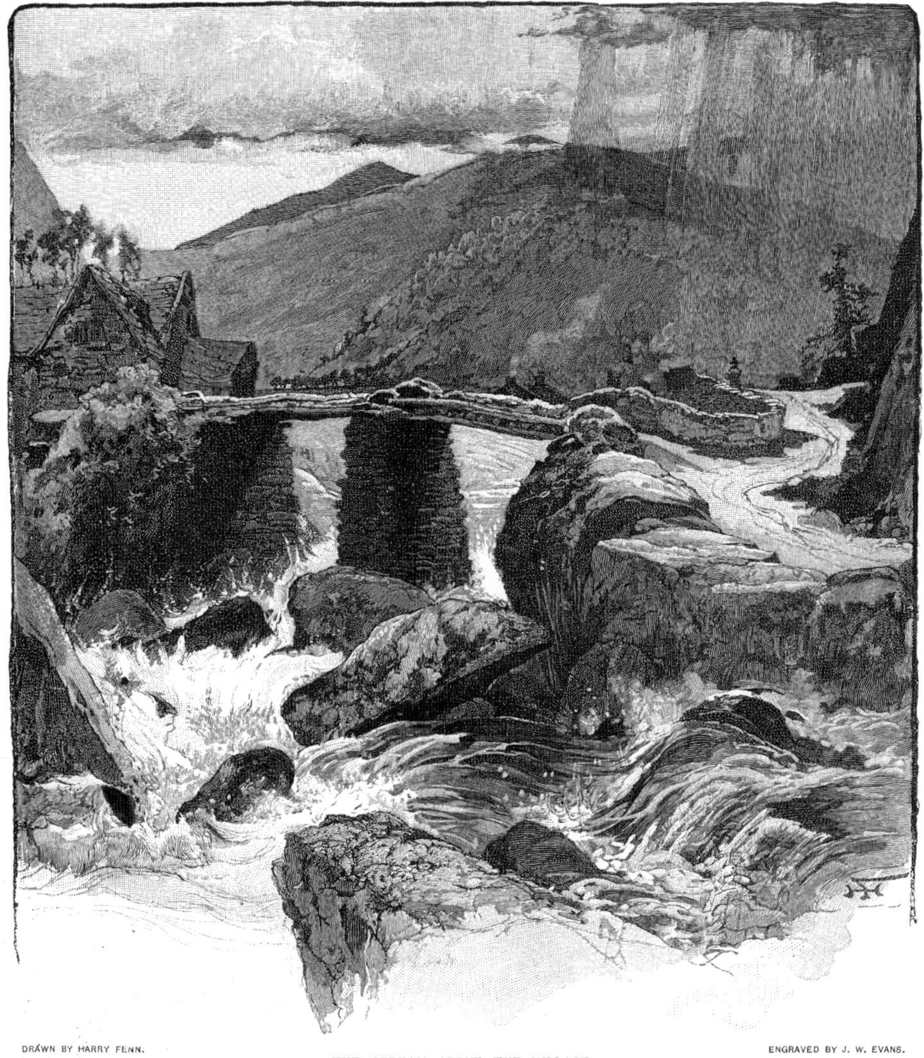

6.31. Harry Fenn, "The Stream above the Village," in "A Summer Month in a Welsh Village" by Susan Nichols Carter. *Century*, April 1894, 861. Halftone with wood engraving by J. W. Evans, 5 13/16" x 5 1/8".

Some of Fenn's later works suggest that he took this criticism to heart. From November 1898 through October 1899 he shared with Castaigne the task of illustrating a series for the *Century* on Alexander the Great written by Benjamin Ide Wheeler, a Greek professor at Cornell University.[97] The editors thought a new biography of Alexander would be timely considering America's recent victories in the Spanish–American War, which resulted, in their opinion, from "the miracle of courage, intelligence, and discipline" and would bring "a grander civilization" to America's new empire.[98] The artists worked according to their specialties: Fenn did the landscapes and Castaigne the historical events.[99] One of

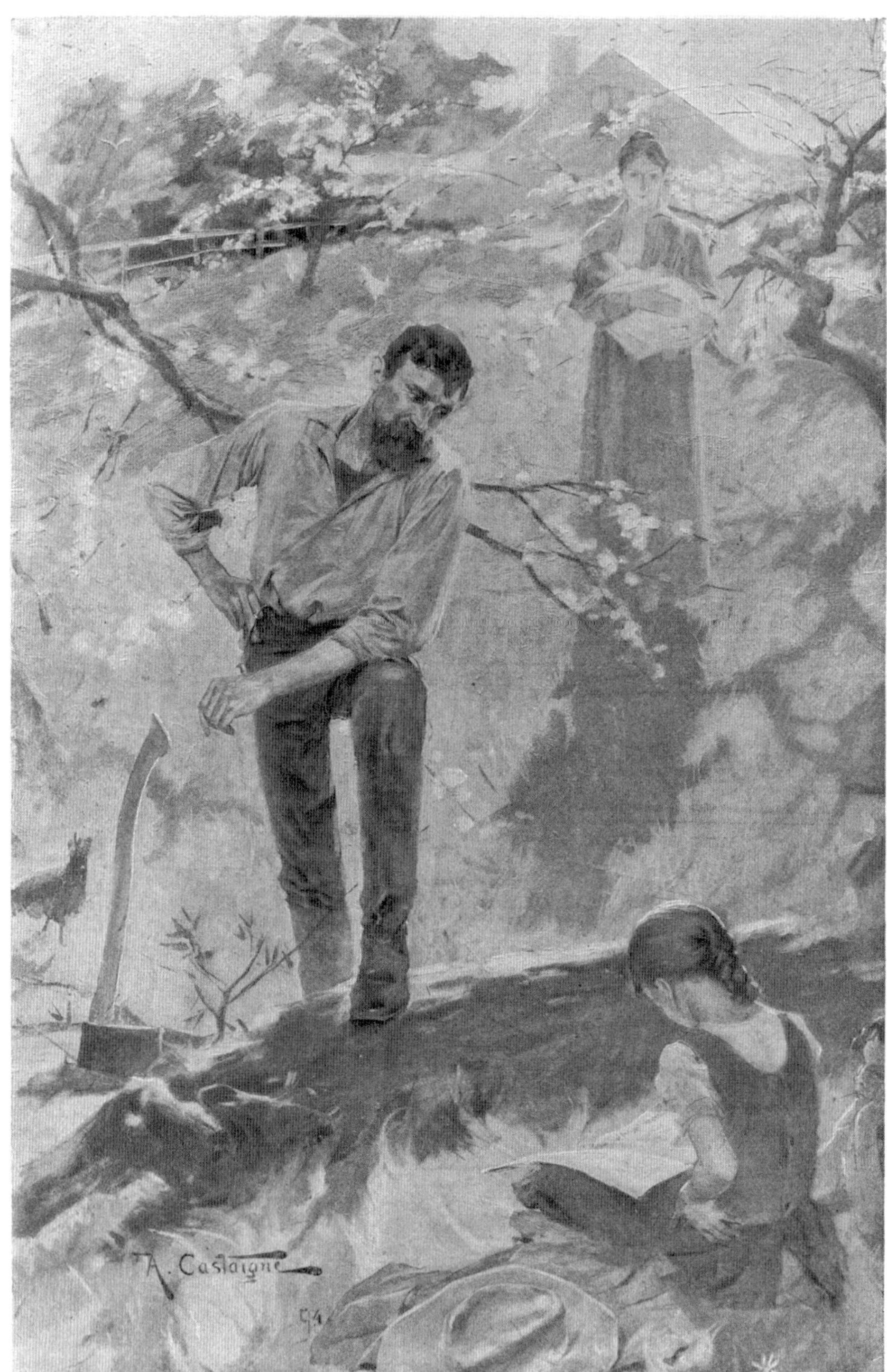

 Challenges and Triumphs

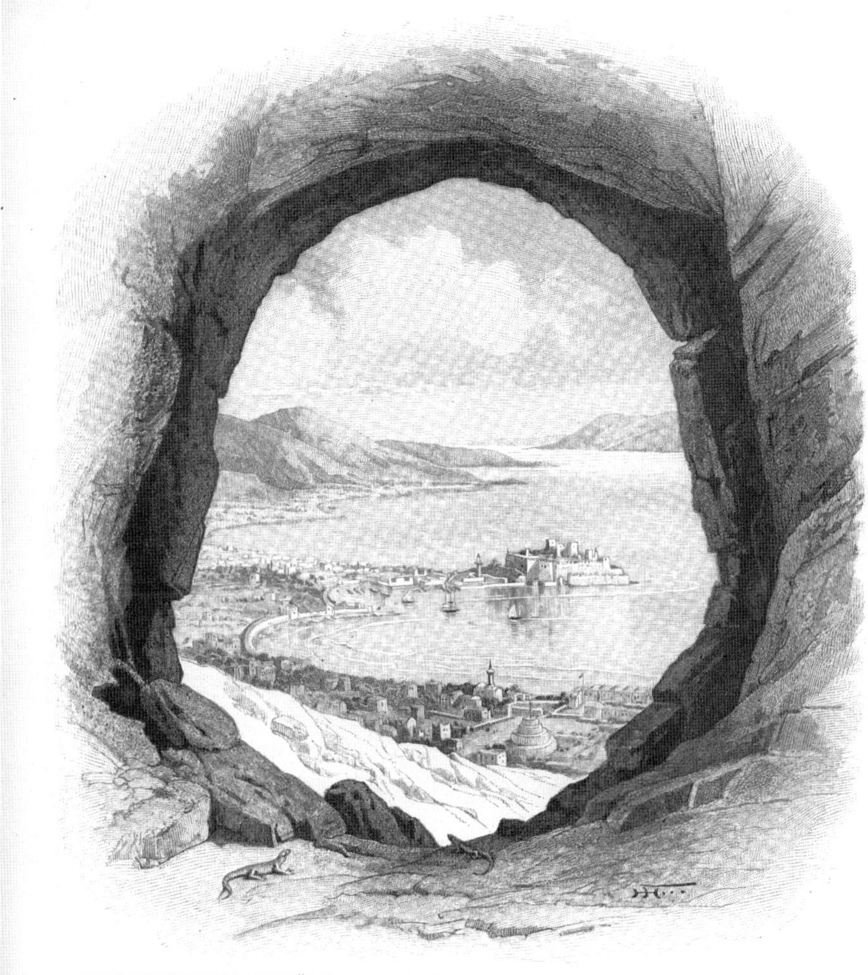

VIEW OF BUDRUM, ANCIENT HALICARNASSUS.

The view is from a rock-cut tomb. The site of the mausoleum (tomb of Mausolus) is indicated by the mound in the foreground surmounted by a flagstaff.

6.33. Harry Fenn, "View of Budrum, Ancient Halicarnassus. The view is from a rock-cut tomb. The site of the mausoleum (tomb of Mausolus) is indicated by the mound in the foreground surmounted by a flagstaff," in "Alexander's Conquest of Asia Minor. Alexander the Great: Fourth Paper" by Benjamin Ide Wheeler. *Century*, February 1899, 559. Halftone with engraving by C. Schwarzburger, approx. 6 1/4" x 5 1/4".

Fenn's images, "View of Budrum, Ancient Halicarnassus" (fig. 6.33), combines a light touch similar to Castaigne's style but with one of his favorite devices, a distant view through an arch or window-like opening. This illustration was printed from a "half-tone plate engraved by C. Schwarzburger."

In this period, the *Century*'s editors were frequently unsatisfied with the results when the halftone process alone was used; one of them, W. Lewis Fraser, complained that the new process was "largely what its name implies—a *half-tone*" because, in his estimation, "the deepest darks cannot be rendered by it, nor the highest lights," resulting in the "loss of a great many of the tones of the original."[100]

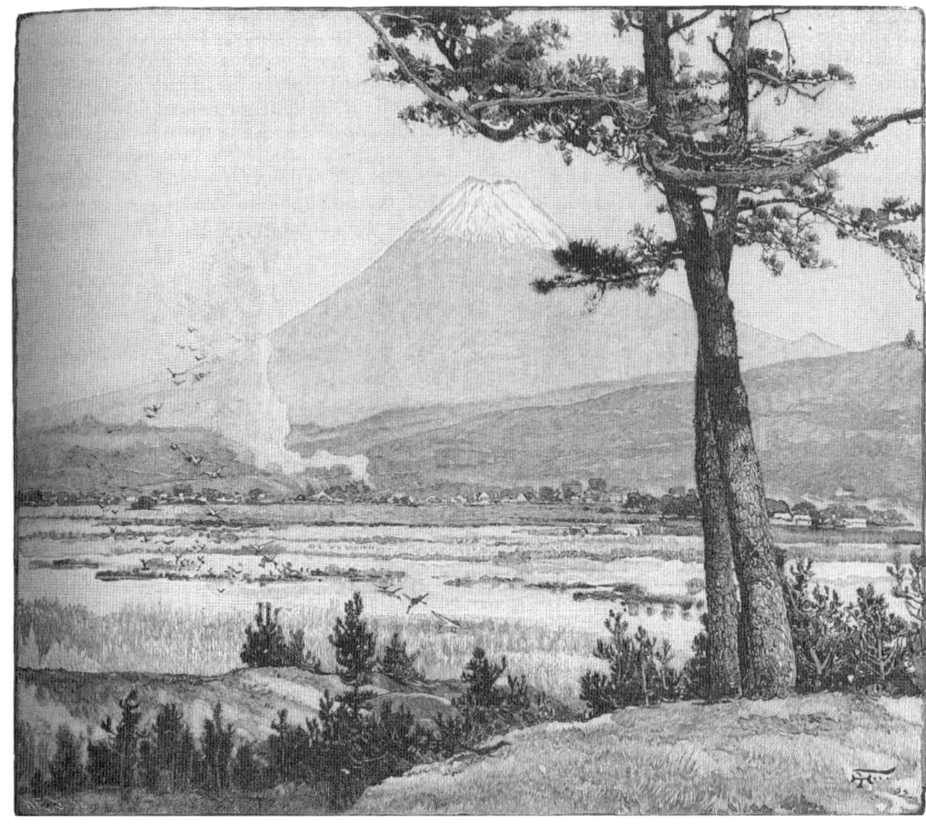

To correct this problem the *Century* often engaged engravers to improve the printing plate, despite the additional expense. Their task was primarily to deepen the grooves in the plate so that ink did not fill in between the dots and to gouge out highlights.[101] An example of a work by Fenn reproduced as a halftone with engraving is "Fuji-San from Omiya" (fig. 6.34), for which he had used watercolor to depict the distant mountain and sky and sharper lines to delineate the foreground trees. In the magazine, the tiny halftone dots reproduced the sky, mountain, and parts of the foreground marsh, whereas H. E. Sylvester's engraved lines represented the trees, birds, and high grass. Fraser explained the relative costs: "First-class wood-engraving is ten times dearer than good half-tone; engraved half-tone costs three or four times as much as unengraved or ordinary half-tone." Then he claimed that the *Century* selected among the various methods "solely with reference to the fidelity with which they reproduce the difficult-to-be-reproduced drawings of to-day."[102] The newer, cheaper periodicals that were reaching a much larger audience, and clearly did take cost into account, used more and more halftones.

 Challenges and Triumphs

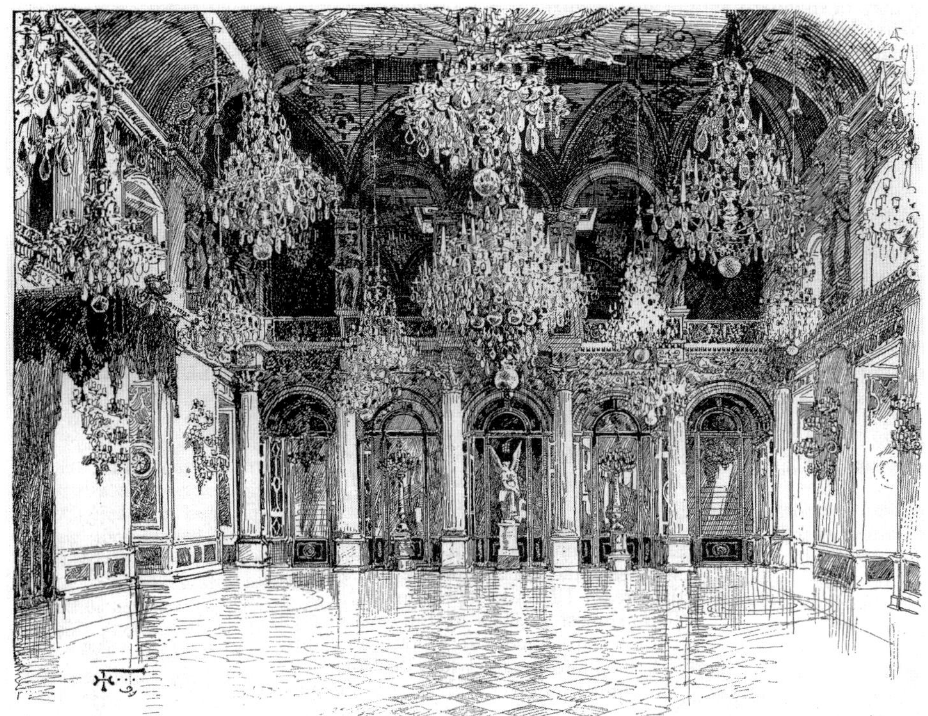

6.35. Harry Fenn, "The White Saloon, Winter Palace, in Which Parliament Is Opened," in "The German Emperor: A Sketch of the First Three Years of His Reign" by Poultney Bigelow. *Century,* August 1891, 491. Process line cut, 4 1/8" x 5 3/16".

Fenn continued to produce crisp line drawings in ink for reproduction as line blocks. Some striking examples for the *Century* are "The White Saloon, Winter Palace, in Which Parliament Is Opened" (fig. 6.35), a virtuoso illustration that appeared in the August 1891 article "The German Emperor," and the "Steps to Santa Trinità dei Monti, Rome, Showing the House, at the Right, Where Keats Died" for the October 1895 article "Keats in Hampstead." Fenn's original drawing for the latter, now in the collection of the Cooper-Hewitt, National Design Museum, shows his skill in using pen and ink to create the illusion of depth and light and shadows (fig. 6.36). The drawing is approximately twice the size of the illustration in the *Century.* For the January 1895 *Scribner's,* he drew the title page for "A Tuscan Shrine," Edith Wharton's story about San Vivaldo, for which he again used a banner-like title. For the magazine's March 1896 article titled "Carnations" by J. H. Connelly, he created virtuoso renderings of flowers that were printed in a deep purple while the text was printed in black, a novel approach at the time. His opening-page design provides a good example of the flourish and drama of these illustrations (fig. 6.37). Also in these years he prepared architectural and landscape images for *Harper's Monthly,* primarily as pen drawings. For

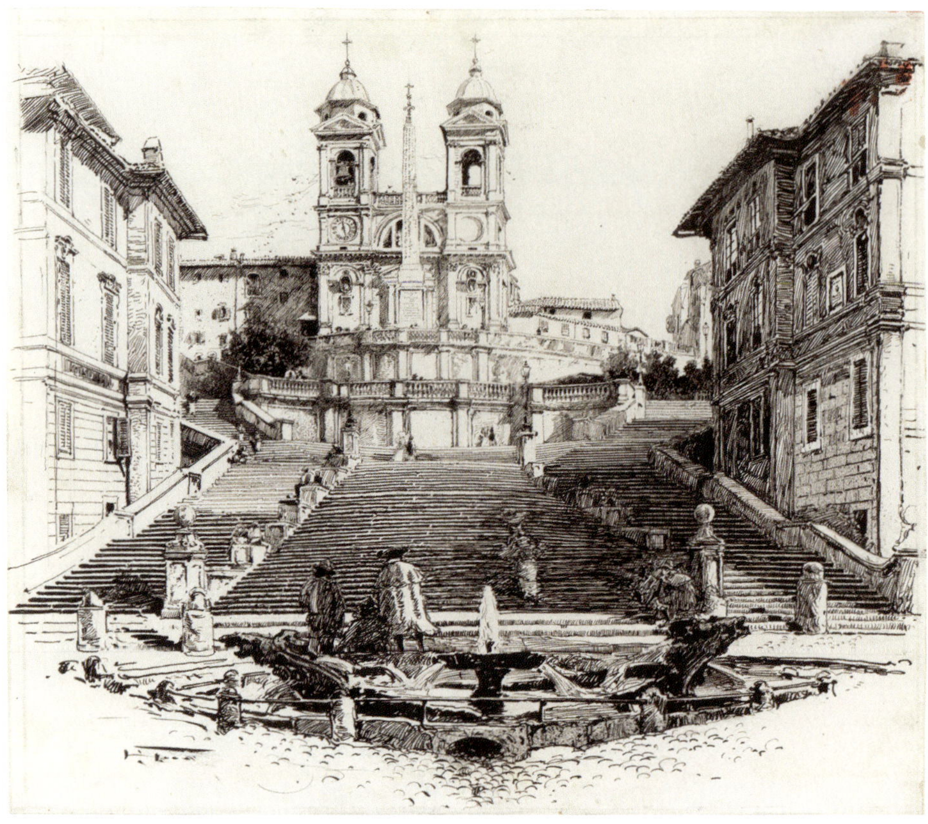

a series in 1899 about George Washington's homes, both Fenn and his son Walter contributed drawings.[103] (See Appendix 1 for additional *Century* and *Harper's Monthly* illustrations.)

Fenn's ability to work in vastly different styles is striking and can be readily appreciated in his illustrations for the *Century* in the 1890s. Such breadth can be seen in two of his designs that both utilize a tripartite format but differ in media, viewpoint, and style. For "Down to Java," Eliza Ruhamah Scidmore's article in the August 1897 issue, he created a detailed close-up of three of its tropical plants— "Frangipani, Sausage-Tree, and Candle-Tree"—done in ink, wash, and gouache, to be reproduced in halftone (fig. 6.38). He supported the author's contention that Java was the finest tropical island in the world, with the best botanical garden, and achieved a dynamic page by playing with three-dimensionality and manipulating the picture plane. Leaves and petals of the lifelike frangipani at the top of the page overlap what appears to be a trompe l'oeil sheet of paper that bears a sketch of the sausage tree; in turn, two of the sausage tree's pods overlap the sketch of the candle

    Challenges and Triumphs

tree below. In contrast to this image is the one he created for the August 1899 issue, when interest in China was still high after the One Hundred Days' Reform. His three-part design for "Chinese River Craft" is more decorative and less realistic. Using both ink and watercolor, he drew a border recalling Chinese furniture motifs to unify distant views of three different boats (fig. 6.39). The illustrations, reproduced by halftone with engraving by Robert Varley, were for Scidmore's article "The River of Tea." The interruption of the border on the lower left of the column of type serves to draw the image and text together.

These contrasting examples provide an opportunity to reflect on how the changing media from the 1860s through the 1890s affected Fenn's illustrations and viewers' perceptions of him as an artist. The process of wood engraving, the primary means of illustrating books and periodicals from early in the century until about 1890, could adequately convey Fenn's skills at composing a subject: his dynamic diagonals, deep perspective, contrasts of light and dark, and interesting juxtapositions of image and type. Yet it was unable to convey the subtlety of his tones to as high a degree. In the 1880s the techniques of the New School engravers achieved better results in interpreting the tones of his watercolors and charcoal drawings. But it wasn't until the 1890s, when line cuts and halftones were able to reproduce artists' work much more directly, that viewers could appreciate his talent with pen and ink and the wide variety of tones—from subtle to bold—in his watercolors. And it is these two new printing processes that would be used to reproduce the designs for his last important poetry project.

6.37. Harry Fenn, opening for "Carnations" by J. H. Connelly. *Scribner's,* March 1896, 313. Process line cut, printed in dark purple, 3 1/4" x 4 7/8". (Alderman Library, University of Virginia Library.)

In Memoriam and Other Books

In 1897 Fenn once again secured a major commission as sole illustrator of a book of poetry. Designing the first profusely illustrated edition of Tennyson's well-loved poem of bereavement, *In Memoriam,* with a lengthy preface by Henry van Dyke,

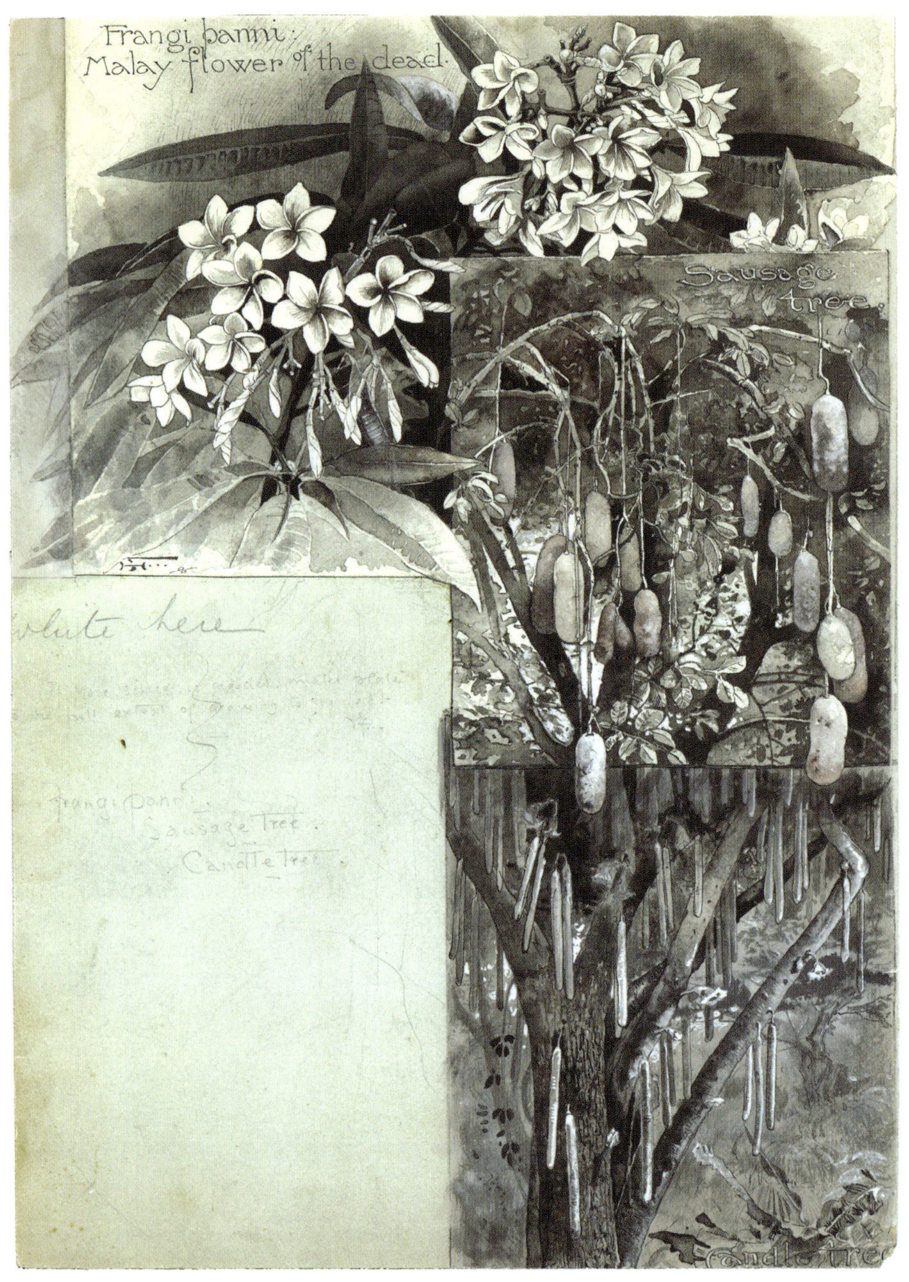

6.38. Harry Fenn, *Frangipani, Sausage Tree, Candle Tree,* ca. 1897. Ink, wash, and gouache, 16 3/4" x 11 1/2". (Private collection.)

was one of his most important late efforts. It was one of three poetry commissions Fenn mentioned on a biographical information sheet requested by the publishers of *The Artists' Year Book;* the other two were *Snow-Bound* and *Gray's Elegy.*[104]

Tennyson had died in 1892, and the 1897 publication of *Alfred Lord Tennyson: A Memoir by His Son* had heightened interest in him and his work.[105] That Fenn knew

Challenges and Triumphs

Tennyson and had once lived near him may have played a role in his selection for this project by the publisher Fords, Howard & Hulbert of New York.[106] The book's execution demonstrates Fenn's remarkable ability to change in his later years; it differs markedly from the Harry Fenn Edition of *Gray's Elegy* of 1883, as well as most of the other poetry books he had worked on, in the way the page designs often give greater attention to the poem's text than to the illustrations. The images do not overpower, or even compete with, the words as much as in earlier books, and the overall design has a simpler, more restrained look, in keeping with the Aesthetic style. The initial capital letters combined with delicate drawings recall the chapter headings Childe Hassam designed for Celia Thaxter's book *An Island Garden,* published by Houghton Mifflin in 1894 (though Hassam's are printed in color), which Fenn likely would have seen. The binding of *In Memoriam* is also strikingly different from the Fenn edition of *Gray's Elegy* (see fig. 5.23); it is almost Japanese in its simplicity, with the title stamped in gold in the upper left quadrant, and tiny floral designs in each corner.[107]

In Memoriam was Tennyson's response to the death of his best friend Arthur Henry Hallam, when Tennyson was only twenty-four. Over a period of several years he chronicled his great grief and gradual recovery through his faith that their souls would be reunited in eternity. The book's design scheme required Fenn to respond to each of the poem's 131 cantos by creating a visual accompaniment that would enrich the reader's experience. In many cases he was remarkably successful, with attractive initials that sometimes coincided with an image of flowers, trees, architecture, and the like (fig. 6.40) He kept the illustrative touches light, in keeping with the spare, rather small typeface arranged in stanzas on about two-thirds of the page. His double-page spread

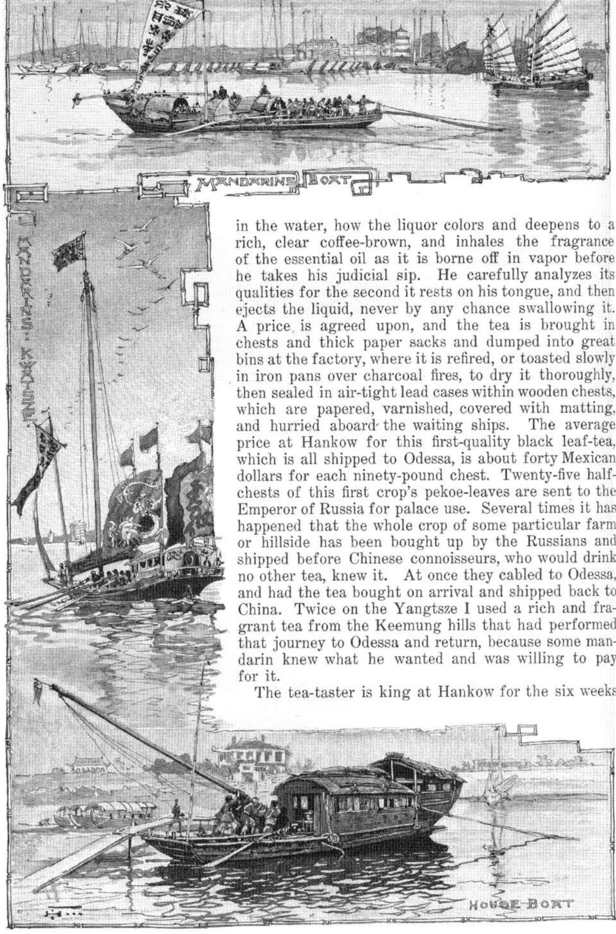

in the water, how the liquor colors and deepens to a rich, clear coffee-brown, and inhales the fragrance of the essential oil as it is borne off in vapor before he takes his judicial sip. He carefully analyzes its qualities for the second it rests on his tongue, and then ejects the liquid, never by any chance swallowing it. A price is agreed upon, and the tea is brought in chests and thick paper sacks and dumped into great bins at the factory, where it is refired, or toasted slowly in iron pans over charcoal fires, to dry it thoroughly, then sealed in air-tight lead cases within wooden chests, which are papered, varnished, covered with matting, and hurried aboard the waiting ships. The average price at Hankow for this first-quality black leaf-tea, which is all shipped to Odessa, is about forty Mexican dollars for each ninety-pound chest. Twenty-five half-chests of this first crop's pekoe-leaves are sent to the Emperor of Russia for palace use. Several times it has happened that the whole crop of some particular farm or hillside has been bought up by the Russians and shipped before Chinese connoisseurs, who would drink no other tea, knew it. At once they cabled to Odessa, and had the tea bought on arrival and shipped back to China. Twice on the Yangtsze I used a rich and fragrant tea from the Keemung hills that had performed that journey to Odessa and return, because some mandarin knew what he wanted and was willing to pay for it.

The tea-taster is king at Hankow for the six weeks

6.39. Harry Fenn, "Chinese River Craft. Mandarin's Boat; Mandarin's Yangtsze House-Boat; Stepping the Mast at Ichang," in "The River of Tea" by Eliza Ruhamah Scidmore. *Century,* August 1899, 556. Halftone engraved by Robert Varley, 7 3/4" x 5 1/16".

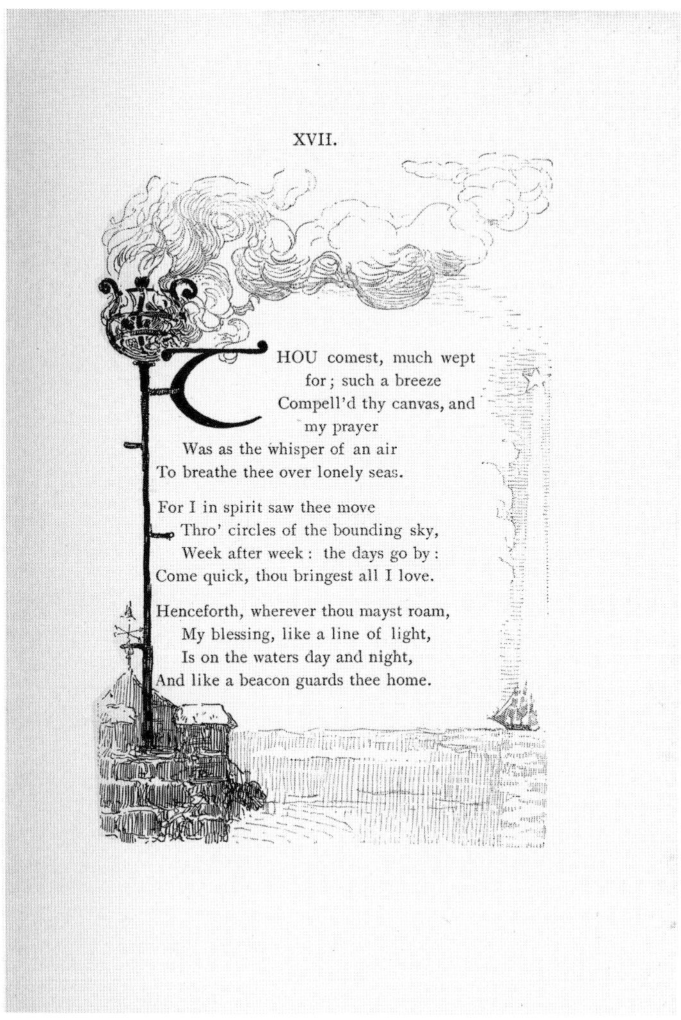

6.40. Harry Fenn, design for canto 17. From Alfred, Lord Tennyson, *In Memoriam* (New York: Fords, Howard & Hulbert, 1897), 37. Process line cut, approx. 5 1/4" x 3 1/4".

of delicate seeds dispersed in the wind illustrates the poet's trust in "the larger hope" despite his observation that "of fifty seeds," Nature "often brings but one to bear" (fig. 6.41). The combination of image and initial letter for canto 130 (fig. 6.42) is striking in its simplicity and abstraction; the circular shape, which appears to divide into at least three planes, relates to at least three elements in the poem: the sun, the power of star and flower, and the words "I prosper, circled with thy voice."

Some of the illustrations were line cuts of ink drawings and some were halftones of watercolors. Four of Fenn's original drawings for the book are now

 Challenges and Triumphs

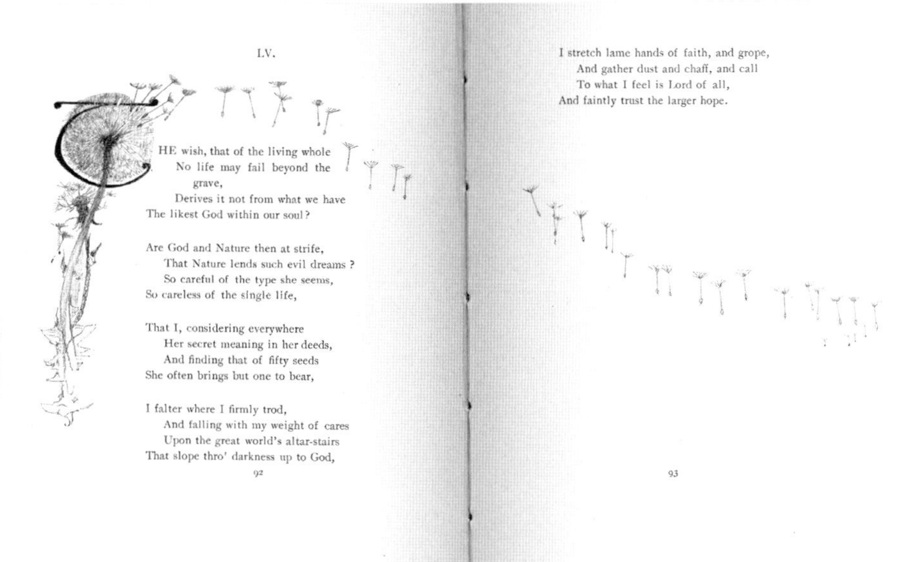

6.41. Harry Fenn, design for canto 55. From Tennyson, *In Memoriam*, 92–93. Halftone, approx. 4" x 9".

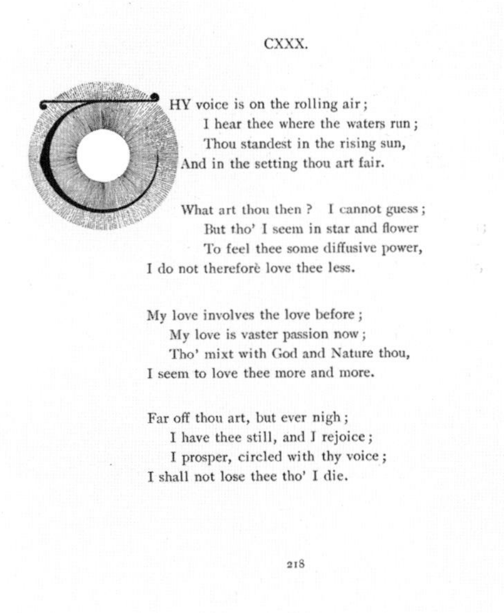

6.42. Harry Fenn, design for canto 130. From Tennyson, *In Memoriam*, 218. Process line cut, approx. 1 3/8" x 1 3/8".

in the collection of the Cleveland Museum of Art; they show how drastically the originals were reduced. For example, his powerful watercolor of a tiger to illustrate "Like Paul with beasts, I fought with Death" measures 10 7/8 by 7 3/4 inches, whereas the image in the book measures a mere 1 1/2 by 1 inch (figs. 6.43, 6.44).[108] The publishers advertised the book in November and December 1897

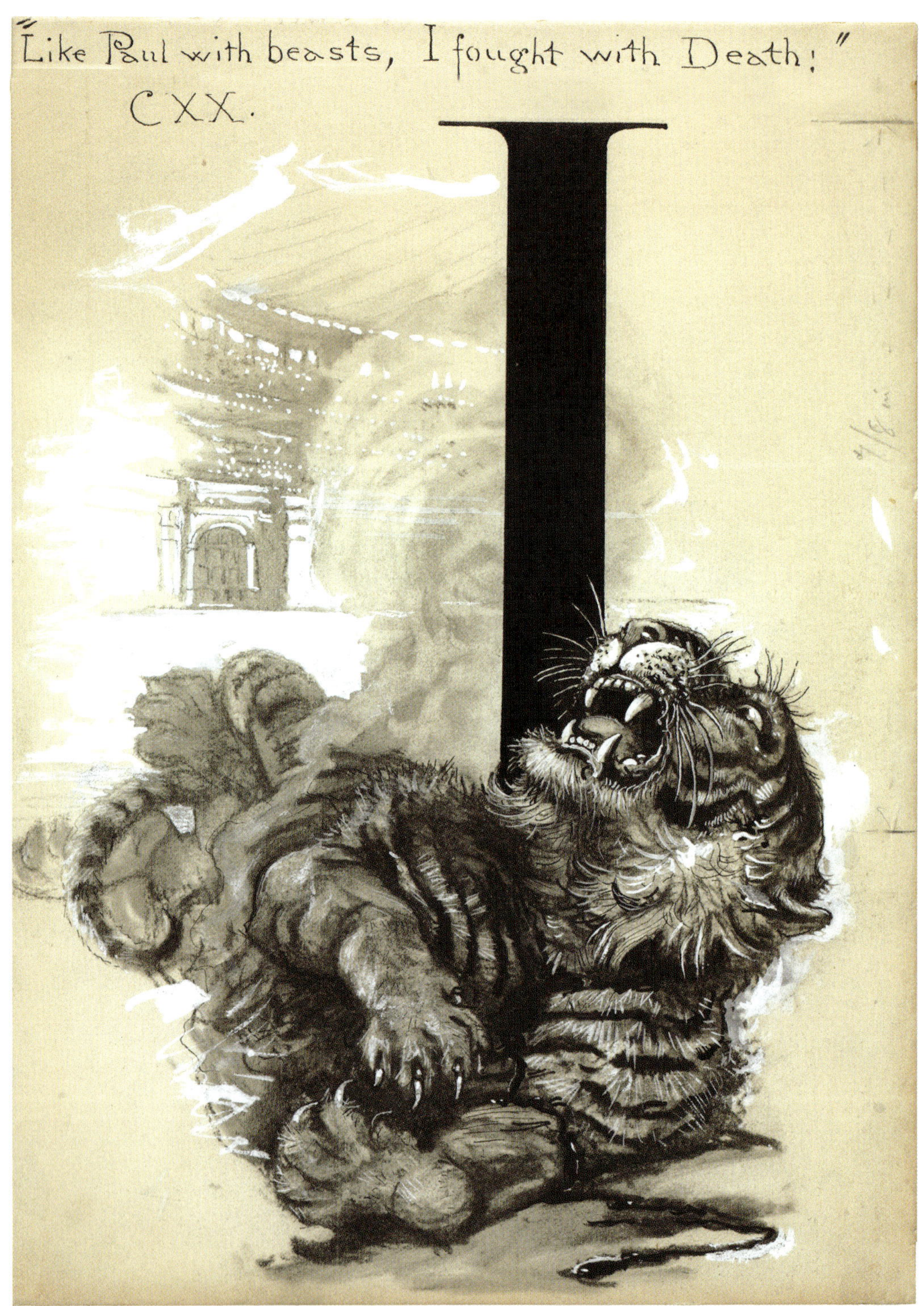

6.43. Harry Fenn, *Tiger*. Pen, ink, and wash, heightened with white, 10 7/8" x 7 3/4".
(The Cleveland Museum of Art. Gift of Rossiter Howard 1928.122.)

as "exquisitely illustrated" by Harry Fenn, "elegantly printed, bound in silk, boxed" for $3.50.[109] They also offered it in "Octavo, silk, gilt top, uncut edges, $3.50" and "In sheets, $3.00. Special bindings to order."[110]

The critical response to Fenn's illustrations ranged from extremely positive to dismissively negative, perhaps indicative of changing attitudes about whether pictures enhanced or detracted from a poetic text, or inspired or constrained the imagination. While some praised the affinity between word and image, a few objected to what they considered Fenn's too literal embellishments. One of the most positive reviewers wrote in the *Independent* that Fenn's drawings "indicate such a close and appreciative study of the poem as to make them an artist's comment on it, as much as Dr. van Dyke's Preface is a critic's. They are . . . alive with the thought, inspiration, emotion and truth which lives in [the book]."[111] Another found that Fenn had successfully translated "into dainty black and white the poet's own word pictures" and "scattered them with taste about the margins and initials of these richly printed pages."[112] *The Chap-Book*'s critic judged the illustrations "alternately excellent and foolish," with some "extremely old-fashioned in their manner" and others "modern and full of delicacy and feeling."[113] *The Critic*'s reviewer found the paper too heavy and objected to "the sort of illustration that gives us a picture of a harp to point the reference to 'one clear harp of divers tones,'" all of which presupposed "a reader absolutely lacking in imagination."[114] Such objections were apparently a minority opinion. The *Bookman* quoted parts of Henry van Dyke's note commending Fenn's illustrations for the comfort they could offer: "Opening windows in the dark walls of grief and looking out upon the silent, lovely consolations of nature. . . . There could be no better notes and illustrations to *In Memoriam* than the pictures of hill and meadow and garden, stream and tree and flower, which have been drawn for this volume by the hand of

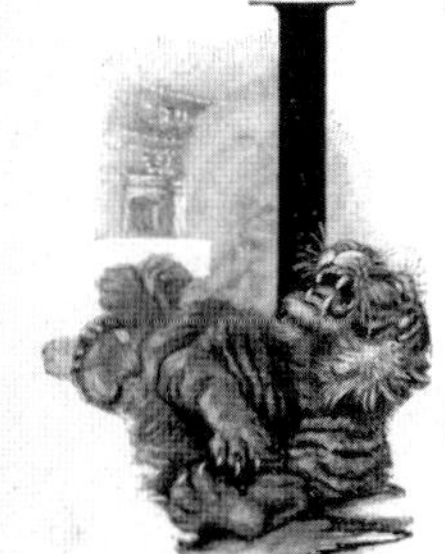

CXX.

I TRUST I have not wasted
   breath :
  I think we are not wholly
   brain,
  Magnetic mockeries ; not
   in vain,
  Like Paul with beasts, I fought
   with Death ;

Not only cunning casts in clay :
  Let Science prove we are, and then
  What matters Science unto men,
At least to me ?   I would not stay.

Let him, the wiser man who springs
  Hereafter, up from childhood shape
  His action like the greater ape,
But I was *born* to other things.

203

6.44. Harry Fenn, design for canto 120. From Tennyson, *In Memoriam*, 203. Halftone, 1 1/2" x 1".

one whose devotion to art is the fruit of his intimacy with Nature, for he has lived with her long and loved her well."[115] This sentiment shows that van Dyke still identified Fenn as a leading interpreter of nature, and many others likely did as well.

After *In Memoriam* it would be a decade before Fenn was given another opportunity to be the sole illustrator of a book.[116] Nevertheless, he continued to contribute to book projects, including *The Complete Writings of Nathaniel Hawthorne,* published in twenty-two volumes by Houghton Mifflin in 1900. Fenn contributed two illustrations for volume 18, *Passages from the American Note-Books:* the frontispiece, "Graylock from the North" (Greylock is a mountain near North Adams, Massachusetts), and "Near Salem Harbor" for the engraved title page. His paintings were reproduced as photogravures.[117] Among the many contributing artists, which included a large number of women, Fenn was the undoubtedly the oldest.[118]

Promoting the Pan-American Exposition in Buffalo

In 1901 Fenn had a chance to illustrate yet another international fair. Even as the United States' new role as a colonial power after the Spanish–American War of 1898 stirred controversy at home and abroad, political and business leaders were once again contemplating sponsoring a fair on the scale of Chicago's in 1893 and larger than the Trans-Mississippi and International Exposition in Omaha, Nebraska, in 1898.[119] A fair promoting—or repairing—friendship in the Americas, North and South, held great appeal. The goals of the 1901 Pan-American Exposition in Buffalo, New York, as stated in the fair's promotional booklet, were to exhibit "the progress and civilization of the nations of the Western Hemisphere, to strengthen their friendship and to inaugurate a new era of social and commercial intercourse with the beginning of the new century."[120] It was the first U.S. world's fair to which European countries were not invited as exhibitors. Clearly, the organizers hoped to foster improvement in the nation's economy through more trade with Latin America and Canada. Buffalo, a major port, was ostensibly selected because "more people" lived "within a day's journey" by train than was true of "any other place in the Western Hemisphere." It was also close to Niagara Falls, always a top tourist attraction and newly equipped with the capacity to generate a vast amount of electricity, some of which would be used to illuminate the fair. Organizers sought to set the Pan-American Exposition apart from the 1893 neoclassical White City through a more symmetrical arrangement of colorful buildings, designed in the California Mission style—an attempt to connect with the architecture of Latin America. The exposition's signature structure was the 375-foot Electric Tower, located at the end of the central axis and serving as the focal point of the nightly illumination that

  Challenges and Triumphs

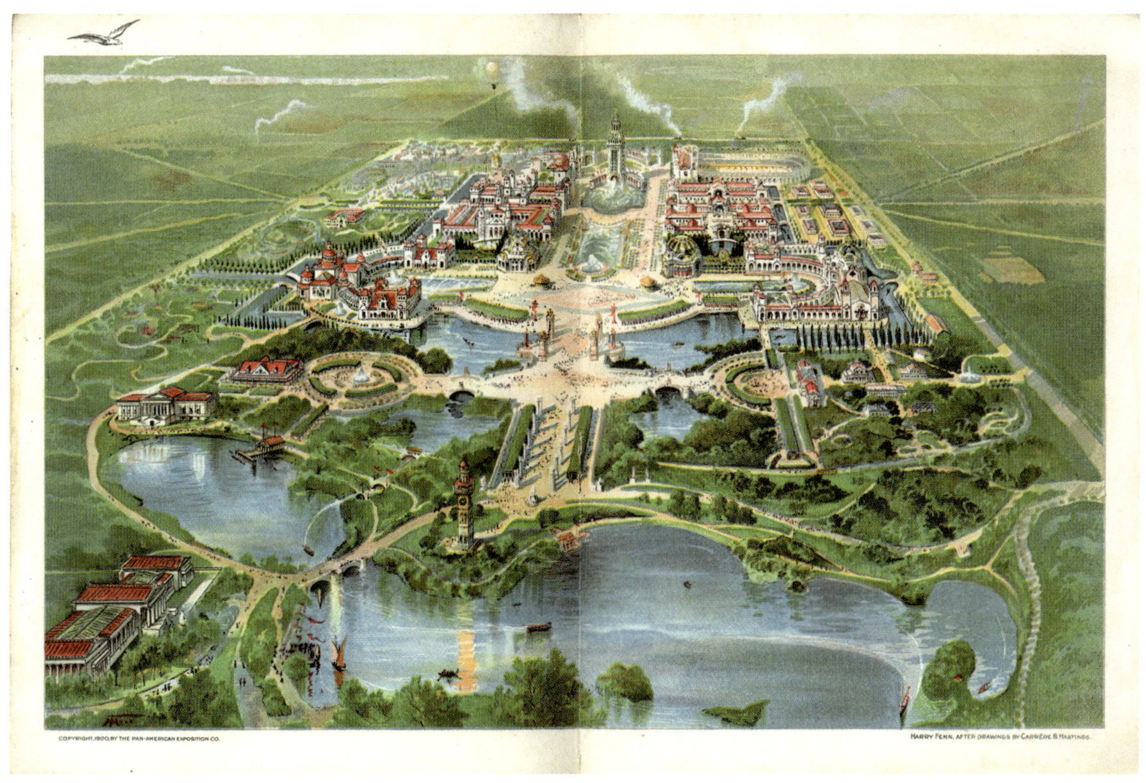

6.45. Harry Fenn, after drawings by Carrère & Hastings, [Bird's-eye View of the Pan-American Exposition, Buffalo]. From *Pan-American Exposition, Buffalo, May 1 to November 1, 1901, Its Purpose and Its Plan* (Pan-American Exposition Co., 1901), centerfold. Chromolithograph by Courier Lithographic Co., Buffalo, N.Y., 7" x 11".

attracted huge crowds at twilight and gave the fair its popular name, the "City of Light." According to David Gray in the *Century:* "Since the world began, this is the first time human eyes have beheld such floods of artificial light as the untiring cataract of Niagara generates for this Exposition."[121]

Fenn exhibited two works at the fair in Group III, the section showing drawings, etchings, engravings, and black and white or monotint paintings. Their titles were "Fuji-San (from Omiya)" (the original of fig. 6.34) and "Interior of Alma-Tadema's Studio" (the original of the *Century* illustration, February 1894, 492), both lent by the Century Company. He was not among the medalists this time. Those honored included many of his younger colleagues: Howard Pyle, Joseph Pennell, Charles Dana Gibson, Maxfield Parrish, William T. Smedley, and W. A. Clark.[122]

Fenn did, however, play a key role in creating imagery for the fair, perhaps even more than he had for the World's Columbian Exposition. His paintings of the colorful buildings and his bird's-eye view of the entire site, after drawings by the architectural firm Carrère & Hastings, were reproduced as chromolithographs in the promotional booklet (fig. 6.45). The bird's-eye view was also issued as a large print, measuring 32 1/2 by 41 inches.[123] After the fair opened in May 1901, Fenn contributed to the *Century*'s feature article, "The City of Light," in the September issue. As with the Chicago fair, his younger colleague André Castaigne prepared the majority of the images, several showing the nighttime illumination. Fenn's two illustrations depicted some of the elaborate structures: "Entrance to the Stadium" and "The Propylea." For these, his much larger watercolors were reproduced by halftone with touch-up engraving. His illustrations for *The Niagara Book* were once more available as well, for Doubleday, Page & Company had issued a new edition to coincide with the exposition that was using Niagara's electric power in such a dramatic fashion.

The Pan-American Exposition failed to gain as much participation by Latin American countries as its organizers had hoped. Then disaster occurred on September 6, when U.S. president William McKinley was shot on the fairgrounds by an anarchist and died eight days later. The fair never recovered and ended up losing about $3 million.[124]

WATERCOLOR EXHIBITIONS—DECORATING AND SHOWING— IN NEW YORK AND BEYOND

During these years of prolific contributions to books and magazines, Fenn continued to fulfill significant responsibilities for the American Water Color Society, complete more watercolors, and seek out new venues for exhibiting his artworks. On November 16, 1892, he was appointed to the committee on decoration for the society's upcoming annual exhibition at the National Academy of Design. He evidently led the committee, for he garnered both the credit and the criticism for the dramatically new setting. Not surprisingly, some of the details sound similar to the Aesthetic-style decorations of Fenn's house. The *Art Amateur*'s commentator liked the decorations, finding them "much more favorable to the pictures than those of recent years. The rooms were hung with light gray, drab or fawn-colored Japanese chintzes; a few fine rugs were displayed over the doors of the galleries; there were some good Japanese bronzes among the plants on the staircase, and that was about all. The pictures gained by the absence of the usual bric-a-brac display. Mr. Harry Fenn, who had charge of the decorations, is to be warmly congratulated on the result."[125] The *New York Times* reviewer, on the other hand, noticed plenty of bric-a-brac and thought the efforts of Fenn, the "decorator in chief," had turned "the austerities of the Academy into frivolous

 Challenges and Triumphs

channels," including "the coquettish chintzes" and "the huge tiger skin." Yet, the reviewer conceded the decorations, as well as the efforts of the hanging committee, had "not been without results," for it appeared the sales would be greater than ever.[126] That year, 1892, Fenn exhibited mainly scenes of the Massachusetts coast (see Appendix 2).

The exhibitions of the American Water Color Society continued to be popular, and apparently Fenn's decorations started a trend, at least for the next few years. According to the *Brooklyn Eagle,* the setting in 1893–94 was "like a dream studio," owing to "the white gallery, with its jars above the door cornices filled with white blossoms, and its gray hung walls and white framed pictures."[127] In 1897 even more elaborate decorations were arranged by Walter Satterlee, and the *Independent* noted that he had "outdone" his predecessors "by the help of loans from the Tiffany Glass Company, and various dealers in antiques, draperies and rugs."[128]

In these years, comments on the paintings Fenn exhibited with the Water Color Society ranged from glibly offhand to extremely positive. In 1894 the *Brooklyn Daily Eagle* critic noted that the figures in *Street Venders in Cairo* were "reflected with true oriental spirit," and his *Banks of Memphremagog* and *Block Island* showed the "range of his work."[129] In 1896, the *New York Times* reviewer said of Fenn only that he was "as dexterous as usual" while praising the popular artist-illustrator E. A. Abbey's *Dawn,* Charles M. McIlhenney's *Evening on the Beach,* and Henry B. Snell's *Docking a Liner,* a Hudson River scene, in keeping with the earlier calls for New York subjects.[130] Nevertheless, Fenn's Middle Eastern subjects received praise the next year. One *New York Times* critic described his *Bâb Tûma, Damascus* as a "strong and carefully painted study of a gateway in the old Eastern city, excellent in composition, delicate in color, and almost photographic in details." The reviewer also praised another of Fenn's paintings, *In the Carpet Bazaar, Damascus,* for its "fine color and the remarkably faithful painting of detail."[131] The small image of it reproduced in the society's catalogue (fig. 6.46) does indeed shows an interesting composition full of intricate patterns of weaving and architectural ornament—a tour de force of precise painting that one hopes will resurface.[132] For the third painting he exhibited in 1897, *A Court of the Alhambra,* Fenn may have worked from sketches from his trip to Granada for *Picturesque Europe.*

In 1899 both of Fenn's exhibited works harked back to his sketches for *Picturesque Europe. An Hour Before the Bull Fight—Seville* was reproduced in the *New York Times* (March 5, 1899); its composition is similar to his illustration "A Ticket in the Shade, Seville Bull-Ring" in volume 3 of *Picturesque Europe.* The

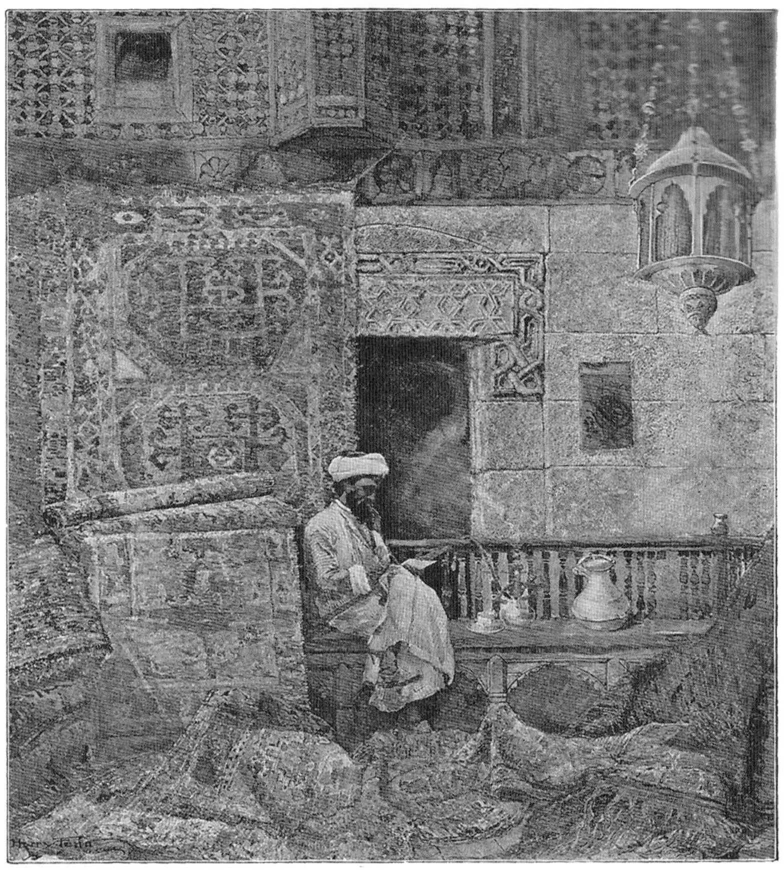

6.46. "85. In the Carpet Bazaar, Damascus.—Harry Fenn, A.W.C.S." *American Water Color Society. Thirtieth Annual Exhibition, Illustrated Catalogue, New York 1897.* Halftone, 4 7/16" x 4".

large watercolor *The Golden Pulpits of Milan* (fig. 6.47) is much like the depiction of the interior of Milan cathedral in the same volume.[133] Comparing the painting with the wood engraving makes us appreciate the power of color, especially Fenn's blues and reds, and demonstrates once again his penchant for using low viewpoints to dramatize height and volume.

In 1898 Fenn again exhibited subjects related to his travels for *Picturesque Palestine: A Street Café, Jerusalem* (unlocated), *A Good Story* (illustrated in the catalogue), and *A Chapter of the Koran,* which is likely the painting reproduced in figure 6.48. Its subject is quite similar to the illustration in volume 2 of *Picturesque Palestine* titled "At School," and both were almost certainly based on a photograph. In this case Fenn created a strikingly beautiful, balanced composition with harmonious colors and interesting details—from the teacher's face to the playful pigeons.[134]

A pair of watercolor paintings by Fenn of Lake Memphremagog, on the border

 Challenges and Triumphs

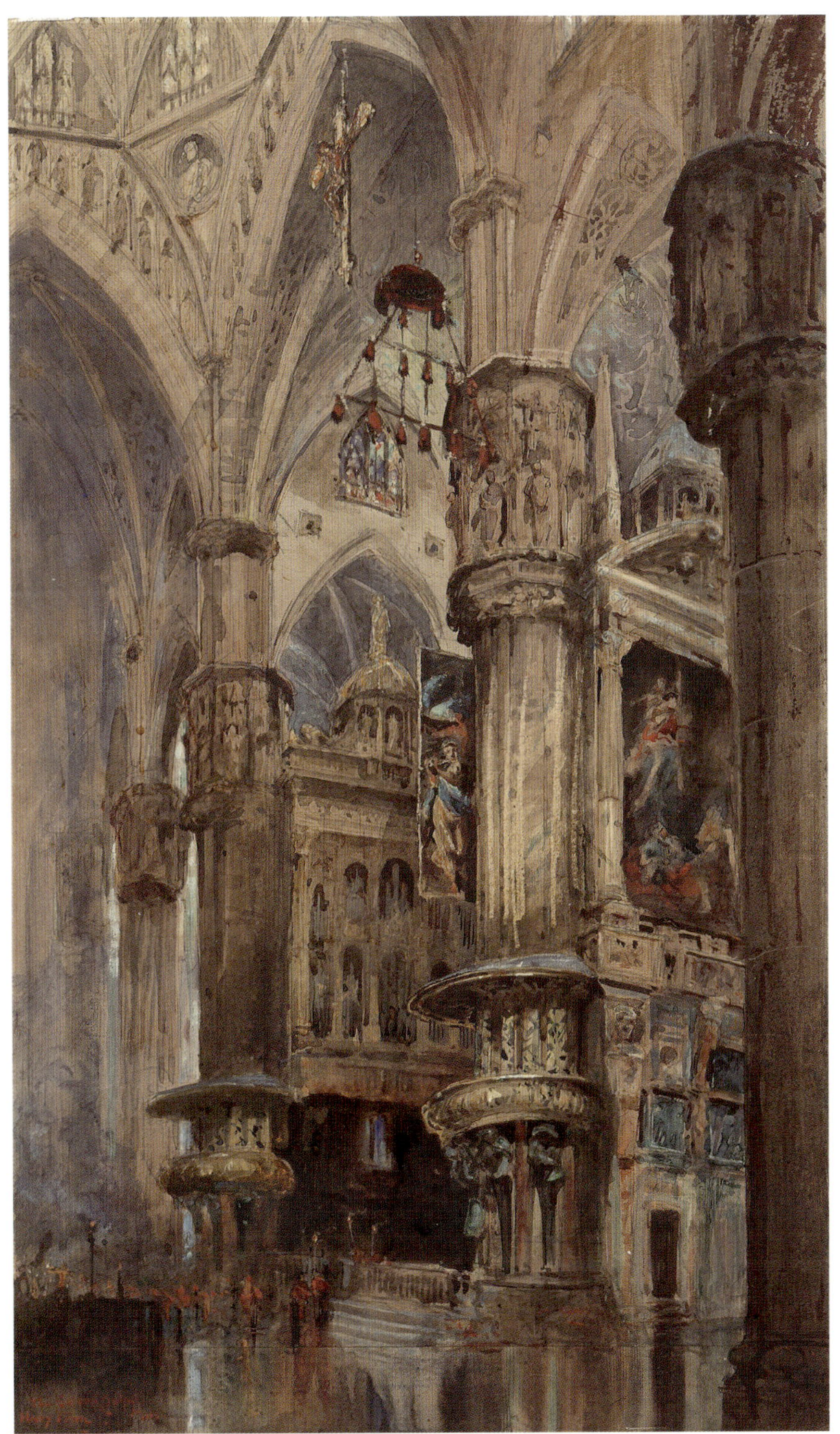

6.47. Harry Fenn. *The Golden Pulpits of Milan*, ca. 1899. Watercolor and gouache, with scratching out on light blue wove paper, approx. 22 1/2" x 12 3/4". (Courtesy of William V. Abt.)

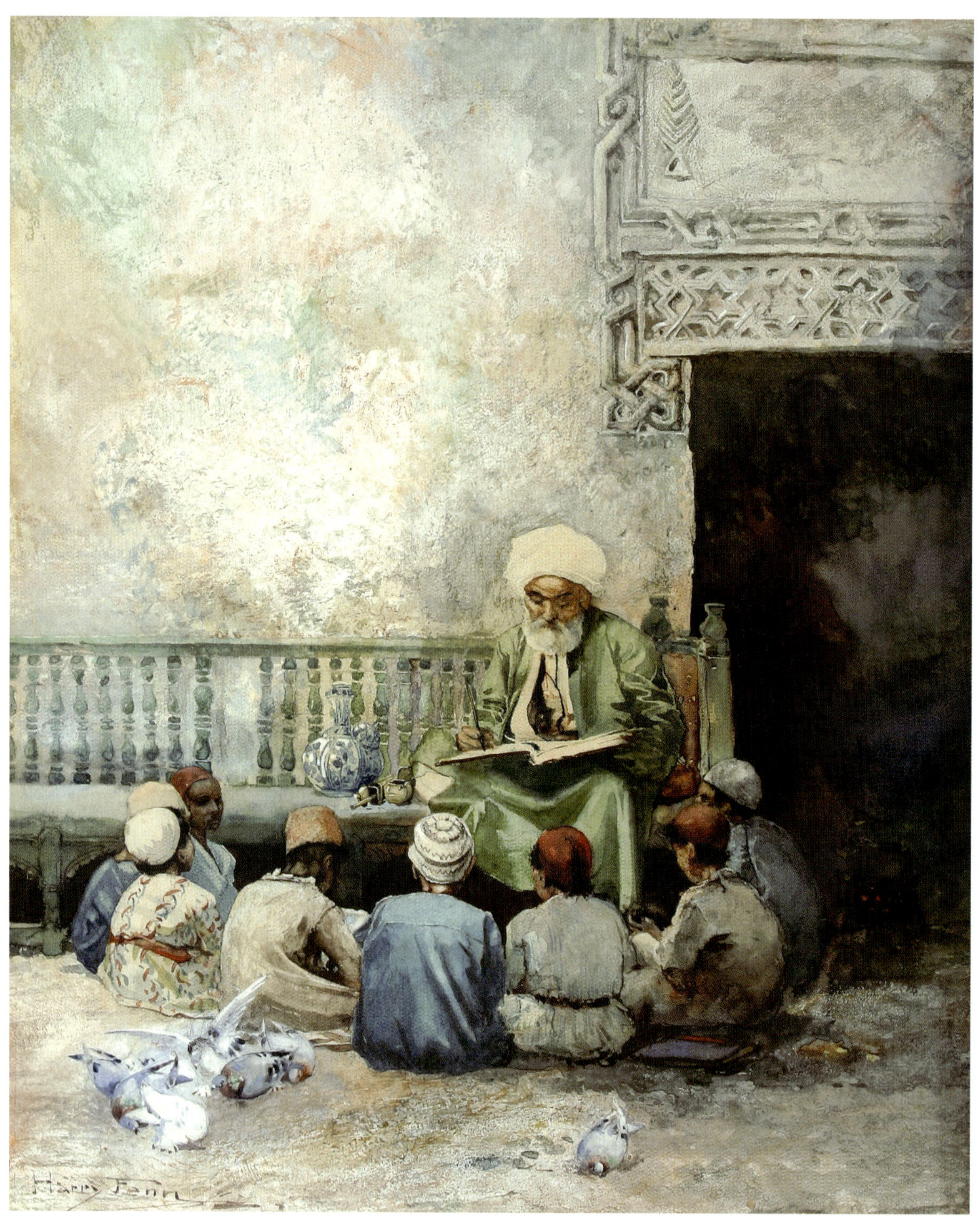

6.48. Harry Fenn. *A Chapter of the Koran*, ca. 1898. Watercolor and gouache on paper, 14" x 12". (Rafael Gallery, New York.)

between Vermont and the province of Quebec, show Fenn taking different approaches to the same subject. The one dated September 21, 1894, is a view across the lake, with vivid fall colors reflected in the water and fog and clouds obscuring the distant mountain, creating that ethereal atmosphere popular in this period (fig. 6.49). This painting may be the one shown at the Chicago Art Institute in 1895 titled *An Autumn Evening on Memphremagog*. The other, which may be the *Banks of Memphremagog* exhibited in the American Water Color Society show in 1894, is a close-up of huge rocks along the lakeshore and a large fallen tree (fig. 6.50). It is in keeping with the focus on the force and vitality of natural processes, ideas that followed the greater acceptance of evolution and other advances in scientific knowledge that emerged at this time. Other artists were also exploring these themes, including Winslow Homer, many of whose late works similarly conveyed nature's powers, but with less attention to precise details than in Fenn's painting.[135]

In this period the professional organization of the art world increased, boosted by the formation of museums, galleries, and associations. Fenn took advantage of this situation by sending works for exhibition in a wide range of venues, including museums in Chicago, Philadelphia, and Buffalo and private galleries such as William Macbeth's in New York. In the winter of 1890–91 he exhibited pen and ink sketches with the Architectural League in its sixth annual exhibition.[136] On December 18, 1891, he was elected a member of the New York Water Color Club, founded the year before, and in 1893 nine of his paintings sold at the club's exhibition.[137] In February 1898 his work and that of younger colleagues, including Howard Pyle and Howard Chandler Christy, appeared at the Avery Galleries in New York in the exhibition *The Revolutionary Pictures,* organized under the auspices of the Daughters of the American Revolution.[138] The paintings and drawings had been commissioned by *Scribner's Magazine* to illustrate its series on the American Revolution by Senator Henry Cabot Lodge and Captain A. T. Mahan running throughout 1898.[139] Clearly, Fenn welcomed opportunities to show his work farther afield as well as in the familiar venues.

FENN IN MONTCLAIR

Closer to home, Fenn was an active member of his community. He continued his participation in the Montclair Art Club, serving as its president in 1899 and continuing to show his works in their exhibitions; these were held in 1894 and 1899, at least, and Fenn's daughter Lillian also contributed.[140] Montclair had attracted quite a few creative individuals and was, according to the *New York Times* in 1894, "the

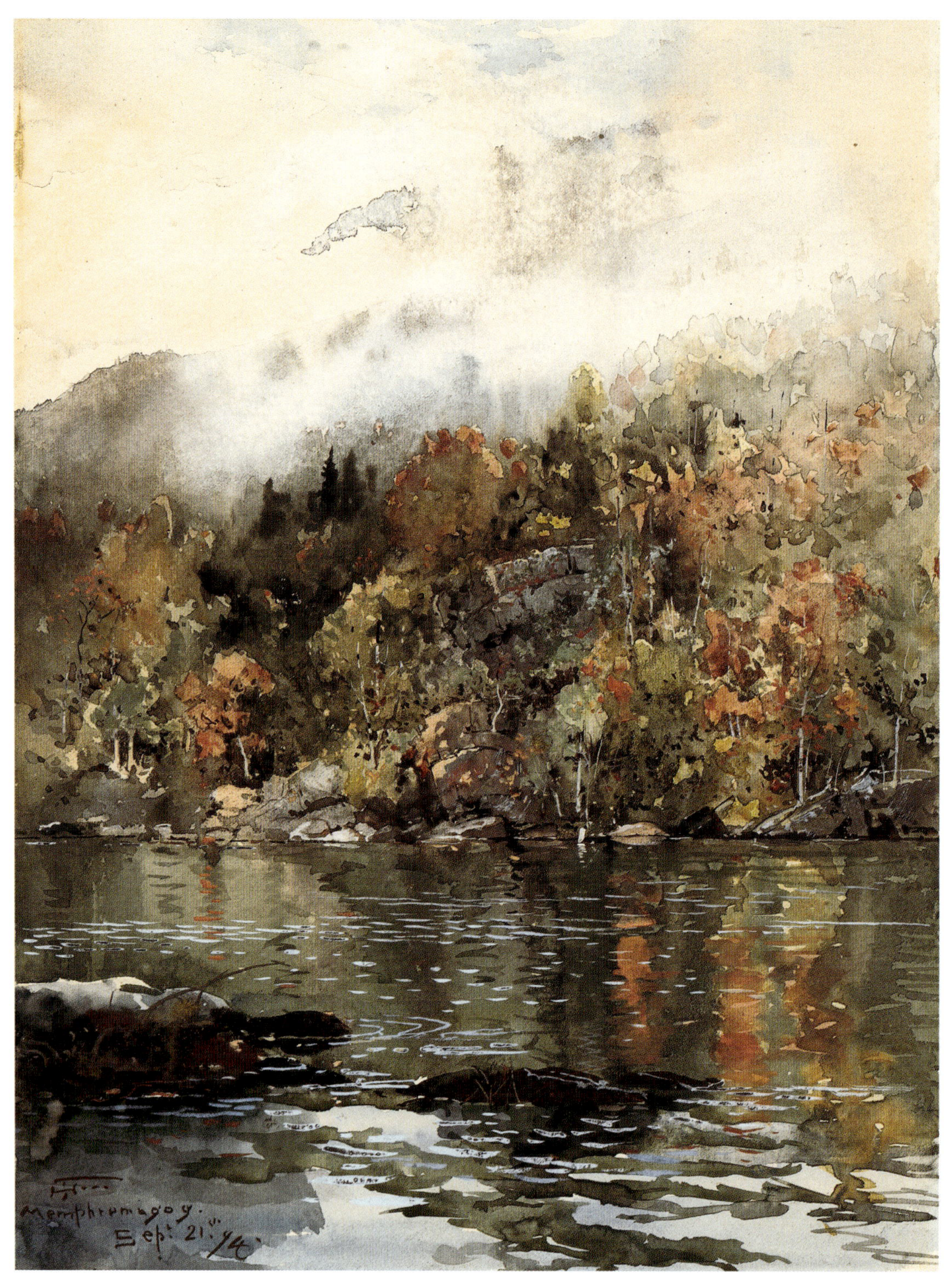

6.49. Harry Fenn, *Lake Memphremagog,* September 21, 1894. Watercolor and gouache, 14 3/4" x 10 7/8". (Courtesy of William V. Abt.)

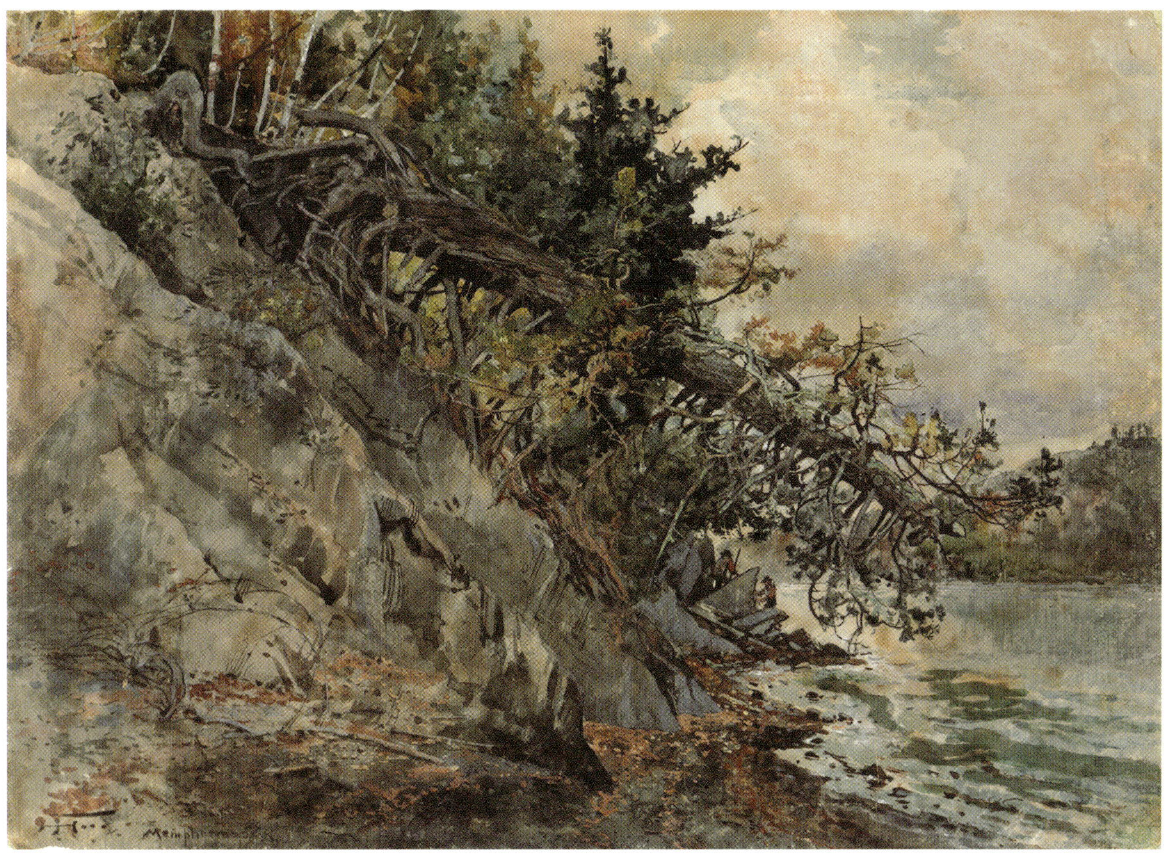

6.50. Harry Fenn, *Lake Memphremagog [Banks of the Memphremagog?]*, ca. 1880s–90s. Watercolor and gouache over graphite, 13 1/2" x 18 5/8". (The Cleveland Museum of Art. Gift of Mr. and Mrs. Noah L. Butkin 1976.115.)

home of more prominent artists and wealthy art connoisseurs, probably, than any other place in New Jersey." The list included the celebrated painters George Inness and his son George Jr., the artist-illustrator F. S. Church, and the sculptor Jonathan Scott Hartley (son-in-law of the elder Inness), as well as such lesser-known painters as Charles Warren Eaton, L. C. Earle, Thomas R. Manley, Walter C. Greenough and his wife, Emilie Koehler Greenough, and Clara McChesney.[141] Among the "wealthy art connoisseurs," the most prominent was the railroad magnate William T. Evans, who collected American art but is not known to have owned works by Fenn. To entertain the town's citizens the Montclair artists arranged "Artists' Tableaux" in the 1890s, in which they sometimes re-created the subjects of well-known paintings with live figures.[142] Fenn and his daughter Lillian also organized bike trips and picnics.[143]

Fenn was acquainted with both Innesses. The father, who was twelve years older than Fenn and whose works were achieving some of the highest prices of any American artist at the time, liked to make long excursions on foot to gather material. In 1891 he and Fenn went on a sketching trip to western New Jersey accompanied by Dr. Samuel C. G. Watkins, a local dentist.[144]

Since building the Cedars in 1885, Fenn had contributed to his hometown in many ways, including by participating in both the art club and a local camera club and by serving on the newly formed Municipal Art Commission, charged with preserving and enhancing Montclair's beauty.[145] He developed a warm friendship with the minister of the First Congregational Church, Amory H. Bradford, and when that church celebrated its twenty-fifth anniversary and Bradford's ministry, Fenn again assumed the decorator's role. On Sunday June 2, 1895, the church was "brightly and gracefully decorated with wreaths and festoons, hanging baskets of flowers, and drooping flags, under the artistic direction of Mr. Harry Fenn."[146] Fenn is further credited with suggesting the design for a new, larger building for Upper Montclair's Union Congregational Church; he made a sketch of the Norman church in Lurgashall, Sussex, that he and Tennyson had attended in the 1870s and gave it to Walter C. Greenough, a member of the building committee.[147] To raise money for the building, in the summer of 1897 Greenough staged "Outdoor Fantasies" that included tableaux of scenes from Shakespeare and the four seasons. Fenn was likely among the participants.[148]

In 1900 the Cedars was home to Fenn and his wife and three of their adult children, all of whom were inclined toward careers in art. Their thirty-eight-year-old son Walter, a painter and illustrator, had recently returned to Montclair after some eight years in California; while there he had bought a ranch and traveled extensively with the Pacific Coast mammalogist Frank Stephens, whose *California Mammals* the younger Fenn illustrated "from studies made from life."[149] Also at home were two of the Fenns' four daughters, thirty-three-year-old Lillian, an aspiring artist,[150] and twenty-year-old Hilda Marguerite, who later became a successful interior decorator.[151] Their two older daughters, Alice Maude and Florence Bessie, had married some years earlier.[152] Mary Fenn's elderly mother, Elizabeth Tompson, also lived with them until her death in 1901.[153] On September 26 of that year the Fenns celebrated in their home the marriage of Hilda to Dudley S. Van Antwerp, an architect.[154]

Fenn's life was full, with work, family, and community responsibilities. In this period he had continued to travel to make sketches and paintings—in California, the South, and the Northeast. His images prepared from photographs pro-

   Challenges and Triumphs

vided information about technological achievements and current events as well as the architecture, culture, and plant growth of faraway lands. Even as an elder statesman in the art world, he touched Americans in both personal and collective ways through a wide range of works, from delicate images of nature intended to assuage grief, as in Tennyson's *In Memoriam,* to large color prints celebrating the nation's accomplishments at two world's fairs. His stamina did not go unnoticed. At age sixty-five, when he attended a dinner at the Salmagundi Club in 1902, "everyone marvel[ed] that the weight of years rests so lightly on him" and that "he still works with unabated skill and vigor."[155]

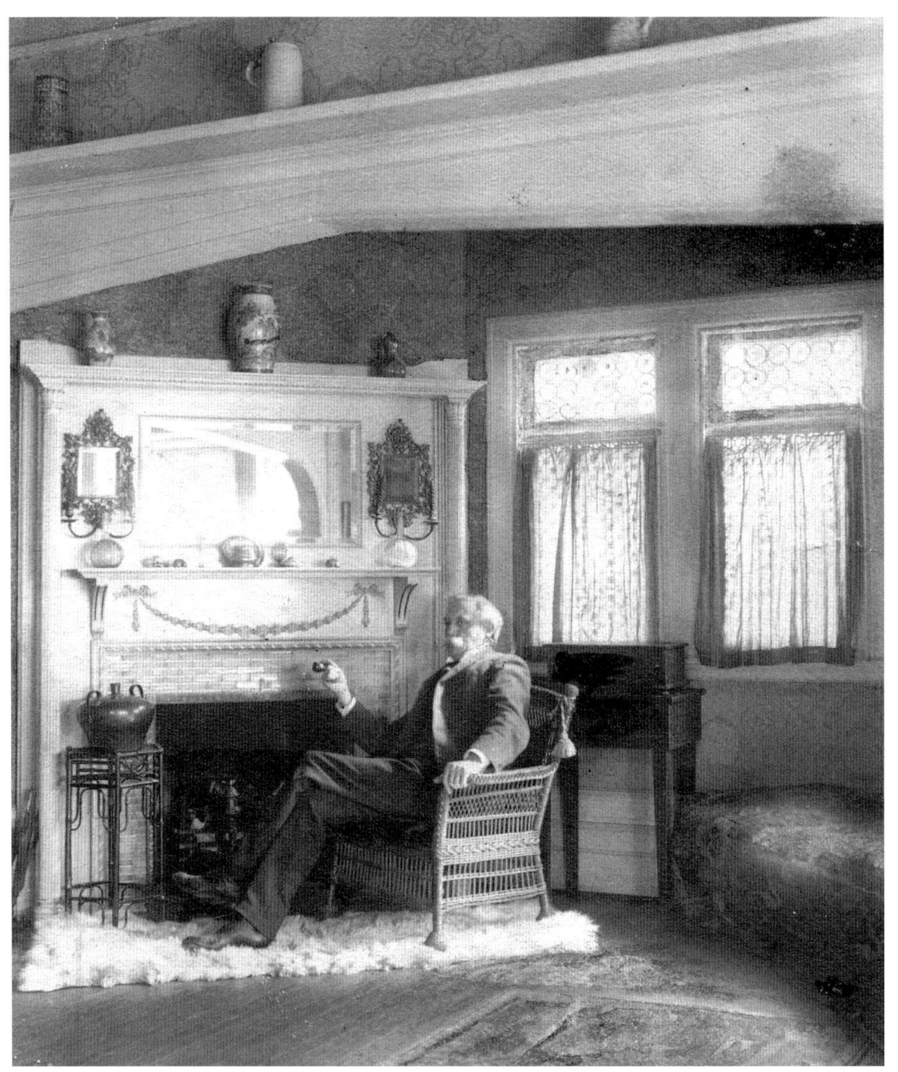

7.1. Photograph of Fenn in the Cedars, Montclair, N.J., ca. 1900. (Courtesy of William V Abt.)

Continuity and Change— 1900–1911, and an Assessment

THE LAST DECADE OF HARRY FENN'S life coincided with the first decade of the twentieth century, with its accelerated pace of innovation and growth in communications, transportation, and industry. Fashions in the art world and in illustrated publications continued to change in ways that positioned Fenn among the more conventional rather than the more innovative. As the technology for making and reproducing photographs improved, the need for artists to accurately depict all aspects of life diminished. They would instead claim different tasks and new roles, encouraged by art critics who increasingly devalued literal representation.[1] Some artists had embraced this change decades earlier; in 1878, for example, Whistler had said: "The imitator is a poor kind of creature. If the man who paints only the tree, or flower, or other surface he sees before him were an artist, the king of artists would be the photographer. It is for the artist to do something beyond this."[2] Fenn's works had long been seen as much more than merely photographic, but he never abandoned forms, details, and colors that corresponded to reality.

By 1903 even his longtime admirer James Henry Moser, who in 1875 had been inspired by Fenn's depictions of Natural Bridge in *Picturesque America,* saw that his approach belonged to an earlier era. In a review of the American Water Color Society's exhibition that year, Moser paid homage to Fenn as one "of the three-score-and-ten men who refuse to grow old, a man who, with F. O. C. Darley [1822–1888], long since gone from the field, is a revered father of the vast tribe of American illustrators." But he focused on the artwork that had won the prestigious William T. Evans Prize, *Sky Scrapers,* by the Philadelphia impressionist Colin Campbell Cooper (1856–1937), known for "his very broad colorful and artistic renderings of architecture." Moser then made these telling remarks about the painting Fenn exhibited: "Mr. Fenn shows

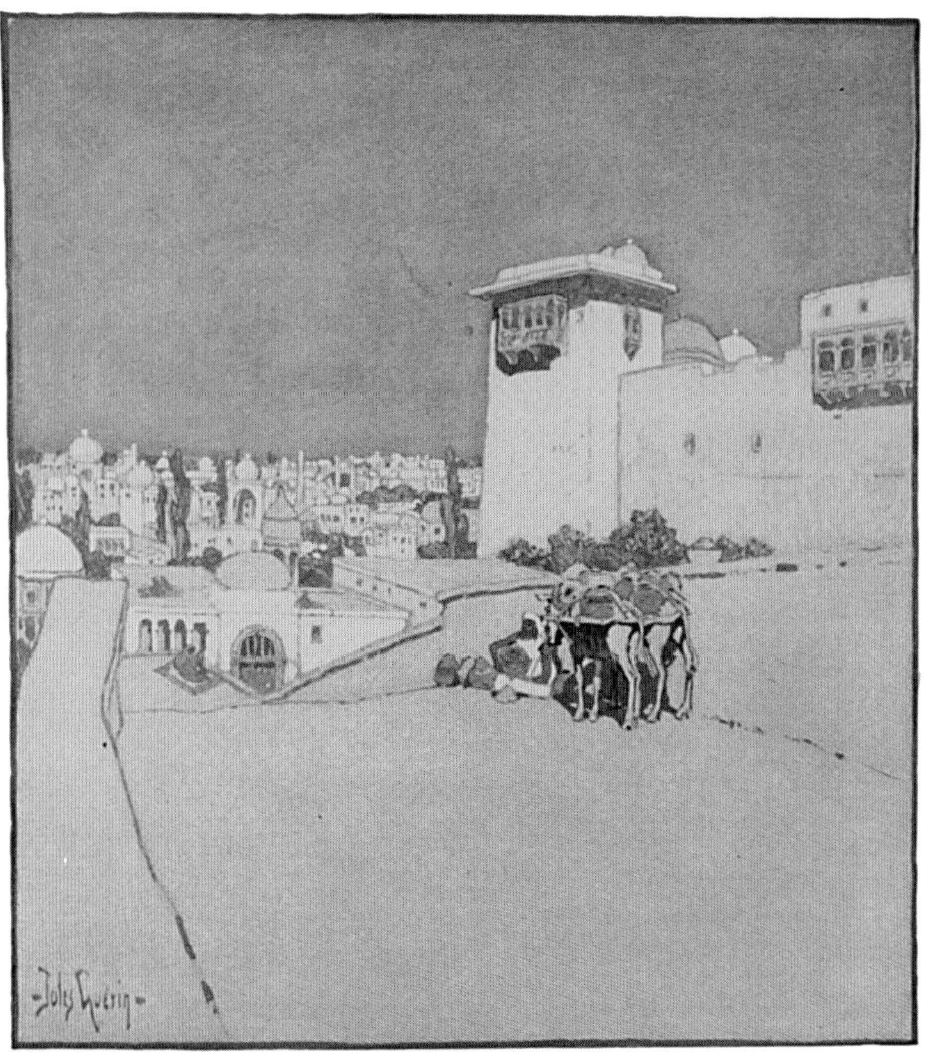

a leafless wood with some children carrying greens along a homeward path—'May Day in the Surry Hills.' It is ingeniously and artistically real in a minute way. One almost never nowadays sees bark and lichens painted with such fidelity."[3] Clearly, the objective exactitude of Ruskinian truth to nature was no longer widely embraced.

Yet Fenn had practiced close observation and more or less exact representation for a lifetime and would not forsake it now. In describing Fenn's depictions of nature, his son-in-law Sidney Brooks sought to combine this outmoded approach with the more recent emphasis on the artist's subjective, emotional response to nature's mystery, saying, "His love of nature was poetically exact, just as his portrayal of it was equally marked with tenderness and fidelity."[4] For more than sixty years Fenn had created compositions that represented places and things with enough credibility

 Continuity and Change

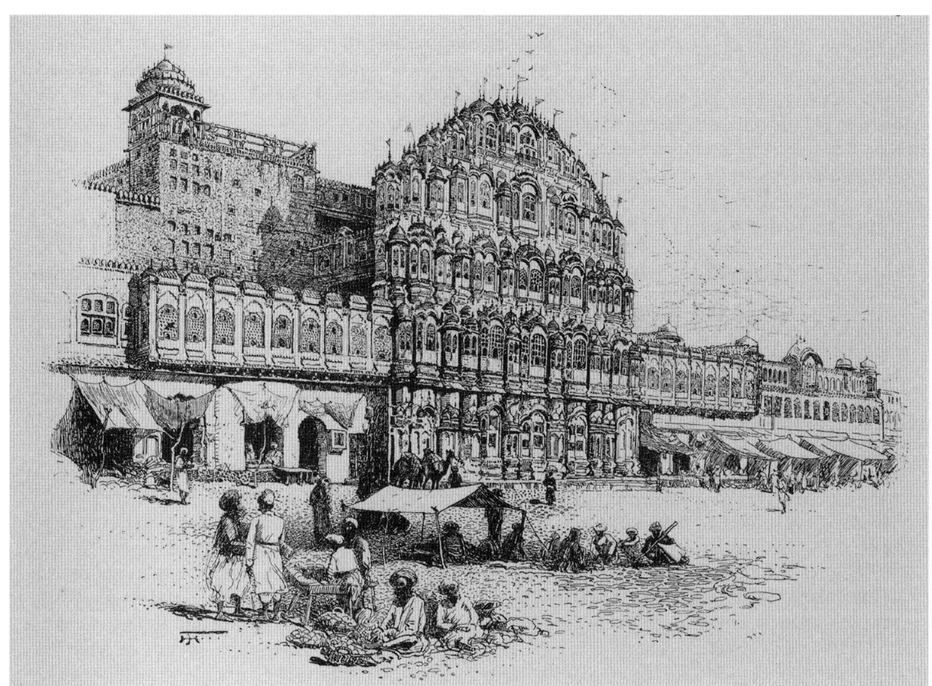

to be accurate, yet sufficient drama and freshness to be considered picturesque or poetic; for him to abandon line and spatial perspective for the contemporary, or "modern," focus on color and increasingly abstract forms would have been too radical a change. And although some embraced Impressionists such as Monet, Pissarro, and Hassam and others responded to the new ways of seeing in works by Cézanne, Munch, Matisse, and Picasso, Fenn's familiar style was still sufficiently appealing to a more conservative audience that publishers continued to hire him.

His staying the course had consequences, however: his colleagues using the newer approaches gained the attention of critics and collectors and garnered the plum commissions. An example of how this situation played out for Fenn is the brief article in the November 1899 *St. Nicholas* titled "The Monkeys of Amber," about Amber fort in Jaipur, India. Of the three illustrations, Fenn supplied one and Jules Guérin (1866–1946) the other two. Guérin had studied at the Art Institute of Chicago and in Paris and specialized in architectural and landscape subjects.[5] His opening image, "The City of Jeypore," a watercolor reproduced by halftone, has subtle shades with large areas of a single tone and little or no detail (fig. 7.2). In contrast, Fenn's ink drawing for "A Street in Jeypore" (fig. 7.3), reproduced by process line cut, renders precisely the intricate details of facades and figures; it provides the type of information that is lacking in Guérin's sparer image. In the table of contents for this volume,

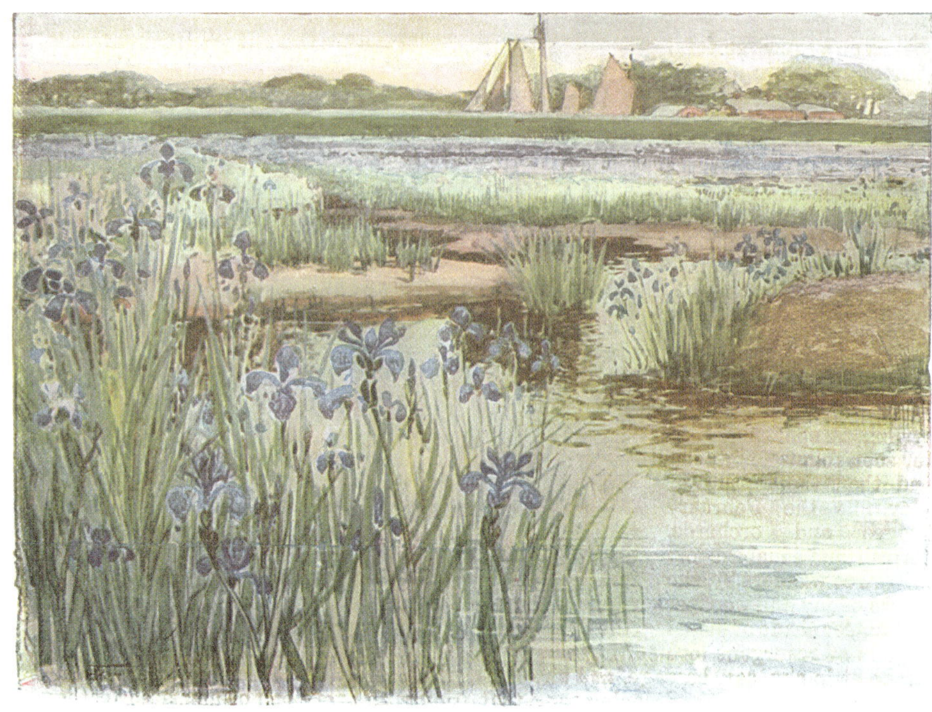

Guérin alone is credited as illustrator, although many who knew Fenn's monogram would recognize his work. Nevertheless, greater prominence was given to the artist whose approach was in keeping with the fashions of the day.[6]

Yet, as we have seen, Fenn took small steps toward the impressionism and soft focus of such American painters as Dwight W. Tryon, John H. Twachtman, Bruce Crane, and George Inness and illustrators like Guérin, Castaigne, and Henry McCarter.[7] This was especially true of his works reproduced by the still-experimental color halftone technology, which began to be used in magazines around the turn of the century. An early color commission was to illustrate "My Midwinter Garden" by Maurice Thompson for the November 1900 *Century,* an issue the magazine advertised as "Superbly Illustrated in Colors," with Fenn's name listed first among the contributing artists in some ads.[8] Still, the color halftones are quite crude, with a limited range of colors that exaggerates their soft quality. One of the more attractive examples, "In a Few Marshy Plots the Glorious Flowers of Iris" (fig. 7.4), gives a hint of the promise of full-color printing and explains why printers were so focused on improving the process. By 1904, when the *Century* regularly included a color frontispiece and two to four other color plates, Fenn's illustration "The Augusta Bridge" (fig. 7.5), printed in color on heavy calendered paper, with the back of the page blank,

   Continuity and Change

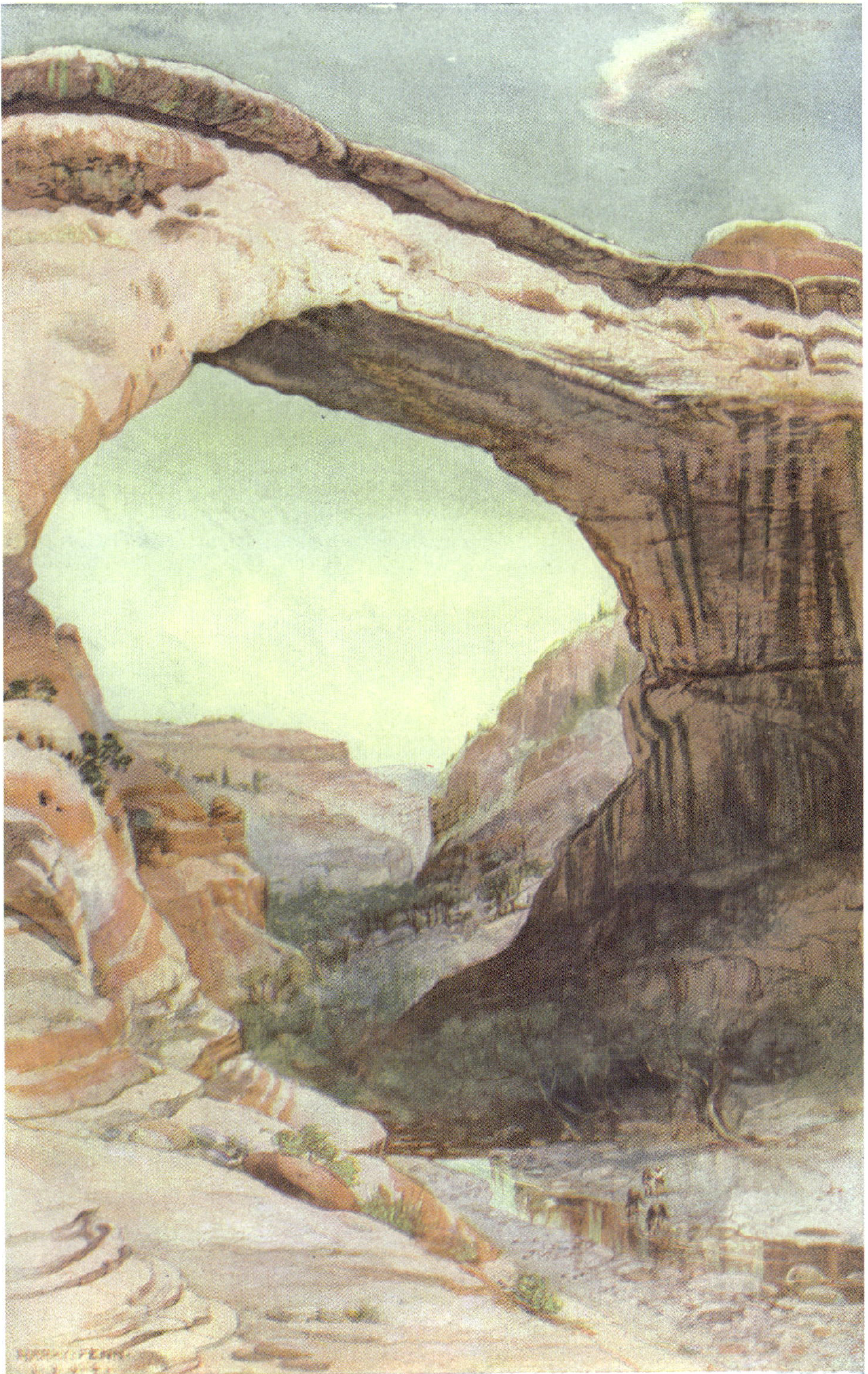

7.5. Harry Fenn, "The Augusta Bridge," in "The Colossal Bridges of Utah: A Recent Discovery of Natural Wonders" by W. W. Dyar. *Century*, August 1904, 507. Color halftone, 7 11/16" x 4 13/16".

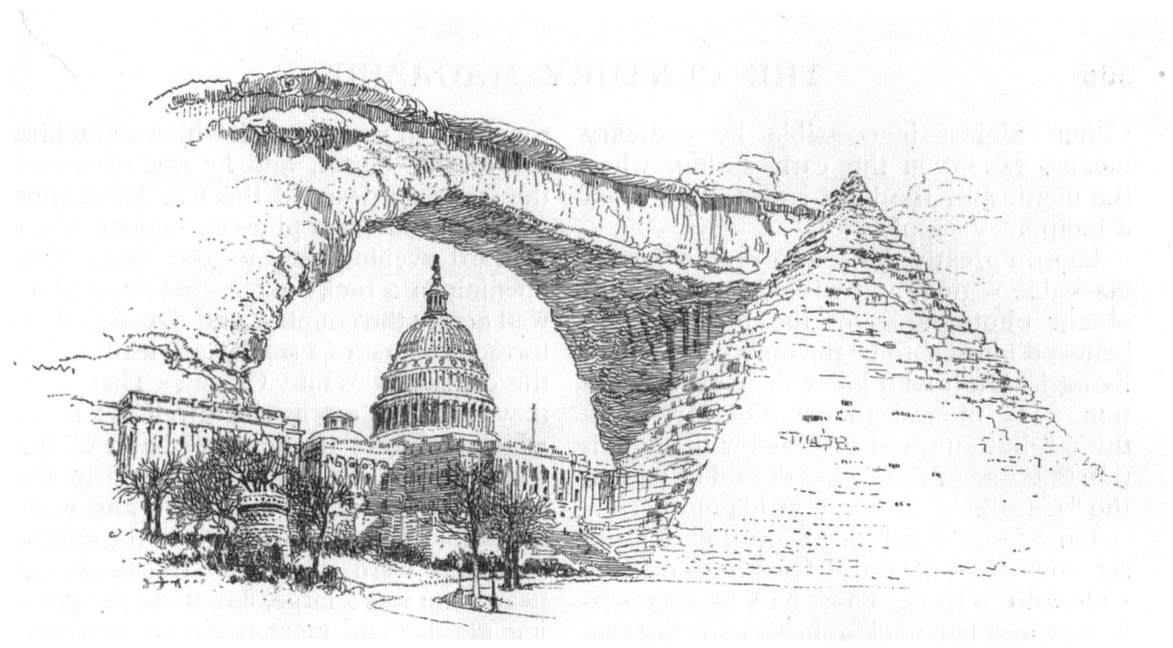

7.6. Harry Fenn, "The Augusta Natural Bridge (See Page 507), Compared with the Capitol at Washington and the Great Pyramid," opening for "The Colossal Bridges of Utah." *Century,* August 1904, 505. Process line cut, approx. 2 1/4" x 5".

was more successful. This "natural wonder" had recently been discovered by "the white race" in Utah;[9] Fenn's full-page depiction accompanied W. W. Dyar's article, "The Colossal Bridges of Utah: A Recent Discovery of Natural Wonders." For the article opening, Fenn created a clever ink drawing showing graphically how the size of the bridge compared with Egypt's pyramids and the U.S. Capitol (fig. 7.6).

"The Augusta Bridge" was Fenn's first and last full-page color plate in the *Century.* The magazine began turning more often to younger artists, especially Jules Guérin, whose color plates for "The Châteaux of Touraine" series appeared from May to July 1905. Another series, "Glimpses of the Summer Girl" (August 1905), featured three color plates by the figure artist Howard Chandler Christy (1873–1952). Color plates by other artists would follow, including those for Eliza Ruhamah Scidmore's article "The Cherry-Blossoms of Japan" (March 1910) by Genjiro Kataoka, who had immigrated to New York from Japan in 1891. *Harper's Monthly* also published color illustrations in this period, but none by Fenn.

Fenn's black and white work for magazines continued to show his creativity and adaptability. The halftone process allowed him to submit finely detailed watercolors for reproduction, as in "Yakutat Indian Camp," based on a photo-

   Continuity and Change

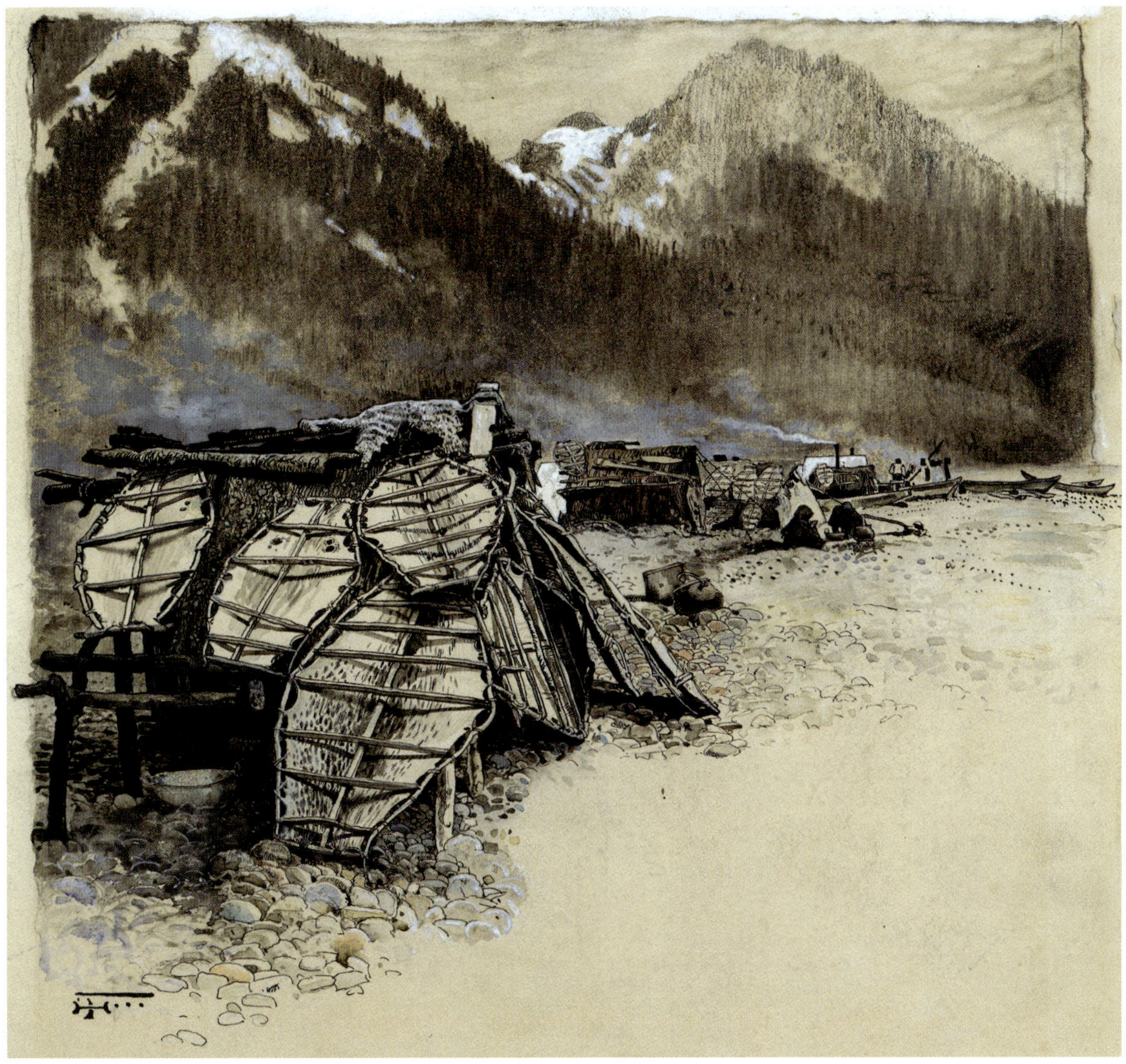

7.7. Harry Fenn, *Yakutat Village*, ca. 1900. Graphite, ink, wash, and gouache, 10 1/4" x 11". (For illustration for "Summer Holidays in Alaskan Waters" by John Burroughs, *Century*, August 1900.) (Private collection.)

graph by Edward Curtis and executed in tones of black, brown, and gray (fig. 7.7). This image illustrated an August 1900 *Century* article by Fenn's friend John Burroughs titled "Summer Holidays in Alaskan Waters," which describes the widely publicized expedition organized by railroad magnate Edward H. Harriman the previous summer that combined hunting adventures and scientific exploration. Although three artists as well as Curtis went along, the *Century* called on Fenn to create effective illustrations based on expedition photographs.[10]

A sampling of Fenn's other *Century* illustrations reproduced by halftones in this period may be seen in an August 1905 article titled "Alpine Climbing in Automobiles" by Sterling Heilig, for which he used a light style more like the works of Castaigne, with dramatic perspective that recalls some of his compositions for the "picturesque" series. Among the most striking are "Combe-Laval, A Cañon Three Quarters of a Mile Deep" (fig. 7.8), a halftone with engraving by R. C. Collins, which has soft grays throughout, and "Les Ecouges: 'Precipices on All Sides of Us'" (fig. 7.9), in which Fenn uses the thrust of the stone guard wall to create a dramatic illusion of depth. An engaging illustration he did for a January 1907 article titled "The Nuisances of Advertising" shows a travel ad on the blank wall of a building, with the caption "Suggestion for the Pictorial Treatment of a Blank Wall / The [chimney] pipe has been transformed into a minaret."

Other *Century* assignments saw Fenn visually reporting on attempts to improve the living conditions of factory workers, as in the article titled "What More Than Wages?" (December 1900), and on new train stations, such as "The Railway Beautiful" (April 1908), for which he depicted fifteen different structures. His commissions to depict historic architecture included an illustration of Dove Cottage, where William Wordsworth lived, which Fenn entwined with flowers for "A Literary Shrine" (May 1900), as well as "The Washington-Craigie-Longfellow House Viewed from the Street" (February 1907).[11] For the four-part series "Historic Palaces of Paris," which began in September 1905, Fenn shared the illustrating tasks with his prominent younger colleagues Guérin and Castaigne.[12] He prepared botanical images for "The Everglades of Florida" (February 1905) and scenes of new technological projects for "America's Agricultural Regeneration of Russia" (August 1901), "The Panama Canal" (November 1905), and "Art in Modern Bridges" (May 1900), as already discussed. (See Appendix 1 for additional *Century* illustrations.)

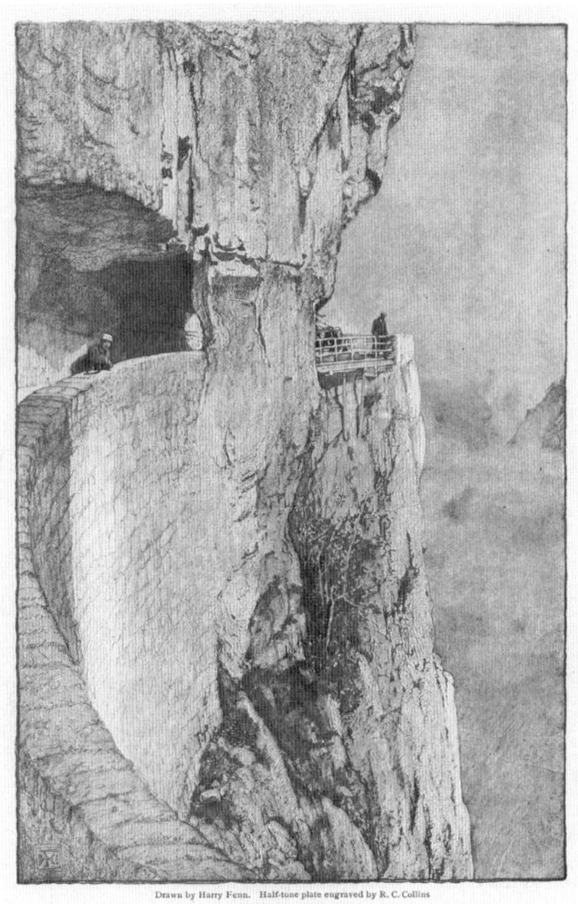

7.8. Harry Fenn, "Combe-Laval, A Cañon Three Quarters of a Mile Deep," in "Alpine Climbing in Automobiles" by Sterling Heilig. *Century*, August 1905, 606. Halftone with engraving by R. C. Collins, approx. 7 5/16" x 4 11/16".

Continuity and Change

For *Harper's Monthly* Fenn illustrated a series of articles on the history of Wall Street written by Frederick Trevor Hill, which appeared between April and September 1908; that year, Harper published the series as a book titled *The Story of a Street: A Narrative History of Wall Street from 1644 to 1908.* By this time Wall Street, with its banks and office buildings, had become the symbol of Manhattan, a sharp contrast to the harbor and docks featured in the New York views Fenn had created for *Picturesque America.*[13] The subject was especially timely, for participation in the stock market was growing despite a liquidity crisis in mid-1907 that led to falling stock prices and had necessitated the intervention of J. P. Morgan and other leading financiers to shore up the system.[14] Increasingly Americans also wanted to know more about wealthy businessmen, a fascination clearly manifested by George Horace Lorimer's popular series "Letters from a Self-Made Merchant to his Son," which first ran in the *Saturday Evening Post* before becoming a best-selling book internationally in 1902.[15] For Harper's *Story of a Street,* Fenn was asked to create images of Wall Street in earlier times, showing figures dressed in historically appropriate dress, a somewhat unusual task for him. Despite his sixteen contributions, mainly watercolors reproduced as halftones printed in brown tones, he was not given credit on the title page or in the list of illustrations. Only his monogram or signature identifies the work as his.

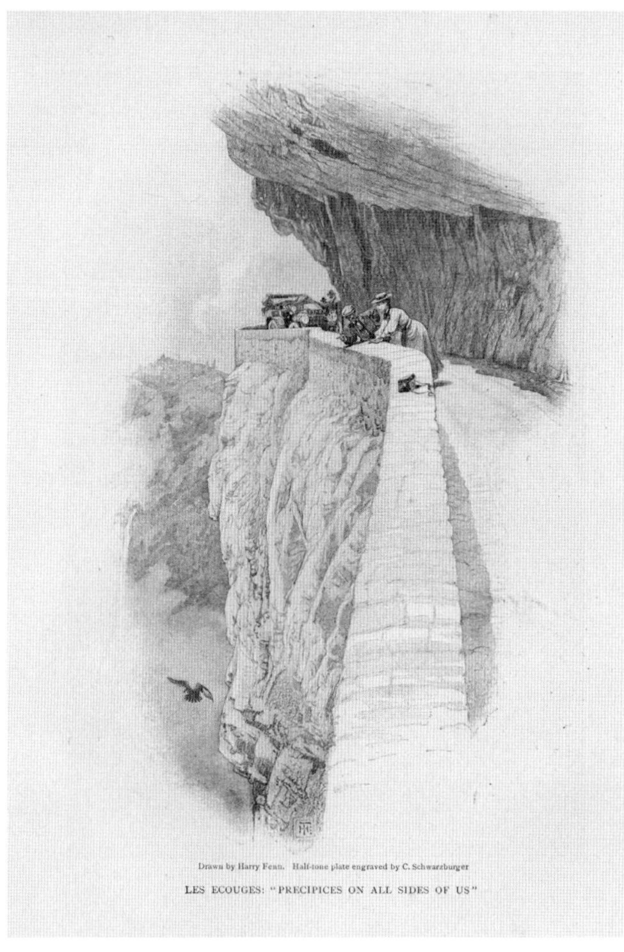

7.9. Harry Fenn, "Les Ecouges: 'Precipices on All Sides of Us,'" in "Alpine Climbing in Automobiles." *Century,* August 1905, 609. Halftone with engraving by C. Schwarzburger, approx. 7" x 4 1/4".

CHANGE

These years also brought great changes in Fenn's personal life. Mary, his wife of four decades, died on June 25, 1902, after suffering from ill health for a long time.[16] She was buried alongside her parents in Evergreens Cemetery in Brooklyn.

Some months later Fenn sold the Cedars, his home in Montclair.[17] His reasons for taking this step are unknown; perhaps the house seemed too large for him after his wife died and his adult children moved away. In 1903, he took a break from the constant pressure to produce illustrations and revisited England. There he rambled "among the old English gardens and all the scenes he had known as a boy and in earlier manhood, making friends as usual wherever he strayed," and "rejuvenating himself as he went from one cherished spot to another."[18] He also spent considerable time doing what he loved best, capturing the beauties of nature. He painted gardens in Surrey, Warwick, and at the Chatsworth estate, as revealed by the catalogue of the 1911 auction held by Anderson Auction house in New York to settle his estate. It included eight watercolors of English subjects, two of which were dated "Sept. 1903" by the artist himself. Besides gardens, his subjects included streetscapes and buildings, notably *Mill Street, Warwick, England; An Old English Manor House;* and *The Sun Dial, Guy's Cliff, Warwick.*

After his return, it is unclear where Fenn lived for the next two years, but by 1906 he was once again living in Montclair with his son and daughter Lillian at 284 Park Street, a house designed by his architect son-in-law Dudley S. van Antwerp.[19] There he painted in a room on the north side of the house, which looked out onto a distant view of fields and gardens.[20] During several summers he also spent time painting in Gloucester, Massachusetts, recording its historic harbor and picturesque coastline. Eighteen watercolors of the region were included in the 1911 auction; their subjects include the harbor, fish houses, the fish wharf, a ship bringing salt from Sicily, Rocky Neck, Eastern Point, the pines of Annisquam, and the old boat yard.[21] Those with dates suggest he was there in 1907, 1908, and 1910.

Fenn continued to exhibit his watercolors until at least 1910, the year before his death, although press coverage of his paintings diminished as the years passed. He showed one or two works, mostly subjects derived from his earlier travels in Europe and the Middle East, in the American Water Color Society's shows until 1905. (See Appendix 2.) He also exhibited in the Salmagundi Club's painting exhibitions, and in some years he donated works to be auctioned for the benefit of the club.[22] In 1902, 1907, 1908, and 1910 he sent works to the annual Exhibition of Water-colors, Pastels and Miniatures by American Artists, organized by the Art Institute of Chicago.[23] In 1904 his painting *Gateway of San Gregorio, Vallalolid* was exhibited at the Louisiana Purchase Exposition in St. Louis,[24] and in 1909 two of his works—*On Eastern Point, Gloucester* and *Bâb-Tûma* (which by now had made the rounds, having been exhibited in the 1897 Water Color Society exhibition)—were displayed at the Buffalo Fine Arts Academy of the Albright Art Gallery.[25] (See Appendix 2.)

 Continuity and Change

Upon turning seventy years old on September 14, 1907, Fenn wrote, "I feel seventeen not to say seven." Evidently, as Moser had noted, he refused to grow old. Indeed, in Fenn's obituary, Sidney Brooks noted: "There was something both of the boy and of the child in him to the end."[26] Fenn's apparently unabated enthusiasm for creating images in midlife and beyond was probably encouraged and supported by the new reproduction processes that allowed him greater autonomy—gradually freeing him from dependence on wood engravers to interpret his work—and that represented his ink drawings and watercolors with greater fidelity. These changes helped to showcase many of Fenn's works in a form that was closer to his autographic sketches. Brooks lamented that, in the years when Fenn had been required to draw meticulous lines on the boxwood blocks for engravers to follow, the "plastic emotion" and "evanescent beauty" of his sketches had been lost. According to Brooks, the painter Sir Lawrence Alma-Tadema (whom Fenn had known while working in England on *Picturesque Europe* and *Picturesque Palestine*) said of Fenn's rapid sketches that they would "make all London sit up" if only he would exhibit them. Brooks too admired his father-in-law's ability to "produce form, atmosphere, and color" in as little as an hour: "He had an almost Japanese certainty of incisive drawing with the brush, a veracity of planes, a fine perception of the poetry of form. He saw the quality of a composition instantly and gripped its essence with a sure, swift touch."[27] Fenn's pleasure in his work continued, despite the diminishing demand for his illustrations as fashions changed. Like most artists, he never gave up creating art for pleasure. One example is the watercolor *At the Greenough Camp,* made in the early morning of September 14, 1897—on which he wrote, "my birthday"—while visiting his Montclair friends at their summer home at Port-Neuf in Quebec (fig. 7.10). Using a limited palette and, in some parts, a thin layer of paint, he effectively captured the sun breaking through the clouds, the mist settling over the lake, and the light falling on a bending tree.

Still, important commissions were to come. Around the time of Fenn's seventieth birthday, Charles Scribner's Sons engaged him to provide all the illustrations for another book, one that allowed him to work in full watercolor at a large scale and to revisit—in memory and, probably, through photographs, his sketches, and *Picturesque Palestine*'s illustrations—some of the Middle Eastern sites where he and Woodward had worked thirty years earlier. The book was *Out-of-Doors in the Holy Land* by Henry van Dyke, minister of the prestigious Brick Presbyterian Church in New York, who had collaborated with Fenn on such projects as *In Memoriam* and authored the hugely successful book *The Story of the Other Wise Man* (1895). Released in 1908 as part of a series the publisher created specially for Van Dyke,

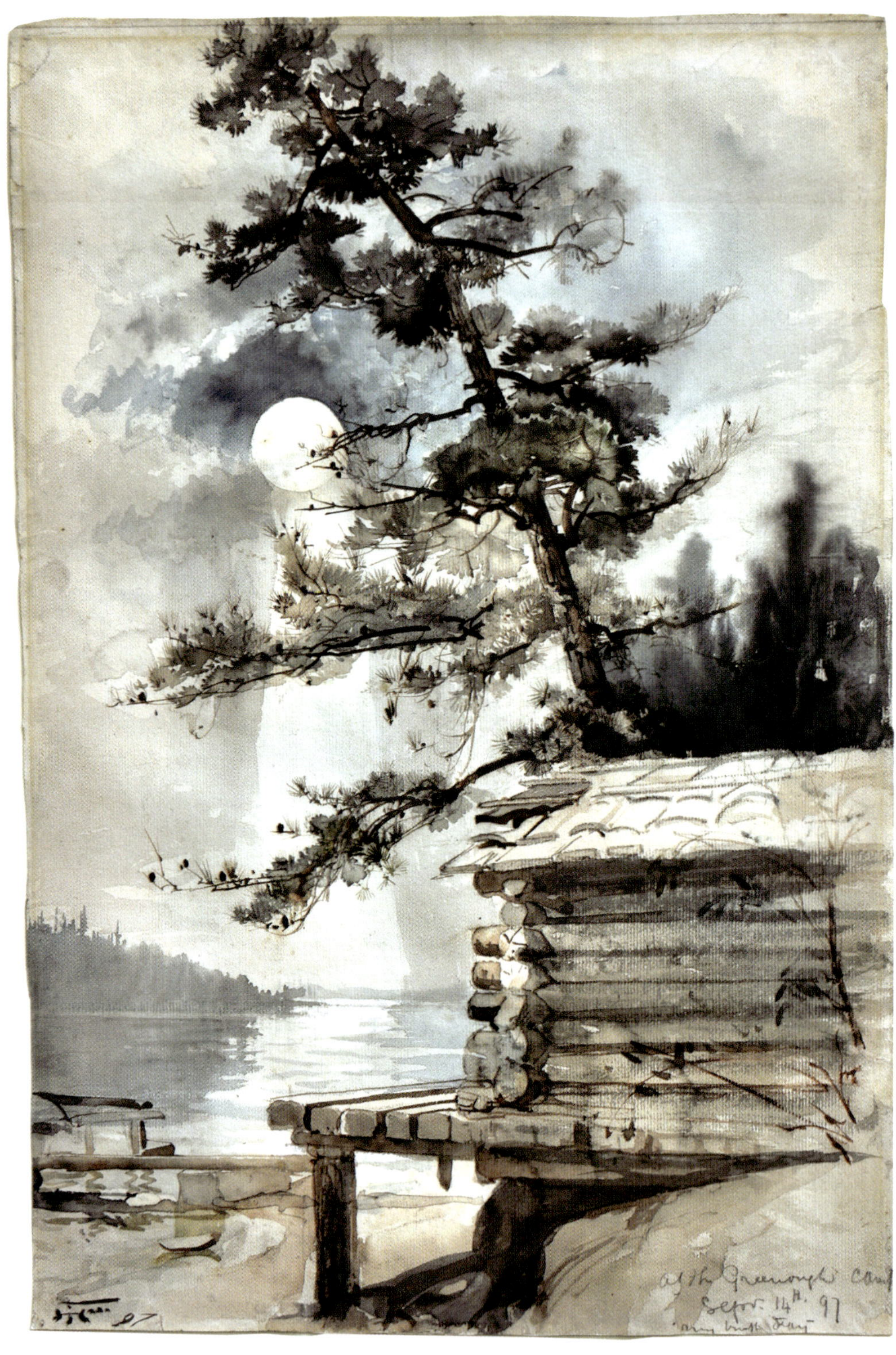

7.10. Harry Fenn, *At the Greenough Camp,* 1897. Watercolor, 22" x 14 ¹/₄". Inscribed in pencil:
"Sept. 14th, '97/my birthday." (Private collection. Photo by Jeanne Campbell.)

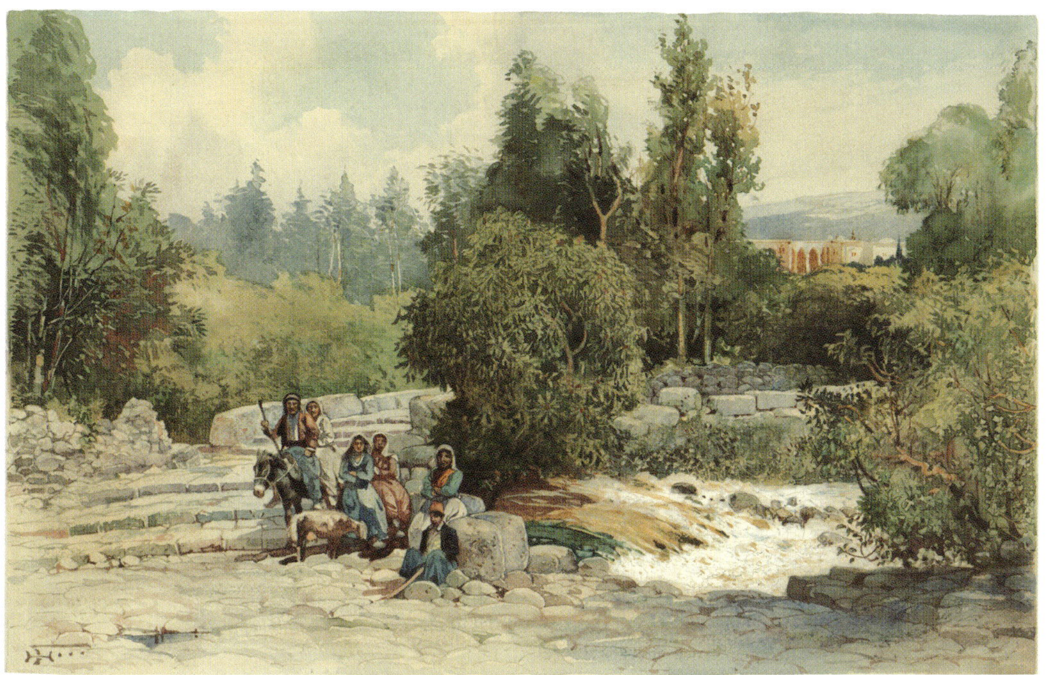

7.11. Harry Fenn, *The Approach to Baniyas,* ca. 1908. Watercolor, gouache, and graphite on paper on board, 9 1/8" x 14". (Houghton Library, Harvard University, MS Typ 192.)

Out-of-Doors in the Holy Land featured an attractive Arts and Crafts–style binding designed by Margaret Armstrong (1867–1944).[28] Van Dyke, like the U.S. president Theodore Roosevelt, espoused a muscular Christianity, emphasizing energetic outdoor activity and athleticism. His travels in the Holy Land had convinced him that Christianity was "an out-of-doors religion" because all its important events took place in the open. In his preface he asks: "How shall we understand it unless we carry it under the free sky and interpret it in the companionship of nature?"[29]

Although Fenn supplied all of the book's illustrations, his name does not appear on the title page or in the list of illustrations—much less on the cover, as it had for the special "Harry Fenn Edition" of *Gray's Elegy in a Country Churchyard* twenty-five years earlier. As was becoming more frequent in this decade, only his monogram at the lower left of the images identifies his work. The twelve images were printed as color halftones measuring approximately 5 3/4 by 3 3/4 inches; they reproduced Fenn's much larger watercolors, six of which are now in the Houghton Library's collection at Harvard University.[30] Despite improvements in color printing, the rather muddy printed illustrations are barely adequate reproductions of Fenn's vivid originals. His watercolor for "The Approach to Baniyas" (fig. 7.11), measuring 9 1/8 by 14 inches, shows his undiminished abil-

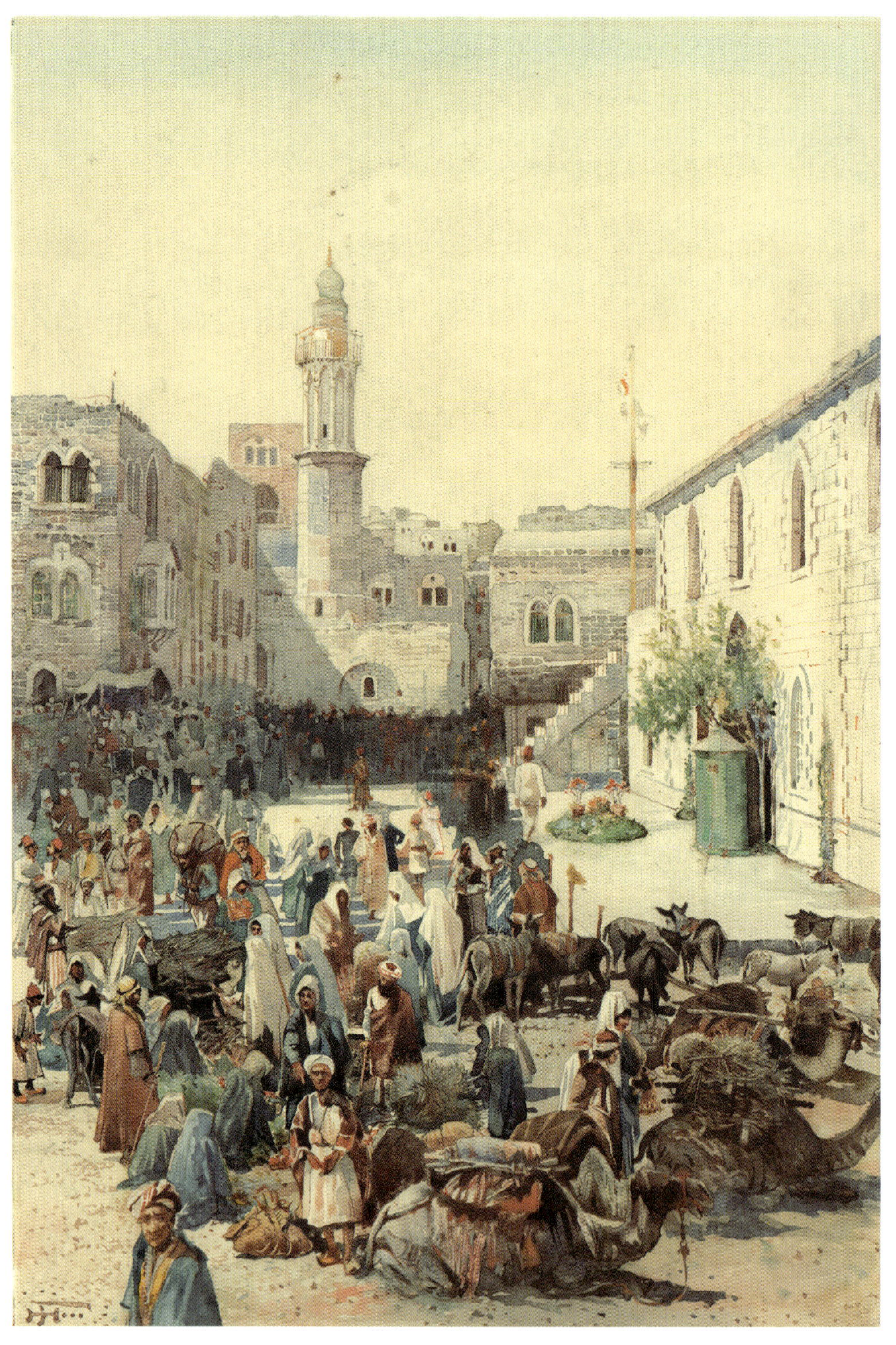

7.12. Harry Fenn, *The Market Place Bethlehem*. Watercolor, gouache, and graphite on paper on board, 13 1/2" x 8 7/8". (Houghton Library, Harvard University, MS Typ 192.)

ity to depict details of nature—from the foliage and water in the middle ground
to the trees and buildings in the background—with impressive chromatic harmony. Furthermore, "The Market-place, Bethlehem" shows his skill in handling
a scene crowded with hundreds of figures that reaches into deep space, suggesting
that even at an advanced age his eyesight and energy remained strong (fig. 7.12).
Several foreground figures (likely based on photographs) gaze directly out at the
viewer, drawing us into the scene.[31]

The book became a best seller, and Scribner's issued several later editions that
also contain Fenn's illustrations.[32] But by 1908, color illustrations were no longer a
novelty, and the distinctive styles of younger artists were drawing more attention.
In a review of illustrated art books in the *Dial,* much more space was devoted to
Otto H. Bacher's *With Whistler in Venice,* H. M. Cundall's *British Water-Colour
Painting* (with fifty illustrations in color), and Robert Hichens's *Egypt and Its
Monuments* (featuring Jules Guérin's illustrations and photographs) than to *Out-
of-Doors in the Holy Land.* The reviewer did praise the volume's imagery, saying that "the unusually beautiful illustrations, in delicate pastel tints, are such as
might adorn a much more expensive book," but failed to mention the name of the
"revered father of the vast tribe of American illustrators" who had made them.[33]

Comparing Guérin's illustrations for *Egypt and Its Monuments,* published by
the Century Company, with Fenn's for *Out-of-Doors in the Holy Land* shows vast
differences in approach. In "The Great Colonnade, Temple of Luxor" (fig. 7.13),
Guérin used planes of colors that are vivid but not naturalistic, patterns of simple
repeating forms, tiny figures as spots of color, and relatively flat space to create a
striking image. In "The Market-place, Bethlehem" (fig. 7.12) by contrast, Fenn
depicted the ancient buildings with considerable precision and realistic color and
used dramatic perspective to create a space accommodating hundreds of figures,
shown dressed mainly in the blue and white garments that he knew from his
visits to be appropriate.Whereas Fenn's objective remained to render a particular
place with accuracy as well as beauty or picturesqueness, Guérin focused on creating a sensual aesthetic experience, leaving it to the book's photographs to provide
the realistic views.

Soon after this publication, the Century Company again turned to Robert
Hichens and Jules Guérin for a series on the Holy Land, which appeared first in
the *Century* magazine, between December 1909 and October 1910, and then as a
book in the same format as *Egypt and Its Monuments,* in late 1910. *The Holy Land*
included eighteen color plates and numerous photographs, also treated as plates,
unlike the smaller photographs in the magazine.[34] Comparing these two books by

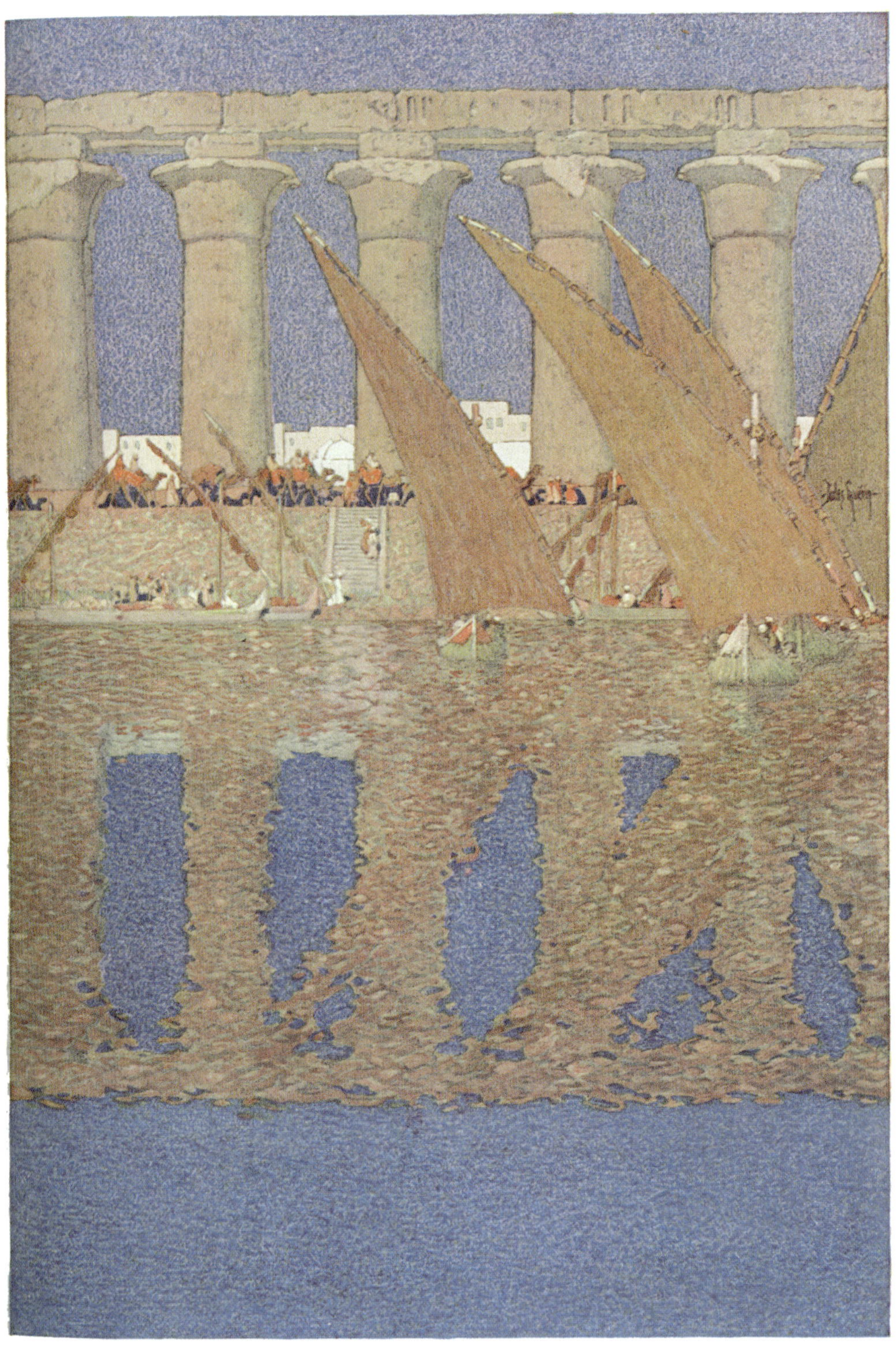

7.13. Jules Guérin, "The Great Colonnade, Temple of Luxor." From Robert Hichens, *Egypt and Its Monuments* (New York: Century Co., 1908), 105. Color halftone, 7 1/2" x 5".

Hichens and Guérin with *Picturesque Palestine,* published some twenty-five years earlier, is instructive. Gone are the steel engravings and hundreds of black and white wood engravings in all shapes and sizes scattered throughout the text. In their place are full-page color artworks and black and white photographs interleaved with the text pages; the images are printed on heavier, smoother paper than the text, with blank versos and tissue guards on which the title of the illustration or photo is printed in red. The text pages are simply but elegantly designed, with the type in black and initial letters, running heads, and page numbers printed in reddish brown. With fewer than three hundred pages, a single author, and a much smaller format (10 1/2 by 7 inches), *The Holy Land* or *Egypt and Its Monuments* provides a reading (and holding) experience that is strikingly different from that of the earlier, more encyclopedic *Picturesque Palestine.* Furthermore, viewing the images in either of the later works—seeing first one of Guérin's vivid interpretations, then a gray-toned, sharp-focused photograph—is rather jarring. Guérin's works draw the eye and invite the reader to linger, whereas the photos offer the facts but often lack contrast, the skies a dull gray. For contemporary audiences the great variety of imagery may well have been appealing, but with the interruptions of the tissue guards and blank versos, an integration of text and images is lacking.

As the century wore on, these two types of pictures—halftones of either artworks or photographs—would be used increasingly within the printing industry but less often within the same book. Publishers of periodicals and less expensive books came to rely more on photographs than on traveling artists to provide visual information about distant places. For deluxe editions, however, they continued to engage artists to create artwork and sometimes to write the text.[35]

In the spring of 1911 Fenn's renowned energy finally began to lag. After suffering from "a combination of diseases," he died at his Park Street home in Montclair on April 21, 1911.[36] After a funeral service at the Watchung Avenue Congregational Church in town, Fenn was buried beside his wife in Evergreens Cemetery, Brooklyn. Beyond a few brief newspaper notices, nothing about his last weeks is known. But the March and April 1911 issues of the *Century* give evidence that Fenn worked up until this last illness, still buoyed by his characteristic confidence to try new approaches. To represent the bricks of fortifications with precision in his illustration of the medieval French town of Carcassonne, which appeared in an article by that name written by George Allan England, Fenn used a pen and ink technique quite different from his usual approach. With its short lines and patterns of dots—resembling some of his younger colleagues' works— the drawing reproduced extremely well as a line block (fig. 7.14). Also among

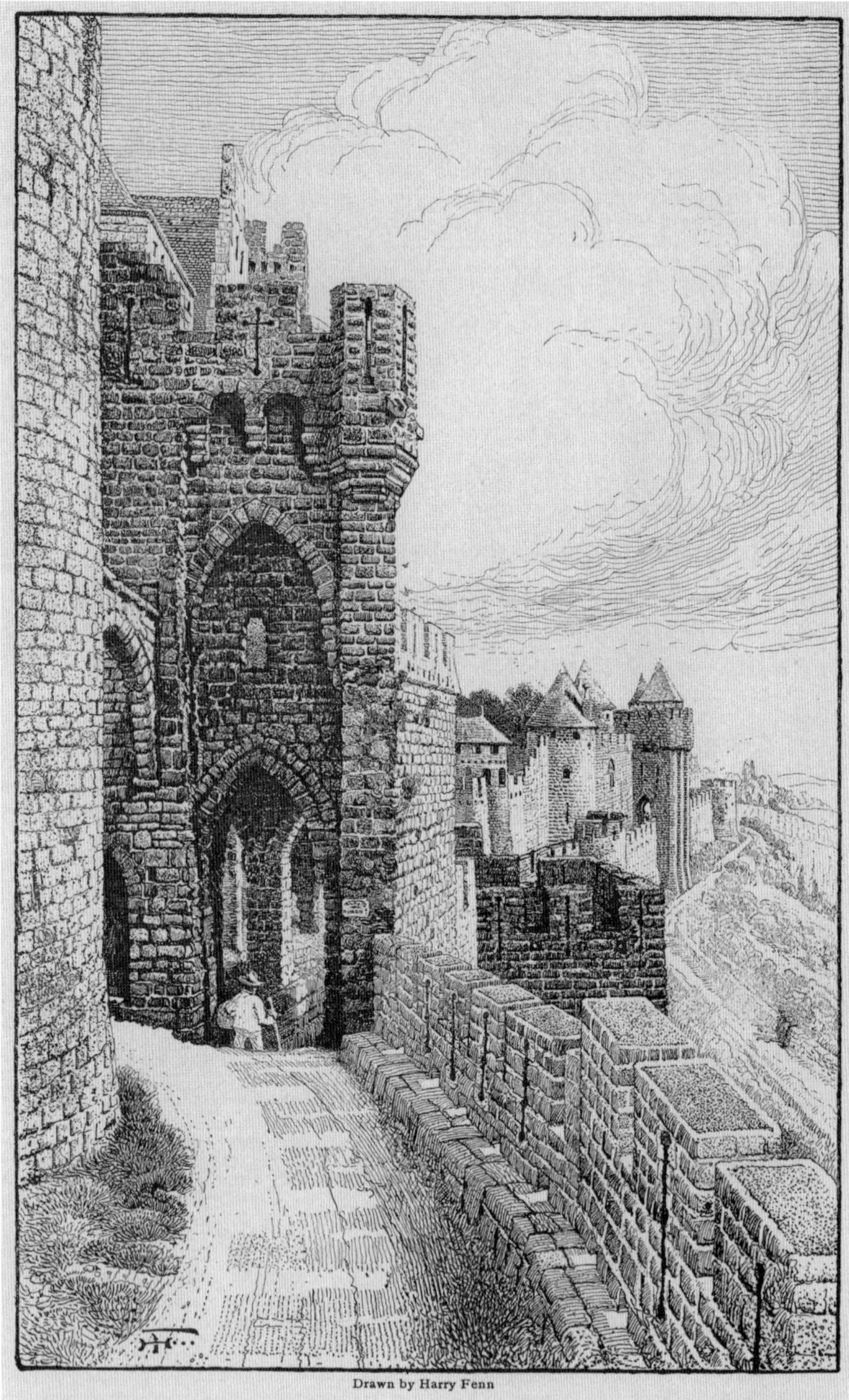

 Continuity and Change

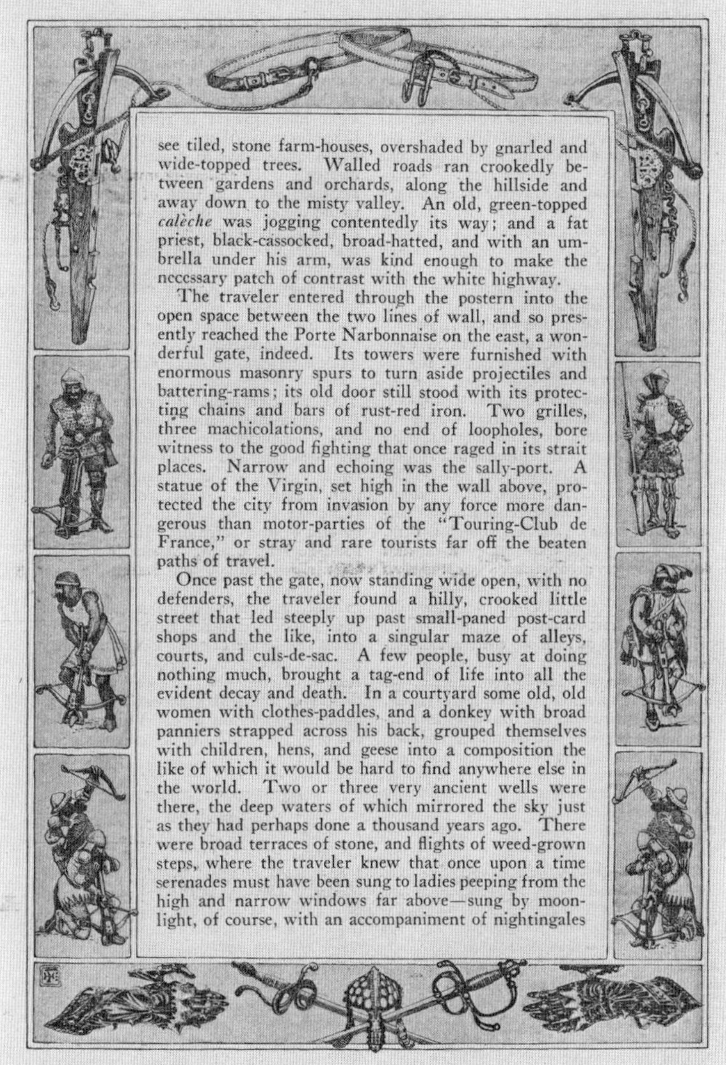

see tiled, stone farm-houses, overshaded by gnarled and wide-topped trees. Walled roads ran crookedly between gardens and orchards, along the hillside and away down to the misty valley. An old, green-topped *calèche* was jogging contentedly its way; and a fat priest, black-cassocked, broad-hatted, and with an umbrella under his arm, was kind enough to make the necessary patch of contrast with the white highway.

The traveler entered through the postern into the open space between the two lines of wall, and so presently reached the Porte Narbonnaise on the east, a wonderful gate, indeed. Its towers were furnished with enormous masonry spurs to turn aside projectiles and battering-rams; its old door still stood with its protecting chains and bars of rust-red iron. Two grilles, three machicolations, and no end of loopholes, bore witness to the good fighting that once raged in its strait places. Narrow and echoing was the sally-port. A statue of the Virgin, set high in the wall above, protected the city from invasion by any force more dangerous than motor-parties of the "Touring-Club de France," or stray and rare tourists far off the beaten paths of travel.

Once past the gate, now standing wide open, with no defenders, the traveler found a hilly, crooked little street that led steeply up past small-paned post-card shops and the like, into a singular maze of alleys, courts, and culs-de-sac. A few people, busy at doing nothing much, brought a tag-end of life into all the evident decay and death. In a courtyard some old, old women with clothes-paddles, and a donkey with broad panniers strapped across his back, grouped themselves with children, hens, and geese into a composition the like of which it would be hard to find anywhere else in the world. Two or three very ancient wells were there, the deep waters of which mirrored the sky just as they had perhaps done a thousand years ago. There were broad terraces of stone, and flights of weed-grown steps, where the traveler knew that once upon a time serenades must have been sung to ladies peeping from the high and narrow windows far above—sung by moonlight, of course, with an accompaniment of nightingales

7.15. Harry Fenn, [Border of Knights and Armor], for "Carcassonne." *Century*, March 1911, 743. Halftone, 7 $^{11}/_{16}$" x 5".

Fenn's six designs for the article is a page in which the text block is surrounded by a border containing images of knights in armor and weapons, similar to recent compositions by George Wharton Edwards, among others (fig. 7.15).

For the April 1911 *Century,* which appeared about two weeks before his death, Fenn had prepared five pen drawings to illustrate "Suburban Gardening." It is noteworthy that although the *Century* had used photographs to illustrate recent articles on gardens, for this piece the editors turned to Fenn.[37] His virtuoso drawing

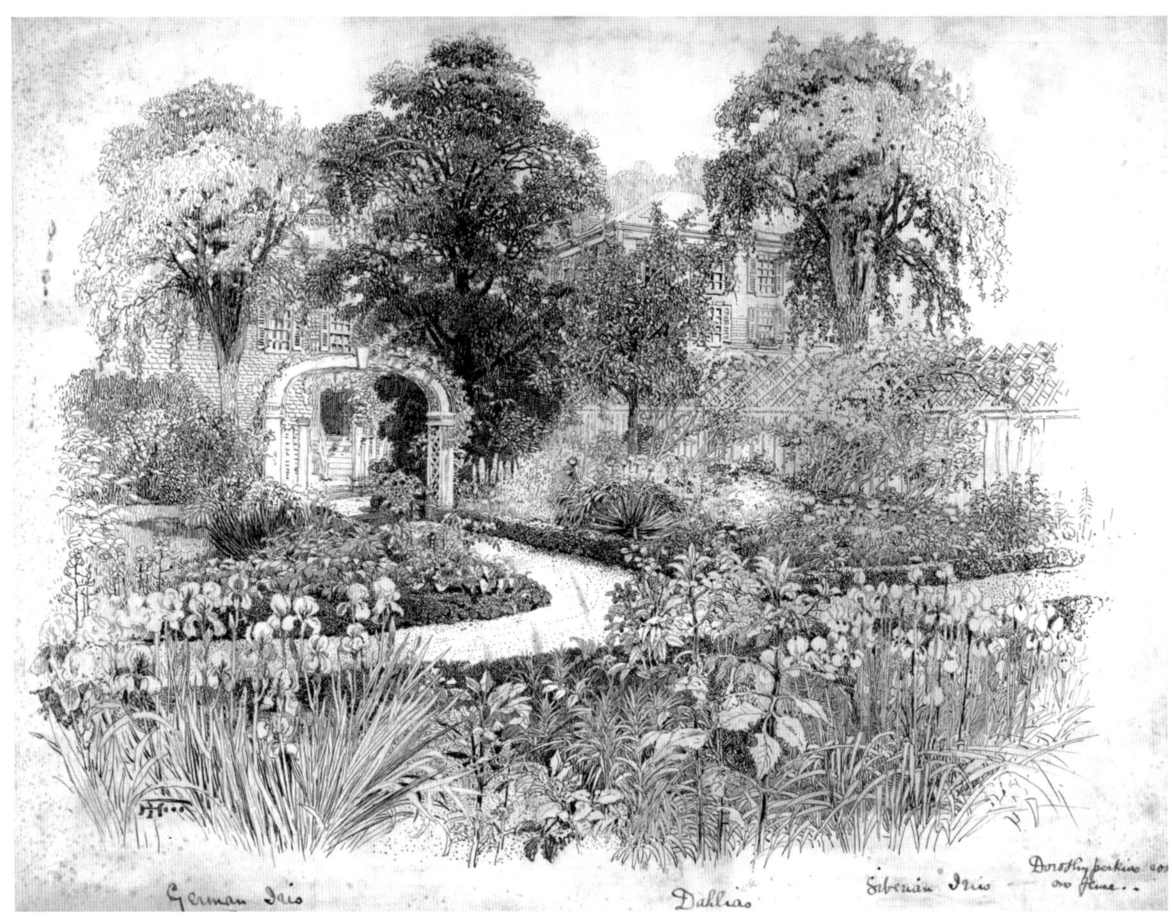

7.16. Harry Fenn, drawing for "Old-fashioned Treatment of a Small Suburban Garden," for illustration for "Suburban Gardening" by Frances Duncan, *Century*, April 1911. Ink on paper, 12 3/4" x 16 1/2". (Private collection.)

for the illustration titled "Old-Fashioned Treatment of a Small Suburban Garden" demonstrates his undiminished skill with the pen (fig. 7.16). The *Century* must also have secured works by Fenn in advance, for his drawing " 'Longwood,' Napoleon's Residence at St. Helena" appeared in the January 1912 issue, and a drawing of a pine branch, marked with his monogram, appeared the next month as the tailpiece for an article by John Muir on Yosemite.[38]

AN ASSESSMENT OF FENN'S CONTRIBUTIONS

Fenn's death was reported in several periodicals, including a brief obituary in the April 23, 1911, *New York Times* titled "Harry Fenn, Artist, Dead in 73d Year." The subtitle, "Made the First Illustrations for Gift Books Produced in This Country," is likely the source of the mistaken but oft-repeated claim that the edition of *Snow-Bound* with Fenn's illustrations was the first gift book published in the United States. In *Outlook* magazine, the notice of his death concluded with: "Among American illustrators no name was better known either in this country or abroad than that of Harry Fenn; and in the history of this department of art he will always remain a striking figure."[39]

On May 13, *Harper's Weekly* ran a much longer tribute, "Harry Fenn: An Appreciation, by a Friend."[40] The anonymous friend thought the daily papers had "done somewhat less than justice to both the artist and the man" and wrote at length about Fenn's "lovable personality" and "winning spirit." The writer also assessed the artist's contributions and legacy in ways that are by now familiar, if not entirely accurate, since numerous books illustrated with wood engravings had preceded *Snow-Bound* and *Picturesque America*. Yet the credit the writer gives Fenn for expanding the field echoes earlier comments about his role:

> To every reader of the leading American magazines, and especially of HARPER'S and the *Century,* his work and its delicacy, finish, and half-poetic atmosphere have been familiar for more than a generation. He was practically the father of black and white illustration in this country, the drawings he made for Whittier's *Snow-Bound* in the sixties and for *Picturesque America,* which followed shortly after, being among the first to be reproduced by the process of wood-engraving. The popularity of the latter of these two volumes may be said, indeed, to have opened up a wholly new field both for artists and publishers, and to have laid the foundations for the extraordinary development which has since taken place in black and white illustration all the world over, and nowhere more conspicuously than in America.

As the writer continues, however, it is clear that a reassessment of the "picturesque" series has taken place, relegating these works to an earlier era:

> But *Picturesque America,* and its successors *Picturesque Europe* and *Picturesque Palestine*—volumes that thirty-odd years ago used to be found on the center-table of every orthodox parlor—by no means give the measure of Mr. Fenn's talents, partly because at the time of their appearance both engraving and printing were in their infancy, and also because Mr. Fenn was afterward active and distinguished as a water-colorist. In the technical history of the art of illustration they will always hold the place that belongs to successful pioneers, but they convey but a meager and inadequate notion of the special grace and verity of the artist's work.

In asserting the importance of Fenn's later work, especially as a "water-color-ist," the writer chooses words similar to those used by Alma-Tadema and Brooks to describe the power of Fenn's sketches and the way the wood-engraving process had disfigured them. The writer regrets that the "life and spirit and exquisite-ness" of Fenn's original sketches were lost "in their reproduced form, mangled and dessicated" in "those primitive days of transferring drawings to the block." This harsh assessment of wood-engraved illustrations during the years when they were most prominent, and when they helped sell countless books, is surprising. The ubiquity by 1911 of the newer technologies—process line cuts and halftone plates—that directly reproduced an artist's original work probably accounts for this judgment; evidently the earlier appreciation of the fine engravers who cut the blocks following Fenn's drawn lines and tones had already receded from memory.

The writer further proclaims that Fenn's works were more than photographic and that he retained "the happy instinct . . . of seizing instantaneously upon the essential spirit and form of his subject and of depicting it with a tender, spontane-ous fidelity which, for all its truthfulness, was never hard or bald or bleakly pho-tographic, but penetrated with a worshipful devotion to nature, and an unfailing apprehension of the appeal of line and light and color." Although only a limited number of Fenn's watercolors have been located, those that are known and repro-duced in this book demonstrate that many of his paintings embody the qualities praised in the obituary; whether they were produced quickly is seldom obvious, however. Like his published illustrations, they benefit from dramatic viewpoints, striking effects of light, and skillful use of line and color. Even when working from photographs, Fenn was adept at selecting from a plethora of details and cre-ating focused and appealing compositions. Regardless of the medium, he created artworks that made scenes of both nature and human artifice seem appealing, and often beautiful.

The public had an opportunity to buy some of these artworks on November 9, 1911, when a "Collection of Water Color Drawings by Harry Fenn" was offered by the Anderson Auction Company to settle his estate. The sale was held at 8:30 p.m. in the Anderson Auditorium, located on Madison Avenue at Fortieth Street in New York, where Fenn's pictures had been on view since November 2. The catalogue listed 82 lots of one item each and included a frontispiece portrait of Fenn and a two-page "Appreciation," which stated: "In this collection which will serve as a memorial exhibition, may be found work covering every period of his long career, showing his tireless devotion to his art. The examples range from the rapid pencil and water colors on tinted paper that won great admiration from Sir Alma-Tadema, to the commanding Italian and Spanish street scenes by which he was represented in last year's exhibitions." The dates of the works ranged from 1871 to 1909 and the sizes from 5 by 8 inches to 17 by 27 inches. Subjects included figures—*A Negro Boy* and *A Boy in Red*—as well as American, European, and Middle Eastern landscapes and city views. The results of the sale must have been disappointing to the family. A brief notice in *American Art News* reported that "some three score of watercolors" sold for a total of $2,058, with $105 the highest price achieved. The notice further described Fenn as "in his day a popular artist and illustrator . . . whose work is now somewhat old fashioned."[41]

In the years after his death, Fenn's work was put before the public on at least two more occasions. In 1913 the Century Company published *Romantic America* by Robert Haven Schauffler in a deluxe edition, its size and format similar to the Hichens–Guérin collaborations but with only one full-color illustration: a frontispiece of the Grand Canyon reproduced from a Maxfield Parrish painting. The remaining illustrative plates, including sixteen by Fenn, were printed in black plus a tone, either pale green or warm beige, on smooth paper with blank versos. Most of Fenn's designs—contained within two chapters, "The Spell of Old Virginia" and "The Old California Missions"—had appeared in the January 1891 *Century,* the issue that had included a probable record thirty-one illustrations by Fenn. But, treated as plates with a tone delineating the sheet on which the drawing appears from the white of the page, and with the elements recombined in some cases, these have quite a new look.[42] One in particular, "The Garden, Santa Barbara" (fig. 7.17), is reproduced at a size much larger than in the magazine and apparently from a new line cut that is much more precise and appealing. It creates the impression of a new work by Fenn two years after his death.

New Yorkers also had a chance to review Fenn's work, including illustrations from *Snow-Bound* and all three books in the "picturesque" series, in a 1916 exhibition of American wood engraving mounted by the prestigious Grolier Club.[43] Those with a special interest in pen and ink rendering and architectural illustration could also have seen examples of his work in manuals such as *Pen-and-Ink and Water-Color Rendering,* first published by the International Correspondence Schools in 1903 and reissued in 1936, as well as in the 1993 revised edition of *The Complete Illustration Guide for Architects, Designers, Artists, and Students.*[44]

During the remainder of the twentieth century, Fenn was much less conspicuous. Occasionally his iconic images appeared, sometimes without attribution, on book jackets, for example, as well as on "The Official 2005 United States Congres-

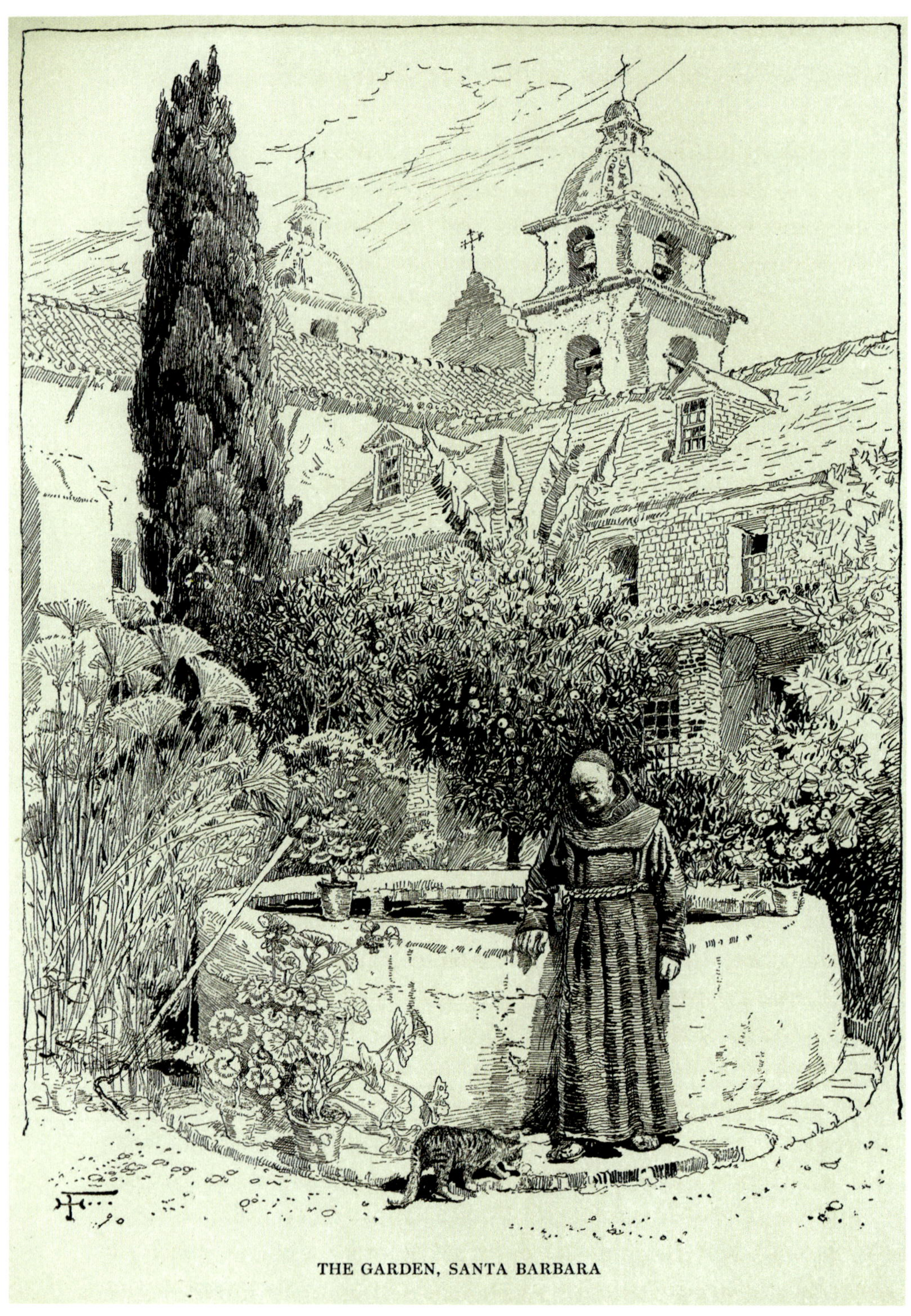

7.17. Harry Fenn, "The Garden, Santa Barbara." From Robert Haven Schauffler, *Romantic America* (New York: Century Co., 1913), 184. Process line cut printed in black, with pale green tone, 7 1/2" x 5 1/4".

sional Holiday Ornament," which reproduced one of his views of the U.S. Capitol. Yet only a scattering of print collectors and those interested in the history of illustration knew his name and his work, and art historians largely ignored prints in books and periodicals. Part of the explanation lies in the changing tastes in the world of art discussed earlier and in the increasing role that photography played in not only publications but also the wider culture. The transformations that photography brought in the late nineteenth and twentieth centuries are analogous to those that digital technology has fostered a century later. Publishers turned to photographs instead of artists for depictions of current events and travel, leaving artists primarily to illustrate fiction, embellish advertisements, and create comic strips. The change can be seen in comments by the irascible Joseph Pennell in his 1925 memoir, *Adventures of an Illustrator*. In it he describes how, in 1880, he had viewed the illustrated magazine as an "art gallery for the world" and thought an illustrator received more publicity from these outlets "than any other artist." By 1917, however, when he returned to the United States after many years in London, his opinion had changed radically. He wrote: "Harper's gave up the task of putting pearls before Americans, and the triumph of the comics is complete, and so is the dry rot of the country, which once was my United States in the art of illustration."[45]

The more even-tempered Fenn died before such drastic changes had taken place, but he had already seen his commissions decrease as publishers used halftone reproductions of photographs to cut costs. Yet, clearly, from the late 1860s through the early 1890s, Fenn had been a prominent, successful, and respected artist whose published works reached a large audience. Why has he not been remembered for his contributions in that period, when he was credited in contemporary accounts as well as in obituaries with opening up "a wholly new field both for artists and publishers," the result of his highly successful designs for wood engravings? Why has one who was called "the Nestor of his guild," "a revered father of the vast tribe of American illustrators," and "practically the father of black and white illustration in this country" been largely forgotten?

To understand the waning of Fenn's reputation requires a consideration of the history of the field of art history, which has largely determined which artists' works are viewed as important. For much of the twentieth century, historians of American visual art focused on oil painting and overlooked the larger field, including graphic artists, illustrators, etchers, and painters in watercolor and pastels. Roger B. Stein described the predominant approach and attitudes with great insight when he answered the question of why the name and reputation of Fenn's younger colleague John Douglas Woodward also disappeared:

Mid-twentieth century efforts to define an American art history worthy of being ranked with the masterpieces of Europe involved privileging oil painting and affirming a modernist history of art as the history of the avant-garde. On these counts Woodward dropped below the art historical horizon. Illustration was deemed a lower and dependent form; the interrelation of image and text and increasingly any hint of referentiality in an image seemed an affront to formalist and abstract values of modernist aesthetics; and even those who argued for the "Americanness of American art" still talked largely in terms of painting. The late phases of Barbizon practice and the work of those Americans who followed their techniques and their vision mostly disappeared from twentieth century accounts. Woodward's fundamentally conservative values and pictorial practice were clearly at war with, for instance, the deconstructive energies of Picasso or Matisse's Fauvist attacks on mimesis.[46]

This privileging of oil painting goes far toward explaining why several other artists who worked as illustrators but also produced oil paintings have maintained a larger role in art history, such as Frederic Remington and Howard Pyle and, in the next generation, John Sloan and Edward Hopper. But Fenn, for whom only a few oil paintings are known, as well as many other graphic artists, remained under the radar until the 1970s and 1980s, when the role of published images of all sorts began to be reexamined and reevaluated. Scholars today are exploring how the pictures in periodicals and books in the nineteenth century shaped the way Americans viewed this country and the wider world, creating a shared culture of impressions, information, and concerns.

Such attention can discover how, for example, no less a cultural force than Henry James assessed the contribution of book and magazine illustrations. Writing in 1889 James states: "If the centuries are ever arraigned at some bar of justice to answer in regard to what they have given, of good or of bad, to humanity, our interesting age (which certainly is not open to the charge of having stood with its hands in its pockets) might perhaps do worse than put forth the plea, 'Dear me! I have given it a fresh interest in black and white.'" He went on to say that such periodical images had the effect of "suppressing intervals and differences, and making the globe seem alarmingly small."[47] Fenn, by his prominence as a leading illustrator of landscapes and cities, made accessible and shaped—through the lens of the picturesque—a world that was overwhelmingly positive, full of natural and architectural beauty, civic amenities, historic monuments, and technological progress. Now, as access to his countless works becomes more available through digital databases and publications about him, the role he played can once more be recognized.

When Fenn first embarked on his mission to "transcribe the beauties of the world," wood engraving was flourishing and the changes that photography would eventually bring were as yet unimagined. He came of age at a time when publishers needed talented and resourceful artists to supply the images desired and demanded by a curious public. As a young immigrant in his adopted country, he acted swiftly and boldly to master the skills necessary and to sell himself as one of a handful of artists best qualified to meet publishers' needs for landscapes and cityscapes. His images of America's scenery and cities nourished and reinforced pride in the nation's landscape and helped reconcile a country divided after the Civil War. By exploiting the medium of wood engraving to create dramatic images and pages that combined pictures and text in fresh ways, he helped popularize illustrated periodicals and books and, in turn, expanded the market for himself and others. Contemporary reactions to his skilled manipulation of the wood-engraved image suggest that his works opened viewers' eyes to that medium's potential for interpreting landscape, much as Ansel Adams's large black and white photographs of the western United States did in the middle of the twentieth century. The admiration for American illustrated periodicals and books both at home and abroad bolstered confidence and pride in the young nation's art and culture. Similarly, Fenn's depictions of Britain and Europe in *Picturesque Europe* and of the Holy Land and Egypt in *Picturesque Palestine* provided many with positive images of these regions and helped forge a society that was more cosmopolitan and outward-looking. While working on such projects, he also participated in founding the American Watercolor Society and prepared paintings in that medium for exhibition and sale to an audience wider than the wealthiest elites.

With the development of printing processes that required new skills, Fenn demonstrated that he was flexible and adaptable enough to learn different techniques and use a greater variety of approaches. He juggled varied assignments for a wide range of publications, treating subjects ranging in scope from bird's-eye views of cities and landscapes to close-ups of plants and insects. His skillful renderings of architecture, particularly in pen and ink, conveyed the appeal and distinction of historic structures as well as new construction—including several of the spectacular world's fairs—serving to bolster pride in American architecture and history while promoting preservation efforts. Like many artists in this period, he tried his hand in many fields—learning to etch, participating in designing and decorating a house, applying his decorative skills to exhibitions and other interiors, and even writing articles. When the halftone process made it possible to reproduce tonal works, Fenn used watercolors and gouache to prepare his illustrations.

A look at the books for which he was the sole illustrator shows clearly how he adapted to changing technologies and styles—from the small, black and white, linear images of *Snow-Bound* to the large pages of *Picturesque America,* with their often dramatically interlocking text and images, to the spare pages of *In Memoriam,* whose delicate illustrations are often combined with decorative initial letters, to the full-color illustrations of *Out-of-Doors in the Holy Land,* packed with detail and information. Even as younger generations schooled in later techniques and styles gradually moved into the limelight and overshadowed him, Fenn continued to produce work that, with its familiar style and obvious skill, found a ready audience among publishers and the public alike.

Throughout a long and amazingly prolific career, Harry Fenn filled the homes and parlor tables of countless Americans with works of art that celebrated the beauty of nature and the cultures of the world. In a period of great upheaval and change, from the Civil War to the growth of the American empire in the years after the Spanish–American War—an era marked by expanding capitalism and labor disputes, new settlements across the continent, scientific discoveries and technological advances, and immigrant groups flocking to American shores—Fenn kept his good humor and kept on preparing illustrations and exhibition watercolors. His overwhelmingly positive images of unchanging mountain peaks and the latest bridges, of old waterways and new automobile roads, of Wall Street, the Bering Strait, and the Great Wall of China promoted optimism, stability, and continuity. He accomplished what he had set out to do, with obvious relish, as noted by his eulogist: "The pursuit and the understanding of Nature and the unveiling of her beauties that others might feel and see them as he did were to Harry Fenn far more than an emotional or artistic delight; they were his religion."[48]

Continuity and Change

Additional Illustrations by Harry Fenn

Note: Listed below are books and periodicals not mentioned in the text that contain illustrations by Harry Fenn. For periodicals, the titles refer to Fenn's images or the articles or poems they illustrate. More nineteenth-century books and periodicals are being digitized every day. If you wish to see Fenn's images in the listed works, I suggest searching for them online in such databases as Google Books and the Making of America (University of Michigan and Cornell University libraries). *An asterisk indicates that the original artwork for an illustration has been located.

1860s and 1870s

BOOKS

Aldrich, Thomas Bailey. *The Story of a Bad Boy.* Boston: Fields, Osgood, 1870. 1 illus. by Fenn, p. 42.

Bryant, William Cullen. *Poetical Works of William Cullen Bryant.* New York: D. Appleton, 1878. Illustrated with 100 engravings from drawings by Harry Fenn, Birket Foster, Alfred Fredericks, and others.

Cary, Alice. *Ballads, Lyrics and Hymns.* New York: Hurd and Houghton, 1866. 2 illus. by Fenn, pp. 19, 149.

Castleman, Harry. *Go-Ahead; or, The Fisher-Boy's Motto.* Philadelphia: Porter & Coates, 1867.

Greeley, Horace. *The Great Industries of the United States.* Hartford: Burr & Hyde, 1872. 1 illus. signed by Fenn, opp. p. 600.

Holland, J. G., ed. *Illustrated Library of Favorite Song.* Illustrated by Harry Fenn and others. New York: Scribner, Armstrong, 1873. 3 illus. by Fenn, pp. 139, 168, 523.

Kellogg, Elijah. *Good Old Times; or, Grandfather's Struggles for a Homestead.* Boston: Lee and Shepard, 1878. 2 illus. signed by Fenn, pp. 33, 106.

Larcom, Lucy. *Childhood Songs.* Boston, James R. Osgood, 1875. 1 illus. by Fenn, p. 40.

Palmer, John Williamson, ed. *Songs of Life, Selected from Many Sources.* New York: Charles Scribner, 1870. 2 illus. by Fenn. pp. 1, 60.

Smith, Samuel Francis. *America: Our National Hymn.* Boston: D. Lothrop, [1879]. Uses wood engravings from *Picturesque America* to illustrate stanzas of "My Country, 'Tis of Thee."

Stiles, Henry Reed. *A History of the City of Brooklyn.* Brooklyn, N.Y.: By subscription, 1867–70. 1 illus. by Fenn in vol. 2, p. 171.

Stockton, Frank Richard. *Round-About Rambles in Lands of Fact and Fancy.* New York: Scribner, Armstrong, 1872. 1 illus. by Fenn, p. 120.

Stowe, Harriet Beecher. *Queer Little People.* Boston: Ticknor and Fields, 1867. 1 illus. by Fenn, p. 86.

Whittier, John Greenleaf, ed. *Child Life: A Collection of Poems.* Boston: Houghton, Mifflin, 1871. 4 illus. by Fenn, pp. 63, 101, 104, 260.

______, ed. *Child Life in Prose*. Boston: J. R. Osgood, 1874. 1 illus. by Fenn, p. 193.
Young, John Russell. *Around the World with General Grant*. New York: American News Co.,
    [1879]. 4 illus. by Fenn, vol. 1: p. 71, opp. p. 321; vol. 2: pp. 176, 186.

PERIODICALS

Appletons' Journal

1869

Apr. 24, May 15, Jun. 12: Art supplement, "New York Illustrated"
Sep. 11: "West Point and the Highlands," steel engraving
Sep. 25: "Fairmount, Philadelphia," fold-out cartoon
Oct. 9: "New England Coast Scene—The Cape Ann Cedar Tree"
Oct. 23: front page, "October"

1870

Apr. 30: "Carthagena in Colombia" by M. L. Dow
Jul. 9: "The Watch as a Growth of Industry" by E. L. Youmans
Nov. 26: front page, "An Autumn Scene"

1871

Jan. 7: front page, "Young America at His Winter Sports"
May 13: "Yosemite Valley, from Mariposa Trail" and "Yosemite Falls"
Aug. 26: front page, "Rock City, Lookout Mountain"
Sep. 23: "Augusta, Georgia"
Dec. 23: front page, "Old Blandford Church"; "The Hudson at Glen's Falls"
Dec. 30: "Christmas at Sea" and, in Christmas supplement, "Christmas at the Antipodes:
    Or, 'Five Thousand Leagues Away'"

1872

Jan. 27: "Schenectady, on the Mohawk"
Feb. 10: "The City of the Future"
Mar. 16: front page, "Cumberland Gap"
Apr. 27: "The Starrucca Viaduct, the Erie Railway"
May 4: front page, "The Light-Ship and Incoming Steamer"
May 11: "The Giant Geyser, Yellowstone Valley"; "Tower Falls, Yellowstone Valley"

The Atlantic Almanac 1868, ed. Oliver Wendell Holmes and Donald G. Mitchell.

Calendar headings for Jun., Aug., Oct. and two illus. from *Snow-Bound*

Harper's New Monthly Magazine

Jan. 1869: first page, "The Silent City at Greenwood" by J. D. Sherwood
Sep. 1869: "Photographs from the High Rockies" by John Samson
Oct. and Nov. 1869: "A Health Trip to Brazil" by Thomas C. Evans

Harper's Weekly

Jul. 24, 1869: "Gettysburg—Culp's Hill," sketched by Theo. R. Davis, signed "H.F."
May 7, 1870: "Winter Scenes in Minnesota"

Hearth and Home

Apr. 10, 1869: illus. of Samuel Colt's home, reprinted from *Armsmear*
Dec. 18, 1869: front page, "Coveting More Land" by Henry Ward Beecher
Jul. 23, 1870: front page, "A Swiss House"

Illustrated Christian Weekly

Apr. 15 and Jun. 17, 1871: "Mount Serbal"; "Mount Sinai"
May 31, 1873: illus. of Trenton Falls from Willis's *Trenton Falls*

Our Young Folks

1865

Feb.: "The Sandpiper"; "Our Country Neighbors" by Harriet Beecher Stowe
Jun.: "The Wild Goose" by J. T. Trowbridge
Jul.: "Farming for Boys"
Nov.: "Farming for Boys"

1866

Feb: vignette of winter
Mar.: "The Battle-Field of Fredericksburg" by J. T. Trowbridge
Jun.: circular illus. of fairy over rainbow
Aug.: "The Daisy's First Winter"
Oct.: "Nutting Song"
Nov.: "The Girl and the Gleaner"
Dec.: reprint of illus. from *The Flower-de-Luce* by Henry Wadsworth Longfellow

1867

Feb., Apr., and Nov.: "Good Old Times" by Elijah Kellogg
Apr.: "Our Violet Girl"
Jul.: "Making Hay"
Aug.: "Summer Morning"
Sep.: "Entering the Ice," after a painting by F. E. Church; "Boat Song"
Oct.: "Beautiful Summer"
Nov.: "The Cove" by Helen C. Week; "November"
Dec.: reprint of illus. from *Snow-Bound;* "In Time's Swing" New Year's illus.

1868

Feb.: "Cast Away in the Cold"; "The Cat's Diary"
May: "The Aurora Borealis" (color), after a painting by F. E. Church
Oct.: frontispiece, "Harvesting"

1869

Feb.: "The Cat's Diary"

Scribner's Monthly

Nov. 1876: "The Charter Oak City" reuses some of Fenn's *Armsmear* illustrations

1880s
BOOKS

Blackmore, R. D. *Lorna Doone.* 2 vols. Cleveland: Burroughs Brothers, 1889.
The Cambridge Book of Poetry and Song, ed. Charlotte Fiske Bates. New York: Thomas Y. Crowell,
    1882.
Carleton, Will. *City Ballads.* New York: Harper and Brothers, 1885. Frontispiece by Fenn.
Lathrop, George Parsons. *Peconic Park: An Exploration of Long Island.* New York: Printed for
    Private Circulation, 1883.
Longfellow, Henry Wadsworth. *The Poetical Works of Henry Wadsworth Longfellow.* Vol. 2.
    Boston: Houghton Mifflin, 1881–83.

Menken, Adah Isaacs. *Infelicia*. Philadelphia: J. P. Lippincott, 1888.

Read, T. Buchanan. *The Poetical Works of T. Buchanan Read.* Rev. ed. Philadelphia: J. B. Lippincott, 1883.

Read, Thomas Buchanan. *The Wagoner of the Alleghanies.* Philadelphia: J. B. Lippincott, 1885.

Scott, Sir Walter. *Marmion.* Boston: James R. Osgood, 1885.

Scudder, Horace Elisha. *Mr. Bodley Abroad.* Boston: Houghton, Mifflin, 1880.

Songs of Christmas. ed. Frances Ridley Havergal. New York: E. P. Dutton, 1885.

Tennyson, Alfred. *The Lady of the Lake.* Boston: J. R. Osgood, 1883.

______. *Lady Clare.* Philadelphia: Porter & Coates, 1884.

______. *The Day Dream.* New York: Dutton, 1886.

______. *The Miller's Daughter.* Philadelphia: J. B. Lippincott, 1889–90.

PERIODICALS

The Century

1882

Sep.: "Thomas Bewick" by Austin Dobson

1883

Aug.: "Under the Olives" by E. D. R. Bianciardi

1884

Apr.: "The New York City Hall" by Edward S. Wilde
May: lead article, "The Salem of Hawthorne" by Julian Hawthorne
May, Jul., and Aug.: "Recent Architecture in America" by Mrs. Schuyler van Rensselaer
*Jun.: "Sailors' Snug Harbor" by Franklin H. North. Original of "A View along the Front," p. 193, is in the Library of Congress Cabinet of American Illustration.
Jul.: "Scenes of Hawthorne's Romances" by Julian Hawthorne
Aug., Sept., Oct.: "On the Track of Ulysses" by W. J. Stillman
Oct.: "Social Conditions in the Colonies" by Edward Eggleston

1885

Mar.: "The Land of the False Prophet" by R. E. Colston
Oct.: "Riverside Park" by William A. Stiles
Nov.: "A Photographer's Visit to Petra" by Edward L. Wilson
Dec.: lead article, "The City of Teherân, First Paper" by S. G. W. Benjamin; "An American Lordship" by George Parsons Lathrop

1886

Jan.: lead article, "The City of Teherân. Second Paper" by S. G. W. Benjamin
Feb.: "Recent Architecture in America, V. City Dwellings" by Mariana G. van Rensselaer
Mar.: "Mountaineering in Persia" by S. G. W. Benjamin
May and Jun.: "American Country Dwellings. VII" by Mrs. Schuyler van Rensselaer
Jun.: "Harvard's Botanic Garden and Its Botanists" by Ernest Ingersoll
Sep.: lead article, "A Summer with Liszt in Weimar" by Albert Morris Bagby
Nov.: begins "Abraham Lincoln: A History" by John G. Nicolay and John Hay; "Lincoln as Pioneer"
Dec.: "Lincoln as Soldier, Surveyor, and Politician"

1887

Jan.: "Comets and Meteors" by S. P. Langley; "Lincoln in Springfield"
*Apr.: "Lincoln, The Territorial Experiment"; "Church and Meeting House before the Revolution" by Edward Eggleston. Fenn's original drawing for "Interior of the Old Goose Creek Church. South Carolina," p. 905, is in the collection of the San Diego Museum of Art, gift of Walter J. Fenn.

Jul.: lead article, "Among the Wild-Flowers" by John Burroughs
Aug.: "Lincoln's Cooper Institute Speech"
Sep.: "The Later Years of Monticello" by Frank R. Stockton
Nov.: lead article, "The Home and Haunts of Washington" by Mrs. Burton Harrison;
"Mount Vernon as It Is" by Sophie Bledsoe Herrick

1888

Apr.: "The American Inventors of the Telegraph" by Franklin Leonard Pope
Jul.: lead article, "Sinai and the Wilderness" by Edward L. Wilson
Nov.: "Where Was The Place Called Calvary?" by Charles S. Robinson
Dec.: "From Sinai to Shechem" by Edward L. Wilson

1889

Jan.: "Round About Galilee" by Edward L. Wilson
Feb.: "Gerome" by Fanny Field Hering
Apr.: "The Inauguration of Washington" by Clarence Winthrop Bowen;
    "Washington at Mount Vernon after the Revolution" by Mrs. Burton Harrison
May: "Round about Jerusalem" by Edward L. Wilson
Jun.: "Certain Forms of Woman's Work for Woman" by Helen Campbell
Dec.: "Selections from Wellington's Letters" by Mary E. Davies Evans

Harper's Bazaar

Dec. 24, 1887: ad suppl., page of illustrations from various books, including one by Fenn from *Bar
    Harbor Days* by Mrs. Burton Harrison
Apr. 21, 1888: "Grand Menan"
Jun. 22, 1889: "Mount Holyoke College and Seminary"

Harper's New Monthly Magazine

1882

Jun.: "Montreal" by C. H. Farnham

1883

Jul.: "Cincinnati" by Olive Logan
Aug.: lead article, "The Heart of the Alleghanies" by George Parsons Lathrop
Oct.: "Last Days of Washington's Army at Newburgh" by J. T. Headley

1884

Mar.: "The Yorkshire Coast" by William H. Rideing

1885

Jul.: "Midsummer on Mount Desert" by Frances L. Mace

1886

Feb.: "Mrs. Wegg's Party on the Kissimmee" by Henri Daugé

1887

Apr.: "The Southern Gateway of the Alleghanies" by Edmund Kirke. Compare these with Fenn's
    Picturesque America illus. of the view from Lookout Mountain, the Tennessee River, and
    Rock City.
May: "The Three Tetons" by Alice Wellington Rollins; "Through the Caucasus, Part II" by Ralph
    Meeker
May: "The Little Crimson Hat," poem by E. F. Lintaber
Sep.: "The South American Yankee" by William Eleroy Curtis

Oct.: "The Smallest of American Republics [Costa Rica]" by William Eleroy Curtis; "A Dead
    Portuguese City in India" by John F. Hurst
Nov.: "A Santa Barbara Holiday" by Edward Roberts

1888

Jan.: "The City of Savannah, Georgia" by I. W. Avery
*Aug.: "A Midsummer Trip to the West Indies. Second Paper" by Lafcadio Hearn. The original
    drawing for Fenn's "In the Jardin des Plantes" is in the Library of Congress Cabinet of
    American Illustration.
Nov.: "A Pink Villa" by Constance Fenimore Woolson. Compare Fenn's view of Sorrento, p. 837,
    with his *Picturesque Europe* illus. 2:447.
Dec.: "The Front Yard" by Constance F. Woolson

Harper's Weekly

1882

Jul. 8: "Breakneck Mountain from the Foot of Cro-Nest, Hudson River.—Drawn by Harry Fenn"

1883

Jul. 14: "Summer Resorts—Mount McGregor.—Drawn by Harry Fenn"

1887

Jan. 1: "San Antonio, Texas.—Drawn by Harry Fenn from Photographs"
Mar. 12: "The Everglades of Florida.—Drawn by Harry Fenn from Sketches by Wolf Harlander";
    "Pushing through the Everglades.—Drawn by Harry Fenn from sketches by Wolf Harlander"
Apr. 9: "The Turpentine Industry.—North Carolina.—Drawn by Harry Fenn"
Apr. 30: "Mount Shasta, California.—Drawn by Harry Fenn from Photographs"
Jun. 11: "Sketches at West Point.—Drawn by Harry Fenn from Photographs"; "The Old Ute
    Reservation, Colorado.—Drawn by Harry Fenn from Photographs by Charles Goodman"
Jul. 16: "Boston Harbor and Its Islands.—Drawn by Harry Fenn"
Jul. 23: "Nahant and Swampscott, Massachusetts Bay.—Drawn by Harry Fenn"
Jul. 30: "Views in and about Marblehead.—Drawn by Harry Fenn"
Aug. 6: "Around Cape Ann.—Drawn by Harry Fenn"
Aug. 20: "Around Kennebunk and Old Orchard Beach.—Drawn by Harry Fenn"
Sep. 3: "Sketches of Camden, Maine, and Its Vicinity.—Drawn by Harry Fenn"
Sep. 10: "An Old Maine Seaport [Castine].—Drawn by Harry Fenn"
Oct. 15: "Mount Desert and Bar Harbor.—Drawn by Harry Fenn"

1888

Aug. 18: "Moosehead Lake, Maine.—Drawn by Harry Fenn"

1889

Jan. 19: "The City of Aspen, Colorado"
May 25: "Representative Scenes and Citizens of the City of Worcester, Massachusetts.—Drawn by
    Harry Fenn, and from Photographs"
Jun. 1: "Scenes in Sicily.—Drawn by Harry Fenn from Photographs"
Nov. 9: "The City of Cleveland, Ohio.—Drawn by Harry Fenn, from Photographs by J. F. Ryder"
Dec. 21: "General View of the City of Cairo"; "On the Outskirts of Cairo with the Pyramids in the
    Distance" for "The Nile Valley" by Charles Chaillé Long

St. Nicholas

Oct. 1883: "Gathering Beech-Nuts"
Nov. 1886: "Boring for Oil"
Feb. 1887: "Among the Gas-Wells"

May 1887: headpiece for "Child-Sketches from George Eliot"
*Jul. 1887: "In English Country" by Frank R. Stockton; drawing for "West Gate," p. 656, in
    private collection
May 1888: "Girard College" by Alice Maude Fenn
Oct. 1888: "Sea Gulls—From the Light-house" by Louie Lyndon

Scribner's Magazine

Apr. 1888: "Gibraltar" by Henry M. Field
Nov. 1889: "Goethe's House at Weimar" by Oscar Browning

The Youth's Companion

Jul. 31, 1887: "A Jaunt in North Wales"

1890–1911
BOOKS

Cleaveland, George A., and Robert E. Campbell. *American Landmarks: A Collection of Pictures of
    Our Country's Historic Shrines.* Boston: Balch Brothers, 1893. Two illus. signed by Fenn: "St.
    John's Church," p. 23; "Washington's Tomb," p. 57.
Grant, George Munro, ed. *The Easternmost Ridge of the Continent.* Chicago: Alexander Belford,
    1899. This book reuses the sections of Munro's *Picturesque Canada* (Toronto: Belden
    Brothers, 1882–84) pertaining to the easternmost provinces. Fenn's contributions are on pp.
    61, 87, 210.
Shackelton, Robert, and Elizabeth Shackelton. *The Quest for the Colonial.* New York: Century,
    1907. "Illustrated with many photographs and with decorations by Harry Fenn"
    (headpieces and tailpieces).
Wilson, Woodrow. *Life of George Washington.* Illus. Howard Pyle, Harry Fenn, and others. New
    York: Harper, 1897.
________. *A History of the American People.* 5 vols. Illus. Harry Fenn and others. New York: Harper,
    1902.

PERIODICALS

The Century

1890

Mar.: "Some Wayside Places in Palestine" by Edward L. Wilson
*May: "Some New Washington Relics" by William Armstrong; "Theodore O'Hara" by Robert
    Burns Wilson. Fenn's drawing "Soldier Monument and Tomb of O'Hara" is in the
    collection of the Brandywine River Museum.
Jun.: lead article, "London Polytechnics and Peoples' Palaces" by Albert Shaw
Aug.: "The Treasures of the Yosemite" by John Muir

1891

Feb. "Fremont in the Conquest of California" by John Bidwell
Mar.: "Résumé of Frémont's Expedition" by M.N.O.
May 1891: "Pioneer Mining in California" by E. G. Waite
Jun. 1891: "Colonel William Byrd of Westover" by Mrs. Burton Harrison; "Women at
    an English University. Newnham College, Cambridge" by Eleanor Field

1892

Feb.: "The Jews in New York.–II" by Richard Wheatley
May: "Homesteads of the Blue Grass" by James Lane Allen
Jun.: "Christopher Columbus. II. In Search of a Patron" by Emilio Castelar

Aug.: lead article, "An Ascent of Fuji the Peerless" by Mabel L. Todd and David P. Todd
Oct.: "What I Saw of the Paris Commune" by Archibald Forbes"; "Architecture of the
World's Columbian Exposition.—V" by Henry Van Brunt
Nov.: "What I Saw of the Paris Commune, II"

1893

Jan.: "The Great Wall of China" by Romyn Hitchcock; "A Winter Ride to the Great Wall of
China" by N. B. Dennys
Feb.: "Life in the Malay Peninsula" by John Fairlie
Apr.: "A Tree Museum [Arnold Arboretum]" by M. C. Robbins
Jul.: "Color in the Court of Honor at the Fair" by Royal Cortissoz; "The Author of 'Gulliver'"
by M. O. W. Oliphant
Aug.: lead article, "Fez, the Mecca of the Moors" by Stephen Bonsal
Sep.: "The Taormina Note-Book" by George E. Woodberry; "The Author of Robinson Crusoe"
by M. O. W. Oliphant
Oct.: "Street-Paving in America" by William Fortune

1894

Feb.: "Laurens Alma-Tadema" by Ellen Gosse
Mar.: "Major André's Story of the 'Mischianza' with a Preface by Sophie Howard"
Apr.: "Driven out of Tibet" by W. Woodville Rockhill
*May: "Hunting an Abandoned Farm in Upper New England" by William Henry Bishop.
Fenn's original for "Waiting for an Artist," p. 86, is in the collection of the Salmagundi Club.
Jul.: "Coasting by Sorrento and Amalfi" by F. Marion Crawford

1895

Jul.: "Bryant and the Berkshire Hills" by Arthur Lawrence
Aug.: "Reminiscences of Literary Berkshires" by Henry Dwight Sedgwick; "A Bit of Italian
Merrymaking" by Mary Scott-Uda
Sep.: "Hunting Customs of the Omaha: Personal Studies of Indian Life" by Alice C. Fletcher;
"Aquatic Gardening" by J. H. Connelly

1896

Jan.: "Tribal Life among the Omahas" by Alice C. Fletcher
*Feb.: lead article, "Certain Worthies and Dames of Old Maryland" by John Williamson
Palmer. Fenn's original drawing for "'Belmont.' near Elkridge, the Seat of the Dorseys of
Maryland. Built in 1738," p. 494, is in the collection of the New Britain Museum of Art.
"Pope Leo XIII and His Household" by F. Marion Crawford
Mar.: "Ways and Means in Arid America" by William E. Smythe
Apr.: "Four Lincoln Conspiracies" by Victor Louis Mason
Jul.: "Glimpses of Venezuela and Guiana" by W. Nephew King
Aug.: "An Island without Death [Miyajima]" by Eliza Ruhamah Scidmore
Oct.: "The Eclipse of Napoleon's Glory" by William M. Sloane; "Glave in the Heart of Africa" by
E. J. Glave
Nov.: "Campaigning with Grant" by Horace Porter

1897

Apr.: "New Conditions in Central Africa" by E. J. Glave
May: lead article, "A Suburban Country Place" by M. G. Van Rensselaer, "With Pictures by Harry
Fenn"; "Bicycling through the Dolomites" by George E. Waring Jr.
Jun.: "A Great Modern Observatory. Harvard's Astronomical Work" by Mabel Loomis Todd;
"Suggested Driveway at the Foot of the Palisades of the Hudson," p. 317, accompanying a
letter by F. P. Albert titled "A Way to Save the Palisades"
Jul.: "Hunting the Jaguar in Venezuela" by William Willard Howard

Aug.: "A Journey in Thessaly" by Thomas Dwight Goodell
Sep.: "Prisoners of State at Boro Boedor" by Eliza Ruhamah Scidmore; "Cruelty in the Congo
        Free State" by E. J. Glave

1898

Jan.: "Maximilian's Empire" by Sara Y. Stevenson
Mar.: "The River Trip to the Klondike" by John Sidney Webb

1899

Jan.: "The Carlyles in Scotland" by John Patrick; "The Sinking of the 'Merrimac,' Part II" by
        Richmond Pearson Hobson
Feb.: "The Sinking of the 'Merrimac,' Part III"
Mar.: "The Sinking of the 'Merrimac,' Part IV"
Jul.: "The Many-Sided Franklin: Franklin's Relations with the Fair Sex" by Paul Leicester Ford
Sep.: "Cruising Up the Yangtsze" by Eliza Ruhamah Scidmore
Oct.: "The Streets of Peking" by Eliza Ruhamah Scidmore

1900

Feb.: "Talks with Napoleon. His Life and Conversation at St. Helena" by B. E. O'Meara
Mar: "The Giant Indians of Tierra del Fuego" by Frederick A. Cook
Sep.: "Troglodyte Dwellings in Cappadocia" by J. R. Sitlington Sterrett
Oct.: "China's 'Holy Land.' A Visit to the Tomb of Confucius" by Ernst von Hesse-Wartegg

1901

Jan.: "Hamlet's Castle" by Jacob A. Riis
Mar.: "Daniel Webster: Second Paper. Webster as Leader of the Opposition" by John Bach McMaster
Jun.: "The Young Men's Christian Association in Europe" by W. S. Harwood
Jul.: "A Notable Masterpiece by Millet" by Frederick Keppel, tailpiece, p. 458
Aug.: "America's Agricultural Regeneration of Russia" by Alexander Hume Ford
Sep.: "Daniel Webster. Fourth Paper" by John B. McMaster, tailpiece, p. 761

1902

Feb.: "A Visit to Mt. Vernon a Century Ago" by W. M. Kozlowski
May: "The Summer Life of the Queen of Rumania" by Zoe De Balatchano

1904

Apr.: "Landmarks of Poe in Richmond" by Charles Marshall Graves
May: "Unhappy Korea" by Arthur Judson Brown
Jul.: "The New West Point" by Sylvester Baxter

1905

Feb.: "The Everglades of Florida, a Region of Mystery" by Edwin Asa Dix and John Nowry
        MacGonigle
May: "The Prize of Rome" by Arthur Hoeber
Sep.: "Historic Palaces of Paris. I. Hotel Monaco" by Count Louis de Perigord and Camille
        Gronkowski
Nov.: "Historic Palaces of Paris. II. Hotel du Prince Eugene (The German Embassy)"; "The
        Panama Canal" by William Barclay Parsons
*Dec.: "Historic Palaces of Paris. III. The Hotel de Crillon." Fenn's original drawing for "The
        Second Salon," p. 261, is in the collection of the Free Library of Philadelphia.

1906

Apr.: "Historic Palaces of Paris. IV. Hotel de la Rochefoucauld-Doudeauville" by Camille
        Gronkowski
Dec.: "Jay Cooke, and the Financing of the Civil War" by Ellis Paxson Oberholzter

1907

Feb.: "Von Moltke's View of Washington's Strategy" by William Milligan Sloane. Fenn's
    illus. "Nassau Hall, Princeton University, A Famous Relic of the Revolution," p. 520, is
    similar in viewpoint, but not in details, to the large watercolor in the Princeton Portrait
    Collection, Princeton University. "The Graves of Three Washingtons" by Henry Codman
    Potter; "The Washington–Craigie–Longfellow House, Washington's Headquarters and
    Longfellow's Home at Cambridge, Mass." by Francis Le Baron
Mar.: lead article, "Early Homes of Longfellow" by Stephen Cammett
Apr.: "A County Thirty-one Years in Rebellion" by Frank Wickizer
*May: "Jamestown, The Cradle of American Civilization" by Thomas Nelson Page; "Garibaldi
    in New York" by Henry Tyrell. The original watercolor for Fenn's illus. "Ruins of the
    Candle-Making Furnace and Caldron at Clifton, Staten Island, as They Appeared about
    1884," p. 179, is in the the Library of Congress Cabinet of American Illustration.
Jun.: "Dueling in Old Creole Days" by Louis J. Meader; "A Haven of Rest, the Home of the Blue
    Nuns at Fiesole" by Helen Zimmern; "Garibaldi in New York" by Henry Tyrrell

1908

May: "A Florentine Roof Garden" by Helen Zimmern
Jun.: "Our Barbarous Fourth" by Mrs. Isaac L. Rice
Sep.: "Andrew Johnson in the White House, Being the Reminiscences of William H. Crook" by
    Margarita Spalding Gerry
Oct.: "The White House Collection of Presidential Ware" by Abby G. Baker

1909

Apr.: "Joseph Jefferson at Home" by Eugénie Paul Jefferson
Jun.: "Saint-Gaudens the Master, the Reminiscences of Augustus Saint-Gaudens" ed. Homer
    Saint-Gaudens

1910

Jan.: "The Outlander" by Mark F. Wilcox
Feb.: "The Preservation of Mount Vernon" by Abby Gunn Baker
Aug.: "Lawn-Tennis, the Queen of Games" by Walter Camp

1911

Mar.: "Carcassonne" by George Allen England
Nov.: "The Great Modern Hospital" by W. Gilman Thompson

Cosmopolitan

1891

Sept.: "The Ladies' New York Club" by Julia Hayes Percy

1892

Jul.: "Sturgeon Fishing in the James" by Charles Washington Coleman
Sep.: "Alligator Hunting with Seminoles" by Kirk Munroe
*Dec.: "A Day with Chivalry" by John B. Osborne. Fenn's original drawing for "A Passage at
    Arms," p. 191, is in the collection of the New York Public Library.

1894

May: "The Silver King at Home" by John Lawrence Wood

1895

Jun.: "The Chautauqua Movement" by H. H. Boyesen

Harper's Bazaar

Feb. 5, 1898: "Spring Days at Atlantic City, New Jersey's Famous All-Year-Round Watering
     Place," with M. Trautschold
Jul. 22, 1899: "The Chicago Women's Athletic Club"

Harper's New Monthly Magazine

1890

Mar.: "John Ruskin: An Essay" by Anne Thackeray Ritchie
Oct.: "Nights at Newstead Abbey" by Joaquin Miller

1891

May: "The Republic of Uruguay" by Theodore Child
Sep.: "London—Plantagenet, II. Princes and Merchants" by Walter Besant

1892

Jan. "London of Charles the Second" by Walter Besant

1895

Mar.: "The Industrial Region of Northern Alabama, Tennessee, and Georgia" by Julian Ralph

1897

May: "Cross-Country Riding" by Casper Whitney

1898

Aug.: "The Convict System in Siberia" by Stephen Bonsal
Sep.: "The Romance of a Mad King" by A. MacKay-Smith
Nov.: "Our Seaboard Islands on the Pacific" by John B. Bennett

1899

Jan.: "The Sultan at Home" by Sidney Whitman
Apr., Jun., Jul.: "The Spanish-American War" by Henry Cabot Lodge.
     Fenn illus. in pts. 3, 5, 6.
*Sep.–Dec.: "The First American [George Washington]: His Homes and Households" by Leila
     Herbert. Fenn's original drawing for "Glassware Used . . ." is in the collection of the San
     Diego Museum of Art, gift of Walter J. Fenn.
Oct.: "The Ascent of Illimani" by Sir Martin Conway
Nov.: "Boston at Century's End" by Sylvester Baxter

1900

Jan.: "The Right Hand of the Continent [California]" by Charles F. Lummis
Feb.: "The Congo States and Central-African Problems" by Demetrius C. Boulger
Mar.: "Germany's First Colony in China [Kiao-chau]" by Poultney Bigelow; "Pretoria Before the
     War" by Howard C. Hillegas
Jul.: "To-day's Science in Europe. II. Professor Ernst Haeckel and the New Zoology" by Henry
     Smith Williams

1901

Jan., Feb., Apr., May, Oct.: "Colonies and Nation. A Short History of the People of the United
     States" by Woodrow Wilson. Fenn illus. in pts. 1, 2, 4, 5, 10.
Jun.: "An Idyl of the Sands" by A. C. Wheeler

1902

Dec.: "The Aztecs of Yesterday and To-day" by Dr. Ales Hrdlicka

1903
Jun.: "The Royal Mother of Ants" by Henry C. McCook

1904
Feb.: "Tailoring Animals" by Henry C. McCook
Mar.: "Crossing a South American Desert" by Charles Johnson Post; "Insect Commonwealth" by
     Henry C. McCook
May: "Aeronautic Spiders" by Henry C. McCook
Jun.: "The Strange Cycle of the Cicada" by Henry C. McCook
Sep.: "The Daintiness of Ants" by Henry C. McCook

1905
May: "Huntress Wasps" by Henry C. McCook
Jul.: "Agricultural Ants" by Henry C. McCook
Nov.: "Insect Herds and Herders" by Henry C. McCook

1906
Jan.: "The Net-Making Caddis-Worm" by Henry C. McCook
Jun.: "Honey-Ants of the Garden of the Gods" by Henry C. McCook
Sep.: "Hunting Wild Bees" by Henry C. McCook

1907
Feb.: "The Story of a Spider" by Henry C. McCook
Sep.: "The Language of Insects" by Henry C. McCook

1908
Apr.–Sep.: "The Story of a Street [Wall Street]" by Frederick Trevor Hill

Harper's Weekly

1890
Mar. 8: "Rimini"
May 24: "The City of Minneapolis"
Aug. 2: "Recent Architecture in New Jersey"

1892
Jun. 11: "Pike's Peak from Colorado Springs"
Aug. 27: "Southampton, L.I." The composite of scenes includes "An Old Southampton landmark
     till 1890," a windmill very like the one in *Picturesque America;* a second drawing shows it
     altered as a dwelling, with the caption: "Its present desecration on Shinnecock hills."

1893
Jan. 14: "Iron in Decorative Design"

1894
*Nov. 24: front page, "The Old Homestead Well." Fenn's original drawing for this illustration is
     in the collection of the Library of Congress Cabinet of American Illustration.

1896
Apr. 11: "Logging-Railroad Ravages around the Head-waters of the Mississippi—Loading a
     Train on One of the Spurs"; "The Happy Hunting-Grounds of the Utes"
Sept. 5: "Sutter's Fort Reconstructed"
Oct. 17: "The Massachusetts General Hospital in Boston"
Nov. 21: "The New Aquarium in Historic Castle Garden, New York. The Tanks and Some of their
     Contents"

Dec. 12: "President Cleveland's Future Home at Princeton, New Jersey"

1897

Jan. 2: "The Grounds and Buildings of the Tennessee Centennial Exposition at Nashville"
Feb. 6: "Buildings of the Tennessee Centennial Exposition at Nashville, to Be Opened May 1"
Mar. 13: "The Evolution of the National Capitol." The image of the capitol at the bottom of the
        page was used for the Official 2005 United States Congressional Holiday Ornament.
Apr. 10: "East and North Facades of the New Brooklyn Institute of Arts and Sciences—McKim,
        Mead, & White, Architects"
Dec. 11: "[The New York Public] Library as It Will Appear When Completed"

1899

Sep. 23: "The United States National Pavilion at the Paris Exposition of 1900"
Oct. 7: "The New Buildings of the University of California as They Will Appear When
        Completed"
Oct. 28: "The Dewey Memorial Hall, Norwich University"

1900

Mar. 24: "The United States Publishers' Building at the Paris Exposition"
Dec. 15: "The Capitol in 1806"

1901

May 4: "Compostella Barracks, Havana, in 1898"

1906

Dec. 15: "May your shadow never grow less," p. 1813, drawing for the seventieth birthday of
        Henry Mills Alden, longtime editor of *Harper's Monthly*. A photo of Fenn at the dinner at
        Harper & Brothers on Nov. 10, 1906, appears on p. 1839.

Harper's Young People

Jan. 30, 1894: *The Round Table,* supplement to *Harper's Young People:* "Sleepy Hollow, Rip's Rock
        and His Staircase"
Mar. 10, 1896: *The Round Table:* "London Tower from the River"

The Ladies' Home Journal

1891

Mar.: "The Princess of Wales at Home," with sketches by Harry Fenn and F. S. Guild
Sep.: "The Valley of the Bow; Looking from the Hotel" in "An Unconventional Holiday" by Lady
        Macdonald (cont. from Aug. issue)

McClure's Magazine

1900

Apr.: "A Tale of a Tub" by Tighe Hopkins

1901

Nov.: "The Romance of Christmas Island" by Flyi Smithbon
Dec. "Lost in the Land of the Midnight Sun" by Augustus Bridle and J. K. Macdonald

1903

July: "The Story of the Snake" by A. W. Rolker
Oct.: "Reclaiming an Ocean Bed: How the Dutch Propose to Drain the Zuyder Zee . . ." by Walter
        Wellman

1906
May: "Reminiscences of a Long Life—Carl Schurz. Part VII. Flight from the Fatherland"

1907
Dec.: "Recollections of Henry Irving" by Ellen Terry

1908
May: "'Olivia' and 'Faust' at the Lyceum" by Ellen Terry

1909
Dec.: "The Secrets of Schluesselburg" by David Soskice

Scribner's Magazine

1890
Jan.: "Water-Storage in the West" by Walter Gillette Bates
Feb.: "Through Three Civilizations" by W. H. Mallock
Apr.: "Tadmor in the Wilderness" by Frederick Jones Bliss
May: "Barbizon and Jean-François Millet" by T. H. Bartlett; "Cooperative Home-Winning" by W. A. Linn; Fenn credited in contents, but illus. unsigned.
Jun.: "Barbizon and Jean-François Millet" by T. H. Bartlett

1891
Apr.: "Ocean Passenger Travel" by John H. Gould
Sep.: "The City of the Sacred Bo-Tree. (Anuradhapura.)" by James Ricalton

1892
May: "Sea and Land" by N. S. Shaler

1893
Feb.: "From Venice to the Gross-Venediger" by Henry van Dyke
May: "The Restoration House" by Stephen T. Aveling

1895
Oct.: "A History of the Last Quarter-Century in the United States. Home Agitations and Foreign Problems" by E. Benjamin Andrew

1898
Feb.: "The Naval Campaign of 1776 on Lake Champlain" by A. T. Mahan

St. Nicholas

1891
Jun.: "A Talk about Wild Flowers" by John Burroughs
Oct.: "Three Trees," poem by Charles H. Crandall

1892
May: "My Troubadour," poem by Charles H. Crandall
*Jul.: "The Scarlet Thorn" by John Burroughs. Fenn's original drawing for the title page is in the collection of the Cooper-Hewitt, National Design Museum.
Dec.: "A Hanging Garden," poem by Edith M. Thomas; "Mark Twain's Big Namesake" by Frank M. Chapman

1893
Jan.: "Boston" by Thomas Wentworth Higginson
Feb.: "The Boyhood of Louis XIV" by Adela E. Orpen
Apr.: "New York" by Edmund Clarence Stedman

Jun.: "City of Groves and Bowers [Washington]" by Frances Hodgson Burnett
Jul.: "Festival Days at Girls' Colleges" by Grace W. Soper; "Chicago" by John F. Ballantyne
*Aug.: "Baltimore" by D. C. Gilman. The original for "Entrance to Druid Hill Park," p. 730, is in
      a private collection.
Oct.: lead article, "The Story of a Grain of Wheat" by W. S. Harwood
Nov.: "New Orleans" by George W. Cable

1894
May: "Some Ancient Musical Instruments" by H. S. Conant
Aug.: "American Bicycles at Mont St. Michel" by Elizabeth Robins Pennell

1896
May: "The Red Bird's Matins," poem by H. G. Bennett; "A Stroll in the Garden of England" by
      John M. Ellicott
Oct.: "The Fire on the Water" by Charles G. D. Roberts; "A Vegetable Ogre" by Eustace B.
      Rogers
Nov.: "How Plants Spread" by Thomas H. Kearney; "The Plimsoll Mark" by J. M. Ellicott
Dec.: "Christmas in Bethlehem" by Edwin S. Wallace

1897
Jan.: "Mirrors of Air" by Tudor Jenks
Feb.: "The Birthplace of President Lincoln" by George H. Yenowine
Mar.: "Animal Tracks in the Snow" by Barney Hoskin
Sep.: "The Street Dogs of Constantinople" by Oswald Garrison Villard
Nov.: "Plants and Their Enemies," by Thomas H. Kearney Jr.

1898
Jan.: "Reasoning out a Metropolis [New York]" by Ernest Ingersoll
Feb.: "Queer American Rivers" by P. H. Spearman
Mar.: "The Great Lakes" by W. S. Harwood; "A Giant Candle" by W. S. Harwood, about the
      Stockholm Exposition, 1897
Apr.: "The Bell-Towers of Italy" by John Ward
May: "A May Colloquy" poem by Mary A. Gillette
Aug.: "The Viking Ship" by Edwin W. Foster; "The Cradle of Cyclones" by J. M. Ellicott

1899
Mar.: "The Wheat That Drowned the City" by E. W. C.
Dec.: "Afternoon Service" by Ian MacLaren

1902
Jun.: "The Castle Garden Aquarium" by Charles L. Bristol
Dec.: "How Uncle Sam Observes Christmas" by Clifford Howard

1903
Mar.: "The City That Lives Outdoors [New Orleans]" by W. S. Harwood

1907
Jul.: "A Message by Fire" by Cullen Bryant Snell
Aug.: "The Spell of the Sea" by Georgiana Homer
Sep.: "An Alpine Adventure" by Grace Wickham Curran

1910
Dec.: "Laddie" by T.H.R.S., illustrated by W. Benda and Harry Fenn.

Harry Fenn's Works Included in Exhibitions

Note: Titles of works are taken from exhibition catalogues; sale price and owner's name, as provided, follow title.

FENN'S LISTINGS IN AMERICAN WATERCOLOR SOCIETY EXHIBITION CATALOGUES, 1867–1910

1867–68: FIRST ANNUAL, WITH THE WINTER EXHIBITION OF THE NATIONAL ACADEMY OF DESIGN
Fenn's address: Montclair, N.J. [hereinafter Fenn's address is given when it indicates a change from Montclair]
378. *Toilers of the Sea,* For Sale
545. *Sketch Near Genoa,* J. T. Fields
546. *Church Porch, Levington, England,* J. T. Fields
590. *Pietra Santa Lucca,* For Sale

1868–69: SECOND ANNUAL, WITH THE WINTER EXHIBITION OF THE NATIONAL ACADEMY OF DESIGN
240, 241, 244, *Proofs of Engravings on Wood—Illus. for Rev. Henry Ward Beecher's* Life of Christ. *Designed by A. L. Rawson; Drawn on Wood by H. Fenn; Engraved by W. J. & H. D. Linton*
490. *A Tomb on the Appian Way, Roman Campagna,* For Sale
543. *Study of Boats, Porto Venice [Venere?], Gulf of Shezzia [Spezia?],* Samuel Wilde
570. *A Winter Study, Montclair, N.J.,* For Sale
594. *A Twilight Study, Near Portland, Me.,* For Sale
616. *By the Well,* For Sale

1869–70: THIRD ANNUAL
353. *A Study Near Florence,* Mrs. Geo. E. Hawes
360. *Study of Wild Pigeons,* For Sale
395. *Roman Grist-Mill on the Tiber,* For Sale

1870–71: FOURTH ANNUAL
472. *The Convent Gate, St. Augustine, Fla.,* The Artist
474. *Home of Howard Payne, author of "Home Sweet Home," East Hampton, L.I.,* The Artist
509. *Sketch on the Ocklawaha River, Fla.,* The Artist
528. *A Winter Study, Montclair, N.J.,* The Artist
529. *Coquina Quarry, Anastasia Island, St. Augustine, Fla.,* The Artist

1872: FIFTH ANNUAL [JANUARY 28, 1872]
309. *Sketch,* For Sale
313. *The Mouth of the St. John's River, Fla.,* For Sale
361. *Study from the Sister Islands, Niagara,* For Sale

1873: SIXTH ANNUAL [MARCH 5, 1873], AND THE ENGLISH COLLECTION OF WATER COLORS & SKETCHES
103. *The Ghetto, Rome,* For Sale
308. *Entrance to Watkins Glen,* Dr. J. W. Pinkham [of Montclair, N.J.]
330. *Cavern Cascade, Watkin's Glen,* Dr. J.W.Pinkham
339. *Goat Island, Niagara*

1874: SEVENTH ANNUAL
Fenn's address: Margate, England
157. *Blue Beads and her Court,* Mrs. W. M. Thompson [Fenn's mother-in-law?]

1875: EIGHTH ANNUAL
Fenn listed as "now in England" [Did not exhibit.]

1876: AT THE CENTENNIAL EXHIBITION: EXHIBITED UNDER HEADING: "AMERICAN SOCIETY OF PAINTERS IN WATER COLORS, OF NEW YORK"
274. *Old Convent Gate, St. Augustine,* Joseph Wilde
329. *Old Fireplace of the Author of "Home, Sweet Home,"* Samuel Wilde
364. *Toilers of the Sea,* Horace Waters
374. *Study of Boats,* Samuel Wilde

1876, 1877: NINTH AND TENTH ANNUALS
[Fenn, still in England, did not exhibit.]

1878: ELEVENTH ANNUAL
Fenn's address: "Egypt"
63. *The Lower Soko, Tangiers, Morocco,* $200 [illustrated in the catalog as *The Soko, Tangiers;* size given as 12 x 18]

288. *Carigan Head, Donegal, Ireland*, $150

1879, 1880, 1881: TWELFTH, THIRTEENTH, AND
FOURTEENTH ANNUALS
[Fenn, still in England, did not exhibit.]

1882: FIFTEENTH ANNUAL
Fenn's address: 7 West 14th St., New York
203. *A Day School in the Shoemaker's Bazaar,
Damascus*, $200
213. *A Bit in North Wales*, T. F. Tompson
[Fenn's brother-in-law?]
216. *The Rialto Market, Venice*, $100
295. *The Market Place, Segovia, Spain*, $80
322. *The Gate of Pardon, Seville Cathedral*, $175
[illustrated; size given as 11 3/4 x 18]
566. *In an English Garden*, $75
[illustrated; size given as 9 1/4 x 14]

1883: SIXTEENTH ANNUAL
Fenn's address: 16 W. 23rd St., New York
*[Fenn listed as a member of the Board of Control
and Jury of Admission, with F. S. Church, Geo. H.
Smillie, Thos. Moran; and on catalogue committee,
with F. S. Church, Walter Shirlaw, and Henry Farrer]*
29. *A Touch of the Gout*, $50
33. *Marshall's Creek, Pa.*, $350
[illustrated; size given as 20 x 29]
117. *The Star Inn, Yarmouth*, $100
128. *A Surrey Cottage*, $100
366. *A Connemara Cabin*, $250
398. *To fetch a Pail of Water*, $125
476. *The Orchard Lane*, $175

1884: SEVENTEENTH ANNUAL
26. *An Autumn Sketch*, $60
203. *The Landing*, $50
304. *A Pennsylvania Bee Colony*, $125
[illustrated; size given as 19 x 10]

1885: EIGHTEENTH ANNUAL
*Fenn's address: 141 St. Mark's Avenue,
Brooklyn, L.I.*
78. *Rye and Sorrel*, $150
[illustrated; size given as 12 x 18]
211. *Ronda*, $150
282. *Gardiner's Island*, $100
410. *The Lone Hand*, $125

1886: NINETEENTH ANNUAL
[Fenn not listed.]

1887: TWENTIETH ANNUAL
Fenn's address: Montclair, N.J.
227. *A Corner of the Studio*, $125
355. *The Green Mosque from the Bazaar
of Meidân, Damascus*, $300
[illustrated; size given as 24 x 29]

1888: TWENTY-FIRST ANNUAL
199. *The Washing Ground of Madrid*
282. *Study of Weeds*, $60
349. *A Doorway in Granada*, $200
[illustrated; size given as 21 x 16]
474. *A Sketch at Montclair*, $75

1889: TWENTY-SECOND ANNUAL
[Fenn on catalogue committee]
54. *The Rialto Market*, $175
[illustrated; size given as 16 x 20]
183. *Low Tide*, $30
233. *Lobster Cove*, $60
399. *A York Harbor Marsh*, $75

1890: TWENTY-THIRD ANNUAL
142. *My Grandmother's Garden*, $150
[illustrated; size given as 21 x 14]
234. *A Bee Village*, $100

1891: TWENTY-FOURTH ANNUAL
651. *The Dome of the Rock, The Mosque of Omar,
Jerusalem*, $250

1892: TWENTY-FIFTH ANNUAL
341. *Marshfield, Mass.*, $85
450. *An Old Colony Road*, $100
526. *Mouth of the Cub River, Green Harbor, Mass.*,
$100
570. *Brant Rock, Mass.*, $75
613. *Green Harbor, Mass.*, $80
663. *Among the Sand Dunes at Brant Rock, Mass.*, $80

1893: TWENTY-SIXTH ANNUAL
*[Fenn listed as a member of the committee on
decorations]*
410. *A Street in Cairo*, $150

1894: TWENTY-SEVENTH ANNUAL
315. *The Banks of Memphremagog*, $100
388. *A Block Island Road*, $75
458. *Street Vendors in Cairo*, $200

1895: TWENTY-EIGHTH ANNUAL
15. *A November Day, Montclair, N.J.*, $75
22. *An Autumn Study*, $50
139. *A Block Island Pastoral*, $100
228. *A Japanese Garden on Lake Memphremagog*, $80

1896: TWENTY-NINTH ANNUAL
180. *A White Day on a Maine Island*, $100
259. *A Surrey Kitchen*, $75

1897: THIRTIETH ANNUAL
*[No prices given from Thirtieth through
Thirty-eighth Annual]*
15. *Bâb Tûma, Damascus*
85. *In the Carpet Bazaar, Damascus*
[illustrated; no size given]
325. *A Court of the Alhambra*

1898: THIRTY-FIRST ANNUAL
69. *A Street Café, Jerusalem*
125. *A Chapter of the Koran*
318. *A Good Story* [illustrated; no size given]

1899: THIRTY-SECOND ANNUAL
185. *An Hour Before the Bull Fight—Seville*
282. *The Golden Pulpits of Milan*

1900: THIRTY-THIRD ANNUAL [HELD AT THE
GALLERIES OF THE WALDORF ASTORIA]
149. *Puetra del Patro Machuca, Alhambra*

1901: THIRTY-FOURTH ANNUAL
180. *The Passamaquoddy Fleet*
219. *St. Gregorio, Valladolid* [illustrated; no size
given]

1902: THIRTY-FIFTH ANNUAL
130. *When the Moors Were in Spain*
131. *A Surrey Cottage*
132. *The Mosque of Tezzir Pasha Akka*

1903: THIRTY-SIXTH ANNUAL
Fenn's address: Salmagundi Club, 14 W. Twelfth St.
92. *May Day in Surrey Hills*

1904: THIRTY-SEVENTH ANNUAL
Fenn's address: 104 W. Forty-ninth Street
91. *Mill Street, Warwick*
90. *A Surrey Garden* [illustrated; no size given]
92. *Ismailia, Egypt*

1905: THIRTY-EIGHTH ANNUAL [HELD AT THE
NATIONAL ARTS CLUB, WHERE SPACE WAS LIMITED;
ONLY 69 WORKS SHOWN]
Fenn's address: 684 St. Nicholas Ave.
20. *The Coast of Antrim, Ireland*
21. *The Silversmith's Bazaar, Damascus*

1906: THIRTY-NINTH ANNUAL
Fenn's address: 284 Park Street, Upper Montclair, N.J.
482. *The Street of Arms, Cairo,* $60
544. *The Oaks of Pelham Bay,* $125

1907: FORTIETH ANNUAL
64. *Market Place, Vittoria,* $150

1908: FORTY-FIRST ANNUAL
456. *After Herring, West Coast of Scotland,* $125
565. *Cottage at Warwick,* $75

1909: FORTY-SECOND ANNUAL
498. *On Eastern Point, Gloucester,* $75
553. *Bab-Juma [sic], A Gate in the Walls of
Damascus,* $175

1910: FORTY-THIRD ANNUAL
74. *Low Tide, Gloucester,* $100
454. *The Mills of Ronda,* $200

1911: FORTY-FOURTH ANNUAL [APRIL 27–MAY 21]
Fenn listed under "Deceased Members"

LISTINGS IN OTHER EXHIBITIONS
(By date of first participation)

NATIONAL ACADEMY OF DESIGN
1864
320. *The Old Basello Florence,* For sale
344. *The Temple of Saturn,* For sale

BROOKLYN ART ASSOCIATION
From Clark S. Marlor, *A History of the Brooklyn
Art Association with an Index of Exhibitions* (New
York: James F. Carr, 1970)

1864 (DECEMBER)
8. *Castle of Chillon,* owner H. Chapman
9. *Carpara Mountains from Via Reggia,* owner
W. M. Thompson [Fenn's father-in-law?]
"Courtship of Miles Standish," by Longfellow
[illustration]

1869 (MARCH)
74. *Study of Boats, Porto Venere, Italy,* ao [artist
owned]
75. *Winter Study, Montclair, N.Y.,* ao
308. *Landscape*

1870 (MARCH)
5. *Study of Wild Pigeons,* fs [for sale]

1873 (MARCH)
150. *The Ghetto, Rome,* fs
151. *Goat Island, Niagara,* fs

1878 (APRIL)
433. *Carigan Head, Donegal, Ireland,* wc
[watercolor] $150
441. *Lower Loko, Tangiers,* wc $200

1882 (MARCH)
89. *The Market Place, Segovia Spain,* wc $80
90. *A Bit of North Wales,* wc $80
91. *A Day School in the Shoe[m]aker Bazaar,
Damascus,* wc $200

1883 (MARCH)
30. *To Fetch a Pail of Water,* wc $125
95. *Connemara Cabin,* wc $250
166. *A Touch of the Gout,* wc $50
197. *A Surrey Cottage,* wc $100

1884 (MARCH)
20. *Merry Day in the Sunny Hills,* wc 4160
231. *An Autumn Sketch,* wc $234
234. *The Landing,* wc $50

1885 (APRIL)
170. *Rye and Sorrel,* wc $100
178. *The Lone Hand,* wc $100
198. *Gardiner's Island,* wc $100
322. *Renda,* wc $125

ARTISTS' FUND SOCIETY
From *The National Museum of American Art's
Index to American Art Exhibition Catalogues from
the Beginning through the 1876 Centennial Year,* vol.
2 (Boston: G. K. Hall, 1986), "Fenn, H.," "Fenn,
Harry," and "Fenn, Henry."

1866, NEW YORK
Chillon, T. F. Thompson [Mrs. Fenn's brother?]
The Bargello, Florence, H. T. Chapman
Margate, H. T. Chapman

1868, PHILADELPHIA
Church Porch, for sale
Near Genoa, for sale

THE BLACK AND WHITE EXHIBITIONS OF THE SALMAGUNDI SKETCH CLUB
From Alexander W. Katlan, *The Black and
White Exhibitions of the Salmagundi Club,
1878–1887* (Flushing, N.Y.: Alexander W. Katlan
Conservator, 2007)

1881 (DECEMBER 1–21, AT GALLERIES OF NATIONAL
ACADEMY OF DESIGN.)
393. *A Study of Gorse*
397. *Coiling Heather and Study of Dead Bracken*
487. *In an English Garden*

1882 (DECEMBER 1–21)
21. *Goldsmith's Deserted Village,* $50
212. *Looking South from Philae, Nile,* $40
463. *The Letter of Admission,* $40

1883 (DECEMBER 1–21)
82. *The Shepherd Lads, Jean Ingelow's "High Tide,"*
$40
83. *October,* $80
84. *The Ploughman,* $80

1884 (DECEMBER 11–23)
[*Harry Fenn on the Hanging Committee, with W. T.
Brundage and Joseph Hartley*]
79. *Old Church, Wilmington, Del.,* Century Co.

BOSTON ART CLUB
From *The Boston Art Club: Exhibition Record,
1878–1909* (Madison, Conn.: Sound View Press,
1991)

1882 (APRIL 28–MAY 27)
129: *An Irish Interior,* wc $200
159: *Market Place, Segovia, Spain,* wc $100
244: *Day School in the Shoemaker's Bazaar,
Damascus,* wc $200

1883
34. *A Touch of the Gout,* wc $40
116. *To fetch a pail of water,* wc $125

1884
62. *Market Scene, Tangiers,* wc $135

1887
39. *The Green Mosque, from the Bazaar of the
Meidan, Damascus,* wc $300, illus.

1888
81. *A Sketch at Montclair,* wc
91. *A Doorway in Granada,* wc
100. *The Washing Ground, Madrid,* wc

1889
114. *Lobster Cove,* wc
179. *Low Tide,* wc

1895
144 *A Japanese Garden on Memphremagog,* wc

1905
255. *A Bit of Color on the East Side,* wc

NEW YORK ETCHING CLUB
From *Index of American Print Exhibitions, 1882–
1940* (Metuchen, N.J.: Scarecrow Press, 1985)

1889 (MARCH 20)
Old Ship Yard, Kennebunkport, Me.
Lobster Cove

THE SALMAGUNDI CLUB PAINTING EXHIBITIONS
From Alexander W. Katlan, *The Salmagundi
Club Painting Exhibitions Records, 1889 to 1939*
(Flushing, N.Y.: Alexander Katlan Conservator,
2008)

1889
49. *The Manasquam River,* $100

1900
20. *Red Oaks, Montclair,* $100
80. *The Seville Bull Ring,* $250

1902

24. *Passamaquody Fleet*, $85

1904

29. *Ursaline convent, New Orleans*

1905

36. *The Rector's Garden, Surry*

1909

29. *After the Rain, Marshfield, Mass.*

ART INSTITUTE OF CHICAGO —
WATERCOLOR EXHIBITIONS

From *The Annual Exhibition Record of the Art Institute of Chicago, 1888–1950,* ed. Peter Hastings Falk (Madison, Conn.: Sound View Press, 1990)

1889

57. *A Still Life Study*, $150

1891

75. *The Dome of the Rock, the Mosque of Omar, Jerusalem,* $200

1892

55. *An Old Colony Road,* $100
56. *Green Harbor, Massachusetts,* $80
57. *Brant Rock, Massachusetts,* $75

1894

78. *A Block Island Road,* $80
79. *The Banks of Memphremagog,* $100

1895

122. *An Autumn Evening on Memphremagog*
123. *Joppa, near Newburyport, Mass.*

1896

139. *A White Day on a Maine Island*
140. *A Silvery Day on the Maine Coast*

1897

147. *A Corner of the Studio*

1898

123. *A Chapter of the Koran*

1899

128. *An Hour Before the Bull Fight, Seville*

1902

163. *St. Gregoria, Vallodolid*

1907

334. *The Street of Arms*
335. *Pigeon Cave*

1908

355. *Market Place, Vittoria*

1910

344. *On Eastern Point, Gloucester*
345. *Bab-Tuma*

1911

391. *Low Tide, Gloucester*

EXHIBITION OF THE SOCIETY OF AMERICAN WOOD ENGRAVERS AT THE MUSEUM OF FINE ARTS, BOSTON

1890 (OCTOBER 2–NOVEMBER 30)
Engraved by H. E. Sylvester:
381. *View,* after Harry Fenn
383. *Interior of the People's Palace, London,* after Harry Fenn
387. *Façade of St. Finbarr's Cork,* after Harry Fenn
Engraved by W. J. Linton:
564. *A Street in Jerusalem,* after Harry Fenn

NEW YORK WATER COLOR CLUB

From catalogues of their exhibitions on microfilm from Archives of American Art, roll N 447

1891, SECOND ANNUAL
110. *Duxbury Meadows*
111. *Joppa, Newburyport, Mass.*
112. *On the Merrimac*

1892, THIRD ANNUAL
322. *York Harbor, Maine,* $150

1893, FOURTH ANNUAL
25. *A Block Island Pond,* $100
146. *In the Sand Dunes of Newburyport,* $75

1895, SIXTH ANNUAL
118. *A Silvery Morning on the Coast of Maine,* $150

1896, SEVENTH ANNUAL
253. *A Corner of the Studio*

1897, EIGHTH ANNUAL
116. *Red Oaks, Montclair,* $75

1906, SEVENTEENTH ANNUAL
307. *Pigeon Cove,* $100

1909, TWENTIETH ANNUAL
278. *East Gloucester*

PENNSYLVANIA ACADEMY OF
THE FINE ARTS

From *The Annual Exhibition Record of the Pennsylvania Academy of the Fine Arts, 1876–1913,* ed. Peter Hastings Falk (Madison, Conn.: Sound View Press, 1988)

1893

26. *Sepulchres of Ferdinand & Isabella, Granada* (black & white)
84. *Kiga* (black & white)
119. *Escutcheon and Fireplace in the Manor-house* (black & white)

139. *Tower of Trinity Church, Boston* (black & white)
145. *General View of Castillo de la Mota* (black & white)
151. *On the Common: Gardiner's Island* (black & white)
153. *First Glimpse of the Kusneh: Petra* (black & white)

1895
453. *Silvery Morning: Coast of Maine* (water color)

1896–97
452. *A Corner of the Studio* (water color)

1898
557. *Red Oaks* (water color)

MONTCLAIR ART CLUB
1894 (MARCH 8)
[Exhibition includes Fenn.]

1899 (NOVEMBER)
[Exhibition includes Fenn and daughter Lillian Fenn.]

MACBETH GALLERIES
1894 (MARCH)
[Exhibition includes Fenn.]

T-SQUARE CLUB OF PHILADELPHIA
From *Catalogue of the Annual Architectural Exhibition, 1899–1900* (viewed on Internet Archive)

1899–1900
The Century Co.:
Harry Fenn
 63. *A Berkshire Interior*
 64. *The Hall, People's Palace, London*
 65. *View of Carpaneto, Birthplace of Leo XIII*
 66. *Interior of Alma Tadema's Studio*

LOUISIANA PURCHASE EXPOSITION, ST. LOUIS
1904
889. *Gateway of San Gregorio, Vallalolid*

TOLEDO MUSEUM OF ART
1908, EXHIBITION OF WATERCOLORS BY ONE HUNDRED AMERICAN ARTISTS
 49. *Market Place, Vittoria*

1909, AMERICAN WATERCOLORS, THE PRIVATE COLLECTION OF MR. G. H. BUEK, OF BROOKLYN
 51. *In Constantinople*

1909, FIFTH ANNUAL EXHIBITION OF WATER COLORS BY AMERICAN ARTISTS
 50. *On Eastern Point, Gloucester*
 51. *Bab-Tuma*

1910, ANNUAL EXHIBITION OF AMERICAN WATER COLOR SOCIETY
 35. *Low Tide, Gloucester*

THE BUFFALO FINE ARTS ACADEMY, ALBRIGHT ART GALLERY
1909 (SEPTEMBER 10–OCTOBER 10), FIFTH ANNUAL EXHIBITION OF SELECTED WATER COLORS BY AMERICAN ARTISTS
 54: *On Eastern Point, Gloucester*
 55. *Bab-Tuma*

DETROIT MUSEUM OF ART
1911 (MARCH 6–26), SIXTH ANNUAL EXHIBITION OF SELECTED WATERCOLORS BY AMERICAN ARTISTS
 35. *Low Tide, Gloucester*

<h1 style="font-family: cursive; font-style: italic;">Notes</h1>

1. EARLY LIFE IN ENGLAND AND NEW YORK

1. James Henry Moser, "Art Topics," *Washington Post,* June 30, 1901.
2. S. G. W. Benjamin, *Art in America: A Critical and Historical Sketch* (New York: Harper & Brothers, 1880), 172.
3. Lowell to J. T. Fields, 1868, quoted in *Letters of James Russell Lowell,* ed. Charles Eliot Norton (New York: Harper & Brothers, 1894), 1:398.
4. Amy Kaplan, *The Social Construction of American Realism* (Chicago: University of Chicago Press, 1988), quoted in Sarah Burns, *Inventing the Modern Artist: Art and Culture in Gilded Age America* (New Haven: Yale University Press, 1996), 13.
5. Lyman Abbott, "The Cradle of Christianity," *Christian Union,* January 19, 1882.
6. F. Hopkinson Smith, *American Illustrators* (New York: Charles Scribner's Sons, 1892), 62.
7. C. M. Fairbanks, "Illustration and Our Illustrators," *Chautauquan: A Weekly Newsmagazine* 13, no. 5 (August 1891): 599. Fairbanks wrote, "In a recent lecture before the Art Students' League in New York upon the subject of illustration, Mr. W. Lewis Frazer [*sic*] [of the *Century*] said that there were practically but three profitable fields of work open to the younger American artists of to-day—portraiture, illustration, and teaching—and of these he thought there was no doubt that illustration presented the most promising field. For in two years past, he said, the American publishers had paid twice as much for illustration as had been paid for paintings in all the American art galleries. Mr. Frazer is in a situation to know what he is talking about."
8. See Michele H. Bogart, *Artists, Advertising, and the Borders of Art* (Chicago: University of Chicago Press, 1995), chap. 1.
9. The New-York Historical Society owns *Storm King & Crow's Nest, New York,* probably from ca. 1870. At least two other oils are in private collections.
10. Catalogues of exhibitions including works by Fenn include *The American Personality: The Artist-Illustrator in the Life of the United States, 1860–1930* (Los Angeles: Grunwald Center for the Graphic Arts, University of California at Los Angeles, 1976); *Battles and Leaders of the Civil War: Drawings from the American Heritage Century Collection* (New York: National Academy of Design, 1982); *American Watercolors from the Metropolitan Museum of Art* (New York: American Federation of Arts in association with Harry N. Abrams, 1991); and *Lines of Thought: American Works on Paper from a Private Collection* (Old Lyme, Conn.: Florence Griswold Museum, 1996).
11. My 1994 study of Fenn's role, as well as that of the other contributing artists and writers, in the production of *Picturesque America* filled in a portion of his story, as did my 2005 article on *Picturesque Palestine, Sinai and Egypt;* see *Creating "Picturesque America": Monument to the Natural and Cultural Landscape* (Nashville, Tenn.: Vanderbilt University Press, 1994); and "Illustration 'Urgently Required': The *Picturesque Palestine* Project, 1878–83," *Prospects* 30 (2005): 181–260. See also Sue Rainey, "Images of the South in *Picturesque America* and *The Great South,*" in *Graphic Arts & the South: Proceedings of the 1990 North American Print Conference,* ed. Judy L. Larson

(Fayetteville: University of Arkansas Press, 1993), 185–215; and Sue Rainey, "Harry Fenn," in *Dictionary of Literary Biography,* vol. 188: *American Book and Magazine Illustrators to 1920,* ed. Steven E. Smith, Catherine A. Hastedt, and Donald H. Dyal (Detroit: Gale, 1998), 95–104.

12. The Historical and Archaeological Section of the Richmond Society, introduction to *Richmond, Surrey, As It Was* (Hendon Mill, Nelson, Eng.: Hendon Publishing, 1976), 2. Fenn's birth date is often given as 1845; however, the baptismal records of the Parish of Richmond, County of Surrey, record that Henry, son of James and Eliza Fenn, was born September 14, 1837, and baptized October 15, 1837.

13. According to the artist's son Walter J. Fenn, his brother James became a merchant in Richmond; Walter J. Fenn, "Biographical Sketch of the Life of Harry Fenn," manuscript, Fenn family papers, 7.

14. An account of Fenn's life in the family's records, likely written by his daughter (it is typed on stationery marked "Hilda Fenn van Antwerp, Interior Decorator"), states that he "was educated in the school of his native town" and received "the conventional instruction" in art "from a local teacher." The brief biography of Fenn in *The M. & M. Karolik Collection of American Water Color Drawings: 1800–1875* (Boston: Museum of Fine Arts, 1962) states that he was "educated at Isleworth and Richmond, England" (1:156).

15. Sketchbook is owned by the family.

16. The original wash drawing for this article is in the collection of the Montclair Art Museum, in New Jersey.

17. The first volume of Ruskin's *Modern Painters* was published in 1843.

18. Harry Fenn, "The Boy and the Bishop," *St. Nicholas,* June 1910, 705–6.

19. For more on this period, see Liza Picard, *Victorian London: The Life of a City, 1840–1870* (New York: St. Martin's Press, 2005), chaps. 17 and 18. According to Picard, "1849 marked the beginning of an economic boom" (214).

20. See Marjorie B. Cohn, *Wash and Gouache: A Study of the Development of the Materials of Watercolor* (Cambridge, Mass.: Center for Conservation and Technical Studies, Fogg Art Museum, and the Foundation of the American Institute for Conservation, 1977), esp. 11–13, 16–18, 50–51.

21. The weekly *Penny Magazine,* published by Charles Knight beginning in 1832, gained a wide circulation and was followed by the *London Journal, Reynolds's Miscellany,* and *Cassell's Illustrated Family Paper;* see Patricia Anderson, *The Printed Image and the Transformation of Popular Culture, 1790–1860* (Oxford: Clarendon Press, 1991), chaps. 2 and 3.

22. Quoted in Eric de Maré, *The Victorian Woodblock Illustrators* (New York: Sandstone Press, 1981), 81. Before 1850, daily newspapers occasionally included pictures, but the time required to produce wood engravings made them impractical for use in creating accurate images of the latest news. See Joshua Brown, *Beyond the Lines: Pictorial Reporting, Everyday Life, and the Crisis of Gilded Age America* (Berkeley: University of California Press, 2002), 11–18.

23. Gerry Beegan, *The Mass Image: A Social History of Photomechanical Reproduction in Victorian London* (Houndmills, Eng.: Palgrave Macmillan, 2008), 54.

24. Jenny Uglow, *Nature's Engraver: A Life of Thomas Bewick* (New York: Farrar, Straus and Giroux, 2006), is an excellent recent biography of Bewick.

25. For an assessment of Bewick's importance in the history of book illustration and art in general, see Charles Rosen and Henri Zerner, "The Romantic Vignette and Thomas Bewick," in *Romanticism and Realism: The Mythology of Nineteenth Century Art* (London: Faber and Faber, 1984), 73–96. The authors credit him with "the invention of the Romantic vignette": "Bewick discarded the clearly limited pictorial field with such natural ease that we are hardly conscious of his having done so. This was nevertheless a revolutionary change" (89).

26. Uglow, *Nature's Engraver,* 350.

27. See Percy Muir, *Victorian Illustrated Books* (New York: Praeger Publishers, 1971), 25.

28. Gerry Beegan, "The Mechanization of the Image: Facsimile, Photography, and Fragmentation in Nineteenth-Century Wood Engraving," *Journal of Design History* 8, no. 4 (1995): 260, 262. Beegan derived these numbers from the Dalziel Archive in the British Museum, which "contains the proofs of the firm's engravings pasted into record books in chronological order" (260).

29. See John Buchanan-Brown, *Early Victorian Illustrated Books: Britain, France, and Germany, 1820–1860* (London and New Castle, Del.: British Library and Oak Knoll Press, 2005), esp. 163–72.

30. For a comparison of several British artists' drawings with wood engravings, see David P. Becker, *Drawings for Book Illustration: The Hofer Collection* (Cambridge, Mass.: Houghton Library, Harvard University, 1980).

31. Electrotypes were made by galvanic action, direct-current electricity in a precipitating cell containing dilute sulfuric acid and copper plates. A beeswax mold of the type or woodcut was covered with a thin coat of graphite and placed in the cell, which was then connected with a galvanic battery. The electric current would slowly deposit a thin copper shell on the mold, which was later backed with type metal to make it extremely durable. See Michael Winship, "Printing with Plates in the Nineteenth-Century United States," *Printing History* 5, no. 2 (1983): 20–21. An earlier process, stereotyping, had adequately duplicated letterpress type but was less successful with wood engravings; see David Tatham, *Winslow Homer and the Illustrated Book* (Syracuse, N.Y.: Syracuse University Press, 1992), 6–7; and Geoffrey Wakeman, *Victorian Book Illustration* (Detroit, Mich.: Gale, 1973), 17–22, 74–75.

32. George Dalziel and Edward Dalziel, *The Brothers Dalziel: A Record of Work, 1840–1890* (1901; reprint, B. T. Batsford, London, 1978), 344.

33. Beegan, "Mechanization of the Image," 262–63. H. M. Cundall, in *Birket Foster, R.W.S.* (London: Adam and Charles Black, 1906), says that, soon after Foster was apprenticed to the wood engraver Ebenezer Landells, the latter discovered "that the boy's ability lay in drawing," but he "continued to do some wood-engraving, and many of his own small drawings were cut by himself" (19).

34. The Dalziels recalled that when the aspiring illustrator Fred Walker asked for advice on drawing on wood, they recommended he copy the works of Foster for landscapes and John Gilbert for figures and probably gave Fenn the same advice; Dalziel and Daziel, *The Brothers Dalziel,* 193.

35. Harry Fenn, "Methods of Illustration," *Palette and Bench,* August 1909, 245. (The article was continued in "Methods of Illustration—Concluded," in the September 1909 *Palette and Bench;* this periodical has been digitized by Google Books.)

36. The sheets were run through two presses, one printing the text and the other the intaglio plates. The books include Samuel Rogers, *Italy* (London: T. Cadell and E. Moxon, 1830), which has been digitized by Google Books; *The Poetical Works of John Milton* (London: John Macrone, 1835); and *The Poetical Works of Sir Walter Scott, Bart* (Edinburgh: R. Cadell, 1841).

37. See, for example, "The Thief and the Dog," 129; the book has been digitized by Google Books. Fenn may also have seen some of the works of French and German artists who prepared designs for wood engravings, such as Tony Johannot, Paul Gavarni, and J. J. Grandville, as well as Adolf Menzel, Otto Speckter, and Ludwig Richter; see Buchanan-Brown, *Early Victorian Illustrated Books,* esp. chaps. 1 and 2.

38. "Harry Fenn: Painter and Illustrator," *American Bookmaker: A Journal of Technical Art and Information* 9, no. 3 (September 1889): 51. This article appears to be based on an interview with Fenn and states: "Mr. Fenn learned the art of wood engraving in the school of the brothers Dalziel. In the meantime he painted and sold some water colors."

39. Dalziel and Dalziel, *The Brothers Dalziel,* 344.

40. "Harry Fenn: Painter and Illustrator," 51.

41. W. J. Fenn, "Biographical Sketch"; he also says the men sailed to New York City, but the Dalziels' account that they went to Canada may be accurate.

42. Thomas Bender, *New York Intellect: A History of the Intellectual Life in New York City, from 1750 to the Beginnings of Our Own Time* (New York: Alfred A. Knopf, 1987), 156. By 1860 printing and publishing vied with food production for second place; the largest industry was textiles and apparel; see Diane Lindstrom, "Economic Structure, Demographic Change, and Income Inequality in Antebellum New York," in John Hull Mollenkopf, *Power, Culture, and Place: Essays on New York City* (New York: Russell Sage Foundation, 1988), 9–10.

43. Brown, *Beyond the Lines,* 22–24.

44. Several monthly magazines published in Philadelphia in the 1840s (including *Godey's Lady's*

Book, Graham's Magazine, Union Magazine, and *Peterson's Magazine*) regularly featured one or two steel engravings or mezzotints of works by American artists; see Cynthia Lee Patterson, *Art for the Middle Classes: America's Illustrated Magazines of the 1840s* (Jackson: University Press of Mississippi, 2010).

45. Benson J. Lossing gives these numbers in *Memorial of Alexander Anderson, M.D.: The First Engraver on Wood in America* (New York: Printed for the subscribers of the New-York Historical Society, 1872); they were first reported in "Dr. Alexander Anderson," *Frank Leslie's Illustrated Newspaper,* November 12, 1870, 133.

46. The definitive work on Anderson is Jane R. Pomeroy, *Alexander Anderson (1775–1870): Wood Engraver and Illustrator; An Annotated Bibliography,* 3 vols. (New Castle, Del., and Worcester, Mass.: Oak Knoll Press and American Antiquarian Society, 2005).

47. Unidentified newspaper clipping, Orr Family Papers, Special and Area Studies Collections, George A. Smathers Libraries, University of Florida, box 4, folder 1.

48. "Introductory Address," *The Pictorial National Library* (1848), 1:15–16.

49. *Cosmopolitan Art Journal* 1 (January 1857): 3, quoted in Brown, *Beyond the Lines,* 7–8, and Frank Luther Mott, *A History of American Magazines, 1850–18* (Cambridge, Mass.: Harvard University Press, 1938), 192.

50. Brown, *Beyond the Lines,* 27. Those that failed included *Ballou's Pictorial Drawing-Room Companion,* the successor to *Gleason's Pictorial Drawing-Room Companion.*

51. See David Tatham, *Winslow Homer and the Pictorial Press* (Syracuse, N.Y.: Syracuse University Press, 2003), chap. 3, esp. 19–21, 28.

52. At first *Gleason's* could not find enough skilled wood engravers, but after Leslie and others joined the staff the quality of pictures improved and circulation increased; Brown, *Beyond the Lines,* 20–21. Brown also provides a detailed history of Leslie and his publications. Back in New York, Leslie was chief engraver for the short-lived *Illustrated News,* which began publication January 1, 1853, and lasted only 11 months. The publishers, P. T. Barnum and Henry D. and Alfred E. Beach, found it exhausting to try to get the news out, complete with illustrations, before the stories were out of date (21).

53. Brown, *Beyond the Lines,* 25–26.

54. Budd Leslie Gambee Jr., "*Frank Leslie's Illustrated Newspaper,* 1855–1860: Artistic and Technical Operations of a Pioneer Pictorial News Weekly in America" (Ph.D. diss., University of Michigan, 1963), 365. Gambee states that Fenn made engravings published in vols. 4, 5, and 6 of *Leslie's,* working either alone or with other engravers, including Speer (he does not give his first name).

55. Harry Fenn, "Methods of Illustration," 245.

56. See "How Illustrated Newspapers Are Made," *Frank Leslie's Illustrated Newspaper,* August 2, 1856. The maximum size of boxwood blocks was approximately 4 by 6 inches; Beegan, "Mechanization of the Image," 258.

57. Fenn, "Methods of Illustration—Concluded," 267.

58. Ibid, 267–68.

59. In his memoir *A World Worth While: A Record of "Auld Acquaintance"* (New York: Harper & Brothers, 1922), the younger illustrator W. A. Rogers (1854–1931) describes going through the "trying-out process" at *Harper's Weekly* and recalls art director Charles Parsons as a hard "taskmaster"; Rogers worked for an entire year "putting in backgrounds, laying out perspectives," with only the occasional chance to draw the main subject (14, 38).

60. Albert Johannsen, *The House of Beadle and Adams and Its Dime and Nickel Novels: The Story of a Vanished Literature* (Norman: University of Oklahoma Press, 1950), 8–9.

61. See Ellen M. Snyder-Grenier, *Brooklyn! An Illustrated History* (Philadelphia: Temple University Press, 1996), 6–7. Population figures are from the website of the U.S. Census Bureau: http://www.census.gov/population/www/documentation/twps0027/tab09.txt.

62. *The Brooklyn City Directory,* for the years ending May 1859, 1860, 1861, 1862, compiled by J. Lain (Brooklyn, N.Y.: J. Lain). Fenn does not appear in Brooklyn directories after May 1862.

His landlord and future father-in-law, William M. Tompson, an engraver on silver, listed his business address at this time as 169 William, a bit farther south in Lower Manhattan.

63. Worthington Whittredge, *The Autobiography of Worthington Whittredge, 1820–1910,* ed. by John I. H. Baur (Brooklyn: Brooklyn Museum Press, 1942), 43.

64. Clark S. Marlor, *A History of the Brooklyn Art Association with an Index of Exhibitions* (New York: James F. Carr, 1970), 5.

65. *Brooklyn Daily Eagle,* November 1, 1860, and November 1, 1861.

66. *Brooklyn Daily Eagle,* December 13, 1858, announced the opening of the Graham Art School and mentioned that Parsons, Herrick, Childs, and H. S. Beckwith were elected officers.

67. *Brooklyn Daily Eagle,* February 23, 1860. Herrick also reported there were 36 members, "of whom five were bank note engravers, five wood engravers, nine general designers, and six historical landscape painters, and the remainder were young men studying the art. . . . The expense of membership was merely nominal, the directors of the Institute providing room, fuel, &c."

68. [Sidney Brooks], "The Late Harry Fenn," [New York] *Evening Post,* May 11, 1911. The family attributed this obituary to Fenn's English son-in-law Sidney Brooks.

69. A wedding date of September 5, 1852, is given in the account of Fenn's life presumably written by his daughter Hilda Fenn van Antwerp (see n. 14), but the year is clearly inaccurate; neither does the September 5 date jibe with travel to England before the birth of a child on August 20, 1862. Perhaps they married in September of 1861.

70. The family name is sometimes spelled Thompson, but I have used the spelling that appears on family gravestones in Evergreens Cemetery, Brooklyn.

71. W. J. Fenn, "Biographical Sketch."

72. "Harry Fenn: Painter and Illustrator," 51.

73. *Illustrated London News,* March 29, 1862, 320. A digital image of this wood engraving can be viewed by searching for "Harry Fenn" on the New York Public Library's site, http://digitalgallery.nypl.org. Many other Fenn illustrations, especially those for *Picturesque Palestine, Sinai and Egypt,* can also be viewed on this site.

74. W. J. Fenn, "Biographical Sketch."

2. GAINING RECOGNITION AS AN ILLUSTRATOR AND WATERCOLOR PAINTER

1. Newspaper clipping identified as "Sunny South, 1876," Orr Family Papers, Special and Area Studies Collections, George A. Smathers Libraries, University of Florida, Gainesville (hereafter "Orr Family Papers"), box 4, folder 1: "Among the very best engravers on wood, in the United States are N. Orr & Co., of New York. They have no superiors, and for many years have stood by general consent at the head of the profession. All American engravers unite in assigning them this position." John Brown, in a June 9 [1890] letter to the editor of the *Sun,* reminisced about artists and engravers congregating at Orr's office (box 4, folder 1). In 1845 the American Institute awarded Orr a silver medal for the best specimen of engraving on wood; Nathaniel Orr to Elisabeth [Holmes], October 27, 1845 (box 3, folder 1).

2. See William Hosley, *Colt: The Making of an American Legend* (Amherst: University of Massachusetts Press, 1996). Hosley points out that the 400-page volume was "the first book-length treatment of a contemporary American mansion" and was "hailed as the 'most splendid Book . . . that was ever printed in this country'" and "exhibited at the World's Fair in Paris in 1867." In her "campaigns of patronage, philanthropy, and works of faithful remembrance," the wealthy young widow "consciously broke new ground . . . creating a new pattern of possibility for American women." Hosley estimates the 500 copies eventually "cost the equivalent today of four hundred thousand dollars," or about $800 per book. The illustrations cost "about twenty-five hundred dollars, the equivalent today of more than one hundred thousand dollars" (192–94).

3. Orr Family Papers, box 3, folder 4.

4. See David Tatham, *Winslow Homer and the Illustrated Book* (Syracuse, N.Y.: Syracuse University Press, 1992), 34–38. From 1857 to 1859, Homer also illustrated books related to the Sunday school movement.

5. The author acknowledged that in writing her inspiring tale of a family overcoming challenges in the White Mountains of New Hampshire she was indebted to the Reverend Thomas Starr King's popular book *The White Hills* (1859).

6. In 1867 he designed the wrapper for *The Illustrated Family Christian Almanac for the United States,* as noted in "A List of American Books Illustrated with Woodcuts," in A. V. S. Anthony, Timothy Cole, and Elbridge Kingsley, *Wood-Engraving: Three Essays* (New York: Grolier Club, 1916), 53 (the books listed were exhibited at the Grolier Club). Some years later, Fenn contributed to another American Tract Society periodical for children, *Apples of Gold,* a weekly started in 1871 and aimed at the youngest readers. The January 1881 issue contained work by Fenn, perhaps reused from earlier sources, for he was then in England.

7. A digitized version of this book may be viewed on Google Books; illus. is on p. 18.

8. Illus. is on p. 74 of the digitized version of the book. The title of the song, as published in sheet music at the time, typically used the plural "Boatmen." For a study of the wide-ranging social power of this and other popular nineteenth-century poems and songs, see Michael C. Cohen, "Contraband Singing: Poems and Songs in Circulation during the Civil War," *American Literature* 82, no. 2 (June 2010): 276–82.

9. Published by O. D. Case & Company, Hartford, and Geo. & C. W. Sherwood, Chicago. Fenn's works appeared in vol. 1: opp. 294, opp. 440, opp. 600; vol. 2: opp. 112, opp. 344, opp. 736, and possibly opp. 432 (unsigned).

10. James D. Hart, *The Popular Book: A History of America's Literary Taste* (1950; reprint, Westport, Conn.: Greenwood Publishers, 1976), 151.

11. Pennell went on to say: "The most awful misfortune that may occur to an illustrator is to be compelled to use the photographs or sketches made by an author," something Fenn would frequently do, without any evidence of complaints; Joseph Pennell, *The Illustration of Books: A Manual for the Use of Students, Notes for a Course of Lectures at the Slade School, University College* (London: T. Fisher Unwin, 1896), 19.

12. *Brooklyn Daily Eagle,* September 5, 1897, in a review of Fenn's illustrations for an article on Borneo that had appeared in the September 1897 issue of the *Century.*

13. In the 1868 edition, Fenn signed two illustrations, and at least four other new ones are probably by him; at least one of these was reused in a feature on the falls that appeared in *Christian Weekly,* May 31, 1873. I have not been able to find information on the artists contributing to the 1851 edition, although Heine could be William Heine (1827–1885), a native of Dresden who immigrated to New York in 1849 and accompanied the Perry Expedition to Japan in 1853–54; see John Neal Hoover, *"Mr. Heine Took a Sketch of the View . . .":* The Career of William Heine, Official Illustrator of the Perry Expedition to Japan and the Far East," *Imprint: Journal of the American Historical Print Collectors Society* 34, no. 1 (spring 2009): 12–23. Much of Trenton Falls has been altered or destroyed by a hydroelectric dam.

14. A digitized version of this book may be viewed on Google Books.

15. A digitized version of this book may be viewed on Google Books. For a sampling of Birket Foster's poetry illustrations, see "Birket Foster: Victorian Illustrator" on the Penn State University Libraries website, https://secureapps.libraries.psu.edu/content/birketfoster. On the cultural roles of poetry reading in this period, see Joan Shelley Rubin, *Songs of Ourselves: The Uses of Poetry in America* (Cambridge, Mass.: Belknap Press of Harvard University Press, 2007).

16. Though today's viewers find La Farge's unconventional British Pre-Raphaelite and Japanese-inspired works striking, they did not start a trend at the time.

17. Other American contributors were William Hart, Sol Eytinge, Charles Barry, and W. J. Hennessy. The 1857 Moxon edition received much attention, especially for the illustrations by members of the Pre-Raphaelite Brotherhood (Holman Hunt, John Everett Millais, and Dante Gabriel Rossetti) engraved by the Dalziel Brothers firm; see Tatham, *Winslow Homer and the Illustrated Book,* esp. chap. 5.

18. [Brooks], "The Late Harry Fenn," *New York Evening Post,* May 11, 1911. This passage brings to mind Fenn's rendition of "Animal Tracks in the Snow," which appeared on two pages of the March 1897 issue of *St. Nicholas,* accompanying a brief article of the same name by Barney Hoskin Standish.

19. See John Buchanan-Brown, *Early Victorian Illustrated Books: Britain, France and Germany, 1820–1860* (London and New Castle, Del.: British Library and Oak Knoll Press, 2005), esp. the design by Phiz (Hablot Knight Browne) on p. 63, as well as the author's emphasis on the use of "stick" borders, or rustic trellising, in German illustration (115–35), and the popularity in Romantic book design of hand-drawn typefaces for chapter openings. Stowe's story was published as a book in 1870, with Fenn illustrations (Boston: Fields, Osgood).

20. Digitized versions of these books may be viewed on Google Books.

21. *Religious Poems,* [93], 99–100.

22. Anthony was a successful engraver in New York before being invited in 1867 "to take charge of the illustrations and engraving of Ticknor and Fields in Boston"; S. G. W. Benjamin, "A. V. S. Anthony," *Our American Artists* (Boston: D. Lothrop, 1881), 63.

23. Harry Fenn, "The Story of Whittier's *Snow-Bound,*" *St. Nicholas,* April 1893, 428.

24. Ibid., 430.

25. Quoted in [Brooks], "The Late Harry Fenn," *New York Evening Post,* May 11, 1911.

26. Harry Fenn, "Methods of Illustration," *Palette and Bench,* August 1909, 246. Fenn indulged in a bit of hyperbole here; only one illustration in *Snow-Bound* could be described as having a dozen figures.

27. He had described Foster as using "India ink or lamp black" on the prepared, whitened surface of the block and then, when it was dry, accenting the forms with lead pencil and the highlights with Chinese white.

28. Quoted in a publisher's advertisement at the back of John Greenleaf Whittier, *Mabel Martin: A Harvest Idyl* (Boston: James R. Osgood, 1876), copy in Special Collections, University of Virginia Library. I have been unable to locate the comment in the *New York Times.*

29. Quoted from Linton's history as first published in *American Art Review* (March–October 1880), July 1880, 376. The history was later published as a book: W. J. Linton, *The History of Wood-Engraving in America* (Boston: Estes and Lauriat, 1882). Linton mentions several gift books published earlier than *Snow-Bound,* including J. G. Holland's *Bitter-Sweet,* with designs by E. J. Whitney, which he deems "not above the level"; John Williamson Palmer's *Folk Songs* (Scribner's, 1866–67); Tennyson's *Enoch Arden,* the drawings of which he found "queer enough," except Darley's; and James Russell Lowell's *Vision of Sir Launfal* (1866–67), illustrated by Sol Eytinge. He also mentions Whittier's *Maud Muller* (Ticknor and Fields, 1866–67), illustrated by W. J. Hennessy.

30. "The Boston Exhibition of Wood-Engravings," *Critic,* January 4, 1882.

31. By one measure, the 2011 equivalents would be $78 and $141 (www.measuringworth.com). Less expensive versions were issued in subsequent years: for example, a "vest pocket" edition (1875) with 10 illustrations for 50 cents.

32. This was probably about 1870; Will H. Low, interview, February 22, 1920, DeWitt McClellan Lockman Papers, roll 503, Archives of American Art, Smithsonian Institution.

33. [Brooks], "The Late Harry Fenn," *New York Evening Post,* May 11, 1911.

34. Of the eight illustrations, Fenn provided four; one is signed by F. O. C. Darley, and three are unsigned but probably copied after Darley. Fenn's illustrations can be seen in a digital edition of the book in the Cornell University Library Making of America Collection (on pp. 72, 80, 112, 136). He may have worked from his imagination, since the edition was rushed to publication. The great success of Murray's book led to an unprecedented number of visitors to the Adirondacks that summer; see Warder H. Cadbury, introduction to William H. H. Murray, *Adventures in the Wilderness,* ed. William K. Verner (Syracuse, N.Y.: Syracuse University Press for the Adirondack Museum, 1970), esp. 39.

35. Horace Bushnell, *Work and Play; or, Literary Varieties* (New York: Charles Scribner, 1864), 16.

36. William H. H. Murray, *Adventures in the Wilderness; or, Camp-life in the Adirondacks* (Boston: Fields, Osgood, 1869), 65.

37. Kathryn Gamble quotes a May 17, 1869, letter from Parsons's daughter-in-law Alice Brigham Parsons to her mother saying that Charles Parsons and Harry Fenn "are very good friends"; Kathryn E. Gamble, introduction to *Charles Parsons and His Domain: An Exhibition of Nineteenth-Century American Illustration, April 6 through April 27, 1958, at the Montclair Art Museum, Montclair, New Jersey* (Montclair, N.J.: By the museum, 1958), 16.

38. The articles these images illustrated were "Photographs from the High Rockies" and "A Health Trip to Brazil" by Thomas C. Evans (in three parts).

39. Because some of the illustrations are unsigned, it is difficult to determine how many are by Fenn.

40. In 1869 the firm's offices were located at 92 Grand St., near Broadway, and in 1872 they moved to 549–551 Broadway, between Spring and Prince Sts.; see Gerard R. Wolfe, *The House of Appleton: The History of a Publishing House and Its Relationship to the Cultural, Social, and Political Events That Helped Shape the Destiny of New York City* (Metuchen, N.J.: Scarecrow Press, 1981).

41. National Academy of Design exhibition records, 1864, nos. 320 and 344.

42. He also exhibited an illustration titled "Courtship of Miles Standish" (which I have been unable to locate); Clark S. Marlor, *A History of the Brooklyn Art Association with an Index of Exhibitions* (New York: James F. Carr, 1970), 188.

43. Pre-1877 Art Exhibition Catalogue Index, Smithsonian American Art Museum, available at http://www.siris.si.edu. Fenn's *Chillon,* owned by T. F. Thompson, likely his brother-in-law, was also exhibited. Whether this was a different painting from the *Castle of Chillon* exhibited in December 1864 is unknown.

44. "A Fine Private Collection," in "Art Notes," *Brooklyn Daily Eagle,* June 9, 1870. Chapman's collection also included some "oil studies by Harry Fenn." Other artists mentioned are William Hart, Nehlig, T. L. Smith, and H. V. Seben of Brussels. A Fenn painting titled *Steps of the Bergello, Florence* sold for $105 in an auction of Chapman's collection at the Leavitt Art Gallery in New York on April 27, 1875; *New York Times,* April 28, 1875. Chapman had also held a sale of his collection in 1873; *New York Times,* February 23, 1873 (no Fenn works are mentioned in this article). The sale of Chapman's collection after his death, held January 27, 28, and 29, 1913, contained no works by Fenn; *Art Collection of the late Col. Henry Thomas Chapman . . .* (New York: Anderson Galleries, Metropolitan Art Association, 1913).

45. Stillman S. Conant, "The Exhibition of Water Colors," *Galaxy,* January 1, 1867, 53–54. Conant's name is given as "Samuel Stillman Conant" and his life dates as "1851–?1885" in Margaret C. Conrads, *Winslow Homer and the Critics: Forging a National Art in the 1870s* (Princeton, N.J.: Princeton University Press in association with the Nelson-Atkins Museum of Art, 2001), 203.

46. Conant, "Exhibition of Water Colors," 59.

47. Thwaites (fl. 1854–71), an illustrator and watercolorist, had illustrated editions of Cinderella, Tom Thumb, Little Red Riding Hood, and other stories in the 1850s and 1860s. After his death, an auction of works in his estate to be held January 10, 1872, was advertised in the *New York Times* on December 19, 1871, as including "a number of paintings and a few sketches by F. O. C. Darley, Harry Fenn and others."

48. "Fine Arts: Opening of the Society of American Painters in Water Colors," *New York Times,* December 20, 1867. "Boughton" refers to George Henry Boughton; "Smilie," to James D. Smillie.

49. "Only a Water-Color," *The Round Table,* February 1, 1868, 69–70.

50. Samuel Wilde's daughter Mary Ellen Wilde gave the painting to the Montclair Art Museum. A similar boat appeared in the steel engraving after Fenn in *Picturesque Europe,* vol. 2, titled "Ventimiglia on the Cornice Road," dated 1876.

51. In the Brooklyn Art Association's spring exhibition in March 1869 Fenn exhibited *Study of Boats, Porto Venere, Italy; Winter Study, Montclair, N.J.;* and *Landscape;* Marlor, *History of the Brooklyn Art Association,* 188.

52. Margaret C. Conrads suggests that "as watercolor became more acceptable as a legitimate medium," the critics "had less tolerance for works that appeared sketchy or incomplete unless they were specifically identified as studies"; Conrads, *Winslow Homer and the Critics,* 89.

53. These were described as "designed by A. L. Rawson; drawn on wood by H. Fenn; engraved by W. J. & H. D. Linton." A chapter of this book, titled "The Overture of Angels," was published by J. B. Ford in late 1869 as a gift edition with two illustrations by Fenn (advertisement, *New York Times,* December 22, 1869). Only the first volume of Beecher's *Life of Jesus, the Christ* was completed (1872), but its sales were "phenomenal," according to the *Publishers' and Stationers' Weekly Trade Circular,* February 1, 1872, 97. After that date, Beecher may have been distracted by the much-publicized accusations of adultery that eventually led to a trial in 1875.

54. Fenn also exhibited *Study of Wild Pigeons* at the Brooklyn Art Association's spring exhibition, in March 1870; Marlor, *History of the Brooklyn Art Association,* 188.

3. POETRY AND *PICTURESQUE AMERICA*

1. Probably as an incentive, the same issue featured the innovation of reproducing sample pages from illustrated books as advertisements.

2. A digitized version of this book may be viewed on Google Books.

3. David Tatham, *Winslow Homer and the Illustrated Book* (Syracuse, N.Y.: Syracuse University Press, 1992), 102. Tatham credits Fields, Osgood, and especially Anthony, with moving in the late 1860s "toward a reform of the gift-book genre" involving greater unity and less inharmonious variety. Fenn's illustrated edition of *Snow-Bound* was an early attempt in this direction.

4. See Doreen Bolger Burke and Catherine Hoover Voorsanger, "The Hudson River School in Eclipse," in *American Paradise: The World of the Hudson River School* (New York: Metropolitan Museum of Art, 1988), esp. 77–83.

5. "The Budget. By M.C.A.," *Independent,* January 13, 1870.

6. See, for example, p. 19 for Homer and p. 29 for Darley. The reviewer for the *Nation,* in contrast, approved of Homer's figures as "simple and natural," judging that they showed "his power, almost unequaled among painters, as a draughtsman of expression" (December 16, 1869, 539), quoted in Tatham, *Winslow Homer and the Illustrated Book,* 103.

7. Whittier to Fields, quoted in John B. Pickard, *Life and Letters of John Greenleaf Whittier* (Boston: Houghton Mifflin, [ca. 1907]), 543. Pickard says the letter was written "while this work was in the hands of the printers" (543).

8. According to the note at the beginning of the book that quotes from Whittier's letter.

9. Hunt drowned on Appledore Island in 1879, an apparent suicide ("William Morris Hunt, Artist," *New York Times,* September 9, 1879); see David Park Curry, *Childe Hassam: An Island Garden Revisited* (Denver, Colo.: Denver Art Museum, 1990); and Ulrich W. Hiesinger, *Childe Hassam: American Impressionist* (Munich: Prestel, 1994). In later years Thaxter offered works by her artist friends for sale in her parlor, which was enlarged in 1887; Curry, *Childe Hassam,* 34, 37.

10. *Letters of John Greenleaf Whittier,* 197.

11. A wood engraving titled "The Drift-Wood Fire" illustrates the section on Celia Thaxter's home in R. H. Stoddard et al., *Poets' Homes: Pen and Pencil Sketches of American Poets and Their Homes* (Boston: D. Lothrop, 1877), 239. The accompanying text describes Thaxter's parlor: "Over the mantel, at one time, was a sketch of herself, laying drift-wood upon the fire. At the time Harry Fenn drew this sketch, the parlor was severely simple, and charming in that simplicity." Fenn would later draw the parlor as it looked in the mid-1880s for the November 1886 issue of *St. Nicholas.* In 1884 Harriet Prescott Spofford mentioned that "water colors by Harry Fenn and Lucy Larcom and Celia Thaxter" hung on the walls in Whittier's home in Amesbury; "Authors at Home. I. John Greenleaf Whittier at Amesbury," *The Critic,* November 1, 1884, 206.

12. In an undated letter, Fenn asked if Whittier wanted to accompany his family to the Isles of Shoals: "Providence permitting we shall be passing thru Newburyport on Thursday or Friday next—En route for the Shoals—will you be ready to go down with us—may we run over to Amesbury and see"; Fenn to Whittier, undated, bMS Am 1844, p. 120, Houghton Library, Harvard University.

13. Quoted in Pickard, *Letters of John Greenleaf Whittier,* 212.

14. With one exception: for William Cullen Bryant's "The Snow-Shower," W. J. Hennessy provided

two figure drawings and Homer D. Martin one landscape. A digitized version of this book may be viewed on Google Books.

15. *Every Saturday,* December 24, 1870, 835.

16. "Editor's Literary Record, Christmas Books," *Harper's New Monthly Magazine,* January 1871, 302. *Songs of Home* was one of four books that reissued the contents, with "additional illustrations," of a large 1867 anthology, *Folk Songs,* ed. John Williamson Palmer. Other titles Fenn contributed to were *Songs of Life* (1870) and *Songs of Nature* (1873).

17. Quoted in Pickard, *Letters of John Greenleaf Whittier,* 228.

18. Ibid., 260.

19. May 12, 1873. Quoted in Pickard, *Letters of John Greenleaf Whittier,* 299.

20. Digital images of this book's pages may be seen on the Internet Archive website: www.archive.org.

21. An October 15, 1870, notice in *American Literary Gazette and Publishers' Circular* identifies the engravers as [W. J.] Linton, [Joseph S.?] Harley, [James] Langridge, [F. W.] Quartley, [John] Filmer, and [John] Karst.

22. "Books and Authors at Home," *Scribner's Monthly,* January 1871, 349. A digitized version of this book may be viewed on Google Books.

23. See the discussion of this book and Homer's illustration of a factory girl, which contrasts with his frequent images of stylish young women at leisure out-of-doors, in Tatham, *Winslow Homer and the Illustrated Book,* 98–101. Tatham thinks the wood engravers "must have taken liberties with Homer's drawing, altering the character and quantity of his line, and especially his distinctive uses of light" in the attempt to achieve "uniform tone and texture to all the illustrations" (101).

24. A digitized version of the book may be viewed on Google Books.

25. For example, *New York Times,* December 11, 1871. Charles Scribner and Co. also put Fenn's name first in the list of illustrators on the title page of *Songs of Home* (1871).

26. "Literature and Art," *Christian Union,* December 25, 1871.

27. Quoted in an ad in the *New York Times,* December 19, 1871.

28. The announced intention of providing extensive coverage of science evidently met with little enthusiasm: the journal's first editor, Edward Livingston Youmans, Appleton's long-time science editor, resigned after little more than a year. In 1872 he became editor of the new, more specialized Appleton publication *Popular Science Monthly,* which did prove successful.

29. Appleton published Spencer's *Education* in 1860 and *First Principles of a New System of Philosophy,* the first volume in *Synthetic Philosophy,* in 1864; see Sue Rainey, *Creating "Picturesque America": Monument to the Natural and Cultural Landscape* (Nashville, Tenn.: Vanderbilt University Press, 1994), 9–11.

30. Kathleen Pyne, *Art and the Higher Life: Painting and Evolutionary Thought in Late Nineteenth-Century America* (Austin: University of Texas Press, 1996), 3; see chap. 1, "The American Response to Darwinism," which begins: "Although *The Origin of Species,* by Charles Darwin . . . was published in 1859 on the eve of the Civil War, it was not until the postwar period of the 1870s that serious opposition to its findings was mounted in America" (11). Pyne goes on to discuss how Darwin's theories that seemed "to deny humankind its special qualities of mind, intelligence, and especially soul" were what most upset American Christians (12). She also discusses Lamarckianism, based on Lamarck's "evolutionary system in which environmental adaptation was the primary mechanism of change" (18); Spencer and many Americans embraced Lamarck's theories.

31. Frederick Hudson, *Journalism in the United States from 1690 to 1872* (New York: Harper & Brothers, 1873), 705. *Hartford Times* review quoted in the *Aldine,* inside back wrapper, December 1871, copy in Special Collections, University of Virginia Library.

32. See Gerry Beegan, *The Mass Image: A Social History of Photomechanical Reproduction in Victorian London* (Houndmills, Eng.: Palgrave Macmillan, 2008), 1–2. Although Beegan's book concerns London and English periodicals, the effects would have been similar in the United States.

33. Examples include an announcement in the December 15, 1869, *New York Times* stating that

Putnam's Magazine would be ready at twelve o'clock that day and another in the December 22, 1869, *New York Times* stating that the January 1870 *Harper's Monthly* would be ready at one o'clock that day.

34. The timing of the illustration's appearance, soon after Celia Thaxter's first "Among the Isles of Shoals" essay in the *Atlantic,* suggests the editor was aware of the interest that piece had aroused and wanted to take advantage of it. Fenn used the same rocky promontory in one of his illustrations for *The Song of the Sower* (p. 33) but reversed it and reworked it as a night scene, with figures representing shipwrecked men who "rejoice again / In the sweet safety of the shore."

35. See David Tatham, *Winslow Homer and the Pictorial Press* (Syracuse, N.Y.: Syracuse University Press, 2003), 162–68. On Waud, see Frederic E. Ray, *Alfred R. Waud: Civil War Artist* (New York: Viking Press, 1974).

36. In his popular *Timothy Titcomb's Letters to Young People* (1858), Holland stressed the importance of character and manners in making one's way in the city; see Mark J. Noonan, *Reading The Century Illustrated Monthly Magazine: American Literature and Culture, 1870–1893* (Kent, Ohio: Kent State University Press, 2010), 1–5, and chap. 1. On Holland, see Robert J. Scholnick, "J. G. Holland and the 'Religion of Civilization' in Mid-Nineteenth Century America," *American Studies* 27 (Spring 1986): 58.

37. Obituary of George S. Appleton, *New York Times,* July 7, 1878, 7. The current editor was either E. L. Youmans or Robert Carter, and the assistant editor was Oliver Bell Bunce, who would play a major role in the project. See Rainey, *Creating "Picturesque America,"* 31, in which I explore this publishing project in more detail, giving attention to the other contributing artists and writers. In the account that follows here, I include new findings and some drawings by Fenn that were unknown to me when the earlier book was written.

38. Idealized Italian landscapes in paintings by Claude Lorrain (1600–1682) had long provided models of the beautiful—balanced compositions of gentle curves, suffused by golden light, with small figures, suggesting humanity in harmony with a benevolent natural order.

39. Many works of the Italian painter Salvator Rosa (1615–1673) depicting threatening storms, wild mountains, and declivities were considered ideal representations of the sublime. In the nineteenth century, many of the landscapes in paintings by J. M. W. Turner in England and Albert Bierstadt and Frederic E. Church in the United States were considered sublime.

40. *American Scenery* was published by the London firm of George Virtue in 30 parts. The book enjoyed wide sales through Virtue's New York office, selling for 75 cents a part, or a total of $22.50. *The Home Book of the Picturesque,* published by George P. Putnam, included essays by well-known American writers, including Bryant, Cooper, and Washington Irving. Other books with views of American scenery are T. Addison Richards's *Landscape Annual* (Leavitt and Allen, 1854) and *The Scenery of the United States* (D. Appleton, 1855), which reused plates from *Meyer's Universum,* an annual published by the Bibliographisches Institut in Hildburghausen, Germany, from 1833 to 1864, and in an English-language edition by Hermann Meyer in New York in 1852–53. The *Ladies' Repository,* a monthly periodical published by the Western Methodist Book Concern (1841–1876), frequently included one or two steel engravings after American landscape paintings.

41. According to Edward W. Earle, in 1867 the average price of stereoscopic views in E. & H. T. Anthony & Co.'s catalogue was $3 per dozen; Edward W. Earle, ed., *Points of View: The Stereograph in America—A Cultural History* (Rochester, N.Y.: Visual Studies Workshop Press, 1979), 40.

42. See Rebecca Bedell, *The Anatomy of Nature: Geology and American Landscape Painting, 1825–1875* (Princeton: Princeton University Press, 2001), 74–83. Alexander von Humboldt, *Cosmos: A Sketch of a Physical Description of the Universe,* trans. E. C. Otté (London: Henry G. Bohn, 1849–52), 2:456.

43. *Appletons' Journal,* April 3, 1869, 27; see also July 2, 1869.

44. The three-part "Novelties of Southern Scenery" appeared October 16, 23, and 30, 1869. The unsigned wood engravings are presumably after works by the author, a well-known travel

writer and landscape painter. Readers also recommended western North Carolina as "a perfect paradise for the landscape artist" and gave directions on how to get there (Letter from "An Artist's Wife," "Table-Talk," July 30, 1870; "Correspondence," from "A Lover of Nature," August 27, 1870). Southern genre scenes featured in *Appletons' Journal* in 1870 were based on drawings by William Ludwell Sheppard, a popular delineator of blacks; "Charcoal Sketches" (February 12) and the four-part "Southern Sketches" (July 2, 9, 23, and August 6).

45. "Fenn, Harry," *National Cyclopedia of American Biography* (New York: James T. White), 6:368. A similar account appears in George and Edward Dalziel, *The Brothers Dalziel: A Record of Work, 1840–1890* (1901; reprint, London: B. T. Batsford, 1978), 344. In this version, after the Englishman's remarks, Fenn said to the representatives of the Appleton firm, "Give me the chance and you shall see what a variety of beautiful material you have got in America." The response was, "Well, you shall have a try if you like. Do a few drawings and let us see."

46. "Harry Fenn," *American Bookmaker* 9, no. 3 (September 1889): front page.

47. *Appletons' Journal,* August 27, 1870, 264.

48. The landscape images included Fenn's foldout cartoon "Descending the Rapids of the St. Lawrence" (July 2); W. M. Cary's "Point Lobos, Cliff House, and Seal Rocks, San Francisco—Moonlight View" (July 16); a steel engraving after W. L. Sonntag, N.A., "Ossipee Valley/New Hampshire" (August 20); unsigned views of Watkins Glen (September 3), "Star Peak, Nevada," and the Mississippi at New Orleans, and Granville Perkins's fold-out of Baltimore and Druid-Hill Park (all September 17); Adirondack scenery by George Smillie (September 24); and unsigned views of Ithaca waterfalls (October 29).

49. *Appletons' Journal,* October 29, 1870, 536.

50. Ibid., November 5, 1870, 563.

51. One of Fenn's obituaries includes this puzzling story: "Through his likeness to Wilkes Booth he was shadowed through the South by detectives, and had to lead them to his home town to establish his identity"; "The Late Harry Fenn," *New York Evening Post,* May 11, 1911. Fenn's likeness to John Wilkes Booth is indeed striking when photographs are compared, but Lincoln's assassin had been killed many years before, in 1865. Perhaps Fenn traveled there earlier.

52. "Miscellaneous Notes," *Christian Advocate,* November 10, 1870.

53. Many books of picturesque views were organized by rivers, among them J. M. W. Turner's *Rivers of France* (London, 1837) and volumes illustrating the Thames and the Rhine.

54. Thomas B. Thorpe, "The St. John's and Ocklawaha Riers, Florida," *Appletons' Journal,* November 12, 1870, 577–84. Rebecca C. McIntyre, "Promoting the Gothic South," *Southern Cultures* 11, no. 2 (summer 2005): 33–61, discusses earlier poems and novels that characterized swamps as sublime settings for Gothic tales of romance and adventure, including those of runaway slaves, such as Harriet Beecher Stowe's *Dred: A Tale of the Great Dismal Swamp* (1856). In an interpretation different from mine, McIntyre concludes that much of the travel literature about the South, including *Picturesque America,* presents the southern landscape as "grotesque" and inferior to the pastoral North.

55. H. E. Colton, "Picturesque America," *Appletons' Journal,* December 17, 1870, 737.

56. Lyell's theory of "uniformitarianism," propounded in his *Principles of Geology* (1830–33), held that slow, ongoing processes such as weathering and erosion had sculpted the earth's surface over eons. Many had come to accept this theory rather than "catastrophism," which held that "geologic change occurs by a series of sudden cataclysmic events (the biblical Flood, for example)"; Bedell, *Anatomy of Nature,* 125; 5–7.

57. A few details show this progression: In the December 17, 1870, issue, Fenn's illustrations of the mountains of North Carolina, "A Farm on the French Broad River, North Carolina" and "Chimney Rock, Hickory-Nut Gap, North Carolina," are printed on calendered paper, but the meager accompanying text is not. By January 7, 1871, Fenn's additional full-page French Broad illustrations, of Mountain Island and a ferry, are printed on regular text paper. The January 28, 1871, issue gives the "Picturesque America" series front-page prominence, with O. B. Bunce's account "A Visit to Mauch Chunk," the picturesque Pennsylvania coal-mining town, appearing

under the series heading; but by July 1, 1871, "Scenes in St. Augustine," illustrated by Fenn, is not identified with the series on the opening page or in the index compiled later for vol. 5.

58. The publisher's announcement appeared directly below the table of contents; he was no doubt aware that the February 18, 1871, *Harper's Weekly* would include industrial scenes of Pittsburgh by Charles Stanley Reinhart. Fenn would depict some of the same subjects, but his images were fundamentally different; see Rina C. Youngner, *Industry in Art: Pittsburgh, 1812 to 1920* (Pittsburgh: University of Pittsburgh Press, 2006): 63–74.

59. See Sarah Burns, *Inventing the Modern Artist: Art and Culture in Gilded Age America* (New Haven: Yale University Press, 1996), chap. 1, on how artists presented themselves. Burns says that artists' portraits in the late 19th century often showed the men smoking cigarettes, linking them to "the borderland spaces of social marginality and deviance" (37). I don't think that assessment applies to Fenn's pipe in this case.

60. Keeler, "The Taking of Pittsburgh. III.—Before the Works," *Every Saturday*, March 18, 1871, 262.

61. For the book *Picturesque America,* Alfred R. Waud illustrated Pittsburgh in the "On the Ohio" section. His images use more distant viewpoints and, although they include plenty of smoke, are less dramatic than Fenn's (2:147–51). Youngner, *Industry in Art,* 75–78, reproduces Waud's views and discusses them.

62. *The Story of the Fountain* appeared in late 1871 for the holiday trade, so Fenn probably worked on it after his trip to Pittsburgh in early 1871.

63. Several of these wood engravings are reproduced and discussed in Youngner, *Industry in Art,* 67–74; "Casting Steel Ingots" (March 11, 1871) and "Top of a Blast Furnace" (March 18, 1871) are reproduced in Rainey, *Creating "Picturesque America,"* 64, 65. Fenn drew larger figures inside the glassworks, and some wear masks to protect their faces from the heat, causing them to look odd; Youngner considers the effects "curious" and "almost mythic" (72 [where this image is reproduced], 73).

64. Keeler, "The Taking of Pittsburgh. IV.—Among the Inhabitants," March 25, 1871, 274.

65. Reproduced in Youngner, *Industry in Art,* 69. Youngner discusses the difficult lives of those living on the slopes above the industries, especially widows and their children—children such as these, according to Keeler (68).

66. "General Jackson at Head-Quarters" (his barber shop) and "General Jackson on Parade" appeared in *Every Saturday,* March 25, 1871, 277, accompanied by Keeler's extensive text describing him (274).

67. "Literary News," *Literary World: A Monthly Review of Current Literature,* March 1, 1871.

68. The notice continued: "Mr. Fenn will this spring visit South Carolina, Georgia, Tennessee and Virginia, after which he will proceed to sections North and West; and when the summer heats are over he will visit other Southern localities. It is the design to illustrate every portion of the Union, in a manner far superior to anything of the kind hitherto attempted. . . . Mr. Fenn, whose vivid and graphic pencil has placed him at the acknowledged head of American draughtsmen, will for the present give his professional labors solely to the pages of APPLETONS' JOURNAL" (360).

69. Henry E. Colton, "East Hampton and Its Old Church," *Appletons' Journal,* March 25, 1871, 346. Bunce would later write the article "Scenes in Eastern Long Island" for the *Picturesque America* book and point out that the old church had been "inexcusably destroyed" since "Mr. Fenn made his sketch," and that the windmills remind "one forcibly of the quaint old mills in Holland which artists have always delighted to paint" (1:254–55). Such coverage would have played a role in this area later becoming a colony for artists, including Thomas Moran and Mary Nimmo Moran, who made etchings of the windmills.

70. Similarities between one of Fenn's illustrations of the French Broad and one of Birket Foster's images in *Birket Foster's Pictures of English Landscape,* published in 1863 with wood engravings by Dalziel Brothers, suggest Fenn was familiar with this publication and used the latter's imagery as a source for some details; see Rainey, *Creating "Picturesque America,"* 141–47, where three works by Fenn are compared with three by Foster.

71. Woodward's illustration appears in 1:278; for a discussion of other approaches Fenn's works may have suggested to the younger artist, see Sue Rainey and Roger B. Stein, *Shaping the Landscape Image, 1865–1910: John Douglas Woodward* (Charlottesville: Bayly Art Museum, University of Virginia, 1997), 28–33.

72. *New York Times,* December 20, 1871.

73. Allan Nevins, *The Evening Post: A Century of Journalism* (New York: Boni & Liveright, 1922), 338, quoted in Thomas Bender, *New York Intellect: A History of the Intellectual Life in New York City, from 1750 to the Beginnings of Our Own Time* (New York: Alfred A. Knopf, 1987), 134.

74. Bryant later recounted that his task was to read the proofs, "correct the language, omit superfluous passages and see that no nonsense crept into the text"; quoted in Parke Godwin, *A Biography of William Cullen Bryant* (New York: D. Appleton, 1883), 2:347. For more on Bryant's involvement with the project, see Rainey, *Creating "Picturesque America,"* 83–85.

75. Arthur Hoeber, "A Century of American Illustration, V.—The Illustrated Subscription Book," *Bookman* 8 (December 1898): 320.

76. See James D. Hart, *The Popular Book: A History of America's Literary Taste* (Westport, Conn.: Greenwood, 1976), 150–52.

77. *Godey's Lady's Book,* July 1871.

78. Rainey, *Creating "Picturesque America,"* 163–74.

79. Beginning in the 1840s with William Henry Fox Talbot's *Pencil of Nature,* several books illustrated with photographs—salt prints, albumen photographs, and even stereographs—were produced.

80. Quotation from 1:iv. Although the renowned William Cullen Bryant was engaged as editor by June 1872, an earlier, unsigned preface, now quite rare, had been distributed with Part One to the earliest subscribers; see Rainey, *Creating "Picturesque America,"* 83–85 and app. B, 309–12, which reproduces the two versions of the preface. Hereafter, all quotations and illustration references to *Picturesque America* are from the original 1872 edition and appear in the text.

81. John Coleman Adams, *William Hamilton Gibson: Artist, Naturalist, Author* (New York: Putnam, 1901), 40–41.

82. For example, James D. Smillie's diary entry for July 20, 1872, states that he asked Harley for "technical suggestions" and saw Bunce and Fenn at the Appleton office, where his drawings were "freely criticized"; Diaries of James D. Smillie, 1865 thru 1872, mfm. roll 2849, Archives of American Art, Smithsonian Institution.

83. Harry Fenn, "Methods of Illustration," *Palette and Bench,* August 1909, 245; the illustration appears in *Palette and Bench,* September 1909, 267. "Flake white" is a lead pigment and can be toxic if not used with care.

84. The wood engraving "Ascending the Ocklawaha River at Night" (1:24) shows several changes from the *Palette and Bench* illustration; in addition to being reversed, it is narrower and has less smoke, a larger tree, and an alligator in the foreground. The relationship between these two works is unclear.

85. Diaries of James D. Smillie, mfm. roll 2850, Archives of American Art, Smithsonian Institution.

86. Ibid. Smillie's cash accounts are at the end of diaries for the years 1872, 1873. Gibson's pay is in Adams, *William Hamilton Gibson,* 42–43. Newspaper salary figures are from "American Journalism," by the editor of *The Leisure Hour,* quoted in "Miscellany," *Appletons' Journal,* June 3, 1871, 661.

87. A. V. S. Anthony, "An Art That Is Passing Away," in A. V. S. Anthony, Timothy Cole, and Elbridge Kingsley, *Wood-Engraving: Three Essays* (New York: Grolier Club, 1916), 20.

88. William Linton, *The History of Wood-Engraving in America* (Boston: Estes and Lauriat, 1882), 37.

89. See Rainey, *Creating "Picturesque America,"* 179–86.

90. Ibid., 186–90.

91. The works are remarkably similar; both are reproduced in ibid., 188–89. Fenn's watercolor is in the M. and M. Karolik Collection, Museum of Fine Arts, Boston.

92. Both Hinshelwood and Hunt had engraved for the *Ladies' Repository,* as had William Wellstood, who also prepared steel engravings for *Picturesque America.*

93. It seems clear he consulted one of Birket Foster's illustrations as a model for the horses and farmer; see "The Watering Place," illus. no. 13 in *Birket Foster's Pictures of English Landscape,* and Rainey, *Creating "Picturesque America,"* 141–47.

94. Temple Emanu-El (1866–68), designed by Leopold Eidlitz and Henry Fernbach, stood at 43rd St. and Fifth Ave. until it was demolished in 1927; Nathan Silver, *Lost New York* (Boston: Houghton Mifflin, 1967), 150.

95. William G. McLoughlin, *The Meaning of Henry Ward Beecher* (New York: Knopf, 1970), 146, 128, 110–13.

96. In *The Influence of Photography on American Landscape Painting, 1839–1880* (New York: Garland, 1977), Elizabeth Lindquist-Cock maintains that painters such as Albert Bierstadt were striving to rival the three-dimensionality of the stereoscope (see esp. chap. 3). For examples of the advice given to photographers about how to manipulate scenes to add charm and picturesque effect, see Richard N. Masteller, "Western Views in Eastern Parlors: The Contribution of the Stereograph Photographer to the Conquest of the West," *Prospects* 6 (1981): 60–62.

97. This influence is suggested by Robert L. McGrath in "The Real and the Ideal: Popular Images of the White Mountains," in *The White Mountains: Place and Perceptions,* exh. cat. (Durham, N.H.: University Press of New England, 1980), 69. McGrath says of Fenn's views of the White Mountains: "It was especially the latter's [Timothy O'Sullivan and William Henry Jackson's] dramatic photographs of the Rockies and Yosemite, which first appeared in the East in the early 1870's, that provided the model for steep precipices, narrow paths, and soaring mountains in Fenn's engravings." Although some photographs served as models for Fenn, the timing would not have been right for Jackson's first photographs of the Rockies, made the summer of 1873, to influence Fenn's White Mountain views in *Picturesque America,* which appeared in parts 7 and 8.

98. Fenn had provided illustrations for Murray's *Adventures in the Wilderness* (1869), as mentioned in chapter 2. On changing attitudes, see T. J. Jackson Lears, "From Salvation to Self-Realization: Advertising and the Therapeutic Roots of the Consumer Culture, 1880–1930," in Richard Wightman Fox and T. J. Jackson Lears, *The Culture of Consumption: Critical Essays in American History, 1880–1980* (New York: Pantheon Books, 1983). According to the authors: "The crucial moral change was the beginning of a shift from a Protestant ethos of salvation through self-denial toward a therapeutic ethos stressing self-realization in this world—an ethos characterized by an almost obsessive concern with psychic and physical health defined in sweeping terms" (4).

99. King, of the California Geological Survey, published his account of climbing Mount Tyndall in the *Atlantic Monthly* beginning in May 1871, and it appeared as a book in 1872. The publishers' trade journal commented: "The mountain fever is the most glorious disease a-going, and it is 'catching from this book' "; *Publishers' and Stationers' Weekly Trade Circular,* February 15, 1874, 141.

100. For more on the messages in the text and images, see Rainey, *Creating "Picturesque America,"* esp. 203–47.

101. In 1872 film was not orthochromatic, that is, it was unable to capture the variety of nature's tonal effects. Greens printed black, and blues were lost entirely. Furthermore, filters that would later enable film to record clouds had not yet been produced, so skies were a monotonous gray. Backgrounds were often lost in overexposure. Assessment based on Estelle Jussim, *Visual Communication and the Graphic Arts: Photographic Technologies in the Nineteenth Century* (New York: R. R. Bowker, 1983), 180.

102. For another example from Fenn's Yellowstone images for *Picturesque America,* see Rainey, *Creating "Picturesque America,"* 165–67.

103. The younger illustrator Edwin Austen Abbey recalled that when he worked in the Harper's Art Department in the early 1870s, thousands of original sketches covering the Civil War were thrown away during office cleanups, including many by Winslow Homer. E. V. Lucas, *Edwin Austen Abbey: Royal Academician; The Record of His Life and Work,* vol. 1, *1852–1893* (New York: Charles Scribner's Sons, 1921), 23.

104. See Rainey and Stein, *Shaping the Landscape Image,* and Rainey, *Creating "Picturesque America";* both books reproduce some of Woodward's drawings for *Picturesque America.* Many of Waud's sketches for the book are in the collection of the Historic New Orleans Foundation; see *Alfred*

R. Waud: Special Artist on Assignment (New Orleans: Historic New Orleans Collection, 1979); "Down the Mississippi," *American Heritage,* June/July 1984, 87–95; and "The Creole Sketchbook of A. R. Waud," *American Heritage,* December 1963, 33–48.

105. The 1867 date on the watercolor raises the possibility that Fenn had traveled to Florida before his commission from *Appletons' Journal* and could have suggested that the state open the series.

106. Fenn's pencil and wash sketch on blue paper of the view from Lookout Mountain, Tennessee, as well as the related wood engraving (to which he added a boat, male hikers, and an artist sketching), are reproduced in Rainey, *Creating "Picturesque America,"* 132,133; chaps. 5 and 6 reproduce examples of preliminary drawings for *Picturesque America* by Woodward, Waud, and others, alongside the corresponding wood engravings.

107. See Rainey, *Creating "Picturesque America,"* 268.

108. An image of this watercolor can be viewed by searching the Collections database on the Metropolitan Museum of Art's website.

109. For an interesting theoretical interpretation of this process, see Gregory Clark, *Rhetorical Landscapes in America: Variations on a Theme from Kenneth Burke* (Columbia: University of South Carolina Press, 2004). Using Burke's "reconception of rhetoric as what constitutes the experience of identification," Clark explores how the shared "symbolic experiences" of viewing the images in works like *Picturesque America* or visiting tourist attractions prompt the "residents of a vast and diverse nation" "to adopt for themselves a common sense of national identity" (8, 15, 38).

110. Quoted in Bunce's "Table-Talk" column, *Appletons' Journal,* May 24, 1873.

111. "Printing and Publishing" ("Extracts from the Report of the French Commission"), U.S. Centennial Commission, *International Exhibition, 1876: Report and Awards, Group 27,* ed. Francis A. Walker (Philadelphia: J. B. Lippincott, 1879), 10:245. On the specially bound copy, see Rainey, *Creating "Picturesque America,"* 358 n. 12.

112. *Publishers' Weekly,* no. 324 (March 20, 1878): 350. The Paris publisher was A. Quantin, and the translator was Benedict-Henry Revoil. The book omitted the steel engravings, Bryant's name as editor, and the names of writers and artists; the contents were presented geographically, and many of the wood engravings were used.

113. Published in Leipzig by Heinrich Schmidt and Carl Günther, the two-volume work was in an even larger format, 14 3/4 x 10 3/4 in.

114. The book was edited by George Monro Grant. Instead of steel engravings, it included fine wood engravings treated as plates, printed on heavier paper, with no printing on the back. Fenn's eight images included five flower studies and one view of rapids near Niagara Falls that could well have been based on a sketch from an earlier trip. Thomas Moran, Robert Swain Gifford, William Hamilton Gibson, and John Douglas Woodward also contributed, as did several Canadian artists. See Rainey, *Creating "Picturesque America,"* 280–81, 360 nn. 24–27; and Allan Pringle, "Thomas Moran: *Picturesque Canada* and the Quest for a Canadian National Landscape," *Imprint: Journal of the American Historical Print Collectors Society* 14, no. 1 (spring 1989): 12–21.

115. William H. Appleton was quoted as stating these figures in the *Chicago Tribune.* He also said the cost, without the printing, was $138,000.

116. It contained 720 pages and cost $3 (30 weekly parts at 10 cents each); see Rainey, *Creating "Picturesque America,"* 288.

117. The minutes of the society record that on November 7, 1871, Fenn exhibited a drawing by Frank [J. or H.?] Smith and nominated him for membership, a motion approved by the Board of Control. It seems likely this artist was F. [Francis] Hopkinson Smith, who became a member in 1872. If indeed Fenn helped Smith attain membership, Smith later returned the favor by writing about how Fenn's success as an illustrator expanded the field for others; American Watercolor Society Papers 1866–1955, mfm. roll N68-8, Archives of American Art, Smithsonian Institution.

118. "The Water-Color Exhibition," *Scribner's Monthly,* April 1871, 686–87.

119. Fanchon, "Exhibition of Water Colors at the Academy," *Chicago Tribune,* April 2, 1871.

120. Carter's description suggests this work was similar to the steel engraving accompanying the Florida section in *Picturesque America;* Susan Nichols Carter, "The Water-Color Exhibition,"

Appletons' Journal, March 2, 1872, 235–36. Fenn's works in this exhibition were also mentioned in a review in the February 21, 1872, *Christian Union,* which described the St. John's River painting as "a capital representation of that desolate yet fascinating coast, with its strange vegetation and interminable stretches of dazzling white beach."

121. *A Collection of Water Color Drawings by Harry Fenn* (New York: Anderson Auction, 1911), 38, entry no. 80.

122. Quoted in *Appletons' Journal,* March 22, 1873, 411.

4. YEARS ABROAD—*PICTURESQUE EUROPE* AND *PICTURESQUE PALESTINE*

1. Timothy Mitchell, *Colonising Egypt* (Cambridge, U.K.: Cambridge University Press, 1988), 6–10.

2. John Urry, *The Tourist Gaze: Leisure and Travel in Contemporary Societies* (London: Sage, 1990), 4.

3. Fenn to Nathaniel Orr, undated, from Gräfenberg House, New Barnet, Herts. Orr Family Papers, box 3, folder 2.

4. *Letters of John Greenleaf Whittier,* ed. John B. Pickard (Cambridge, Mass.: Belknap Press of Harvard University Press, 1975), 261. In a letter of November 11, 1869, to Thaxter, Whittier had also reported that Mrs. Fenn was "dangerously sick" (203).

5. Fenn to Mrs. Holmes, Montclair Sunday, undated, private collection.

6. Fenn to Nathaniel Orr, Gräfenberg House, New Barnet, Hertfordshire, undated, Orr Family Papers, box 3, folder 2.

7. John Douglas Woodward (hereafter JDW) to his mother, July 20, 1876, Woodward Papers, Valentine Richmond History Center, Richmond, Va. (Hereafter all JDW letters are referred to by names and dates only.)

8. "Notes," *Appletons' Journal,* February 28, 1874, 284.

9. *Philadelphia Inquirer,* March 5, 1874.

10. "Art," *Appletons' Journal,* February 28, 1874, 284.

11. "The Fine Arts," *New-York Herald Tribune,* January 29, 1874. Elizabeth Thomson may have submitted the painting at his request.

12. *Study of Boats,* dated 1868, was listed as being owned by Samuel Wilde, so it seems likely it is the painting now in the Montclair Art Museum (see fig. 2.13): it is similar to the steel engraving titled "Ventimiglia on the Cornice Road" in *Picturesque Europe,* 2:opp. 161.

13. John Moran, "The American Water-Colour Society's Exhibition," *Art Journal* (London), New Series 4 (1878): 92.

14. The firm was founded by John Cassell, and in 1855 Thomas Dixon Galpin and George William Petter became part owners; see Simon Nowell-Smith, *The House of Cassell, 1848–1958* (London: Cassell, 1958), esp. 85. Its U.S. office was at 596 Broadway, near the Appleton office building at numbers 549–551.

15. A digitized version of vol. 1 of the C., P. & G edition may be viewed on the Canadian Libraries Internet Archive website.

16. Bayard Taylor, ed., *Picturesque Europe* (New York: D. Appleton, 1875–79), 1:iii. (Hereafter, unless otherwise noted, all quotations and illustration references to *Picturesque Europe* are from the American edition and appear in the text.)

17. The entire announcement is reproduced in Sue Rainey, *Creating "Picturesque America": Monument to the Natural and Cultural Landscape* (Nashville, Tenn.: Vanderbilt University Press, 1994), app. D, 319.

18. It is clear from Woodward's letters that his plan to travel to Constantinople was abandoned after war was declared between Russia and Turkey in 1877. JDW to Virginia Minor, July 8, 1877.

19. Fenn's name appears in the table of contents as a contributor to other sections, but it is difficult to identify specific works by him in these sections.

20. Lucy H.[Hamilton] Hooper, "From Abroad, Paris, February 29, 1876," *Appletons' Journal,* March 25, 1876, 412.

21. [Sidney Brooks], "The Late Harry Fenn," *New York Evening Post,* May 11, 1911.

22. Fenn to Nathaniel Orr, undated, Orr Family Papers, SASC, Smathers.

23. This sum would be roughly equivalent to $2,000 in 2007. Fenn's colleague John Douglas Woodward would ask for more and got £24 a week; JDW to his mother, May 21, 1876.

24. JDW to his mother, January 27, 1878. On Woodward's life and career, see Sue Rainey and Roger B. Stein, *Shaping the Landscape Image, 1865–1910: John Douglas Woodward* (Charlottesville: Bayly Art Museum, University of Virginia, 1997).

25. Many of the illustrations are signed "Whymper," identifying the firm, but not the particular engraver who did the work. Woodward's letters indicate that he and Fenn were dissatisfied with the firm's work. JDW to his mother, February 3 and September 15, 1878.

26. "Picturesque Europe," *Art Journal* (New York), January 1877, 19. The sale of Fenn's works after his death included a painting titled *The Rialto, Venice,* dated 1875; see *A Collection of Water Color Drawings by Harry Fenn* (New York: Anderson Auction, 1911), 23, entry no. 39.

27. JDW to his mother, September 3, 1876.

28. In vol. 3, the same figure appears in images on pp. 380 and 389, and another figure is repeated on pp. 389 and 392; a figure on p. 388 is reversed on p. 392. The illustrations of figures in Constantinople were definitely based on photographs since it was too dangerous for Woodward to travel there; see *Picturesque Europe,* 3:312, 314, 317.

29. A notice in the December 19, 1875, *Chicago Daily Tribune* announced that *Picturesque Europe* "is now ready," published by subscription, and that "parties desiring to examine or subscribe for the above elegant work will be called upon by sending their address to . . . the Tribune office." It seems likely that, after the wood engravings had been cut and the text typeset in London, electrotypes were made and shipped to Appleton's office in New York for printing. It is possible, however, that printed sheets were shipped from London to New York. Neither scenario explains why the Appleton edition began appearing sooner than the British edition published by C., P. & G.

30. *Appletons' Journal,* August 21, 1875, 248. The notice stated: "Some of the canvassers of this work have, with great effrontery, declared to those whom they have approached that Appleton & Co. have abandoned their design, and that the work offered is substituted therefore, under which plausible but altogether false representation they have secured many subscribers." The work referred to may have been John Sherer, *Europe Illustrated: Its Picturesque Scenes and Places of Note,* 2 vols. (London: London Printing and Publishing Co., [1876–79]), which included numerous steel engravings by English artists, many or all reused from previous publications.

31. "Report of Mr. James W. Wilcox, Chairman of the Board of Judges of Group XIII, Applying to Printing Presses," *New York Times,* December 14, 1876. The presses exhibited for "fine cut-work" were from "Messrs. Potter & Co., Hoe & Co., and Messrs Cottrell & Babcock." The illustrations were likely the wood engravings, since the article refers to the printing of sheets on continuous rolls of paper. The cylinder presses that printed newspapers on such rolls were considered "to rank among the great feats of the mechanic arts."

32. December 20, 1879.

33. December 14, 1879.

34. An advertisement in the February 3, 1876, *Times* (London) noted: "In a few days will be published, after many years of preparation the first part of a most superbly illustrated Fine Art Work, entitled Picturesque Europe."

35. "Christmas Books," *Times* (London), December 12, 1876.

36. Nowell-Smith, *House of Cassell,* 101. The University of Virginia Libraries Special Collections owns the version bound in red leather. According to one online currency converter, in 1879, 50 guineas had the buying power of $5,488.22 in 2012, and 20 guineas had the buying power of $2,195.29 in 2012.

37. The price of 18/- (shillings) for each volume is listed in the catalogue at the back of the reduced-size C., P. & G. edition of *The Holy Land* with lithographs after designs by David Roberts.

38. *Europa pintoresca* was published in two volumes by Montaner y Simon, in Barcelona. This book included many of the original wood engravings, but no steel engravings, as well as selections from the text, in translation.

39. "Catalogue of the Whole of the Original Water-Colour Drawings, made for the well-known works, 'Picturesque Europe' and the 'Illustrated Shakespeare,' Published by Messrs. Cassell, Petter, Galpin, and Co. Including Seventeen Works of Birket Foster," photocopy of the original (with notations of prices realized), Getty Research Institute, Los Angeles. Regarding the "drawings," the catalogue states that the publishers "reserve the copyright for their reproduction in black and white, in any size not exceeding 15 in. by 12 in"; "Goupil" is noted as a purchaser of several items, raising the question of whether Goupil & Cie and other purchasers may have planned to produce prints larger than those in *Picturesque Europe*. Perhaps as Fenn receives greater attention, some of his works from this sale will resurface.

40. Charles Wilson, ed., *Picturesque Palestine, Sinai and Egypt,* 2 vols. (New York: D. Appleton and Company, 1881–1883). A digitized version of vol. 1 may be viewed on the Internet Archive of the University of Toronto. (Hereafter, all quotations from and illustration references to *Picturesque Palestine, Sinai and Egypt* are from the American edition and appear in the text.)

41. The firm had also issued Francis Frith's important series of photographs, *Egypt and Palestine* (1858–1860), and an 1860 edition of the Bible illustrated with steel engravings. James S. Virtue's partner, Frederic Daldy, had previously been involved in selling the photographs made by the Palestine Exploration Fund and in publishing sermons and devotional works by Christian ministers.

42. The territory denoted by the familiar, historic term *Palestine* had long been part of the Ottoman Empire; located in western Greater Syria, it encompassed the two administrative units ruled from Damascus and Sidon. See John Davis, *The Landscape of Belief: Encountering the Holy Land in Nineteenth-Century American Art and Culture* (Princeton: Princeton University Press, 1996); Yehoshua Ben-Arieh, *Painting in the Holy Land in the Nineteenth Century* (New York: Hemed, 1997); and Sue Rainey, "Illustration 'Urgently Required': The *Picturesque Palestine* Project, 1878–83," *Prospects: An Annual of American Cultural Studies* 30 (2005): esp. 183–85.

43. E. W. Lane's translation of *The Thousand and One Nights* was published in London in 1840; see Rainey, "Illustration 'Urgently Required,'" 183–85.

44. See Naomi Shepherd, *The Zealous Intruders: The Rediscovery of Palestine* (London: Collins, 1987), 90. Thomson's book popularized the earlier work by the American biblical scholar and linguist Edward Robinson, *Biblical Researches in Palestine, Mount Sinai and Arabia Petraea* (1841). Robinson ignored the sites long identified by Roman Catholic and Eastern Orthodox traditions and used the biblical text and local place names as his guide.

45. Published in London by F. G. Moon and lithographed by Louis Haghe. In 1855–56, smaller-format, less-expensive versions, with the lithographs reduced photographically, were published in London by Day & Son and in New York by D. Appleton.

46. See Gerald R. Wolfe, *The House of Appleton* (Metuchen, N.J.: Scarecrow, 1981), 47.

47. The scientists included James McCosh and Joseph LeConte; see George Cotkin, *Reluctant Modernism: American Thought and Culture 1880–1900* (New York: Twayne Publishers, 1992), chap. 1. Cotkin asserts: "Whether scientists or theologians, most American thinkers in the period 1880–1900 used Darwinism, as well as other doctrines of evolutionary development, to support and extend traditional beliefs" (2).

48. See Neil Asher Silberman, *Digging for God and Country: Exploration, Archeology, and the Secret Struggle for the Holy Land, 1799–1917* (New York: Alfred A. Knopf, 1982), chap. 11, esp. 108, 115.

49. An excerpt from this book also appeared in the February 18, 1871, *Appletons' Journal.*

50. *Illustrated Christian Weekly,* April 29, 1871.

51. For the classic discussion of this attitude and its repercussions, see Edward Said, *Orientalism* (New York: Pantheon, 1978).

52. Joseph P. Thompson, "Concluding Appeal," *Palestine Exploration Society,* no. 1 (July 1871): 34–35; quoted in John Davis, "Picturing Palestine: The Holy Land in Nineteenth-Century American Art and Culture" (Ph.D. diss., Columbia University, 1991). The American Palestine Exploration Society had trouble finding skilled surveyors and raising sufficient funds (the economic downturn of 1873 did not help). It was quiescent by 1878, and its map of the Moab area was not detailed enough to be useful for exploration.

53. Appleton had published the first American editions of Darwin's *On the Origin of Species* (1859) and *Descent of Man* (1871); Huxley's *Man's Place in Nature* (1863), *Lessons in Elementary Physiology* (1866), and *Lay Sermons and Addresses* (1870); and the works of William Tyndall. The firm also published works that presented opposing theories or sought to reconcile science and religion, such as the geology professor Joseph Le Conte's *Religion and Science* (1873).

54. John James Moscrop, *Measuring Jerusalem: The Palestine Exploration Fund and British Interests in the Holy Land* (New York: Leicester University Press, 2000), 2.

55. To maintain access to markets for grain and other commodities, much diplomatic maneuvering and even declarations of war had been required between 1776 and 1816 to work out treaties with the Barbary States of North Africa; see Fuad Sha'ban, *Islam and Arabs in Early American Thought: The Roots of Orientalism in America* (Durham, N.C.: Acorn, 1991), 65–81.

56. See D. H. Finnie, *Pioneers East: The Early American Experience in the Middle East* (Cambridge: Harvard University Press, 1967), 70–81; Ruth Kark, *American Consuls in the Holy Land, 1832–1914* (Jerusalem: Magnes, 1994); and Lester I. Vogel, *To See a Promised Land; Americans and the Holy Land in the Nineteenth Century* (University Park: Pennsylvania State University Press, 1993), esp. chap. 6.

57. Hilton Obenzinger, *American Palestine: Melville, Twain, and the Holy Land Mania* (Princeton: Princeton University Press, 1999), 161, 38, 190. He also points out that Bayard Taylor and Mark Twain, who had visited both regions, frequently compared them in their writings.

58. Among the wood engravers, the names of [Joseph S.] Harley and W. H. Morse appear frequently; others are H. Linton, Lauderback, P. Meeder, J. Filmer, and W. F. Dana. Of the wood engravers, only Whymper and Dalziel are definitely known to have been working in England: Josiah Wood Whymper (1813–1903) had been the manager and chief wood engraver for *Picturesque Europe,* and Dalziel was the signature of the prominent London firm where Fenn had served as an apprentice in the 1850s.

59. JDW to his mother, September 14, 1877.

60. JDW to his mother, December 9, 1877.

61. JDW to his mother, January 27, 1878.

62. JDW to his mother, February 3 and 18, 1878; in the earlier letter, Woodward wrote: "no blocks of mine will ever find their way into his [Whymper's] hands if I can prevent them."

63. JDW to his wife, February 22, 1878. In this letter, Woodward tells her that $12 weekly would be deposited in his "Palestine" account.

64. JDW to his wife, February 22, 1878.

65. Dean Stanley, *Lecture on the History of the Jewish Church,* pt. 1 (London, 1863), 11. Shepherd, in *Zealous Intruders,* points out the prevalence of this approach and its problems (89–94).

66. See also Fenn's "Character Sketches" from the *Quarterly Illustrator,* January 1894, 167, reproduced in Rainey, "Illustration 'Urgently Required,'" 211.

67. See *Rolla Floyd: Letters from Palestine, 1868–1912* (n.p., 1981).

68. Such luxurious camps were not unusual; see Mark Twain's description in *The Innocents Abroad* (1869; reprint, New York: Penguin, 1966), 322–23; and Vogel, *To See a Promised Land,* chap. 3.

69. JDW to his mother, Joppa [Jaffa], March 3, 1878.

70. JDW to his wife, March 6, 1878.

71. JDW to his wife, March 24, 1878.

72. JDW to his wife, March 17, 1878.

73. JDW to his mother, March 22, 1878.

74. JDW to his wife, March 12, 1878.

75. JDW to his mother, March 22, 1878.

76. Fenn's inscription reads: "(Luke IX.51)/(Matt. XVI 13.20 XVII 1.13)." The work is reproduced in *American Watercolors from the Metropolitan Museum of Art* (New York: By the museum, 1991), no. 79; an image of it may be seen by searching the Collections database on the museum's website.

77. JDW to his wife, March 24, 1878.

78. JDW to his wife, March 31, 1878.

79. Ibid.

80. Two of the many earlier representations are reproduced in Rainey and Stein, *Shaping the Landscape Image,* one by J. M. W. Turner based on a sketch by C. Barry, in Thomas Hartwell Horne, *The Biblical Keepsake* (1835), and one by W. H. Bartlett, in his *Walks About the City and Environs of Jerusalem* (1844). The climax of Herman Melville's long poem *Clarel* (1876) is set at Mar Saba.

81. JDW to his wife, April 14, 1878.

82. Since many of Woodward's sketches from this journey still exist, we know that in most cases he made careful pencil renderings and added watercolor or gouache, as he did for three of his Mar Saba works. He also occasionally made highly finished watercolors, one of which was the basis for the steel engraving titled "Mar Saba, Valley of the Kedron" (1:opp. 149). Another, *The Dead Sea and Mountains of Moab from the Convent of Mar Saba,* is similar to a wood engraving. These works are reproduced in color in Rainey and Stein, *Shaping the Landscape Image,* 71, 72.

83. "Picturesque Palestine," *Art Journal* (London) 8, no. 22 (1882): 300.

84. JDW to his wife, April 14 and May 31, 1878; JDW to his mother, July 28, 1878.

85. JDW to his wife, May 6, 1878.

86. JDW to his wife, May 10, 1878.

87. Compare, for example, the images on the following pages: 1:237 and 2:192; 1:60 and 1:61, 294; and 1:106 and 1:334, 367. For more on the use of photographs as sources for figures in *Picturesque Palestine,* see Rainey, "Illustration 'Urgently Required,'" 208–17. See also Carney E. S. Gavin, *The Image of the East: Nineteenth-Century Near Eastern Photographs by Bonfils from the Collection of the Harvard Semitic Museum,* with 10 microfiches (Chicago: University of Chicago Press, 1982); and *In Arab Lands: The Bonfils Collection of the University of Pennsylvania Museum* (Cairo: American University in Cairo Press, 2000). There is no indication from Woodward's letters that Fenn and Woodward were aware the photographers often "preferred docile paid models to the unpredictable peasantry," as Naomi Shepherd and others have pointed out; see Shepherd, *Zealous Intruders,* 189–90.

88. According to Marjorie Balge (conversation with author, May 2011), intentionally flattening the picture plane in this way can be viewed as a small step toward the flat picture plane seen in much of modern art.

89. See Siegfried Wichmann, *Japonisme: The Japanese Influence on Western Art Since 1858* (London: Thames and Hudson, 1981), 224–25; reproduced on p. 225 is a circa-1880 Staffordshire plate whose decoration of a rectangular landscape resting in a spray of flowers is similar to many illustrations in *Picturesque Palestine.*

90. "Picturesque Palestine," London *Times,* September 23, 1881.

91. JDW to his wife, May 19, 1878; to his motehr, June 2, 1878.

92. Fenn to Mrs. Rand, undated, Montclair Art Museum archives, Montclair, N.J.

93. JDW to his mother, June 21, 1878.

94. Harry Fenn, "There Were Giants in Those Days," *St. Nicholas* 25, no. 12 (October 1898): 1028–32.

95. Details of their hasty departure and Fenn's family members' conditions are in JDW to his mother, June 21, July 14 and 28, 1878.

96. JDW to his mother, August 4, 1878.

97. Comments about this period are in JDW to his mother, August 25, September 8 and 15, 1878. Notices in the "Money-Market and City Intelligence" feature of the *Times* (London) for August 23, 27, and 31, 1878, confirm the firm's financial difficulties: its liabilities were more than £171,000, although its assets were stated by the firm "to be considerable"; at meetings with creditors, liquidators of the estate were appointed and "the business [was] to go on under the guidance of trustees capable of working it into a better position" (August 31, 1878).

98. JDW to his mother, December 22 and 28, 1878; January 5, 1879. Stanley recommended George Grove, his colleague in the PEF, to serve as editor; it is unknown whether Grove was approached by the Appleton firm.

99. Details of their trip are in JDW to his wife, January 11, 1879. On January 20, 1879, Woodward wrote to his wife: "It is perfectly astonishing how a thing gets about in the East. I found out later that they knew all about the failure of Virtue. We were not even aware of their knowing Virtue was interested in the book."

100. JDW to his mother, January 20, 1879.

101. The water carrier on the left is similar to (though reversed from) the one in the wood engraving titled "The Necropolis of Asyût" (2:418).

102. JDW to his wife, February 15, 1879.

103. Ibid.

104. JDW to his wife, April 7, 1879.

105. JDW to his wife, April 6 and 20, 1879.

106. JDW to his mother, March 31, 1879.

107. [Brooks], "The Late Harry Fenn, *New York Evening Post,* May 11, 1911. Woodward's account is tamer in a March 31, 1879, letter to his mother, except for the stormy crossing: "Five Englishmen came over to Ayun Musa to spend the day. They . . . said there was no quarantine and it was only red tape to extract baksheeh and that we had better leave everything and attempt to cross with them. So, ordering everybody to stay there until they heard from us, we walked down to the water, about two miles, passed right through the quarantine camp by a score of sentinels, out on a long pier and got into the boat. It was so rough . . . we were from four until 10 o'clock that night, beating against a fierce head wind without seeming able to make any progress. I think they discovered our escape soon after we left, for two soldiers followed us along the shore for some time."

108. JDW to his wife, April 20, 1879.

109. Ibid.

110. JDW to his mother, May 4, 1879.

111. Harry Fenn, "Silk & Cedars: A Scramble in the Lebanons," *St. Nicholas* 26, no. 4 (April 1897): 467–70.

112. JDW to his mother, June 15, 1879.

113. See Rainey, "Illustration 'Urgently Required,'" 227–44, for more on the writers and the contents of their texts. Rogers was the sister of the British consul and well known for her 1862 book *Domestic Life in Palestine;* Merrill was "Archaeologist of the American Palestine Exploration Society," according to *Picturesque Palestine*'s prospectus.

114. See Rainey, "Illustration 'Urgently Required,'" 229.

115. Many followed Sir Christopher Wren in believing that Gothic architecture was derived from Islamic architecture of the Middle East; see Kenneth Paul Bendiner, "The Portrayal of the Middle East in British Painting, 1835–1860" (Ph.D. diss., Columbia University, 1979). Bendiner discusses this notion in relation to David Roberts's interest in depicting architecture (133–38).

116. The only images that could be interpreted as akin to the eroticism of orientalist paintings are three that show women with nose rings and/or partially bared breasts (1:32, 271; 2:209), although the artists chose to make these unattractive rather than alluring.

117. See Silberman, *Digging for God and Country,* 44–45; and Alexander Schölch, *Palestine in Transformation, 1856–1882: Studies in Social, Economic, and Political Development,* trans. William C. Young and Michael C. Gerrity (Washington, D.C.: Institute for Palestine Studies, ca. 1993), 63.

118. They obtained a recommendation for *Picturesque Palestine* from Gustav Gottheil, the rabbi of New York's Temple Emanu-El; he regarded it as a "most welcome guide and lucid interpreter" of the Bible. Portions of a November 3, 1881, letter from him are quoted with other "Recommendations" on the back of some of the late part covers; see Rainey, "Illustration 'Urgently Required,'" 258 n. 176.

119. The British Mandate ended in 1948 with the establishment of Israel.

120. Palestine Park and the "Jerusalem" at the St. Louis fair are discussed in Davis, *Landscape of Belief,* 88–97; and in John Davis, "Holy Land, Holy People? Photography, Semitic Wannabes, and Chautauqua's Palestine Park," *Prospects: An Annual of American Cultural Studies* 17 (1992).

121. See notices announcing the publication in "Art Notes," *New York Times,* May 31, 1881. "Picturesque Palestine," *Times* (London), September 23, 1881; "Illustrated Books," *Times* (London), December 26, 1881.

122. Quoted on the backs of some part covers.

123. "Picturesque Palestine," *Times* (London), September 23, 1881.

124. Lyman Abbott, "The Cradle of Christianity," *Christian Union,* January 19, 1882, 73–74.

125. It has been described as "the most important nineteenth-century book of illustrations of the Holy Land"; Yehoshua Ben-Arieh, *Painting in the Holy Land in the Nineteenth Century* (New York: Hemed, 1997), 245.

126. *La Terre Sainte,* published serially in 1882–84 by E. Plon, Paris, was written by Victor Guérin (1821–1890), leader of several French government expeditions; it used *Picturesque Palestine*'s illustrations without mentioning the artists' names. The German publication, *Palästina in Bild und Wort: Nebst der Sinaihalbinsel und dem Lande Gosen* (Stuttgart: Deutsche Verlags-Anstalt, 1883–84), edited by Georg Ebers (1837–98) and Hermann Guthe (1849–1936), was a loose translation of *Picturesque Palestine*'s text and reused most of that book's wood engravings. What, if any, business arrangements the publishers had with Appleton and Virtue is unknown, although clearly they had access to electrotypes of the wood engravings.

127. "Picturesque Palestine," *New York Evangelist,* December 13, 1883.

128. In 1868, for example, 250 Americans passed from Jaffa to Jerusalem, whereas in 1910 the number was 1,600; David Klatzer, "American Christian Travelers to the Holy Land, 1821–1939" (Ph.D. diss., Temple University, 1987), 22.

129. Including *The Poetical Works of Longfellow,* vol. 2 (Houghton Mifflin, 1882), and subsequent works published by *Picturesque Palestine*'s publishers: Stanley Lane-Poole's *Cairo: Sketches of Its History, Monuments and Social Life* (London: J. S. Virtue, 1898); and two Appleton works in their World's Great Books series: Sir John Mandeville's *Voyages and Travels* (1899) and Alexander William Kinglake's *Eothen* (1899).

130. Alice Maude Fenn, "Among the Red Roofs of Sussex," *Century* 30, no. 5 (September 1885): 709–23. Images of the house may be seen in the digitized version of this article on the Cornell University Library Making of America Collection website.

131. Alice Maude Fenn, "The Borderlands of Surrey," *Century* 24, no. 4 (August 1882): 483–94; Fenn's illustrations include one of Tennyson's house (489). "Among the Red Roofs of Sussex," *Century* 30, no. 5 (September 1885): 709–23, includes Fenn's illustrations of the rented farmhouse (711), its kitchen (710), and his studio (714).

132. [Brooks], "The Late Harry Fenn." Fenn composed an illustration of Tennyson walking along a road, titled "Lane from Farringford to Beacon Down. The Poet's Favorite Walk,"; see Edith M. Nicholl, "A Little Girl's Glimpse of Tennyson," *St. Nicholas,* November 1899, 11.

133. Fenn to James Russell Lowell, Linchmere, February 18, 1881, bMS Am 148 3, p. 113, Houghton Library, Harvard University.

5. NEW CLIENTS, NEW TECHNOLOGIES, AND A NEW HOME—THE 1880s

1. Fenn's son Walter gives September 30, 1881, as the date of their return; Walter J. Fenn "Biographical Sketch of the Life of Harry Fenn," manuscript, Fenn family records, 5. He describes the house on pp. 9–11.

2. In the *U.S. Art Directory and Yearbook* for 1882, Fenn's address is listed as 7 W. 14th St.; in 1884 it is 16 W. 23rd St. The 1883–84 directory gives his home address as 403 Adelphi St., Brooklyn. It is unknown whether the number of the Tompsons' house had changed or the Fenns were residing in a neighboring house. In 1885, Fenn's address in the American Water Color Society catalogue is 141 St. Mark's Ave., Brooklyn, about ten blocks south of Adelphi St.

3. Letter of John Douglas Woodward to his mother, February 24, 1884, Woodward papers, Valentine Richmond History Center, Richmond, Virginia.

4. "Montclair in the 1870's: A Place for Artists," undated unidentified newspaper clipping, quoting a description of Fenn in the January 5, 1878, *Montclair Times.* He was also said to be "an earnest Christian, a model parent, a rare companion, with a heart open to every good work." This view is somewhat at odds with the opinion of Charles Parsons's daughter-in-law Alice Brigham Parsons, who, after spending an evening with the Fenns, wrote to her mother on May 1, 1869: "They are very refined and cultivated people and very exclusive and do not mingle with the people in the town"; Kathryn E. Gamble, introduction to *Charles Parsons and His Domain* (Montclair, N.J.: Montclair Art Museum, 1958), 16.

5. Sarah Burns, *Inventing the Modern Artist: Art and Culture in Gilded Age America* (New Haven: Yale University Press, 1996), 2.

6. Sean Dennis Cashman, *America in the Gilded Age: From the Death of Lincoln to the Rise of Theodore Roosevelt* (New York: New York University Press, 1984), chap. 1.

7. Ibid.

8. See Candice Millard, *Destiny of the Republic: A Tale of Madness, Medicine, and the Murder of a President* (New York: Doubleday, 2011), esp. 234. Fenn would contribute to an album of artworks assembled for Garfield's young daughter, Mollie, now owned by the Archives of American Art, Smithsonian Institution. See Fenn's contribution as reproduced in Ann Prentice Wagner, "Art for a President's Daughter: Mollie Garfield's Album," *Archives of American Art Journal,* 45, nos. 1–2 (2005): 2–17; his drawing of a spider in its web is on p. 15.

9. Peter Bermingham, *American Art in the Barbizon Mood* (Washington, D.C.: Smithsonian Institution Press, 1975), 69. The new magazines included the *Art Journal, Art Amateur, American Art Review,* and a New York edition of the *Magazine of Art,* published by Cassell & Co. In 1883 *Art Age* and *Art Folio* were launched. See Frank Luther Mott, *A History of American Magazines, 1865–1885,* vol. 2 (Cambridge: Harvard University Press, 1938), 184–85.

10. Bermingham, *American Art in the Barbizon Mood,* 14.

11. Clarence Cook, "The New World's Fair," *New York Daily Tribune,* May 10, 1876; Susan Nichols Carter, "Art at the Exhibition," *Appletons' Journal,* June 3, 1876, 726, and "Paintings at the Centennial Exhibition," *Art Journal* (New York), August 1876, 218. Carter mentions especially Leighton's *Summer Moon* and Hunt's *Self-Portrait.*

12. Frank Duveneck, Frank Currier, William Merritt Chase, Walter Shirlaw, Otto Bacher, and others had studied at the Royal Academy in Munich in the early 1870s; see Michael Quick, "Munich and American Realism," in *Munich and American Realism in the 19th Century* (Sacramento, Calif.: E. B. Crocker Art Gallery, 1978), 22–36.

13. Ibid., 31. A feature titled "A Peasant Painter—Jules Bastien-Lepage," by Ripley Hitchcock, opened the November 1887 issue of the children's magazine *St. Nicholas.*

14. For an account of the conflict between the younger artists, many of whom were from patrician families, and the members of the National Academy of Design, see Saul E. Zalesch, "Competition and Conflict in the New York Art World, 1874–1879," *Winterthur Portfolio* 29, nos. 2/3 (Summer/Autumn 1994): 103–20.

15. H. Barbara Weinberg, introduction to G. W. Sheldon, *Hours with Art and Artists* (ca. 1882; reprint, New York: Garland Publishing, 1978), 9.

16. Kathleen A. Foster, "Makers of the American Watercolor Movement: 1860–1890" (Ph.D. diss., Yale University, 1982), 29–30.

17. The article mistakenly denotes it as the sixteenth annual exhibition; "The Water-Color Society," *Harper's Weekly,* February 4, 1882.

18. Other of Fenn's exhibited works, all unlocated, appear from their titles to be related to published illustrations; for *A Day School in the Shoemaker's Bazaar,* see *Picturesque Palestine,* 1:394; *The Rialto Market, Venice,* see *Picturesque Europe,* 2:233 or 235; *The Market Place, Segovia,* see *Picturesque Europe,* 2:380.

19. See Edward Kaufman, "Architecture and Travel in the Age of British Eclecticism," in *Architecture and Its Image: Four Centuries of Architectural Representation, Works from the Collection of the Canadian Centre for Architecture* (Montreal: Canadian Centre for Architecture, 1989), 59–85.

20. Clarence Cook, "The Art Gallery. The Water-Color Society's Exhibition," *Art Amateur,* March 1882, 75. Cook's comments on Thomas Moran, immediately following, show how tastes have changed since Cook's time: He wrote that Moran "will continue to paint us the Yellowstone region, and make drawings that are as disagreeable in color as they are incredible. Because Nature does impossible and outlandish things occasionally, or did in her salad days, must we needs mortify the ancient dame by pulling her gaudy youthful 'duds' out of her trunks and showing them to the public? Nature made these fantastic mountains to please her first-born monsters, the ichthyosaurus, the pterodactyl, and the rest who were, we take it color-blind; she never thought of us, who are not color-blind at all."
21. See Thomas P. Bruhn, *American Etching: The 1880s* (Storrs, Conn.: William Benton Museum of Art, 1985). For details of the etching revival movement as seen through the life of Peter Moran, see David Gilmore Wright, *Domestic and Wild: Peter Moran's Images of America* (Baltimore, Md.: Creo Press, 2010).
22. "The Water-Color Society," *Harper's Weekly,* February 2, 1882.
23. Entry dated May 6, 1882, "Smillie Diarie," Smillie Papers, reel #2851, Archives of American Art, Smithsonian Institution. My thanks to W. Dale Horst for this information.
24. Fenn's etchings are listed in *Catalog of the New York Etching Club Exhibition Held at the National Academy of Design, N.Y. Feb. 4–March 20, 1889;* see Raymond L. Wilson, *Index of American Print Exhibitions, 1882–1940* (Metuchen, N.J.: Scarecrow Press, 1988). The Parrish Art Museum, Southampton, N.Y., owns a work titled *Lobster Cove,* ca. 1889 (showing a building, a dock, and an arching tree), which is illustrated in Alicia G. Longwell, *First Impressions: Nineteenth-Century American Master Prints* (Southampton, N.Y.; Parrish Art Museum, 2010). An etching on silk by Fenn titled *Lobster Cove, Cape Ann* was offered on eBay July 30, 2004; perhaps other etchings by him will surface in the future. Fenn also did at least one monotype, for Child's Gallery, Boston, had one in stock as of January 2012.
25. Two examples are *Poets and Etchers* (Boston: James R. Osgood, 1882) and the so-called Zuyder Zee edition of *Holland and Its People* by Edmondo de Amicus (New York: G. P. Putnam's Sons, 1885), with etchings by R. Swain Gifford, Charles A. Platt, Samuel Colman, Joseph Pennell, and Charles A. Vanderhoof. The most expensive version of this edition was advertised at $25, "with extra proofs of etchings on satin"; *New York Times,* December 16, 1884.
26. Walter Shirlaw (1838–1909) had played a controversial role in the New York art scene before Fenn's return. He was the first president of the Society of American Artists and resigned his membership in the National Academy of Design when the Academy failed to elect other society members as associates in 1879; Zalesch, "Competition and Conflict," 114–15, 117.
27. The *New York Times,* March 12, 1883, stated that Fenn said "he only accepted the candidacy after much urging, and time [had] only deepened his disinclination to enter into any contest."
28. "Rewards of Painters," *New York Times,* October 1, 1882.
29. "The Water-Color Exhibition," *Harper's Weekly,* February 3, 1883.
30. Ibid. The society's exhibition was the subject of a children's book by Lizzie W. Champney, wife of artist James Wells Champney, titled *John Angelo at the Water Color Exhibition* (Boston: D. Lothrop, 1883), "with illustrations by members of the American Water Color Society." Two young boys discuss the merits of various paintings—one likes works with more finish, the other likes works by "impressionists." Fenn's *Marshall's Creek, Pa.* is reproduced on p. 24. I am grateful to Selma Avdicevic for bringing this book to my attention. In 1882 and 1883 Fenn also exhibited with the Philadelphia Society of Artists.
31. Quoted from "the *Pictorial World* and *Life*" in *Studio* 2 (July 1883): 46–47, in a column signed by "Porcupine." The American Water-Color Exhibition, arranged by a Mr. Hamlet S. Philpot, was displayed in "the drawing room of the Egyptian Hall, immediately over the Dudley Gallery."
32. E.W.M., "The Watercolor Exhibition in New York," *Boston Daily Evening Transcript,* February 14, 1884. The black-and-white wood engraving "Pennsylvania Bee Colony" in the society's catalogue and on the front page of the March 1884 *Art Amateur* sheds no light on the controversial coloring. Fenn exhibited two other works at this exhibition; see app. 2 for the listings for 1884 and 1885.

33. It was shown in the Watercolor Exhibition of the Boston Art Club; "The Watercolor Exhibition," *Boston Daily Evening Transcript,* Apr. 18, 1884.

34. Perhaps these unlocated works were similar to the illustrations titled "Dead Bracken" (p. 486) and "Gorse or Furze" (p. 488) that accompany Alice Maude Fenn's article "The Borderlands of Surrey," *Century,* August 1882.

35. Alexander Katlan, "The Salmagundi Club: A Prestigious History," *American Arts Quarterly,* winter 1997, 34–37. The Black and White Exhibitions, held from 1878 to 1887, were open to all artists, including women (although membership was limited to men); see Alexander W. Katlan, *The Black and White Exhibitions of the Salmagundi Sketch Club, 1878–1887* (Flushing, N.Y.: Alexander W. Katlan Conservator, 2007). Interest in these exhibitions declined in the 1880s, perhaps because, as the processes for reproducing ink and watercolor drawings improved, there was less difference between the original artwork and the printed image; see W. H. Shelton, *The Salmagundi Club Being a History of Its Beginning as a Sketch Class, Its Public Service as a Black and White Society, and Its Career as a Club from MDCCCLXXI to MCMXVIII* (New York: Houghton Mifflin, 1918), 46. Fenn was elected to the hanging committee of the Salmagundi Club in 1883, along with W. T. Brandage and J. A. S. Monks. His formal admission to the club was in March 1891, when he was proposed by Charles Yardley Turner, president of the club from 1889 to 1893, and seconded by Alexander C. Morgan and Thomas Moran, who served as president from 1893 to 1896; see Alexander W. Katlan, *The Salmagundi Club Painting Exhibition Records 1889 to 1939* (Flushing, N.Y.: Alexander Katlan Conservator, 2008). I am grateful to Alexander W. Katlan for this information; thanks also to Bob Mueller, chair of the Salmagundi Club curatorial committee.

36. "Men of Ideal Worlds," *Brooklyn Daily Eagle,* November 25, 1883. A letter from Fenn to the writer Edward Eggleston in 1894 suggests that he tried the medium at least once: "The drawings have all been made for some days. But in an evil moment I was tempted to make the ship burning business a Black & White *oil* and the pure blacks refuse to dry—The moment they condescend to be obliging I will send the lot to 806 B.W. [Broadway]"; MSS: Edward Eggleston Letters, 1868–1902, Indiana State Library. I have been unable to identify the illustration in question.

37. These auctions are described in John Ott, "How New York Stole the Luxury Art Market: Blockbuster Auctions and the Bourgeois Identity in Gilded Age America," *Winterthur Portfolio* 42, nos. 2/3 (Summer/Autumn 2008): 138–41.

38. Ibid., 141. In *John Angelo at the Water Color Exhibition,* Champney includes a discussion about the differences in prices realized between European oils and American watercolors. One of the boys says: "The ugly high-priced foreign pictures can only be bought by a few rich swells, you see, while people who are just comfortably off can afford to buy the really nice work of our own American artists instead of the photographs and engravings which used to be the best they could have" (27).

39. Ott, "How New York Stole the Luxury Art Market," 146–48. The American Art Association's auctions provided stiff competition for the National Academy of Design's exhibitions; according to Ott: "The NAD's revenues from their annual salons peaked in 1882, the last year before the debut of the AAA" (137).

40. Washington Gladden, quoted in Theodore P. Greene, *America's Heroes: The Changing Models of Success in American Magazines* (New York: Oxford University Press, 1970), 73; Gladden was "speaking about Roswell Smith, business manager and part-owner of the *Century.*"

41. Irene Tichenor describes the process as follows: "The key to making wood engravings ready for printing lay in a system of 'overlays.' This term (potentially confusing to the uninitiated) referred to layers of tissue *under* the paper (and, hence, laid *over* the surface against which the back of the paper rested before printing). These layers were meticulously cut out in varying shapes to give more pressure to darker areas and less to lighter. De Vinne was not the originator of the process by any means. . . . While he took his cue from others, De Vinne experimented with paper overlays until he perfected the technique. He also used a 'peeled overlay' technique in which a three- or four-ply cardboard was scraped and cut to give less pressure to 'gray' areas and even less to white

ones"; Irene Tichenor, *No Art without Craft: The Life of Theodore Low De Vinne, Printer* (Boston: David R. Godine, 2005), 60. See also Theodore L. De Vinne, "The Printing of 'The Century,'" *Century,* November 1890, 87–99; overlaying is described on pp. 94–96 and in De Vinne's earlier article, "The Growth of Wood-cut Printing. II," *Scribner's Monthly,* May 1880, 39–43.

42. *St. Nicholas* was launched by Scribner in 1873; see Susan R. Gannon, Suzanne Rahn, and Ruth Anne Thompson, eds., *St. Nicholas and Mary Mapes Dodge: The Legacy of a Children's Magazine Editor, 1873–1905* (Jefferson, N.C.: McFarland, 2004), 31, 82.

43. Theodore Peterson, *Magazines in the Twentieth Century,* 2nd ed. (Urbana: University of Illinois Press, 1964), 5. In "The Printing of 'The Century,'" De Vinne describes a massive web press built for the Century Co. by R. Hoe & Co. that could print 32 pages, front and back, and cut and fold them. This press was used to print the pages without illustrations and the ads; for illustrations, smaller, slower stop-cylinder presses were used, as well as a new Hoe web press designed especially to print illustrations that could do the work of four stop-cylinder presses (93–94).

44. This was the Postal Act of March 3, 1879; Peterson, *Magazines in the Twentieth Century,* 2, 98.

45. Ibid., 150.

46. Greene, *America's Heroes,* 71. Such individuals are sometimes referred to as "Mugwumps."

47. "Notes," *Critic,* December 8, 1883.

48. *Harper's Christmas: Pictures and Papers, Done by the Tile Club and Its Literary Friends; Specimen of Harper & Brothers Printing; A Souvenir of the New Orleans Exposition,* [December] 1882, 3; a copy is in Special Collections, University of Virginia Library.

49. Joseph Pennell, *The Adventures of an Illustrator* (Boston: Little, Brown, 1925), 58.

50. "Magazine Miscellany," *Christian Union,* February 1, 1883, 100.

51. This use of photography to create an image on the woodblock for the engraver to follow had gradually become more widespread. Stephen P. Rice says that the technique was "sometimes called 'photoxylography'" and asserts that "the art editor of *Scribner's* was making regular use" of it by the mid-1870s; Stephen P. Rice, "Photography in Engraving on Wood," *Common-place* 7, no. 3 (April 2007), n.p., http://www.common-place.org. Arthur Hoeber wrote that, by 1876, the use of photography on the block had become "an accomplished fact"; Arthur Hoeber, "A Century of American Illustration," *Bookman* 8 (November 1898): 323. For a description of the process, see Thomas W. Smillie, "Photographing on Wood for Engraving," *Smithsonian Miscellaneous Collections,* vol. 47 (Washington, D.C.: Smithsonian Institution, 1905), 497–99.

52. See William H. Brandt, *Interpretive Wood-Engraving: The Story of the Society of American Wood-Engravers* (New Castle, Del.: Oak Knoll Press, 2009). In 1887 the society produced a portfolio titled *Engravings on Wood by Members of the Society of American Wood-Engravers* (Harper). It sent proofs of the 25 engravings in the portfolio, plus 77 more, to the 1889 Exposition Universelle in Paris; the same works toured the United States afterward, exhibited first in New York at the Grolier Club and then in several other cities (86–89). *Exhibition of the Society of American Wood-Engravers,* the catalogue for the show held at the Museum of Fine Arts, Boston (October 2–November 30, 1890), lists four works by Fenn, but in this case the focus was on the engravers: H. E. Sylvester engraved "View," "Interior of the People's Palace, London," and "Façade of St. Finbarr's, Cork"; W. J. Linton engraved "A Street in Jerusalem."

53. Linton's first diatribe against the New School approach was "Art in Engraving on Wood," *Atlantic Monthly,* June 1879, 705–15.

54. Arthur Hoeber, "A Century of American Illustration, IV.—Departures in Engraving; VI.—Influence of the European Students" *Bookman* 8 (December 1898): 317, 322–23.

55. Quoted in "Wood-Engraving and The Century Prizes," *Century,* June 1882, 230.

56. "Art," *Churchman,* August 27, 1881, 238.

57. The illustrator is not named, and I have not identified the monogram.

58. The building, at 33 E. 17th St., was completed in 1881, after the Century Co. became independent of Scribner's, and the magazine's offices were on the fifth floor; see Robert A. M. Stern, Thomas Mellin, and David Fishman, *New York 1880: Architecture and Urbanism in the Gilded Age* (New York: Monacelli Press, 1999), 441–43.

59. Letter from Dr. Holland, editor of *Scribner's Magazine,* to Philip Gilbert Hamerton, quoted in Philip Gilbert Hamerton, *The Graphic Arts: A Treatise on the Varieties of Drawing, Painting and Engraving* (New York: Macmillan, 1882), 326 fn.

60. Quoted in William Fayal Clarke, "An Appreciation [of Alexander W. Drake]," in Alexander W. Drake, *Three Midnight Stories* (New York: Century, 1916), 109; on Drake's role at the *Century,* see Arthur John, *The Best Years of the* Century (Urbana: University of Illinois Press, 1981), 77–78.

61. See, for example, "She knew not her husband stood watching her" and "Side by side, hand in hand" in both the 1883 Thomas Y. Crowell edition of *Lucile,* illustrated by F. T. Merrill, and the 1892 Crowell edition.

62. The engraver's monogram looks like "WM," possibly that of W. H. Morse; thanks to William H. Brandt for this suggestion.

63. Fenn and his daughter Alice Maude also collaborated in 1886 on two articles for the London *Art Journal:* "The Hudson River," no. 7 (July): 198–202, and "Niagara," no. 8 (August): 237–41. Alice Maude writes from the viewpoint of a visitor from Britain; for these illustrations Fenn may have reworked some of his sketches or illustrations for *Picturesque America.* Father and daughter also collaborated on a piece for the May 1888 *St. Nicholas,* "Girard College," 509–15, about a boarding school for "poor white male orphans" in Philadelphia founded by the French immigrant Stephen Girard; one of Fenn's illustrations, "A Ball Game on the Play-grounds, Girard College," includes many figures and was probably based on a photograph, as the others could have been.

64. "Gallery and Studio," *Brooklyn Daily Eagle,* September 20, 1885. Fenn also prepared illustrations of England for the July 1887 issue of *St. Nicholas;* they accompanied a "Personally Conducted" tour "In English Country" by Frank. R. Stockton, one of a series of twelve by the writer.

65. Estelle Jussim uses the term *process line engraving* for this method in her excellent *Visual Communication and the Graphic Arts: Photographic Technologies in the Nineteenth Century* (New York: R. R. Bowker, 1983). Bamber Gascoigne describes the process of making "line blocks, etched, with photography (warm rinse)" as follows: "A zinc plate was coated with light-sensitized gelatin and a negative of the artwork was placed upon it for exposure. The transparent lines of the image hardened the gelatin on the plate, but the unexposed gelatin could be rinsed away in warm water. . . . When the lines had been coated to make them fully acid-resistant, the white areas were etched down to the necessary depth. Once the acid-resist was cleaned from the raised surfaces, the block was ready for printing—though for some time improvements were usually made by hand with the engraving tool"; Bamber Gascoigne, *How to Identify Prints* (New York: Thames and Hudson, 1986), section 33, f (n.p.). According to David Woodward, "the honour for this invention must go to Charles Gillot, who had improved the technique sufficiently for commercial use by 1872"; David Woodward, "The Decline of Commercial Wood-Engraving in Nineteenth-Century America," *Journal of the Printing Historical Society,* no. 10 (1974–75): 57–83. He states that another advantage over wood engraving was that "large sized illustrations could be printed from one line-block, where wood-engravings required a number of small blocks bolted together" (67–68). Earlier use of process line blocks to reproduce Fenn's ink drawings appears in the March 1884 *Century:* "Old State House, Boston," 688.

66. Pennell, *Adventures of an Illustrator,* 68. He declared that *Harper's Weekly* was not considered a rival.

67. Fenn's first commission for Harper after his return was a front-page image for the July 1, 1882, *Harper's Weekly:* "Breakneck Mountain, from the Foot of Cro'Nest, Hudson River" illustrated an article on the history and picturesque charm of the Hudson River valley.

68. *New York Times,* January 21, 1883.

69. *The Critic,* January 20, 1883, 55.

70. Quoted from "The Spectator," *New York Times,* March 26, 1882. It is also noteworthy that the styles of both Fenn and Foster were familiar enough that such comments needed no further explanation.

71. Some eighty proofs of illustrations printed on heavy paper, without text, now in the possession of William Abt, suggest that the publishers provided Fenn with proofs of each image to approve or perhaps comment on.

72. Fenn's original drawing for "View on the Powow River" in this article can be viewed by searching the Library of Congress website, http://www.loc.gov/pictures.

73. At least three of the Adirondack images (those on pp. 217, 223, and 225 of *Harper's Monthly*) were reused in Henry P. Wells, *City Boys in the Woods; or, A Trapping Venture in Maine* (New York: Harper & Brothers, 1890). The image on p. 223, as well as two other works by Fenn, appeared in the trade catalogue of the Henry C. Squires company, *Descriptive Catalogue and Price-List of Sportsmen's Supplies . . .* (New York: By the company, 1890), 125; the booklet was praised as "probably" the finest example ever produced "in the whole range of trade literature" (*The Decorator and Furnisher* 15, no. 5 [February 1890]: 166). Presumably the company bought electrotypes of previously printed illustrations to embellish its catalogues; the one example I have seen states on its title page: "With many illustrations by the most eminent and well-known artists in America" and lists Frederic Remington, W. Hamilton Gibson, Childe Hassam, Thomas Moran, A. B. Frost, and others, but not Fenn. Fenn's illustrations were also reused in almanacs. One example is the 1883 *Almanack* "Illustrated by Celebrated Artists" that was published by William Resor & Co., Cincinnati, Ohio; Fenn's designs illustrate January through June, and his wood engravings from *Snow-Bound* embellish the "Encyclopaedia of Quotations" in the back.

74. In most cases the name of the photographer is given below the image, lower left, and that of the engraver, lower right.

75. Robert Underwood Johnson, *Remembered Yesterdays* (Boston: Little, Brown, 1923), 208, quoted in Timothy P. Caron, "'How Changeable Are the Events of War': National Reconciliation in the *Century Magazine*'s 'Battles and Leaders of the Civil War,'" *American Periodicals* 16, no. 2 (2006): 155.

76. See Caron, "'How Changeable Are the Events of War,'" and Janet Gabler-Hover, "The North-South Reconciliation Theme and the 'Shadow of the Negro' in the *Century Magazine*," in Kenneth M. Price and Susan Belasco, eds., *Periodical Literature in Nineteenth Century America* (Charlottesville: University of Virginia Press, 1995). Mark J. Noonan finds that the *Century*'s fiction related to the Civil War, especially by Mark Twain, presented narratives different from that of the series; Mark J. Noonan, *Reading* The Century Illustrated Monthly Magazine: *American Literature and Culture, 1870–1893* (Kent, Ohio: Kent State University Press, 2010), chap. 7, "Reading the War of *The Century*."

77. Quoted in Stephen W. Sears, ed., *The American Heritage Century Collection of Civil War Art* (New York: American Heritage Publishing, 1983), 12.

78. Gilder, "The 'Century' War Series," *Century,* March 1885, 788.

79. Sears, *Civil War Art,* 12.

80. See Sears, *Civil War Art,* for information on many of the participating artists and reproductions of their original drawings for the series; he considers Fenn "the most skilled of the artists," aside from Homer and Pennell (39).

81. The drawing is reproduced in Sears, *Civil War Art,* 31.

82. He urged them to "*make* [your lines] *more open and heavier than you find them in any of the magazines!*"; Ernest Knaufft, "Pen Drawing for Photo-Engraving. XI.," *Art Amateur,* May 1890, 119–20.

83. *Brooklyn Daily Eagle,* August 23, 1885.

84. Sears, *Civil War Art,* pl. 150; also published in vol. 3 of the *Battles and Leaders of the Civil War* book. The Tennessee State Museum owns three of Fenn's original works for the project: "The Cumberland River from Fort Donelson," "Gunboats at Fort Donelson" (pl. 59 in Sears) and "Lookout Mountain" (pl. 281 in Sears). James C. Kelly, *Civil War Drawings from the Tennessee State Museum* (Tennessee State Museum Foundation, 1989).

85. Bruce Catton, foreword to Sears, *Civil War Art,* 9.

86. Joseph Pennell, *Pen Drawing and Pen Draughtsmen* (London: Macmillan, 1889), 302.

87. Quoted in the account of Fenn's life attributed to his daughter Hilda Fenn van Antwerp in the Fenn family papers.

88. Pennell, *Pen Drawing and Pen Draughtsmen,* 310.

89. William Welles Bosworth, "William Rotch Ware, 1848–1917," *American Architect* 111 (May 2, 1917): 274; I have been unable to find out more about the competition mentioned in Ware's obituary.

90. A "new" Old South Church had been completed in 1876, and White feared the old building would be demolished (687–88). The same drawing (at a smaller size) was used to illustrate Thomas Wentworth Higginson's article "Boston" in the April 1892 *St. Nicholas.*

91. A few months later Fenn drew historic buildings in Salem, Mass., to illustrate two articles by Julian Hawthorne related to his father, Nathaniel Hawthorne: "Salem of Hawthorne" opened the May 1884 issue, and "Scenes of Hawthorne's Romances" appeared in July. For these Fenn introduced variety with framing devices and insets to show objects not visible from the viewpoint he had chosen.

92. Not long after, the magazine began publishing the "plantation myth fiction" of Thomas Nelson Page and others; see Noonan, *Reading* The Century, esp. 133–44.

93. In a letter dated August 24[?], 1885, to S. R. Koehler, Fenn wrote: "As I start very shortly for an extended sketching tour in the south, I shall be glad of the check" (S. R. Koehler Collection, Syracuse University Library). The only other records of this trip I have located are (1) a one-sentence notice in the November 28, 1885, *Harper's Weekly* reporting that Fenn became seriously ill at Louisville, Ky., while on a trip with Burroughs and "received the kindly ministrations of the nuns of that city"; and (2) a notice in the May 29, 1886, *Critic:* "Col. McDowell, of Ashland, Lexington, has named a fancy colt after Harry Fenn, in memory of a recent visit of the artist to the old home of Henry Clay. Among the new colts the closest rival of Harry Fenn is [the Dutch/British painter] Alma-Tadema." This trip might also have provided material for some of the Civil War series views of Lookout Mountain and Chattanooga. Fenn and John Burroughs collaborated on a July 1887 *Century* article titled "Among the Wildflowers," but the flowers described and depicted were not ones they would have seen on their trip. For the June 1891 *St. Nicholas* Fenn illustrated Burroughs's article "A Talk about Wild Flowers."

94. See Howard Mumford Jones, *The Age of Energy: Varieties of American Experience, 1865–1915* (New York: Viking Press, 1970), 37.

95. S. G. W. Benjamin, *Art in America: A Critical and Historical Sketch* (New York: Harper & Brothers, 1880), 178–79.

96. His renderings appear most prominently in part 1, "Public Buildings," May 1884; part 4, "Churches," January 1885; part 5, "City Dwellings," February 1886; and part 7, "American Country Dwellings. I," May 1886. His drawing for "Ames Memorial Town-Hall, North Easton, Mass." (May 1884) is in the collection of the Metropolitan Museum of Art, New York, acc. no. 1996.461. The drawing for "Interior of St. Stephen's Church, Lynn, Mass." (January 1885) is reproduced in the Christie's catalogue *Property from the Estate of E. Maurice Bloch, Part II, New York, Wednesday, January 9, 1991,* lot 185; several Fenn drawings were offered in this sale. Fenn's drawing for "House of Mrs. Mary Hemenway, Manchester, Mass." (May 1886) is in a private collection. His drawing "House of Samuel Coleman, Esq., Newport, R.I." (June 1886) is also reproduced in the Christie's catalogue *Property of the Estate of E. Maurice Bloch,* lot 182. In June 1884 Fenn illustrated an article titled "Sailors' Snug Harbor," about a home for aged sailors on Staten Island; one of his original works for this article is in the Cabinet of American Illustration of the Library of Congress, and a digital image of it appears on the library's website.

97. Mariana Schuyler van Rensselaer, "Churches," *Century,* January 1885, 328. Van Rensselaer approves of the use of paint rather than "the chisel" for the colorful interior decoration (330–32), but the black and white illustration cannot show this.

98. "Illustrated Holiday Books," *Nation,* December 13, 1883: 491.

99. A review of Ingelow's poem in the December 5, 1883, *Continent: An Illustrated Weekly Magazine* begins: "Though ten thousand schoolgirls bring their budding elocutionary powers to bear on Jean Ingelow's pathetic poem, 'The High Tide on the Coast of Lincolnshire, 1571,' no repetition dulls its charms, and Roberts Brothers have done a service to every lover of the tender, sorrowful ballad in illustrating it for the holiday season." Fenn's floral designs for Tennyson's *Lady Clare* (Philadelphia: Porter & Coates, 1884) were praised in the *Critic,* December 13, 1884,

which stated: "[They] would add a grace to any poem. They are in a style peculiarly appropriate to Tennyson's muse."

100. Other artists who participated in one or more of these books include J. Appleton Brown, Thomas Moran, Childe Hassam, F. B. Schell, F. S. Church, E. H. Garrett, F. Dielman, F. Hopkinson Smith, A. B. Frost, Mary Hallock Foote, J. Douglas Woodward, and Henry Sandham.

101. An ad in *Literary World,* December 1, 1883, publicized "illuminated covers, with fringed borders, Christmas card style, with box, $1.75; flexible morocco, or tree calf, $4.00; Royal 8vo edition (ca. 9 1/8 by 6 5/8") beautifully bound in cloth, $3.00; antique morocco, or tree calf, $8.00." The larger-format edition was printed on even heavier paper, with blank versos.

102. In the large paper edition, on which the pages are printed only on one side, these two images do not appear side by side.

103. "Editor's Literary Record," *Harper's New Monthly Magazine,* January 1884, 321. "Illustrated Holiday Books," *Nation,* December 13, 1883, 492.

104. "Art," *Churchman,* August 27, 1881, 17. The writer mentions as unnecessary two illustrations of a story by Constance Fenimore Woolson titled "Anne" in the August 1881 *Harper's Monthly.* A later critique of illustrations that "give the letter . . . and not the spirit" of the text and "are apt to stunt, if they do not kill, the imagination" appeared in "Over-Illustration," *Harper's Weekly,* July 29, 1911, 6.

105. "Illustrated Books," *Lippincott's Magazine,* January 1884.

106. See Hollister Sturges, ed., *The Rural Vision: France and America in the Late Nineteenth Century* (Omaha, Nebr.: Joslyn Art Museum, 1987). Writers such as Thomas Hardy, Émile Zola, and Leo Tolstoy treated similar subjects; see "Rural Scenes," in Robert Rosenblum, Maryanne Stevens, and Ann Dumas, *1900: Art at the Crossroads* (New York: Solomon R. Guggenheim Museum, 2000), 282.

107. "Illustrated Holiday Books," *Nation,* December 13, 1883, 492; "Books for the Holidays," *Dial,* December 1883, 200; "Editor's Literary Record," 321.

108. According to measuringworth.com, using the CPI index, the 2011 equivalent of $10,000 in 1872, when Fenn was working on *Picturesque America,* would be approximately $190,000.

109. John Douglas Woodward to his mother, February 24, 1884, Woodward Papers, Valentine Richmond History Center, Richmond, Va. The original address was 177 N. Mountain Ave., but after Fenn sold the house it was moved downhill, and its current address is 208 North Mountain Ave.; "Individual Structure Survey Form, Historic Sites Inventory No. 0713372," Historic Preservation Section, Trenton, N.J. It has undergone many alterations over the years. In 2009 the new owner launched a blog about the house and its restoration: thecedarsofmontclair.blogspot.com.

110. Ficken came to America in 1869 and started practicing architecture in New York in 1878; see "Ficken, Henry Edwards," *Who Was Who in America,* vol. 1 (Chicago: Marquis-Who's Who, 1942), 367. Ficken's partner was Charles D. Gambrill; *New York Times,* September 14, 1880; February 22, 1882; and June 27, 1929 (Ficken's obituary). Ficken designed the Hoboken Ferry Terminal (1883–86), Proctor's Theater in Manhattan (1888), and a house at 135 W. 81st St. (1886–88); see Stern et al., *New York 1880,* 81, 677, 757.

111. Eileen Michels says that Ficken was "among the best perspective delineators working in this country in 1876," with works appearing frequently in *American Architect.* "Ficken established himself successfully as an architect in New York by 1883 after steady work as a draftsman with first Potter and Robertson and then Charles Smith"; Eileen Michels, "Late Nineteenth-Century Published American Perspective Drawing," *Journal of the Society of Architectural Historians* 31, no. 4 (December 1972): 294–95.

112. "Mr. Harry Fenn's House," in *Artistic Country-Seats,* ed. George William Sheldon (New York: D. Appleton, 1886), 1:13. On the shingle style, see books by Vincent J. Scully; the earliest is *The Shingle Style: Architectural Theory and Design from Richardson to the Origins of Wright* (New Haven: Yale University Press, 1955).

113. *Harper's Weekly,* September 26, 1885, 627.

114. Champney also covered George Inness senior and junior, who like Fenn were in Montclair, as well as Will H. Low in Milton, N.Y.; Thomas Moran in Easthampton, L.I.; Percy Moran in Greenport, L.I.; Samuel Colman in Newport, R.I.; Eastman Johnson in Nantucket. Mass.; R. Swain Gifford and William Sartain in Nonquitt, Mass.; and Elbridge Kingsley and his "studio car."

115. Lizzie W. Champney, "The Summer Haunts of American Artists," *Century,* October 1885, 848. In addition to his own studio, Fenn illustrated those of Samuel Colman, Eastman Johnson, and George Fuller; Bierstadt's Malkasten had burned to the ground in 1882.

116. Preface to *In Pursuit of Beauty: Americans and the Aesthetic Movement* (New York: Metropolitan Museum of Art and Rizzoli, 1986), 19; see esp. Roger B. Stein's insightful essay, "Artifact as Ideology: The Aesthetic Movement in Its American Cultural Context," 23–51.

117. See Kristin L. Hoganson, *Consumers' Imperium: The Global Production of American Domesticity, 1865–1920* (Chapel Hill: University of North Carolina Press, 2007), esp. chap. 1. Hoganson emphasizes that women sought to create homes that "demonstrated a familiarity with the wider world" (14) and relates the use of imported items to the growth of imperialism.

118. Katherine C. Grier, *Culture and Comfort: People, Parlors, and Upholstery, 1850–1930* (Rochester, N.Y.: Strong Museum, 1988), 188–92.

119. The 1876 exposition also provided what was for many a first look at Japanese people, buildings, and gardens, for Japan had been closed to the West until the mid-19th century. As Neil Harris has written: "Japanese exclusion meant that, except for a few sailors and shipwrecked civilians, there was absolutely no interaction between Japan and the United States before the mid nineteenth century, and very little information about Japan diffused in this country before the Centennial Exhibition of 1876"; Neil Harris, *Cultural Excursions: Marketing Appetites and Cultural Taste in Modern America* (Chicago: University of Chicago Press, 1990), 30, 35. According to Sylvia L. Yount, "Until the Centennial, most Americans tended to think of Japan and China as an indistinguishable 'Orient'"; Sylvia L. Yount, "'Give the People What They Want': The American Aesthetic Movement, Art Worlds, and Consumer Culture, 1876–1890" (Ph.D. diss., University of Pennsylvania, 1995), 75. As Gabriel P. Weisberg points out: "At no site at the fairground was acknowledgment given to the importance of the Japanese print tradition, a heritage that was already igniting the passionate interest of numerous Europeans. Works on paper, which exerted a lasting impact on American art and craftsmanship later in the century, were totally absent from the fair's halls, even though there were already available in New York and Boston from dealers—albeit not in huge quantities"; Weisberg, "Japonisme: The Commercialization of an Opportunity," in Julia Meech and Gabriel P. Weisberg, *Japonisme Comes to America: The Japanese Impact on the Graphic Arts, 1876–1925* (New York: Harry N. Abrams, in association with Jane Voorhees Zimmerli Art Museum, Rutgers, State University of New Jersey, 1990), 19. The French exhibit included porcelain decorated with Japanese motifs, a "tendency" that "had been well established throughout France since the mid-1860s" (Weisberg, "Japonisme," 19). Hannah Sigur discusses Japan's involvement in world's fairs, an important focus of the Meiji government; Hannah Sigur, *The Influence of Japanese Art on Design* (Salt Lake City, Utah: Gibbs Smith, 2008), chap. 2.

120. See Sarah Burns, "The Price of Beauty: Art, Commerce, and the Late Nineteenth-Century American Studio Interior," in David C. Miller, ed., *American Iconology: New Approaches to Nineteenth-Century Art and Literature* (New Haven: Yale University Press, 1993), 209–38.

121. Several artists' studios had been depicted and described in G. W. Sheldon, *Hours with Art and Artists* (New York: D. Appleton, 1882), 171–82, including those of Samuel Colman, Louis C. Tiffany, R. Swain Gifford, and W. M. Chase. In 1884 Appleton published *Artists at Home* edited by F. G. Stephens, with photographs of the sitting rooms or studios of select English artists; it was published in London the same year by Sampson Low, Marston, Searle, and Rivington. See also *In Pursuit of Beauty,* esp. Roger B. Stein, "Artifact as Ideology," 24–25, 38–46, and Marilynn Johnson, "The Artful Interior," 111–41.

122. In her book *Beauty in the Household* (New York, 1882), the painter Maria Oakey Dewing rec-

ommended the hue: "Yellow is, in truth, warmth itself. . . . [It is] a color that can be contrasted with various shades of itself more unerringly than any other color"; quoted in Doreen Bolger Burke, "Painters and Sculptors in a Decorative Age," in *In Pursuit of Beauty,* 299–300.

123. "The Home of Mr. Harry Fenn," *Art Amateur,* November 1896, 127. One of Fenn's drawings of the home's interior is owned by the Library of Congress Prints and Photographs Division, Cabinet of American Illustration, and may be viewed online by searching http://www.loc.gov/pictures.

124. See Ronald G. Pisano, *The Tile Club and the Aesthetic Movement in America* (New York: Harry N. Abrams, in association with the Museums at Stony Brook, 1999).

125. "The Home of Mr. Harry Fenn."

126. Fenn to S. R. Koehler, July 24–25, 1885, and August 24–26, 1885, box 1, Syracuse University Library.

127. George William Sheldon, prefatory note, in *Artistic Country-Seats.*

128. "Mr. Harry Fenn's House," in *Artistic Country-Seats,* 13–15. The March 19, 1887, *Scientific American* also ran a brief article on Fenn's house, "Suburban House of a New York Artist," reusing the exterior view and the view of the hall.

129. The binding of the first edition of *Ben-Hur* featured a decoration of flowers similar to Fenn's and Woodward's in *Picturesque Palestine,* with leaves and blossoms overlapping the title block; it is pictured in Eugene Exman, *The House of Harper: One Hundred and Fifty Years of Publishing* (New York: Harper and Row, 1967), 149.

130. The material from the series was eventually published as a book, *In Scripture Lands: New Views of Sacred Places* (New York: Charles Scribner's, 1890). Fenn's illustrations for the series often enhance the photographs they were based on; see, for example, "The Parable of the Sower," in which four sketches of different types of soil are entwined with stalks of wheat (*Century,* January 1889, 421).

131. Two of Fenn's ink drawings for this article are now in the collection of the Cooper-Hewitt National Design Museum, Smithsonian Institution, New York: "Ewer of Solid Silver . . ." (p. 725) and "Example of Old Persian Carving in Brass" (p. 728). The original drawing for "Minaret of Small Mosque in Teherân" (p. 718) is owned by the Delaware Art Museum, Wilmington.

132. The author, listed as Henry W. Jessup, is almost certainly Henry H. Jessup, an American missionary to Syria who had written for *Picturesque Palestine* and published two books, *Women of the Arabs* (1873) and *Syrian Home Life* (1874). The opening of his article is typically condescending: "If the little Arabs are heathen, they are at least picturesque heathen."

133. Compare "Old Bridge at Banias" (p. 427) in *Harper's Monthly* with the steel engraving in *Picturesque Palestine* 1:opp. 353 (and also with Fenn's 1878 watercolor at the Metropolitan Museum of Art: *Caesarea Philippi (Banias),* see chapter 4, note 76).

134. The illustration was for Frederick Jones Bliss, "Tadmor in the Wilderness," about Palmyra (*Scribner's Magazine,* April 1890, 406); F. Hopkinson Smith later chose to reproduce it as an example of Fenn's work in his book *American Illustrators* (New York: Charles Scribner's, 1892), 64. Also for *Scribner's,* which had launched in 1887, Fenn contributed illustrations to the April 1888 article on Gibraltar by Henry M. Field; for two of these he reworked his *Picturesque Europe* images of the famous rock; compare "The Sunset Gun" (457) with *Picturesque Europe* (3:258); and "Catalan Bay, on the East Side of Gibraltar" (460) with *Picturesque Europe* (3:244). Reworking images was an approach Fenn used more often in his later years.

135. When Parsons retired in 1890, Fenn was one of many artists who submitted an original work for a portfolio presented to him, which is now in the collection of the Montclair Art Museum. Fenn's contribution was a watercolor titled *The Pines of Ravenna.*

136. Tom Gretton, "Signs of Labour-Value in Printed Pictures after the Photomechanical Revolution: Mainstream Changes and Extreme Cases around 1900," *Oxford Art Journal* 28, no. 3 (2005): 378–79.

137. James D. Kornwolf, "American Architecture and the Aesthetic Movement," in *In Pursuit of Beauty,* 376–77.

138. "Round about Behring's Straits," *Harper's Weekly,* February 12, 1887, 111.

139. See Dona Brown, *Inventing New England: Regional Tourism in the Nineteenth Century* (Washington, D.C.: Smithsonian Institution Press, 1995), 5–9.

140. "The West Side," *Harper's Weekly,* January 26, 1889, 67–68.

141. Harry Fenn, "From Owen Sound to Mackinac," *Harper's Weekly,* October 5, 1889, 795.

142. See Rowland Elzea, "The Golden Age of American Illustration and Its Sources," *The Golden Age of American Illustration, 1880–1914* (Wilmington: Delaware Art Museum, 1972), 15. Estelle Jussim, in *Visual Communication,* comments that Pyle's illustrations "were reproduced not by facsimile wood engraving, as has been claimed, but by process line engraving" (115).

143. John Ruskin's ideas inspired this movement; see Ellen Mazur Thomson, *The Origins of Graphic Design in America, 1870–1920* (New Haven: Yale University Press, 1997), 31–33.

144. Such was the case with E. P. Dutton's edition of Tennyson's *Day Dream,* to which Fenn contributed (reviewed in *Art Amateur,* November 1885); Estes and Lauriat's edition of Tennyson's *Fairy Lilian and Other Poems* (1888); and Sir Walter Scott's *Christmas in the Olden Time* (Cassell, 1887), also with Fenn contributions.

145. As advertised in the *Critic,* September 29, 1883.

146. The color printing used an early halftone process. A more expensive edition bound in morocco antique and tree calf leather, priced $15, had "a picture of the great Preacher stamped in gold" on the front cover; *Church Review,* January 1886, 294.

147. See the review of *The Sermon on the Mount* in *Church Review,* January 1886, and comments about over-illustration in "'Childe Harold' Illustrated," *Art Amateur,* December 1885. (An earlier instance of a cover design by Fenn printed in color is the 1883 Christmas issue of *Youth's Companion;* I have been unable to locate a copy, which is somewhat surprising since an ad in the December 19, 1883, *Western Christian Advocate* states that the publisher will give "this Christmas Number free to any one who subscribes now. They are printing 350,000 copies to supply the demand for it.")

148. For these, he could have consulted his recent sketches from the "watering-place" excursions, as well as his earlier sketches and illustrations for *Picturesque America;* he definitely reworked a couple of his illustrations for the poem "Midsummer on Mount Desert" in the July 1885 *Harper's Monthly.* A digitized version of *Bar Harbor Days* may be viewed on Google Books.

149. Estelle Jussim, in *Visual Communication,* describes the process this way: "Called the most beautiful of all photo technologies, it depends for its effects on the richness of ink available to all intaglio processes.... Based on the properties of aquatint, in which reticulation of a powder on a metal plate provides a variety of dot structures, photogravure is etched and produces a 'print' in terms of book illustration" (344). Once photogravure was developed for preparing illustrations, steel engraving, already outmoded, was largely abandoned.

150. The publishing of elaborate illustrated books was moving beyond the eastern centers of New York and Boston. For the holiday trade in 1889, a Cleveland firm produced a heavily illustrated edition (possibly 2 vols.) of R. D. Blackmore's *Lorna Doone.* One review called the publisher, Burrows [Burroughs] Brothers Co., "one of the great book houses of the west"; *Magazine of Western History,* December 1889, 232. Another noted: "The initials adorning the opening of each chapter show equally careful and conscientious work. Heavy paper, wide margins, and handsome binding make a most harmonious whole"; *Chautauquan,* January 1890, 507. Fenn contributed only four illustrations; those who provided many more include Henry Sandham, Charles Copeland, George Wharton Edwards, Harper Pennington, Irving R. Wiles, and G. E. Graves.

151. See Sue Rainey, "*Picturesque California:* How Westerners Portrayed the West in the Age of John Muir," *Common-place* 7, no. 3 (April 2007), n.p., http://www.common-place.org. After this online article was completed, Erika Esau confirmed that *Picturesque California* was printed in New York, based on information in an article on the J. Dewing Co. that appeared in the December 6, 1889, *San Francisco Chronicle,* which states: "Two years ago an art printing establishment was opened by the company in New York city for the issuance of this work [*Picturesque California*]" (5).

152. The two illustrations listed are in vol. 2, pp. 84 and 54, respectively. "Hotel Del Monte and Grounds" (1:opp. 44) is a full-page photogravure of Fenn's original, presumably a watercolor. An impression of this photogravure, with watercolor and gouache applied by hand and Fenn's bold signature in pencil in the margin, suggests that the publisher provided Fenn, and presumably the other artists, with unbound impressions of their works to keep, give as gifts, or sell; the impression described is now in the Robert B. Honeyman Jr. Collection of Early Californian and Western American Pictorial Material, Bancroft Library, University of California, Berkeley, and can be viewed online by searching the Online Archive of California, http://www.oac.cdlib.org.

153. The book was offered in different bindings: parchment paper, $1.50 and "drawing-paper tied with ribbon, $2.50." According to the April 1888 *Art Amateur,* one option was sumptuous: "The firm publishes what appears to be a pincushion of white satin decorated with lilies and forget-me-nots and put up in a box with stamped paper edges."

154. *Literary World,* December 8, 1888, 449. A second collaboration was titled *Sea Vistas in Many Climes,* also published by Stokes in 1888 and marketed as a gift book for Christmas. The two books were issued at $3.50 each in an unusual vellum cloth binding "covered with graceful designs of shells, grasses, etc. outlined with gold and filled in with pink and blue"; *Publishers Weekly,* September 22, 1888, 296, 340. Skelding was the niece of the painter Susie M. Barstow (1836–1923).

155. Fenn's image "Sea of Galilee from Tiberias" is extremely close to the wood engraving after John Douglas Woodward's design "Mosque of Tiberias" in *Picturesque Palestine,* 1:300.

156. It was announced as "an exhibition in white and gold"—referring to the mats and frames surrounding the works. The October 19, 1889, *New York Times* listed the painters as "Misses Maud Humphrey and Susie B. Skelding and Messrs. Percy and Paul Moran, Harry Fenn, James Symington, J. M. Barnsley, C. R. Grant, H. W. McVickar, and Hamilton Gibson." A notice in the November 1889 *Art Amateur* omits Skelding but adds Amy Cross and Margaret Ruff. Montezuma, "My Note Book," *Art Amateur,* November 1889.

157. According to Eugene Exman in *House of Harper,* in his dealings with the Harper firm Howard Pyle "received $100 for a page illustration in the *Magazine* if the drawing was returned to him—$150 if it was retained" (117). Valuing the original works prepared for illustrations in this period constitutes a change from the common practice during wood engraving's heyday of discarding preliminary sketches.

158. "The American Water-Color Society," *Harper's Weekly,* February 5, 1887, 99; eight works by other artists were also reproduced. Fenn also exhibited *A Corner of the Studio* ($125), probably a depiction of his new studio at the Cedars.

159. "Art Notes," *Boston Daily Evening Transcript,* April 16, 1887.

160. Mrs. Schuyler Van Rensselaer, "The Academy Water-Color Landscapes and Etchings," *Independent,* February 16, 1888; see also "Fine Arts," *Nation,* February 23, 1888, 163. Fenn also exhibited *A Study of Weeds* ($60), *A Doorway in Granada* ($200), and *A Sketch at Montclair* ($75); American Watercolor Society exhibition records, American Watercolor Society Archives, Salmagundi Club, New York. Fenn was appointed to the catalogue committee again for the 1889 exhibition, along with Percy Moran and Henry Farrer (Meeting of November 12, 1888, American Watercolor Society Papers, 1866–1955, microfilm roll N68-8, Archives of American Art, Smithsonian Institution).

161. "Fine Arts," *Brooklyn Eagle,* April 6, 1885, 6. Fenn also exhibited *The Lone Hand* at the 1885 American Water Color Society exhibition; records of AWCS.

162. Fenn drew a similar—perhaps identical—young woman wearing a hat and carrying a parasol to illustrate his daughter Alice Maude's article "Among the Red Roofs of Sussex," *Century,* September 1885, 717.

163. See Robert R. Preato, "Whistler's Aesthetics and Japanese Design: Their Combined Influence on American Painting, 1880–1917," in *La Femme: The Influence of Whistler and Japanese Print Masters on American Art, 1880–1917,* by Gary Levine, Robert R. Preato, and Francine Tyler

(New York: Grand Central Art Galleries, 1983), 30–95. Preato discusses the painting shown in figure 5.38 on p. 74, and it is pictured on p. 75.

164. See Sarah Burns, "Fighting Infection: Aestheticism, Degeneration, and the Regulation of Artistic Masculinity," chap. 3 in *Inventing the Modern Artist: Art and Culture in Gilded Age America* (New Haven: Yale University Press, 1996).

165. "Harry Fenn. Painter and Illustrator," *American Bookmaker: A Journal of Technical Art and Information,* September 1889, 51–52.

6. CHALLENGES AND TRIUMPHS—THE 1890s AND BEYOND

1. See Judy Crichton, *America 1900: The Turning Point* (New York: Henry Holt, 1998), 4, 22.

2. Dennis Cashman, *America in the Gilded Age: From the Death of Lincoln to the Rise of Theodore Roosevelt* (New York: New York University Press, 1984), 12–14; and Robert Higgs, *The Transformation of the American Economy, 1865–1914: An Essay in Interpretation* (New York: John Wiley, 1991), 46–48.

3. Frederick Emory, "Our Commercial Expansion," *Munsey's,* January 1900, quoted in Crichton, *America 1900,* 30.

4. Ibid.

5. This number was double that of any preceding decade, according to Edwin Emery and Michael Emery, *The Press and America: An Interpretative History of the Mass Media* (Englewood Cliffs, N.J.: Prentice-Hall, ca. 1975), 200.

6. Kristin L. Hoganson reports that about 50,000 U.S. tourists went to Europe in 1880, compared to "roughly 125,000" by 1900; Kristin L. Hoganson, *Consumers' Imperium: The Global Production of American Domesticity, 1865–1920* (Chapel Hill: University of North Carolina Press, 2007), 171. Chap. 4, "Girdling the Globe: The Fictive Travel Movement and the Rise of the Tourist Mentality," describes women's travel clubs, of which she has identified more than 320 in existence between 1890 and 1920; many club members read such books as John Stoddard's 10-volume Travel Series and attended lectures illustrated with stereopticon, or "magic lantern," slides.

7. F. Hopkinson Smith, *American Illustrators* (New York: Charles Scribner's, 1892), 49.

8. The photographs were by the Detroit Photographic Co.

9. This series was published 1901–7 by Arthur Livingston in New York. Another was published by Illustrated Postal Card Co. (New York–Leipzig); called "private mailing cards," these had "Picturesque America" and the name of the place printed below the photographic image. A message could be written on the side with the picture (only the address was permitted on the other side). On the reaction of contemporary critics to the postcard, see Neil Harris, *Cultural Excursions* (Chicago: University of Chicago Press, 1990), 344–45.

10. Charles Dana Gibson, *Americans* (New York: R. H. Russell, 1900).

11. See, for example, C. M. Fairbanks, "Illustration and Our Illustrators," *Chautauquan: A Weekly Newspaper* 13, no. 5 (August 1891): 597–601; William A. Coffin, "American Illustration of Today," *Scribner's,* January, February, and March 1892, mentions Fenn on the last page of the last article (349); and Ernest Dressel North, "A Group of Young Illustrators," *Outlook* 63, no. 14 (December 2, 1899): 791–97. The women mentioned in these articles include Rosina Emmet Sherwood, Alice Barber [Stephens], Mary Hallock Foote, Genevieve and Maude Cowles, a Miss Green, and a Miss Corey. On Foote, see Sue Rainey, "Mary Hallock Foote: A Leading Illustrator of the 1870s and 1880s," *Winterthur Portfolio* 41, no. 23 (Summer/Autumn 2007): 97–139.

12. Fairbanks, "Illustration and Our Illustrators," 600.

13. These figures appear in an ad in the November 1890 *Century.* According to David Clayton Phillips: "By 1893, with a circulation of 700,000, the *Ladies' Home Journal* was the most popular and most profitable magazine in the country. Originally an 8-page magazine that sold for 50 cents a year, by 1893 the *Journal* offered 32 pages for a dollar [a year]. . . . Over the course of the same ten

year period, the revenue earned from advertising had grown from \$200 to \$4,000 per page"; David Clayton Phillips, "Art for Industry's Sake: Halftone Technology, Mass Photography, and the Social Transformation of American Print Culture, 1880–1920" (Ph.D. diss., Yale University, 1996), 53.

14. See "The Making of an Illustrated Magazine," *Cosmopolitan,* January 1893, 259–72, for an inside account of the challenges in producing an illustrated magazine. At that time circulation was 150,000, and the previous issue had included 91 pages of paid advertising. Pictures of many of the editors, writers, and illustrators are included, with Harry Fenn on p. 261. On the contents of the *Cosmopolitan,* see Richard Ohmann, *Selling Culture: Magazines, Markets, and Class at the Turn of the Century* (London: Verso, 1996), 226–27.

15. Tom Gretton, "Signs for Labour-Value in Printed Pictures after the Photomechanical Revolution: Mainstream Changes and Extreme Cases around 1900," *Oxford Art Journal* 28, no. 3 (2005): 376. Gretton points out that "screened half-tone plates became the dominant printed-picture technology in the course of the 1890s, and retained that position until the digital revolution a century later." David Reed provides a longer explanation: "A diamond-ruled lattice on a transparent sheet was interposed between a plate coated with a light-sensitive emulsion and a negative of the original during exposure to a light source. . . . The light passed through the negative and the screen to reach the plate and the edge-effect of the lattice deflected the rays. Thus, a very dark area on the original object was converted to a translucent area on the negative. . . . Conversely, bright areas of the original created dense sites on the negative which only passed a little light while the plate was being exposed. These faint rays were focused by the lattice as relatively small dots of light on the plate emulsion. . . . Once the plate had been exposed, the development and etching of the plate transformed the latent image, which was composed of dots of varying sizes, into a delicate relief of metal. Thus, if the quality of such printed images was consequent upon the efficient transfer of ink from tiny pinnacles of etched metal, it is evident that the quality of the paper surface was a critical element in getting the best from the plate"; David Reed, *The Popular Magazine in Britain and the United States 1880–1960* (London: The British Library, 1997), 28–29.

16. Reed, *Popular Magazine,* 28; he states that by 1880 the S. D. Warren firm of Boston owned the largest paper mill in the world and in 1881 became the first manufacturer of coated paper on a commercial scale in the United States. Theodore De Vinne, "The Printing of 'The Century,'" *Century,* November 1890, describes earlier methods of smoothing paper, noting that "pressing each sheet through hot plates" was "too expensive to be considered for magazines." Therefore, from about 1870 the method "of smoothing a sheet in a web by passing it through stacks of calendaring rollers" was used by the magazine (and probably for *Picturesque America*'s sheets as well); but this method sometimes made the paper "transparent and so hard that it would not properly receive the ink." The new approach added a soluble filling to the paper during the manufacturing process, which resulted in an "absolutely uniform surface readily smoothed by the calendering rollers. . . . No other paper can show with such clearness the whole scale of color from the palest gray to the intensest black" (88).

17. Reed, *Popular Magazine,* 36.

18. In 1893 the price of *Scribner's, Frank Leslie's Popular Monthly,* and *Cosmopolitan* was 25 cents. In July of that year, *Cosmopolitan* cut its price to 12 1/2 cents but had increased it to 15 cents by January 1894; Reed, *Popular Magazine,* 66.

19. Phillips, "Art for Industry's Sake," 38; he notes that, "by the turn of the century, *Munsey's* claimed the largest circulation of any magazine in the world" (60–61).

20. Theodore Peterson, *Magazines in the Twentieth Century,* 2nd ed. (Urbana: University of Illinois Press, 1964), 14–15.

21. Quoted in Michael Leja, "The Illustrated Magazines and Print Connoisseurship in the Late 19th Century," *Block Points* 1 (1993): 67. Leja points out: "Whereas *Century* was prudish and puritanical, rarely reproducing nudes, *Munsey's* . . . campaigns to increase circulation in the 1890s mark an early systematic use of the female nude, as rendered in European academic painting and thereby insulated as 'art,' as a marketing tool in the new mass culture" (67–69).

22. Ohmann, *Selling Culture,* 29.

23. Peterson, *Magazines in the Twentieth Century,* 10.

24. Quoted in Eugene Exman, *The House of Harper: One Hundred and Fifty Years of Publishing* (New York: Harper & Row, 1967), 183; chaps. 18 and 19 concern the failure and reorganization. Appleton also had financial difficulties about the same time, having tied up too much capital "in subscription sales"; see Gerard R. Wolfe, *The House of Appleton* (Metuchen, N.J.: Scarecrow Press, 1981), chap. 16, "Reorganization and Retrenchment."

25. Ohmann, *Selling Culture,* 29.

26. Smith, *American Illustrators,* 62.

27. No plates by Fenn were included in the Scribner's portfolios, which were produced while he was still in England; *Portfolio of Proof Impressions Selected from Scribner's Monthly and St. Nicholas* (New York: Scribner, 1879), and *Proofs from Scribner's Monthly and St. Nicholas: Second Series* (New York: Scribner, 1881).

28. Publisher's notice, *Quarterly Illustrator,* January 1893. Fenn's work was reproduced in the following issues: vol. 1, no. 4 (October–December, 1893): 283; in a feature on Fenn, "Glimpses of Picturesque Places," by George Parsons Lathrop, vol. 2, no. 6 (April–June, 1894): 166–69; vol. 2, no. 7 (February 1895, after title changed to the *Monthly Illustrator*): 163, photo of Fenn, 192. This periodical has been digitized by JSTOR. See also Ellen Mazur Thomson, *The Origins of Graphic Design in America, 1870–1920* (New Haven: Yale University Press, 1997), 57.

29. See Michele H. Bogart, *Artists, Advertising, and the Borders of Art* (Chicago: The University of Chicago Press, 1995), chap. 1, "The Problem of Status for American Illustrators," esp. 35. (I do not agree with Bogart's interpretation of the field of illustration as "a woman's field" in this period.)

30. I have not been able to determine when Fenn joined. He is listed among "Deceased Members" in *The Society of Illustrators, 1901–1928* (New York: Society of Illustrators, 1928), 30.

31. In fact, when the Century Co. published *The Century Gallery* in 1893, reproducing "Selected Proofs from the Century Magazine and St. Nicholas," Fenn was not included; however, it did feature works by younger illustrators and painters, as well as old masters, reproduced mainly by New School wood engravers. Thanks to William Brandt for this information.

32. Joseph Pennell, *Pen Drawing and Pen Draughtsmen* (London: Macmillan, 1889), chap. 2, esp. 21, 32, 42.

33. W. A. Rogers, *A World Worth While: A Record of "Auld Acquaintance"* (New York: Harper & Brothers, 1922), 122–23. This would have been about 1875–78; Abbey left for England in 1878.

34. Jaccaci claimed: "When Vierge began his career of illustrator, the wood-engravers were painstaking artisans who hugged with the same affection and lack of discrimination unimportant as well as important facts. . . . In not only inspiring, but personally training his engravers, Vierge . . . is the father of a school of engravers who, permeating their work with light, color, and refreshing unexpectedness of treatment, putting playfulness, and character, and feeling into it, have infused with vigorous life an art which had grown old, stiff, and mechanical" (201).

35. *Brooklyn Daily Eagle,* August 23, 1885. Pennell's illustrations for "Italy, from a Tricycle" by Elizabeth Robbins Pennell (his wife), in the March and April 1886 *Century,* are especially charming.

36. See Appendix 1 for the other. On attitudes toward the *Ladies' Home Journal,* see Ohmann, *Selling Culture,* 28.

37. Siegfried Wichmann describes "composite formats" in Japanese art as using disparate forms, such as circles, rectangles, fan shapes, etc., in conjunction, "one format within another. The style was more subtle than this, however: the secondary formats contained within the principal pictorial structure could also be cut-off, overlapped, or arranged in distinctive progression as desired"; Siegfried Wichmann, "Composite Formats," *Japonisme: The Japanese Influence on Western Art since 1858* (New York: Harmony Books, ca. 1981), 224.

38. Fenn's drawing for this image was reproduced in Christie's catalogue *American and European Works on Paper from the Estate of E. Maurice Bloch, Part I, New York, Tuesday, June 19, 1990,* item 110; several works by Fenn were up for auction.

39. Fenn to Turnure, March 1892, Harper Collection, roll no. N709, Archives of American Art, Pierpont Morgan Library (hereafter Harper Collection).

40. Fenn to Schell, December 5, 1890, Harper Collection.

41. Fenn's pen and ink drawing for the illustration "Pier and Shelter-tower of the New York Central Railway Bridge over the Harlem River, New York City" (p. 18 in the *Century*) is reproduced in *The American Personality: The Artist-Illustrator of Life in the United States, 1860–1930* (Los Angeles: Grunwald Center for the Graphic Arts, University of California at Los Angeles, 1976), 80.

42. Fenn to Schell, January 28, 1890, Harper Collection. Given all the minute architectural detail, this assignment may have been the one he alludes to when writing that he couldn't say when he would finish since he was very busy and "it is a dose and will have to be taken in pilules."

43. Fenn to Schell, Deal Beach, N.J., July 4, 1890, Harper Collection.

44. Fenn to Richard Watson Gilder, March 22, 1895, Century Company Collection—Correspondence of *The Century Magazine,* Ms. Div., Archives of American Art, New York Public Library (hereafter Century Collection). I have not found an article on the topic Fenn suggested, but the August 1895 *Century* includes "Reminiscences of the Literary Berkshires" by Henry Dwight Sedgwick, illustrated by Fenn and featuring the writers who lived or vacationed in a different county of Massachusetts, including Catherine Maria Sedgwick, Fanny Kemble, and many others.

45. Fenn to "My dear Mr. B—[?]," Century Collection. Fenn went on to suggest how to treat Memphis and the pyramids in Egypt. For the series on Alexander, Fenn provided numerous landscape images; Louis Loeb and André Castaigne drew historical incidents, and photographs supplied the remaining images.

46. Fenn to Schell, n.d., Harper Collection. The illustration appears on p. 788 of the *Monthly.*

47. Fenn to Edward Eggleston, [1894], Mss: Edward Eggleston #S410, Indiana State Library. I have been unable to determine the illustration he was working on.

48. See Linda Henefield Skatlet, "The Market for American Painting in New York: 1870–1915" (Ph.D. diss., Johns Hopkins University, 1980), iv, 205; and Gwendolyn Owens, "Art and Commerce: William Macbeth, The Eight and the Popularization of American Art," in *Painters of a New Century: The Eight & American Art,* by Elizabeth Milroy (Milwaukee, Wis.: Milwaukee Art Museum, 1991), 61–85.

49. Fenn to William Macbeth, n.d., NMc6 Macbeth Gallery correspondence 1894–1914, Archives of American Art, New York Public Library (hereafter NYPL).

50. Two watercolors from this vacation were included in the November 9, 1911, auction of Fenn's works: No. 11, "Brant Rock, Massachusetts Coast" (dated August 1891; 7 1/2 x 14 1/2 in.); and "Green Harbor, Mass." (dated 1891; 12 x 14 1/2 in.), of the waterfront just across from Brant Rock. See *A Collection of Water Color Drawings by Harry Fenn* (New York: Anderson Auction, 1911).

51. Fenn to F. B. Schell, [September 1891], Harper Collection. Fenn's movements can be mapped as follows: In a letter dated July 1891 Fenn informed Schell that after July 10 he would be "c/o Miss C. M. Pierce, Lyman Cottage, Brant Rock, Mass." and asked for the latest date he could send the "Old London" images, likely pen drawings for process line blocks destined to illustrate the *Harper's Monthly* articles "London Plantagenet II, Prince and Merchants" (September 1891) and perhaps "The London of Charles the Second" (January 1892). In a letter dated September 1891, Fenn informed Schell he would be with Mrs. Spofford at Newburyport for "a week or ten days" and then return to Brant Rock. And in the letter mentioning duck hunting, Fenn informed Schell that he would soon be back in Montclair. (All letters, Harper Collection.)

52. Fenn to William Macbeth, August 26, 1893, NMc 6, Macbeth Gallery correspondence, 1894–1914, Archives of American Art, NYPL.

53. The painting is reproduced in Carl Little and Arnold Skolnick, *The Art of Monhegan Island* (Rockport, Me.: Down East Books, 2004), 14. In subsequent years Monhegan would become known as an artists' colony; Robert Henri first went there in 1903, and his students included Rockwell Kent, Edward Hopper, Randall Davey, and George Bellows. See Susan Danly, "Monhegan Island: 'Colony in Rock,'" in Thomas Denenberg, Amy Kurtz Lansing, and Susan Danly, *Call of the Coast, Art Colonies of New England* (Portland, Me., and Old Lyme, Conn.: Portland Museum of Art and Florence Griswold Museum, 2009), 80–87.

54. See Matthew Schneirov, *The Dream of a New Social Order: Popular Magazines in America, 1893–1914* (New York: Columbia University Press, 1994), 67–72.

55. On April 24 Fenn wrote that he had been in bed "with rheumatic gout suffering the tortures of Inferno" since the retirement dinner for Charles Parsons (on April 15): "My feet are in such a state that I don't expect to get boots on for a week or ten days"; Fenn to F. B. Schell, April 24, 1890, Harper Collection. On June 18 his wife wrote on his behalf from Deal Beach, N.J., because he was "unable to work"; Marian Fenn to Schell, June 18, 1890, Harper Collection.

56. T. S. van Dyke, "Southernmost California," in John Muir, ed., *Picturesque California* . . . (San Francisco: J. Dewing, 1888–89), 4:188.

57. See Kevin Starr, *Americans and the California Dream, 1850–1915* (New York, 1973), esp. chap. 6. Starr says of Benjamin Cummings Truman's 1884 book *Homes and Happiness in the Golden State of California:* "Truman's suggestion of a California life under one's own fruit trees caught the theme which dominated promotional pamphleteering at the turn of the century: that California would witness a return of the middle class to the land" (201).

58. Starr, *Americans and the California Dream,* 125.

59. Fenn to F. B. Schell, October 27, 1890, Harper Collection.

60. The double-page spread Fenn had prepared for the May 18, 1889, *Harper's Weekly* titled "Pre-Historic Arizona" may have whetted his appetite to see these regions.

61. According to Kevin Starr, "Bidwell's wheat, the main product of the Rancho, won the gold medal at the Paris International Exposition in 1878 for being judged the finest grain in the world"; Starr, *Americans and the California Dream,* 197.

62. Fenn's drawing "The Truckee Meadow" for the illustration on p. 127 is in the Robert B. Honeyman Jr. Collection of Early Californian and Western American Pictorial Material, Bancroft Library, University of California, Berkeley (hereafter Honeyman Collection); it may be viewed digitally by searching the Online Archive of California, http://www.oac.cdlib.org.

63. For more on Remington, see Peggy and Harold Samuels, *Frederic Remington: A Biography* (Garden City, N.Y.: Doubleday, 1982), 126–27; and Peter Hassrick, *Frederic Remington: Paintings, Drawings, and Sculpture in the Amon Carter Museum and the Sid W. Richardson Foundation Collection* (New York: Harry N. Abrams in association with the Amon Carter Museum of Western Art, 1973), 30–31.

64. The illustration is on p. 166. The article also includes "The Old Cuartel at Monterey" (180) signed "W. J. Fenn," Harry's son Walter, suggesting that he was also in California at the time. In his own account of his life, Walter Fenn says that he lived in California from 1892 to 1898 and "purchased a ranch there," although he was sometimes mistaken about dates; see "The Fenn Family," appended to "Biographical Sketch of the Life of Harry Fenn," manuscript, Fenn family papers.

65. Fenn's drawings for the two illustrations on p. 397, "Mission of San Fernando, Los Angeles" and "Cloisters and Bell of San Fernando," are in the Honeyman Collection and may be viewed digitally by searching the Online Archive of California, http://www.oac.cdlib.org.

66. The June 1891 issue included "A Miner's Sunday in Coloma. (From the Writer's California Journal, 1849–50.)" by Charles B. Gillespie. Fenn's watercolor drawing for "Coloma in 1857 . . ." (265) is in the Honeyman Collection and may be viewed digitally by searching the Online Archive of California, http://www.oac.cdlib.org.

67. Fenn's ink and gouache drawing for the illustration titled "Sweetwater Dam, California: A Representative Work of Irrigation" (95) is in the collection of the Free Library of Philadelphia.

68. Robert W. Rydell, John E. Findling, and Kimberly D. Pell, *Fair America: World's Fairs in the United States* (Washington: Smithsonian Institution Press, 2000), 30–32. On May 4, 1886, a demonstration for an eight-hour workday by a small group of anarchists drew a crowd of some 1,500; when police tried to disperse them, a bomb exploded and a riot ensued in which seven officers and four others were killed and more than 100 were wounded. After a trial in which no evidence was produced to link them to the bomb, eight anarchists were convicted of inciting violence, and four were hanged. See *Columbia Encyclopedia,* 3rd ed., s.v. "Haymarket Square riot."

69. Sarah Burns, *Inventing the Modern Artist: Art and Culture in Gilded Age America* (New Haven: Yale University Press, 1996), 32.

70. Rydell et al., *Fair America,* 32–36, 41. According to the authors, "When most of the fair was destroyed in 1894 by a fire of mysterious origins, the fair acquired a unique mystique that would perpetuate its memory" (41). Most of the buildings were built as temporary structures, except for the Fine Arts Building (for fire safety reasons) (34).

71. "The Artists' Innings," *Dallas Morning News,* June 5, 1894.

72. DeYoung was second vice president of the national commission for the fair and a member of its Board of Control. Fenn's original ink drawing for "The Lagoon" is in the Prints, Drawings, and Photographs Collection, NYPL.

73. Fenn's original ink drawing for an illustration in this article, "A Corner of the Agricultural Building," is in the Prints, Drawings, and Photographs Collection, NYPL.

74. Fenn did provide one full-page view of the Fisheries Pavilion (October 1892) and an opening illustration of the Port of Seville for one part of a *Century* series on Christopher Columbus (June 1892).

75. Ensign John M. Ellicott, U.S.N., "Columbus at La Rábida," *St. Nicholas,* May 1893, 509–11. Fenn's ink drawing for this illustration, made from a photograph according to the table of contents, is in the Honeyman Collection; a digital image may be viewed on the Bancroft Library's website. After the fair, Spain donated its exhibition hall to Chicago, and it is now a children's hospital; "History of La Rabida," La Rabida Children's Hospital, http://www.larabida.org/about-us-history.

76. *Washington Post,* May 6 and 20, 1894. The *Knoxville Journal* used the publication to promote sales, encouraging readers to "cut out Ten 'Book of the Builders' Coupons, of different dates, and present them at our Art Department with Twenty-five Cents" to secure a copy of the first number; *Knoxville Journal,* April 11, 1894.

77. Fenn's view of the West Terrace was also included in *World's Columbian Exposition* (Chicago: Edwin D. Weary, 1894), which consisted of 24 leaves of plates measuring 41 x 51 cm.

78. A digital image of the part cover may be viewed by searching for "The Art of the World" on the website of the Spencer Museum of Art, University of Kansas.

79. For the fair in Nashville, Fenn contributed to the following articles: "The Grounds and Buildings of the Tennessee Centennial Exposition at Nashville," *Harper's Weekly,* January 2, 1897, with an illustration titled "The Negro Building"; and "Buildings of the Tennessee Centennial Exposition at Nashville, To Be Opened on May 1," *Harper's Bazaar,* February 6, 1897, with "The Women's Building". For the 1900 Paris Exposition his illustrations include "The United States National Pavilion at the Paris Exposition of 1900," *Harper's Weekly,* September 23, 1899; and "The United States Publishers' Building at the Paris Exposition," *Harper's Weekly,* March 24, 1900. Fenn also made ink drawings of the Jamestown Exposition in Virginia in 1907; see the Christie's catalogue "American and European Works on Paper from the Estate of E. Maurice Bloch, Part 1; Tuesday, June 19, 1990," lot 118, two drawings. The one reproduced appeared in the May 1907 *Century,* opening Thomas Nelson Page's article on the exposition, "Jamestown, the Cradle of American Civilization."

Another important architectural complex depicted by Fenn was Columbia University, in Manhattan, with Low Library, completed in 1897, as the centerpiece. Fenn's original ink drawing (16 x 23 ¾") is in the collection of Avery Drawings and Archives, Columbia University; the New York Public Library's Print Collection owns an impression of the 1903 print reproducing this drawing, published by R. Haider (sheet size, 16 5/8 x 24 5/8").

80. *Chicago Tribune,* August 19, 1893. This newspaper article incorrectly lists Fenn among the artists who received a medal for watercolors. The fair's official publication lists Fenn among those awarded a medal for "Works in Black and White," along with Gilbert Gaul, A. B. Wenzell, Frederick Remington, W. T. Smedley, A. B. Frost, Carlton T. Chapman, Thule De Thulstrup, W. Hamilton Gibson, Edwin A. Abbey, Howard Pyle, Will H. Low, A. C. Redwood, A. Castaigne, C. S. Reinhart, Robert Blum, R. F. Zogbaum, C. D. Gibson, Jos. Pennell, W. S.

Metcalf, Elizabeth Nourse, and Caroline A. Lord; *Revised Catalogue, Department of Fine Arts* (Chicago: W. B. Conkey, 1893), 15. Unfortunately, Fenn's "diploma" has not been located.

81. "The Fine Arts Exhibit," in Rossiter Johnson, ed., *History of the World's Columbian Exposition,* vol. 3, *Exhibits* (New York: D. Appleton, 1897–98), 400.

82. I have not found this drawing reproduced in the *Century.*

83. Fenn's other exhibited works were "Escutcheon and Fireplace in the Manor House, Gardiner's Island" (pen drawing; *Century,* December 1885); "Castillo de la Mota, near Medina, Spain" (wash drawing); "Tower of Trinity Church, Boston" (black and white; *Century,* January 1885); "Rousseau's House and Stairs to Studio, at his Death, 1867" (black and white; *Scribner's,* June 1890); "East End of Ganne's Hotel in Barbizon" (black and white; *Scribner's,* May 1890); and "On the Common, Gardiner's Island" (black and white; *Century,* December 1885). For the full list of artworks exhibited, see "United States: Pen and Ink, Charcoal, Black and White and Other Drawings," *World's Columbian Exposition, 1893: Official Catalogue,* pt. 10, *Department K., Fine Arts* (Chicago: W. B. Conkey, 1893), 45.

84. W. D. Howells, Mark Twain, and Nathaniel S. Shaler, *The Niagara Book* (Buffalo, N.Y.: Underhill and Nichols, 1893), n.p.

85. *Critic,* November 4, 1893, 286.

86. Digital images of these watercolors may be viewed on the Albright-Knox Art Gallery's website: http://www.albrightknox.org/collection/search/. None of the compositions are similar enough to Fenn's Niagara illustrations for *Picturesque America* to suggest he reworked them for this project.

87. In December 2, 1893, the *Literary World*'s reviewer wrote: "The Appleton Press has never done finer work, and the seventy or more full-page illustrations by Harry Fenn and from photographs are admirably executed" (416). Another instance of a publisher featuring Fenn prominently with little justification beyond marketing occurred with *The Reign of Law: A Tale of the Kentucky Hemp Fields* (New York: Macmillan, 1900), by the Kentucky local-color novelist James Lane Allen (1849–1925). Although largely forgotten today, the book became a best seller as "a brilliant defense of Evolution," dealing with a young man's crisis of faith followed by a new understanding of a loving God (*New York Times* ad, November 8, 1900; and review, June 30, 1900). Fenn collaborated with J. C. Earl, and even though both their names appeared prominently on the title page and in ads, of the 9 illustrations in the book only 4 are reproductions of artworks, whereas 5 are halftones of photographs. Of the 4 designs, 3 are signed by both artists, with Fenn presumably having drawn the rather indistinct landscape settings and Earl the figures. This is a rare instance of Fenn collaborating with another artist in this way. The illustrations are not very attractive, although the *Brooklyn Daily Eagle* wrote that Fenn and Earl had "caught the author's spirit in their pictures" (June 30, 1900). The most successful image is "Into Its Largeness, Its Woodland Odors, and Twilight Peace" (opp. 312), with a strong female figure standing by bold tree trunks. A digitized version of this book may be viewed on Google Books.

88. Gib Prettyman explores how articles on new technologies introduced readers "to the increasingly differentiated features of the world," enabling them not only to feel educated but also to distinguish themselves from the workers involved—as part of the middle class; Gib Prettyman, "*Harper's Weekly* and the Spectacle of Industrialization," *American Periodicals* 11 (2001): 24–48.

89. A few months later, Fenn illustrated two articles on China by Eliza Ruhamah Scidmore for the *Century:* "Cruising Up the Yangtsze" (September 1899) and "The Streets of Peking" (October 1899). For the October 1900 issue, he illustrated "China's 'Holy Land': A Visit to the Tomb of Confucius" by Ernst von Hesse-Wartegg.

90. Susan R. Gannon, "'Here's to *Our* Magazine!': Promoting *St. Nicholas* (1873–1905)," in Susan R. Gannon, Suzanne Rahn, and Ruth Anne Thompson, eds. *St. Nicholas and Mary Mapes Dodge: The Legacy of a Children's Magazine Editor, 1873–1905* (Jefferson, N.C.: McFarland, 2004), 85.

91. *Chicago Daily Tribune,* November 21, 1896; *Brooklyn Daily Eagle,* December 14, 1896; *The Literary World,* November 28, 1896; *New York Observer and Chronicle,* October 8, 1896. The book's title page states: "With Drawings by Harry Fenn after Sketches by the Author."

92. Harry Fenn, "Travelers of the Sky," *St. Nicholas,* January 1894, 230–31.

93. Harry Fenn, "How Plants Spread," *St. Nicholas*, November 1896, 16.

94. The Museum of New Brunswick owns Fenn's watercolor for the illustration titled "At the Brink of the Grand Falls, Showing the Crest of the Incline. (From a Photograph)" for the article "The Grand Falls of the Labrador," p. 651.

95. Kathleen Pyne, *Art and the Higher Life: Painting and Evolutionary Thought in Late Nineteenth-Century America* (Austin: University of Texas Press, 1996), 85–86. See also the essays in Marc Simpson, ed., *Like Breath on Glass: Whistler, Inness, and the Art of Painting Softly* (Williamstown, Mass.: Sterling and Francine Clark Institute, 2008).

96. "The Illustrator; Hints Suggested by New Publications," *Art Amateur,* May 1894, 169. The writer (perhaps Ernest Knauff, who had given advice on ink drawings for the line-cut process in the same magazine) did point out that "while Mr. Fenn's drawings have been interpreted by various engravers on wood, those of Castaigne have been reproduced in fac-simile by the half-tone process." Fenn was again compared unfavorably with Castaigne by a critic in the *Brooklyn Daily Eagle* who preferred the "grace and softness and sense of diffused light" of Castaigne's drawings of the siege of Tyre for the April 1899 *Century,* stating that Fenn's "lines seem hard" in contrast (20).

97. Wheeler was also president of the University of California from 1899 to 1919.

98. [Richard Watson Gilder], "Topics of the Time," *Century,* October 1898, 955.

99. They each contributed approximately the same number of illustrations, but Castaigne's were full page, and Fenn's were not. Louis Loeb and August Will also contributed, and photographs of statues, coins, etc., were used as well.

100. W. Lewis Fraser, "A Word about the Century's Pictures," *Century,* January 1895, 479.

101. See David Woodward, "The Decline of Commercial Wood-Engraving in Nineteenth-century America," *Journal of the Printing Historical Society* 10 (1974–75): 70–71.

102. Fraser, "Century's Pictures," 479.

103. The series by Leila Herbert, titled "The First American: His Homes and his Households," ran September–December 1899. A. I. Keller contributed the figure illustrations, and Fenn's monogram is on most of the depictions of buildings; several other illustrations are by his son.

104. The form was filled out by Fenn for Art League Publishing Co., Chicago, after 1897. In response to "What special books illustrated," Fenn listed "Pict. Am., Pict. Europe, Pict. Palestine, Sinai, and Egypt—Whittiers Snow Bound, Grey's Elegy, Tennyson's In memoriam & & &"; Albert Duveen Collection, Archives of American Art, Smithsonian Institution.

105. *Alfred Lord Tennyson* was published in New York and London by Macmillan in 1897, written by Hallam Tennyson, baron (1852–1928). Since its initial publication in 1850, *In Memoriam* had appeared in numerous editions published by British and American firms.

106. The *Brooklyn Daily Eagle* mentioned Fenn's acquaintance with Tennyson in at least two notices about the book, September 12, 1897, and December 19, 1897. The fact that Fenn had previously illustrated pieces Henry van Dyke had written might also have played a role. These included "From Venice to the Gross-Venediger" (*Scribner's Magazine,* February 1893) and "Ampersand" (*Harper's Monthly,* July 1885).

107. This is true of the leather-bound copy I have seen.

108. The other three are the drawing of daffodils for the title page; the illustration on p. 67; and the title and landscape scene for canto 123 on p. 208.

109. Advertisement, *New York Times,* December 11, 1897.

110. Advertisement, *Outlook,* November 27, 1897.

111. *Independent,* December 9, 1897, 23.

112. "Among New Books," *Chicago Tribune,* December 8, 1897.

113. *Chap-Book,* December 1, 1897, 82. A writer in the *Dial,* December 1, 1897, liked the landscapes but found the "merely decorative drawings, initial letters . . . perhaps a little stiff" (338).

114. *Critic,* November 20, 1897, 302.

115. "Some Holiday Publications," *Bookman,* December 1897, 370.

116. Fenn contributed to a publication honoring Eugene Field, who died in 1895; his drawings

illustrated Field's poem "When I Was a Boy." The publication was intended to raise money for a monument dedicated to Field. *Field Flowers* (Chicago: Monument Fund Committee, [1896]). Fenn also contributed to Woodrow Wilson's *Life of George Washington* (Harper & Brothers, 1897), advertised in December 1896 as illustrated by Howard Pyle, Harry Fenn, and others. Fenn did the architectural views and landscapes; Pyle illustrated the people.

117. This set provides yet another example of how publishers marketed a variety of editions at different prices. In the most expensive "Autograph Edition," limited to 500 copies, the signature of Hawthorne's daughter Rose Hawthorne Lathrop was pasted on the endpapers of vol. 1, and the frontispiece of each volume was signed by the artist. Vol. 18 contains two frontispieces: Fenn's "Graylock from the North" is printed first in color and then in black and white, with his signature in pencil below the black and white photogravure plate.

118. Among the artists were Mary Ayer, B. West Clinedinst, Maude Cowles, Edmund H. Garrett, Jules Guérin, Childe Hassam, Albert Herter, Eric Pape, E. C. Peixotto, Howard Pyle, Frank E. Schoonover, Jessie Wilcox Smith, Alice Barber Stephens, and Sarah S. Stilwell.

119. Another neoclassical White City with lagoons was created for the exposition in Omaha, but it was considerably smaller than the one in Chicago. The *Century*'s feature was illustrated entirely by halftones of photographs; Albert Shaw, "Trans-Mississippians and Their Fair at Omaha," *Century,* October 1898, 836–52. As at the 1901 Pan-American Exposition, the nightly illuminations were a popular feature.

120. *Pan-American Exposition, Buffalo, May 1 to November 1, 1901: Its Purpose and Its Plan* (Buffalo: Pan-American Exposition, 1901), n.p. [first page of text]. Several years earlier Fenn had contributed to *Harper's Monthly* features by Theodore Child that fed the interest in Latin America: "The Republic of Uruguay," May 1891, 906–27; and "Up the River Paraná," about a boat trip through Argentina, June 1891, 32–45. For the December 1895 issue, Fenn contributed a view of Caracas, Venezuela, for "The Paris of South America" by Richard Harding Davis, 104–15.

121. David Gray, "The City of Light," *Century,* September 1901, 675.

122. *Catalogue of the Exhibition of Fine Arts, Pan-American Exposition, Buffalo, 1901* (Buffalo: David Gray, 1901), 164, x.

123. The NYPL owns a copy of this large print. The image as printed on the sheet measures 27 ½ by 38 ½ inches.

124. See Rydell, Findling, and Pelle, *Fair America,* 48–52, for information on the Pan-American Exposition, including the focus on the Philippines, one of the colonies recently acquired by the United States as a result of the Spanish–American War, and its "racially encoded hierarchical design," with "darker, so-called cruder colors at the perimeter" giving way "to gradually lighter, finer shades in the center of the site" (48). In the midway, called "the Pan," there was a Filipino village where visitors rode "in carts pulled by water buffalo" (50).

125. "The Exhibition at 'The Academy,'" *Art Amateur,* March 1893, 98. The New York Etching Club once again exhibited with the American Water Color Society, and the reviewer opined: "We cannot say that as a body the club is improving. It contains too many members to whom etching offers merely a convenient way of multiplying impressions of their sketches." J. H. Twachtman was singled out as an exception.

126. *New York Times,* February 25, 1893.

127. *Brooklyn Daily Eagle,* February 11, 1894. In 1896 the decorations, arranged by C. Y. Turner and W. H. Lippincott, again sound similar to Fenn's, as described with approval by the *New York Times* reviewer (February 1, 1896).

128. The writer continued: "The walls are covered with Japanese draperies separated from the frieze of contrasting color by a gold picture molding. Some of the over-doors are treated shrine-wise, a Madonna in the center of one, and queer little wooden figures hold long swags of amber beads. Plaques in yellow iridescent glass form centers of ornament along the frieze of one room, in another are combinations of gilded palm leaves, in a third are ribboned wreaths of gilt"; Sophia Antoinette Walker, "Fine Arts: The Water Color Society," *Independent,* February 11, 1897, 7.

129. *Brooklyn Daily Eagle,* February 11, 1894. The next year the same paper's reviewer had harsher words for Fenn, tempered by some approval: "Harry Fenn, in spite of his mannerism, strikes a good note, now and again. His 'November Day, Montclair,' contains all his wiry tree growth and a certain mosaic opacity, but the colors fit into each other with judgment and the tone is autumnal" (February 3, 1895).

130. *New York Times,* February 1, 1896.

131. "The Water Color Exhibition," *New York Times,* February 6, 1897.

132. A similar watercolor by Fenn titled *The Rug Merchant,* dated 1899, was reproduced in Christie, Manson & Woods International, *American Watercolors, Drawings, Paintings, and Sculpture of the 19th and 20th Centuries, . . . March 14, 1986* (New York: Christie's, 1986).

133. Pages 133, 93.

134. Page 385. Fenn used a textured paper to help depict the rough surface of the walls and ground. The same appears to be true of *The Good Story* from its appearance as reproduced in the American Water Color Society catalogue. He also signed both paintings with the distinctively different signature shown in figure 6.49.

135. See Elizabeth Johns, *Winslow Homer: The Nature of Observation* (Berkeley: University of California Press, 2002), chap. 4, esp. 135–40.

136. Susan Hayes Ward, "Fine Art: The Sixth Annual Exhibition of the Architectural League," *Independent,* January 8, 1891, 10. Some of Fenn's drawings were sent by the Century Co. to an exhibition of the T-Square Club in Philadelphia in conjunction with the Architectural League of America in late 1899; Alfred Morton Githens, "The T-Square Club Exhibition," *American Architect and Building News,* January 13, 1900, 13 (see Appendix 2 for a list of works). In 1893, the year of the World's Columbian Exposition, he exhibited with the Art Institute of Chicago and in 1894 at the Albany Club, for the benefit of the Child's Hospital (*New York Times,* April 16, 1894).

137. Proceedings of the New York Water Color Club, reel N68-9, Archives of American Art, Smithsonian Institution. In November 1897 he participated in the club's eighth annual show, held in galleries of the American Fine Arts Society, 215 W. 57th St.

138. *Bookman,* March 1898. The exhibition had already been mounted in Hartford, Providence, Boston, and other cities; participating artists included B. W. Clinedinst, F. C. Yohn, E. C. Peixotto, and Carlton T. Chapman.

139. Fenn's only contributions were to Mahan's article "The Naval Campaign of 1776 on Lake Champlain," February 1898. E. C. Peixotto did most of the landscape and architectural illustrations for Lodge's articles. Lodge's *Story of the Revolution* was published in 2 vols. by Charles Scribner's Sons in 1898.

140. "The Art Club Exhibition," *Montclair (N.J.) Times,* December 9, 1899, 5, cited in *The Montclair Art Colony Past and Present* (Montclair, N.J.: Montclair Art Museum, 1997), 15 n. 74.

141. *New York Times,* March 8 and 10, 1894; see also *Montclair Art Colony* and *The Greenoughs of Montclair,* a pamphlet published by the Montclair Art Museum, 1993.

142. In February 1895, Fenn "posed" John Singer Sargent's *Carmencita* (1890)—at a time when Sargent's portraits were acclaimed in Paris and the United States—and two other tableaux not identified with paintings titled "Love Versus Riches" and "Envy"; *Montclair (N.J.) Times,* February 16, 1895.

143. Diane Pietrucha Fischer, "The Inness Colony of Montclair," in Montclair Art Museum, *Montclair Art Colony,* 11.

144. William H. Gerdts, *Painting and Sculpture in New Jersey* (Princeton, N.J.: Van Nostrand, 1964), 154; Elliott Daingerfield, "Inness: Genius of American Art" in Adrienne Baxter Bell, ed., *George Inness: Writings and Reflections on Art and Philosophy* (New York: George Braziller, 2006), 213. S. C. G. Watkins, "Reminiscences of George Inness, the Great Painter, As I Knew Him," *Montclair (N.J.) Times,* April 14, 1928; reprinted in S. C. G. Watkins, *Reminiscences of Montclair* (New York: A. S. Barnes, 1929), 112.

145. "Municipal Art Commission," *Montclair (N.J.) Times,* May 2, 1908, cited in *Montclair Art Colony,* 15 n. 77.

146. *Outlook,* June 15, 1895: 1044. In 1902, the Rev. Bradford dedicated his book, *Messages of the Masters: Spiritual Interpretations of Great Paintings* (New York: Thomas Y. Crowell) to Fenn: "To Harry Fenn / My Dear Mr. Fenn / You will be surprised to find your name on this page, but that does not matter so long as I have the privilege of here expressing my admiration for you as an artist, my gratitude for your long-continued friendship, and my appreciation of your lofty and noble manhood. / Trusting that you will pardon my presumption, / I remain, My Dear Mr. Fenn,/Very sincerely yours, / Amory H. Bradford."

147. The architects were Cody, Berg & See; Chandler B. Grannis, *Century of a Modern Church: A Centennial History of Union Congregational Church, United Church of Christ, 1881–1981* (Upper Montclair, N.J.: Union Congregational Church U.C.C., 1983), 17.

148. Ibid., 19. Fenn's great grandson William Abt heard stories of tableaux, and another family member owns an apparent self-portrait of Fenn in Elizabethan dress.

149. *California Mammals* (San Diego: West Coast Publishing, 1906). Stephens and his wife Kate were instrumental in establishing the San Diego Museum of Natural History; "Katherine 'Kate' Stephens," San Diego Museum of Natural History, http://www.sdnhm.org/history/kstephens/index.html. In his account of his own life in "The Fenn Family," appended to "Biographical Sketch of the Life of Harry Fenn," Walter J. Fenn recounts that after studying a year in Paris and at the Art Students League in New York, he "became an illustrator for magazines. He was, at different times, art manager of the American and Outing Magazines published in New York. Also art manager of McClure's newspaper syndicate." He was in California from 1892 to around 1900, where he owned a ranch near Ballena, in San Diego County, with a large apiary. He returned to California in 1921, residing first in La Jolla, and from 1932 in Chula Vista. He was also a published poet; Walter J. Fenn, "The Fenn Family," and typescript of two biographies of W. J. Fenn, Fenn family papers. One of these biographies was "published in Chula Vista Star, 1940," and the other in *The Biographical Dictionary of Contemporary Poets of America* (New York: Avon House, 1938).

150. In an undated letter to William Macbeth, Lillian Fenn asked if she could place "a small water color study of violets" in his gallery for sale; Macbeth Gallery correspondence 1894–1914, NMC6, Ms. Div., Archives of American Art, NYPL. Walter J. Fenn recounted that Lilly did not marry: "She has been an accomplished carver in wood, designer of jewelry, and pastelle and watercolor painter. She gave instruction to a number of pupils"; Fenn, "Fenn Family."

151. According to her brother; Fenn, "Fenn Family."

152. Alice Maude married Charles Coffin of Brooklyn, a member of the New York Produce Exchange; they made their home in Montclair, and Alice became an interior decorator. Florence Bessie married a journalist, Allan Forman of Brooklyn; after his death she married Sidney Brooks, "a prominent English journalist," and lived in London; Fenn, "Fenn Family."

153. Information from the Twelfth Census of the United States, 1900 Population Schedule, Montclair, Essex County, New Jersey, Enumeration District 205, sheet 1 B.

154. *New York Times,* September 27, 1901.

155. James Henry Moser, "Art Topics," *Washington Post,* December 14, 1902.

7· CONTINUITY AND CHANGE—1900–1911, AND AN ASSESSMENT

1. See J. M. Mancini, *Pre-Modernism: Art-World Change and American Culture from the Civil War to the Armory Show* (Princeton: Princeton University Press, 2005), esp. chap. 3. Mancini discusses some of the critics in this period and states: "By undermining the legitimacy of common, everyday experience as a guide to artistic judgments, critics delegitimized representation as an aesthetic goal" (116).

2. Quoted in Marc Simpson, "Whistler, Modernism, and the Creative Afflatus," in *Like Breath on Glass: Whistler, Inness, and the Art of Painting Softly* (Williamstown, Mass.: Sterling and Francine Clark Art Institute, 2008), 38.

3. James Henry Moser, "Art Topics," *Washington Post,* April 26, 1903.

4. [Sidney Brooks], "The Late Harry Fenn," *New York Evening Post,* May 11, 1911.

5. See Mark A. Hewitt, "Jules Guérin and the American Renaissance," in *Jules Guérin: Master Delineator,* exh. cat. (Houston, Tex.: Rice University, 1983). Guérin prepared illustrations for Daniel Burnham and Edward Bennett's 1909 *Plan of Chicago* and for the design competition for the Lincoln Memorial in 1911–12. He also painted murals in the Lincoln Memorial and many other buildings in the 1920s.

6. This was a change from a few years earlier, when Fenn and Pennell illustrated "American Bicyclers at Mont St. Michel" for the August 1894 *St. Nicholas;* in that case, the table of contents for vol. 21, no. 2 noted the article was illustrated by "H. Fenn and others." But by 1910, when the *Century* published an overview of illustration titled "Forty Years of This Magazine: A Survey of 'The Century's' Progress in the Arts of Illustration" (November), no example of Fenn's work was included.

7. Sadakichi Hartmann considered McCarter "the most modern of illustrators," with "traces of Beardsley" and "the Japanese" in his style, among other elements; Hartmann, *A History of American Art,* 2 vols. (Boston, L. C. Page, 1902), 2:123. For an example of his work, see "An Easter Hymn," *Scribner's,* April 1895, 422–28.

8. See, for example, the *Chicago Tribune,* November 24, 1900.

9. W. W. Dyar, "The Colossal Bridges of Utah," *Century,* August 1904, 505.

10. The Curtis photograph Fenn used for "Yakutat Indian Camp" is owned by the University Libraries, University of Washington, and may be viewed digitally by searching the library's website, http://content.lib.washington.edu. A comparison of the photograph and the illustration shows that, once again, Fenn improved the composition by including the tops of the mountains, increasing the contrast, and pulling the distant structures closer. He drew two other illustrations for this article. The artists who went on the expedition were Frederick S. Dellenbaugh, Louis A. Fuertes, and R. Swain Gifford; two of the article's illustrations were by Gifford.

11. The article on the house that had been Washington's headquarters and Longfellow's home in Cambridge, Mass., was by Francis Le Baron. For the same issue, he also drew Nassau Hall at Princeton for an article about the Revolutionary War written by William Milligan Sloane, "Von Moltke's View of Washington's Strategy"; its frontal view is similar but not identical to Fenn's large (24 3/4 x 42 3/4 in.) watercolor of the building dated 1900 and now in the Princeton Portrait Collection, Princeton University Art Museum.

12. The articles appeared in September, November, and December 1905 and April 1906. In each one Guérin and Castaigne had a full-page image reproduced as a halftone with engraving, whereas Fenn had one or two images, either line cuts or halftones. Fenn's original ink drawing for "The Second Salon" of the Hotel de Crillon (December 1905) is in the collection of the Free Library of Philadelphia.

13. Rebecca Zurier, *Picturing the City: Urban Vision and the Ashcan School* (Berkeley: University of California Press, 2006), 50.

14. See T. J. Jackson Lears, *Rebirth of a Nation: The Making of Modern America, 1877–1920* (Harper Perennial, 2010), 291–300.

15. See John Tebbel, *The American Magazine: A Compact History* (New York: Hawthorn Books, 1969), 190–91.

16. Walter J. Fenn gave two other dates for his mother's death in the Fenn family papers: June 30, 1903, in his "Biographical Sketch of the Life of Harry Fenn" (p. 7) and June 25, 1903, in the "Fenn Family Record." The date given in the text was taken from her tombstone. Family stories relate that Mary Fenn was somewhat of an invalid after falling from a hammock and hurting her back (date unknown).

17. Fenn paid the $144 tax on the house in 1901; no tax on the house was listed for 1902. Town of Montclair, Tax Duplicate, 1901, 1902, Montclair Public Library, Montclair, N.J. Thanks to William T. Fischer at the library.

18. "Harry Fenn: An Appreciation, by a Friend" (unsigned obituary), *Harper's Weekly,* May 13, 1911. Fenn probably visited his daughter Florence Bessie and her husband, Sidney Brooks, on this trip; see Walter J. Fenn, "Biographical Sketch of the Life of Harry Fenn," Fenn family papers.

19. Walter J. Fenn, "Biographical Sketch," 6. Harry Fenn gave two addresses on a biographical form he filled out for Art League Publishing Co., Chicago, sometime after 1897: The Majestic, 145th St. and St. Nicholas Ave., New York City, and the Salmagundi Club, 14 W. 12th St., New York; Albert Duveen Collection, Archives of American Art, Smithsonian Institution. Walter J. Fenn wrote in the family photo album that he and Lillian lived in the new house with their father for five years (until his death in 1911).

20. Edwin A. Ulrich to Mrs. John C. Colwell (Montclair Art Museum), Harry Fenn papers, Montclair Art Museum. In the letter Ulrich describes the Park St. house and the view out Fenn's "picture painting window."

21. See *A Collection of Water Color Drawings by Harry Fenn* (New York: Anderson Auction Co., 1911).

22. The proceeds from auctioned works were split 50/50, half to the club and half to the artist; Alexander W. Katlan, *The Salmagundi Club Painting Exhibition Records, 1889 to 1939* (Flushing, N.Y.: Alexander Katlan Conservator, 2008). In 1910 Fenn painted a mug for the Salmagundi Club auction, and it is among those presently in the club's collection; the location of another mug painted in 1900 is unknown (thanks to Robert Mueller for this information).

23. The catalogues show Fenn's works as follows: 1902, *St. Gregoria, Valladolid;* 1907, *The street of arms* and *Pigeon cave;* 1908, *Market place, Vittoria;* 1910, *On Eastern Point, Gloucester* and *Bab-Tuma.*

24. Two of Fenn's exhibited works were sold, according to "Sales and Sales Prices," *Brush and Pencil* 16 no. 1 (July 1905): 28.

25. In these years a selection of works from the American Water Color Society's exhibitions was sent to various venues around the country. For example, *The Sixth Annual Exhibition of Selected Water Colors by American Artists,* drawn from the spring 1910 exhibition of the American Water Color Society plus "numerous works secured directly from the studios of artists since then," was on display at the Detroit Museum of Art March 6–26, 1911. The show included Fenn's *Low Tide, Gloucester.* In 1906 Fenn was represented at the Silas L. George Gallery, Watertown, N.Y., in the "first competitive" (*New York Times,* March 25, 1906).

26. [Brooks], "The Late Harry Fenn."

27. Ibid.

28. A digital image of the binding may be viewed on the American Trade Bindings Digital Library website of the University of North Carolina, Greensboro, http://libcdm1.uncg.edu.

29. Henry van Dyke, preface to *Out-of-Doors in the Holy Land* (New York: Charles Scribner's Sons, 1908), xi–xii. For a discussion of this book, see David Klatzker, "Sacred Journeys: Jerusalem in the Eyes of American Travelers before 1948," in *Jerusalem in the Mind of the Western World, 1800–1948,* vol. 5, *With Eyes toward Zion,* ed. Yehoshua Ben-Arieh and Moshe Davis (Westport, Conn.: Praeger, 1997), 49–50.

30. This book has been digitized on several websites, and images of the illustrations are readily accessible.

31. A photograph of the market square, Bethlehem, by American Colony Photographers with a similar crowd of people and camels in the foreground was clearly Fenn's main source for this watercolor; it is reproduced in *From Jerusalem with Love: A Fascinating Journey through the Holy Land with Art, Photography, and Souvenirs, 1799–1948* (Amsterdam: Uitgeverij Waanders, [2010]), 131. Fenn selected a narrower format and a higher viewpoint than in the photograph.

32. Editions were issued in 1911, 1912, 1914, 1915, 1919, 1920, 1921, 1930, and as recently as 1977; Copp Clark Co., Toronto, also issued the book, in 1916.

33. "Illustrated Art Books," *Dial,* December 1, 1908, 408–9. One of Fenn's illustrations for *Out-of-Doors in the Holy Land,* "The Ruins of Jerash," was reproduced in the article "Representative Book Illustration" in the *Printing Art: An Illustrated Monthly Magazine of the Art of Printing and of the Allied Arts* 3 (September 1908–February 1909): opp. 170. The comment on the illustrations was that they "admirably supplement the writer's vivid descriptions, constituting one of the best types of book work in colors."

34. The book may have included two color plates that didn't appear in the *Century:* "Men of Galilee" and "Tiberias and the Sea of Galilee"; on the other hand, these plates could have been missing from the bound volume of the *Century* that I examined. Most of the photographs in the book are credited to Underwood and Underwood, a firm that had produced early stereographic photos of the Holy Land.

35. Ernest Peixotto wrote and illustrated a series of books for Charles Scribner's Sons, ranging from *By Italian Seas* in 1906 to *Through Spain and Portugal* in 1922; George Wharton Edwards wrote and illustrated three books for Moffat, Yard & Co., New York, followed by a series for Penn Publishing Co., Philadelphia, that ranged from *Vanished Towers and Chimes of Flanders* in 1916 to *Constantinople* in 1930. In the same years, the London firm of Adam and Charles Black published books about different regions that contained color plates of paintings by Mortimer Menpes and other British artists.

36. Death notices in different newspapers give varying accounts of the length of Fenn's illness: the *New York Times* said six weeks ("Harry Fenn, Artist, Dead in 73d Year," April 23, 1911); the *Newark (N.J.) Evening News,* April 22, 1911, reported "about six months."

37. The article was written by Frances Duncan. Articles illustrated by photographs include "A Garden of Romance: Mrs. Tyson's, at Hamilton House, South Berwick, Maine" (September 1910) and "A Garden of the Heart, 'Green Alley,' The Home of Cecilia Beaux" (October 1910).

38. "Three Adventures in the Yosemite," 661.

39. "A Veteran Artist," *Outlook,* May 6, 1911, 98.

40. "Harry Fenn: An Appreciation," *Harper's Weekly,* May 13, 1911, 10.

41. "Fenn Watercolor Sale," *American Art News* 10, no. 6 (November 18, 1911): 5.

42. "The Powder Magazine at Jamestown a Generation Ago" is printed with the beige tint and appears to be a new halftone, for the dots are much smaller than they were in the *Century* (January 1891, 331). Fenn's drawings of Westover plantation reproduced in *Romantic America* first appeared in the *Century* article "Colonel William Byrd of Westover, Virginia" (June 1891). Other artists who contributed to *Romantic America* include Henry Guy Fangel, Joseph Pennell, André Castaigne, and Anna Bosworth Greene, among others.

43. A. V. S. Anthony, Timothy Cole, and Elbridge Kingsley, *Wood-Engraving: Three Essays* (New York: Grolier Club, 1916). This publication includes "A List of American Books Illustrated with Woodcuts" detailing the works that were exhibited.

44. Larry Evans, *The Complete Illustration Guide for Architects, Designers, Artists, and Students* (1982; reprint, New York: Van Nostrand Reinhold, 1993); Fenn and Pennell are featured in the chapter "Early Masters of Rendering," and five of Fenn's architectural illustrations are reproduced (2–5, 17).

45. Joseph Pennell, *Adventures of an Illustrator* (Boston: Little, Brown, 1925), 358. Color comics in newspapers had been introduced by the 1890s. "Hogan's Alley" began in the New York *World* in 1894 and became very popular, contributing to a great increase in circulation; William R. Taylor, *In Pursuit of Gotham: Culture and Commerce in New York* (New York: Oxford University Press, 1992), 83. In the July 29, 1911, *Harper's Weekly* an article titled "Over-Illustration" complained about "the pictorial squalor . . . of the Sunday newspapers, of which the Funny Page is the dreariest monstrosity ever foisted upon a patient and long-suffering public" (6).

46. Roger B. Stein, "Shaping the Landscape Image," introduction to *Shaping the Landscape Image, 1865–1910: John Douglas Woodward,* by Sue Rainey and Roger B. Stein (Charlottesville: Bayly Art Museum, University of Virginia, 1997), 8.

47. Henry James, "Our Artists in Europe," *Harper's Monthly,* June 1889, 50, 58. The same article was published as "Black and White" in James's *Picture and Text* (New York: Harper and Brothers, 1893).

48. "Harry Fenn: An Appreciation."

S$_{UE}$ R$_{AINEY}$ is a historian of American graphic arts, with particular interest in the artists who drew landscapes and cityscapes for periodical and book illustrations. She holds degrees from Duke and Columbia universities. From 1996 to 2009 she was editor of *Imprint: Journal of the American Historical Print Collectors Society.* Her book *Creating "Picturesque America": Monument to the Natural and Cultural Landscape* (1994) won the Charles C. Eldredge Prize of the Smithsonian American Art Museum and the Ewell L. Newman Book Award of the American Historical Print Collectors Society. Her 1997 publication co-authored with Roger B. Stein, *Shaping the Landscape Image, 1865–1910: John Douglas Woodward,* also won the Ewell L. Newman Book Award. Rainey lives in Charlottesville, Virginia.